with the
of

see also P.W. van der Horst, "Pseudo-Phocylides Revisited," Journal for the Study of the Pseudepigrapha 3 (1988) 3-30

THE SENTENCES
OF
PSEUDO-PHOCYLIDES

STUDIA
IN VETERIS TESTAMENTI
PSEUDEPIGRAPHA

EDIDERUNT

A. M. DENIS et M. DE JONGE

VOLUMEN QUARTUM

P. W. VAN DER HORST

THE SENTENCES
OF
PSEUDO-PHOCYLIDES

LEIDEN
E. J. BRILL
1978

THE SENTENCES
OF
PSEUDO-PHOCYLIDES

With Introduction and Commentary

BY

P. W. VAN DER HORST

LEIDEN
E. J. BRILL
1978

Published with financial support from the Netherlands Organization for the Advancement of Pure Research (Z.W.O.)

ISBN 90 04 05707 2

Copyright 1978 by E. J. Brill, Leiden, The Netherlands

All rights reserved. No part of this book may be reproduced or translated in any form, by print, photoprint, microfilm, microfiche or any other means without written permission from the publisher

PRINTED IN THE NETHERLANDS

manibus patris
זכרונו לברכה

TABLE OF CONTENTS

Preface IX
List of Abbreviations XI

Introduction
   1. History of the Research on Pseudo-Phocylides 3
   2. The Authenticity of the Poem 55
   3. The Pseudonym 59
   4. The Teaching of Pseudo-Phocylides 64
   5. The Author's Purpose 70
   6. The Genre of the Poem 77
   7. Date and Provenance 81
   Appendix: The Interpolation in *Oracula Sibyllina* II and
     the Manuscripts 84

Text and Translation 87
Commentary 105

Bibliography 263
Concordance 281
Index of Subjects 289
Index of Biblical Passages 292

PREFACE

This book is about an interesting Jewish poem from the time of Jesus, a work which deserves more attention than it has hitherto received. In order to further discussion about this writing, an extensive "Forschungsbericht" (focusing upon the scholarly discussion from 1856 to 1976) forms the main part of the Introduction, providing what is hoped to be a useful survey of work done on Pseudo-Phocylides by previous scholars. The subsequent six chapters concerning the various problems posed by the poem are short; I have refrained from seeking a solution for all of them, firstly because the material dealt with turned out to be of such a nature as to make clear conclusions impossible, and secondly because an attempt at solving these problems would itself have taken another five (if not ten) years. Therefore, possible solutions are only sketched, so that much is left to the reader's ingenuity. There is no chapter on the Formgeschichte and Traditionsgeschichte of ancient gnomic literature in general, but such a chapter can hardly be written in the present state of affairs, and comprehensive coverage would require a team of specialists.

The main emphasis of the book is on the Commentary. A host of parallels from Greek, Latin, Jewish, and Christian literature is adduced in order to clarify the spiritual affinities of Ps-Phoc. To keep the book readable for classicists who may be interested in the subject, all quotations from rabbinic sources have been given in English; and the few quotations in Hebrew have been provided with a translation.

Of the scholars who have helped me during the five years of research on Ps-Phoc., either by giving me valuable hints or by supporting me in other ways, I will mention only the most important. First of all, Prof. Dr. W. C. van Unnik, under whose guidance this book grew into a dissertation accepted by the Faculty of Theology at the University of Utrecht. To my great sorrow he died some months before the publication of this book. We lost in him not only a man of great learning, but also a man with a warm and endearing personality. To Prof. J. Reiling, Prof. W. J. Verdenius, Prof. Th. C. de Kruijf, Prof. D. Young (the most recent editor of the text of Ps-Phoc., who died so suddenly in 1973), Dr. G. Mussies and Dr.

P. Staples I am indebted for helping me in various ways to make the book what it is now. I also thank Prof. M. de Jonge and Father A.-M. Denis for accepting this book for the series Studia in Veteris Testamenti Pseudepigrapha.

Utrecht, Faculty of Theology   P. W. v. d. H.

LIST OF ABBREVIATIONS

Abbreviations of biblical books, apocrypha, pseudepigrapha, rabbinic treatises, Early Christian writings, names of classical authors and their works have such a wide currency that they need no explanation; otherwise they can easily be found in any of the greater lexica or encyclopedias. Abbreviated titles of books and articles are given in full form in the Bibliography.

AJP	American Journal of Philology
Ant. Class.	Antiquité Classique
ARW	Archiv für Religionswissenschaft
BHH	Biblisch-historisches Handwörterbuch
CBQ	Catholic Biblical Quarterly
CIG	Corpus Inscriptionum Graecarum
CII	Corpus Inscriptionum Iudaicarum
CIL	Corpus Inscriptionum Latinarum
Class. Quart.	Classical Quarterly
Class. Rev.	Classical Review
CPJ	Corpus Papyrorum Judaicarum
Enc. Jud.	Encyclopaedia Judaica
FGH	Fragmente der griechischen Historiker
HTR	Harvard Theological Review
HUCA	Hebrew Union College Annual
IDB	Interpreter's Dictionary of the Bible
ILS	Inscriptiones Latinae Selectae
JBL	Journal of Biblical Literature
JHS	Journal of Hellenic Studies
JJS	Journal of Jewish Studies
JQR	Jewish Quarterly Review
JSHRZ	Jüdische Schriften aus hellenistisch-römischer Zeit
JSJ	Journal for the Study of Judaism
JTS	Journal of Theological Studies
K-G	Kühner-Gerth (see Bibliography)
LCL	Loeb Classical Library
LSJ	Liddell-Scott-Jones (see Bibliography)
LThK	Lexikon für Theologie und Kirche
MGWJ	Monatsschrift für Geschichte und Wissenschaft des Judentums
NTS	New Testament Studies
OCD	Oxford Classical Dictionary
Philol.	Philologus
PW (RE)	Pauly-Wissowa's Realencyklopädie der classischen Altertumswissenschaft
RAC	Reallexikon für Antike und Christentum
REJ	Revue des Études Juives
Rev. Bib.	Revue Biblique
RGG	Religion in Geschichte und Gegenwart
Rhein. Mus.	Rheinisches Museum für Philologie
RHPhR	Revue d'Histoire et de Philosophie Religieuses

Riv.	Rivista di Filologia e Istruzione Classica
RSR	Recherches de Science Religieuse
SVF	Stoicorum Veterum Fragmenta
ThR	Theologische Rundschau
TLZ	Theologische Literaturzeitung
TWNT	Theologisches Wörterbuch zum Neuen Testament
ZAW	Zeitschrift für die alttestamentliche Wissenschaft
ZNW	Zeitschrift für die neutestamentliche Wissenschaft
ZPE	Zeitschrift für Papyrologie und Epigraphik
ZRGG	Zeitschrift für Religions- und Geistesgeschichte
ZThK	Zeitschrift für Theologie und Kirche

INTRODUCTION

CHAPTER ONE

HISTORY OF THE RESEARCH ON PSEUDO-PHOCYLIDES

From the sixteenth to the eighteenth century (Sylburg, Scaliger)

For more than 15 centuries no one has doubted the authenticity of the didactic poem that was written under the name of Phocylides, an Ionic bard who lived in the middle of the 6th century B.C. in Miletus.[1] Though probably little known in antiquity,[2] the poem enjoyed great popularity in the later Middle Ages in view of the rich manuscript tradition. Nobody was disturbed by the fact that in this piece of pagan poetry numercus reminiscences of the Old Testament were to be found. On the contrary, in all naïvety one rejoiced that the "natural reason" of a pagan could agree to such a great extent with the Word of God.[3] In a 15th century ms. Phocylides' poem is preceded by an iambic eulogy, in which it is said about him that he

ὡς χριστομύστης, ὡς ἀπόστολος μέγας,
ὡς ἀκροατὴς τῶν θεοῦ θεσπισμάτων,
καὶ μυσταγωγὸς τῶν ἀρίστων πρακτέων,
εὐαγγελικῶς ταῦτα λαλεῖ καὶ γράφει
εὔχρηστα τυγχάνοντα τοῖς ἐν τῷ βίῳ.[4]

So, although the Biblical reminiscences were clearly seen, this induced nobody to doubt the authenticity of the poem. This remained so in the 16th century, during which the poem's popularity

---

[1] On the real Phocylides see Ahlert, "Phokylides", *PW(RE)* XX 1 (1941), 503-505; Bielohlawek, *Hypotheke und Gnome* (1940), 14-20; Eckermann, "Phokylides", in Ersch-Gruber, *Allgemeine Encyhlopädie* III. Section, 24. Band (1848), 482-485. N.B. All the references in abbreviated form are given in full in the Bibliography.

[2] The poem is quoted for the first time by Stobaeus (5th cent. A.D.).

[3] Bernays, "Über das phokylideische Gedicht", *Ges. Abh.* I (1885), 193: "Je häufigere und vernehmlichere Anklänge an die Bibel bemerkt wurden, desto herzlicher freute man sich, in dem unbefangenen Glaube, hier abermals einen hellen Beweis zu gewinnen, dass das ungefälschte Zeugnis der Natur aus dem Munde der edlern Heiden im wesentlichen gleichlaute dem göttlichen Gnadenwort der Bibel". Still in 1840 Hewett wrote: "Many of the instructions contained in this poem tho(ugh) the product of a Heathen, from the bare light of Nature, are in effect to be found in the Law given by God to his people" (*The Preceptive Poem of Phocylides*, Watford 1840, 3).

[4] Quoted from Bergk, *Poetae Lyrici Graeci*, II⁴ (1882), 79.

was at its zenith. After the first printed edition in 1495 (in Venice), it was edited numerous times in the 16th century.⁵ The poem was considered very useful for the education of the youth, since it combined lofty morals, that were in agreement with the Bible, with literary beauty. It became a favourite schoolbook.⁶

It was not until 1591 that the first doubts about the authenticity of the poem arose. In his edition of gnomic poets, Friedrich Sylburg hesitatingly wonders whether the unmistakably Biblical passages in the poem should not be considered to be Jewish and Christian interpolations. But he does not exclude the possibility that Phocylides, just like Pythagoras, had had a Hebrew master.⁷

It was only in 1606, however, that the great Joseph Scaliger for the first time levelled thorough criticisms against the general acceptance of the authenticity of our gnomic poem. In his *Animadversiones in Chronologica Eusebii* ⁸ he says: The real Phocylides wrote short γνῶμαι preceded by the *sphragis* (Scaliger calls it *gnorisma*) καὶ τόδε Φωκυλίδεω. "At iste vulgaris perpetuum carmen scripsit non apposita illa veteri nota" (88). Moreover, this poem is quoted nowhere and never in antiquity, as contrasted with the real Phocylides. Scaliger, then, surmises that the author was a Jew or a Christian, and that he "aut unum ex Hellenistis Alexandrinis fuisse, cuiusmodi multi praestantissimi floruerunt sub Ptolemaeis, aut, quod vero propius, Christianum" (88). He tries to prove this by demonstrating that the poet undoubtedly knew the LXX; he points out the striking agreements between Ps-Phoc. 84f. and Deut. XXII 6f. and between Ps-Phoc. 139, 147f. and

---

⁵ Fürst, *Bibliotheca Judaica* III (1863), 96f., enumerates more than 40 editions just from the 16th century, apart from many translations. Cf. also J. A. Fabricius, *Bibliotheca Graeca* I, Hamburg 1790⁴, 706-720.

⁶ Bernays, *op. cit.*, 192: "Während des sechszehnten Jahrhunderts waren sie (sc. the hexameters of Ps-Phoc.) von Gross und Klein gekannt als ein Gegenstand früher Knabenlectüre".

⁷ F. Sylburg, *Epicae elegiacaeque minorum poetarum gnomae*, Frankfurt 1591. The identical 1659 edition is used here (now entitled *Theognidis, Phocylidis, Pythagorae, Solonis et aliorum poemata gnomica*); ibid. p. 163: "Adeo multi hujus poematii versus tales sunt ut non tam ex ethnica (Pythagorea in primis) quam ex Judaica et Christiana philosophia promanasse videantur. Ac fieri potuit, ut quemadmodum Pythagoras et ceteri veteres philosophi, ita et hic vel ab Hebraeis, vel ab Hebraeorum discipulis aut sectatoribus aliqua sui poematii praecepta desumpserit. Nisi forte ab Hebraeis et Christianis nonnulla praecepta huic poematio inserta, ut eo majorem juventuti fructum afferre possent".

⁸ Printed in his *Thesaurus Temporum*, Leiden 1606.

Ex. XXII 31, Lev. XXII 8. Further, he asserts that in v. 140 (κτῆνος δ' ἢν ἐχθροῖο πέσῃ καθ' ὁδόν, συνέγειρε) Ps-Phoc. has modified the ordinance in Deut. XXII 4 in a Christian sense, by prescribing help in raising up not only the pack-animal of an ἀδελφός, but also that of an ἐχθρός. "In quo non Iudaeum, sed Christianum agnoscas, quum addidit ἐχθροῖο" (89). This is a curious error on the part of Scaliger, since Ex. XXIII 5 says: ἐὰν δὲ ἴδῃς τὸ ὑποζύγιον τοῦ ἐχθροῦ σου πεπτωκὸς ὑπὸ τὸν γόμον αὐτοῦ, οὐ παρελεύσῃ αὐτό, ἀλλὰ συνεγερεῖς αὐτὸ μετ' αὐτοῦ.[9] But this was not his only argument for assuming Christian authorship. He quotes vv. 102-108 (on the resurrection and after-life) and on these lines he comments abruptly and without giving any proof: "Vide hic plane doctrinam Christianam" (89).[10] Therefore he concludes simply: "Noli igitur putare hoc carmen illius Phocylidis esse, sed ἀνωνύμου Christiani" and "totam illam poesim falso hactenus Phocylidae attributam" (89). This statement does not restrain Scaliger from giving expression to his great admiration for the poem in the oft quoted and much criticized remark "Neque vero puto ullius veterum carmen extare, quod cum poesi huius Phocylidis (si modo ei id nomen fuit) aut elegantia, aut nitore, aut cultu verborum conferri possit" (89). It should be borne in mind that Scaliger probably means by *veteres* the ancient *Christian* authors.[11]

One of the consequences of Scaliger's proof of the unauthenticity of the poem was a rapid decline of interest in Ps-Phoc.[12] In spite of Scaliger's own appeal to his readers to test his surmises,[13] the number of editions and translations declined,[14] and serious research on the poem as he wanted it actually failed to materialize for two and a half centuries. Scaliger's thesis that the poem is Christian is repeated uncritically without anybody examining his proofs

---

[9] Bernays, *op. cit.* 196-198, who was very amused by this error, assumed that Scaliger has quickly seen the mistake since he omitted this passage in the second impression of the book (Amsterdam 1608).

[10] In the Commentary it will be shown that these verses have no special Christian character.

[11] So rightly Bernays, *op. cit.* 195 n.1. See the criticisms of Scaliger's remark by Bernhardy, *Grundriss der griechischen Literatur* II (1867) 520 and Goram, "De Pseudo-Phocylide", *Philologus* 14 (1859), 111.

[12] See F. Susemihl, *Geschichte der griechischen Literatur in der Alexandrinerzeit* II (1892) 642 n. 63: "Dann kühlte sich der Eifer ab, seitdem man die Fälschung erkannt hat".

[13] *Animadversiones* 89.

[14] As can be seen in Fürst, *op. cit.* 96ff.

for it, which are very weak in fact.[15] It is useless to enumerate all those who have subsequently occupied themselves with Ps-Phoc. in the 17th and 18th centuries, since they put forward no new points of view. The literature can easily be found in Fürst, *Bibl. Jud.* III 96ff.

The nineteenth century (Bernays, Bergk, Harnack, Sebestyén, Wendland)

It was only in 1856 that research on the nature and origin of this poem got a new impulse, namely from the book *Ueber das phokylideische Gedicht* of the great Jewish-German scholar Jacob Bernays.[16] Bernays begins with an extensive discussion of Scaliger's thesis,[17] the strong and weak aspects of which he demonstrates. The dependence upon the LXX is an established fact; but then it is strange that the poem now and then speaks of θεοί.[18] Bernays emends these passages in such a way, however, that this offensive terminology disappears,[19] and those passages in which the terms Οὐρανίδαι and μάκαρες occur are interpreted by him in such a way that they deal with the forces of nature.[20] So the monotheistic character of the poem is beyond all doubt. After an elaborate discussion of the anti-Hellenic character of v. 49 (see my Comm.) and some other passages, Bernays takes up the question of a possibly Christian origin of the poem.[21] He shows that the author

---

[15] So e.g. Wachler, Rohde, Hewett, Brunck (see Bibliography). Brunck 152 dated the poem to the end of the 4th century A.D., probably to avoid the difficulty, already felt by Scaliger, that Ps-Phoc. is quoted neither by Clement of Alexandria nor by Eusebius. It seems that Isaac Vossius, in his book *De Oraculis Sibyllinis* (London 1685) 237, which unfortunately was inaccessible to me, was the only one to defend a purely Jewish origin of the poem, without exerting any influence with his thesis (see Fabricius *Bibl. Gr.* I⁴ 721 and Susemihl, *op. cit.* 643 n. 63). G. Sartorius, *Analysis grammatica carminum Phocylidis et Pythagorae*, Görlitz 1617, still gratuitously assumed the authenticity of the poem. L. Wachler was the first to call the author Pseudo-Phoc. in his *Dissertatio inauguralis philologica de Pseudo-Phocylide*, Rinteln 1788.

[16] See on him the fascinating studies by A. Momigliano, *Jacob Bernays* (Meded. der Kon. Ned. Akad. van Wet., Afd. Lett., N.R. XXXII 5), Amsterdam 1969, and H. I. Bach, *Jacob Bernays*, Tübingen 1974.

[17] *Op. cit.* 194-199. I refer to the pagination of the reprint of the essay in Bernays' *Gesammelte Abhandlungen* I, Berlin 1885, 192-261.

[18] "in heidnischer Mehrzahl" (199).

[19] See my Commentary on vv. 98 and 104.

[20] Vv. 71, 75, 163. See *op. cit.* 206ff. (In a long note on p. 206f., Bernays tried to demonstrate the Aristotelian character of vv. 59, 64 and 68).

[21] *Op. cit.* 215ff.

does not have any knowledge of Christianity, and those words and passages which suggest a Christian character appear on closer scrutiny to be Byzantine corrections and interpolations.[22] Scaliger did not see sharply enough here, for only v. 152 could already have opened his eyes to the non-Christian character of the poem.[23]

Bernays next discusses the long insertion of a part of the Pseudo-Phocylidea into the second book of the *Oracula Sibyllina*.[24] This interpolation clearly disrupts the course of that book. It does not occur, moreover, in the older mss. of *Or. Sib*. But it must have been an early insertion, since Suidas already knew it.[25] The fact that the interpolation stands in a Christian context and the interpolator also tried to give the interpolation a Christian character by making additions and modifications, should induce nobody to see Ps-Phoc. as a Christian author.

In a long paragraph, Bernays next deals with the problem posed by the character of the poem.[26] The first question he raises is: If Ps-Phoc. is a Jew, why did he not combat idolatry? This question can only be answered if one knows why he did include some Old Testament commandments and others not. It appears from the poem itself that Ps-Phoc. has included only such commandments as concern the "Moral des Privatlebens oder des öffentlichen nach seinen nicht die jüdische Nationalität berührenden Seiten", but excluded "alles was mit dem Sonderwesen der jüdischen Nationalität zusammenhängt; ferner alles Rituelle, das sich nicht mit dem Verstande abfindet" (227).[27] Hence, Ps-Phoc. never mentions any injunction against idolatry. The beginning of the poem illustrates this principle well. It is a selective rendering of the Decalogue, from which the second commandment, on idolatry, and the tenth, on sabbath-rest, have been omitted. Vv. 8-41 are

---

[22] So o.g. v. 129 (see my Comm.) and the reading παρθενίην in v. 13 which was changed by Bernays into παρθεσίην, a conjecture he did "mit derjenigen Sicherheit das Richtige getroffen zu haben, welch in dergleichen Fällen aus dem blossen Gefühle entspringt" (220).

[23] V. 152 runs μὴ κακὸν εὖ ἔρξῃς· σπείρειν ἴσον ἔστ' ἐνὶ πόντῳ.

[24] *Op. cit.* 222ff. Vv. 5-79, into which the interpolator himself has in turn made interpolations, have been inserted between *Or. Sib.* II 55 and 149. How extensive the interpolations within the interpolated part of Ps-Phoc. are, is apparent from the fact that this section of 75 verses occupies 94 verses in *Or. Sib*.

[25] Suidas s.v. Φωκυλίδης· ... εἰσὶ δ' ἐκ τῶν Σιβυλλιακῶν κεκλεμμένα.

[26] *Op. cit.* 226ff.

[27] Bernays calls these respectively the מצות שכליות (Verstandes-Gesetze) and the מצות שמעיות (Gehorsams-Gesetze), but these are medieval terms.

mainly based upon that chapter of Leviticus "welcher in neuen wie in alten Zeiten mit Recht für das Gegenstück des Dekalogs angesehen wird" (228), viz. chapter 19. In a long passage (228-233), Bernays lists the parallels between Lev. 19 and Ps-Phoc. 8-41.[28] Which parts of Lev. 19, however, have been omitted? Again, those on the sabbath, on idolatry and on sacrifices. In vv. 42-82 Bernays sees "eine Spruchsammlung allgemein ethischer Art, geordnet nach den Haupttugenden, wie sie in den Philosophenschulen benannt und behandelt zu werden pflegten" (234). Vv. 83-85 undeniably derive from the O.T., but vv. 86-131 are a series of loosely strung maxims of various provenance. In vv. 132-152, the influence of the Pentateuch is again perceptible, but the lines have to be regrouped,[29] and the text often emended. Of vv. 153-174 (on the value of labour) Bernays says: "Überall klingen hier ausgewählte biblische Sprüche zusammen mit Gnomen von echt classischer Einfachheit" (241). The passage 175-198 is based upon Lev. 18 and is "eine Auswahl der biblischen Bestimmungen über die geschlechtlichen Verhältnisse, zugleich mit einigen Strafreden gegen solche Laster, zu deren ausdrückliche Verfolgung die mosaische Gesetzgebung in der jüdischen Sitte keinen Anlass fand, die aber bei den übrigen Völkern, classischen wie nichtclassischen, nur zu offenkundig im Schwange gingen" (242). In the remaining passages on family life (vv. 199-230), clear borrowings from the O.T. are again to be found. From the closing sentences (229-230) it appears that Ps-Phoc. "seine Arbeit für nichts Anderes hielt und auch für nichts Anderes wollte gehalten wissen, als für das, was sie ist: für eine zwar aus biblischen Quellen geschöpfte, aber jedes positiv biblischen Elements entkleidete Anleitung zu sittlichem Leben" (248).

Bernays' final chapter deals with the time and place of origin of the poem (248-254). The *terminus post quem* is the compilation of the LXX. The *terminus ante quem* is the middle of the second century A.D., after which no one can simply ignore Christianity. The absence of any trace of N.T. influence demands a date before 150 A.D. But "das deutliche Absehen auf Besserung der Heiden" also urges a date before 70 A.D. So the time of origin is somewhere between the middle of the second century B.C. and the middle of

---

[28] These parallels can be found in the Commentary.
[29] Bernays 237 proposed the order: 132-8, 143-4, 140-2, 145, 139, 147-151, 146, 152.

the first century A.D., a period that also constitutes the hey-day of Jewish pseudepigraphy. The name Phocylides was chosen by the author as a pseudonym since "verbindungsloses Nebeneinanderstellen der Sprüche als bezeichnende Eigenthümlichkeit des phokylideischen Stils anerkannt war" (250).[30]

The most probable place of origin is Alexandria, a city where anatomy was practised (alluded to in v. 102) and where a considerable number of hellenized Jews lived. Especially in that city the combating of idolatry did not make any sense, since "dort inniger als in den übrigen heidnischen Ländern die ausgearbeitetste Idololatrie mit allen Lebensverhältnissen verwachsen war" (251). In this connection Bernays refers to Josephus' interpretation of Ex. XXII 27 (*Ant*. IV 207; *C.Ap*. II 237), where this verse is taken to mean that the heathen gods may not be blasphemed.[31]

Nevertheless, in the end Bernays severely criticizes Ps-Phoc. for his silence on idolatry, which is forbidden after all in the Noachian laws to which the poem is so clearly related.[32] Probably it is precisely this serious omission that was the cause of the absence of quotations from it in the Church Fathers. For Byzantine pedagogues, however, this poem was a deliverance from the dilemma "entweder schlechtes Griechisch oder heidnische Sitten mit der Jugend zu tractiren" (254). In an appendix Bernays presents a critical text-edition (254-261).

The reason why Bernays' study has been dealt with at such length is because his work has retained its predominance up to the present day. In essentials his view has remained unchallenged. As we shall see, the arguments of those who differ fundamentally from Bernays are less convincing. After 1856, critics mainly differed from him in the interpretation of details;[33] but his basic thesis, that the poem is a Jewish-Hellenistic pseudepigraphon, still seems unassailable. Subsequent modifications and additions to his work can now be reviewed.[34]

---

[30] In this connection Bernays refers to Dio Chrys. XXXVI 12. This text is quoted below.

[31] On this see G. Delling, "Josephus und die heidnischen Religionen", in: *Studien zum N.T.*, 1970, 45-52.

[32] Here Bernays' own Jewish point of view becomes evident.

[33] My own criticisms of Bernays will become clear in the Commentary.

[34] In 1856 the second volume of Alexandre's monumental edition of Or. Sib. also appeared. In this volume (entitled *Excursus ad Sibyllina*), Alexandre devotes a section (pp. 401-409) to the long insertion of Ps-Phoc. into the second book, about which he thinks that this is done "ab ipso

The first scholar after Bernays to occupy himself with Ps-Phoc. was Goram [35] who, in an article of 1859, wants to do no more than give some additions and corrections to Bernays' study. He begins by refuting once more Scaliger's thesis that the poem must be viewed as Christian on the basis of vv. 102-108, and shows that this whole passage can be explained from he LXX.[36] Thereafter he tries to demonstrate that several passages of *Sapientia Salomonis* form the basis of numerous verses in Ps-Phoc.[37] Goram then submits that Ps-Phoc. was written in the same time as *Sap. Sal.*, which he regards as a writing of Aristobulus. Hence he dates Ps-Phoc. between 150 and 130 B.C.[38] In his view, the verses about trade, shipping, jurisdiction, and anatomy clearly point to an Alexandrian origin.[39] Ps-Phoc. has also borrowed much from Greek literature, especially from Theognis and Pindar; and in many verses a mixture of Jewish and Greek wisdom is to be found.[40] His main sources are the Pentateuch, Proverbs, Sap. Sal. and Sirach, mixed with Greek wisdom; but he omits everything typically Jewish.[41] Finally, Goram proposes a number of emendations, many of them unnecessary and forced. As will be shown later, also his dating is contestable. And many of his parallels from the LXX

Sibyllista" (408) in view of the fact that in the verses before and after the insertion several allusions are made to Ps-Phoc. On Ps-Phoc. he says that many lines betray a Christian origin (e.g. 10, 11, 13, 54, 103). "Quod ... in iis quaedam, imo plura christiana sunt, inde tuto colligitur expurgati Phocylidis editionem vel omnino christianam fuisse, vel si judaica, serius a Christianis retractatam" (406). He concludes that the poem is most probably "compositum a Judaeis primum, deinde a Christianis recognitum, et fortasse non semel nec uno modo retractatam ad usum praecipue scholarum" (408). Bernays had seen things more sharply here.

Only in passing can the long review of Bernays' book by L. Schmidt in *Jahrbücher für classische Philologie* 3 (1857), 510-519, be indicated. Schmidt agrees to a great extent with Bernays' interpretation, but he criticizes his Jewish bias. Furthermore, he finds that Bernays reckons too little with interpolations, "denn von jeher hat kein Zweig der Poesie der Interpolation einen so weiten Spielraum geboten wie der gnomische" (514). Schmidt proposes a number of very ingenious emendations, metatheses and atheteses of verses; see the Comm.

[35] O. Goram, "De Pseudo-Phocylide", *Philologus* 14 (1859), 91-112.
[36] *Art. cit.* 92-94.
[37] *Art. cit.* 95-97. He regards Sap. Sal. as the source of e.g. vv. 45, 65-7, 70, 71-5, 86-90, 129, 131.
[38] *Art. cit.* 98.
[39] *Art. cit.* 100f.
[40] On pp. 101ff. Goram gives a number of parallels from Greek literature and LXX (on which see the Comm.).
[41] "Omnia Iudaeis singularia consulto tacuit" (109).

are far-fetched and unconvincing. Nevertheless, his article corroborates Bernays' point of view.[42]

In 1867 Bernhardy devoted a number of pages in his *Grundriss der griechischen Literatur* to Ps-Phoc.,[43] which he characterizes in the following way: "Der Verfasser war mittelmässig, sein Sprachschatz verräth wenig Poesie, die Sprache hat Mängel und Eigenheiten einer späteren Zeit, der Vortrag is nüchtern und selten durch einigen Glanz der Rhetorik (wie v. 71-75, 160-174) oder durch Wortfülle gehoben, der Versbau folgt dem gemeinen Mechanismus und kennt weder Wohlklang noch rhythmischen Wechsel, die Lehren sind ohne Zusammenhang und passende Gliederung an einander gereiht, mehrmahls auch durch Wiederholung oder jüngere Zusätze verwirrt; schon hieran empfindet man den scharfen Widerspruch mit den aphoristischen Formen des alten Spruchdichters" (518). The poem "gehört einem aufgeklärten jüdischen Verfasser, welcher von den trennenden Unterschieden der Nationalität absah und den Griechen die Moral, die gesetzlichen Vorschriften des Alten Testaments in ihrer Reinheit mild und ohne jeden polemischen Misston empfahl" (518). "Niemand weiss aus Alexandrinischer Zeit einen gleich berechnenden und aufgeklärten Juden der laxen Observanz, der überall vor dem Heidentum behutsam ausbiegt, um nirgend mit den Götzendienst oder Hellenismus zusammenzustossen. Das konnte nur ein Mann der grossen Welt sein" (522). But "seinen Zweck hat er doch verfehlt, da weder das Alterthum noch belesene Kirchenväter davon für ihre Zwecke Gebrauch machten; auch finden wir keinen gelehrten heidnischen Leser" (522). Bernhardy thinks that Goram's dating to the second century B.C. is too early.[44] According to him,

---

[42] The same applies to the translation (with Introduction) of Ps-Phoc. by W. Binder, *Die Elegien des Theognis nebst Phokylides' Mahngedicht und Pythagoras' Goldenen Sprüchen; Deutsch im Versmasse der Urschriften*, Stuttgart 1859, 67-78. According to Binder, the poem is definitely Jewish. But he has no desire, as Bernays had, to explain away anything that does not fit in with that. "Die wenigen polytheistischen Überreste sind wohl Folge des fingirten Ursprunges von dem heidnischen Griechen Phokylides, oder eines in der Weltstadt Alexandria allwärts geläufigen Synkretismus" (69). Quite curiously Binder consciously does not follow in his translation the Greek text exactly, "im Interesse unsers deutschen Sittlichkeitsgefühls" (70 n. 1)!

[43] *Grundriss* II 1, Halle 1867³, 517-523. In former editions, which were inaccessible to me, Bernhardy held another view, which he modified under Bernays' influence.

[44] *Op. cit.* 522. His reason for this is weak: v. 149 (μαγικῶν βίβλων ἀπέχεσθαι) could not be well situated in that period.

the number of later additions is great. The poem is an aggregate of older and younger components and especially the passages with a more rhetorical usage are of later date. But also some verses that are metrically bad and grammatically incorrect "thäte man Unrecht dem ersten Verfasser anzurechnen" (523).[45] According to Bernhardy several hands had already revised the poem before the Byzantine period.[46]

The next important contributions to the discussion came from Theodor Bergk.[47] His article in *Philologus* of 1882 mainly consists of textcritical considerations on the poem. The great number of variants in the text of Ps-Phoc. is surprising. "Selten wird man auf so engem Raume eine so grosse Zahl von Verderbnissen jeder Art wahrnehmen" (580). One might expect that the poem had been handed down rather undamaged, since the interpretation did not cause serious difficulties, "aber es war im Mittelalter ein Schulbuch, wurde eifrig gelesen und fleissig abgeschrieben: eben deshalb, aber vielleicht mehr noch, weil es der Bildungsstufe der Byzantiner recht gemäss war, weil man sich hier vollkommen heimisch fühlte, entschlug man sich des Respectes, den man vor classischen Schriftwerken im allgemeinen sich bewahrte" (580). In the Introduction to his critical edition (*PLG* II[4], 74-81) Bergk discusses, besides the

---

[45] To these later additions Bernhardy reckons among others vv. 21, 22' 42-47, 68, 77, 79, 98, 133, 157, 158, 164ff., 210, mostly unnecessarily as will be seen.

[46] In the next ten years, 3 minor contributions appear: A. Hart, "Die Pseudo-Phokylideia und Theognis im Codex Venetus Marcianus 522", *Neue Jahrbücher für classische Philologie* 14 (1868), 331-336, says that there are so many mss. of Ps-Phoc. that it is recommendable to exclude the useless mss. from the critical apparatus. He lists the variants from the ms. mentioned in the title, that shows a deviant order of the verses, as had already been surmised by Bernays. In his *Die Flavius Josephus beigelegte Schrift über die Herrschaft der Vernunft*, Breslau 1869, 161-163, J. Freudenthal protests against Bernays' view that vv. 59, 64 and 68 betray wide reading in Aristotle (see above p. 6 n. 20 and the Comm.). H. Graetz, *Geschichte der Juden* III[3], Leipzig 1878, completely agrees with Bernays. He only specifies the date: "Der Umstand, dass der Verf. gegen die Ehelosigkeit spricht (V. 175-6), weist ihn in die Kaiserzeit, da diese in Folge der Bürgerkriege überhandgenommem und auch ausserhalb Italiens grassirt hat" (633; not conclusive). J. B. Feuling - H. D. Goodwin, *Phocylides. Poem of Admonition translated with Introduction and Commentary*, Andover (Mass.) 1879, was unfortunately inaccessible to me.

[47] Th. Bergk, "Kritische Beiträge zu dem sog. Phokylides", *Philologus* 41 (1882), 577-601; *Poetae Lyrici Graeci* II, Leipzig 1882[4], 74-109 (textedition with introduction); cf. also his edition in *Anthologia Lyrica*, Leipzig 1883[3], 28-35; *Griechische Literaturgeschichte* II, Berlin 1883, 298-302.

mss. tradition, the views of Bernays and Goram. He agrees in the main with Bernays, but he criticizes his thesis that the pseudonym Phocylides had been chosen because "etiam ille varia praecepta nullo fere vinculo inter se apta ediderit" (75 n. 1). Bergk objects that the real Phocylides only wrote short maxims of one or two lines without connecting them with one another, whereas in the case of Ps-Phoc. we have a "carmen perpetuum". By this, Bergk does not want to deny that the original author himself choose this pseudonym, for he attacks the view of Bernays and Goram that vv. 1-2 (the lines where the name Phocylides occurs) were added by a later hand. The author certainly did need a pseudonym in order to reach the Greeks.[48]

A surprisingly new thesis of Bergk is that one should not speak of an insertion of part of Ps-Phoc. into *Or. Sib.* II, but, on the contrary, of an omission in those mss. of *Or. Sib.* that do not contain this passage; "poterat enim librarius, cum animadvertisset integrum Phocylidis poema superstes esse, ut suo labori parceret, haec omittere" (77). This matter has been discussed more fully by other scholars, as will be shown later. Finally, Bergk enumerates the nine different superscriptions of the poem in the several mss.[49]

In the posthumously edited second part of his *Griechische Literaturgeschichte* (1883), Bergk emphasizes that there is not any trace of Christian influence in the poem, but that the author obviously was an Alexandrian Jew, who mixed Jewish and Greek concepts whilst very carefully avoiding anything typically and exclusively Jewish. Vv. 102-115 where the resurrection of the dead and immortality of the soul are combined, are a striking example.[50] "Der Verfasser accommodirt sich sogar der Anschauungsweise seiner Leser so weit, dass er keinen Anstand nimmt, von Himmlischen oder Seligen zu sprechen, wenn er die Naturmächte oder Naturkörper erwähnt (71, 75, 163)" (299). The author clearly wrote with the pagans in view. Hence the pseudonym Phocylides. If he

---

[48] *PLG* 78. In passing, Bergk points to the curious fact that Bernays both athetizes vv. 1-2 and wants to maintain the name Phocylides. On the authenticity of vv. 1-2 see ch. 3 and the Comm.

[49] *PLG* 78. These nine superscriptions are: Φωκυλίδου ποίημα νουθετικόν, Φωκυλίδου γνῶμαι, Φωκυλίδου γνῶμαι ποίησις ὧδε τοῦ Φωκυλίδου ὀρθοποδηγοῦσα πρὸς τὸ βέλτιον, Φωκυλίδου ἀργυρᾶ ἔπη ἡρωϊκά, Φωκυλίδου φιλοσόφου ποίησις ὠφέλιμος, Φωκυλλίδου ποίησις ὠφέλιμος, Φωκυλίδου ποίημα, Φωκυλίδους ποίησις πάνυ ὠφέλιμος· τὰ λεγόμενα ἀργυρᾶ, Φωκυλλίδου γνωμικοῦ ὡραῖα.

[50] *Griech. Lit.* II 299f.

had written for Jews, he would have chosen the name Solomon.[51] The language and metrics of the poem are often awkward and the author found no response in antiquity.[52]

In 1884 there appeared a short study by J. Sitzler,[53] in which, besides making some proposals for emendation of the text, he examines the use of the combination *muta cum liquida* in Ps-Phoc. It then appears that the author makes an arbitrary use of "position", that is: before *muta cum liquida* he lets the preceding syllable be long or not.[54] "Halten wir nun diese Resultate mit denen die sich aus den übrigen Epikern ergeben, zusammen, so folgt auch hieraus deutlich, dass unser Gedicht der spätern Zeit angehört. Besonders springt in die Augen die Ähnlichkeit zwischen unserm Dichter und Nikandros, vielleicht eben deshalb, weil beide der didaktischen Richtung angehören" (51).[55]

In 1883 the *Didache* was published for the first time. This constituted a turning-point in the research on Ps-Phoc. Especially the first chapters of the Did., I-VI (the part with the Two Ways doctrine), showed many conspicuous parallels to Ps-Phoc.[56] The first to point that out, though without elaborating it, was Hermann Usener in his Preface to Bernays' *Gesammelte Abhandlungen*, which were published in 1885.[57] This indication was immediately taken up by Harnack in his review of Bernays' collected essays.[58] According to Harnack, the agreements between Did. and Ps-Phoc. again made the question of the poem's origin a debatable point. He admits that the first chapters of Did. have undergone a strong Jewish-hellenistic influence; but, nevertheless, Bernays' thesis of a Jewish origin seems to him to be wrong. The phrase ὀπίσω δὲ θεοὶ τελέθονται in v. 104 should have made Bernays aware of the Christian nature of the poem instead of inducing him to the conjecture

---

[51] *Op. cit.* 301. Another reason why Bergk refused to athetize vv. 1-2 is that the poem could hardly begin with v. 3. He does not see a reason either to reject the whole prooemium, vv. 1-7 (301 n. 17).

[52] Below (p. 39 n. 151) I shall return to Bergk's mistaken remark (302 n. 20) that the scholiast on Aristophanes' *Nubes* had already seen through the unauthenticity of the poem (so already Bernays 234 n. 2).

[53] "Zu den griechischen Elegikern", *Jahrbücher für classische Philologie* 30 (1884), 48-53.

[54] E.g. ἀνυβρίστως (157) with short υ, but ὕβριζε (189) with long υ.

[55] Nicander lived in the second century B.C.

[56] See e.g. A. von Harnack, *Geschichte der altchristlichen Literatur* I 1 (1893), 89 and the Comm.

[57] 2 vols., Berlin 1885. Usener in vol. I, p. V-VI.

[58] *Theologische Literaturzeitung* 10 (1885), 159-161.

νέοι for θεοί (see above p. 6 n. 19). That men become gods after death is an early Christian thought; cf. Theophilus *Ad Autol.* II 27 ... εἰ ῥέψῃ ἐπὶ τὰ τῆς ἀθανασίας τηρήσας τὴν ἐντολὴν τοῦ θεοῦ, μισθὸν κομίσηται παρ' αὐτοῦ τὴν ἀθανασίαν καὶ γένηται θεός. Harnack concludes: "Da ... das Gedicht unzweifelhaft auf biblische Grundlage ruht, da also nur gefragt werden kann, ob es jüdisch oder christlich ist, so ist auf christlichen Ursprung zu entscheiden; denn, soviel mir bekannt, ist die jüdische Philosophie nie so sehr auf die Antike eingegangen, dass sie die Menschen, welche die Unsterblichkeit erlangt haben, als *theoi* bezeichnet hat" (160).[59] The weakness of Harnack's thesis—he could interpret only one verse in a Christian sense—no doubt became clear to himself, for in his later *Geschichte der altchristlichen Literatur* he reckoned with the possibility that vv. 103-4 could have been an interpolation.[60]

In the same year, 1885, Harnack received support from James Rendel Harris. In his book *The Teaching of the Apostles and the Sibylline Books*,[61] the latter concluded on the basis of the parallels between Did. and Ps-Phoc. that Ps-Phoc. in part actually is a metrical rendering of Did., and hence a Christian writing. This position was strongly attacked in 1887 by F.X. Funk in his *Doctrina duodecim apostolorum*.[62] Funk concedes that there are striking similarities; but he adds that this by no means proves that Ps-Phoc. drew on Did., for in Ps-Phoc., for example, every indication of a Two Ways doctrine and also the Golden Rule are missing as well as many other essential rules of the "pars moralis" of the Did.[63] Hence "Pseudophocylides Doctrinam non legisse videtur" (XXI). Harris replied in the same year. In his book *The Teaching of the*

---

[59] Actually this is a revival of Scaliger's theory, partly even with the same arguments.

[60] *Gesch.* 1 2, Leipzig 1893, 863f.: "Die meisten Gelehrten halten es für jüdisch, doch wäre um Vers 104 willen christlicher Ursprung wahrscheinlich, wenn diese Stelle nicht interpolirt ist". And *ibid.* II 1, Leipzig 1897, 589: "Das Gedicht enthält einen Stoff, der den Juden und Christen gemeinsam ist. Da alle evangelischen und christlichen Merkmale in dieser poetischen Moralpredigt fehlen, wird man jüdischen Ursprung für wahrscheinlicher halten. Allein dann muss V. 104 eine christliche (heidnische?) Interpolation sein".

[61] Cambridge 1885. Unfortunately, this book was inaccessible to me. The data were taken from his later book *The Teaching of the Apostles*, London-Baltimore 1887.

[62] *Doctrina duodecim apostolorum. Canones apostolorum ecclesiastici ac reliquae doctrinae de duabus viis expositiones veteres*, Tübingen 1887.

[63] *Op. cit.* XVIII-XXII.

Apostles,⁶⁴ he reproaches Funk for objecting too much by means of "arguments from the silence of the Phocylidist" (45). That Ps-Phoc. omitted so much is not significant, for Did. itself omitted nothing less than the commandment to honour one's parents. Moreover, the author of *Or. Sib.* II clearly put the passage from Ps-Phoc. into a Two Ways framework (II 150). Therefore, Harris concludes: "It seems to me ... that it is still possible ... to maintain that Ps-Phocylides is either a metrical simplification of our Teaching, or a versification of an earlier book of Discipline with which our own Teaching is not altogether unconnected" (46). So Harris cautiously adds an alternative, for the weakness of his original position is apparent, though Funk offered no alternative of his own.⁶⁵

In 1892, F. Susemihl devoted a paragraph to Ps-Phoc. in his great work on Hellenistic literature.⁶⁶ He presents a concise but good survey of the research on Ps-Phoc. from 1591 to 1891. In the end he subscribes to Bernays' view. He calls our poem a "matte(s) und in vulgärer Sprache abgefasste(s) Spruchgedicht, in welchem den Heiden, aber in höchst vorsichtig zurückhaltender, jeden Anstoss und daher auch namentlich jede Polemik gegen den Götzendienst vermeidender, ebendeshalb aber auch höchst abgeblasster Weise altttestamentliche Moral gepredigt wird" (639f.). It was probably written in Alexandria (see v. 102) round the beginning of our era.

In the same year three other minor contributions to the study of Ps-Phoc. were published. Two of them are short but valuable studies on the manuscript tradition, by A. Ludwich and W. Kroll,⁶⁷ in which they demonstrate that only a few of the very many mss. of Ps-Phoc. are of any great value. A third short contribution is a passage in an article by C. F. G. Heinrici,⁶⁸ in which he signalizes a

---

⁶⁴ See note 61.

⁶⁵ In B. Stade - O. Holtzmann, *Geschichte des Volkes Israel* II, Berlin 1888, 305-9, Holtzmann discusses Ps-Phoc. He agrees almost completely with Bernays.

⁶⁶ *Geschichte der griechischen Literatur in der Alexandrinerzeit* II, Leipzig 1892, 639-44.

⁶⁷ A. Ludwich, *Lectiones Pseudophocylideae*, Königsberg 1892; W. Kroll, "Zur Überlieferung der Pseudophocylidea", *Rheinisches Museum* 47 (1892), 457-9. Though these contributions (and others) should be mentioned, in general it will not be necessary to trouble the reader too much with textual problems. These matters have been studied only in passing, because this is not intended to be a critical edition of the text. I rely upon the recent critical edition by Young (see below).

⁶⁸ "Die urchristliche Überlieferung und das Neue Testament", *Theologische Abhandlungen Carl von Weizsäcker gewidmet*, Freiburg i.B. 1892, 321-52.

number of agreements between Ps-Phoc. and the N.T., and then wonders whether the Greek, the Old Testament, or the Christian element preponderates in the poem.[69] But the agreements mentioned by Heinrici are either very weak or wholly absent,[70] and one wonders how Heinrici could have seen Christian influence. The old position of Scaliger is still persistent.

That is apparent again from a contribution by A. Dieterich in 1893. In his book on the recently discovered *Apocalypse of Peter* [71] he, too, points out the relationship between Did. and Ps-Phoc. He then demonstrates that there is a conspicuous parallelism between the (lists of) types of sinners in Did., Ps-Phoc., *Or. Sib.* and *Apoc. Petri*.[72] This list ultimately derives from a Stoic "Lasterkatalog", but has undergone Christian influence. As regards Ps-Phoc., Dieterich thinks it quite probable that there is in the poem an old core from the real Phocylides, but that this core has undergone all kinds of accretion and revision in the course of the centuries, especially since the third century B.C. under the influence of Stoic ethics; but also Orphic-Pythagorean, Jewish, and Christian influences contributed to the present form of the poem.[73] The period in which it took its final form in this shape falls between 80 and 130 A.D. Dieterich's conclusion is that Ps-Phoc., Did., *Or. Sib.* II and *Apoc. Petri* are part of the "ägyptisch-christliche Literatur, hauptsächlich der ersten Hälfte des zweiten Jahrhunderts" (190).

In 1895 a monograph on Ps-Phoc. by the Hungarian K. Sebestyén appeared.[74] This scholar first discusses the place of Ps-Phoc. in Medieval, Byzantine schools and education and gives a short survey of the most important studies on Ps-Phoc. since Sylburg. Then he declares that he broadly agrees with Bernays.[75] The spirit of Moses infuses the whole poem, but the aim of the author forbade him to put the rather obvious Jewish commandments in the forefront, because in that case he would have failed prematurely

---

[69] *Art. cit.* 333.

[70] See also the criticisms by Rossbroich, *De Pseudo-Phocylideis*, Münster 1910, 20.

[71] *Nekyia. Beiträge zur Erklärung der neuentdeckten Petrusapokalypse*, Leipzig-Berlin 1893, 1913² (repr. Darmstadt 1969).

[72] *Op. cit.* 176f.

[73] *Op. cit.* 180f. Thus he says on vv. 100-108: "Jüdische und pythagoreisch-stoische Unsterblichkeitsauffassung scheint mir da unvermittelt nebeneinander zu stehen" (181 n. 2).

[74] *A Pseudo-Phokylides*, Budapest 1895. Reverend H. G. van der Graaf kindly translated this booklet for my use.

[75] *Op. cit.* 1-6.

to attain his goal, which was to influence the Greeks. He carefully guarded his assumed identity, though to almost every verse there may be found parallels from Pentateuch or from Proverbia, Sirach and Sapientia. The poem does not contain any original thought, and the extent to which Ps-Phoc. makes use of themes in Greek literature and philosophy is wholly determined by his O.T. convictions. An Alexandrian origin is most probable in view of the prohibition of the dissection of corpses, the description of the sea and navigation, etc.[76] Next, Sebestyén enumerates a great number of parallels from the O.T., many of them new ones from Prov., Sir. and Sap. Sal.[77] The prooemium of the poem (vv. 3-7) is a kind of program, because it is a short rendering of the Decalogue, from which the typically Jewish commandments have been omitted. In dating the poem Sebestyén goes his own way. With Goram, he takes the date of composition of Sap. Sal. as *terminus post quem*; but, widely differing from Goram (who dated Sap. Sal. to the middle of the second century B.C.), he dates Sap. Sal. to about 40 A.D., since in his opinion chapters 2 and 3 reflect the sufferings of the Jews in Alexandria during the reign of Caligula. Hence, Ps-Phoc. originated in the second half of the first century A.D. During the short persecution under Caligula, many Jews apostatized, but others then strongly championed their faith, e.g. the author of Sap. Sal. Ps-Phoc. belongs to those who had apostatized, but who, nevertheless, in their hearts wanted to belong to the Jewish community. He wrote this poem in the confidence that in this way he could facilitate things for the Jews by bringing the heathen to a more human way of life.[78] Sebestyén concludes his book with a concise philological commentary.[79] Apart from the dating of the poem, this book actually offers no new points of view.

New points of view are indeed provided by P. Wendland in his study "Die Therapeuten und die philonische Schrift vom beschaulichen Leben" of 1896.[80] He is the first to point out the striking similarities between Ps-Phoc., some passages in Philo's *Hypothetica* (as preserved in Eusebius' *PE* VIII 7) and Josephus' *C.Ap.* II 188-219. He says that these three writings offer "eine Zusammen-

---

[76] *Op. cit.* 7-12.
[77] *Op. cit.* 13-17. It should be said that many of these parallels are far-fetched.
[78] *Op. cit.* 21-29.
[79] *Op. cit.* 32-41. See my Comm.
[80] *Jahrbücher für classische Philologie*, Supplementband 22 (1896), 693-772.

stellung der wichtigsten jüdischen Gesetzesbestimmungen, deren Auswahl durch wesentlich gleiche, vorwiegend moralische Gesichtspunkte bestimmt ist, die kein rein sachliches Interesse hat, sondern die den Standpunkt des Gesetzes als im allgemeinen identisch mit den sittlichen Anschauungen auch der Heiden und darum leicht annehmbar erscheinen lässt" (709). Wendland presents a list of agreements between these three writings.[81] Further, he points out that Ps-Phoc., just like Philo, borrows all kinds of ideas from the popular philosophical diatribe. "Das Verhältnis zu Philo und Josephus wie zur Diatribe machen es sehr wahrscheinlich, dass das pseudophokylideische Gedicht im ersten Jahrhundert nach Chr., also in der Blütezeit der Diatribe entstanden ist" (712). This selecting of commandments and prohibitions from the O.T. with the exclusion of particularistic ideas and ceremonial laws is typical of Jewish apologetics. One put commandments together not so much to exhort people to keep them as to demonstrate the excellence of the Jewish law.[82] In a nutshell Wendland pointed out two new elements, which will always remain part of the discussion; first, the agreements with passages from Philo's *Hyp.* and Josephus' *C.Ap.*; and secondly, the influence of the diatribe.[83]

The twentieth century

a) from 1900 to 1925 (Lincke, Ludwich, Seeberg, Klein, Rossbroich, Beltrami)

In 1903 K. F. A. Lincke contributed to the discussion in a highly curious way with his book *Samaria und seine Propheten*. Though

---

[81] *Op. cit.* 709-712. For a similar list see also E. Kamlah, "Frömmigkeit und Tugend. Die Gesetzesapologie des Josephus C. Ap. 2, 145-295", in: *Josephus-Studien für Otto Michel*, Göttingen 1974, 228-9. Kamlah says that Josephus presents "das Judentum seinen aufgeklärten Lesern in einem griechischen Gewand ... als eine reine, weithin humane Philosophie von hohem metaphysischen, moralischen und praktischen Wert" (220).

[82] *Op. cit.* 713f.

[83] Only in passing the short article of N. G. Dossios, "Über einige Varianten zu den Pseudophocylidea", *Philologus* 56 (1897), 616-620, can be mentioned, in which the *variae lectiones* of one 16th century ms. are listed. Also A. A. Zanolli's book *De Pseudophocylidea*, Venice 1902, is not discussed here since it was not available to me. It is only known to me from Ludwich's review in the *Berliner philologische Wochenschrift* 23 (1903), 1153-5, who extensively points out the innumerable serious mistakes in the author's Latin (even in the book's title, note the femininum); about the contents he only says that it "kritisch-exegetischer Natur ist und dem Leser ebenso viele Überraschungen bietet wie die Form" (1155). From Farina, *Silloge pseudophocilidea*, Naples 1962, we learn that Zanolli mostly agrees with Bernays.

the title does not suggest it, Ps-Phoc. is nevertheless very extensively discussed in this book. The core of his theory is, in his own words, the following: "Das Phokylideische Gedicht ist ein persisches Sittengesetz in griechischer Sprache. Phokylides ist der ins Griechische übersetzte Zarathustra" (59). Lincke strongly emphasizes the cultural unity of the whole ancient Near East (Ionia, Israel, Egypt, Persia) under Persian rule. After the Persian conquest of Asia Minor, Parsism spread there very quickly and strongly influenced the religion and philosophy of the Ionian Greeks, especially in their cultural centre Miletus. Thus people like Xenophanes, Pythagoras and Phocylides became the bearers of Parsistic ideas.[84] On the basis of the great similarity of contents between the fragments of the real Phocylides and the so-called Pseudo-Phocylidean poem, it must be concluded that the latter is authentic. Phocylides was very influential. He influenced e.g. Theognis, Pindar, Aristophanes, but above all Plato. He himself, however, was strongly influenced by Pythagoras; hence the presence of Pythagorean ideas on monotheism, immortality, faithfulness in friendship, justice and concord in Phocylides' poem. But still stronger are the Parsistic influences on Phoc., e.g. in matters of judgment after death, God's wisdom, universal monotheism and other subjects. The poem is "das Denkmal der moralischen Eroberungen des Perserreiches zur Zeit der grossen Könige" (60).

Lincke concedes that there are striking parallels with several parts of the Pentateuch, especially Lev. 19, but also Lev. 18 and Exod. 22 and 23.[85] But these similarities can be fully explained by the great influence of Parsism in Palestine after 538 B.C. Phocylides and the Pentateuch have the same spiritual background. "Die Weisheitslehre des Phokylides wird bei der Erklärung des A.T. nicht mehr zu umgehen sein. Die Religion des Dekalogs ist auch die Religion des Phokylides, des Pythagoras und Zarathustras" (99). Ultimately, it can be assumed that Phocylides served as a model for some parts of the "Mosaic" law, especially for Lev. 19. In Lincke's judgment, Phocylides compares favourably with the author of the Holiness-code, who remains too narrowly nationalistic Jewish, whereas Phocylides' poem is "ein Lehrbuch des universal-ethischen Monotheismus" (75). "Das *heno*theistische Frömmigkeitsideal, das der Levitenkodex aufstellt, ist nicht eben

---

[84] *Op. cit.* 40ff.
[85] *Op. cit.* 64ff.

so rein sittlich bestimmt, wie das Rechtschaffenheitsideal des *Mono*theisten Phokylides" (sic!, 75).

Further, Lincke sees great similarities between Phoc. and the Essenes as described by Philo and Josephus.[86] That is not surprising, however, because the Essenes were a very old tribe from Samaria, where as early as the sixth century B.C. a school of prophets was founded, which was "eine Frucht der Vereinigung des persisch-griechischen Geistes mit schlicht essenischer Frömmigkeit" (137). The main product of this prophetic school was Sap. Sal., which shows strong similarities to Phocylides. Here, too, Parsism is the clue to the solution of the problems raised by similarities.

It is not surprising that nobody has ever taken the trouble to refute Lincke's theories. As Schürer says,[87] it would require a whole book to prove Lincke wrong. Moreover, the fancifulness and far-fetchedness of his theories are too obvious to need demonstration. As will be seen, this was not Lincke's only attempt to defend the authenticity of our poem.

In 1904, A. Ludwich again contributed to the research on Ps-Phoc.[88] As in 1892,[89] he first discusses problems of manuscript tradition. He points out that vv. 1-2 (with the *sphragis*) not only do not occur in many mss., but that also in the mss. that do have these verses the title of the poem is sometimes put between v. 2 and v. 3. The question of whether the first two lines are an integral part of the poem is still very difficult.[90] Subsequently, Ludwich discusses very extensively the value of Ψ for the textual tradition of Ps-Phoc.[91] Ψ is the symbol for a mss. group of *Or. Sib.* II into which vv. 5-79 of Ps-Phoc. have been interpolated, verses which in turn underwent manifold interpolations: 22 lines have been inserted between them in Ψ, some have been omitted. These 22 lines are in Ludwich's view so much worse in language, style and metre than Ps-Phoc. that there is not the slightest doubt that they derive from a later hand. Many of these interpolations are certainly not

---

[86] *Op. cit.* 109ff.

[87] In a short review of Lincke's book in the *Theol. Lit. Zeit.* 28 (1903), 708-710.

[88] A. Ludwich, "Über das Spruchbuch des falschen Phokylides", *Programm Königsberg* 1904, 1-26; idem, "Quaestionum pseudophocylidearum pars altera", *ibid.* 27-32.

[89] See above p. 16 n. 67.

[90] See the discussion of this problem in the Comm. *ad loc.*

[91] *Spruchbuch* 7-18.

consistent with the character of the poem, especially the obviously Christian passages. Furthermore, the passage does not fit into *Or. Sib.* II when considered as a whole. The interpolator (in a double sense) from beginning to end shows himself to be an "unfähiger Stümper" (12). Agreements between mss. of Ps-Phoc. and Ψ' are, therefore, not to be trusted. The extent of Ψ's influence on a ms. determines the latter's value. Ludwich declares that there is only one ms. (V = Vindobonensis, 13th-14th cent.) that was not influenced by Ψ'; hence this is the best ms. of Ps-Phoc. On the basis of this ms. Ludwich proposes a number of emendations.[92]

In his second contribution, Ludwich objects to Bergk's athetizings and Bernays' transpositions of lines (see the Comm.). These cannot be supported in any way. "Von einer ordnenden Hand, die das Spruchbüchlein logisch zu gliedern versucht hätte, ist nicht die leiseste Spur zu bemerken" (28). The safest way is to follow the mss. tradition as far as possible.[93] More important is Ludwich's resistance to Bernays' attempt to get rid of the plural θεοί in some verses in order to save the monotheistic character of the poem. From these very passages Ps-Phoc. appears to have a polytheistic conviction. Οὐρανίδαι and μάκαρες (in vv. 71, 75, 163) fit in with this conclusion very well. So Ps-Phoc. was not a Jew! Since every other typically Jewish element is lacking as well, that must be an established fact. Furthermore, there is no trace of Christian influence; therefore the author must have been a pagan Greek who knew the LXX.[94] "Unser Spruchgedicht enthält grösstentheils griechische Vorstellungen gemischt mit einigen semitischen Sitten- und Vernunftlehren" (32). Finally, Ludwich remarks (probably against Dieterich): "Sprache und Kunststil des ursprünglichen Gedichtes tragen übrigens einen durchaus einheitlichen Charakter und bieten für die Annahme verschiedener Verfasser nicht den allergeringsten Anhaltspunkt" (32).

In a review of Ludwich's treatises,[95] W. Kroll agrees with him in nearly all respects. "Auch damit bin ich einverstanden, dass er (gegen Bernays) die jüdische Konfession des Dichters nicht für erwiesen ansieht; doch möchte ich nicht so zuversichtlich wie er behaupten, dass er ein heidnischer Grieche gewesen ist: einen

---

[92] *Spruchbuch* 20-26.
[93] *Quaestiones* 27-29.
[94] *Quaestiones* 29-32.
[95] *Berliner Philologische Wochenschrift* 25 (1905), 241-243.

hellenisierten Juden von einem judaisierenden Hellenen zu scheiden, ist in solchen Fällen kaum möglich" (243).[96]

In 1906, A. Seeberg opened a new perspective for the research on Ps-Phoc. He takes up again the problem, already posed in 1885, of the agreements between Ps-Phoc. and the Didache, but now in a much wider perspective. In his book *Die beiden Wege und das Aposteldekret*[97] he develops further a thesis already put forward in his earlier work *Der Katechismus der Urchristenheit*.[98] His thesis is that the so-called Two Ways doctrine originally was a Jewish proselyte-catechism, and was later taken over by Christians with some modifications as baptismal instruction. Seeberg now tries to trace the contents of the Jewish Two Ways doctrine by comparing a number of early Christian writings. The most important features appear to be the incorporation of almost the whole of Lev. 19 into this document, and also the combination of the Golden Rule with commandments from the Decalogue, in which it is notable that the commandment to honour one's parents is always put *after* the commandments of the second table. It is Ps-Phoc. who demonstrates that this Two Ways doctrine already existed in Judaism in pre-Christian times. "Das pseudophokylideische Gedicht weist in seinem ersten Teil (v. 3-24) eine enge Anlehnung an die Wege auf" (25). Vv. 3-8 are an enumeration of commandments from the Decalogue occurring in the Two Ways (with the honouring of one's parents after the commandments of the second table); and to vv. 9-24 there are numerous parallels in Lev. 19 and in the rest of the Two Ways doctrine.[99] This fits in excellently with Bernays' thesis about Lev. 19 as the main source of this part of the poem.[100] In the rest of the poem too there are traces of the Two Ways.[101] Seeberg finds a proof of the correctness

---

[96] Cf. A. Dieterich's more critical remarks in *ARW* 8 (1905), 501. The article on Ps-Phoc. by S. Krauss in the *Jewish Encyclopedia* X (New York-London 1905), 255-6, offers no new points of view. Krauss almost completely agrees with Bernays and regards the author as an Alexandrian Jew who wrote the poem between 150 B.C. and 150 A.D. for the purpose of propaganda.

[97] Leipzig 1906.

[98] Leipzig 1903, repr. München 1966 (in the series Theologische Bücherei). Cf. also his later book *Die Didache des Judentums und der Urchristenheit*, Leipzig 1908.

[99] On pp. 27-30 Seeberg presents many of these parallels.

[100] Quite curiously, Seeberg consistently speaks of Bernay (sic.). This occurs so often that it cannot be regarded as a printer's error.

[101] A striking example is mentioned by Seeberg on p. 30 n. 1: "Vergleicht man Aristides *Apol.* 15, 3-7 mit dem pseudophokylideischen Gedicht, so ergibt sich dass fast alles in diesem wiederkehrt".

of his thesis in the fact that the author of *Or. Sib.* II still knew the connection between Ps-Phoc. and the Two Ways, because in his own interpolations into that part of Ps-Phoc. which he had himself incorporated into it, the influence of the Two Ways is quite clear. The whole Ps-Phoc. passage has been put there into a Two Ways framework. The Golden Rule combined with (parts of) the Decalogue belonged to the instruction of proselytes; hence also the Two Ways doctrine belonged to it. So Ps-Phoc. is partly based upon Jewish instruction of proselytes.[102]

An article of 1908 by the Italian A. Beltrami [103] should be mentioned in passing. In it he lists a great number of parallels to about 70 percent of the lines of Ps-Phoc. both from the Old and the New Testament. Many of his references are wrong since the "vestigia" (see the title) are very farfetched, especially in the case of N.T. texts. Beltrami's theory of the Essene origin of our poem will be discussed later (see p. 31).

In 1909, the visionary Lincke gave a second contribution to the discussion with an article on "Phokylides und die Essener".[104] The agreements between Ps-Phoc. and Essene doctrines as described by Philo and Josephus, already signalized by him in 1903, are here discussed and elucidated in Lincke's very own way. The Essenes were an old tribe that lived in Northern Palestine as early as the time of Rechab. Here they were strongly influenced, already in the sixth century B.C., by Pythagoras whose monotheism, belief in immortality and the harmony of spheres are also found in Phoc. (our Ps-Phoc.). The Holiness-Code (Lev. 17-26) is to a great extent based upon Phoc., and the Decalogue, the youngest part of the Pentateuch, is in its turn an excerpt of the Holiness-Code. So Phoc. is an ancestor of the Decalogue! Therefore "gebührt dem Lehrgedichte des milesischen Pythagoreers ein Ehrenplatz in der allgemeinen Religions- und Kulturgeschichte, besonders in der Geschichte des Christentums" (136). The universalistic

---

[102] On pp. 94-102 ("Josephus und die jüdischen Wege") Seeberg tries to corroborate his theory by using numerous parallels from Josephus, where the latter demonstrably draws on a Two Ways document. Throughout his book, Seeberg wants to demonstrate for more than 20 percent of our poem an origin in the Two Ways doctrine.

[103] "Ea quae apud Pseudo-Phocylidem Veteris et Novi Testamenti vestigia deprehenduntur", *Rivista di Filologia e Istruzione Classica* 36 (1908), 411-423.

[104] *Die Grenzboten (Zeitschrift für Politik, Literatur und Kunst)* 68 (1909), 128-138.

tendency of the Decalogue is due to Persian influence. The Essenes, too, demonstrate in their ethics a strong Persian tendency thanks to Phocylides' influence, whose only God is Ahura Mazda and whose ethics is Zoroastrian. So: Zoroastrian = Pythagorean = Essene, and the central figure in all these complex cultural connections is Phocylides with his influential gnomic poem. It can be seen again that Lincke is bewitched by his own pan-Zoroastrianism.

In the same year there appeared an important book written by the Stockholm Rabbi G. Klein.[105] Klein argues that in Israel there had always been, alongside the priest with his Torah, the Sage (*chakam*) with his more universalistic attitude. Especially after Ezra's nationalistic legislation, there was opposition from these Sages (e.g. the books Jona, Ruth). The only thing the Sage wanted to do was to shed light on all aspects of life from his religious point of view, and that for all people, without the name Israel coming from his lips. This universal ethics, also called the Way, later got the name *Derek Erez* (lit. "the way of the world" = correct behaviour). "In dieser sollten die für alle Menschen gültigen ethischen Normen zusammengefasst werden" (62). *Derek Erez* is "die mittels der Vernunft erkannte und vom Gewissen eines jeden Menschen bezeugte Norm der Sittlichkeit. Mit einem Worte: Derek Erez ist identisch mit 'natürlicher Religion'" (63). Only for pagans had *derek erez* an independent value; for Israel the Torah was always valid too. These universalistic tendencies in Israel were very much frustrated by the great wars of 66 and 132 A.D., after which these attempts to humanize the pagan world declined strongly.[106]

Subsequently, Klein discusses some Derek Erez tractates of a later date (*Tanna debe Eliahu, Orchoth Chajjim, Aboth de Rabbi Nathan, Derek Erez Zuta* and *Rabba*),[107] but with the remark "Als Träger dieser Lehre durch die Welt bewährten sich die alexandrinischen Missionäre besser als die palästinischen" (80), he turns

---

[105] *Der älteste christliche Katechismus und die jüdische Propagandaliteratur*, Berlin 1909.
[106] *Op. cit.* 8-65.
[107] *Op. cit.* 66-142. To this chapter apply the criticisms by J. E. Crouch, *The Origin and Intention of the Colossian Haustafel*, Göttingen 1972, 16 n. 16: "the major weakness of Klein's study is ... his occasional willingness to project late sources back into an earlier period". Cf. also W. D. Davies, *Paul and Rabbinic Judaism*, London 1955², 134f. Klein is defended by H. J. Schoeps, *Paulus*, Tübingen 1959, 236f.

to Philo. He says that Philo's treatises *De humanitate* and *Hypothetica* (*ap.* Eus. *PE*) are compendia of *derek erez* commandments. *Hypothetica* centers upon "die Besprechung solcher jüdischen Gebote, deren Befolgung er auch einem nichtjüdischen Leserkreis ...'anraten' (ὑποτίθεσθαι, cf. ὑποθήκη) konnte" (84). Also Josephus' *Contra Apionem* draws on traditional *derek erez* materials.[108] Klein concludes: "Aus dem Angeführten ergibt sich, dass ein Bedürfnis vorhanden war, kurze Kompendien behufs Bekehrung der Heiden zu verfassen. Im Vordergrund der Predigt stand natürlich die Lehre von den Wegen Gottes. Als Einführung in dieselbe und als Vorbereitung auf dieselbe wurden zunächst moralische Lehren und soziale Tugenden, in Palästina Derek Erez oder noachidische Gebote genannt, vorgetragen. Diese Lehren wurden an die goldene Regel angeknüpft. Mit dieser verband man auch andere, den Heiden bekannte, natürliche Moralvorschriften. Diesen wurde ein monotheistisches Gepräge aufgedrückt, indem sie als 'ungeschriebene' Gesetze des einen Gottes, für die ganze Menschheit bestimmt, angesehen wurden" (93f.).

In the next chapter [109] Klein discusses Ps-Phoc. His thesis is as follows: "Den ältesten Katechismus für die Heiden besitzen wir im pseudophokylideischen Gedicht" (143). Bernays' reproach that the prohibition of idolatry should not have been omitted by Ps-Phoc. is dismissed by Klein: Bernays misjudges the task that Ps-Phoc. has set himself. It is historically demonstrable that in missionary practice idolatry was not aggressively attacked. According to rabbinic halaka idolatry should be ridiculed or mocked; but the universalistic missionaries have consciously dissociated themselves from this nationalistic halaka. Keeping the commandments was more important than the right view of God. "In diesem Geiste arbeitete auch Phokylides. Ihm war es hauptsächlich darum zu tun, eine Anleitung zum sittlichen Leben zu geben. Ruhig und sachgemäss, ohne Angriffe auf das Heidentum, legt er die Gesetze des moralischen Monotheismus dar. Wie die Chakamim der Bibel nimmt er auf Israel keine Rücksicht, kennt er kein spezifisch israelitisches Gebot. Und was er mit seiner Arbeit bezweckt, das sagt er unzweideutig am Schlusse seines Gedichtes: vv. 229-230 [quotation of these lines]. So verheisst denn auch Phokylides, dem Psalmisten (Ps. 34) gleich, demjenigen, der vom bösen weicht,

---

[108] Cf. Wendland's observations (1896), above p. 18f.
[109] *Op. cit.* 143-150.

d.h. nach ihm, der den 'Weihen der Gerechtigkeit' gemäss lebt, ein langes Leben" (147). Klein then quotes a number of parallels to Ps-Phoc. from *derek erez* literature,[110] from which it appears, in his view, that Ps-Phoc. knew not only the written but also the oral (Palestinian) doctrine. This *derek erez* material also lies behind Didache I-VI and other early Christian writings in which the Two Ways doctrine plays a role. So Ps-Phoc. is a Greek version of a *derek erez* catechism. "Ausgerüstet mit diesem Katechismus, wenden sich die jüdischen Missionäre an die Heiden, um sie zur Sinnesänderung zu bewegen. Was aber sollte der Endzweck dieser Bekehrung sein? Wollte man die Heiden zu Juden machen? Nach meinem Dafürhalten hat man in der vorchristlichen Zeit sich diese Frage gar nicht vorgelegt. Denkt man sich einen Teil der Missionare als Fortsetzer der Chakamim, so kam es auch ihnen auf den Namen Israel nicht an. Die Hauptsache war den Heiden die Augen zu öffnen, sie zur Besinnung auf sich selbst zu bringen, ihnen ein sittliches Ideal einzuschärfen. Zeuge des ist das Gedicht des Phokylides, das sich so wenig wie die Weisheitsliteratur um speziell jüdische Gebote kümmert" (244). To conclude, Klein's book presents an important new theory for understanding the poet's purpose.

In the same year Schürer proposed a different theory.[111] Against Ludwich he defends the Jewish origin of the poem. About the author's purpose he says: "Der Verfasser will zunächst nur für die jüdische Moral wirken. Die beiden religiösen Grundideen des Judentums, die der Einheit Gottes und der künftigen Vergeltung, sind zwar auch bei ihm vorhanden, und er tritt auch indirekt für dieselben ein. Aber er tut es in so zurückhaltender Weise, dass man sieht, es ist ihm in erster Linie doch nur um die Moral zu tun" (619). It is precisely this restriction to morals that makes Schürer doubt whether the author intended to win over pagan readers to his ideas.[112] "Dann sollte man ein stärkeres Hervortreten der jüdischen Anschauungen erwarten. Schreibt dagegen ein Jude für Juden, so ist die Beschränkung auf die Moral leichter verständlich,

---

[110] *Op. cit.* 150-153.

[111] *Geschichte des jüdischen Volkes im Zeitalter Jesu Christi* III, Leipzig 1909⁴, 617-622.

[112] Contrast Schürer's own position in the first edition of his work 35 years earlier (under the title *Lehrbuch der neutestamentlichen Zeitgeschichte*, Leipzig 1874), where he says: "Es (sc. the poem) hat ... den Zweck, heidnische Leser zum Judenthum zu bekehren" (642).

weil dann die gemeinsamen religiösen Anschauungen als selbstverständlich vorausgesetzt werden" (619). This leads Schürer to consider whether the ascription of the poem to Phocylides (in vv. 1-2) was added by a later hand; because it would have taken a rather eccentric Jew indeed to write for fellow Jews under a pagan pseudonym. But Schürer himself concedes that "die ganze sprachliche Form des Gedichts" (the Ionic!) speaks against this theory.

In 1910 the first line by line commentary on Ps-Phoc. was published. It was written by Martin Rossbroich,[113] a pupil of Wilhelm Kroll. This important book is divided into an introduction (pp. 3-25), a commentary (pp. 25-102), and an epilogue (pp. 102-103). Rossbroich's interpretation of the individual verses will be dealt with in the Commentary. Here attention will be given to his Introduction and to the character of his commentary as a whole.

His chapter *De re metrica* (3-10) is interesting only in so far as a metrical analysis of the poem demonstrates that Ps-Phoc. shows many resemblances *in metricis* to later epic poetry, and also that on metrical grounds it is improbable that more than one author has worked at the poem. In the chapter *De vocibus* (10-16) Rossbroich tries to show that Ps-Phoc.'s vocabulary agrees to a great extent with that of authors from the Hellenistic and Roman period. He discusses 55 words from the poem and illustrates their usage by citing passages from many Greek authors. More important is the chapter *De auctore* (16-23), in which Rossbroich attacks Bernays. In his view, the poem is by no means a rephrasing of ethical principles from the O.T. omitting all nationalistic-Jewish aspects, because the poem is hardly Jewish at all. In vv. 71-75 the stars are called gods and that seems to exclude a Jewish origin. A Christian origin or redaction can also be excluded. Yet it is quite clear that the LXX has played some part in the poem's origin. But the agreements with the LXX do not prove that the author was a Jew. The author must have been a "proselyte".[114] The frequent use of θεός (once εἷς θεός) shows that the author was a worshipper of a θεὸς ὕψιστος. But the presence of polytheistic traits combined with reminiscences of the O.T. strongly suggests that the author was a proselyte (read: God-fearer). This hypothesis explains both the

---

[113] *De Pseudo-Phocylideis*, diss. Münster 1910.

[114] "Ego ... astricte contendo auctorem fuisse προσήλυτον" (21). From what follows, it appears that by προσήλυτος Rossbroich means a σεβόμενος, a "God-fearer". This wrong identification is made very often; see Moore, *Judaism* I 326ff.

pagan and the Jewish elements. "Auctorem abscondere et opprimere suam religionem dici non iam necesse est" (23). In the last chapter of the Introduction, *De aetate auctoris* (23-25), Rossbroich states that the *terminus ante quem* is the beginning of the third century A.D., when the second book of *Or. Sib.* was composed, and that the *terminus post quem* is 50 B.C. because Posidonian influences are traceable in the poem. Since there is also strong influence from the Stoic-Cynic diatribe that flourished in the first century A.D., the poem probably originated in that century.

Rossbroich's commentary on the text is characterized by a continuous attempt to demonstrate that where earlier scholars assumed LXX influence, nevertheless a non-Jewish origin of the verses concerned is more probable. The very few Jewish parallels he quotes are only from the LXX, Philo and Josephus (never from pseudepigrapha or early rabbinic literature). Furthermore, he heavily emphasizes the Cynic (and Stoic) character of many maxims and the influence of Posidonius.[115] Rossbroich continually points out that the poem does not show any principle of composition and that the author often put together heterogeneous and dissimilar materials in a very clumsy way, sometimes even in one verse.

An important, critical review of Rossbroich's book was written by J. Sitzler.[116] On Rossbroich's treatment of metrics he says: "Man darf nicht vergessen, ... dass wir es hier nicht mit einem eigentlichen Dichter zu tun haben, sondern nur mit einem Manne, der die dichterische Form, so gut es eben ging, wählte, um seinen Lehren mehr Eingang zu verschaffen" (449). More serious, however are his criticisms of the proselyte-hypothesis. The so-called polytheistic verses (71-75, 104, 163) cannot indeed have been written by a Jew, but not by a proselyte either. There were two kinds of proselytes, the first of which were obliged to keep all Jewish commandments, the second only the Noachian laws, which contained, however, the prohibition of idolatry. Yet the whole poem clearly has a Jewish character. It should, therefore, be assumed that these typically non-Jewish verses are spurious: vv. 71-75 are already missing in the *Vorlage* of *Or. Sib.* II (intentional omission is an unjustified surmise [117]), v. 104 disrupts the sequence of 103 and

---

[115] This, of course, is quite compatible with the Posidonius-rage of the first quarter of the twentieth century.

[116] *Wochenschrift für klassische Philologie* 29 (1912), 449-457.

[117] Rossbroich 19 reasons the other way round: the fact that the author of *Or. Sib.* II omits vv. 71-75 proves that Ps-Phoc. is no Jew.

105, and v. 163 is lacking in some mss. So not one of these un-Jewish lines is authentic. Hence the author may have been a common Jew, who did not intend to propagandize for Judaism but only wanted to give instruction for every day practice. Sitzler protests against Rossbroich's heavy accentuating the influence of the diatribe: "... im ganzen Gedicht findet sich nicht *ein* Gedanke, der den Stoikern oder Kynikern ausschliesslich angehörte" (452). Furthermore, Posidonius' influence has been exaggerated by Rossbroich: "Viel wahrscheinlicher ist, ... dass unser Dichter seine griechische Weisheit aus Sammelwerken, Gnomologien geschöpft habe. Das Bezeichnende in seinem Gedicht ist entschieden das Jüdische, und deswegen halte ich den Dichter für einen mit der griechischen Literatur bekannten Juden" (452).

Thereafter, Sitzler discusses the incoherency of the poem and he points out that this is a common phenomenon in gnomologies. "Die Verfasser begnügen sich damit, Gedankengruppen ohne scharfe Abgrenzung zu bilden und innerhalb dieser je nach Neigung oder Möglichkeit die Vorschriften kurz zu geben oder weiter auszuführen. Beide Merkmale zeigt auch unser Gedicht" (452). Sitzler then points out that these characteristics facilitated the omission and interpolation of verses. The mss. of Ps-Phoc. certainly prove that. Rossbroich's reproach of incoherency between lines and passages is unjustified in so far as he should have investigated whether verses have fallen out or been added. He could have done this by studying the Ψ-tradition of *Or. Sib.* In this group of mss. a much more coherent tradition can be found than in our mss. of Ps-Phoc. In Ψ there is no question of omissions and interpolations, but of an older type of text which is more original.[118] On the basis of Ψ Sitzler then proposes a large number of athetizings, emendations and metatheses, which are often original but mostly unprovable and unnecessary. His high estimation of Ψ has found few followers (there is but one exception).[119]

Lincke, who has already been mentioned, contributed in 1911

---

[118] Hereby Sitzler took a position diametrically opposed to earlier investigators (e.g. Bernays, and esp. Ludwich), who had demonstrated that ψ has no value as a witness for the text of Ps-Phoc.

[119] On Kurfess (1939) see below. Here it may be observed briefly that Sitzler (following Bernays 234 n. 2) wrongly takes the view that the scholion on Aristophanes' *Nubes* 240 points to a "Nachweisung der Unechtheit" (456) already in antiquity. We shall return to this below in connection with Dornseiff (see p. 39 n. 151).

for the third and last time to the research of Ps-Phoc. in an article entitled "Phokylides, Isokrates und der Dekalog".[120] On the basis of a number of parallels between the pseudo-Isocratic *Ad Demonicum* and Ps-Phoc. he concludes that the poem already existed before the fourth century B.C. Therefore it must be authentic. It proclaims the new ethics of Pythagoras. The agreements with the Decalogue and Lev. 19 can be explained by the far-reaching influence of Pythagorean ethics upon several nations in the ancient world. Phocylides' poem is "ein Denkmal der Ethik des Pythagoras und ihres Einflusses auf die mosaische Schriftstellerei" (442). Apart from the (very weak) argument for the authenticity of the poem on the basis of agreements with *Ad. Dem.* the article adds nothing new to what he had already stated in his former publications. None of Lincke's contributions has ever been taken seriously by other scholars.[121]

In 1913 Beltrami, whose collection of Biblical parallels to Ps-Phoc. (1908) has already been mentioned, tried to demonstrate the Essene origin of the poem.[122] He begins his article with an attempt to prove that originally the poem consisted of six rounded "ecloghe morali", which were lost by transposition of lines in the course of the transmission of the text. These eclogues successively dealt with religious duties, justice, moderation, humanity, self-restraint and duties towards one's children. Under this division Beltrami tries to distribute every verse. Then follows a great number of parallels from Philo and Josephus to each of these six eclogues, several of which are very far-fetched.[123] He intends to show by this that Ps-Phoc. has his roots in Hellenistic Judaism. Subsequently he supports this by demonstrating a number of similarities between Ps-Phoc. and Josephus' (and Philo's) description of the Essenes.[124] He thinks Ps-Phoc. is an adherent of that sect. The Essenes were strongly influenced by Greek ideas, as was Ps-Phoc. However, Beltrami does not question the historical reliability of Josephus' account. Moreover, his parallels are to a great extent

---

[120] *Philologus* 70 (1911), 438-442.
[121] It can be mentioned only in passing that F. Rudisch, "Zur Überlieferung der Pseudophocylidea", *Wiener Studien* 35 (1913), 386-88, merely discusses the variant readings in a 15th century ms. from Vienna.
[122] "Spirito giudaico e specialmente essenico della silloge pseudofocilidea", *Rivista di Filologia e Istruzione Classica* 41 (1913), 513-48.
[123] *Art. cit.* 520-42.
[124] *Art. cit.* 543-8.

commonplaces and he adduces no parallels from Ps. Phoc. to the typically Essene elements in Josephus' account. So his thesis is very weak.[125]

In the same year, another Italian author, J. Raspante, proposed a still more radical theory concerning the original form of the poem.[126] According to Raspante, the original poem consisted of only 90 verses, 30 clusters of 3 lines, subdivided into 15 triads on duties towards others plus 15 triads on duties towards oneself and members of the family. He supposes that this poem was written in the beginning of the Hellenistic era by a pagan Greek, but later rewritten and expanded by an Alexandrian grammarian, a Stoic

---

[125] Beltrami gets some support from E. Zeller, *Philosophie der Griechen* III 2, Leipzig 1923[5], 291 n. 3, who sees in vv. 71-5 and 102-8 ideas related to those of the Essenes. For Zeller's theory about the Essenes see *ibid.* 307-377. But see the criticisms by O. Stählin in Christ-Schmid, *Gesch. der griech. Lit.* II 1, München 1920[6], 622 n. 7: "Der Versuch Beltramis, essenischen Ursprung nachzuweisen, ist ebensowenig überzeugend wie seine Aussonderung von einer Anzahl 'moralischer Eklogen', die den Grundstock der ursprünglichen Sammlung gebildet haben sollen". Cf. also W. Bousset (-H. Gressmann), *Religion des Judentums*, Tübingen 1926[3], 462 n. 1: "In der gesammten uns erhaltenen späteren jüdischen Literatur kann man kaum eine Schrift, so oft das auch versucht ist, der essenischen Sekte zuweisen. Es findet sich zwar überall hier und da einiges, was man essenisch nennen könnte. Aber es findet sich auch in allen spezifisch Nichtessenisches. Und gerade die besonderen Eigentümlichkeiten des essenischen Ordens finden sich nirgends".
How sloppily Beltrami works is apparent, for instance, when he quotes Jos. *Bell*. II 136 σπουδάζουσι δ' ἐκτόπως περὶ τὰ τῶν παλαιῶν συντάγματα, μάλιστα τὰ πρὸς ὠφέλειαν ψυχῆς καὶ σώματος ἐκλέγοντες, and calls this passage the "luogo di capitale importanza per l'ammissione della mia tesi che il probabile compositore dell' attuale silloge pseudofocilidea sia stato un Ebreo esseno. Cfr. v. 228-230" (544). But he does not say that Josephus' text goes on as follows: ἔνθεν αὐτοῖς πρὸς θεραπείαν παθῶν ῥίζαι τε ἀλεξητήριοι καὶ λίθων ἰδιότητες ἀνερευνῶνται. Thackeray, in a note in the Loeb-edition (vol. II p. 374), rightly remarks that the text is about charms or amulets. Zeller (*Philos*. III 2, 333) says that probably magic books are meant here. This has nothing at all to do with vv. 228-230 of Ps-Phoc. and is even incompatible with v. 149 φάρμακα μὴ τεύχειν, μαγικῶν βίβλων ἀπέχεσθαι. So the "luogo di capitale importanza" for Beltrami's thesis fails to stand.
He defended this same thesis more elaborately in his book *Studi pseudofocilidei*, Florence 1913. Unfortunately, this book was not available to me. From Farina (see below) it can be learned that Beltrami has called the original poem a *summarium* of Hesiod's *Erga* here on the basis of agreements between the *Erga* and Ps-Phoc. 153-174, lines which Beltrami considers as the nucleus of the poem.

[126] *Sulla composizione e sull' autore del Carme Pseudofocilideo*, Catania 1913. Unfortunately, this book was also inaccessible to me. I know about the contents only from the reviews by L. Cohn, *Sokrates* 3 (1915), 234-7, and by J. Sitzler, *Wochenschr. für klass. Philol.* 33 (1916), 699-702.

philosopher, a Hellenistic Jew, and a Byzantine Christian.[127] Consequently, 140 lines do not belong to the original poem, including every verse with O.T. allusions. The Jewish character is, therefore, wholly secondary. Also many repetitions and the incoherency of the poem are due to these later interpolators. The critics (Cohn, Sitzler) remark that Raspante's poem of 90 lines still suffers from the same defect as the poem of 230 lines, as it has been handed down, viz. the same kind of incoherency and repetitions. Moreover, several lines concocted by Raspante from parts of other lines are still less acceptable than the ones in the poem in its present form. Both Cohn and Sitzler think it is still most probable that the poem was written, more or less in its present form, by a hellenized Jew in the first century A.D. Raspante's theory is sheer arbitrariness.[128]

Criticism of Raspante is also found in the work of Otto Stählin who, in 1920, devoted a paragraph to Ps-Phoc. in his chapter on Hellenistic-Jewish literature in W. von Christ's *Geschichte der griechischen Literatur*.[129] "An der Einheitlichkeit des Gedichtes ist nicht zu zweifeln; weder Sprache noch Inhalt berechtigen zur Annahme verschiedener Verfasser" (622). Stählin feels somewhat attracted to Rossbroich's "proselyte"-hypothesis, since traces of Greek ways of thought as well as dependence on the Jewish Law can certainly be explained in such a way. About the relation to the Didache he says that both writings drew upon a common Jewish source. The poem is "ein interessantes Zeugnis für jenes Zusammenfliessen jüdischer und griechischer Gedanken, bei dem die Herkunft der einzelnen Teile oft nicht mehr festgestellt werden kann" (622).

---

[127] Following the rendering by Cohn. According to Sitzler: by a Stoicizing Alexandrian grammarian, afterwards by Jews and Christians.

[128] In 1914 a book by N. G. Dossios (cf. n 83 on p. 19) appeared, *Quelques variantes dans les Phokylideia d'après un manuscrit du 17ᵉ siècle de Janina (Épire)*, Le Puy-en-Velay 1914. Again this book was inaccessible to me, but the title indicates that it is of minor importance for our purpose. During the First World War, no studies on Ps-Phoc. appeared. It may be mentioned here that Otto Weinreich in his *Stiftung und Kultsatzungen eines Privatheiligtums in Philadelpheia in Lydien*, Sitzungsberichte der Heidelberger Akademie der Wissenschaften, Phil.-hist. Klasse XVI, 1919, 58f., points out a number of striking agreements between the precepts on the inscription of this little sanctuary (= Dittenberger, *Sylloge* III 985, second century B.C.) and Ps-Phoc. (prohibition of murder, wiles, magic, abortion and several sexual sins). The material is insufficient to draw conclusions. The parallels will be noted in the Comm.

[129] *Gesch*. II 1, München 1920⁶, 621f.

Stählin assumes that the poem was written in the first century A.D.[130]

b) *From 1925 to 1945 (Guttmann, Dornseiff, Kroll)*

In a book dated 1925, *Ecclesiastes and the Early Greek Wisdom Literature,* Harry Ranston attempted to demonstrate that there is an old, authentic core in Ps-Phoc.[131] He enumerates some parallels between Qoheleth and Ps-Phoc. and concludes: "The evidence strongly points to some connexion" (82). He also states that it is not probable that Ps-Phoc. has drawn upon Qoheleth, since this O.T. book was one of the disputed books of the O.T. canon till the end of the first century A.D. "If then the author of the Pseudo-Phokylideia is endeavouring to set before Greek readers what to him are important elements in O.T. thought, it is surprising that he used a book so disputed as Ecclesiastes. To many Jews it could not be regarded as in any way typically Jewish" (82f.). Hence, it must be assumed that the similarities are to be explained by Qoheleth's borrowing from Ps-Phoc., or rather from Phocylides. Presumably the poem contains a core of authentic maxims of the real Phocylides which have been used by both Qoheleth and Ps-Phoc. This old core has later been expanded by an Alexandrian Jew.[132]

Though strictly speaking it is not a contribution to the research on Ps-Phoc., the third edition of Bousset's masterpiece *Die Religion des Judentums im späthellenistischen Zeitalter* [133] is worth mentioning here. Bousset refers only four or five times to Ps-Phoc., but always so that his position in Judaism, especially Hellenistic Judaism, becomes very clear. Ps-Phoc. fits in very well with the total picture of Hellenistic Judaism as it is drawn by Bousset. However,

---

[130] Though it is not my intention to deal with the history of the text and text-editions, yet the first critical edition of the poem since Bergk, by E. Diehl in his *Anthologia Lyrica,* Leipzig 1923, may be mentioned here with honour. This edition was revised by R. Beutler in 1950 and by D. Young in 1960 (1971²). It had a much better manuscript basis than Bergk's edition.

[131] *Op. cit.,* cap. III (Ecclesiastes and Phokylides), 79-84.

[132] Criticisms of Ranston are made by K. Galling, "Stand und Aufgabe der Kohelet-Forschung", *Theologische Rundschau* N.F. 6 (1934), 361-6 (esp. against Ranston's thesis of Qohelet's dependence on Theognis).

[133] Tübingen 1926³, edited by H. Gressmann (= 1966⁴, edited by E. Lohse). In the matters to be discussed this third impression is not different from the first in 1903. When calling this book a masterpiece, I am well aware of its limitations and defects and of the serious criticisms levelled against it.

he emphasizes that the non-particularistic attitude, as we find it in Ps-Phoc. and sometimes in Philo and Josephus, remains exceptional in the whole Jewish culture of those days. The average Jew certainly was different from that, also in the Diaspora.[134] He also points out a tendency to "Verflachung" and "Utilitarismus" in later Jewish Wisdom maxims, e.g. the (Syriac) Sentences of Menander, Ps-Phoc. and also in the Testaments of the Twelve Patriarchs and the ethical maxims of some early rabbis.[135] Bousset also remarks that the ethics of Hellenistic Judaism passed by national and public life and mainly concentrated upon the private and social life of the individual, being therein primarily prohibitive (cf. the frequent μή in Ps-Phoc.).[136] Therefore, Bousset's book is of great importance for locating the poem of Ps-Phoc. in its cultural context.

In 1927, an important contribution came from the Jewish scholar M. Guttmann in his book *Das Judentum und seine Umwelt*. In a discussion of the Noachian laws [137] he remarks that the important thing about these commandments is that they undeniably have universal traits. They are prescripts from which anything nationally or geographically or historically distinct has been stripped. The following passages deserve to be quoted in full: "Aus dem Noachidenprinzip erklärt sich am einfachsten die Bewegung der 'Gottesfürchtigen'. Darin, dass man Heiden für die Grundlehren vom einzigen Gott und für eine auf Sittenreinheit und Gerechtigkeit sich aufbauende Ethik gewinne, die ja mit den Noachidengeboten identisch sind, sah das gesetzestreue Judentum keinen Akt des Proselytismus im religionspolitischen Sinne, keine Vergrösserung des synagogalen Machtbereichs, sondern einen vom jüdischen Gemeinschaftsinteresse ganz unabhängigen rein religiösen Selbstzweck. Da nun einmal die Tora eine Urgesetzgebung für die ganze Menschheit enthält, so hält der Israelit die Menschheit für verpflichtet, dieser Urgesetzgebung zu gehorchen, und fühlt auch sich selbst dazu verpflichtet die Menschheit darüber aufzuklären, und in diesem Sinne auf sie einzuwirken. Das ist der feste Punkt von dem man auszugehen hat, wenn man die jüdische Propaganda richtig verstehen will. Die Versuche, in der weitver-

---

[134] *Op. cit.* 136.
[135] *Op. cit.* 411.
[136] *Op. cit.* 421ff.
[137] *Op. cit.* 98ff.

zweigten 'Gottesfürchtigen'-Bewegung jüdischerseits eine Art von Proselytenmacherei, oder wie manche sich ausdrucken, eine Art von Seelenfängerei zu erblicken, sind ganz verfehlt. Schon der Name 'Gottesfürchtiger', den der neugewonnene Gläubige erhält, schliesst jeden glaubenspolitischen Gesichtspunkt aus. Das erste, wodurch die Zugehörigkeit eines Anhängers zur Kirche dokumentiert wird, ist zweifellos die Benennung, die ihm beigelegt wird, und gerade die Benennung ist hier neutral. 'Gottesfürchtiger' ist jeder, der Gott fürchtet bzw. verehrt, ohne Rücksicht auf seine Zugehörigkeit zum Judentum" (110f.). "Dieser Eifer (sc. zur Gewinnung von 'Gottesfürchtigen') hat mit dem konfessionellen Moment so wenig zu tun, dass sich der Jude als solcher nicht selten in einen unsichtbaren Hintergrund zurückzieht, ein Pseudonym annimmt und unter heidnischer Maske an die Heiden herangeht" (111). Then on Ps-Phoc.: "Freilich haben wir es hier mit einer religiösen Propaganda zu tun, sie ist aber keine konfessionelle. Ein jüdischer Autor, der es so gut versteht, das spezifisch jüdische, oder sagen wir konfessionelle, aus einer speziell der religiösen Propaganda gewidmeten Schrift fernzuhalten, dass er anderthalb Jahrtausend unerkannt geblieben ist, muss ein anderes Ideal gehabt haben als das eines konfessionellen Proselytenmachers. Nicht Juden wollte er aus den Heiden machen, sondern 'Gottesfürchtige' oder fromme Noachiden. Diese sich selbst verleugnende Propaganda führt unmittelbar oder mittelbar auf den altjüdischen Grundsatz zurück, dass es eine Uroffenbarung gebe, der die ganze Menschheit sich unterordnen müsse, und dass es verdienstlich, ja, heilige Pflicht sei, die Menschheit zu ihrem Gotte zurückzuführen" (112). It can be seen here how the thesis of Klein (1909) is worked out (without involving the catechism and the *derek erez* literature in the discussion, probably rightly). Guttmann's very clear statements about the intention of Ps-Phoc. are important, because they have exerted a great influence on some later scholars who have worked on Ps-Phoc.[138]

---

[138] E.g. on J. E. Crouch, *The Origin and Intention of the Colossian Haustafel*, Göttingen 1972, 93, who cites also Guttmann, *op. cit.* 134: "Das Ziel der jüdischen Propaganda war ... nicht auf Proselytenmacherei eingestellt, sondern auf Verbreitung von Ideen und Satzungen, die das Judentum als universal, als der ganzen Menschheit bestimmt lehrte". Criticisms of Guttmann came from E. L. Dietrich, "Die 'Religion Noahs', ihre Herkunft und ihre Bedeutung", *Zeitschrift für Religions- und Geistesgeschichte* 1 (1948), 306: "Die Meinung Guttmanns, dass von den Noachidischen Geboten aus

Only for the sake of completeness must mention be made of the two following translations, one German, by Riessler in 1928,[139] and one English, by Easton in 1932.[140] Neither translation is very reliable; Riessler's because it is based upon the outdated edition of Bergk, and also because he sometimes simply gives a wrong translation; and Easton's since it is more a paraphrase than a translation and based upon Bergk's text as well. Neither of these scholars presents new points of view. Only Easton points out the importance of the poem for New Testament studies: "The maxims ... are important as showing that precedents existed in the non-Christian world for the ethical combinations made so freely in the Pastoral Epistles, II Peter and the Apostolic Fathers, particularly Hermas" (222).[141]

In 1933 S. Spinner made a new attempt to prove the authenticity of the poem in his book *Herkunft, Entstehung und antike Umwelt des hebräischen Volkes*.[142] According to Spinner, there was, long before the Persian wars, an intensive spiritual contact between the Hebrew people and the Greeks, among other things by way of the great Jewish settlements in Asia Minor. The Jews who lived there had already made a Greek translation of parts of the Old Testament. Probably as early as the seventh century B.C. the Greeks could take cognizance of the contents of the Mosaic laws. These several partial translations were later (in the third century B.C.) revised

---

die jüdische Mission und der Proselytismus der hellenistischen Zeit vorgegangen sei, ja dass diese Gebote ihre treibende Kraft gewesen seien, ist ... irrig; denn nicht der Proselyt, sondern der *ger toschab*, der Heide blieb, aber unter Juden wohnte, war der Gegenstand der noachidischen Tafel". That the Noachian laws concerned (only) the *ger toshab* is, however, a very onesided statement; see *Enc. Jud.* XII (1971), 1190.

[139] P. Riessler, *Altjüdisches Schrifttum ausserhalb der Bibel*, Heidelberg 1928, (repr. 1966), 862-870, with notes on 1318-1321.

[140] B. S. Easton, "Pseudo-Phocylides", *Anglican Theological Review* 14 (1932), 222-228.

[141] In 1930 appeared P. Fiebig's short article on Ps-Phoc. in *RGG* IV² 1239, in which he subscribes to Klein's theory: "Wahrscheinlich gehört es in die Reihe jüdischer Schriften, die das für alle Menschen Verbindliche darstellen wollen; vgl. die Grundschrift der Apostellehre und die Derek-ereṣ-Traktate".

[142] In a chapter with the significant title "Semitisch und Arisch. Semitischer Einfluss in Kleinasien, Griechenland und Italien, desgleichen im Osten in Parthien, Baktrien, Ariana, sowie Einfluss der hebräischen Kultur auf die Grundlagen der Geistesentwicklung Griechenlands und Italiens. Die älteren kleinasiatisch-griechischen Teilübersetzungen biblischer Schriften und die von ihr ausgegangene geistige Befruchtung" (380-494).

and combined so as to form the LXX. Actually these earlier translations exerted a powerful influence upon several great personages in Greek cultural history, e.g. Hesiod, Aesopus, Pythagoras, Democritus, Anaxagoras, Xenophanes. "Wenn man sich auf den realen Boden der Geschichte, die keine Wunder kennt, stellt und die griechische Geistesentwicklung von den ionischen Naturphilosophen bis Plato in ihrem Kausalnexus betrachtet, muss jeder Unbefangene die Einwirkung von jüdischer Seite her zugeben" (486). Only on this presupposition can one explain the agreements between Phocylides and the O.T. Of course, later revision by a Jew cannot be excluded; but it is at least equally plausible that the real Phocylides in the sixth century B.C. composed this poem under the influence of Greek translations of the O.T. (487f.). According to Spinner, the proof of the existence of these translations comes from the Letter of Aristeas.[143]

In 1939, A. Kurfess published an article about the interpolation of Ps-Phoc. 5-79 into Ψ, a mss. group of *Or. Sib.*[144] He begins with criticisms of Rossbroich's proselyte-hypothesis. "Das stoische und Kynische Kolorit das R. in diesen Versen finden wollte, ist nicht derart, dass man auf einen Griechen schliessen müsste. Das Jüdische ist jedenfalls vorherrschend" (171). Kurfess concedes that a number of verses (e.g. 70-75) can hardly have been written by a Jew, but the absence of such verses in Ψ may indicate that they are not an original part of the poem. Kurfess criticizes Geffcken's opinion [145] that the omission of verses of Ps-Phoc. in Ψ is secondary and the additions interpolated. The mss. of this group may be very good textual witnesses for Ps-Phoc. On the basis of a number of "Texterweiterungen" in Ψ, Kurfess tries to demonstrate that precisely

---

[143] *Ep. Arist.* 30 and 313-6. The interpretation of the first passage is disputed, the historical reliability of the second extremely doubtful. See Meisner *ad loc.* (in JSHRZ), S. Jellicoe, *The Septuagint and Modern Study*, Oxford 1968, 51 and Fraser, *Ptolemaic Alexandria* II 956f. n. 2; see further note 153 on p. 40. The related attempt of A. Marmorstein ("A Greek Lyric and a Hebrew Poet", *Jewish Quarterly Review* 37 (1946-47), 169-173) to explain the supposed influence of Isaiah upon Alcaeus (6th cent. B.C.) may be mentioned in passing. He points out that there were Greek hirelings in Nebuchadnezzar's army (in this case also Alcaeus' brother). Through these channels knowledge of the O.T. could have penetrated into the Greek world even before the LXX came into existence. This explanation looks less unacceptable than Spinner's one.

[144] "Das Mahngedicht des sogenannten Phokylides im zweiten Buch der Oracula Sibyllina", *ZNW* 38 (1939), 171-181.

[145] Geffcken edited *Or. Sib.*, Leipzig 1902; also Kurfess, München 1951.

these so-called insertions clarify the text of Ps-Phoc. Thus he keeps *Or. Sib.* II 59, where idolatry is combated, in his text, without seeing, however, that stylistically it connects very awkwardly with v. 60 = Ps-Phoc. 8.¹⁴⁶ Kurfess goes so far as to change the order of lines in the mss. of Ps-Phoc. in order to get a more smoothly running text in Ψ. He concludes: "So wage ich die ketzerische Ansicht, dass Sib. (Ψ) noch ein älteres, vollkommeneres Exemplar benutzt hat" (177). Finally, there follows a translation of *Or. Sib.* II 34-153 in order to show that "die Überlieferung in Sib. besseren Zusammenhang aufweist" (177).

Quite apart from the fact that the incorrectness of this position had already been convincingly demonstrated by Ludwich in 1904,¹⁴⁷ it is very curious indeed that Kurfess nowhere mentions Sitzler, who had already proposed exactly the same theory in 1912.¹⁴⁸

In the same year, the famous polymath Franz Dornseiff contributed to the discussion.¹⁴⁹ In his book on "Echtheitsfragen" he devotes a chapter to "Pseudo"-Phokylides.¹⁵⁰ Dornseiff begins by pointing out the almost word for word agreement between Ps-Phoc. 87 and Aristophanes' *Vespae* 725f. He assumes that Aristophanes is quoting here and he takes that passage to be the oldest evidence for the existence of our gnomic poem. Furthermore, he points out the tribute paid to Phoc. by Isocrates and judges it to be improbable that (the real) Phocylides' "Einzelgnomen" won him this fame. Therefore, he assumes that the poem is authentic.¹⁵¹

---

¹⁴⁶ The text then runs: μηδὲ μάτην εἴδωλα σέβου· τὸν δ' ἄφθιτον αἰεί] πρῶτα θεὸν τίμα, μετέπειτα δὲ σεῖο γονῆας.

¹⁴⁷ See above p. 21. See also the criticisms by Keydell (below p. 41 n. 161) 27f.

¹⁴⁸ See above p. 30. In Kurfess' later article "Oracula Sibyllina I/II", *ZNW* 40 (1941), 151-165, Ps-Phoc. is mentioned only in passing when Kurfess dates *Or. Sib.* II to the same period as Ps-Phoc., "d.h. ungefähr in die Zeit unmittelbar vor oder nach Christi Geburt" (162).

¹⁴⁹ *Echtheitsfragen antik-griechischer Literatur. Rettungen des Theognis, Phokylides, Hekataios, Choirilos*, Berlin 1939.

¹⁵⁰ *Op. cit.* 37-51.

¹⁵¹ In this connection he takes issue with Bernays' interpretation of a scholion on Aristophanes' *Nubes* 240. This scholion runs: Φωκυλίδης ἐν μὲν τοῖς αὑτοῦ ποιήμασι κατὰ τὴν συνήθειαν τοὺς χρεωφειλέτας χρήστας καλεῖ λέγων οὕτως · χρήστης κακοῦ ἔμμεναι ἀνδρὸς φεύγειν, μή σέ γ' ἀνιήσῃ παρὰ καιρὸν ἀπαιτέων (= Phoc. fr. 6). ἐν ἐκείνῳ μέντοι ἀντὶ τοῦ δανειστὴς λαμβάνεται· μηδέποτε χρήστης πικρὸς γένῃ ἀνδρὶ πένητι (= Ps-Phoc. 83). Bernays 234 n. 2 writes: "Diese Worten scheinen aus einer Nachweisung der Unechtheit unseres Phokylides zu stammen, denn nur so lässt sich die Wendung ἐν ἐκείνῳ μέντοι erklären; sie müssen aus einer Zeit stammen, da der echte

What has been identified as Stoic characteristics in this poem has, in his opinion, parallels in early Greek literature. Dornseiff then gives a paraphrase of the poem with some explanatory notes.[152] He also refers to parallels in the O.T., but denies that it can be proved that the LXX was the *Vorlage*. According to Dornseiff it is quite possible that in the second half of the sixth century B.C. in Miletus a poem was written with numerous Biblical allusions. For ever since 722 B.C. there had been a Jewish diaspora. And later in the Persian empire the position of the Jews was favourable. Aramaic was understood everywhere and Jews were everywhere. So in Miletus Jews and Greeks could exchange ideas in Aramaic. Moreover, there are clear indications that by the first half of the sixth century B.C. there was a Greek translation of the Pentateuch.[153] So Phocylides could have read parts of the O.T. in a translation that stood in the same relation to the LXX as the Vetus Latina to the Vulgate. Finally, Dornseiff remarks that nobody has succeeded in demonstrating on linguistic grounds that Phocylides' poem is late.[154]

Phokylides noch erhalten war, also aus keiner sehr späten". Bergk (see p. 14 n. 52) and Sitzler (see p. 30 n. 119) accept this interpretation. But Dornseiff 38 says: "Der Scholiast ... hat bloss angemerkt: 'Dieses Wort kommt auch mal in der Bedeutung 'Schuldner' vor, bei Phokylides. In dessen Gnomai V. 83 heisst es freilich wieder 'Gläubiger' wie bei Aristophanes'". However, the truth is more complex. Only the first half of the scholion (up to the quotation of Phoc. fr. 6) is a *scholium vetus*. Only that part is in the codices. The second part (ἐν ἐκείνω μέντοι κτλ.) is not in any codex but turns up only in the *editio Aldina* of 1498. It is an addition by Musurus, the compiler of the scholia of this edition. It is very doubtful whether Musurus wanted to distinguish in this way between a real and a pseudo-Phocylides. Prof. W. J. W. Koster, to whom I am indebted for this information (in a letter of 14.10.1972), thinks Musurus did not. Note that the *Aldina* reads ἐν τοῖς αὐτοῦ ποιήμασι, not, as Diehl reads in the *app. crit.* to Phoc. fr. 6, αὐτοῦ. [Only after the completion of this book I saw that in the recent edition of the scholia by Holwerda (Groningen 1977) the scholion runs: Φωκυλίδης δὲ κατὰ τὴν συνήθειαν τοὺς χρεωφειλέτας χρήστας καλεῖ λέγων· χρήστας κακοὺς ἔμμεναι ἀνδρὸς φεύγειν μή γε ἀνιήσειε διδούς, παρὰ καιρὸν ἀπαιτέων (p. 59)].

[152] *Op. cit.* 39-48.
[153] Dornseiff (50) refers here to Aristobulus *apud* Clem. Alex. *Strom.* I 22, 150 (93, 3f. St.) and to *Ep. Arist.* 30, both passages of rather dubious historical reliability. See the discussion of both texts by A. Pelletier, *Lettre d'Aristée à Philocrate*, Paris 1962, 118 n. 3, and esp. N. Walter, *Der Thoraausleger Aristobulos*, Berlin 1964, 88ff. See also p. 38 n. 143 above.
[154] Dornseiff makes here a curious error: he reacts to Goram who drew attention to the late form ἀπόλειψον, with the remark: "dieses Verbum gebraucht aber schon Homer" (51). He obviously failed to grasp that Goram means that a sigmatic aorist of λείπω (ἔλειψα instead of ἔλιπον) is a feature of late Greek.

Dornseiff's theory has been widely criticized. His most important critics are the following. Howald in a review,[155] characterized Dornseiff's "Grundanschauung" as follows: "D. ist des Glaubens, dass die ältere griechische Kulturanschauung aus ihrer Isolation befreit werden und ganz in die Kultur Vorderasiens hineingestellt werden müsse" (665).[156] But his only proof for the poem's early existence, viz. the so-called quotation from Phocylides in Arist. *Vesp.* 725, does not hold since Ps-Phoc. 83 has to be athetized. Diehl had already done so in 1923 on the basis of the mss. tradition. A. von Blumenthal's review [157] is also very critical. He regards the existence of a Greek translation of the Pentateuch in the sixth century B.C. as extremely improbable.[158] The language of the poem really does show traces of a late origin. This is also Herter's opinion.[159] He remarks, moreover, that the fragments of the real Phocylides do not show any traces of O.T. influence. He states: "Ein Mann, der dem AT so stark verpflichtet ist wie der Verfasser dieser Gnomensammlung, würde in Milet im 6. Jhdt. so einsam darstehen, dass ich mich nicht entschliessen kann, ihn für den echten Phokylides zu halten" (19). Nor has Eltester been convinced.[160] Among other things he wonders whether the Ionian Greeks in the Persian empire did learn so much Aramaic. In his opinion the use of Ps-Phoc. in *Or. Sib.* II is corroborative evidence of its Jewish-Hellenistic origin. Keydell,[161] too, rejects Dornseiff's position: "Das Gedicht ist nach Inhalt und Sprache hellenistisch" (27). As far as the present writer knows, after Dornseiff

---

[155] *Deutsche Literaturzeitung* 61 (1940), 663-668.
[156] See e.g. Dornseiff's collected essays *Antike und alter Orient. Kleine Schriften I*, Leipzig 1959². Indeed, the problems broached here by Dornseiff are still under discussion. See e.g. the publications of Cyrus Gordon (*Before the Bible*, London 1962) and Michael Astour (*Hellenosemitica*, Leiden 1965).
[157] *Gnomon* 19 (1943), 289-293.
[158] He rightly explains the quotation from Aristobulus in Clem. Alex. as an attempt "um Platons und Pythagoras' angebliche Abhängigkeit vom Pentateuch glaubhaft zu machen" (291 n. 4). Cf. also 293 n. 3: "Wer die Existenz einer griechischen Übersetzung des A.T. im 6., 5. und 4. Jh. behauptet, muss auch die Frage beantworten, für wen eine solche Übersetzung bestimmt war. Gab es denn schon judengriechische Gemeinden?".
[159] *Theol. Lit. Zeitung* 66 (1941), 17-19.
[160] *ZNW* 39 (1940), 243.
[161] "Die griechische Dichtung der Kaiserzeit", *Jahresbericht über die Fortschritte der klassischen Altertumswissenschaft* 272 (1941), 1-71, esp. 27f. Cf. A. Momigliano, *Alien Wisdom*, 1975, 78.

the authenticity of the poem has no longer been defended.[162]

The next contribution is W. Kroll's article on Ps-Phoc. in Pauly-Wissowa's *Realencyklopädie*.[163] Speaking about contradictions, repetitions and in general the bad composition of the poem he says: "Dieser Mangel an Disposition eignet zum Teil der Gattung, beruht aber auch auf mangelnder Fähigkeit des Autors und auf Kompilation seiner Regeln aus verschiedenen Quellen" (505). There are four sets of verses that draw on Jewish wisdom,[164] but in these sets there is also pagan material and vice versa (e.g. 84f. is Jewish). "Der Monotheismus wagt sich nicht viel weiter hervor als etwa auch bei gebildeten Heiden" (506). Ps-Phoc. is not dependent upon the Didache, because there is not a single reference to the Two Ways in the poem. More important is Wendland's reference to the Jewish ὑποθῆκαι that are based not only on the O.T. but also on the worldly wisdom of the pagan *Umwelt* and that are known from Philo's *Hypothetica* and Josephus' *C.Ap.* II 188-219. Many admonitions in Ps-Phoc. derive from popular philosophy, especially "die mehrfach auftretende Mahnung zur Genügsamkeit und Mässigung" (508). The author also draws on older collections of sentences, to which he owes his knowledge of Theognis and the Branchidae oracle (v. 162). "Bisweilen erhebt er sich durch einen gewissen Schwung über die Ebene der ὑποθῆκαι, so in der Schilderung der arbeitsfreudigen Ameisen und Bienen v. 164ff."

---

[162] Though it concerns only two short remarks in a large tome, the judgement that the famous Utrecht professor of Ancient History H. Bolkestein passed on Ps-Phoc. in his *Wohltätigkeit und Armenpflege im vorchristlichen Altertum*, Utrecht 1939, 429, cannot be overlooked. Here he calls Ps-Phoc. "das interessanteste Literaturdenkmal griechisch-orientalischen Synkretismus" and he remarks in note 1: "Rossbroich meint in vielen Punkten stoischen Einfluss feststellen zu können. In Wirklichkeit steckt auch viel altgriechisches Gedankengut darin, das mit allerlei orientalischen, ägyptischen, persischen und auch jüdischen Auffassungen zu einem monströsen Mischmasch vereinigt ist, wie eine genaue Analyse z.B. von Vers 99-108 deutlich ergibt. Es ist völlig zwecklos, sich die Frage vorzulegen, was für ein Landsmann oder wes Geistes Kind der Zusammensteller dieses Mischmaschs war: eine eigene Persönlichkeit ist darin nicht zu entdecken". Cf. p. 73: "Eine Welt scheidet diese echt-griechische Lebensweisheit (sc. of the real Phocylides) von jenen farblosen Lektionen, Erzeugnissen eines kraftlosen Synkretismus, die kurz vor oder nach dem Anfang unserer Zeitrechnung in Alexandrien in metrische Form gebracht und unter dem berühmten Namen des Phocylides herausgegeben worden sind".

[163] *RE* XX 1 (Stuttgart 1941), 505-510. Kroll had already worked on Ps-Phoc. before; see above p. 16 n. 67 and p. 22 n. 95.

[164] Vv. 3-39, 140-149, 170-188, 220-227.

(509). The author has mastered the epic usage rather well. He was no propagandist for Judaism ("Bernays' These ... ist heute allgemein aufgegeben", 509), and certainly not an Essene (against Beltrami). The poem should be dated between 50 and 150 A.D. These are the essential points of Kroll's position.

It is noticeable that Kroll does not give a clear answer to the question of whether the author was a Jew or not. He probably did that on purpose,[165] though the fact that he indicated verses which he thinks are "völlig unjüdisch" (507) suggests that he seriously doubted the Jewishness of the author. The agreements with the position of his pupil Rossbroich (1910) are clear, especially in his stressing the Hellenistic elements at the cost of the Jewish ones.

From 1945 to 1975 (Lewis, Alon, Farina, Crouch)

After Kroll's article there was a long silence on the subject of Ps. Phoc. The first publication to deal with Ps-Phoc. after the Second World War seems to be an article published in 1953 by J. J. Lewis.[166] Lewis finds Ps-Phoc. an interesting instance of Jewish apologetics. "Its purpose is obviously to commend the central doctrines to Greek readers" (295), but what Philo did for the educated, Ps-Phoc. does "for the man-in-the-street whose knowledge was conveyed and expressed through the aphorisms of gnomic teaching" (295). Then Lewis tries to describe more or less systematically Ps-Phoc.' doctrine under the following headings: 1. Doctrine of God. 2. Doctrine of Man. 3. The Moral Ideal. 4. Social Relationships. 5. Social Questions. He tries to class as many lines of the poem as possible under these five headings. This seems, however, to be an almost impossible task.[167] The most important details of this presentation are the following.

There is only one God, who is just, wise, almighty and provident. The human mind is his image. God judges and rules the deceased, and demands mutual mercifulness from all men. The polytheistic references are "impossible to reconcile with the conceptions of Jewish orthodoxy" (295), but here it becomes "evident that there is no clearly thought out and coherent doctrine of God but an

---

[165] Cf. his statement in *Berl. Phil. Woch.* 25 (1905), 243, quoted above p. 22f.

[166] "The Teaching of Pseudo-Phocylidea", *The London Quarterly and Holborn Review*, October 1953, 295-298.

[167] It is, for instance, significant that Lewis does not devote a word to the sexual ethics which play such a great part in the poem.

intermingling of two different outlooks and conceptions" (296). The same applies to the doctrine of man, for as to what happens at death three theories are given: 1. There is a bodily resurrection for the departed. 2. The spirit proceeds to the halls of Hades where all, rich and poor alike, are made equal. 3. The body is turned into dust and the spirit is released into the upper elements. "No attempt is made in the poem to harmonize these points of view nor is any description given of the nature of life after death" (296). The fact that the author devotes much more attention to warning against evils than to picturing the good life shows that he assumes "that human nature is unstable and biased toward evil." But "behind all these precepts is the confident assumption that, if he so desires, man's will is strong enough for him to reject the evil and cleave to the good. There is no teaching upon the need for forgiveness nor for divine aid in conquering evil" (296). The "Moral Ideal" of Ps-Phoc. is wisdom, both in the Jewish and in the Greek sense, with a strong emphasis upon moderateness, self-restraint and hard work. As to the social relationships, "the writer reveals a keen sense of the value and obligation of home and family relationships" (297). He stresses good relations within the family, also with regard to slaves and even animals. Outside the family one should seek worthy friends. Under the heading "Social Questions" Lewis remarks: "The poem deals with such social conditions as may have existed in the locality where it was produced. Excessive wealth and luxury are condemned". "Stress is laid upon the value of law and order". "In all social questions the poem advocates fairness and equality for all. Each man must be given his due" (297). In his conclusion Lewis says that the poem "provides a fair picture of what must have been an advanced type of Jewish thinking within the Greek environment probably at Alexandria about the beginning of the second century B.C." (297).[168] From a religious point of view, the poem has little profundity and is somewhat superficial. "The teaching is generally external and utilitarian and far more concerned with individual than with social life. Little interest is displayed in the wider affairs of the nation" (298). Though most precepts deal with "commonplace needs and situations ... it reaches a high standard" (298).

---

[168] This very early dating is linked up with Lewis' view that the poem is used by Ps-Aristeas and Philo who constitute, therefore, a *terminus ante quem*. Lewis returns to this matter again in 1966; see below p. 48 n. 184.

Finally, Lewis puts forward his own theory about the origin of the poem. Comparison with Theognis, he says, "indicates a strong possibility that both are dependent upon a common source which, in the absence of other sources, may well have been the actual teachings of the Milesian poet Phocylides" (298). He supports Ranston's thesis [169] that Ps-Phoc. "might contain genuine material". "It is not improbable that this Greek-speaking Alexandrian Jew somewhere between 250-160 B.C. selected probably from an oral tradition some of the teaching of Phocylides to which he added the precepts of the Jewish Law, sending the composite work out to the Greek public under the authority of the name of the Milesian sage" (298).

Though Lewis' article is sometimes superficial, it has the merit of trying to systematize the ideas of Ps-Phoc. and of demonstrating in this way some of the weaknesses of the poem.[170]

In an article written in Hebrew [171] the Israeli scholar G. Alon compares Ps-Phoc. with Did. I-VI and denies that the poem has anything to do with the Noachian commandments (against Bernays, Klein and Guttmann) since the prohibition of idolatry, which is central in the Noachian commandments, is lacking here.[172] This can only be explained on the assumption that Ps-Phoc. did not write for pagans but for Jews. The poem is a presentation of the principles of Jewish life as compared to the heathen way of life (hence the many agreements with the Two Ways document behind Did. I-VI). The poet, speaking here in the name of an ancient Greek author, seeks to demonstrate to the Jews who are engrossed in Hellenistic culture and imitate its manners and deeds, that even an ancient Greek writer of great acclaim recognizes Jewish moral requisites. The author wants to bring them back to

---

[169] See above p. 34.

[170] In 1954 appeared P. Dalbert's book *Die Theologie der hellenistisch-jüdischen Missionsliteratur unter Ausschluss von Philo und Josephus*. Dalbert explicitly refuses to include Ps-Phoc. in his research, since he seriously doubts whether the author was a Jew. He refers to Harnack, Schürer, Rossbroich, Kroll (9f.). "Pseudo Phokylides vermittelt Lebensweisheit der hellenistischen Diatribe, die auch alttestamentliche Weisheit in sich aufgenommen hat" (10).

[171] ההלכה שבתורת י״ב השליחים (= The Halakah in the Teaching of the Twelve Apostles), in his *Studies in Jewish History in the Times of the Second Temple, the Mishnah and the Talmud* (in Hebrew), I, Hakibbutz Hameuchad 1957 (1967²), 274-294. Prof. David Flusser drew this article to my attention and my colleague Huub van de Sandt assisted me in reading it.

[172] *Art. cit.* 277.

good deeds in an indirect way. He need not mention abandonment of idolatry since this Jewish position was taken for granted in any case, even by these hellenized Jews. Alon goes on to situate Ps-Phoc. within a current in ancient Judaism which tended to reduce the Torah to a limited set of ethical principles, which were meant for the Jews. He cites some texts to support this,[173] among which those N.T. texts where the love of one's neighbour (Lev. XIX 18) is said to be the fulfilment of the whole Torah (Gal. V 14; Jas. II 8; cf. Mk. XII 31 parr.). Alon does not deny that such summaries of the Torah were used for propaganda purposes, e.g. in Philo's *Hyp.* and Josephus' *C.Ap.*, but that is not the case with Ps-Phoc.[174] This is a stimulating contribution which seems to solve at least the problem of the author's purpose.[175]

Though not strictly belonging to the history of research on Ps-Phoc., the following two publications from 1961 should nevertheless be mentioned. Firstly, D. G. Castanien's article "Quevedo's Translation of the Pseudo-Phocylides",[176] in which he discusses the strongly paraphrasing "expanded translation"[177] of this poem by the seventeenth century Spanish author Francisco de Quevedo. This article shows how, in a period when Scaliger's views had not yet become known to everyone, Ps-Phoc. was admired and how one did one's best to make the poem as accessible as possible to a broad public. Secondly, there appeared in 1961 an important new (Teubner) edition of Ps-Phoc. in Douglas Young's revision of a part of Diehl's *Anthologia Graeca*.[178] This edition is the most reliable one that is now available. It underlies the present Commentary.[179]

---

[173] *Art. cit.* 278f.

[174] *Art. cit.* 279.

[175] It should be noted in this connection that in 1957 V. Tcherikover for the first time proposed his thesis that all Jewish-Alexandrian literature was meant not for the Gentiles but for the Jews ("Jewish Apologetic Literature Reconsidered", in *Symbolae R. Taubenschlag dedicatae* III, Wratislawa 1957, 169-193).

[176] *Philological Quarterly* 40 (1961), 44-52.

[177] The translation consists of 594 hendecasyllabic lines.

[178] *Theognis, Ps-Pythagoras, Ps-Phocylides, Chares, Anonymi Aulodia, Fragmentum Teleiambicum*, post E. Diehl iterum edidit Douglas Young, Leipzig 1961. A second edition, with some addenda, was published in 1971. Till his sudden death on 23 October 1973, Young was professor of Greek at the University of North Carolina in Chapel Hill. During 1972 and 1973 the present author had a fruitful contact with him, as will appear in the Comm.

[179] Young's text is also printed in A. M. Denis, *Fragmenta Pseudepigraphorum quae supersunt graeca*, Leiden 1970, 149-156.

From 1961 to 1972 some articles on Ps-Phoc. appeared in encyclopedias. Since all of them are very concise and offer no new points of view, they need only be mentioned briefly in a footnote.[180]

In 1962 the Italian classicist A. Farina published an edition of Ps-Phoc. with an introduction, translation and concise commentary.[181] In the introduction, Farina asserts that the poem is composed not by a single author, but by a large number of authors. The poem has grown during the course of centuries. By association of ideas and formal similarity of words it was expanded more and more by anyone who wanted to add something to it. It is a mistake to look for an original core and then to blame interpolators for the disorder. All have interpolated! Hence there is no need either to try to find an original order of the lines. We have to retain the present form of the poem.[182] So it is probably true that beginning (vv. 1-2) and end (vv. 229-230) of the poem have been added in a late stage (thus also the name Phocylides), but nevertheless these lines should be left as they are. The whole prooemium is a good summary of the motifs that are treated in the poem. Collecting parallels from Greek and Latin authors and the Bible is a waste of time, for the poem contains only eternal, timeless truths which may be found anywhere. What is important is the practical nature of the poem, and its purpose is "osservare la vita nel suo aspetto normale e pratico" (13). The main motifs of the poem are: labour, justice, concord. The fact that the origin and character of the

---

[180] E. Lohse, "Phokylides", *RGG*³ V, Tübingen 1961, 362, still doubts whether the author was a Jew or a Christian. But in his *Umwelt des Neuen Testaments*, Göttingen 1971, 89f., he unhesitatingly assumes a Jewish origin. J. Schmid, "Pseudo-Phokylides", *LThK* VIII, Freiburg 1963, 867f. C. Schneider, "Phokylides", *BHH* III, Göttingen 1966, 1463f. M. S. Hurwitz, "Pseudo-Phocylides", *Enc. Jud.* XIII, Jerusalem 1971, 1335f. Both Hurwitz and Schneider stress more the connections with the Wisdom literature (Prov., Sir., Sap. Sal.) than with the Pentateuch. Both prefer a dating in the first century B.C. (whereas Schneider in his *Kulturgeschichte des Hellenismus* I, München 1967, 892 dates it much later: "erst nachhellenistisch und von Musonius Rufus oder einem seiner Geistesverwandten beeinflusst"). R. Keydell, "Phokylides", *Der Kleine Pauly* IV, München 1972, 806f. dates it to the first or second cent. A.D. He sees as main sources of Ps-Phoc. Lev., Deut., Prov., Jewish ὑποθῆκαι, Theognis and popular philosophic themes.

[181] *Silloge Pseudofocilidea* (Collana di studi greci 37), Naples 1962.

[182] The result of the application of this theory is that in his edition of the text Farina does not athetize any line, not even those lines that are found in only one ms., for in his view even the most recent Byzantine copyist adding a line is a legitimate co-author.

writing are so difficult to determine and that contradictions within the poem are demonstrable is to be explained on the basis of the multiple authorship of the poem. It should be assumed that there has been a very long period of growth, perhaps beginning as early as the sixth century B.C.,[183] after which one reader after another has expanded the poem "per gusto di erudizione o per semplice associazione di idee" (15). This proces was undoubtedly influenced by collections of sentences already existing such as those of Hesiod, Theognis, the Seven Sages, Ps-Isocrates' *Ad Demonicum*, Proverbs and Sirach. Farina also presents a kind of "Forschungsbericht" which is very incomplete and confused. His commentary on the Greek text is very brief. Moreover, the *cruces interpretum* are completely ignored. He presents an arbitrary choice of parallels (against his own better judgement!) from classical authors. What is noticeable here is that many of these are from Horace and Ovid, but none from the LXX. It is clear that Farina's work is of little help.

In 1966 J. J. Lewis contributed a second article to the discussion in which he tries to demonstrate that there are many obvious parallels between Ps-Phoc. and the Letter of Aristeas, especially in the table-talk section.[184] "A close association exists between the two works, not to be accounted for by any suggestion of dependence upon a common source, since the parallel teaching involves both Greek and Jewish ideas". "The most reasonable conclusion is that Aristeas probably drew from the poem ideas which formed starting-points for his own table-talk discussions" (56). Aristeas' purpose was identical with that of Ps-Phoc., viz. "to commend the moral teaching of the Torah to the Greek world" (56). But actually many of Lewis' parallels are farfetched and his proof of Aristeas' dependence is very weak.[185]

---

[183] "si puo ben ritenere che alcune sentenze siano molto antiche e risalgono, forse, allo stesso poeta milesio", 14f. The authors of the poem date from the sixth cent. B.C. to the Middle Ages.

[184] "The Table-Talk Section in the Letter of Aristeas", *NTS* 13 (1966/7), 53-6. For his former publication see above p. 43 with n. 166.

[185] Crouch (see p. 50 note 193) suggests (75f.) that Ps-Aristeas grouped his table-talk section round the Stoic καθῆκον-scheme, which might explain the agreements with Ps-Phoc. Cf. p. 99: "Obviously, Lewis' thesis is false if one can demonstrate the existence of a common source in which both Greek and Jewish ideas have been combined. We have seen that such was the case with the Hellenistic Jewish propaganda". On this theory of Crouch see below p. 50ff.

In 1970 A. M. Denis gave a short but good survey of the problems concerning Ps-Phoc. and of the several theories proposed in his *Introduction aux pseudépigraphes grecs d'Ancien Testament*.[186] Denis himself has doubts about the origin of the poem. "Deux emplois du pluriel 'les dieux' (v. 98?, 103-104) ne s'opposeraient pas à l'origine juive de l'auteur, bien que finalement, l'on ne puisse guère décider avec certitude s'il était juif ou païen" (218).[187]

In 1972 Martin Hengel published a long article, "Anonymität, Pseudepigraphie und 'literarische Fälschung' in der jüdisch-hellenistischen Literatur",[188] in which he devotes a paragraph to Ps-Phoc.[189] His criticisms of Kroll are important. The latter sees Jewish influence in only a few passages.[190] Against this Hengel says: "der jüdische Einfluss geht durch das ganze Gedicht, das eine Einheit bildet. Kroll unterschätzt den überwiegend jüdischen Gesamtcharakter der Schrift" (296 n. 3). The author was undoubtedly a Jew. The poem is strongly stamped by O.T. Wisdom traditions. "Dass sich in dem Gedicht auch starke Anklänge an die griechische Gnomik finden, ist bei dem internationalen, universalethischen Charakter gerade auch der jüdischen Weisheitsdichtung selbstverständlich" (297). The frequent use of θεός, the severe sexual and family ethics and also the warning against magic are wholly in accordance with the Jewish way of life in the Diaspora. "Das Gedicht ist von seiner Moral her etwa mit den Test. der 12 Patr. verwandt" (297). The absence of exclusively Jewish characteristics is to be explained on the basis of the Wisdom character of the poem and from its pseudepigraphic dress. Herein Ps-Phoc. is in full agreement with the falsified quotations from classical authors.[191] The closing lines of the poem (229f. ταῦτα δικαιοσύνης μυστήρια κτλ.) show "wie der Schwerpunkt der jüdischen Frömmigkeit in der Diaspora ganz auf der Ethik lag. Dies erklärt auch ihre Missionserfolge" (298). Later, in another context, Hengel remarks: "Das Niveau der Fälschungen war verschieden. Die Klassikerfragmente

---

[186] *Op. cit.* 215-9. The views of modern scholars are not always presented correctly by Denis.

[187] Yet Denis has printed the text of Ps-Phoc. in his simultaneously published edition of the fragments of the Jewish pseudepigrapha (see Bibl.).

[188] In *Pseudepigrapha* I, Entretiens sur l'antiquité classique XVIII, Vandœuvres-Geneva 1972, 231-308. This volume contains the lectures (and discussions) of the September 1971 session of the Fondation Hardt.

[189] *Op. cit.* 296-298.

[190] See above p. 42 n. 164.

[191] See the collection in Denis, *Fragmenta* 161-173.

machen einen dürftigen Eindruck. Pseudophokylides ist dagegen so gut gelungen, dass man zweifelte, ob es sich um eine jüdische Fälschung handelte" (313).[192]

In the same year James Crouch's dissertation on the Colossian *Haustafel* was published.[193] In a discussion of Stoic and Jewish lists of duties he demonstrates that Ps-Phoc. has been influenced by "Stoic codes", albeit probably indirectly. Exactly the same influence is also found in Philo's *Hypothetica* (*ap*. Eus. *PE* VIII 7) and Josephus' *C.Ap*. II 190-219. Philo and Josephus both intend to give a summary of Jewish laws to pagan readers. "The material offered, however, exceeds in many instances the legal injunctions of the Pentateuch and contains materials found in Greek ethical codes. Consequently, it is not possible to explain the similarity between Philo and Josephus on the basis of a common dependence upon the Old Testament. Neither is the theory that Josephus used Philo satisfactory to explain the parallels between the two, for the disposition of materials in *C.Ap*. varies from that in *Hyp*. Furthermore, Pseudo-Phocylides offers a good deal of material common to the others, and in a number of instances he shares material with only one of them. ... Laws dealing with sexual offences constitute an important section in each of the passages under consideration. There is no attempt, however, to reproduce completely the O.T. laws (Lev. 18; 20). Instead, a representative selection is given in each case, a fact which makes the agreement among the three works even more striking" (84). After presenting a list of parallels between these three treatises [194] Crouch remarks: "On the basis of this brief summary of material common to Philo, Josephus and Ps-Phocylides it would appear that we are dealing with a body of ethical material which cannot be attributed directly to any one of these writers. Furthermore, this material was gathered prior to all three of them and constituted a source from which each drew for his own particular purpose" (88). In order to explain in what kind of "Sitz im Leben" such a body of ethical material could come into being, Crouch refers to the work of Klein (1909),[195] whose idea of an elaborated Jewish catechism is, it is true, not

---

[192] In the discussion (pp. 309-329) Hengel defended the authenticity of vv. 1-2 over against Wolfgang Speyer, *op. cit*. 324. See my Comm. *ad loc*.

[193] *The Origin and Intention of the Colossian Haustafel* (FRLANT 109), Göttingen 1972.

[194] *Op. cit*. 84-88. All these parallels can be found in the Comm.

[195] See above p. 25f.

taken over by him, but whose argument for the existence of "a tradition in Judaism which was interested in propagating ethical monotheism" (89) he deems important. Klein was right in "his basic thesis that there was a widespread Jewish missionary activity which promoted ethical monotheism and that we can observe something of its purpose and methodology in material which has its origin in late Judaism" (89). Ps-Phoc. belongs to this material. He drew on "a store of ethical material which was in current use in the Jewish missionary activity" (90). What is significant about this material is that it "presents only 'laws' which could be expected to find a sympathetic hearing with non-Jews" (90). According to Crouch this missionary activity reached its zenith in the Roman period. For the background of this activity he refers especially to the considerations of Guttmann, whose views have already been discussed.[196] "The original impulse and intention of the Jewish mission lay ... not in an extension of 'Judaism' as a national and religious cult but in the proclamation of the one God and his universal, ethical standards" (94). Hence, the clear traces of the Noachian laws in Ps.Phoc., Philo and Josephus,[197] alongside traces of the unwritten laws of Greek ethics. "Both were regarded as expressions of a primitive code of ethics which was valid for the entire human race" (96). The Jewish propagandists "felt free to make use of anything which was morally superior and could be counted on to win a sympathetic hearing for the message of ethical monotheism. Consequently, we find a significant amount of material in later Hellenistic Jewish works which is of Greek origin" (97). The difference between Philo and Josephus on the one hand, and Ps-Phoc. on the other, is that the first call their material Jewish, whereas Ps-Phoc. "identifies neither himself nor his material. He prefers to remain anonymous in the hope that his message will receive a more sympathetic hearing" (98).

Crouch has been allowed to speak extensively for himself because in this book a kind of growing *communis opinio* concerning a number of problems is clearly presented. It succeeds in situating Ps-Phoc. within a specific movement. A theory based upon the data furnished by Wendland, Klein and Guttmann seems to be one that could well explain the enigmatic phenomena posed before us by the poem of Ps-Phoc.

---

[196] See above p. 35f.

[197] E.g. the injunctions against sexual sins, emasculation, the eating of blood, robbery, etc. (Crouch 95).

The latest publication (1975) on Ps-Phoc. is Felix Christ's article "Das Leben nach dem Tode bei Pseudo-Phokylides" [198]. Christ finds in vv. 99-115 "eine erstaunlich entwickelte individuelle Eschatologie" (140). After a translation of these lines and a very brief commentary (mentioning only Jewish parallels) he tries "dem Passus als ganzem einen einheitlichen Sinn abzugewinnen". In Christ's opinion, Ps-Phoc. has a trichotomic anthropology (body-soul-spirit). With this corresponds a kind of trichotomic cosmology: earth (grave)-Hades-air. At death the body goes into the earth (vv. 99f., 103, 107); the soul remains with the dead and lives in Hades (vv. 105, 109-115); the spirit is taken up into the air (108) as God's loan and image (106). "Bei der Auferstehung kommt der Körper aus Erde und Grab heraus, verbindet sich mit der Seele, die aus dem Urgrab des Hades aufsteigt, und wird vom Geist belebt, der aus der Luft von Gott herabsteigt, um den Körperschatten ans Licht zu führen". "Zwischen Tod und Auferstehung befinden sich also Geist, Seele und Leib in drei verschiedenen Zwischenzuständen" (145). This theory is said to have Greek and Jewish parallels and also to shed light on the "Aufenthalt Jesu im *Triduum*" (146). The "Begründung" of after-life in Ps-Phoc. is hard to discover. The poem as a whole creates the impression that only the just ones will attain to this goal, whereas vv. 99-115 suggest that the different parts of the dying "sozusagen automatisch an ihre Plätze aufgrund anthropologischer-kosmologischer Gesetze und Notwendigkeiten (gelangen)" (146). It might be possible to extract a "theologische Begründung" from v. 111.

Though Christ's essay is an intelligent attempt to discover a "Sinneinheit" in the "synkretistische Amalgam" (147) of vv. 99-115, there is a suspicion that he might have gone too far in harmonizing and ironing out the differences in the diverse ideas which in these lines stand so "unausgeglichen" beside one another. The treatment of the same passage by Cavallin [199] is preferable, because he does more justice to the text by taking more account of what Nock called "the widespread tendency of language about the afterlife to admit inconsistencies".[200] Cavallin indeed speaks of

---

[198] *Theol. Zeitschr.* 31 (1975), 140-9. The same subject is also treated by H. C. C. Cavallin in *Life After Death* I, Lund 1974, 151-5, a book on the views of after-life in ancient Judaism.
[199] See previous note.
[200] *Essays* I 507 n. 19.

"unharmonized juxtaposition of contradictory ideas about after-life" (153). After his analysis of vv. 99-115 he concludes that Ps-Phoc. "manages to combine a literalistic resurrection language with a clear dichotomic anthropology, based upon Gen. 1-3, which he interprets in a Hellenizing or, perhaps, a Stoicizing way, with the reference to the spirit's or soul's reception by the air" (153).[201] As Cavallin's book demonstrates, this "unharmonized juxtaposition of contradictory ideas about after-life" is a characteristic feature of ancient Jewish literature. To find so subtle a system in Ps-Phoc. as Christ does is probably to read into the text more than there is.

Conclusion

The writing and reading of this "Forschungsbericht" is not a very encouraging activity. It seems that almost every conceivable theory can be advanced about Ps-Phoc. Every possible theory has already been put forward about him. The only really constant element in the discussion is the unanimous acknowledgement of agreements with the O.T.[202] But apart from that it would seem that Ps-Phoc. is too elusive to come to a *communis opinio* about him. Nevertheless, it could be said that in the course of the last 120 years enough has become known about him to situate him more or less clearly in the cultural history of antiquity. The present Commentary is intended to be a further contribution in that direction, utilizing the valuable studies of our predecessors in this process. In this connection it should, therefore, be pointed out that a second characteristic of the history of research on Ps-Phoc. is that many authors appear to be badly informed about what their forerunners had already asserted about the same subject. Because of this, several doublets occurred or theories have been defended that had already been convincingly refuted long before.[203]

Although many scholars have occupied themselves with Ps-Phoc. since 1856, there remain some gaps in the research. Firstly, it is striking that regarding the problem of authenticity remarks

---

[201] In this connection it should be said that one of the causes of Christ's over-subtle interpretation is probably that he failed to see that in Hellenistic Jewish writings ψυχή and πνεῦμα are very often used indiscriminately; see Bousset, *Religion* 400f. and the Comm. *ad loc.*

[202] Purposely I do not say: dependence upon the O.T., for people like Lincke reverse the relationship.

[203] One example is Kurfess (1939). Even Rossbroich is not acquainted with several studies published before 1910.

have now and then been made on the linguistic aspects of the text, but that no one has ever systematically examined the author's vocabulary. If it could be shown that he uses a great number of words or forms that came into common use only in the Hellenistic period, the authenticity of the poem would become really indefensible.[204]

Secondly, little research has been done on the motive for the choice of the pseudonym Phocylides. An inquiry into the way that Phocylides was spoken or written about in antiquity can probably shed some light on this question.[205] Among other things, these two points can be clarified to a certain extent in the following sections.

In spite of all the research which has been done on Ps-Phoc., one of the most important aspects of the poem still remains puzzling, viz. its purpose. Several ingenious attempts have already been made to put Ps-Phoc. into a setting in which his poem made sense. Is he a pagan writing for pagan readers? Is he a Jew writing for Jewish readers? Is he a Jew writing for pagan readers? Or does he belong to yet another category? No really satisfactory answer has ever been found to this question. Nor is it possible to answer it in this book. Perhaps the materials collected together in the Commentary will provide other scholars with some of the ingredients needed to facilitate the solution of this vexing problem.

One thing has become clear from the history of research on Ps-Phoc., viz. that the material we are dealing with is not of such a nature as to admit absolutely certain solutions and results. The greatest caution should therefore be exercised in arriving at conclusions.[206]

[J. H. Charlesworth's book *The Pseudepigrapha and Modern Research* (Missoula 1976) came to my attention too late to be included in this survey. See his discussion of Ps-Phoc. on pp. 173-5.]

---

[204] What Rossbroich 10ff. has done in this respect is insufficient.

[205] Perhaps one of the causes why this problem has been neglected was doubt about the authenticity of vv. 1-2.

[206] All the problems appertaining to Ps-Phoc. have been so amply mooted in this "Forschungsbericht" that the next chapters can be short. I will only indicate briefly my own point of view on the problems now already known.

CHAPTER TWO

THE AUTHENTICITY OF THE POEM

From the previous section it has become clear that after Scaliger not many scholars have defended the authenticity of the poem, i.e., have maintained that it was written by Phocylides (middle of the sixth century B.C.). Yet it is useful not to accept uncritically the *communis opinio* on this point, but rather to investigate systematically (but briefly) the facts that tell against its authenticity.

In the first place, there is the matter of the author's language. He tries to write in the old Ionic dialect of Phocylides and succeeds in doing so to a great extent.[1] Yet there is in his poem a considerable number of words and word-forms that occur or even can occur only in the Hellenistic period.[2] A single example is, of course, not decisive,[3] but when there are about 30 examples in a poem of such a limited size, doubts concerning its authenticity become very serious.[4] The following words and word-forms are concerned:[5]

V. 1 ταῦτα in the sense of the classical τάδε (see the Comm. *ad loc.*).

V. 3 γαμοκλοπέω is a *hapax*,[6] but γαμοκλόπος and γαμοκλοπίη do not occur before the first cent. A.D.

---

[1] On the great skill often demonstrated in imitating language and style of a much earlier author see W. Speyer, *Die literarische Fälschung im heidnischen und christlichen Altertum*, München 1971, 45.82.85.

[2] See J. Wackernagel, *Sprachliche Untersuchungen zu Homer*, Göttingen 1916, 178-200 ("Spuren der zeitgenössischen Sprache bei den nachhomerischen Epikern"), esp. 178: "obwohl die Konstanz des Stils in keiner Gattung der griechischen Literatur grösser ist als im Epos, hat doch kein Epiker es zu Stande gebracht, innerhalb einer längeren Reihe von Versen seine sprachliche Umwelt völlig zu verleugnen und zu verstecken". This is also valid for didactic poetry (since Hesiod).

[3] Wackernagel, *op. cit.* 191: "Das Fehlen (sc. eines Wortes) in ältern Texten kann leicht auf Zufall beruhen".

[4] There are still about 25 other words that occur only at the end of the fifth or in the fourth cent. B.C., but these have of course less weight. Moreover, 30 cases of words and forms occurring only in the third cent. or later would seem to me to carry more than enough weight for the present case.

[5] The evidence was gathered from the Greek Lexicon of Liddell and Scott. Of course the spurious lines have been omitted from this survey.

[6] Hapaxes, of which there are several in the poem, do not of course count in themselves, but they do if directly related words also occur only in late texts, as in the present case.

V. 13 παρθεσίη occurs only once elsewhere in a Hellenistic poem (see Comm.).
V. 15 ἑτερόζυγος occurs since the third cent. B.C.
V. 23 ἔλεος in the sense of "alms" occurs only in and after the LXX.
V. 24 ἄστεγος since the third cent. B.C.
V. 26 ἀπερίστατος since the second cent. B.C.
V. 49 πετροφυής since the first cent. B.C.
V. 73 ὕψωμα since the first cent. A.D.
V. 77 ἀπόλειψον is a sigmatic aorist of ἀπολείπω which is typically Hellenistic, though there is one (dubious) instance in Aristophanes fr. 695, which may be of Antiphanes fr. 35 (fourth cent. B.C.). It is certainly impossible in the sixth cent. B.C.
V. 89 χωρεῖν in the sense of "to grasp" occurs only in Hellenistic texts. Of ἀδίδακτος there is one instance in Demosthenes (after 350 B.C.), further only in Hellenistic texts.
V. 96 ἀκατάσχετος since the second cent. B.C.
V. 99 ἀτάρχυτος since the third cent. B.C.
V. 135 κλόπιμος since the first cent. A.D.
V. 138 ἐπιδεύης, if correct, may be a newly created active form to a middle verb, a phenomenon which is typical of later Greek (see Comm.).
V. 140 συνεγείρω since the LXX.
V. 147 θηρόβορος only here and in Manetho Astrologus (fourth cent. A.D.).
V. 156 σκυβάλισμα is a *hapax*, but σκύβαλον occurs since the third cent. B.C. and σκυβαλίζω since the first cent. B.C.
V. 157 φαγέοις is probably the optative of a present φαγέειν, which occurs further only in the very late *Anonymus in Eth. Nic.*
V. 161 γεηπονίη (= γεωπονία) only in Hellenistic texts.
V. 164 μύχατος since the third cent. B.C.
V. 166 πλήθω in a transitive sense only in Hellenistic poets.
V. 167 νεοτριβής only since the first cent. A.D.
V. 178 μοιχικός only since the first cent. A.D.
V. 190 ἄθεσμος since the first cent. B.C.
V. 191 συνεύαδον only here and in Apoll. Rhod.
V. 193 ἀκάθεκτος since the first cent. B.C.
V. 199 πολυχρήματος only in Hellenistic texts.
V. 201 γειαρότης since the second or first cent. B.C.

V. 202 ὑψιτένων is a *hapax* but ὑψιτενής and ὑψιτενέω occur only after the first cent. A.D.

V. 217 δυστήρητος since the first cent. A.D.

Perhaps some of these examples could be dropped should some of these words eventually turn up in new texts of an earlier date. On the other hand, forms like ἔστωσαν (v. 39) actually may belong to the category of Hellenistic forms, though there are some instances in Euripides; in any case it is extremely improbable that such a form of the third person plural imperative was used as early as the sixth cent. B.C.[7] The general impression would hardly change, and that is that the language and vocabulary of Ps-Phoc. show many characteristics of Hellenistic usage. No wonder that as great an authority on later Greek poetry as Rudolf Keydell says: "Das Gedicht ist nach Inhalt und *Sprache* hellenistisch"[8] (italics added).

But that is not all. As the quotation from Keydell already indicates, several aspects of the contents of the poem also point to a period much later than that of the real Phocylides. First and foremost, the unmistakable influence of the O.T. upon the poem should be mentioned. If the far-fetched theory of Lincke[9] that Phocylides has had an important influence upon the coming-into-being of several parts of the O.T. is rejected, it must be assumed that our author has written his poem after the LXX had been completed. For the other theory that Phocylides' knowledge of the O.T. in the sixth cent. B.C. is due to a partial, old, pre-LXX translation of the O.T., a theory based upon some remarks in Ps-Aristeas and Aristobulus, has, from a historical point of view, no basis at all. It is not necessary here to demonstrate that these passages in Ps-Aristeas and Aristobulus have been inspired by purely apologetic motives and hence have no historical value whatsoever. Other scholars have already shown that convincingly, and the reader may be referred to their studies.[10] It may be added that there is no trace of O.T. influence in the fragments of the real

---

[7] See R. Kühner - F. Blass, *Griech. Gramm.* I 2 (1892), 51.
[8] R. Keydell, "Die griechische Dichtung der Kaiserzeit. 1930-1939", *Jahresbericht etc.* 272 (1941), 27.
[9] See above pp. 19f., 24f.
[10] See the publications of Walter, Pelletier, Jellicoe, and Fraser mentioned above on p. 38 n. 143 and p. 40 n. 153.

Phocylides, as Herter rightly remarked (against Dornseiff).[11] Consequently, when O.T. reminiscences are found in the poem in the great majority of the verses (as the Commentary will amply illustrate), the hypothesis of LXX influence upon our author seems to be the most plausible one, the more so since there are some typical LXX words (e.g. συνεγείρω) in the poem. This fact also points to a period of origin long after the real Phocylides.

But there is still more. Alongside clear influence of the LXX, there are undeniable traces of Stoic influence to be seen in the poem. This influence is less predominant than that of the LXX, but (as will be demonstrated in the Commentary) for instance vv. 63-67 cannot be explained except on the assumption that the author knew Stoic theories, albeit perhaps at second hand.[12] This, too, tells strongly against the authenticity of the poem, as does the fact that vv. 124-128 are conceivable only after Protagoras and v. 59 only after Crantor (see the Comm.).

These factors (the language, the influence of the LXX and Stoicism) make it impossible to maintain that the poem was written by the real Phocylides. Why, then, does his name appear above the poem? [13]

---

[11] *TLZ* 66 (1941), 17-19.

[12] Rossbroich's attempt to find the influence of Posidonius everywhere can be regarded as unsuccessful. See above p. 29 with n. 115 and p. 30 (Sitzler).

[13] The above-said does not prove Farina's theory of multiple authorship to be wrong, but there is not the slightest reason to accept it. See also Stählin's remarks in Christ's *Gesch. der griech. Lit.* 622.

CHAPTER THREE

THE PSEUDONYM

Under this heading the question of why the author assumed a pseudonym (see for that the Chapter on the purpose of the poem, ch. 5) is not discussed; rather, why he has chosen this particular pseudonym. But first attention should be given to the question of whether the author actually chose this name himself or whether a later hand added it. For in several mss. vv. 1-2, which mention the name Phocylides (the so-called *sphragis*), are missing. And, as Speyer[1] has demonstrated, it frequently happened that a pseudonym was attributed to an originally anonymous work later in the tradition. In another context Speyer remarks that in Ps-Phoc. indeed vv. 1-2 are "erst im Laufe der Überlieferung vor die anonym umlaufende Spruchsammlung gestellt worden".[2] But it can be objected that it is hardly imaginable that a Jewish-Hellenistic author wrote these lines in this old-fashioned Ionic dialect *without* attributing them to an earlier authority. As Schürer[3] already said, "die ganze sprachliche Form" of the poem tells in favour of the authenticity of vv. 1-2. Moreover, it cannot be imagined that the poem would begin with v. 3 without a preamble.[4] Another important argument to retain vv. 1-2 is the clear correspondence between these lines and vv. 229-230 (the last two lines of the poem), which has been indicated particularly by Kranz.[5] The correlation between beginning and end in literary works with a *sphragis* is a common phenomenon. Though the omission of vv. 1-2 in a number of mss. cannot be wholly explained, it may be surmised that scribes may have omitted these lines temporarily to add them later in capital letters with ornamentation as a title or subtitle; and this would lead to the omission in several mss. (see also the Comm. *ad. loc.*).[6]

---

[1] W. Speyer, *Die literarische Fälschung* ... 7, esp. 40.
[2] *Pseudepigrapha* I (Entretiens XVIII), Geneva 1972, 324.
[3] *Geschichte* III⁴ (1909), 619.
[4] Bergk, *Griech. Lit. gesch.* II (1883), 301 n. 17, had already observed this.
[5] W. Kranz, "Sphragis", *Rhein. Mus.* 104 (1961), 100. This, too, had already been pointed out by Bergk, *PLG* II⁴ (1882), 78.
[6] The fact that Ps-Phoc. is quoted for the first time only by Stobaeus (fifth cent. A.D.) does not imply that the poem has been unknown or anonymous before that time. E.g. the well-known Teles, too, is quoted for the first time by Stobaeus; see Dudley, *History of Cynicism* 84f.

When it is assumed that it was the author himself who actually chose the pseudonym Phocylides, then one should ask what sort of associations were attached to this name in antiquity. It has been suggested that Phocylides was an unknown name.[7] But though that applies to modern times, it surely does not to antiquity as will become apparent from the following testimonia.[8]

Plato *Resp.* 407a7: here Phoc. fr. 9 is quoted freely to witness that we must ἀρετὴν ἀσκεῖν. At 407b3 that is called Φωκυλίδου παρακέλευμα.

Isocrates *Ad Nicoclem* 42f.: though people know that the works of great poets are χρησιμώτατα by their counsels (συμβουλεύοντα), yet they do not like to listen to them. (43) σημεῖον δ' ἄν τις ποιήσαιτο τὴν Ἡσιόδου καὶ Θεόγνιδος καὶ Φωκυλίδου ποίησιν. καὶ γὰρ τούτους φασὶ μὲν ἀρίστους γεγενῆσθαι συμβούλους τῷ βίῳ τῷ τῶν ἀνθρώπων, ταῦτα δὲ λέγοντες αἱροῦνται συνδιατρίβειν ταῖς ἀλλήλων ἀνοίαις μᾶλλον ἢ ταῖς ἐκείνων ὑποθήκαις.

Aristotle *Polit.* IV 11, 1295b34 quotes Phoc. fr. 12 to support his argument, introducing it by καλῶς ηὔξατο Φωκυλίδης.

Cicero *Epist. ad Att.* IV 9, 1 writes about Pompeius: *Multa mecum de re publica sane sibi displicens, ut loquebatur (sic est enim in hoc homine dicendum), Syriam spernens, Hispaniam iactans, hic quoque, ut loquebatur; et, opinor, usquequaque, de hoc cum dicemus, sit hoc quasi καὶ τόδε Φωκυλίδεω* ("with the same proviso 'as he said', which I think must be inserted everywhere when he is mentioned, like the tag 'this too by Phocylides' ").[9]

Strabo X 5, 12 (487), speaking of the island Leros, quotes the well-known first fragment of Phoc.: καὶ τόδε Φωκυλίδεω· Λέριοι κακοὶ κτλ.

Dio Chrysostom II 5 calls the poems of Phocylides and Theognis δημοτικά (popular) and συμβουλεύοντα καὶ παραινοῦντα τοῖς πολλοῖς καὶ ἰδιώταις. Dio Chrysostom XXXVI 9ff. is a long passage on Phocylides. In a conversation somebody who does not want to hear about any poet other than Homer is asked in fun whether he thinks that Homer is the best poet or Phocylides. When he says that

---

[7] So e.g. Hengel, in *Pseudepigrapha* I 324 (see above p. 59 n. 2).

[8] References to the most important texts can be found in W. Pape-G. Benseler, *Wörterbuch der griechischen Eigennamen* II, Braunschweig 1911³ (repr. Graz 1959), 1657. Only the most significant texts are mentioned, and in a chronological order.

[9] An important feature of Phocylides' style is that he "sealed" most of his sentences with the opening hemistich καὶ τόδε Φωκυλίδεω.

he does not even know the name Phocylides, Dio replies: (11) τὸν δὲ Φωκυλίδην ὑμεῖς μὲν οὐκ ἐπίστασθε, ὡς λέγεις· πάνυ δὲ τῶν ἐνδόξων γέγονε ποιητῶν.... (12) καὶ γάρ ἐστιν οὐ τῶν μακράν τινα καὶ συνεχῆ ποίησιν εἰρόντων, ὥσπερ ὁ ὑμέτερος μίαν ἑξῆς διέξεισι μάχην ἐν πλείοσιν ἢ πεντακισχιλίοις ἔπεσιν, ἀλλὰ κατὰ δύο καὶ τρία ἔπη αὐτῷ καὶ ἀρχὴν ἡ ποίησις καὶ πέρας λαμβάνει. Dio also says that Phoc. rightly προστίθησι τὸ ὄνομα αὐτοῦ καθ' ἕκαστον διανόημα, ἅτε σπουδαῖον καὶ πολλοῦ ἄξιον ἡγούμενος, wholly otherwise than Homer. (13) As an example fr. 4 (on Nineveh) is quoted and qualified as ταῦτα τὰ ἔπη ἐσθλά, and (in 15) Dio says about it: ἐμοὶ δοκεῖ σφόδρα καλῶς λέγειν ὑπὲρ τῆς πόλεως. Furthermore, Dio stresses (in 13ff.) the usefulness of Phocylides' poetry (συνέφερε, ὠφελεῖ).

Plutarch *Rect. rat. aud.* 13, 45B: μέμψαιτο δ' ἄν τις Ἀρχιλόχου μὲν ὑπόθεσιν, Παρμενίδου δὲ τὴν στιχοποιίαν, Φωκυλίδου δὲ τὴν εὐτέλειαν (economy), Εὐριπίδου δὲ τὴν λαλιάν, Σοφοκλέους δὲ τὴν ἀνωμαλίαν ... ἕκαστός γε μὴν ἐπαινεῖται κατὰ τὸ ἴδιον τῆς δυνάμεως, ᾧ κινεῖν καὶ ἄγειν πέφυκεν (*ibid*. 18, 47E Plutarch illustrates his argument with fr. 14, introduced by ὥς φησι Φωκυλίδης). Cf. *Lib. educ.* 5, 3F: Plato gives some good pieces of advice for the education of children, κινδυνεύει δὲ καὶ Φωκυλίδης ὁ ποιητὴς καλῶς παραινεῖν λέγων· (fr. 13).

Athenaeus *Deipnosoph.* X 428B: here Phoc. fr 11 is quoted amongst citations from Hesiod, Theognis and the three great tragedians. *Ibid.* XIV 620C: Chamaeleon says in his book "On Stesichorus" μελῳδηθῆναι ... οὐ μόνον τὰ Ὁμήρου, ἀλλὰ καὶ τὰ Ἡσιόδου καὶ Ἀρχιλόχου, ἔτι δὲ Μιμνέρμου καὶ Φωκυλίδου.

Phrynichus *Ecl.* 336 (p. 463 Rutherford) quotes Phoc. fr. 5 to illustrate a typically Ionic usage.

Clement of Alexandria *Strom.* V 127, 4 quotes Phoc. fr. 16 amongst citations from Archilochus, Orpheus, Philemon, Sophocles and Pindar.[10]

Iulianus Apostata *Contra Galil.* fr. 224 (p. 203 Neumann) *apud* Cyrill. Alex. *Adv. Iul.* VII 224 (= *PG* 76, 841D) ὁ σοφώτατος Σολομῶν παρόμοιός ἐστι τῷ παρ' Ἕλλησι Φωκυλίδῃ ἢ Θεόγνιδι ἢ Ἰσοκράτει; πόθεν;

Cyrillus' reaction *ibid*. 225 (PG 76, 844C) εἶτα μακροῦ μεταξὺ γεγονότος καιροῦ (sc. after Solomon) ... Φωκυλίδης καὶ Θέογνις ἐγενέσθην. συγγεγράφασι δὲ καὶ αὐτοὶ χρηστομαθῆ, ψιλὰ καὶ κεκομψευ-

---

[10] The whole of this passage from Clement is taken over word for word by Eusebius in *PE* XIII 13, 54.

μένα, όποιά περ άν και τίτθαι κορίοις, και μην και παιδαγωγοί φαίεν άν νουθετούντες τα μειράκια.

Libanius *Epist.* 1473, 6 μηδέ τοιούτους ημάς άποφαινέτω χρήστας, οίους φεύγειν παραινεί Φωκυλίδης (fr. 6). *Ibid.* 1512, 1 και γαρ τούτου (sc. χορού) μετέσχηκε Φωκυλίδη πειθόμενος μετά χρήματα λόγων άψάμενος (possibly an allusion to fr. 9).

Themistius *Or.* 24, 307c: quotation of Soph. *O.R.* 4f. and then: αλλά Φωκυλίδης τά τε άλλα αληθώς λέγει και ότι σμικρά πόλις μετά φρονήσεως επί σκοπέλου κατοικούσα κρείττων Νίνου αφραινούσης (fr. 4).

Stobaeus quotes several fragments of Phoc. which he thinks useful: fr. 2 in IV 22, 192; fr. 3 in IV 29, 28; fr. 7 in IV 15, 6; fr. 9 in II 15, 8.[11]

Stephanus Byz. *Ethnica* s.v. Μίλητος (p. 452 Meineke) mentions Phocylides among the famous Milesians, together with Thales, Timotheus, etc.

Suda *Lex.* s.v. Φωκυλίδης· Μιλήσιος, φιλόσοφος, σύγχρονος Θεόγνιδος. ήν δε εκάτερος μετά χμζ' έτη των Τρωϊκών, ολυμπιάδι γεγονότες νθ'. έγραψεν έπη και ελεγείας, παραινέσεις ήτοι γνώμας· άς τινες Κεφάλαια επιγράφουσιν. εισί δε εκ των Σιβυλλιακών κεκλεμμένα.[12]

Tzetzes on Aristoph. *Ran.* 931: όθεν άριστως και Φωκυλίδης φησί· fr. 8.

It is not difficult to gather from this collection of ancient testimonia about Phoc. that his fame was greater than is commonly assumed. He is always quoted with great approval (καλώς, άρίστως). He is often bracketed together with the very great poets (Hesiod, Theognis, the great tragedians, etc.). By several authors he is even abundantly praised and recommended for the useful wisdom that one can draw from his poetry. From the first half of the fourth century B.C. till well into the Middle Ages the name Phocylides is regarded as a guarantee for wise and useful counsel for daily life.[13] If it was someone's concern to propagate wise and useful advices

---

[11] Under the name Phocylides, Stobaeus quotes Ps-Phoc. vv. 111 and 113 in III 3, 27 and vv. 125-130 (omitting v. 129) in III 3, 28.

[12] The title Κεφάλαια (meaning "main points, principal matters") does not occur in the extant mss. of Ps-Phoc. Suda's remark that Phoc. has stolen his verses from the Sibylline oracles is, of course, based upon the assumption of the great antiquity of these oracles.

[13] On the fame of Phocylides in antiquity see also A. Croiset-M. Croiset, *Histoire de la littérature grecque* II (1890) 157; G. A. Gerhard, *Phoinix von Kolophon* (1909) 254f.; J. M. Edmonds, *Elegy and Iambus* (LCL) I (1931) 23; K. Bielohlawek, *Hypotheke und Gnome* (1940) 16ff.

for daily life, the name Phocylides was a pre-eminently appropriate pseudonym.[14] Possibly the choice of this pseudonym was also influenced by the fact that in fr. 4 Phocylides expresses a negative opinion about Nineveh, which may have been (mis)understood as a Biblical allusion.[15]

---

[14] It is amusing to mention here that the Frisian scholar Jan Fokkes (= son of Fokke) at Holwerd, who was professor of Philosophy in Franeker from 1639 to 1651, called himself Johannes *Phocylides* Holwarda (on him see S. Galama, *Het Wijsgerig Onderwijs aan de Hogeschool te Franeker 1585-1811*, Franeker 1954, 91-100. I owe this reference to my colleague Dr. A. de Groot who also added that there were many more people who called themselves Phocylides in the 17th and 18th centuries).

[15] W. Nestle-W. Liebich, *Gesch. der griech. Lit.* I, Berlin 1961³, 47: "Die Erwähnung des Falles der üppigen Weltstadt Niniveh in einem seiner Sprüche (Fr. 4D) bildete wohl den Anlass zur Fälschung eines grösseren Lehrgedichts auf den Namen dieses Dichters..." (cf. Zeph. II 13, etc.).

CHAPTER FOUR

THE TEACHING OF PSEUDO-PHOCYLIDES

What is the nature of the practical ethics propagated by Ps-Phoc.? After all that has been said in the chapter on the history of the research, it is not necessary to repeat that Ps-Phoc. preaches a kind of universally valid ethics that could be assented to by any right-minded man in antiquity.[1] His primary sources [2] are the LXX (especially the Pentateuch and the Wisdom literature) and Greek gnomological traditions; also the popular diatribe might be men-

---

[1] J. P. Audet, "La sagesse de Ménandre l'Égyptien", *Rev. Bibl.* 59 (1952), 79, writes that the whole ethics of the Syriac Sentences of Menander could be summarized by the words of Plutarch in *Lib. educ.* 10, 7D-E. Apart from some polytheistic elements, this applies also to Ps-Phoc. The passage runs: διὰ γὰρ ταύτην (= φιλοσοφίαν) ἔστι καὶ μετὰ ταύτης γνῶναι τί τὸ καλὸν τί τὸ αἰσχρόν, τί τὸ δίκαιον τί τὸ ἄδικον, τί τὸ συλλήβδην αἱρετόν, τί τὸ φευκτόν· πῶς θεοῖς πῶς γονεῦσι πῶς πρεσβυτέροις πῶς νόμοις πῶς ἀλλοτρίοις πῶς ἄρχουσι πῶς φίλοις πῶς γυναιξὶ πῶς τέκνοις πῶς οἰκέταις χρηστέον ἐστί· ὅτι δεῖ θεοὺς μὲν σέβεσθαι, γονέας δὲ τιμᾶν, πρεσβυτέροις αἰδεῖσθαι, νόμοις πειθαρχεῖν, ἄρχουσιν ὑπείκειν, φίλους ἀγαπᾶν, πρὸς γυναῖκας σωφρονεῖν, τέκνων στερκτικοὺς εἶναι, δούλους μὴ περιυβρίζειν· τὸ δὲ μέγιστον, μήτ' ἐν ταῖς εὐπραγίαις περιχαρεῖς μήτ' ἐν ταῖς συμφοραῖς περιλύπους ὑπάρχειν, μήτ' ἐν ταῖς ἡδοναῖς ἐκλύτους εἶναι μήτ' ἐν ταῖς ὀργαῖς ἐκπαθεῖς καὶ θηριώδεις. Cf. Crouch, *Origin* 70.

[2] That Ps-Phoc. also used other sources than the ones mentioned in the text, is very probable. For instance, there is a rather striking difference in vocabulary between vv. 1-174 and vv. 175-230. The latter passage, because of its agreements with the N.T. *Haustafeln*, was already thought to derive from an earlier source (see esp. Crouch, *Origin*). But besides that, the following particularities can be noted: the article is used 28 times in 1-174, only 1 or 2 times (v. 179 is a dubious case) in 175-230; in v. 73 the participle of εἰμι is ἐών, in 204 it is ὤν; ἐν and ἐνί occur 10 times in 1-174, not once in 175-230; ἐπί is used 2 times in 1-174, but 6 times in 175-230; θεός occurs 10 times in 1-174, only once in 175-230; κατά is used 6 times in 1-174, not once in 175-230; μηδέ is used 6 times in 1-174, but 14 times in 175-230; μήτε is used 14 times in 1-174, only once in 175-230; πᾶς is used 21 times in 1-174, but only once in 175-230. All this may be due to a source.

It is impossible to treat here at length the very complicated and difficult question of Ps-Phoc.'s sources. Besides the sources already mentioned, one may be more or less certain that he used a) materials that were (later?) also used in Two Ways documents (see esp. Seeberg), and b) materials that were also used by Philo and Josephus in their apologies for the Jewish Law (see Wendland). These are rather vague and elusive entities, about which it is hard to say anything definite. Geffcken (*Zwei griechische Apologeten*, Leipzig-Berlin 1907, XL) rightly sighed: "wer kann die Quellen der Pseudophokylideia bestimmen?".

tioned.³ It may be that these Greek elements reached him only in Jewish dress, so that he had no first-hand knowledge of his Greek sources. But, on the other hand, the diatribe and gnomologies were so well-known among the people ⁴ that first-hand knowledge definitely will not have been impossible for our author.

In the Commentary both Jewish and Greek parallels to most of the verses can be found. A relatively small number of lines has only Jewish or only Greek parallels. It is likely that this small number of cases can be reduced still further on the basis of a more exhaustive use of the available Jewish and Greek literature. Nevertheless, it is surely significant that even those lines to which only Greek (or Roman) parallels have been noted do not reveal a single thought which is really un-Jewish (see vv. 21, 25, 27, 49, 51-2, 55-6, 59-60, 65-7, 95-6, 121, 123, 143, 162-3, 191, 200, 201-4, 227). On the other hand, however, a number of verses for which only Jewish parallels could be noted, has typically Jewish, sometimes very un-Greek themes, e.g. the strong concern for the poor and needy (vv. 10, 19, 22-3, 29), the concern for strangers (vv. 39ff.), the injunction not to take the motherbird from the nest together with its nestlings (vv. 84-5), the bodily resurrection of the dead (vv. 103-4), the warning against eating meat from a torn animal (vv. 147-8), the great value of manual labour (vv. 153ff.), the severe sexual ethics (esp. vv. 186-190), not to speak ill of a slave to his master (v. 226).

But, as already stated, the author mostly took from the O.T. only ethical statements that were not specifically Jewish. As with the Wisdom teachers in Israel, the name Israel does not pass his lips and anything particularistic has been omitted. Hence, no word about the sabbath, circumcision, ritual purity and suchlike. The fact that the author remained unrecognized as a Jew till the end of the sixteenth century is significant in this respect.

---

³ Cynic influence, detected in so many places by Rossbroich, has been exaggerated. Much of it is common in the Hellenistic world. It is difficult to determine the extent of Cynic influence on later authors. See D. R. Dudley, *History of Cynicism*, London 1937, 114 and Heinemann, *Philons griechische und jüdische Bildung*, Breslau 1932, 547f.

⁴ The popular ethical-philosophical preachers could be heard on every street-corner (Wendland, *Die hellenistisch-römische Kultur*, Tübingen 1912²⁻³, 75ff.), and gnomologies were used at school (see J. Barns, "A New Gnomologium", *Class. Quart.* 44 (1950), 132ff. and esp. K. Horna, *PW Suppl.* VI (1935), 78).

As to his use of the O.T., it is noteworthy that the author, although he generally picks his precepts at random from all parts of the O.T., also incorporates a great part of one specific chapter of the Pentateuch into his poem, viz. Lev. XIX.[5] After a kind of summary of the Decalogue in vv. 3-8 (omitting the introductory formula "I am the Lord, your God, etc." and the commandments concerning the sabbath and idolatry), there follows a passage (vv. 9-41) in which a great part of the precepts of Lev. XIX is presented (again, omitting the repeated "I am the Lord, your God" and the precepts concerning sabbath, idolatry and cult). This can only be explained by assuming that for Ps-Phoc. Lev. XIX was a kind of summary of the Torah or a counterpart of the Decalogue. Other sources for this view, it is true, are late. In Sifra Qedoshim, Parasha I (on XIX 1), it is said: "This section [sc. Lev. XIX] was spoken in the assembly. Why was it spoken in the assembly? Because the majority of the principles of the Torah are attached to it" (p. 380 in the Jerusalem 1967/8 edition of Torat Kohanim). In Lev. Rabbah XXIV 5 we read: "R. Ḥiyya taught: This section [sc. Lev. XIX] was spoken in the presence of a gathering of the whole assembly, because most of the essential principles of the Torah are attached to it. R. Levi said: Because the Ten Commandments are included therein".[6] Though these statements are from the third century A.D. and later, it is not impossible that what is expressed in them is much older.[7] Some small indications in that direction can possibly be found in the considerable importance Philo attached to Lev. XIX (in *Spec. leg.* he quotes from this chapter 17 times); also in the fact that Lev. XIX 18 ("You must love your neighbour as yourself") is called several times in the N.T. the central commandment of the whole Torah, or is mentioned in immediate connection with commandments of the Decalogue or the Shema (Mt. XIX 18f.; XXII 37-40; Mk. XII 31; Lk. X 27;

---

[5] The first to note this was Bernays (228-234), see above p. 8.

[6] Viz. the first commandment in v. 2, the second in v. 4, the third in v. 12, the fourth in v. 3, the fifth in v. 3, the sixth in v. 16, the seventh in v. 10, the eighth in v. 11, the ninth in v. 16, the tenth in v. 18. See on this passage W. Bacher, *Die Agada der palästinischen Amoräer* II (1896) 369.

[7] Prof. David Flusser thinks that these statements reflect an early, pre-mishnaic tradition (letter of 2.9.77). Cf. the striking case of the combination of circumcision and name-giving on the eighth day after birth (Luke I 59 and II 21) which is only mentioned in Jewish literature for the first time in Pirqe de R. Eliezer (ninth cent. A.D.), whereas it is certainly a much older use as appears from the N.T.; see Billerbeck II 107.

Rom. XIII 9; Gal. V 14) which has Jewish parallels.[8] One might tentatively conclude that in Judaism at the beginning of our era Lev. XIX was regarded as a central chapter in the Torah.[9]

Though Ps-Phoc. has adopted many precepts from the Pentateuch, the spirit of his writing is more congenial to the Wisdom literature.[10] There, too, we see a constant search for a universal ethics which shuns particularistic elements and is not averse to the good and useful elements in the ethics of the surrounding peoples. It was especially G. Klein (1909) who emphasized that Ps-Phoc. must be regarded as a Wisdom teacher. This point is dealt with below (sections 5 and 6).

What, then, are the contents of the poem? These are hard to summarize, because the enumerative and incoherent character of the poem does not allow its thoughts to be systematized. Furthermore, it is not necessary to itemize all the author's ethical statements here. The most important topics of the poem are: justice, honesty, moderation, faithfulness, care for the poor and the helpless, the usefulness of labour and of marriage, the danger of sexual sins.

A little more should be said of the author's statements about God and man. The only wise and almighty God (54) must be honoured before anything else (8). God is the source of our prosperity, and therefore he demands that the rich share their riches with the poor (29). He hates perjury (17) and will punish in judgement those who have judged evilly (11). He provided every creature with a means of defence, man with the faculty of thinking and speaking (125-128). Man's spirit is God's image (106). All this implies (though it is nowhere explicitly stated) that God is the creator of the universe, which is a harmonious whole (71-74). God is not only the ruler of the world, but also of the nether-world (111). The problem of the so-called "polytheistic" verses (75, 98, 104, 163), that have often been a stumbling-block, has been exaggerated. One verse (98) must obviously be emended, whilst two others (75, 163)

---

[8] See Billerbeck I 353ff. and cf. Berger, *Gesetzesauslegung Jesu* I (1972) 80ff. The theories of Seeberg, Carrington and Selwyn (see Bibliography) about the existence of a catechism for proselytes based upon Lev. XIX have never been proved.

[9] It should also be mentioned that Lev. XVIII and XX form the basis of Ps-Phoc. 179ff. This series of precepts has other Jewish parallels as well.

[10] Several scholars have classified Ps-Phoc. among Wisdom poetry, e.g. Baumgartner 229f., Berger 47, Hengel (1972) 297 (see Bibliography). It is significant that the author assumes the epithet σοφώτατος (v. 2) which traditionally belongs to Solomon, the father of Wisdom literature.

imply nothing more than the ascription of personality to the heavenly bodies (which is common in Jewish texts). Only in v. 104 it might be suspected that the author has gone rather far in adapting himself to pagan views, without becoming really un-Jewish.[11] For detailed discussion the reader may be referred to the commentary on these passages.

The author's "anthropology" has several O.T. elements as well. Man is made out of the dust of the earth, to which he eventually returns; but his spirit, which is God's image, again ascends into the air (vv. 106-8). The author issues innumerable warnings against evil-doing [12] so that it may be concluded that according to him human nature is inclined to evil. But nowhere is God's forgiveness and help spoken of; so the author apparently thinks that man's will is strong enough to reject evil and to do what is good. As already stated, labour is of great importance for man (153-174) and also marrying and begetting children (175f.). Sex is only for procreation and not for all kinds of lustful pleasures, which are extensively mentioned and repudiated (177-194). Moderation and self-restraint in all things are very important (36, 69, 76, 98, 145). Ps-Phoc. also emphasizes good relationships in the family: between husband and wife (195-7); between parents and children (207-9); between masters and slaves (223-7); also between friends (218). One should try to change even an enemy into a friend (140-2).

Ps-Phoc. has no systematic thoughts on life after death. In the passage concerned (99-115), several seemingly contradictory notions are loosely juxtaposed, as if the author felt no inconsistencies. Thus e.g. he preaches the bodily resurrection of the dead (103f.), but also the immortality of the soul (115). This phenomenon, however, has many parallels in ancient Judaism, as Cavallin demonstrated in his dissertation.[13] It is noticeable here that the bodily resurrection is mentioned so clearly, for actually this is almost the only totally un-Greek and typically Jewish element in the poem. One could say: here the author betrays himself. Was he, after all, so "orthodox" that he could not omit a mention of this important Jewish tenet? Vv. 147f., where eating

---

[11] Here, it should be realized that in the immediately preceding words (103f.) the author speaks about the bodily resurrection of the dead, such an un-Greek thought that Ps-Phoc. possibly tries to neutralize its effect.

[12] μή, μηδέ and μήτε occur about 85 times.

[13] *Life After Death* I, Lund 1974; see my review in *Bijdragen* 36 (1975), 330f.

meat cut or torn from a living animal is forbidden, raise a similar question, for this prohibition, too, is typically Jewish (though there is perhaps a vague Pythagorean parallel). Maybe the author has incorporated this precept under the influence of a source (e.g. a list of Noachian laws, cf. Sahn. 56a).[14]

Since almost any religious foundation of his ethics is lacking in Ps-Phoc., the poem as a whole makes a somewhat superficial impression. Maybe that is the reason of the fact that the Church Fathers never quote it, contrary to other Jewish pseudepigrapha.[15]

---

[14] One could also refer to vv. 84f. (= Deut. XXII 6f.), to which there is not any Greek parallel. Of vv. 84f. and 147f. I. G. Matthews, *Apologetic* 10 says they are "Jewish interpolations in an old Grecian writer" [sic!].

[15] The many similarities of Ps-Phoc. and the New Testament are not treated here; see besides the Commentary my article "Pseudo-Phocylides and the New Testament", *ZNW* 69 (1978) (forthcoming).

CHAPTER FIVE

THE AUTHOR'S PURPOSE

The most difficult problem posed by our poem is the question why the author wrote it. What intention did he have when he wrote down these ethical precepts? What did he aim at, or rather, who was he aiming at? Whom did he hope to reach with his sentences and what did he hope to achieve by it?

Though there is hardly any doubt about the Jewishness of the author, almost everything typically Jewish has been avoided in this poem. It looks as if the author did his utmost to conceal his Jewishness. The single lines which might betray his Jewish beliefs (84f., 103f., 147f.) were probably not meant by the author to reveal himself as a Jew. That would contradict the whole tendency of the poem, namely, to pass on O.T. ethical principles in a hidden way, so as to obscure their origin. The only thing that is said about the origin of these precepts is that they are "counsels of God", revealed to men by Phocylides (v. 1). It would seem to be impossible that Ps-Phoc. believed that he could convert people to Judaism by this poem. This is even more implausible in the light of the fact that the author has chosen a non-Jewish pseudonym. But what then did he want? Theoretically, there are four possibilities. 1. The author did not want anything; he wrote the poem just for the sheer pleasure of doing it, as a kind of exercise in versification. 2. The author wrote for his fellow Jews, to encourage or to entertain them. He wanted to say to them by means of this poem, with this pseudonym: Look, Greek ethics in essentials agrees with the Torah, so don't be ashamed of your own tradition and don't be afraid that you lack anything important when remaining Jewish. Or the author wrote to satisfy a literary need of the Jews. 3. The author wrote for a pagan public, not in order to convert them to Judaism, but only to make "sympathizers", that is to say, to win over people to a standpoint more sympathetic to Judaism so as to break through the isolation of the Jews in the Hellenistic and Roman world. Or, more modestly, he wrote solely to humanize the pagan world. He only wanted to inculcate in heathen minds some fundamental and universally valid precepts, hoping that society would become more livable by that. 4. The author was a "God-fearer", someone on the borderline between paganism and Judaism, trying to win over people to his own way of life.

As to the first possibility, there is not anyone who defends it and it seems to be a very improbable thesis. Nobody will write, purely for fun and without any other intention, a poem in the old Ionic dialect and with such a clear and definite selective principle. The second possibility (that the author wrote for his co-religionists) deserves more serious attention. Tcherikover defends the thesis that all Jewish Hellenistic literature "was meant not for the Gentiles but for the Jews"; he is followed in this by Walter and Hengel.[1] They believe that "Jewish Alexandrian literature was directed inwards and not outwards" (so Tcherikover 182) and that the aim was "die Befriedigung des literarischen Bedarfs der griechischsprechenden Juden selbst" (so Hengel, *Pseud.* 306). However, strict proofs for this thesis have not been furnished by any of these three scholars.[2]

Nevertheless, the application of a similar thesis (independent of these scholars) to Ps-Phoc. by Alon[3] yielded a most attractive result. He claims that all the features of the poem can be explained on the assumption that the author makes an ancient Greek wisdom poet hold out to hellenized Jews a more or less current presentation of the (ethical) principles of the Torah in order to check further decline into a non-Jewish way of life. The poet says, as it were, that by remaining Jewish a Jew does not miss anything important in Greek culture, for already a highly esteemed early Greek author fully agreed with the principles of the Jewish way of life. This theory explains the use of a pseudonym, the absence of the prohibition of idolatry (for this is supposed to be self-evident even among thoroughly hellenized Jews), and the generally non-proselytizing

---

[1] V. Tcherikover, "Jewish Apologetic Literature Reconsidered", *Symbolae R. Taubenschlag dedicatae* III, Wratislawa 1957, 169-193 (quotation on p. 178f.); N. Walter, *Der Thoraausleger Aristobulus*, Berlin 1964, 44 and esp. "Frühe Begegnungen zwischen jüdischem Glauben und hellenistischer Bildung" (1964) 375f. (Walter will defend this stance in respect of Ps-Phoc. in his forthcoming German translation of Ps-Phoc. for the series Jüdische Schriften aus hellenistisch-römischer Zeit); M. Hengel, *Judentum und Hellenismus*, Tübingen 1973², 129f., also in *Pseudepigrapha* I, Geneva 1972, 306f., and *Juden, Griechen und Barbaren*, Stuttgart 1976, 138f.
[2] So, rightly, W. Speyer, *Die literarische Fälschung im heidnischen und christlichen Altertum*, München 1971, 158-160.
[3] See above p. 45 n. 171.

character of the poem. Therefore, this is a more probable thesis than the theory about the literary needs of hellenized Jews, because those needs could be satisfied in other and better ways than by pseudepigraphy; think, e.g., of the Moses drama of Ezekiel the Tragedian. But even Alon's theory cannot be strictly proved, and it needs more unambiguous evidence than just this one poem. However, it cannot be disproved either and it deserves serious consideration.[4]

One could also consider the interesting possibility [5] that Ps-Phoc. was a Jew who wrote for Jewish schoolboys. It is a well-known fact that in the ancient schools the young children, after mastering the writing of letters, syllables and words, began to exercise in writing short sentences, and these were mostly γνῶμαι.[6] School-exercisebooks have been preserved [7] in which one can see that collections of sentences (gnomologies) from Homer, Hesiod, Theognis were used for calligraphic exercises. Ziebarth thinks that Phocylides (the real) was also used for this purpose.[8] The aim was, of course, not only to teach the children to write neatly, but also to acquaint them (almost unconsciously) with the ethical ideas of these famous authors.[9] Ps-Phoc. may have served the same or a similar purpose for Jewish children. (It should be noted that the text from Plutarch

---

[4] It may be added that, if Alon's thesis is right, then Brockington's remark (in "The Problem of Pseudonymity", *JTS* n.s. 4 (1953), 19) that a Jew addressing himself to Jews with Wisdom literature was almost bound to assume the pseudonym Solomon, needs correcting.

[5] This possibility was suggested to me by Prof. W. C. van Unnik in a private communication.

[6] See E. Ziebarth, *Aus dem griechischen Schulwesen*, Leipzig 1914², 127f., 130f. H. I. Marrou, *Histoire de l'éducation dans l'antiquité*, Paris 1960⁵, 218. M. P. Nilsson, *Die hellenistische Schule*, München 1955, 12. 15.

[7] Collected by E. Ziebarth, *Aus der antiken Schule*, Bonn 1913², esp. 6f. and 22f.

[8] *Aus dem griechischen Schulwesen* 131.

[9] See Sen. *Epist.* 33, 7 *ideo pueris et sententias ediscendas damus et has quas Graeci chrias vocant, quia complecti illas puerilis animus potest qui plus adhuc non capit*. See the discussion of this text by F. H. Colson, "Quintilian I 9 and the Chria in Ancient Education", *Class. Rev.* 35 (1921), 150-4. A. Dihle ("Posidonius' System of Moral Philosophy", *JHS* 93 (1973), 50) formulates one of the Stoic principles of education as follows: "Praecepta as a medium of moral education have to be applied to children, to beginners in the struggle for virtue, and to persons intellectually incapable of getting a philosophic instruction. Those persons must be guided by the authority of a teacher, by the influence of moral examples, and by the fascination of well formulated sentences, because they can't ... understand the reasons for which something is called good and something bad".

quoted above (p. 64 n. 1) is from a treatise on the education of children!). Though, again, one can neither prove nor disprove it. But the use of a heathen pseudonym can hardly be explained on this assumption.

Is the third possibility more probable? As is known from the first chapter, especially the two Jewish scholars Klein (1909) and Guttmann (1927) have proposed this solution, followed among others by Crouch (1972). They assume that in antiquity there was a universalistic, Jewish propaganda movement which was not intent on making proselytes, but only on inculcating in pagans a number of universally valid ethical precepts. The aim of this movement was no more (and no less) than the humanizing of pagan society. Ps-Phoc. is supposed to belong to this movement. In this connection they referred to possible sources and parallels like the Noachian commandments, the *Derek Erez* literature and some passages in Philo's *Hypothetica* and Josephus' *Contra Apionem*, where the same universalistic tendendy is said to be discernible.[10] The appeal to *Derek Erez* treatises (by Klein) has rightly been rejected by Guttmann and Crouch, since these writings are all several centuries later than Ps-Phoc. and it is hard to discover with certainty really old elements in them. Klein's parallels, moreover, were often very far-fetched. However, even the appeal to the Noachian laws, though they are demonstrably old (cf. Jub. VII 20)[11], does not solve many problems, From the seven Noachian commandments[12], two central ones do not occur at all in Ps-Phoc., viz., to refrain from blasphemy and from idolatry.[13] The other five

---

[10] See for all this above pp. 25ff., 35f., 50f.
[11] See L. Finkelstein, "Some Examples of Maccabean Halaka", *JBL* 49 (1930), 21-25; E. L. Dietrich, "Die 'Religion Noahs', ihre Herkunft und ihre Bedeutung", *ZRGG* I (1948), 310.
[12] As is well-known, the exact number of Noachian commandments varies considerably in the various rabbinic sources, but it is commonly assumed that the list of seven as represented e.g. in Sanh. 56a has some claim to be original. These seven rules are: to establish courts of justice; to refrain from blasphemy, idolatry, adultery, bloodshed, robbery, and eating flesh cut from a living animal.
[13] That nothing is said against idolatry might be explained by a tradition occurring in Philo (*Spec. leg.* I 53) and Josephus (*Ant.* IV 207), which says not to scold the gods of the pagans, on the basis of the (wrong) LXX translation of Ex. XXII 27 θεοὺς οὐ κακολογήσεις. See on this matter G. Delling, "Josephus und die heidnischen Religionen", *Studien zum N.T.* (1970) 45-52.

do occur here and there in a more or less concealed way, "mais, à part ces rapprochements, on ne peut pas trouver, dans tout ce long poème, deux phrases consécutives qui coïncident avec des préscriptions noachidiques. Le poème est impregné d'un esprit monothéiste et humanitaire non équivoque, mais cet esprit va beaucoup plus loin que les lois noachidiques établis par les rabbins".[14] As to the materials common to Philo, Josephus and Ps-Phoc.[15], the great difference is that in Philo and Josephus the universally valid precepts, drawn both from the O.T. and Greek ethical codes, appear in recognizably Jewish contexts, whereas in Ps-Phoc. they do not. What can be said of this material (which presents only precepts that could be expected to find a sympathetic hearing with non-Jews) is that it "was gathered prior to all three of them and constituted a source from which each drew for his own particular purpose".[16] But which "particular purpose" Ps-Phoc. had can hardly be deduced on the basis of this material, whereas Philo and Josephus leave no doubt as to what their "particular purpose" was, viz. to show to their pagan readers the high level of Jewish law. This difference from Ps-Phoc. is substantial. In Ps-Phoc. there is not the slightest hint of apologetics or propaganda for the Jewish law *as Jewish law*, let alone a missionary aim. When Crouch, following Klein and Guttmann, says that "there was a widespread Jewish missionary activity which promoted ethical monotheism",[17] one cannot but ask for more clear and unambiguous evidence of this "widespread" movement. Probably there were indeed Jews who had abandoned the ritual precepts in their propaganda. The attitude of the Jewish merchant Ananias towards Izates, king of Adiabene, testifies to this. See Jos. *Ant.* XX 41: "The king could, Ananias said, worship God even without being circumcised if indeed he had fully decided to be a devoted adherent of Judaism, for it was this that counted more than circumcision". This isolated case cannot, however, be a proof of the existence of a

---

[14] S. Krauss, "Les préceptes des Noachides", *Rev. Ét. Juives* 47 (1903), 32f. The attempt by F. Siegert ("Gottesfürchtige und Sympathisanten", *JSJ* 4 (1973), 125) to find the seven Noachian commandments in the opening lines of Ps-Phoc. cannot be regarded as successful. Cf. also Alon, "The Halakah..." 277.

[15] These agreements had already been seen by Wendland in 1896, see above p. 18f.

[16] Crouch, *Origin* 88.

[17] *Origin* 89.

"widespread movement".¹⁸ Moreover, Ananias *did* try to win Izates over to Judaism, whereas Ps-Phoc. definitely does nothing of the sort. The passages in Philo and Josephus and also the Noachian commandments are parallel to Ps-Phoc. only in so far as they show that there was a tendency in some Jewish circles to summarize the essentials of the Torah in a set of reasonable, sensible and universally valid rules for human conduct.¹⁹ Given this tendency Ps-Phoc. is consistent with it, but with this difference: he is so modest as to conceal even the origin of these rules (and also his own person, by his pseudonym). He only says they derive from God (v. 1).

What he wanted to attain by this procedure does not become very clear. He cannot have made proselytes, not even "God-fearers", because even for that aim the Jewishness of the poem is too concealed. It could well be that by this means he could have achieved no more than this: people whom he influenced came unknowingly to stand closer to Judaism, became unconscious

---

¹⁸ Though H. Hegermann in Leipoldt-Grundmann, *Umwelt* I 310, remarks: "Angestrebt wurde an sich der volle Übertritt des Heiden zum jüdischen Glauben, seine Gewinnung zum Proselyten. In Ansätzen muss es aber eine zweite Auffassung gegeben haben, nach der man nicht unbedingt alle Heiden zu Juden machen wollte. Das zeigt die ausdrückliche Erklärung des jüdischen Kaufmanns, der das Königshaus in Adiabene für das Judentum gewann, dass man den wahren Gott auch verehren könne, ohne durch Beschneidung ein voller Jude geworden zu sein. Diese vereinzelte, von Josephus ablehnend kommentierte Äusserung wird man durchaus ernst nehmen dürfen angesichts der grossen Gruppen von sog. Gottesfürchtigen, die vor allem in der Apostelgeschichte des Lukas sichtbar werden. Denn diese stehen ja auf dem Boden ebensolcher Auffassung".

¹⁹ On this tendency to summarize the Torah see Moore, *Judaism* II 86-8; Sanders, *Paul* 112-4; and esp. K. Berger, *Die Gesetzesauslegung Jesu* I (1972), 56-257. Cf. *ibid.* 38ff. on the tendency to "Verengung des Inhaltes [sc. of the Torah] und die faktische Weglassung weitester Teile der atl. Gesetzessammlungen" (for which he refers to Sir., Ps. Sal., Sap. Sal., Ps-Phoc. and Ps-Men.). "Dem entspricht positiv die Einbeziehung griechischer Tugend- und Lasterbegriffe unter dem Gesetzesbegriff" (39). That often occurs when "justice" is seen as a recapitulation of the whole Torah. "Zu Beginn und am Ende dieser Aufzählungen erscheint sehr oft der allgemeine Hinweis auf 'Recht und Gerechtigkeit', deren Entfaltung dann die Einzelforderungen sind. Die gesammte Reihe ist eine Art Summe der Gerechtigkeit und des sozialen Verhaltens, eine Tora im Kleinen mit Angabe der für wichtig gehaltenen Forderungen" (40). Ps-Phoc. is a good example of this with δίκη in v. 1 and δικαιοσύνη in v. 229, meant as leading motive of the whole poem.

"sympathizers" [20] of a sort. Perhaps this was all Ps-Phoc. wanted?

The fourth solution of the problem posed by this poem would be to assume, *pace* Rossbroich (1910), that it was written by a "God-fearer", that is, a heathen who had not become a Jew (therefore not a proselyte, as Rossbroich erroneously calls him), but who observed a number of important Jewish commandments and customs, and could be found on the fringe of the Jewish community. Ps-Phoc. is supposed to tell by this poem to his fellow men that the ethical rules he observes were already propagated by the great Phocylides and are hence worthwhile. However, we do not have any other evidence for the existence of literature written by "God-fearers", that category of people on the borderline between Judaism and paganism.[21] This does not mean, of course, that such literature has not existed at all. This question should, therefore, be left open.

It must be confessed that it is impossible to choose between the three latter possibilities, all of which can neither be proved nor disproved. We need new materials to get more light on this problem. For the present moment, we must rest content with the fact that the exact purpose of our author is still somewhat enigmatical.[22]

---

[20] On this category, as distinct from "Godfearers", see L. H. Feldmann, "Jewish 'Sympathizers' in Classical Literature and Inscriptions", *Transactions and Proceedings of the American Philological Association* 81 (1950), 200-208, and esp. F. Siegert, "Gottesfürchtigen und Sympathisanten", *JSJ* 4 (1973), 109-164.

[21] In this connection, reference should be made to J. P. Audet, "La sagesse de Ménandre l'Égyptien", *Rev. Bibl.* 59 (1952), 55-81, who maintains that the (Syriac) Sentences of Menander (a gnomic collection showing many resemblances to Ps-Phoc.) are the work of a "God-fearer". The borderline position of "God-fearers" between Judaism and paganism is well illustrated by Juvenal *Sat.* XIV 96-110.

[22] It should be admitted here that, whereas at first the Klein-Guttmann -Crouch position seemed to me to be the most plausible solution, the Alon-Walter thesis gradually appeared to be more attractive and convincing. But one cannot unreservedly take sides. "Bleibt zu fragen, ob die grob gemusterte Landkarte vom frühen Judentum nicht noch für differenziertere Gruppierungen und Konzeptionen Raum bieten müsste" (E. Brandenburger, "Himmelfahrt Moses", in *JSHRZ* V 2 (1976) 65f.).

CHAPTER SIX

THE GENRE OF THE POEM

The poem of Ps-Phoc. has been called a Wisdom-poem, a didactic poem, and a gnomology (i.e. a collection of sentences, a *Spruchsammlung*). All these categorizations are equally right and equally wrong. Ps-Phoc. belongs to all these genres, but cannot be identified with one of them.

As a Jewish writing this poem belongs to Wisdom literature. A sketch of the manifold manifestations of the Old Testament Wisdom literature cannot be given here—the reader can be referred to the abundant relevant literature [1]—, but this much should be said here: Wisdom in Israel is all about the art of living. Wisdom embraces all kinds of practical insights for everyday life. It was in the first instance a practical philosophy of the good life and of the personal and ethical standards needed to attain it. Its main topics are modesty, self-control, honesty, reliability, diligence, careful speech, respect for superiors, concern for truth and justice.[2] Its rules of conduct have a certain universal validity, because they do not have a specific Israelite character. For that reason, Wisdom literature had a great capacity for absorbing all kinds of foreign influences. In O.T. Wisdom texts, many traces have been found of Egyptian, Babylonian, Persian, Edomite and Greek ideas which the Israelite Sages thought valuable enough to adopt into their own writings, be it with frequent modification.[3] Among the several poetic forms of Wisdom literature, poems can also be found that

---

[1] The following is only a random selection of publications where references to further literature can be found. S. H. Blank, "Wisdom", *IDB* IV (1962) 852-861. O. Eissfeldt, *Einleitung in das Alte Testament*, Tübingen 1964³, 109ff. 166ff. G. von Rad, *Weisheit in Israel*, Neukirchen 1970. R. B. Y. Scott, *The Way of Wisdom*, New York 1971. W. Zimmerli, *Grundriss der alttestamentlichen Theologie*, Stuttgart 1975², 136-146. J. L. Crenshaw (ed.), *Studies in Ancient Israelite Wisdom*, New York 1976. Crenshaw writes significantly (p. 22): "It is at present neither possible to write a chronological history of the development of wisdom literature nor to place each of the forms within its proper setting".
[2] See R. B. Y. Scott, "The Study of Wisdom Literature", *Interpretation* 24 (1970), 29.26.
[3] Eissfeldt, *op. cit.* 111ff., esp. 115.

are "eine lose Aneinanderreihung einzelner Sprüche",[4] of which the best-known example is the collection in Prov. X 1-XXII 16. This collection consists of 375 single sentences, which have little or no mutual connection and coherence. Sometimes they are arranged on the basis of similar content, sometimes they are put together because there are certain formal similarities. But mostly no ordering principle can be discerned and each single line has to be looked at on its own.[5]

It is obvious to every reader of Ps-Phoc. that what is said here of Wisdom poetry also applies to this poem. That need not be illustrated here. It is no wonder, therefore, that the books from the O.T. which show most parallels to Ps-Phoc. are Proverbia and Sirach (though the affinity of spiritual climate is less great with Sirach, who shows his Jewishness much more than does the author of Prov.). An important formal difference is that the typical O.T. form of a Wisdom sentence, viz. the *parallelismus membrorum*,[6] is dropped by Ps-Phoc., who chose another way of expressing his ideas.

This brings us to our second category, the didactic poem. Ps-Phoc. writes in dactylic hexameters. In Greek poetry this metre was reserved for two genres, epic and didactic poetry. Both genres also had their own specific dialect, scil. a kind of Homeric and Hesiodic Ionic. Both these features, the hexameter and the Ionic dialect, are part of the make-up of Ps-Phoc.'s poem. There is no doubt that Ps-Phoc. wanted to place himself into the long tradition of Greek didactic poetry, which began with Hesiod and lasted till far in the Roman period.[7]

For the ancient Greeks, Hesiod was the originator not only of didactic poetry, but also of the γνώμη, the sentence.[8] This brings

---

[4] Eissfeldt, *op. cit.* 167.
[5] Eissfeldt, *op. cit.* 640f.
[6] Eissfeldt, *op. cit.* 76f. Needless to say, the typically Jewish theological elements in some Wisdom books are dropped by Ps-Phoc.
[7] For a short survey see R. A. B. Mynors, "Didactic Poetry", *OCD* (1949) 277f. One difference between Ps-Phoc. and other didactic poets is that they mostly deal with a single subject, e.g. farming (Hesiod, Menecrates) or medicine (Marcellus of Side) or astronomy (Aratus, Manetho) or geography (Dionysius Periegetes), whereas Ps-Phoc. deals with many subjects at the same time, albeit all of them ethical.
[8] On this and the following see K. Horna, "Gnome, Gnomendichtung, Gnomologien", *PW Suppl.* VI (1935) 74-90 (88-90 are additions by Kurt von Fritz).

us to the third category, for in a number of mss. our poem is superscribed Φωκυλίδου γνῶμαι, and as a matter of fact more than half of the verses in Ps-Phoc. have parallels in Greek gnomic literature. Again, I shall not try to sketch the history of this branch of Greek literature. The preliminary work for the writing of such a history has not yet been done, and it would require more than a life-time to do it. It is a field beset with enormous difficulties and complexities.[9] The following remarks will suffice on this occasion.

The γνώμη, a short sentence giving a rule for conduct in daily life,[10] is already found in Hesiod's *Opera et Dies*. But that is not a gnomic poem. The first instance we have of a poem that is wholly made up of γνῶμαι is that of Theognis (mid sixth century B.C.), though he probably was not the first to write a whole piece of poetry consisting of ethical maxims (cf. the Χείρωνος ὑποθῆκαι). After him, there are other gnomic poets like Phocylides, Chares, Phoinix and also some of the Presocratic philosophers. One of these philosophers, Democritus, played an important part in the development of the prose γνώμη, a genre of which we have a well-known instance in Ps-Isocrates' *Ad Demonicum* (second half of the fourth century B.C.). As early as in the fifth century B.C. people began to make collections of sentences, primarily meant for the needs of elementary education at school, "in dem als Schreib- und Lesevorlagen, sowie als Diktatstoffe aus den Dichtern passende Sentenzen ausgewählt wurden. Auch für die Unterweisung der reiferen Jugend in Moral und praktischer Lebensweisheit wurden Gnomensammlungen in reichem Masse verwendet" (Horna 78).[11] Especially

---

[9] See Horna, *art. cit.* 87.
[10] Aristotle *Rhet.* II 21 gives the following definition: ἔστι δὲ γνώμη ἀπόφανσις, οὐ μέντοι περὶ τῶν καθ' ἕκαστον, οἷον ποῖός τις Ἰφικράτης, ἀλλὰ καθόλου, καὶ οὐ περὶ πάντων, οἷον ὅτι τὸ εὐθὺ τῷ καμπύλῳ ἐναντίον, ἀλλὰ περὶ ὅσων αἱ πράξεις εἰσὶ καὶ αἱρετὰ ἢ φευκτά ἐστι πρὸς τὸ πράττειν. Most of the definitions in the later so-called *progymnastici* derive from Aristotle (or Anaximenes), See e.g. Hermogenes, *Progymn.* 4 (in Spengel, *Rhet. Gr.* II 7) γνώμη ἐστὶ λόγος κεφαλαιώδης ἐν ἀποφάνσει καθολικῇ, ἀποτρέπων τι ἢ προτρέπων ἐπί τι, ἢ ὁποῖόν ἐστι ἕκαστον δηλῶν. Nicolaus Sophistes, *Progymn.* 4 (Spengel III 463) τὴν ἀπόφανσιν εἶναι... καθολικήν, συμβουλήν τινα καὶ παραίνεσιν ἔχουσαν πρός τι τῶν ἐν βίῳ χρησίμων. The differences between *gnome, apophthegma, chria, apomnemoneuma, homoioma, hypotheke*, etc. need not be discussed here; see Horna, *art. cit.* 75f. and von Fritz, *ibid.* 88f.
[11] See also Ch. 5 above, p. 72. Cf. Aeschines III 15 διὰ τοῦτο γὰρ οἶμαι παῖδας ὄντας τὰς τῶν ποιητῶν γνώμας ἐκμανθάνειν, ἵν' ἄνδρες ὄντες αὐταῖς χρώμεθα. One may think of the way Ps-Phoc. was used in the Middle Ages and in the 16th century; see above p. 1.

in Hellenistic times, this collecting of wise maxims from poets and philosophers was very much in vogue. For instance, Chrysippus, the great Stoic, promoted it very strongly and made himself a *thesaurus sententiarum*.[12] One could also refer to Epicurus' *Kyriai doxai* and Porphyry's *Ad Marcellam*, to mention two examples of other philosophical schools. The two poets whose works were most plundered for *gnōmai* were Euripides and Menander. An important characteristic of such collections was, of course, their "Zusammenhanglosigkeit". Sentences were simply juxtaposed with no clear connection with either previous or following verses. It was only sometimes that they were arranged alphabetically or more or less thematically; but mostly that was not the case, exactly as in O.T. Wisdom poetry. This principle of loose arrangement facilitated the adoption of all kinds of materials and the intermingling of the writer's own creations and traditional sentences (and, of course, it also facilitated interpolation). As it appears from Isocr. *Ad. Nicocl.* 43 (quoted above in chapter 3) that Phocylides' sentences were also regarded as very useful for educational purposes, it can readily be understood that a person writing under this name wrote his didactic Wisdom poem in the form of a gnomology in order that it could be used in schools. In this way he could already exercise influence on young children. It should be added that our poem is not such a totally disconnected whole as many gnomologies and O.T. Wisdom poems. There seems to be some arrangement of the materials in it, as I have tried to indicate by 15 headings (see the Comm.). Sometimes the thematic connection is very clear (e.g. 153ff., 175ff.), sometimes less so.

It has been shown that our poem partly participates in the characteristics of all three genres. The genres of Wisdom poetry and of *gnōmai* have an important point of agreement in their practical and educational purposes. Ps-Phoc. translated these purposes in the form of a didactic poem with a content which may be called gnomic Wisdom.[13]

---

[12] See on this esp. the works of Elter (see Bibliography).
[13] A more detailed "formgeschichtliche" investigation of Ps-Phoc. on this point will only be possible when the whole genre is much more fully investigated.

CHAPTER SEVEN

DATE AND PROVENANCE

Though the dates that have been attributed to this poem over the years vary from the sixth century B.C. to the fourth century A.D., there is a growing consensus to ascribe it to the period between 200 B.C. and 150 A.D. What has to be considered is whether it is possible to determine the time of origin more precisely. This is difficult, however, since in the whole poem there is not a single reference to political events or circumstances that might help us further. Nevertheless, there are some features of language and content that make it possible to narrow down the above-mentioned period.

Ps-Phoc. uses about 30 words (or word-forms) which are not attested in Greek literature before the third century B.C.[1] and about 15 of these do not occur in texts before the first century B.C. This might suggest 100 B.C. as a *terminus post quem*.[2] The same date is suggested by the fact that Ps-Phoc. knew the LXX, not only the Pentateuch (which is evident in more than half of the verses), but unmistakably also the Prophets and the Wisdom literature.[3] The influence of Stoicism on the author is also undeniable.[4] In itself this Stoic influence only indicates that the poem was written after 300 B.C., but the mental affinity, in several parts of the poem, especially with first century A.D. Stoics like Musonius Rufus, Seneca and Hierocles strongly points to the Imperial period.[5] This period is also suggested by the many agreements with Philo and by similarities with the "diatribe" of the popular philo-

---

[1] See above p. 55ff.
[2] Of course, this evidence is too scanty to base a firm conclusion upon it. But in combination with the following arguments these facts get their due weight.
[3] See the Comm. The unmistakable allusions to Jer. IX 22 in v. 53 and to Prov. VI 6-8c in vv. 164-174 are very clear instances.
[4] E.g. in vv. 63-67 where Ps-Phoc. distinguishes between different types of anger, zeal and love, which are Stoic distinctions.
[5] C. Schneider, *Kulturgeschichte des Hellenismus* I, München 1967, 892 even asserts that Ps-Phoc. is "von Musonius Rufus oder einem seiner Geistesverwandten beeinflusst".

sophical-ethical preachers, who were most active in the early Roman period.⁶

This cumulative evidence seems to favour a date between 50 B.C. and 100 A.D. Moreover, if one takes into account the fact that the poem was probably written in Alexandria (see below), then it may be suggested that the most probable date for its origin is within the period during which the relations between Jews and Greeks in Alexandria were not too tense. In the particular period under consideration that means the reigns of the two emperors Augustus (30 B.C.-14 A.D.) and Tiberius (14-37 A.D.). It can hardly be imagined that after the anti-Jewish pogroms in Alexandria during the reign of Caligula (37-41 A.D.) ⁷ an Alexandrian Jew could have maintained such a great openness towards pagan culture. Therefore, the most probable date would seem to be somewhere between, say, 30 B.C. and 40 A.D.⁸ Needless to say, this does not mean that another dating is impossible.⁹ But on this assumption the characteristics of the poem can best be explained.

That Alexandria is to be preferred as the city where the poem probably originated is actually based on only a single line (v. 102), where it is said that it is not right to dissect a human body. As far as we know, it was only in Alexandria that human anatomy was studied by means of dissection.¹⁰ This is, of course, no definite proof that the poem was written there; but that city is at least the context where such a prohibition makes most sense. And since in other respects as well the poem is congruent with Jewish Hellenistic culture in Alexandria as it is known from other sources,¹¹ that city

---

⁶ See P. Wendland, *Therapeuten* 712 n. 2 with reference to his "Philo und die kynisch-stoische Diatribe" in Wendland-Kern, *Beiträge zur Gesch. der griech. Phil. und Rel.*, Berlin 1895, 1-75. Cf. also W. Capelle-H. I. Marrou, "Diatribe", *RAC* III (1957), 996.

⁷ See E. Schürer, *The History of the Jewish People in the Age of Jesus Christ* I (new ed. by G. Vermes and F. Millar), Edinburgh 1973, 388ff.

⁸ Cf. the dating by A. Kurfess, *ZNW* 40 (1941), 162: "ungefähr in die Zeit unmittelbar vor oder nach Christi Geburt". F. Christ, *Theol. Zeitschr.* 31 (1975), 140: "aus der Zeit Jesu". Ch. Guignebert, *Le monde juif vers le temps de Jésus*, Paris 1935, 258; etc.

⁹ Another dating should probably have to be earlier, not later.

¹⁰ See L. Edelstein, "The History of Anatomy in Antiquity", in *Ancient Medicine*, Baltimore 1967, 247-301. F. Kudlien, "Anatomie", *PW Suppl.* XI (1968), 38-48. See further the Comm. *ad loc.*

¹¹ Cf. the remarks on universalistic tendencies which were characteristic of Alexandrian Judaism by H. F. Weiss, "Zur Frage der historischen Voraussetzungen der Begegnung von Antike und Christentum", *Klio* 43-45

has the best chance of being the place of origin.[12] It should be added, however, that we know very little about other Jewish communities in the Diaspora.

(1965), 310-316; also L. H. Feldmann, "The Orthodoxy of the Jews in Hellenistic Egypt", *Jewish Social Studies* 22 (1960), 215-237 and P. M. Fraser, *Ptolemaic Alexandria* I, Oxford 1972, 282ff.

[12] See e.g. W. Kroll, "Phokylides (2)", *PW* XX 1 (1941), 507; P. M. Fraser, *Ptolemaic Alexandria* II, Oxford 1972, 539.

APPENDIX

THE INTERPOLATION IN *ORACULA SIBYLLINA* II AND THE MANUSCRIPTS

The commentary which follows is based upon the latest critical edition by Young (1971), to whose choise and rejection of variant readings I generally adhere. Hence text-critical problems will be discussed only when they have exegetical relevance. The "interpolated interpolation" of Ps-Phoc. 5-79 in *Or. Sib.* II (Ψ) is also regarded as a text-critical problem, and I do not think that, as a whole, it effects the exegesis of Ps-Phoc. I assume with Bernays,[1] Geffcken,[2] Ludwich,[3] and Keydell[4] that a Christian interpolator has been at work in *Or. Sib.* which implies that I reject the theory of Sitzler[5] and Kurfess[6] to the effect that Ψ has preserved a much older text-form than the extant mss. of Ps-Phoc., although the interpolation cannot have been inserted at a very late date: the Suda (s.v. Φωκυλίδης) already says: ... εἰσὶ δ' ἐκ τῶν Σιβυλλιακῶν κεκλεμμένα, which, though wrong, indicates at any rate that its author knew this insertion. And Geffcken narrows it down by adducing the Theosophy of Tübingen: "Die Theosophie zeigt ... öfter, wenn auch nicht überall, Anlehnung an die Lesarten von Ψ, also fällt in letzter Instanz die Entstehung dieser Überlieferung vor die Abfassungszeit der Theosophie, d.h. etwa vor den Ausgang des 5. Jahrhunderts (n. 2: Damit wäre denn auch der Einschub der Phokylidea II 56-148 chronologisch halbwegs fixxiert)".[7]

Why these lines have been inserted into *Or. Sib.* II, we can only guess. It is clear at any rate that the interpolator thought that this material lent itself well to his propagandistic purpose, albeit with some modifications, the most conspicuous of which is the omission of vv. 70-75, one of the supposed polytheistic passages. An investi-

---

[1] *Über das phokylideische Gedicht* (1856) 223ff.
[2] *Die Oracula Sibyllina* (1902) XLV ff.
[3] *Spruchbuch* (1904) 9.
[4] *Jahresbericht* 272 (1941), 27f.
[5] *Woch. für klass. Phil.* 29 (1912), 449ff.
[6] *ZNW* 38 (1939), 171ff.
[7] *Op. cit.* XLIII.

gation into the motives of the interpolator, however, does not belong to a study of Ps-Phoc. but is best left to students of *Or. Sib.*[8]

The critical editions of the text of Ps-Phoc. by Diehl and Young are mainly based upon five important mss. (there are many more, but all of them inferior).[9] These mss. are:

M (in Paris)	10th century
B (in Oxford)	10th century
P (in Paris)	12th century
L (in Florence)	13th century
V (in Vienna)	13/14th century

---

[8] A translation of *Or. Sib.* II 56-148 by J. Geffcken can be found in E. Hennecke, *Neutestamentliche Apokryphen*, Tübingen-Leipzig 1904, 339-341 (no longer in Hennecke-Schneemelcher II (1964), due to the influence of Kurfess who deals with *Or. Sib.* in this volume).

[9] See Young pp. XVIff.; also Denis, *Introduction* 216.

TEXT AND TRANSLATION

ΦΩΚΥΛΙΔΟΥ ΓΝΩΜΑΙ

Young
p. 95
Ταῦτα δίκησ' ὁσίῃσι θεοῦ βουλεύματα φαίνει
Φωκυλίδης ἀνδρῶν ὁ σοφώτατος ὄλβια δῶρα.

μήτε γαμοκλοπέειν μήτ' ἄρσενα Κύπριν ὀρίνειν
μήτε δόλους ῥάπτειν μήθ' αἵματι χεῖρα μιαίνειν.
5 μὴ πλουτεῖν ἀδίκως, ἀλλ' ἐξ ὁσίων βιοτεύειν.
p. 96 ἀρκεῖσθαι παρ' ἐοῖσι καὶ ἀλλοτρίων ἀπέχεσθαι.
ψεύδεα μὴ βάζειν, τὰ δ' ἐτήτυμα πάντ' ἀγορεύειν.
πρῶτα θεὸν τιμᾶν, μετέπειτα δὲ σεῖο γονῆας.

πάντα δίκαια νέμειν, μὴ δὲ κρίσιν ἐς χάριν ἕλκειν.
10 μὴ ῥίψῃς πενίην ἀδίκως, μὴ κρῖνε πρόσωπον·
ἢν σὺ κακῶς δικάσῃς, σὲ θεὸς μετέπειτα δικάσσει.
μαρτυρίην ψευδῆ φεύγειν· τὰ δίκαια βραβεύειν.
παρθεσίην τηρεῖν, πίστιν δ' ἐν πᾶσι φυλάσσειν.
μέτρα νέμειν τὰ δίκαια, καλὸν δ' ἐπίμετρον ἁπάντων.
p. 97 σταθμὸν μὴ κρούειν ἑτερόζυγον, ἀλλ' ἴσον ἕλκειν.
16 μὴ δ' ἐπιορκήσῃς μήτ' ἀγνῶς μήτε ἑκοντί·
ψεύδορκον στυγέει θεὸς ἄμβροτος ὅστις ὀμόσσῃ.
σπέρματα μὴ κλέπτειν· ἐπαράσιμος ὅστις ἕληται.
μισθὸν μοχθήσαντι δίδου, μὴ θλῖβε πένητα.
20 γλώσσῃ νοῦν ἐχέμεν, κρυπτὸν λόγον ἐν φρεσὶν ἴσχειν.
μήτ' ἀδικεῖν ἐθέλῃς μήτ' οὖν ἀδικοῦντα ἐάσῃς.

πτωχῷ δ' εὐθὺ δίδου μὴ δ' αὔριον ἐλθέμεν εἴπῃς·
πληρώσει σέο χεῖρ'. ἔλεον χρῄζοντι παράσχου.
ἄστεγον εἰς οἶκον δέξαι καὶ τυφλὸν ὁδήγει.
25 ναυηγοὺς οἴκτιρον, ἐπεὶ πλόος ἐστὶν ἄδηλος.
χεῖρα πεσόντι δίδου, σῶσον δ' ἀπερίστατον ἄνδρα.
p. 98 κοινὰ πάθη πάντων· ὁ βίος τροχός· ἄστατος ὄλβος.
πλοῦτον ἔχων σὴν χεῖρα πενητεύουσιν ὄρεξον.

THE SENTENCES OF PHOCYLIDES

Vv. 1-2 *Prologue*

These counsels of God by His holy judgments
Phocylides the wisest of men sets forth, gifts of blessing.

Vv. 3-8 *Summary of the Decalogue*

Commit not adultery nor rouse homosexual passion,
stitch not wiles together nor stain your hands with blood.
5 Do not become unjustly rich, but live from honourable means.
Be content with what you have and abstain from what is another's.
Tell not lies, but speak always the truth.
Honour God first and foremost, and thereafter your parents.

Vv. 9-21 *Exhortations to Justice*

Always dispense justice and stretch not judgment for a favour.
10 Cast the poor not down unjustly, judge not partially.
If you judge evilly, God will judge you thereafter.
Flee false witness; arbitrate justice.
Watch over a deposit, and in everything keep faith.
Give a just measure, good is an extra full measure of all things.
15 Make a balance not unequal, but weigh honestly.
Do not commit perjury, neither ignorantly nor willingly.
The immortal God hates a perjurer, whosoever it is who has sworn.
Do not steal seeds; cursed is whosoever takes them.
Give the labourer his pay, do not afflict the poor.
20 Take heed of your tongue, keep your word hidden in your heart.
Neither wish to do injustice, nor therefore allow another to do injustice.

Vv. 22-41 *Admonitions to Mercy*

Give to the poor man at once, and do not tell him to come tomorrow.
You should fill your hand. Give alms to the needy.
Receive the homeless in your house, and lead the blind man.
25 Pity the shipwrecked, for navigation is unsure.
Extend your hand to him who falls, and save the helpless one.
Suffering is common to all; life is a wheel; prosperity is unstable.
When you have wealth, stretch out your hand to the poor.

ὧν σοι ἔδωκε θεός, τούτων χρήζουσι παράσχου.
30 ἔστω κοινὸς ἅπας ὁ βίος καὶ ὁμόφρονα πάντα.
  [Αἷμα δὲ μὴ φαγέειν, εἰδωλοθύτων ἀπέχεσθαι.]
  Τὸ ξίφος ἀμφιβαλοῦ μὴ πρὸς φόνον, ἀλλ' ἐς ἄμυναν.
  εἴθε δὲ μὴ χρήζοις μήτ' ἔκνομα μήτε δικαίως·
  ἢν γὰρ ἀποκτείνῃς ἐχθρόν, σέο χεῖρα μιαίνεις.
35 Ἀγροῦ γειτονέοντος ἀπόσχεο μὴ δ' ἄρ' ὑπερβῇς.
Young [πάντων μέτρον ἄριστον, ὑπερβασίαι δ' ἀλεγειναί.]
p.99 [κτῆσις ὀνήσιμός ἐσθ' ὁσίων, ἀδίκων δὲ πονηρά.]
  μηδέ τιν' αὐξόμενον καρπὸν λωβήσῃ ἀρούρης.
  Ἔστωσαν δ' ὁμότιμοι ἐπήλυδες ἐν πολιήταις·
40 πάντες γὰρ πενίης πειρώμεθα τῆς πολυπλάγκτου,
  χώρης δ' οὔ τι βέβαιον ἔχει πέδον ἀνθρώποισιν.

  Ἡ φιλοχρημοσύνη μήτηρ κακότητος ἁπάσης.
  χρυσὸς ἀεὶ δόλος ἐστὶ καὶ ἄργυρος ἀνθρώποισιν.
  Χρυσέ, κακῶν ἀρχηγέ, βιοφθόρε, πάντα χαλέπτων,
45 εἴθε σε μὴ θνητοῖσι γενέσθαι πῆμα ποθεινόν·
  σεῦ γὰρ ἕκητι μάχαι τε λεηλασίαι τε φόνοι τε,
  ἐχθρὰ δὲ τέκνα γονεῦσιν ἀδελφειοί τε συναίμοις.

p.100 Μὴ δ' ἕτερον κεύθῃς κραδίῃ νόον ἀλλ' ἀγορεύων,
  μηδ' ὡς πετροφυὴς πολύπους κατὰ χῶρον ἀμείβου.
50 πᾶσιν δ' ἁπλόος ἴσθι, τὰ δ' ἐκ ψυχῆς ἀγόρευε.
  Ὅστις ἑκὼν ἀδικεῖ, κακὸς ἀνήρ· ἢν δ' ὑπ' ἀνάγκης,
  οὐκ ἐρέω τὸ τέλος. βουλὴ δ' εὐθύνεθ' ἑκάστου.
  Μὴ γαυροῦ σοφίῃ μήτ' ἀλκῇ μήτ' ἐνὶ πλούτῳ·
  εἷς θεός ἐστι σοφὸς δυνατός θ' ἅμα καὶ πολύολβος.
55 Μὴ δὲ παροιχομένοισι κακοῖς τρύχου τεὸν ἧπαρ·
  οὐκέτι γὰρ δύναται τὸ τετυγμένον εἶναι ἄτυκτον.
  Μὴ προπετὴς ἐς χεῖρα, χαλίνου δ' ἄγριον ὀργήν·
  πολλάκι γὰρ πλήξας ἀέκων φόνον ἐξετέλεσσεν.

Of that which God has given you, give of it to the needy.
30 Let all of life be in common, and all things be in agreement.
[Do not eat blood; abstain from food sacrificed to idols.]
If you gird on a sword, let it be not to murder but to protect.
But may you not need it at all, neither without the law nor justly.
For if you kill an enemy, you stain your hand.
35 Keep off the field of your neighbour, be thus not a trespasser.
[Moderation is the best of all, excesses are grievous.]
[Honest acquisition is useful, but unjust acquisition is bad.]
Do not damage fruits that are growing on the land.
Strangers should be held in equal honour with citizens.
40 For we all experience the poverty that makes one wander;
and the land has nothing constant for men.

Vv. 42-47 *Love of Money and its Consequences*

Love of money is the mother of all evil.
Gold and silver are always a lure for men.
Gold, originator of evil, destroyer of life, crushing all things,
45 would that you were not a desirable calamity to mortals!
For your sake there are battles and plunderings and murders,
and children become the enemies of their parents and brothers
                           (the enemies) of their kinsmen.

Vv. 48-58 *Honesty, Modesty, and Self-Control*

Hide not a different thought in your heart while uttering another.
Change not yourself according to the spot like a polyp that clings
                           to the rock.
50 Be sincere to all, speak what is in your heart.
Whoever wrongs wilfully is a bad man, but if he does so under
                           compulsion,
I shall not pass sentence. For it is each man's intention that is
                           examined.
Pride not yourself on wisdom nor on strength nor on riches.
The only God is wise and mighty and at the same time rich in
                           blessings.
55 Vex not your liver with bygone evils;
for what has been done can no more be undone.
Be not rash with your hands, but bridle your wild anger.
For often someone who has dealt a blow has unintentionally com-
                           mitted a murder.

Ἔστω κοινὰ πάθη· μηδὲν μέγα μηδ' ὑπέροπλον.
Young 60 οὐκ ἀγαθὸν πλεονάζον ἔφυ θνητοῖσιν ὄνειαρ·
p. 101 ἡ πολλὴ δὲ τρυφὴ πρὸς ἀμέτρους ἕλκετ' ἔρωτας·
ὑψαυχεῖ δ' ὁ πολὺς πλοῦτος καὶ ἐς ὕβριν ἀέξει.
θυμὸς ὑπερχόμενος μανίην ὀλοόφρονα τεύχει.
ὀργὴ δ' ἐστὶν ὄρεξις, ὑπερβαίνουσα δὲ μῆνις.
65 ζῆλος τῶν ἀγαθῶν ἐσθλός, φαύλων δ' ὑπέρογκος.
τόλμα κακῶν ὀλοή, μέγ' ὀφέλλει δ' ἐσθλὰ πονεῦντα.
σεμνὸς ἔρως ἀρετῆς, ὁ δὲ Κύπριδος αἶσχος ὀφέλλει.
ἡδὺς ἄγαν ἄφρων κικλήσκεται ἐν πολιήταις.
μέτρῳ ἔδειν, μέτρῳ δὲ πιεῖν καὶ μυθολογεύειν.
69ᵇ πάντων μέτρον ἄριστον, ὑπερβασίαι δ' ἀλεγειναί.

70 Μὴ φθονέοις ἀγαθῶν ἑτάροις, μὴ μῶμον ἀνάψῃς.
ἄφθονοι Οὐρανίδαι καὶ ἐν ἀλλήλοις τελέθουσιν.
οὐ φθονέει μήνη πολὺ κρείσσοσιν ἡλίου αὐγαῖς,
οὐ χθὼν οὐρανίοισ' ὑψώμασι νέρθεν ἐοῦσα,
οὐ ποταμοὶ πελάγεσσιν. ἀεὶ δ' ὁμόνοιαν ἔχουσιν·
75 εἰ γὰρ ἔρις μακάρεσσιν ἔην, οὐκ ἂν πόλος ἔστη.
p. 102 Σωφροσύνην ἀσκεῖν, αἰσχρῶν δ' ἔργων ἀπέχεσθαι.
μὴ μιμοῦ κακότητα, Δίκη δ' ἀπόλειψον ἄμυναν.
Πειθὼ μὲν γὰρ ὄνειαρ, Ἔρις δ' ἔριν ἀντιφυτεύει.
μὴ πίστευε τάχιστα, πρὶν ἀτρεκέως πέρας ὄψει.
80 νικᾶν εὖ ἔρδοντας ἐπὶ πλεόνεσσι καθήκει.
Καλὸν ξεινίζειν ταχέως λιταῖσι τραπέζαις
ἢ πλείσταις δολίαισι βραδυνούσαις παρὰ καιρόν.
Μηδέποτε χρήστης πικρὸς γένῃ ἀνδρὶ πένητι.
μηδέ τις ὄρνιθας καλιῆς ἅμα πάντας ἑλέσθω,
85 μητέρα δ' ἐκπρολίποις, ἵν' ἔχῃς πάλι τῆσδε νεοσσούς.
Μηδέποτε κρίνειν ἀδαήμονας ἄνδρας ἐάσῃς.
[μηδὲ δίκην δικάσῃς, πρὶν ⟨ἂν⟩ ἄμφω μῦθον ἀκούσῃς.]

Vv. 59-69 *Moderation in All Things*

Let your emotions be moderate, neither great nor overwhelming.
60 Excess, even of good, is never a boon to mortals.
Great luxuriousness draws one to immoderate desires.
Great wealth is conceited and grows to insolence.
Anger that steals over one causes destructive madness.
Rage is a desire, but wrath surpasses it.
65 Zeal for good things is noble, for bad things excessive.
Daring in bad deeds is ruinous, but greatly strengthens a man who
works at good deeds.
Love of virtue is noble, but love of passion increases shame.
A man who is too simple is called foolish among the citizens.
Eat and drink in moderation, be moderate in your talk.
Moderation is the best of all, excesses are grievous.

Vv. 70-96 *The Danger of Envy and Other Vices*

70 Do not envy others their goods, do not fix reproach upon them.
The heavenly ones also are without envy toward each other.
The moon envies not the sun his much stronger beams,
nor the earth the heavenly heights though it is below,
nor the rivers the seas. They are always in concord.
75 For if there were strife among the blessed ones, heaven would not
stand firm.
Practise self-restraint, and abstain from shameful deeds.
Do not imitate evil, but leave vengeance to justice.
For persuasiveness is a boon, but strife begets only strife.
Trust not too quickly, before you shall see exactly the end.
80 It is proper to surpass your benefactors with still more benefactions.
It is better to present guests with a simple meal quickly
than with a large number of elaborated courses[1] drawn out beyond
the appropriate time.
Never be a relentless creditor to a poor man.
One should not take all the birds from a nest at the same time.
85 But leave the mother-bird behind, in order to get young from her
again.
Never allow ignorant men to sit in judgment.
[Do not pass a judgment before you have heard the word of both
parties.]

---

[1] reading θαλίαισι

Young
p. 103   τὴν σοφίην σοφὸς εὐθύνει, τέχνας δ' ὁμότεχνος.
         οὐ χωρεῖ μεγάλην διδαχὴν ἀδίδακτος ἀκουή.
   90   οὐ γὰρ δὴ νοέουσ' οἱ μηδέποτ' ἐσθλὰ μαθόντες.
         Μὴ δὲ τραπεζοκόρους κόλακας ποιεῖσθαι ἑταίρους·
         πολλοὶ γὰρ πόσιος καὶ βρώσιός εἰσιν ἑταῖροι
         καιρὸν θωπεύοντες, ἐπὴν κορέσασθαι ἔχωσιν,
         ἀχθόμενοι δ' ὀλίγοις καὶ πολλοῖς πάντες ἄπληστοι.
   95   Λαῷ μὴ πίστευε, πολύτροπός ἐστιν ὅμιλος·
         λαὸς <γὰρ> καὶ ὕδωρ καὶ πῦρ ἀκατάσχετα πάντα.

         Μὴ δὲ μάτην ἐπὶ πῦρ καθίσας μινύθῃς φίλον ἦτορ.
         μέτρα δὲ τεῦχ' ἔθ' ἑοῖσι· τὸ γὰρ μέτρον ἐστὶν ἄριστον.
         γαῖαν ἐπιμοιρᾶσθαι ἀταρχύτοις νεκύεσσιν.
  100   μὴ τύμβον φθιμένων ἀνορύξῃς μηδ' ἀθέατα
         δείξῃς ἠελίῳ καὶ δαιμόνιον χόλον ὄρσῃς.
         οὐ καλὸν ἁρμονίην ἀναλυέμεν ἀνθρώποιο·
p. 104   καὶ τάχα δ' ἐκ γαίης ἐλπίζομεν ἐς φάος ἐλθεῖν
         λείψαν' ἀποιχομένων· ὀπίσω δὲ θεοὶ τελέθονται.
  105   ψυχαὶ γὰρ μίμνουσιν ἀκήριοι ἐν φθιμένοισιν.
         πνεῦμα γάρ ἐστι θεοῦ χρῆσις θνητοῖσι καὶ εἰκών·
         σῶμα γὰρ ἐκ γαίης ἔχομεν κἄπειτα πρὸς αὖ γῆν
         λυόμενοι κόνις ἐσμέν· ἀὴρ δ' ἀνὰ πνεῦμα δέδεκται.
         Πλουτῶν μὴ φείδου· μέμνησ' ὅτι θνητὸς ὑπάρχεις·
  110   οὐκ ἔνι εἰς Ἅιδην ὄλβον καὶ χρήματ' ἄγεσθαι.
         πάντες ἴσον νέκυες, ψυχῶν δὲ θεὸς βασιλεύει.
         κοινὰ μέλαθρα δόμων αἰώνια καὶ πατρὶς Ἅιδης,
         ξυνὸς χῶρος ἅπασι, πένησί τε καὶ βασιλεῦσιν.
         οὐ πολὺν ἄνθρωποι ζῶμεν χρόνον, ἀλλ' ἐπίκαιρον·
  115   ψυχὴ δ' ἀθάνατος καὶ ἀγήρως ζῇ διὰ παντός.

p. 105   [οὐδεὶς γινώσκει, τί μετ' αὔριον ἢ τί μεθ' ὥραν.
         ἄσκοπός ἐστι βροτῶν θάνατος, τὸ δὲ μέλλον ἄδηλον.]
         Μήτε κακοῖσ' ἄχθου μήτ' οὖν ἐπαγάλλεο χάρμῃ·

A wise man keeps straight wisdom, and a fellow-craftsman crafts.
An untrained ear cannot grasp important teaching.
90 For those who have never learned good things do not understand.
Make not parasitic flatterers your friends.
For there are many friends of eating and drinking,
who are time-servers whenever they can satiate themselves,
but discontented all of them with little and insatiable with much.
95 Trust not the people, the mob is fickle.
For the people and water and fire are all uncontrollable.

Vv. 97-115 *Death and After-Life*

Sit not in vain beside the fire, weakening your heart.
Be moderate in your grief,[2] for moderation is the best.
Let the unburied dead receive their share of earth.
100 Do not dig up the grave of the deceased, neither expose
to the sun what may not be seen, lest you stir up the divine anger.
It is not good to dissolve the human frame.
For in fact we hope that the remains of the departed will soon come
to the light again out of the earth. And afterwards they become gods.
105 For the souls remain unharmed in the deceased.
For the spirit is a loan from God to mortals, and his image.
For we have a body out of earth, and when afterwards we are resolved
again into earth we are but dust; but the air has received our spirit.
When you are rich do not be sparing; remember that you are mortal.
110 It is impossible to take riches and money with you into Hades.
All alike are corpses, but God rules over the souls.
Hades is our common eternal home and fatherland,
a common place for all, poor and kings.
We humans live not a long time but for a season.
115 But our soul is immortal and lives ageless forever.

Vv. 116-121 *The Instability of Life*

[Nobody knows what will be after tomorrow or after an hour.]
[The death of mortals cannot be foreseen, and the future is uncertain.]
Let not evils dismay you nor exult in success.

---

[2] reading γόοισι

πολλάκις ἐν βιότῳ καὶ θαρσαλέοισιν ἄπιστον
120 πῆμα καὶ ἀχθομένοισι κακοῦ λύσις ἤλυθεν ἄφνω.
καιρῷ λατρεύειν, μὴ δ' ἀντιπνέειν ἀνέμοισιν.

Μὴ μεγαληγορίῃ τρυφῶν φρένα λυσσωθείης.
εὐεπίην ἀσκεῖν, ἥτις μάλα πάντας ὀνήσει.
ὅπλον τοι λόγος ἀνδρὶ τομώτερόν ἐστι σιδήρου·
125 ὅπλον ἑκάστῳ νεῖμε θεός, φύσιν ἠερόφοιτον
ὄρνισιν, πώλοις ταχυτῆτ', ἀλκήν τε λέουσιν,
ταύρους δ' αὐτοχύτως κέρα ἕσσεν, κέντρα μελίσσαις
Young ἔμφυτον ἄλκαρ ἔδωκε, λόγον δ' ἔρυμ' ἀνθρώποισιν.
p. 106 [τῆς δὲ θεοπνεύστου σοφίης λόγος ἐστὶν ἄριστος.]
130 βέλτερος ἀλκήεντος ἔφυ σεσοφισμένος ἀνήρ·
ἀγροὺς καὶ πόλιας σοφίη καὶ νῆα κυβερνᾷ.

Οὐχ ὅσιον κρύπτειν τὸν ἀτάσθαλον ἄνδρ' ἀνέλεγκτον,
ἀλλὰ χρὴ κακοεργὸν ἀποτρωπᾶσθαι ἀνάγκῃ.
πολλάκι συνθνήσκουσι κακοῖσ' οἱ συμπαρεόντες.
135 Φωρῶν μὴ δέξῃ κλοπίμην ἄδικον παραθήκην·
ἀμφότεροι κλῶπες, καὶ ὁ δεξάμενος καὶ ὁ κλέψας.
Μοίρας πᾶσι νέμειν, ἰσότης δ' ἐν πᾶσιν ἄριστον.
ἀρχόμενος φείδου πάντων, μὴ τέρμ' ἐπιδεύῃς.
μὴ κτήνους θνητοῖο βορὴν κατὰ μέτρον ἕληαι.
140 κτῆνος δ' ἢν ἐχθροῖο πέσῃ καθ' ὁδόν, συνέγειρε.
πλαζόμενον δὲ βροτὸν καὶ ἀλίτροπον οὔποτ' ἐλέγξεις.
βέλτερον ἀντ' ἐχθροῦ τεύχειν φίλον εὐμενέοντα.
p. 107 Ἀρχόμενον τὸ κακὸν κόπτειν ἕλκος τ' ἀκέσασθαι.
[ἐξ ὀλίγου σπινθῆρος ἀθέσφατος αἴθεται ὕλη.
145 Ἐγκρατὲς ἦτορ ἔχειν, καὶ λωβητῶν δ' ἀπέχεσθαι.
φεῦγε κακὴν φήμην, φεῦγ' ἀνθρώπους ἀθεμίστους.]
Μὴ δέ τι θηρόβορον δαίσῃ κρέας, ἀργίποσιν δέ

Many times in life incredible calamity comes suddenly
120 to the confident and release from evil to the vexed.
Accommodate yourself to the circumstances, do not blow against
                                                                the winds.

Vv. 122-131   *Speech and Wisdom, Man's Distinction*

Become not mad in your mind by revelling in boastfulness.
Practise speaking of good words, which will greatly benefit all.
Speech is to man a weapon sharper than iron.
125 God allotted a weapon to every creature; the capacity to fly
to birds, speed to horses, and strength to the lions;
he clothed the bulls with their self-growing ³ horns, he gave stings
to the bees as a natural means of defence, but reason to man as
                                                              his protection.
[But speech of the divinely inspired wisdom is best.]
130 Better is a wise man than a strong one.
Wisdom directs the course of lands and cities and ships.

Vv. 132-152   *Avoidance of Wickedness and Virtuous Life*

It is unholy to hide a wicked man so as to prevent his being brought
                                                               to trial;
but one must turn away an evildoer forcibly.
Those who are with the bad often die together with them.
135 Accept not from thieves a stolen, unlawful deposit.
Both are thieves, the one who receives as well as the one who steals.
Render to all their due; impartiality is best in every way.
In the beginning be sparing with all things, lest in the end you
                                                               come short.
Take not for yourself a mortal beast's ration of food.
140 If a beast of your enemy falls on the way, help it to rise.
Never expose a wandering man and a sinner.
It is better to make a gracious friend instead of an enemy.
Nip the evil in the bud and heal the wound.
[By a tiny spark a vast wood is set on fire.]
145 [Keep your heart restrained and abstain from disgraceful things.]
[Flee an evil report; flee lawless men.]
Eat no meat that is torn by wild animals, but leave the remains

---

³ reading αὐτοφύτως

λείψανα λεῖπε κυσίν· θηρῶν ἄπο θῆρες ἔδονται.
Φάρμακα μὴ τεύχειν, μαγικῶν βίβλων ἀπέχεσθαι.
150 Νηπιάχοις ἀταλοῖς μὴ ἄψῃ χεῖρα βιαίως.
Φεῦγε διχοστασίην καὶ ἔριν πολέμου προσιόντος.
Μὴ κακὸν εὖ ἔρξῃς· σπείρειν ἴσον ἔστ' ἐνὶ πόντῳ.

Ἐργάζευ μοχθῶν, ὡς ἐξ ἰδίων βιοτεύσῃς·
πᾶς γὰρ ἀεργὸς ἀνὴρ ζώει κλοπίμων ἀπὸ χειρῶν.
155 [τέχνη ⟨γὰρ⟩ τρέφει ἄνδρα, ἀεργὸν δ' ἴψατο λιμός.]
μὴ δ' ἄλλου παρὰ δαιτὸς ἔδοις σκυβάλισμα τραπέζης,
ἀλλ' ἀπὸ τῶν ἰδίων μισθῶν φαγέοις ἀνυβρίστως.
Young εἰ δέ τις οὐ δεδάηκε τέχνης, σκάπτοιτο δικέλλῃ.
p. 108 ἔστι βίῳ πᾶν ἔργον, ἐπὴν μοχθεῖν ἐθέλησθα.
160 ναυτίλος εἰ πλώειν ἐθέλεις, εὑρεῖα θάλασσα·
εἰ δὲ γεηπονίην μεθέπειν, μακραί τοι ἄρουραι.
οὐδὲν ἄνευ καμάτου πέλει ἀνδράσιν εὐπετὲς ἔργον
οὐδ' αὐτοῖς μακάρεσσι· πόνος δ' ἀρετὴν μέγ' ὀφέλλει.
μύρμηκες γαίης μυχάτους προλελοιπότες οἴκους
165 ἔρχονται βιότου κεχρημένοι, ὁππότ' ἄρουραι
λήϊα κειράμεναι καρπῶν πλήθωσιν ἀλωαί.
οἱ δ' αὐτοὶ πυροῖο νεοτριβὲς ἄχθος ἔχουσιν
ἢ κριθῶν, αἰεὶ δὲ φέρων φορέοντα διώκει,
ἐκ θέρεος ποτὶ χεῖμα βορὴν σφετέρην ἐπάγοντες
170 ἄτρυτοι· φῦλον δ' ὀλίγον τελέθει πολύμοχθον.
κάμνει δ' ἠεροφοῖτις ἀριστοπόνος τε μέλισσα
ἠὲ πέτρης κοίλης κατὰ χηραμὸν ἢ δονάκεσσιν
p. 109 ἢ δρυὸς ὠγυγίης κατὰ κοιλάδος ἔνδοθι σίμβλων
σμήνεσι μυριότρητα κατ' ἄγγεα κηροδομοῦσα.

175 Μὴ μείνῃς ἄγαμος, μή πως νώνυμνος ὄληαι·
δός τι φύσει καὐτός, τέκε δ' ἔμπαλιν, ὡς ἐλοχεύθης.
Μὴ προαγωγεύσῃς ἄλοχον σέο τέκνα μιαίνων·
οὐ γὰρ τίκτει παῖδας ὁμοίους μοιχικὰ λέκτρα.
μητρυιῆς μὴ ψαῦε τὰ δεύτερα λέκτρα γονῆος·
180 μητέρα δ' ὡς τίμα τὴν μητέρος ἴχνια βᾶσαν.
μηδέ τι παλλακίσιν πατρὸς λεχέεσσι μιγείης.

to the swift dogs. Animals eat from animals.
Make no potions, keep away from magical books.
150 Do not apply your hand violently to tender children.
Flee dissension and strife when war is drawing near.
Do no good to a bad man; it is like sowing in the sea.

Vv. 153-174 *The Usefulness of Labour*

Work hard so that you can live from your own means.
For every idle man lives from what his hands can steal.
155 [A craft maintains a man, but an idle man is oppressed by hunger.]
Eat not the left-overs of another man's meal,
but eat without shame from what you have earned yourself.
And if someone has not learned a craft, he must dig with a mattock.
Life has every kind of work, if you are willing to toil.
160 If you want to sail and be a mariner, the sea is wide.
And if you want to cultivate land, the fields are large.
There is no easy work without toil for men,
not even for the blessed. But labour gives great increase to virtue.
The ants having left their homes, deeply hidden under the earth,
165 come in their need of food, when the fields
fill the threshing floors with fruits after the crops have been reaped.
They themselves have a load of freshly threshed wheat
or barley—and bearer always follows bearer—,
and from the summer harvest they supply their food for the winter,
170 being indefatigable. This tiny folk is hard-working.
The bee toils, traversing the air, working excellently,
either in the crevice of a hollow rock or in the reeds,
or in the hollow of an ancient oak, within their nests,
in swarms at their thousand-celled combs, building with wax.

Vv. 175-227 *Marriage, Chastity and Family Life*

175 Remain not unmarried, lest you die nameless.
Give nature her due, beget in turn as you were begotten.
Do not induce your wife to prostitution, defiling your children;
for the adulterous bed brings not sons in your likeness.
Touch not your stepmother, your father's second wife;
180 but honour her as a mother, because she follows the footsteps of
                                                    your mother.
Do not have intercourse with the concubines of your father.

μηδὲ κασιγνήτης ἐς ἀπότροπον ἐλθέμεν εὐνήν.
μηδὲ κασιγνήτων ἀλόχων ἐπὶ δέμνια βαίνειν.
μηδὲ γυνὴ φθείρῃ βρέφος ἔμβρυον ἔνδοθι γαστρός,
185 μηδὲ τεκοῦσα κυσὶν ῥίψῃ καὶ γυψὶν ἕλωρα.
μηδ' ἐπὶ σῇ ἀλόχῳ ἐγκύμονι χεῖρα βάλῃαι.
μηδ' αὖ παιδογόνον τέμνειν φύσιν ἄρσενα κούρου.
Young μηδ' ἀλόγοις ζῴοισι βατήριον ἐς λέχος ἐλθεῖν.
p. 110 μηδ' ὕβριζε γυναῖκα ἐπ' αἰσχυντοῖς λεχέεσσιν.
190 μὴ παραβῇς εὐνὰς φύσεως ἐς Κύπριν ἄθεσμον·
οὐδ' αὐτοῖς θήρεσσι συνεύαδον ἄρσενες εὐναί.
μηδέ τι θηλύτεραι λέχος ἀνδρῶν μιμήσαιντο.
μηδ' ἐς ἔρωτα γυναικὸς ἅπας ῥεύσῃς ἀκάθεκτον·
οὐ γὰρ ἔρως θεός ἐστι, πάθος δ' ἀίδηλον ἁπάντων.
195 Στέργε τεὴν ἄλοχον· τί γὰρ ἡδύτερον καὶ ἄρειον,
ἢ ὅταν ἀνδρὶ γυνὴ φρονέῃ φίλα γήραος ἄχρις
καὶ πόσις ᾖ ἀλόχῳ, μηδ' ἐμπέσῃ ἄνδιχα νεῖκος;
Μὴ δέ τις ἀμνήστευτα βίῃ κούρῃσι μιγείη.
Μὴ δὲ γυναῖκα κακὴν πολυχρήματον οἴκαδ' ἄγεσθαι·
200 λατρεύσεις ἀλόχῳ λυγρῆς χάριν εἵνεκα φερνῆς.
ἵππους εὐγενέας διζήμεθα γειαρότας τε
ταύρους ὑψιτένοντας, ἀτὰρ σκυλάκων πανάριστον·
p. 111 γῆμαι δ' οὐκ ἀγαθὴν ἐριδαίνομεν ἀφρονέοντες.
οὐ δὲ γυνὴ κακὸν ἄνδρ' ἀπαναίνεται ἀφνεὸν ὄντα.
205 μηδὲ γάμῳ γάμον ἄλλον ἄγοις ἔπι, πήματι πῆμα.
μηδ' ἀμφὶ κτεάνων συνομαίμοσιν εἰς ἔριν ἔλθῃς.
Παισὶν μὴ χαλέπαινε τεοῖσ', ἀλλ' ἤπιος εἴης.
ἢν δέ τι παῖς ἀλίτῃ σε, κολουέτω υἱέα μήτηρ
ἢ καὶ πρεσβύτατοι γενεῆς ἢ δημογέροντες.
210 Μὴ μὲν ἐπ' ἄρσενι παιδὶ τρέφειν πλοκάμους ἐπὶ χαίτης.
μὴ κορυφὴν πλέξῃς μήθ' ἅμματα λοξὰ κορύμβων.
ἄρσεσιν οὐκ ἐπέοικε κομᾶν, χλιδαναῖς δὲ γυναιξίν.
Παιδὸς δ' εὐμόρφου φρουρεῖν νεοτήσιον ὥρην·
πολλοὶ γὰρ λυσσῶσι πρὸς ἄρσενα μεῖξιν ἔρωτος.
215 παρθενικὴν δὲ φύλασσε πολυκλείστοις θαλάμοισιν,
μὴ δέ μιν ἄχρι γάμων πρὸ δόμων ὀφθῆμεν ἐάσῃς.
κάλλος δυστήρητον ἔφυ παίδων τοκέεσσιν.

Approach not the bed of your sister, a bed to turn away from.
Nor go to bed with the wives of your brothers.
A woman should not destroy the unborn babe in her belly,
185 nor after its birth throw it before the dogs and the vultures as a prey.
Lay not your hand upon your wife when she is pregnant.
Cut not a youth's masculine procreative faculty.
Seek not sexual union with irrational animals.
Outrage not your wife for shameful ways of intercourse.
190 Transgress not for unlawful sex the natural limits of sexuality.
For even animals are not pleased by intercourse of male with male.
And let not women imitate the sexual role of men.
Do not deliver yourself wholly unto unbridled sensuality towards your wife.
For 'eros' is not a god, but a passion destructive of all.
195 Love your own wife, for what is sweeter and better
than whenever a wife is kindly disposed toward her husband till old age
and a husband towards his wife, without strife interfering as a dividing force?
Let no one violently have intercourse with maidens without wooing.
Bring not as wife into your home a bad and wealthy woman.
200 You will be a slave of your wife because of the baneful dowry.
We seek noble horses and strong-necked bulls,
ploughers of the earth, and the very best of dogs.
Yet we fools do not strive to marry a good wife;
nor does a woman reject a bad man when he is rich.
205 Add not marriage to marriage, calamity to calamity.
Nor permit yourself strife with your kinsfolk about possessions.
Be not harsh with your children, but be gentle.
And if a child sins against you, let the mother cut her son down to size,
or else the elders of the family or the chiefs of the people.
210 If a child is a boy, do not let locks grow on his head.
Braid not his crown nor make cross-knots at the top of his head.
Long hair is not fit for men, but for voluptuous women.
Guard the youthful beauty of a comely boy;
because many rage for intercourse with a man.
215 Guard a virgin in firmly locked rooms,
and let her not be seen before the house until her wedding-day.
The beauty of children is hard for their parents to guard.

Young
p. 112
[Στέργε φίλους ἄχρις θανάτου· πίστις γὰρ ἀμείνων.]
Συγγενέσιν φιλότητα νέμοις ὁσίην θ' ὁμόνοιαν.
220 αἰδεῖσθαι πολιοκροτάφους, εἴκειν δὲ γέρουσιν
ἕδρης καὶ γεράων πάντων· γενεῇ δ' ἀτάλαντον
πρέσβυν ὁμήλικα πατρὸς ἴσαις τιμαῖσι γέραιρε.
 Γαστρὸς ὀφειλόμενον δασμὸν παρέχειν θεράποντι.
δούλῳ τακτὰ νέμοις, ἵνα τοι καταθύμιος εἴη.
225 στίγματα μὴ γράψῃς ἐπονειδίζων θεράποντα.
δοῦλον μὴ βλάψῃς τι κακηγορέων παρ' ἄνακτι.
λάμβανε καὶ βουλὴν παρὰ οἰκέτου εὖ φρονέοντος.

 Ἁγνείη ψυχῆς, οὐ σώματός εἰσι καθαρμοί.
 Ταῦτα δικαιοσύνης μυστήρια, τοῖα βιεῦντες
230 ζωὴν ἐκτελέοιτ' ἀγαθὴν μέχρι γήραος οὐδοῦ.

[Love your friends till death, for faithfulness is a good thing.]
Show love to your kinsmen and pious unanimity.
220 Revere those with grey hair on the temples and yield your seat
and all privileges to old persons. To an old man of equal descent
and of the same age as your father give the same honours.
Provide your slave with the tribute he owes to his stomach.
Apportion to a slave what is appointed so that he will be as you wish.
225 Insult not your slave by branding him.
Do not hurt a slave by slandering him to his master.
Accept advice also from a kindly disposed slave.

Vv. 228-230 *Epilogue*

Purifications are for the purity [4] of the soul, not of the body.
These are the mysteries of righteousness; living thus
may you live out a good life, right up to the threshold of old age.

---

[4] reading ἀγνείη

COMMENTARY

Vv.	1-2	Prologue	107
Vv.	3-8	Summary of the Decalogue	110
Vv.	9-21	Exhortations to Justice	117
Vv.	22-41	Admonitions to Mercy	128
Vv.	42-47	Love of Money and its Consequences	142
Vv.	48-58	Honesty, Modesty and Self-Control	146
Vv.	59-69	Moderation in all Things	153
Vv.	70-96	The Danger of Envy and Other Vices	161
Vv.	97-115	Death and After-Life	179
Vv.	116-121	The Instability of Life	195
Vv.	122-131	Speech and Wisdom, Man's Distinction	198
Vv.	132-152	Avoidance of Wickedness and Virtuous Life	203
Vv.	153-174	The Usefulness of Labour	216
Vv.	175-227	Marriage, Chastity and Family Life	225
Vv.	228-230	Epilogue	258

Vv. 1-2   *Prologue*

1-2   Ταῦτα δίκησ' ὁσίησι θεοῦ βουλεύματα φαίνει
Φωκυλίδης ἀνδρῶν ὁ σοφώτατος ὄλβια δῶρα.

These counsels of God by His holy judgments
Phocylides the wisest of men sets forth, gifts of blessing.

ταῦτα: the first word of the poem already betrays its Hellenistic origin. In the classical period, the demonstrative in a *sphragis* always was a form of the pronoun ὅδε (τόδε, τάδε, ἥδε, ὧδε), e.g., Hes. *Theog.* 24, Theogn. 19f., Alcmaeon fr. B 1, Herod. *praef.* 1, Hecataeus FGH 1F1 (texts in Kranz, *Sphragis* 44-5 and Schmalzriedt, *Peri Physeōs* 32-6); cf. esp. in Phocylides καὶ τόδε Φωκυλίδεω at the beginning of most of his sentences. Though οὗτος referring to what follows need not be Hellenistic (see LSJ *s.v.* C I 2 and K-G I 646), its occurrence in a *sphragis* definitely is Hellenistic. On the disappearance of ὅδε in later Greek and the assumption of its functions by οὗτος see Mussies, *Morphology of Koine Greek* 179f.

δίκησ' ὁσίησι: Young's text as it stands is hard to render. The function of this dative is unclear. Possibly δίκησ' ὁσίησι indicates the way or form in which God's βουλεύματα are made known to man. Diehl reads δίκησ' ὁσίοισι with most mss., referring to ἄγριον ὀργήν in v. 57 for the masculine gender of the adjective, but cf. δίκη ὁσίη in Theogn. 132. Keydell, *Jahresbericht* 272 (1941), 27 suggests ταῦτα Δίκης ὁσίοισι θεοῦ βουλεύματα: "die Δίκης βουλεύματα entsprechen den Δικαιοσύνης μυστήρια am Schluss (229), von den ὅσιοι αὐτοῦ in Beziehung auf Gott ist in der Septuaginta oft die Rede". Cf. Dornseiff, *Echtheitsfragen* 39 n. 2 "φαίνει verlangt einen Dativ, in dem mitgeteilt wird, wem gezeigt wird". Rossbroich's conjecture ταῦτ' ἀδίκοις ὁσίοις τε is very attractive, since in vv. 5 and 37 ἄδικος and ὅσιος are also opposites (see for ὅσιος extensively J. C. Bolkestein, *Ὅσιος en Εὐσεβής*, 1936, *passim*, and esp. Terstegen, ΕΥΣΕΒΗΣ *en* ΟΣΙΟΣ, 1941, *passim*, and Van der Valk, 'Zum Worte ὅσιος', *Mnem.* 1942, 113-140). For the frequent combination of δίκαιος and ὅσιος see LSJ *s.v.* ὅσιος; Schmidt, *Ethik* I 308; Dihle, *Der Kanon der zwei Tugenden, passim*, and esp. Berger, *Gesetzesauslegung Jesu* I 143-165.

θεοῦ βουλεύματα: θεοῦ may belong to the preceding words, but βουλεύομαι is frequently used of God in the LXX. This expression is reminiscent of the etymology of the word *Sibylla* as reported by Varro *ap.* Lact. *Div. Inst.* I 6, 7 σιούς *deos, non* θεούς *et consilium non* βουλήν, *sed* βούλλαν *appellabant Aeolico genere sermonis; itaque Sibyllam dictam esse quasi* θεοβούλην (for other similar texts see Nikiprowetzky, *La troisième Sibylle* 2 n. 5). Perhaps θεοῦ βουλεύματα = θεοῦ βουλήματα, for that expression see Jos. *Ant.* II 304 and Bauer *s.v.* βούλημα. No doubt Ps-Phoc. means the Torah here (see Berger, *Gesetzesauslegung Jesu* I 47). By means of these words the author claims great authority for the rules of conduct he gives in this poem.

φαίνει: Kranz, *Sphragis* 100 compares Theocr. IX 28 Μοῖσαι..., φαίνετε δ' ᾠδάν, τὰν τόκ' ἐγώ κτλ. and Apoll. Rhod. IV 782 φαῖνέ τε μῦθον. See LSJ *s.v.* A I 1 b.

Φωκυλίδης: the "seal" (σφραγίς) of the poem, often used in classical literature to claim the work as inalienable property; so very frequently in the work of Phocylides (καὶ τόδε Φωκυλίδεω). On this see Kranz, *Sphragis, passim.* Kranz emphasizes the correlation between the beginning and the end in works with a *sphragis.* This could well be a point in favour of the "authenticity" of vv. 1-2 (see below). For Phocylides' fame in antiquity see Introd., pp. 59ff.

ἀνδρῶν ὁ σοφώτατος: these words are offensive to some scholars, e.g. Farina 33: "tono troppo superbo" (in his view incompatible with v. 53). But Dornseiff 39 sees here "wahrhaft gross-königlichen parsischen Stolz" (!) and compares the inscription mentioned by Herodotus IV 91 where Darius calls himself ἀνὴρ ἄριστός τε καὶ κάλλιστος πάντων ἀνθρώπων. Perhaps it would be better to compare another *sphragis*, Theogn. 19-24, v. 23 πάντας δὲ κατ' ἀνθρώπους ὀνομαστός, but admittedly the expression in Ps-Phoc. is more pompous and self-assertive. A closer verbal parallel is the Delphic oracle's statement about Socrates as mentioned by Ps-Justin *Coh. ad gentes* 36 ἀνδρῶν ἁπάντων Σωκράτης σοφώτατος (cf. Plato *Apol.* 21a ἀνεῖλεν οὖν ἡ Πυθία μηδένα σοφώτερον εἶναι, and see Otto *ad loc.* in *Corp. Apol.* II (1849²), 111f.). Is Ps-Phoc. polemizing here against the elevation of Socrates? Or does he rather transfer to himself an epithet of Solomon, the originator of Wisdom poetry according to Jewish tradition, who was often regarded as the wisest of all men by the Jews? See *Test. Sal.* rec. D IV 6 (p. 92, 20 McCown) σοφώτατε Σολομῶν, *ibid.* Tit. Mss. V W (p. 99, 5 McCown) διαθήκη τοῦ σοφωτάτου Σολομῶντος, also in the subscription of ms. V (p. 99,

9 McC.). Eus. *PE* XI 5, 4 (II p. 11, 15 Mras) ὁ σοφώτατος παρὰ τοῖσδε Σολομῶν. Cf. 3 Kings V 11 ἐσοφίσατο ὑπὲρ πάντας τοὺς ἀνθρώπους and Jos. *Ant*. VIII 24: God gave Solomon σοφίαν οἵαν οὐκ ἄλλος τις ἀνθρώπων ἔσχεν οὔτε βασιλέων οὔτ' ἰδιωτῶν. See further E. Lohse, *TWNT* VII 462. It is very remarkable that this tradition is used by the emperor Julian when he compares Solomon (unfavourably) to Phocylides (!), *Contra Galil*. fr. 224C (p. 203, 6f. Neumann, *ap*. Cyrill. Alex. *Adv. Iul.* VII 224) ὁ σοφώτατος Σολομῶν παρόμοιός ἐστι τῷ παρ' "Ελλησι Φωκυλίδῃ ἢ Θεόγνιδι ἢ 'Ισοκράτει; πόθεν; (see Peretti, *Teognide nella tradizione gnomologica* 115f.). It is quite probable, therefore, that Ps-Phoc. assumes a traditional predicate of Solomon.

ὄλβια δῶρα: apposition to βουλεύματα. On ὄλβιος see C. de Heer, ΜΑΚΑΡ etc., *passim*. The expression is Homeric, *Od*. XIII 41f. Cf. *Or. Sib.* II 53 δώσει (sc. God) πλούσια δῶρα. Bergk, *PLG* II⁴ 78 remarks: "nimis iners additamentum", and surmises a corruption of 'Ολβιοδώρου (Phoc., son of Olbiodorus); quite unnecessarily.

Some scholars have contended that vv. 1-2 are not an original part of the poem. Bernays 247 n. 2 was the first to athetize them as being a Byzantine addition in clumsy Greek. He is followed in this by Rossbroich 25ff., Sebestyén 32f. and Speyer, *Entretiens* XVIII (*Pseudepigrapha* I), 324. The "authenticity" (that is, the belonging to the original poem) is defended by Bergk, *Gr. Lit. gesch.* II 301 n. 17 and *PLG* II⁴ 77, Beltrami, *Rivista* 41 (1913) 513, Keydell, *Jahresbericht* 272 (1941) 27, Young (see *app. crit.*) and Hengel, *Entretiens* XVIII, 324. Quite apart from reasons of style and content, the problem is that these verses are missing in a number of mss. (see Ludwich, *Spruchbuch* 6). How is that to be explained? Indeed, the most simple solution seems to be to assume that the verses were originally not there, but are a later addition. Then it has to be assumed that the poem was anonymous at first. Rossbroich 26 does make this assumption ("Primo igitur hanc syllogam sine ullo auctoris nomine exstitisse credo"). He admits that the addition of vv. 1-2 must have taken place early, for Stobaeus quotes some lines from this poem under the name Phocylides. However, it would be hard to imagine that a Jew wrote this poem in this clearly old-fashioned style without giving it the name of an ancient authority; cf. Schürer, *Gesch.* III⁴ 619: "die ganze sprachliche Form" argues against it. And it is still more unimaginable that he should begin the poem baldly with v. 3; Bergk, *PLG* II⁴ 77: "plane ἀκέφαλον foret poema". Cf. also Sitzler, *Wochenschrift für klass. Philol.* 29 (1912), 455. One may surmise that scribes have omitted vv. 1-2 temporarily to add them later in capital letters with ornamentation, as a title or subtitle; and this would lead to the omission in several mss. (Or perhaps a critical scribe might have had doubts about the authenticity of the poem which were so serious that he omitted the verses with the name of Phocylides?) See also Introduction p. 59. Bergk 78, Keydell 27 and Kranz 100 point to the correlation between vv. 1-2 and 229-230, the final verses. This is another indication of the originality of the prologue.

Vv. 3-8   *Summary of the Decalogue*

3-4 μήτε γαμοκλοπέειν μήτ' ἄρσενα Κύπριν ὀρίνειν
μήτε δόλους ῥάπτειν μήθ' αἵματι χεῖρα μιαίνειν.

Commit not adultery nor rouse homosexual passion.
Stitch not wiles together nor stain your hands with blood.

γαμοκλοπέειν (the *infinitivus pro imperativo* is very frequent in Ps-Phoc.): hapax, but γαμοκλόπος occurs in some late texts, e.g. *Anth. Pal.* IX 475, Tryphiodorus 45, Nonnus *Dionys.* III 377, and γαμοκλοπίη in *Or. Sib.* II 52 and V 430; cf. also κλεψίγαμος in *Or. Sib.* II 258 and III 204. Other compounds with γαμο- are also of late date, see LSJ 337. For the firm prohibition of adultery in the O.T. see Ex. XX 13 (= Deut. V 17) οὐ μοιχεύσεις, Deut. XXII 22-4; Prov. V 20; VI 24.29; VII 5; Sir. IX 9; etc. (see Epstein, *Sex Laws* 199ff.; for rabbinic material further Billerbeck I 295ff. and Schechter, *Aspects* 224ff.). N.T. *passim* (see Hauck, art. μοιχεύω κτλ., *TWNT* IV 737ff.). Cf. Did. II 2, V 1, Herm. *Mand.* IV 1. This prohibition was one of the Noachian laws, see Sanh. 56a. Adultery was universally condemned in antiquity, see Delling, "Ehebruch", *RAC* IV 666-677. E.g. Dittenberger, *Syll.* III 985, 26ff. ἄνδρα παρὰ τὴν ἑαυτοῦ γυναῖκα ἀλλοτρίαν ἢ ἐλευθέραν ἢ δούλην ἄνδρα ἔχουσαν μὴ φθερεῖν, and Mus. Ruf. XII (p. 64, 4ff. H.) συμπλοκαὶ δ' ἄλλαι αἱ μὲν κατὰ μοιχείαν παρανομώταται κτλ. Polemics against sexual sins play an important role in Jewish-Hellenistic literature (see vv. 177ff.); cf. Berger, *Gesetzesauslegung Jesu* I 307ff. The LXX already puts the prohibition of adultery in the Decalogue before that of murder (against MT) so that it is the first commandment of the second table; see Bousset, *Religion* 425 with n. 3. Philo emphasizes this, *Spec. leg.* III 8 ἐν δὲ τῇ δευτέρᾳ δέλτῳ πρῶτον γράμμα τοῦτ' ἐστίν· οὐ μοιχεύσεις. Decal. 121 ἀπὸ μοιχείας ἄρχεται, μέγιστον ἀδικημάτων τοῦτ' εἶναι ὑπολαβών (cf. Heinemann, Philons Bildung 278). This explains why Ps-Phoc. mentions adultery in the first place and only thereafter (v. 4) murder. This sequence of the commandments is also found in the N.T., Lk. XVIII 20; Rom. XIII 9; Jas. II 11; but cf. 1 Tim. I 9ff. ἀνδροφόνοις, πόρνοις, ἀρσενοκοίταις κτλ. (on this problem of sequence see Reicke, Die zehn Worte 21ff.).

ἄρσενα Κύπριν ὀρίνειν: ἄρσενα, adj. instead of the genit. of the noun, see K-G. I 261f. Κύπρις, originally = Aphrodite, in poetry metaph. for "love, passion", e.g. Eur. Bacch. 773, Arist. Eccl. 772, Men. Mon. 231, in our poem also in vv. 67 and 190. ὀρίνειν passim in Hom. in expressions like θυμὸν ὀρίνειν. This prohibition is not from the Decalogue, but see Lev. XVIII 22 μετὰ ἄρσενος οὐ κοιμηθήσῃ κοίτην γυναικός, cf. XX 13. In the N.T. Rom. I 27, 1 Tim. I 10 etc. Cf. Did. II 2 οὐ παιδοφθορήσεις, and Barn. XIX 4 (from the Two Ways). Judaism abhorred homosexuality, see Preuss, Prostitution 470ff., Billerbeck ad Rom. I 27, Heinemann, Philons Bildung 283f. Jos. C.Ap. II 199 τὴν δὲ (sc. μῖξιν) πρὸς ἄρρενας ἀρρένων ἐστύγηκε (sc. ὁ νόμος). Philo Hyp., ap. Eus. PE VIII 7, 1 (429, 19f. Mr.) ἐὰν παιδεραστῇς, ἐὰν μοιχεύῃς, ἐὰν βιάσῃ παῖδα (ἄρρενα μὲν μηδὲ λέγε, ἀλλὰ κἂν θήλειαν), . . . θάνατος ἡ ζημία. Or. Sib. III 764 μοιχείας πεφύλαξο καὶ ἄρσενος ἄκριτον εὐνήν and V 430 οὐδὲ γαμοκλοπίαι καὶ παίδων Κύπρις ἄθεσμος are striking parallels to v. 3 (see also the texts collected by Geffcken on Or. Sib. II 73). From these texts it is clear that adulterous and homosexual relations are often mentioned together. This is also the case in non-Jewish texts, e.g. the passages from Mus. Ruf. XII and Ditt. Syll. III 985 quoted above. Though in general homosexuality was much more accepted (and even defended) in the Greek world than among the Jews (see Licht, Sittengeschichte 244-294; Dover, Greek Popular Morality 205ff.), there were critical voices, esp. in the Stoic-Cynic literature; see Gerhard, Phoinix 141ff.; e.g. Heracl. Epist, VII p. 70, 2 Attridge; Juv. Sat. III 134; 164f. Rossbroich 29 onesidedly explains v. 3b against this background. For further material see the Comm. on vv. 190 and 214, where this theme recurs.

V. 3 is quoted anonymously in Floril. Monac. 12 (Meineke, Stob. IV 268).

δόλους ῥάπτειν: Or. Sib. II 119; cf. Hom. Il. VI 187 δόλον ὑφαίνειν; Od. XVI 379 φόνον ῥάπτειν, 423 κακὰ ῥάπτειν, see further LSJ s.v.

ῥάπτειν. For δόλος see Bauer s.v. Deut. XXVII 24 ἐπικατάρατος ὁ τύπτων τὸν πλησίον αὐτοῦ δόλῳ, Ex. XXI 14 (further Hatch-Redpath s.v.); Or. Sib. III 38.191; Mk. VII 22 δόλος in a catalogue of sins, etc. Ditt., Syll. III 985, 17 δόλον μηθένα μήτε ἀνδρὶ μήτε γυναικὶ εἰδότες.

αἵματι χεῖρα μιαίνειν: cf. v. 34 ἢν γὰρ ἀποκτείνῃς ἐχθρόν, σέο χεῖρα μιαίνεις. For μιαίνειν see Hauck in TWNT IV 647-9. It is often combined with αἵματι. ibid. 647 n. 2 and LSJ s.v. Kaibel, Epigr. Gr. 713, 9 οὐ χεῖρα φόνοισι μιάνας. Probably v. 4b renders Ex. XX 15 (= Deut. V 18) οὐ φονεύσεις. On bloodshed as one of the cardinal sins in rabbinic literature see Billerbeck I 254ff. and Schechter, Aspects 226-232.

On the whole of vv. 3-4 cf. the combination of μοιχεία, φόνος and δόλος in Sap. Sal. XIV 25f. and in Barn. XX 1 (in the Two Ways section).

It is probable that vv. 3-8 are a free rendering of the (second table of the) Decalogue, in which the original order of the commandments is not maintained. (One might compare 1 Tim. I 9-10 which also shows "Berührungen mit dem Dekalog", thus Dibelius-Conzelmann ad loc., who refer to Apoc. Bar. gr. IV 17, VIII 5, XIII 4). The first to indicate this was Bernays (227f.) who said that vv. 3-7 are a selection from the Decalogue. Cf. Crouch. Origin 88 n. 20 "His opening verses are clearly intended to be a parallel to the Decalogue". The probability of this suggestion is confirmed by the fact that the inverse order of the first two commandments of the second table (οὐ μοιχεύσεις—οὐ φονεύσεις) is found here in the same way as in the LXX, Philo and the N.T. If it is valid also for vv. 5-8 (which is less certain), that would be an argument against the view that vv. 3-7 are "Eindringlinge", so Sitzler, Wochenschr. für klass. Phil. 29 (1912), 455 and others. See further below ad v. 8.

5 μὴ πλουτεῖν ἀδίκως, ἀλλ' ἐξ ὁσίων βιοτεύειν.
Do not become unjustly rich, but live from honourable means.

πλουτεῖν ἀδίκως: Theogn. 146; cf. 1155f. οὐκ ἔραμαι πλουτεῖν οὐδ' εὔχομαι, ἀλλά μοι εἴη ζῆν ἀπὸ τῶν ὀλίγων μηδὲν ἔχοντι κακόν (imitated by Or. Sib. II 109f., see Geffcken ad loc.). Democr. fr 78 χρήματα πορίζειν μὲν οὐκ ἀχρεῖον, ἐξ ἀδικίης δὲ πάντων κακίον. Ps-Isocr. Ad Dem. 38 μᾶλλον ἀποδέχου δικαίαν πενίαν ἢ πλοῦτον ἄδικον. Thales ap. Diog. Laert. I 37 μὴ πλούτει κακῶς. Men. Mon.

421 καλῶς πένεσθαι μᾶλλον ἢ πλουτεῖν κακῶς (cf. Men. gnom. pap. V 1, p. 9 Jaekel). Texts of this kind have a firm place in the gnomic tradition of the Greeks. See also the collection in Stob. III 10 (III pp. 408ff. W-H) περὶ ἀδικίας [καὶ φιλαργυρίας καὶ πλεονεξίας] and Delling, art. πλεονεξία, *TWNT* VI 266ff.; Dover, *Greek Popular Morality* 110ff., 170ff. Bernays 228 sees here a reference to the Decalogue, Ex. XX 14 (= Deut. V 19) οὐ κλέψεις (cf. Lev. XIX 13 οὐχ ἁρπάσεις), but Job XX 15 πλοῦτος ἀδίκως συναγόμενος ἐξεμεσθήσεται is a better parallel. (For later Jewish texts see Cronbach, "Social Ideals" 144). However, in view of the dependence of vv. 3-4 upon the Decalogue, Bernays may be right. But the language has in any case been moulded by the Greek gnomological tradition.

The μὴ-ἀλλὰ pattern also in vv. 156f. and 207. It is a traditional pattern, cf. Ps-Isocr. *Ad Dem.* 9f., 1 Thess. II 1-8, Eph. V 15. It is frequent in gnomologies, e.g. Men. *Mon.* 458, 481, 497. Cf. A. J. Malherbe, "Hellenistic Moralists and the New Testament" § 3 (as yet unpublished).

ἐξ ὁσίων βιοτεύειν: cf. v. 153 ὡς ἐξ ἰδίων βιοτεύσῃς. Anon. simil. 65 (Mullach, *Fr. Phil. Gr.* I 491) ἱδρὼς μὲν ὁ ἐκ τῶν γυμνασίων εὐσχημονέστερος, πλοῦτος δ᾽ ὁ ἐκ τῶν ἰδίων πόνων. For ὅσιος = δίκαιος see Schmidt, *Ethik* I 308; Bolkestein, "Ὅσιος 70; Terstegen, ΕΥΣΕΒΗΣ 121, who translates ἐξ ὁσίων by "van eerlijk gedreven zaken". This exhortation was probably not beside the point in Alexandria, where trade flourished (see Fraser, *Ptolemaic Alexandria* I 132-88; for Jewish traders in Alexandria see Fuchs, *Juden Aegyptens* 56ff.). But in general great care should be taken when drawing conclusions about the situation of the readers from traditional parenetic material (see Dibelius, *Der Brief des Jakobus* 13ff.; Thyen, *Stil* 86). For Greek and Jewish views on wealth see Hauck, art. πλοῦτος, *TWNT* VI 316-24 (316f. literature). There is a very strong emphasis on justice in Ps-Phoc. (9, 12, 14f. etc.).

With v. 5 the long insertion of Ps-Phoc. 5-79 into *Or. Sib.* II 56-148 begins, on which see Introd. pp. 84f.

6 ἀρκεῖσθαι παρ᾽ ἐοῖσι καὶ ἀλλοτρίων ἀπέχεσθαι.

Be content with what you have and abstain from what is another's.

V. 6 is closely parallel to v. 5. ἀρκεῖσθαι παρ᾽ ἐοῖσι: so the most important mss. M and V. It is the *lectio difficilior* when compared with Diehl's conjecture παρεοῦσι (supported by Rossbroich 30 and Keydell (1931) 93). But the following passages seem to favour

Diehl's conjecture. Democr. fr. 191 τοῖς παρεοῦσιν ἀρκέεσθαι. Teles p. 11, 5 H. ἀρκεῖσθαι τοῖς παροῦσιν, p. 38, 10 ἀρκούμενος τοῖς παροῦσι, p. 41, 12 etc. Dio Chrys. XXX 33 ἀρκεῖσθαι τοῖς παροῦσιν. Dio Cassius XXXVIII 8, 3 τοῖς παροῦσιν ἀρκεῖσθαι, XXXVIII 38, 1 ἠρκέσθησαν τοῖς παροῦσιν. Hebr. XIII 5 ἀρκούμενοι τοῖς παροῦσιν. Cf. Philo *Spec. leg.* IV 5 τοῖς οὖσιν οὐκ ἀρκούμενος and Ps-Isocr. *Ad Dem.* 29 στέργε τὰ πάροντα. This evidence, combined with the fact that ἀρκεῖσθαι is always followed by a simple dative without παρά casts doubt upon Bergk's *lectio* which has been adopted by Ludwich (*Spruchbuch* 20) and Young. Bergk's reference to Hierax *ap.* Stob. III 9, 54 (III p. 367 W-H) ἀρκοῦ τοῖς αὑτοῦ καὶ μὴ διάρπαζε τὰ τῶν πλησίον does not support his reading, though it is a good parallel to v. 6. Ludwich asserts that παρόντα and ἀλλότρια are no real opposites, but cf. Xen. *Symp.* IV 42 οἷς γὰρ μάλιστα τὰ παρόντα ἀρκεῖ, ἥκιστα τῶν ἀλλοτρίων ὀρέγονται. Moreover, ἀρκεῖσθαι τοῖς παροῦσιν had become a proverbial expression for: 'to be content with what you have' (Gerhard, *Phoinix* 56f.: "Schlagwörter der (kynischen) Sekte"). Admittedly, παρ' ἐοῖσι is the *lectio difficilior* (is παρά added *metri causa*?) and it is hard to cut the knot.

On the Jewish ideal of "Genügsamkeit in allen Dingen" cf. Bousset, *Religion* 424 with n. 6; see e.g. *Test. Iss.* IV 2 ὁ ἁπλοῦς χρυσίον οὐκ ἐπιθυμεῖ, τὸν πλησίον οὐ πλεονεκτεῖ, βρωμάτων ποικίλων οὐκ ἐφίεται, ἐσθῆτα διάφορον οὐ θέλει. 1 Tim. VI 6.8 (ἀρκεῖσθαι, cf. III 14). Bernays 228 refers to Ex. XX 17 (= Deut. V 21) οὐκ ἐπιθυμήσεις κτλ. . . . τοῦ πλησίον σου (cf. Did. II 3, Barn. XIX 6: from the Two Ways).

καὶ ἀλλοτρίων ἀπέχεσθαι: καί is adversative; see Denniston, *Gr. Part.* 292 and Verdenius, *Mnem.* IV 8 (1955), 15. ἀπέχεσθαι is frequent in Ps-Phoc. (31, 35, 76, 145, 149). It is a common term in Jewish and Christian paraenesis, see Bauer *s.v.* But cf. Xen. *Cyrop.* VI 13 ἀπέχονται τῶν ἀλλοτρίων. Isocr. *Nicocl.* 49 ἀπέχεσθε τῶν ἀλλοτρίων. Epict. III 7, 11 ἀπέχεται τῶν ἀλλοτρίων. This theme is, of course, both Jewish and Greek; see Heinemann, *Philons Bildung* 420ff. Rossbroich 30 refers to *Gnom. Byz.* 191 ὁ τῷ κατὰ φύσιν ἀρκούμενος πλούτῳ τοῦ τὰ πολλὰ μὲν κεκτημένου, πλείονα δὲ ἐπιθυμοῦντος πολύ ἐστι πλουσιώτερος· τῷ μὲν γὰρ οὐδὲν ἐλλείπει, τῷ δὲ καὶ ὧν κέκτηται πολλῷ πλείονα, cf. *ibid.* 195. See also (the Jewish) Ps-Men. *ap.* Clem. Alex. *Strom.* V 119, 2 (Denis, *Fragm.* p. 170, 13ff.).

The combination of licentiousness and covetousness in vv. 3-6 is also found in Eph. IV 19, V 3.5; there, these are the principal vices of the heathen. On its traditional Jewish character see Gnilka *ad loc.* Cf. Mk. VII 21-22, where nearly all the vices enumerated in vv. 3-6 occur: ... πορνεῖαι, κλοπαί, φόνοι, μοιχεῖαι, πλεονεξίαι, πονηρίαι, δόλος, ἀσέλγεια.

7 ψεύδεα μὴ βάζειν, τὰ δ' ἐτήτυμα πάντ' ἀγορεύειν.
Tell not lies, but speak always the truth.

A truth too general to need much comment. Dornseiff's characterization in *Echtheitsfragen* 40: "persisch" is very odd. βάζειν: a poetic verb (see LSJ *s.v.*). ἐτήτυμα ἀγορεύειν is Homeric, *Od.* I 174 (on ἐτήτυμος see Luther, *Wahrheit* etc. 51ff.). Democr. fr. 225 ἀληθομυθέειν χρεών, ὃ πολὺ λώϊον. Solon (in Snell, *Sieben Weisen* 96) μὴ ψεύδου, ἀλλ' ἀλήθευε. Men. *Mon.* 849 ψεῦδος μέγιστόν ἐστιν ἀνθρώποις κακόν. Floril. duo graeca I 40 (p. 9 Schenkl) τὸ ψεῦδος μίσει ἵνα σοι ἡ ἀλήθεια συνεθίζηται. See also the many texts in Stob. III 11 (III p. 429-443 W-H) περὶ ἀληθείας and III 12 (p. 444-453) περὶ ψεύδους. Xenocrates, Theophrastus, Chrysippus and other philosophers wrote treatises περὶ ψεύδους; see Speyer, *Fälschung* 95 n.1. From the O.T. compare Prov. XXI 3 ποιεῖν δίκαια καὶ ἀληθεύειν ἀρεστὰ παρὰ θεῷ. Sir. VII 13 μὴ θέλε ψεύδεσθαι πᾶν ψεῦδος (cf. XX 24-26). Zech. VIII 16 λαλεῖτε ἀλήθειαν ἕκαστος πρὸς τὸν πλησίον αὐτοῦ, etc. Test. Dan V 2. More Jewish texts in Billerbeck *ad* Eph. IV 25. Texts from Philo in Conzelmann, *TWNT* IX 596. Eph. IV 25 ἀποθέμενοι τὸ ψεῦδος λαλεῖτε ἀλήθειαν ἕκαστος μετὰ τοῦ πλησίον αὐτοῦ. Did. II 5 οὐκ ἔσται ὁ λόγος σου ψευδής. Herm. *Mand.* III 1.3; VIII 5.9 etc. For pagan, Jewish and Christian material see Conzelmann, *TWNT* IX 590-599 (with extensive bibliography). Carrington's suggestion (*Primitive Christian Catechism* 15) that Ps-Phoc. forbids here the cult of idols ("if by *pseudea* he means idols") is wrong. For adverbial πάντα ("in all points, wholly; always") see LSJ *s.v.* D4 and Bauer *s.v.* 2a δ.

Berger, *Gesetzesauslegung Jesu* I 272f. sees in vv. 3-7 one of the "dekalogähnliche Lasterkataloge im Judentum" (see his list of other examples 273), here rendering the 6th, 5th, 7th and 10th Commandment; cf. Philemon *ap.* Clem. Alex. *Strom.* V 14, 119, 2 (see Berger 270-276 on the function of the Decalogue as "Zusammenfassung der Sozialgebote" in Jewish propaganda).

8 πρῶτα θεὸν τιμᾶν, μετέπειτα δὲ σεῖο γονῆας.

Honour God first and foremost, and thereafter your parents.

Exhortations to honour God and parents are very common both in Greek and Jewish literature. This injunction was one of the "unwritten laws" in Greek ethics; see Schmidt, *Ethik* II 141ff.; Bolkestein, *Wohltätigkeit* 79f., 118f.; J. W. Hewitt, "Gratitude to Parents in Greek and Roman Literature", *AJP* 52 (1931), 30-48; Crouch, *Origin* 39f.; Dodds, *The Greeks and the Irrational* 60 n. 101; Praechter, *Hierokles* 45ff.; Wendland, *Anaximenes* 86; Wefelmeier, *Die Sentenzensammlung der Demonicea* 78ff. Xen. *Mem.* IV 4, 19f. (in a discussion of the "unwritten laws") παρὰ πᾶσιν ἀνθρώποις πρῶτον νομίζεται θεοὺς σέβειν. — οὐκοῦν καὶ γονέας τιμᾶν πανταχοῦ νομίζεται; — καὶ τοῦτο, ἔφη. Ps-Isocr. *Ad Dem.* 16 τοὺς μὲν θεοὺς φοβοῦ, τοὺς δὲ γονεῖς τίμα. Cleobulus *ap.* Boissonade, *Anecd. Gr.* I 135 θεὸν σέβεσθαι, γονέας αἰδεῖσθαι. Men. *Mon.* 322 θεὸν προτίμα, δεύτερον τοὺς σοὺς γονεῖς, cf. 525f. Polyb. VI 4, 4 θεοὺς σέβεσθαι, γονεῖς θεραπεύειν. Eur. fr. 853 θεούς τε τιμᾶν τούς τε φύσαντας γονῆς. Cf. Hes. fr. 170; Pind. *Pyth.* VI 23-7; Men. fr. 600 and gnom. pap. VIII 5 (p. 13 J.), XIII 17f. (p. 17 J); Aristot. *EN* IX 2, 8, 1165a24; Plut. *Lib. educ.* 10, 7E; Ps-Pyth. *Carm. aur.* 1-4; Ael. Arist. 13 p. 297 Dind. and many more texts in Stob. IV 25 (IV p. 619ff. W-H).

In the O.T., these commandments seldom occur in this combination. Prov. I 7-8 and Sir. VII 27-31 come close to it. Separately they often occur: *ad* 8a: Prov. VII 1; Sir. I 14ff.; Deut VI 5 etc.; *ad* 8b: Ex. XX 12 (= Deut. V 16) τίμα τὸν πατέρα σου καὶ τὴν μητέρα σου. Lev. XIX 3; Prov. XXIII 22-5; XIX 26; XXVIII 24; Sir. III 1-6; Tob. IV 3ff.; in the N.T. Eph. VI 2 etc. But the combination does occur in later Jewish texts, e.g. *Or. Sib.* III 593f. τιμῶσι μόνον τὸν ἀεὶ μεδέοντα ἀθάνατον καὶ ἔπειτα γονεῖς. Jos. *C. Ap.* II 206 γονέων τιμὴν μετὰ τὴν πρὸς θεὸν δευτέραν ἔταξε (sc. ὁ νόμος). Men. gnom. syr. 2 "Vor allem sollst du Gott fürchten und Vater und Mutter ehren" (tr. Schulthess). Cf. Philo *Spec. leg.* II 235, *Decal.* 51; Ep. Arist. 234; Jub. VII 20; Vita Aesopi 109 (rec. G, p. 69 Perry); etc. See for more texts (Jewish and Greek) Berger, *Gesetzesauslegung Jesu* I 284-7. For Rabbinic remarks on the honouring of parents (e.g. Qidd. 31a) see Heinemann, *Philons Bildung* 254 n. 1; Bacher, *Agada Tann.* I 112; cf. Bousset, *Religion* 426.

Many scholars have suspected that v. 8 was originally the beginning of the poem, and that vv. 3-7 were inserted by a later hand, e.g. Rossbroich 31; Kroll, *PW* XX 1, 505. Appeal is often made to *Carm. aur.* 1ff. that begins with ἀθανάτους μὲν πρῶτα θεοὺς ... τίμα, ... σούς τε γονεῖς τίμα. Wefelmeier, *Sentenzensammlung* 80: "In der Tat beginnt eine Reihe überlieferter Sammlungen mit der Götterverehrung und schliesst an sie die Ehrung der Eltern an" (other examples in n. 4). But if vv. 3-8 are a kind of paraphrase of the Decalogue, this view is improbable. The fact that the Ψ insertion in *Or. Sib.* II begins with Ps-Phoc. 5 also argues against it. (Before v. 8 Ψ has its first clumsy interpolation: μηδὲ μάτην εἴδωλα σέβου, τὸν δ' ἄφθιτον αἰεὶ | πρῶτα θεὸν τιμᾶν κτλ.).

Vv. 9-21 *Exhortations to Justice*

9 πάντα δίκαια νέμειν, μὴ δὲ κρίσιν ἐς χάριν ἕλκειν.
Always dispense justice and stretch not judgement for a favour.

δίκαια νέμειν: Plato *Polit.* 301D (δίκ. διανέμ.); Aristot. *EN* 1137a13; *Or. Sib.* I 272.295; II 49. For this use of ἕλκειν LSJ give no parallels.

For ἐς χάριν (or πρὸς χάριν) see Soph. *O.R.* 1351 (cf. 1152); Isocr. *Ad. Nicocl.* 4; Ael. Arist. 46, p. 158 and 169 Dind. and LSJ s.v. VI 2a. Cf. Theocr. V 69 ἐν χάριτι κρίνειν τινά, to decide from partiality to one. In the LXX, εἰς χάριν occurs only in Jud. VIII 23, X 8; cf. πρὸς χάριν Prov. VII 5; Ezek. XII 24. The expressions mostly mean "to do a favour, to gain favour". Here, this expression is clearly a warning against partiality, as is so often the case in the O.T., e.g. Ex. XXIII 1-3; Deut. I 17, XVI 18-20; Sir. XI 7, XIX 13-17. Bernays refers to Lev. XIX 15 οὐ ποιήσετε ἄδικον ἐν κρίσει. See further *ad* v. 10. For Greek texts on the impartiality of judges see Hirzel, *Themis* 417f. (417: "Der Richter soll ohne vorgefasste Meinung an sein Geschäft gehn, beiden Parteien das gleiche Wohlwollen (εὔνοια) entgegenbringen (Isokr. 15, 21. Dem. 18, 2 u. 7. 19, 1 u. 228) oder vielmehr, wie das sein Eid formulierte, in keinerlei sich durch Gunst und Abgunst (οὔτε χάριτος ἕνεκα οὔτε ἔχθρας) bestimmen lassen").

It is uncertain whether one has to think here in terms of the activities of a court of justice (for the Jewish tribunals in Alexandria see Tcherikover, *CPJ* I 32f.) or of "rein privates κρίνειν" (so Geffcken, *Apologeten* 88, who compares John VII 24 μὴ κρίνετε κατ' ὄψιν, ἀλλὰ τὴν δικαίαν κρίσιν κρίνετε). Vv. 10-12 favour the first interpretation. Berger, *Gesetzesauslegung Jesu* I 343 calls vv. 9-12 a "Richterspiegel".

10 μὴ ῥίψῃς πενίην ἀδίκως, μὴ κρῖνε πρόσωπον.

Cast the poor not down unjustly, judge not partially.

ῥίψῃς: Rossbroich, Diehl and others read τρίψῃς with reference to Hes. *Op*. 250f. σκολιῇσι δίκῃσιν ἀλλήλους τρίβουσιν. Cf. also Amos VIII 4 ἐκτρίβοντες ... πένητα. Bernays 216 n. 1 reads θλίψῃς referring to v. 19 μὴ θλῖβε πένητα. Bergk proposes ῥέψῃς: "i.e. iudicem cavere oportet, ne praeter ius atque fas pauperis causa superior fiat", with reference to Ex. XXIII 3 πένητα οὐκ ἐλεήσεις ἐν κρίσει and Lev. XIX 15 οὐ ποιήσετε ἄδικον ἐν κρίσει, οὐ λήψῃ πρόσωπον πτωχοῦ. But ῥίψῃς is tenable; cf. Ps. L 11, LXX 9 μὴ ἀπορρίψῃς με (for ῥίπτω = ἀπορρίπτω see LSJ *s.v.* IV). The line means: "you must not favour a rich man above a poor one". It is to be seen in connection with v. 9.

πενίην = πένητα(ς), cf. 62 πλοῦτος = πλούσιοι; Sir. XVI 8 τῆς παροικίας = τῶν παροίκων. Men. gnom. syr. 19 "Und die Armut (= die Armen) verachte nicht" (tr. Schulthess). See K-G I 10-11. ἀδίκως is to be taken with μὴ ῥίψῃς πενίην, not with the following, so wrongly LSJ 1533 and Farina 34. Farina (following Bergk) says ἀδίκως is superfluous in v. 10a because the oppression of the poor is always unjust, but he fails to see that the same would be the case when ἀδίκως is taken with v. 10b. Apparently he does not know the O.T. background of the expression κρίνειν πρόσωπον.

μὴ κρῖνε πρόσωπον = judge without respect of persons. At the background is the O.T. expression *naśa' panim* = λαμβάνειν πρόσωπον, to treat with partiality, to favour, e.g. Lev. XIX 15 (quoted above) and Sir. IV 27 μὴ λάβῃς πρόσωπον δυνάστου, Deut. I 17, XVI 19; Prov. XXIV 23; Aboth de R. Nathan (rec. A) X 1. N.T. 1 Pet. I 17 τὸν ἀπροσωπολήμπτως κρίνοντα, Mt. XXII 16 etc. Cf. Barn. XIX 4. (Alexandre on *Or. Sib.* II 62: Hebraica loquendi forma, Graecis insolens, certe apud profanos auctores vix usquam obvia [right], et quae vel sola christianam prodat Phocylidis interpolationem [wrong]).

This verse (and see 19, 22f., 29) indicates "a typically Jewish concern for the poor" (Crouch, *Origin* 86). Ex. XXIII 6 οὐ διαστρέψεις κρίμα πένητος ἐν κρίσει αὐτοῦ (cf. v. 3). Prov. XXII 22 μὴ ἀποβιάζου πένητα, πτωχὸς γάρ ἐστιν, cf. XVIII 5, XXIV 23, XXXI 9; Sir. IV 1-6 etc.; for more texts see Beltrami (1908) 412. Philo

Jos. 72 ἐὰν οὖν δικάζειν δέῃ, δικάσω μήτε πλουσίῳ προσθέμενος διὰ τὴν περιουσίαν μήτε πένητι διὰ τὸν ἐπὶ ταῖς ἀτυχίαις ἔλεον, ἀλλὰ τὰ τῶν κρινομένων ἀξιώματα καὶ σχήματα παρακαλυψάμενος ἀδόλως βραβεύσω τὸ φανησόμενον δίκαιον. See the expression πενήτων ἄνομοι κριταί in Did. V 2 and Barn. XX 2 (from the Jewish Two Ways). On the Jewish view of poverty as a severe suffering see e.g. Billerbeck I 818f. etc. (Reg. *s.v.* Armut). and the paragraph "The Woes of the Poor" in Cronbach, "Social Ideals of the Apocrypha" 125-131. There are no parallels to v. 10a in the Greek moralists. On this difference between Greek and Jewish ethics see Bolkestein, *Wohltätigkeit und Armenpflege* 129 and *passim*.

11 ἢν σὺ κακῶς δικάσῃς, σὲ θεὸς μετέπειτα δικάσσει.
If you judge evilly, God will judge you thereafter.

The interpretation of this line depends upon the meaning of μετέπειτα. Does it mean: after your evil judgement?; or: in the after-life? (cf. the similar problem in 1 Thess. IV 6). If Ps-Phoc. means no more than that in this life God's judgment will come upon anyone who judges evilly, that is the current O.T. way of understanding God's punishments of evildoers (cf. Hos. VII 12; IX 1-6; Amos I 3ff.; Jer. VI 16-21). But possibly Ps-Phoc. means God's judgment in the hereafter, which, though hardly an O.T. tenet (but cf. Eccl. XI 9 γνῶθι ὅτι ἐπὶ πᾶσι τούτοις ἄξει σε ὁ θεὸς ἐν κρίσει), was a common belief among both Greeks and Jews in antiquity. For the Greek view see Ruhl, *De mortuorum iudicio, passim*; Rohde, *Psyche* I 308ff.; Cumont, *After Life* 170ff.; Nilsson, *Gesch. der griech. Rel.* II² 239ff.; Hengel, *Judentum und Hellenismus* 361 n. 551. For the Jewish view Bousset, *Religion* 293ff.; Moore, *Judaism* II 287ff.; Billerbeck, Register *s.v.* Gericht. If judgment in the hereafter is meant here, this verse alludes to one of the very few "dogmas" of ancient Judaism, see Bousset, *Religion* 192f. (not, as Alexandre (on *Or. Sib.* II 63) asserts, to the Christian doctrine).

For the sentiment of this verse cf. Prov. XVII 15 ὃς δίκαιον κρίνει τὸν ἄδικον, ἄδικον δὲ τὸν δίκαιον, ἀκάθαρτος καὶ βδελυκτὸς παρὰ τῷ θεῷ. *Or. Sib.* IV 183 καὶ τότε δὴ κρίσις ἔσσετ', ἐφ' ᾗ δικάσει θεὸς αὐτός. Matt. VII 2 ἐν ᾧ ... κρίματι κρίνετε κριθήσεσθε. Luk. VI 37 καὶ μὴ κρίνετε, καὶ οὐ μὴ κριθῆτε· καὶ μὴ καταδικάζετε, καὶ οὐ μὴ καταδικασθῆτε. Sextus 183 ὁ κρίνων ἄνθρωπον κρίνεται ὑπὸ τοῦ θεοῦ (cf. 184 μείζων ὁ κίνδυνος δικαζομένου δικαστῇ).

12 μαρτυρίην ψευδῆ φεύγειν· τὰ δίκαια βραβεύειν.

Flee false witness; arbitrate justice.

μαρτυρίην ψευδῆ φεύγειν may mean "do not give false witness", but the context suggests the meaning "do not allow yourself to be influenced by false witness". This, of course, implies the prohibition of false witnessing, which is often found in the O.T., e.g. Ex. XX 16 οὐ ψευδομαρτυρήσεις κατὰ τὸν πλησίον σου μαρτυρίαν ψευδῆ (= Deut. V 20), cf. Deut. XIX 15-19; Prov. XXI 28 μάρτυς ψευδὴς ἀπολεῖται, XXV 18, etc. Philo *Decal.* 138.172. Because this prohibition also occurs in Did. II 3 (cf. V 1), Aristides *Apol.* XV 4 and related early Christian texts, Audet (*Didache* 291) asserts that Ps-Phoc. 12a (and 16f.) "dépendent ici d'une récension du *Duae viae* déja en circulation", which is unnecessary. For some passages in Greek literature see LSJ s.v. ψευδομαρτυρία, Bauer 1763 (and cf. *falsum testimonium* in Plautus *Rudens* prol. 13, *Menaechmi* 839).

τὰ δίκαια βραβεύειν: Philo *LA* I 87 βραβεύει τὸ δίκαιον, cf. *Jos.* 72 quoted under v. 10; Mus. Ruf. VIII (p. 33, 8 H) τὰ δίκαια βραβεύειν; *Or. Sib.* II 45 ἁγνὸς γὰρ Χριστὸς τούτοις τὰ δίκαια βραβεύσει. Ael. Arist. XLVI 27 K. Ludwich, *Spruchbuch* 20, unnecessarily reads τὰ δίκαι' ἀγορεύειν with his favourite ms. V.

13 παρθεσίην τηρεῖν, πίστιν δ' ἐν πᾶσι φυλάσσειν.

Watch over a deposit, and in everything keep faith.

All mss. read παρθενίην (virginity), but Bernays 220 has pointed out that this must be a Byzantine (Christian) corruption of παρθεσίην (deposit; cf. παραθήκη in v. 135) as is also the case in *Anth. Pal.* VII 37, 2. This conjecture has been generally accepted (Ludwich, *Quaest.* 27, is an exception) since it fits much better the trend of the whole poem, esp. vv. 175ff. (Berger, *Gesetzesauslegung Jesu* I 325 wrongly interprets παρθεσίην as virginity!). Bernays 228 sees Lev. XIX 11 (οὐ κλέψετε, οὐ ψεύσεσθε, οὐ συκοφαντήσει ἕκαστος τὸν πλησίον) as the source of this verse, which is not impossible but not probable either. Lev. V 20-26 and Ex. XXII 6-12 forbid the touching of or lying about the deposit of a neighbour; cf. Ezek. XVIII 7. See also Jos. *Ant.* IV 285 παρακαταθήκην δὲ ὥσπερ ἱερόν τι καὶ θεῖον χρῆμα ὁ παραλαβὼν φυλακῆς ἀξιούτω ("le parole di Giuseppe sembrano suggerite da Pseudofoc.", Beltrami, *Riv.* 41 (1913) 537, unnecessarily) and Philo's expositions on this matter in *Spec. leg.* IV 30ff. (with the comments of Heinemann, *Philons*

Bildung 424ff.). Rabbinic texts on this subject are discussed by Marmorstein, "Das Motiv vom veruntreuten Depositum in der jüdischen Volkskunde", *MGWJ* 78 (1934), 183-195.
For the formulation of v. 13 see Ps-Isocr. *Ad Dem.* 22 τήρει τὰς παρακαταθήκας. Also παρ. φυλάσσειν occurs, e.g. *Vita Aesopi* 109 rec. G, p. 69 Perry and in the N.T. 1 Tim. VI 20; 2 Tim. I 12.14. On παρα(κατα)θήκη see Spicq, *Ep. Past.* I 580f. (bibliography!). The Jewish rules concerning deposits are discussed in *Baba Metzia* III 1-12. Pittacus *ap.* Boissonade, *Anecd. Gr.* I 139 παρακαταθήκην ἀπόδος, cf. Aristot. *EN* V 8, 1135b4ff. Cic. *Tusc.* III 17. To return a deposit intact was a commonly accepted rule in antiquity, see P. Frezza, Παρακαταθήκη 139-172 and Taubenschlag, *Law* 349ff. Pliny *Ep.* X 96, 7 about the Christians: ... *ne fidem fallerent, ne depositum appellati abnegarent* (cf. Aristides *Apol.* XV 4 with Geffcken 87f. *ad loc.*). This combination of παρα(κατα)θήκη and πίστις occurs both in this verse and also in Ps-Plato *Defin.* 415d παρακαταθήκη· δόμα μετὰ πίστεως (although in another sense; see LSJ *s.v.* I 3b).

πίστιν ... φυλάσσειν: Soph. *O.C.* 626 τὸ σὸν πιστὸν φυλάσσειν, Polyb. XVIII 41 διεφύλαξε τὴν πίστιν, also with τηρεῖν, e.g. Polyb. VI 58, 4 τετηρηκέναι τὴν πίστιν. (For the parallelism of τηρεῖν and φυλάσσειν cf. in the N.T. John XVII 12). Here πίστις means faithfulness (as in 218), see Lührmann, "Pistis im Judentum" 25f.: "Es ist ... auffällig, dass der durch die LXX-Übersetzung gewonnene Inhalt von πιστεύειν und πίστις in der uns erhaltenen griechischsprachigen jüdischen Literatur nur sehr zögernd aufgenommen wird. Ps-Hekatäus und Ps-Phokylides (13; 218?) verwenden πίστις in der Bedeutung 'Treue', ... πιστεύειν in der Bedeutung 'vertrauen' (79)". Cf. Epict. II 4, 1 ὁ ἄνθρωπος πρὸς πίστιν γέγονεν καὶ τοῦτο ὁ ἀνατρέπων ἀνατρέπει τὸ ἴδιον τοῦ ἀνθρώπου. For more passages from Greek literature see Bultmann, *TWNT* VI 175-182.

14-15 μέτρα νέμειν τὰ δίκαια, καλὸν δ' ἐπίμετρον ἁπάντων.
σταθμὸν μὴ κρούειν ἑτερόζυγον, ἀλλ' ἴσον ἕλκειν.

Give a just measure, good is an extra full measure of all things.
Make a balance not unequal, but weigh honestly.

μέτρα δίκαια: Deut. XXV 14f. οὐκ ἔσται ἐν τῇ οἰκίᾳ σου μέτρον καὶ μέτρον, μέγα ἢ μικρόν· ... μέτρον ἀληθινὸν καὶ δίκαιον ἔσται σοι. Lev. XIX 35f. (quoted below). Philo *LA* III 165 ... ἵνα μέτροις δικαίοις χρωμένη μὴ ἀδικῇς, *Hyp.* in Eus. *PE* VIII 7, 8 (431, 3f. Mr.)

μὴ ζυγὸν ἄδικον ἀνθυποβάλλειν, μὴ χοίνικα ἄμετρον, μὴ νόμισμα ἄδικον (cf. *Quis heres* 162). Jos. *C. Ap.* II 216 ἀλλὰ καὶ περὶ μέτρων εἴ τις κακουργήσειεν ἢ σταθμῶν, ἢ περὶ πράσεως ἀδίκου καὶ δόλῳ γενομένης ... πάντων εἰσὶ κολάσεις κτλ. (see Crouch, *Origin* 86). Cf. *Or. Sib.* III 237 (μέτρα δίκαια). These injunctions are also found frequently in the Wisdom literature, e.g. Prov. XI 1, XVI 11, XX 10.23; Sir. XLII 4, and in the prophets, e.g. Amos VIII 4ff., Hosea XII 8, Micha VI 11, Ezek. XLV 10. The LXX origin of these vv. is very clear (see also Young in *app. crit.*). Even Rossbroich 34 admits this.

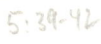

καλὸν δ' ἐπίμετρον ἁπάντων: ἐπίμετρον is something added to make a good measure (LSJ *s.v.*; first instance in Theophr.). "Give a baker's dozen for 12" (Young, letter of 6.10.1972). Many have tried to emend the text: Bernays 219 n. 2 states: "Die Krämerzugabe, ἐπίμετρον, wird durch den ... Zusammenhang unweigerlich verlangt. Aber das Schlusswort ἁπάντων ist allerdings matt. Ich glaube, es steckt ἐπαντλεῖν darin ... 'Hinzuschöpfen' sagt der Verfasser, weil er hier vom Messen des Flüssigen redet; im folgenden Vers (15) spricht er vom Wegen des Festen". Ludwich, *Spruchbuch* 16 reads καλὸν δ' ἐπὶ μέτρον ἀπαντᾶν, "schön ist es, zu seinem Maasse zu kommen". Kurfess, *ZNW* 1939, 176 prefers the reading of *Or. Sib.* (Ψ) ἅπασι, "schön ist eine Zugabe bei allem". But the text can be kept as it is (see the translation). The ἐπίμετρον is the μέτρον καλὸν πεπιεσμένον σεσαλευμένον ὑπερεκχυννόμενον of Luk. VI 38 (see Casaubonus *ad loc.* in Wettstein, *N.T.Gr.* I, Amsterdam 1751, 696: "cumulus in mensura aridorum est id quod excedit legitimam mensuram, et hostoriolo solet abradi. Seneca vocat accessionem. Non vacat de pretio quaeri, plus in accessionibus fuit. Id vocant Latini auctarium, Graeci ἐπίμετρον)". Rossbroich 34f. says "quonam modo δίκαια μέτρα et ἐπίμετρον inter se cohaereant non video", and suggests that v. 14b originated from a wrong interpretation of Hes. *Op.* 349f. εὖ μὲν μετρεῖσθαι παρὰ γείτονος, εὖ δ' ἀποδοῦναι, αὐτῷ τῷ μέτρῳ, καὶ λώιον, αἴ κε δύνηαι (cf. 396f. ἐγὼ δέ τοι οὐκ ἐπιδώσω, οὐδ' ἐπιμετρήσω), unnecessarily.

σταθμὸν μὴ κρούειν ἑτερόζυγον: Lev. XIX 35f. οὐ ποιήσετε ἄδικον ... ἐν μέτροις καὶ ἐν σταθμίοις καὶ ἐν ζυγοῖς· ζυγὰ δίκαια καὶ στάθμια δίκαια καὶ χοῦς δίκαιος ἔσται ὑμῖν. If Lev. XIX is also the source here, then the word ἑτερόζυγος (which is to be taken proleptically here) may have been suggested by Lev. XIX 19, though it has another sense there. For Philo and Josephus see above and also *Spec. leg.* IV 193 on the demand of justice from οἱ σταθμία καὶ ζυγὰ καὶ μέτρα διαχειρίζοντες ἔμποροι καὶ κάπηλοι καὶ ἀγοραῖοι, cf. 194 ζυγὰ δίκαια καὶ σταθμία καὶ μέτρα παρασκευάζεσθαι (for the terminology cf. Ael. Arist. 46, 29 K. σταθμά τε καὶ ζυγὰ καὶ μέτρα καὶ τὸ ἐν τούτοις δίκαιον). On σταθμὸν κρούειν (lit. to strike the balance) see Schmidt, *Synonymik* III 290, and cf. κρουσιμετρέω and κρουσιμέτρης, LSJ *s.vv.*

ἴσον ἕλκειν: "die Waage im Gleichgewicht halten", Kurfess, *ZNW* 1939, 178. See σταθμὸν ἕλκειν in Herod. I 50; cf. Hom. *Il.* VIII 72. It can be said both of the man who weighs and of the thing weighed.

The occurrence of these injunctions in Ps-Phoc., Philo's *Hyp.* and Jos.*C.Ap.* makes it probable that they are drawn from a store of ethical material which all three of them had as a common source (see Introduction p. 18f., 50f., 74).

16-17 **μὴ δ' ἐπιορκήσῃς μήτ' ἀγνῶς μήτε ἑκοντί ·**
ψεύδορκον στυγέει θεὸς ἄμβροτος ὅστις ὀμόσσῃ.

Do not commit perjury, neither ignorantly nor willingly.
The immortal God hates a perjurer, whosoever it is who has sworn.

These two lines should be dealt with together as a unity. μὴ δ' ἐπιορκήσῃς: Theogn. 1195f. μήτι θεοὺς ἐπίορκος ἐπόμνυθι· οὐ γὰρ ἀνεκτὸν ἀθανάτους κρύψαι χρεῖος ὀφειλόμενον. Cf. Hes. *Theog.* 231f. Soph. fr. 431 calls perjury εἰς θεοὺς ἁμαρτάνειν (see Rohde, *Psyche* I 65 n. 1 and 2). Men. *Mon.* 347 θεὸν ἐπιορκῶν μὴ δόκει λεληθέναι. Cf. Pind. *Ol.* II 65-7; Arist. *Ran.* 145ff., esp. 150 and the collection of texts in Stob. III 27 περὶ ὅρκου (III p. 611-6 W-H) and III 28 περὶ ἐπιορκίας (III p. 616-26 W-H). The Greek view of perjury is discussed by R. Hirzel, *Der Eid* 75ff. Cf. Schmidt, *Ethik* II 3ff.; Dover, *Popular Morality* 248ff.

μήτ' ἀγνῶς μήτε ἑκοντί: Arist. *Rhet.* I 13, 1373b33-5 ἀνάγκη πάντα τὰ ἐγκλήματα ἢ πρὸς τὸ κοινὸν ἢ πρὸς τὸ ἴδιον εἶναι, καὶ ἢ ἀγνοοῦντος καὶ ἄκοντος ἢ ἑκόντος καὶ εἰδότος. Sebestyén 35 proposes εἰκαῖος instead of ἑκοντί, unnecessarily; cf. the similar adverb ἐθελοντί. Perhaps there is an allusion here to the O.T. distinction between sinning inadvertently (בשגגה) and sinning presumptuously (ביד רמה), Num. XV 29f. (LXX ἀκουσίως and ἐν χειρὶ ὑπερηφανίας), cf. 1 QS VIII 17-24. On this distinction see Billerbeck II 264 and Spicq, *Ép. Past.* I 342. Cf. further Hauck, *TWNT* II 467.

O.T. prohibitions of perjury: Ex. XX 7 (= Deut. V 11) οὐ λήμψῃ τὸ ὄνομα κυρίου τοῦ θεοῦ σου ἐπὶ ματαίῳ. οὐ γὰρ μὴ καθαρίσῃ κύριος τὸν λαμβάνοντα τὸ ὄνομα αὐτοῦ ἐπὶ ματαίῳ. Lev. XIX 12 οὐκ ὀμεῖσθε τῷ ὀνόματί μου ἐπ' ἀδίκῳ. Cf. Sir. XXIII 11, Ps. Sal. IV 4, Sap. Sal. XIV 28f., Apoc. Bar. Gr. IV 17. N.T. 1 Tim. I 10 (cf. Matt. V 33; Jas. V 12 with Dibelius *ad loc.*: "ein völliges Eidverbot setzt sich im Judentum wohl schon mit Rücksicht auf das A.T. nicht durch; Ps-Phok. 16 hat nur das Verbot des Meineids"). Philo discusses the matter in *Spec. leg.* II 26ff. 252; IV 40; *Decal.* 86ff. (with Heinemann's remarks, *Philons Bildung* 92-4). Did. II 3 οὐκ ἐπιορκήσεις (Audet, *Did.* 291: from *Duae Viae* doctrine).

ψεύδορκον στυγέει θεός: Lewis, "Teaching" 295: "a typically Jewish anthropopathism", but Dornseiff, *Echtheitsfragen* 40: "die hinzugefügte göttliche Bedrohung ist Umschreibung von "Ich bin Jahwe" [sc. from Lev. XIX 12], liegt aber auch vom griechischen her nahe, vgl. Theognis 1195 [quoted above]". It may be, however, a rendering of the Decalogue's "the Lord will not leave unpunished the man who misuses his name" (Ex. XX 7), though admittedly a threatening is also implied in the texts from the Greek authors quoted above. Perjury is, in any case, a direct offence against the deity, who is involved by it in human evil.

ὅστις ὀμόσσῃ: God is no respector of persons. (Deut. X 17, Rom. II 11).

Between vv. 17 and 18 Ψ inserts: ἐξ ἀδίκων ἔργων δῶρον χερὶ μή ποτε δέξῃ.

18 σπέρματα μὴ κλέπτειν· ἐπαράσιμος ὅστις ἕληται.

Do not steal seeds; cursed is whosoever takes them.

Though σπέρματα is read in all the mss., several scholars reject it. Bernays 229 reads τέρματα μὴ κλέπτειν and interprets it as "do not move your neighbour's boundary stones", referring to Deut. XXVII 17 ἐπικατάρατος ὁ μετατιθεὶς ὅρια τοῦ πλησίον. He is followed by Sebestyén, Seeberg (*Die beiden Wege* 28), Riessler, and Easton. Beltrami, *Riv.* 1913, 527f. reads κέρματα (coins), referring to Jos. *C.Ap.* II 216. These emendations are unconvincing and unnecessary. Those who retain σπέρματα explain it in divergent ways. Dieterich, *Nekyia* 176 interprets it as a prohibition of masturbation (rightly refuted by Rossbroich 35). Sitzler, *Wochenschr.* 29 (1912), 454 thinks the verse forbids child-stealing (so already Geiger, *Jüd. Zeitschr. f. Wiss. und Leben* 4 (1866) 55f.), "denn nur ein solcher rechtfertigt die Worte ἐπαράσιμος ὅστις ἕληται, vgl. Ex. 21, 17; Deut. 24, 7." He is followed by Kurfess, *ZNW* 38 (1939) 173f. "keine Knaben rauben", namely in order to organize paederastic brothels. Both support this thesis by referring to the two lines that follow upon v. 18 in Ψ', where ἀρσενοκοιτεῖν is forbidden. But their view of Ψ' is untenable, see Introduction p. 84. Kurfess moreover refers to 1 Tim. I 10 where homosexuals and kidnappers are mentioned together. Berger, *Gesetzesauslegung Jesu* I 330, curiously interprets σπέρματα as "Juden". Weinreich, *Stiftung* 59 says v. 18 forbids abortion.

It is more natural, however, to interpret σπέρματα as seeds or the yield of seeds. Cf. *Anth. Pal.* IX 89 τοῖς γαίης σπέρμασι, "with the products of earth" (said of corn-stalks), and LSJ s.v. I 1. Sartorius, *Analysis grammatica* (1617) 20 already explains it in this sense, but he thinks the verse is about stealing by magical means. So too Bergk *ad loc.* and Farina 35, who refers to the *Twelve Tables* VIII 5 where the stealing of fruits by means of magic (*qui fruges excantassit*) is condemned; cf. Mommsen, *Strafrecht* 772f. The idea of magic might explain the cursing formula ἐπαράσιμος κτλ. But the verse may simply mean, as does v. 38, keeping away from fruits that are growing on the land. See Klein, *Der ält. christl. Kat.* 86f. who refers to Philo *Hyp.* in Eus. *PE* VIII 7, 6 (p. 430, 18-20 Mr.) ἃ μὴ κατέθηκεν, μηδ' ἀναιρεῖσθαι, μηδ' ἐκ πρασιᾶς μηδ' ἐκ ληνοῦ μηδ' ἐξ ἅλωνος· μὴ θημῶνος ὑφαιρεῖσθαι μέγα ἢ μικρὸν ἁπλῶς μηδέν (in VIII 7, 7 (431, 2f. Mr.) μὴ σπέρμα ἀφανίζειν probably alludes to *coitus interruptus* or to the use of contraceptives). Cf. Rossbroich 35 who, after having discussed every possibility, concludes: "Nihil aliud igitur restare puto nisi, ut dicamus auctorem re vera semina agricolae significasse. Ineptum illud quidem est, sed contextus hic omnino non conspicitur". This is correct. See also Alexandre on *Or. Sib.* II 71: ". . . scriptum hoc esse in satores improbos qui semina sibi credita suffurantur".

After v. 18 Ψ' inserts: εἰς γενεὰς γενεῶν, εἰς σκορπισμὸν βιότοιο. μὴ ἀρσενοκοιτεῖν, μὴ συκοφαντεῖν, μήτε φονεύειν,

19 μισθὸν μοχθήσαντι δίδου, μὴ θλῖβε πένητα.
Give the labourer his pay, do not afflict the poor.

Here "a typically Jewish concern for the poor" (Crouch, *Origin* 86) can again be seen. On this see Billerbeck IV 536ff. ("Die altjüdische Privatwohltätigkeit") and 559ff. ("Die altjüdischen Liebeswerke"). The passage Hes. *Op.* 370 μισθὸς δ' ἀνδρὶ φίλῳ εἰρημένος ἄρκιος ἔστω (referred to by Farina 35) is only a remote parallel. But cf. Men. gnom. pap. IX 4 πένητα μὴ παρίδῃς, *Mon*. 376, 542. The notion of special duties towards the poor is underdeveloped in Greek ethics; see Bolkestein, *Wohltätigkeit und Armenpflege* 67ff. and Skemp, "Service to the Needy in the Graeco-Roman World", *Service in Christ* 17-26. The adjective φιλοπένης in *Corp. Inscr. Iud.* 203 is characteristically Jewish.

The O.T. source of v. 19a is possibly Lev. XIX 13 οὐ μὴ κοιμηθήσεται ὁ μισθὸς τοῦ μισθωτοῦ παρὰ σοὶ ἕως πρωί (cf. Tob. IV 14) or Deut. XXIV 14 οὐκ ἀπαδικήσεις μισθὸν πένητος (with the comments in Jos. *Ant.* IV 288). See the rabbinic texts in Billerbeck I 832; add *Derek Erez Rabba* II 28. Cf. in the N.T. 1 Tim. V 18 ἄξιος ὁ ἐργάτης τοῦ μισθοῦ αὐτοῦ (Lk. X 7), Jas V 4 ὁ μισθὸς τῶν ἐργατῶν ... ὁ ἀφυστερημένος ἀφ' ὑμῶν κράζει. A discussion of the theme "die Beraubung des Tagelöhners" in Jewish and Christian literature can be found in Berger, *Gesetzesauslegung Jesu* I 382-4. For v. 19b see Amos VIII 4 οἱ ἐκτρίβοντες (*v.l.* ἐκθλίβοντες) ... πένητα. Lev. XXV 17 μὴ θλιβέτω ἄνθρωπος τὸν πλησίον. Prov. XIV 21.31; XVII 5; XXII 22; Sir. IV 1-6 (v. 4 θλιβόμενον). *Or. Sib.* III 630 τὴν δὲ δικαιοσύνην τίμα καὶ μηδένα θλῖβε, cf. III 241-5. Herm. *Mand.* VIII 10 χρεώστας μὴ θλίβειν καὶ ἐνδεεῖς.

20 γλώσσῃ νοῦν ἐχέμεν, κρυπτὸν λόγον ἐν φρεσὶν ἴσχειν.

Take heed of your tongue, keep your word hidden in your heart.

Bernays 230 says that this verse contradicts the plea for openness in vv. 48-50; therefore he reads κρύπτων λόγον ἐν φρεσὶν ἴψῃ and translates the whole verse "Habe deine Sinnesmeinung auf der Zunge; hältst du das Wort in der Brust versteckt, so schadest du nur". In his view, the source of this verse is Lev. XIX 17 οὐ μισήσεις τὸν ἀδελφόν σου τῇ διανοίᾳ σου. He is followed by Sebestyén 34, Riessler 863, Dornseiff 40. But contradictions are no proof of text-corruption in a poem with traditional parenetic materials. Bergk, *Philol.* 41 (1882) 589f. links κρυπτόν to νοῦν: "beim reden verbirg deine gesinnung (gedanken), sei zurückhaltend in deinen äusserungen"; cf. Bergk in *PLG* II[4] *ad loc.*: "sententia haec est: si loqueris, consilium tuum occulta: verba pectore sint recondita; i.e. cave eloquaris, quidquid in mentem venit". Sitzler, *Wochenschr.* 29 (1912) 455 (taking κρυπτόν with λόγον, cf. the *v.l.* κρυπτὸν ... λόγον in Aesch. *Choeph.* 773) more rightly translates: "in der Zunge habe Verstand, verborgen im Herzen halte das Wort, d.h. sprich verständig, nicht vorschnell". Cf. Rossbroich 36: "praeceptum linguae temperare". But νοῦν ἔχειν (mostly followed by a preposition) means "to have one's mind directed to something", so the translation "take heed of" is better.

There are several parallels in the Greek gnomological tradition. Theogn. 421f. πολλοῖσ' ἀνθρώπων γλώσσῃ θύραι οὐκ ἐπίκεινται ἁρμόδιαι. Ps-Isocr. Ad Dem. 41 πᾶν ὅτι ἂν μέλλῃς ἐρεῖν πρότερον ἐπισκόπει τῇ γνώμῃ. Chilo ap. Diog. Laert. I 70 τὴν γλῶτταν μὴ προτρέχειν τοῦ νοῦ (cf. Boissonade, Anecd. Gr. I 138; Snell, Sieben Weisen 98; Sternbach, Gnom. Vat. 167 note). The Jewish Wisdom literature, however, also has comparable texts. Prov. XXI 23 ὃς φυλάσσει τὸ στόμα αὐτοῦ καὶ τὴν γλῶσσαν, διατηρεῖ ἐκ θλίψεως τὴν ψυχὴν αὐτοῦ. Eccles. V 1 μὴ σπεῦδε ἐπὶ στόματί σου καὶ καρδία σου μὴ ταχυνάτω τοῦ ἐξενέγκαι λόγον (cf. Jas. I 19; III 1ff.). Sir. XXI 26 ἐν στόματι μωρῶν ἡ καρδία αὐτῶν, καρδία δὲ σοφῶν στόμα αὐτῶν (cf. XIX 10; XX 5). Maxims of Ahikar (syr.) 2, 3, 52, 53, 54. Barn. XIX 8 οὐκ ἔσῃ πρόγλωσσος (in the Two Ways section). For the use of κρυπτόν cf. Test. Rub. I 4 ... εἴπω ... ὅσα ἔχω ἐν τῇ καρδίᾳ μου κρυπτά.

After v. 20 Ψ' inserts: ὀρφανικοῖς χήραις ἐπιδευομένοις δὲ παράσχου.

21 μήτ' ἀδικεῖν ἐθέλῃς μήτ' οὖν ἀδικοῦντα ἐάσῃς.

Neither wish to do injustice, nor therefore allow another to do injustice.

On μήτε ... μήτε οὖν see K-G II 158. Bergk reads ἐθέλοις with some mss., since μή + opt. is more frequent in this poem, but see vv. 48 and 97. The thought expressed in this verse is very common. In any lexicon (e.g. Bauer s.v. ἀδικέω) parallels may be found, but for the formulation see esp. Menander's sentence in Boissonade, Anecd. Gr. I 153 ἀνὴρ δίκαιός ἐστιν οὐκ ἀδικεῖν θέλων (cf. Mon. 37f. and Philemon fr. 94, 1f.) and Ael. Arist. II 270 Behr οὐ μόνον αὐτὸς οὐκ ἀδικήσει, ἀλλ' οὐδ' ἕτερον ἐάσει. ... μήτ' ἀδικήσει μήτε ἕτερον ἐάσει. Cf. Democr. fr. 38 καλὸν μὲν τὸν ἀδικέοντα κωλύειν, εἰ δὲ μή, μὴ ξυναδικέειν, and fr. 261 ἀδικουμένοισι τιμωρεῖν κατὰ δύναμιν χρὴ καὶ μὴ παριέναι. On the duty of βοηθεῖν τοῖς ἀδικουμένοις in Greek ethics see Bolkestein, Wohltätigkeit 90f. Bernays 231 thinks the source is Lev. XIX 16 οὐκ ἐπιστήσει ἐφ' αἵματι τοῦ πλησίον σου, which is very improbable. Lincke, Samaria 71 and Dornseiff, Echtheitsfragen 40 refer to Ex. XXIII 7 ἀπὸ παντὸς ῥήματος ἀδίκου ἀποστήσει κτλ. Cf. Jos. Ant. XII 291 τὸ γὰρ μηδὲν ἀδικεῖν ἰσχυρὰ δύναμις. But the doubleness of the prohibition should be stressed: neither to do injustice nor to allow it.

Bernhardy, *Grundriss* 522 says that v. 21 is one of those clumsy verses which has been added by a later hand; so also Goram 112, unnecessarily (Farina 36 mistakenly blames Bernays for this athetizing). Sebestyén 35 reads ἀδικεῖν τιν' ἐάσῃς following the critical remarks on the hiatus made by Bernays 231 n.1 But hiatus is common in this poem.

Vv. 22-41   *Admonitions to Mercy*

22   πτωχῷ δ' εὐθὺ δίδου μὴ δ' αὔριον ἐλθέμεν εἴπῃς.
Give to the poor man at once, and do not tell him to come tomorrow.

εὐθύ: Brunck 154: "Peccavit pius auctor huius carminis: εὐθύ non adhibitur ἐπὶ χρόνου" (cf. Bernhardy, *Grundriss* 523 "sprachlich anstössig"). Indeed some mss. (M,P) read εὐθύς. But that is metrically impossible. Moreover, εὐθύ is sometimes used of time, see LSJ s.v. εὐθύς B I 3. Ps-Phoc. uses ἐλθέμεν in 22 and 182, ἐλθεῖν in 103 and 188 (both also found in Homer). Bernays 231 thinks that vv. 22-30 are an elaboration of Lev. XIX 9f., which is unlikely. This verse is more reminiscent of Lev. XIX 13 (quoted under v. 19); but there it is said that one cannot wait till tomorrow to give the labourer his money, whereas here it is about the poor in general. The best parallel and probably the source is Prov. III 27f. μὴ ἀπόσχῃ εὖ ποιεῖν ἐνδεῆ, ἡνίκα ἂν ἔχῃ ἡ χείρ σου βοηθεῖν· μὴ εἴπῃς Ἐπανελθὼν ἐπάνηκε καὶ αὔριον δώσω, δυνατοῦ σου ὄντος εὖ ποιεῖν. Cf. Sir. IV 3 μὴ παρελκύσῃς δόσιν προσδεομένου. For more texts see under 19; Beltrami 1908; Nissen, *Gott und der Nächste* 267ff. ("Wohltätigkeit"), esp. 269 n. 758 (cf. 227 n. 583). See also Did. IV 8 οὐκ ἀποστραφήσῃ τὸν ἐνδεόμενον, IV 7 and Barn. XX 2 (from the Two Ways); but there is no emphasis on the immediateness of the giving there. There are hardly any non-Jewish parallels. Rossbroich 36 quotes from *Floril. duo graeca* I 31 (p. 8 Schenkl) ταχὺς γίνου πρὸς εὐεργεσίαν. It would be better to compare *ibid.* I 9 (p. 6 Sch.) δυνάμενος χαρίζεσθαι μὴ βράδυνε, ἀλλὰ δίδου, ἐπιστάμενος μὴ εἶναι τὰ πράγματα μόνιμα. But these texts are more remote than Prov. III 27f.

23   πληρώσει σέο χεῖρ'. ἔλεον χρῄζοντι παράσχου.
You should fill your hand. Give alms to the needy.

In the text as it stands it is hard to see who or what the subject of πληρώσει is. The *v.ll.* πληρώσεις and πληρώσας are clearly secondary, though πληρώσας is adopted by some scholars, e.g. Lincke, *Samaria* 167 and Farina 36 ("fill your hand and give"). Ludwich, *Spruchbuch* 20 links πληρώσεις to v. 22: μηδ' αὔριον ἐλθέμεν εἴπῃς πληρώσεις· σέο χεῖρ' ἐλέου (so one ms.) χρήζοντι παράσχου: "sage nicht, morgen würde seine Befriedigung erfolgen; reiche deine Hand dem, der Mitleid begehrt". Then πλήρωσις is the bodily satisfaction given by food and drink. Diehl suggested πλήρης εἰ σέο χείρ, ἔλεον κτλ. or πληρωθεὶς σέο χεῖρ'. It is also possible to read πληρώσεις ἕο χεῖρ', "you should fill his hand", with a LXX *futurum pro imperativo* like ἀγαπήσεις τὸν πλησίον σου ὡς σεαυτόν, Lev. XIX 18 (cf. v. 141) and epic ἕο for οὗ. One could also take πληρώσει as a 2nd p. sing. ind. fut. med.: "you must fill your hand". So one need not change anything in the mss. tradition. Young (letter of 6.10. 1972) renders his own text: "It (the immediate giving to a beggar of v. 22) will fill your hand"; God will reward your charity (hence the high point after v. 22 in his ed.). It is, however, hard to decide what is exactly meant here; probably something like: you should give with full hands (to the poor of v. 22). (The LXX πληροῦν τὴν χεῖρα, rendering מלא יד, obviously has nothing to do with this verse; there it means "to consecrate").

ἔλεον χρήζοντι παράσχου: here, ἔλεος is masculine as in classical Greek, in the LXX ἔλεος is neuter. In normal Greek ἔλεος means "pity". Though this was mostly seen as a virtue by the ancient Greeks (Schmidt, *Ethik* II 290f.; Dover, *Popular Morality* 195ff.; Burkert, *Mitleidsbegriff, passim*), in Hellenistic philosophy, esp. the Stoa, it belonged to the vices (Pohlenz, *Stoa* II 83; Greeven, *Hauptproblem* 147; Bodson, *Morale sociale* 71; Bolkestein, *Wohltätigkeit* 142f.). See e.g. Teles VII p. 55, 7f. Hense φόβος καὶ ἀγωνία καὶ ὀργὴ καὶ ἔλεος. Diog. Laert. VII 111 ἔλεον, φθόνον, ζῆλον, ζηλοτυπίαν, κτλ. But here in Ps-Phoc. it most probably has the typically Jewish sense "alms". ἔλεος = ἐλεημοσύνη. ἔλεον παρέχειν = ποιεῖν ἐλεημοσύνην (= עשׂה צדקה); e.g. Ezek. XVIII 19 δικαιοσύνην καὶ ἔλεος ἐποίησεν (cf. XVIII 21). Bolkestein, "Almosen", *RAC* I 301: "Die Bedeutungsverengerung ἔλεος, ἐλεημοσύνη von "Mitleid" zu "Barmherzigkeit gegen Arme", "Armengabe" hat sich im griechischsprechenden Orient vollzogen, in der Literatur zuerst in LXX (Prov. 21, 26; Dan. 4, 24 (27)); aber auch anderswo (ps-Phoc. 23; Or. Sib. II, 80-82)". Cf. Bolkestein, *Wohltätigkeit* 428f., esp. 429 n. 2 where he points out that the interpolator of *Or. Sib.* II (80ff.) interpreted ἔλεος in Ps-Phoc. 23 as ἐλεημοσύνη since he proceeds with ὃς δ' ἐλεημοσύνην παρέχει, θεῷ οἶδε δανείζειν. ῥύεται ἐκ θανάτου ἔλεος, κρίσις ὁππόταν ἔλθῃ. οὐ θυσίην, ἔλεος δὲ θέλει θεὸς ἀντὶ θυσίης. ἔνδυσον οὖν γυμνόν, μετάδος πεινῶντ' ἄρτων σῶν. On ṣedaqa = δικαιοσύνη = ἐλεημοσύνη see also Cronbach, "Social Ideals" 132f. and Rosenthal, "Sedaka, Charity", *HUCA* 23 (1950/1), 411ff. On the centrality of this concept in Judaism see Bousset, *Religion* 141 ("ein Grundpfeiler religiös-sittlichen Lebens"); Billerbeck I 387f., IV 536ff. On the difference in valuation of pity and commiseration of the poor between Hellenistic philosophy and Judaism see Bergmann, "Stoische Philosophie und jüdische Frömmigkeit" 164f. and Glatzer, *Hillel* 81; further Bultmann, *TWNT* II 474ff. Only some examples: Test. Ben. IV 4 τὸν πένητα ἐλεεῖ (sc. ὁ ἀγαθὸς ἄνθρωπος). Test. Zab. VII 3 ... δοῦναι τῷ χρῄζοντι. Tob. IV 16 πᾶν, ὃ ἐὰν περισσεύσῃ σοι, ποίει ἐλεημοσύνην. Prov. III 27 (quoted under 22); Sir. IV 1, VII 32, XXIX 1f. 8f., etc.; 5 (=4) Esdr. II 20. Cf. also Barn. XX 2 οὐκ ἐλεοῦντες πτωχόν (in the Two Ways section). More passages in Cronbach, "Social Ideals" 131ff. Of course, benevolence was also a Stoic duty, e.g. Sen. *Ep.* 81, *Benef.*, *passim*; see Rossbroich 37, who also quotes *Gnom. Byz.* 10 θεῷ ὅμοιον ἔχει ἄνθρωπος τὸ εὖ ποιεῖν, ὅταν τὸ εὖ ποιεῖν μὴ καπηλεύηται and *ibid.* 117 ξένοις μεταδίδου καὶ τοῖς δεομένοις ἐκ τῶν ἐνόντων. ὁ γὰρ μὴ διδοὺς δεομένοις οὐ λήψεται δεόμενος. Cf. Gildemeister, "Pythagorassprüche in syrischer Überlieferung", *Hermes* 4 (1870), 92 (sent. 51).

24 ἄστεγον εἰς οἶκον δέξαι καὶ τυφλὸν ὁδήγει.
Receive the homeless in your house, and lead the blind man.

Ad 24a: Is. LVIII 7 πτωχοὺς ἀστέγους εἴσαγε εἰς τὸν οἶκόν σου. Cf. Job XXXI 32 ἔξω δὲ οὐκ ηὐλίζετο ξένος. The sheltering of homeless people was one of the most important g^emiluth ḥasadim among the Jews, see Billerbeck IV 565ff. and Ginzberg, *Legends*, Reg. *s.v.* Hospitality (though, sheltering of homeless people is, of course, more than hospitality). See for instance the stress laid on Abraham's all-embracing hospitality in the opening-passage of Test. Abr. I (Rec. A); also Aboth de R. Nathan (Rec. A) VII 1. In the N.T. see Rom. XII 13 and Hebr. XIII 2 (φιλοξενία). Cf. Arist. *Apol.* XV 7 ξένον ἐὰν ἴδωσιν ὑπὸ στέγην εἰσάγουσιν (sc. the Christians). Hermas *Mand.* VIII 10 φιλόξενον εἶναι. Rossbroich 37 says: "praeceptum Iudaeorum proprium videtur esse", but hospitality was at least deemed important among the Greeks; see Bolkestein, *Wohl-*

tätigkeit 224ff. But in this case Is. LVIII 7 probably is the source of Ps-Phoc.

Ad 24b: Bernays 231 thinks 24b is a paraphrase of Lev. XIX 14 ἀπέναντι τυφλοῦ οὐ προσθήσεις σκάνδαλον. One may better compare Deut. XXVII 18 ἐπικατάρατος ὁ πλανῶν τυφλὸν ἐν ὁδῷ (so Beltrami (1908) 414). Cf. Job XXIX 15 ὀφθαλμὸς ἤμην τυφλῶν. But exact parallels are missing (also in the N.T. and early Christian literature; see Michaelis, *TWNT* V 103 n. 14). For the terminology cf. Matt. XV 14 τυφλὸς δὲ τυφλὸν ἐὰν ὁδηγῇ (XXIII 16; Lk. VI 39; Rom. II 19); also Test. Rub. II 9 ὁδηγεῖ ὡς τυφλὸν ... But in Ps-Phoc. it is not meant metaphorically but literally. Thackeray (in a note to his translation of Jos.*C.Ap.* II 211 ὁδοὺς φράζειν) refers to Juvenal who accuses the Jews of *"non monstrare vias"* (*Sat.* XIV 103f.), but this has nothing to do with the leading of blind people; ὁδοὺς φράζειν was one of the Buzygian laws (on which see *ad* 99; see Bolkestein, *Een geval van sociaal-ethisch syncretisme* 25). Farina 36 wrongly refers to Cic. *Off.* III 13, 54. The change from an aorist imperative to a present imperative is purely for the sake of variation. Both are meant as general commands (cf. v. 26). In this respect there is no consistency in this poem. In some cases metrical reasons may have played a part.

25   ναυηγοὺς οἴκτιρον, ἐπεὶ πλόος ἐστὶν ἄδηλος.

Pity the shipwrecked, for navigation is unsure.

This verse has no O.T. parallels (Israel was not a sea-faring people). Dornseiff 40 boldly remarks "dies dürfte milesisch sein"; it may indeed point to a coastal town. Rossbroich 38 refers to Dio Chrys. VII 52 ἠλέησα δὲ πολλάκις ναυαγοὺς ἀφικομένους καὶ τῇ σκηνῇ ὑπεδεξάμην (cf. Ps-Phoc. 24a!), but interprets the verse as a warning against (coastal) piracy: "noli male tractare naufragos conservatos ut praedo maritimus vel praedo litoris". This is reading too much into the text (cf. also Farina 36f.). To illustrate the mood of v. 25b Beltrami (1913) 535 compares Posidippus fr. 22 *ap.* Athen. IV 154f. ὁ μὴ πεπλευκὼς οὐδὲν ἑόρακεν κακόν· τῶν μονομαχούντων ἐσμὲν ἀθλιώτεροι. Cf. Plato *Epigr.* 15. See further Windisch on 2 Cor. XI 26 (κίνδυνοι ἐν θαλάσσῃ), and esp. W. Kroll, "Schiffahrt", *PW* 2A (1923), 412-414. One should bear in mind that there were no navigation-instruments (like compass, sextant and log) in antiquity.

26 χεῖρα πεσόντι δίδου, σῶσον δ' ἀπερίστατον ἄνδρα.
Extend your hand to him who falls, and save the helpless one.

ἀπερίστατος: orig. "not stood around", hence "solitary", "helpless"; a word of late occurrence (first instance in Polyb. VI 44, 8). Rossbroich 38: "Versus 26 tam late patet, ut locum similem indagare difficile sit". The references of Bernays, Beltrami and Dornseiff to parallel passages in the LXX (Lev. XXV 35, Ezek. XVIII 7) are all beside the point. But the sentiment is Jewish, though not exclusively. See Prov. XXII 22 μὴ ἀτιμάσῃς ἀσθενῆ ἐν πύλαις, cf. XXI 13. Berger, *Gesetzesauslegung Jesu* I 374 mentions Ps-Phoc. 21-26 as a traditional Jewish "soziale Reihe", which has many parallels in Jewish literature (see the long list *ibid*. 369-381). V. 26 is the last one of a series of injunctions to help people who have been afflicted by misfortune in some way.

27 κοινὰ πάθη πάντων · ὁ βίος τροχός · ἄστατος ὄλβος.
Suffering is common to all; life is a wheel; prosperity is unstable.

κοινὰ πάθη πάντων (κοινὰ πάθη occurs in v. 59 in the sense of "moderate emotions"): for κοινός with genitive see Aesch. *Prom*. 1092, *Pers*. 132, *Eum*. 109; Pind. *Nem*. I 32; Ael. Arist. 52, p. 586 Dindorf κοινὸς ἁπάντων ὁ κίνδυνος. The thought is common: Ps-Isocr. *Ad Dem*. 29 κοινὴ γὰρ ἡ τύχη. Men. *Mon*. 10 ἄνθρωπος ὢν μέμνησο τῆς κοινῆς τύχης, *ibid*. 114 νόμιζε κοινὰ πάντα δυστυχήματα. Boissonade, *Anecd. Gr*. I 121 μηδενὶ συμφορὰν ὀνειδίσῃς· κοινὴ γὰρ ἡ τύχη καὶ τὸ μέλλον ἀόρατον. Cf. Eur. *Suppl*. 226.

ὁ βίος τροχός: the wheel of life is a very common image in antiquity (Diehl's accentuation τρόχος = "circular race", is wrong). See the collection of (Rabbinic, Indian and Greek) materials in G. Kittel, *Die Probleme des palästinischen Spätjudentums und das Urchristentum* 141-168; further the commentaries of Ropes and Dibelius on James III 6 (τὸν τροχὸν τῆς γενέσεως = τοῦ βίου) and the additional material in Büchsel, *TWNT* I 682f. and Nock, "Orphism or Popular Philosophy", *Essays* I 507 n. 15 (more lit. in Bauer *s.v.*). A selection of Greek texts may suffice here (there are no O.T. examples): Soph. fr 871, 1-2 ἀλλ' οὑμὸς αἰεὶ πότμος ἐν πυκνῷ θεοῦ|τροχῷ κυκλεῖται καὶ μεταλλάσσει φύσιν, cf. Eur. fr. 415, 3. Anacreontea 30, 7 τροχὸς ἅρματος γὰρ οἷα βίοτος τρέχει κυλισθείς. Hdt. I 207 κύκλος τῶν ἀνθρωπηίων ... πρηγμάτων. *Paroem. Gr*. II 87 τροχὸς τὰ ἀνθρώπινα· ἤτοι εὐμετάβολα (with the notes *ad loc.*).

Boiss., *Anecd.* I 19 γέλα, τοῦ βίου τὸν τροχὸν ὁρῶν ἀτάκτως κυλιόμενον, *ibid.* I 87 τροχός τίς ἐστιν ἀστάτως πεπηγμένος ὁ μικρὸς οὗτος καὶ πολύτροπος βίος. cf. *ibid.* I 50. Plut. *Vita Numae* XIV 5 τοῖς Αἰγυπτίοις (!) τροχοῖς αἰνίττεταί τι καὶ διδάσκει παραπλήσιον ἡ μεταβολὴ τοῦ σχήματος, ὡς οὐδενὸς ἑστῶτος τῶν ἀνθρωπίνων, ἀλλ' ὅπως ἂν στρέφῃ καὶ ἀνελίττῃ τὸν βίον ἡμῶν ὁ θεός, ἀγαπᾶν καὶ δέχεσθαι προσῆκον. Cf. the similar remarks of Dionysius Thrax *ap.* Clem. Alex. *Strom.* V 8, 45, 4-6. Dibelius, *Jak.* 240, rightly says: "der Ausdruck hatte wohl schon seinen orphischen Charakter verloren und war zu einer geläufigen Wendung für des Lebens Auf und Ab geworden". His suggestion (*ibid.* 239) that Ps-Phoc. 27 is "wahrscheinlich von einem älteren Gnomiker entlehnt", may be right.

ἄστατος ὄλβος: again, a very common thought, closely linked up with the former (see the expression ἄστατος τροχός in Mesomedes *Hymn. in Nemesin* 7). Pind. *Pyth.* III 105f. ὄλβος οὐκ ἐς μακρὸν ἀνδρῶν ἔρχεται σῶς. Eur. *Phoen.* 558 ὁ δ' ὄλβος οὐ βέβαιος, ἀλλ' ἐφήμερος (spurious?, cf. Ps-Plut. *Cons. ad Apoll.* 5, 104A), *Herc. Fur.* 511f. Ps-Plut. *Cons. ad Apoll.* 5, 103F οὐκ ἐνθυμούμενοι τὸ τῆς τύχης ἄστατον (cf. Jos. *Ant.* XX 57 τὸ τῆς τύχης ἄστατον)καὶ ἀβέβαιον, οὐδ' ὅτι ῥᾳδίως τὰ ὑψηλὰ γίγνεται ταπεινὰ καὶ τὰ χθαμαλὰ πάλιν ὑψοῦται ταῖς ὀξυρρόποις μεθιστάμενα τῆς τύχης μεταβολαῖς. Plut. *Puer. educ.* 8, 5D πλοῦτος δὲ τίμιον μέν, ἀλλὰ τύχης κτῆμα, ἐπειδὴ τῶν μὲν ἐχόντων πολλάκις ἀφείλετο, τοῖς δ' οὐκ ἐλπίσασι φέρουσα προσήνεγκε. Boiss., *Anecd.* I 164 ὅρα τὸν ἀστάθμητον ἄστατον βίον.

Rossbroich 39 says that this verse is an expression of the "opinio propria aetatis Alexandrinae atque posteritatis"; Ranston, *Ecclesiastes* 80, remarks: "Is not this in the spirit of Koheleth?". Both views are not wrong, but too narrow, as the parallels show.

28 πλοῦτον ἔχων σὴν χεῖρα πενητεύουσιν ὄρεξον.
When you have wealth, stretch out your hand to the poor.

This verse reflects a really Jewish sentiment. Some parallels may be found under v. 23. Cf. further Deut. XV 11 ἀνοίγων ἀνοίξεις τὰς χεῖράς σου τῷ ἀδελφῷ σου τῷ πένητι. Sir. VII 32 πτωχῷ ἔκτεινον τὴν χεῖρά σου (the expression ἐκτείνειν τὴν χεῖρα is very frequent in the LXX). Prov. XXXI 20 χεῖρας δὲ αὐτῆς διήνοιξεν πένητι, καρπὸν δὲ ἐξέτεινεν πτωχῷ. Men. gnom. syr. 63 (transl. Schulthess) "Wenn du Geld hast und Vermögen besitzest, so sei bescheiden und freundlich und mitteilsam und tue nicht gross". Cf. Lk. III 11 ὁ ἔχων δύο χιτῶνας μεταδότω τῷ μὴ ἔχοντι. Jos. *C. Ap.* II 291 calls τὴν τῶν ὄντων κοινωνίαν one of the essentials of the Law. From the Greek side cf. Men. *Mon.* 478 μέμνησο πλουτῶν τοὺς πένητας ὠφελεῖν. *Gnom. Byz.* 117 (quoted under v. 23) with Wachsmuth *ad loc.* Gerhard, *Phoinix* 113ff. has some material of Cynic origin on the right use of riches. On πενητεύειν see Schmidt, *Synonymik* IV 391.

It is unclear why Amstutz, ΑΠΛΟΤΗΣ 75, sees "eine ganz bestimmte Auffassung von Bodenbesitz" behind vv. 28-30 (on the basis of Test. Iss. III 6-8 and Test. Zab. VII 2, quoted below under v. 29).

29 ὧν σοι ἔδωκε θεός, τούτων χρῄζουσι παράσχου.
Of that which God has given you, give of it to the needy.

This is one of the very few verses in Ps-Phoc. in which charity has a religious basis, since God is viewed as the giver of all riches from which one has to give to the poor. Cf. Deut. XV 14b καθὰ εὐλόγησέν σε κύριος ὁ θεός σου, δώσεις αὐτῷ (sc. τῷ ἀδελφῷ σου). Test. Zab. VII 2 ἐξ ὧν παρέχει ὑμῖν ὁ θεός, ἀδιακρίτως πᾶσι σπλαγχνιζόμενοι ἐλεᾶτε. See also the references in Nissen, *Gott und der Nächste* 166 n. 299 and for rabbinic texts on God as the giver of riches Billerbeck I 820.824; III 657. From early Christian literature cf. Did. I 5 παντὶ τῷ αἰτοῦντί σε δίδου καὶ μὴ ἀπαίτει· πᾶσι γὰρ θέλει δίδοσθαι ὁ πατὴρ ἐκ τῶν ἰδίων χαρισμάτων. Herm. *Mand.* II 4 ἐκ τῶν κόπων σου ὧν ὁ θεὸς δίδωσίν σοι πᾶσιν ὑστερουμένοις δίδου ἁπλῶς. Sextus *Sent.* 242 ἃ προῖκα λαμβάνεις παρὰ θεοῦ, καὶ δίδου προῖκα. Cf. Men. *Mon.* 198 δίδου πένησιν ὡς λάβῃς θεὸν δότην.

30 ἔστω κοινὸς ἅπας ὁ βίος καὶ ὁμόφρονα πάντα.
Let all of life be in common, and all things be in agreement.

The exact meaning of the first half of this verse is unclear. Some scholars (Sartorius 33; Beltrami, *Riv.* 1913, 530; Farina 37) think it is an exhortation to have all things in common like the Pythagoreans (Iambl. *Vita Pyth.* 29f., 81, 168), the Essenes (Jos. *Ant.* XVIII 20) and the early Christians (Acts II 45, Did. IV 8). Beltrami, therefore, regards this verse as one of the proofs of the Essene origin of the poem. But Rossbroich 40 thinks: "praeceptum est de humanitate" and suggests that κοινός means here "kind, affable" (see LSJ *s.v.* IV 3b; e.g. Athen. VI 253D τῇ πρὸς πάντας φιλανθρωπίᾳ κοινός) and βίος "mode of life, manner of living". That may be right, but, in view of the preceding verses, the meaning is more probably that one should share with one another the vitally important things needed to stay alive; cf. Barn. XIX 8 κοινωνήσεις ἐν πᾶσιν τῷ πλησίον σου, καὶ οὐκ ἐρεῖς ἴδια εἶναι.

ὁμόφρονα πάντα: One should not only share one's goods with others, there should also be unity of mind and feeling; note the emphasis on ὁμόνοια in vv. 74 and 219 (there lit.).

Kurfess, *ZNW* 1939, 179 wrongly adopts the reading of Ψ (= Or. Sib. II 90) κοινὸς πᾶς ὁ βίος μερόπων, ἄνισος δὲ τέτυκται. After this, Ψ inserts the following six lines (91-96): μήποτε ἄνδρα πένητα ἰδὼν σκώψῃς ἐπέεσσιν | μηδὲ κακῶς γε προσείπῃς μωμητόν τινα φῶτα. | τὸ ζῆν ἐν θανάτῳ δοκιμάζεται· εἴ τις ἔπραξεν | ἔκνομον ἢ δίκαιον, διακρίνεται εἰς κρίσιν ἐλθών. | μηδὲ φρένας βλάπτειν οἴνῳ μηδ' ἄμετρα πίνειν. | αἷμα δὲ μὴ φαγέειν, εἰδωλοθύτων δ' ἀπέχεσθαι (see v. [31]).

31 [αἷμα δὲ μὴ φαγέειν, εἰδωλοθύτων ἀπέχεσθαι.]
Do not eat blood; abstain from food sacrificed to idols.

This verse is an interpolation, since only one inferior ms. contains it. Moreover, as Bergk *ad loc.* already remarked, this verse is "omnino ab huius poematis instituto alienus, cuius scriptor nusquam aperte Graecae gentis sacra reprehendit". Also Klein, *Ält. christl. Katech.* 174 points out that the use of the word εἰδωλόθυτον is incompatible with the tendency of the poem when considered as a whole. And Ludwich, *Spruchbuch* 9 asserts that the author would never use φαγέειν, but either φαγεῖν or φαγέμεν, just as he writes ἐλθεῖν or ἐλθέμεν. The defence of the authenticity of the verse by Beltrami, *Riv.* 1913, 525 and by Kurfess, *ZNW* 1939, 179 is wholly unconvincing (Kurfess maintains the verse because Ψ has it; in Or. Sib. II this line suits the context much better).

Lev. XIX 26a MT לא תאכלו על־הדם could have been the Vorlage of v. 31a but the LXX translates μὴ ἔσθετε ἐπὶ τῶν ὀρέων, reading ההרם, cf. Ezek. XVIII 6.11.15; XXII 9. But cf. Lev. III 19 πᾶν αἷμα οὐκ ἔδεσθε (= VII 26; cf. XVII 10) and Deut. XII 16 τὸ αἷμα οὐ φάγεσθε (cf. XII 23-25; XV 23). However, the most probable source of v. 31 is Acts XV 29 ἀπέχεσθαι εἰδωλοθύτων καὶ αἵματος (cf. XXI 25). In the LXX εἰδωλόθυτος occurs only in 4 Macc. V 2. It is a typically early Christian term (though of Jewish origin) occurring also in 1 Cor. VIII 1.4.7.10; X 19; Apoc. II 14.20. Did. VI 3 ἀπὸ δὲ εἰδωλοθύτου λίαν πρόσεχε (on the basis of this passage, belonging to the Two Ways section, Seeberg, *Die beiden Wege* 38ff., says this injunction belonged to a Jewish "Two Ways" catechism and therefore the verse may be original). But note also the Pythagorean rules in Diog. Laert. VIII 13.20.22. Although weakly attested, this verse must have been inserted rather early, viz. in a time when the prescriptions of the apostolic decree were still practised.

32-34 τὸ ξίφος ἀμφιβαλοῦ μὴ πρὸς φόνον, ἀλλ' ἐς ἄμυναν.
εἴθε δὲ μὴ χρήζοις μήτ' ἔκνομα μήτε δικαίως.
ἢν γὰρ ἀποκτείνῃς ἐχθρόν, σέο χεῖρα μιαίνεις.

If you gird on a sword, let it be not to murder but to protect.
But may you not need it at all, neither without the law nor justly.
For if you kill an enemy, you stain your hand.

In v. 32 ἄμυνα means "protection", in v. 77 "vengeance". Lincke, *Samaria* 68 and Dornseiff, *Echtheitsfragen* 40 suggest that the source of this verse is Lev. XIX 16b οὐκ ἐπισυστήσῃ ἐφ' αἷμα τοῦ πλησίον σου, but that is improbable. One could compare Matt. XXVI 52 πάντες γὰρ οἱ λαβόντες μάχαιραν ἐν μαχαίρῃ ἀπολοῦνται, but a better parallel is Sextus, *Sent.* 324 σίδηρον ἀνδροφόνον ἄριστον μὲν ἦν μὴ γενέσθαι, γενόμενον δὲ σοὶ μὴ νόμιζε εἶναι, which probably means: no military service for you (see Chadwick *ad loc.*, p. 177). This might be the sense of these verses in Ps-Phoc. which are quoted by Chadwick as a "near parallel" (*ibid.*). Cf. the Jewish(?) Men. gnom. syr. 4 (transl. Schulthess) "Töte nicht, und deine Hände sollen nicht tun, was hässlich ist, denn das Schwert liegt in der Mitte (= hindert)". (But this translation is uncertain; see Audet, *Rev. Bibl.* 59 (1952) 59 n. 2).

In v. 33 the μήτ' ἔκνομα μήτε δικαίως is difficult. Rossbroich 41 comments: "Iusta causa commotum gladium stringere quemquam vetare non potest auctor. Ut immunditiam evitet, nemini opus est omittere, quominus iuste vi vim illatam defendat? ... quomodo auctor potest dicere ἀλλ' ἐς ἄμυναν et postea μήτε δικαίως? An iniuriam faciunt homines, si se defendunt?" The author possibly reasons as follows: Use of the sword is only allowed ἐς ἄμυναν, for then it is δικαίως, but it is to be hoped that you will never need it (optat. χρήζοις!), for even δικαίως using the sword, even justified self-defence, stains your hands, when somebody is killed. This seems to be a rather exceptional point of view in antiquity. The rule μήθ' αἵματι χεῖρα μιαίνειν in v. 4 is very strictly applied here; cf. 5 Esdr. I 26. There is undeniably a pacifistic ring about these verses. Beltrami, *Riv.* 41 (1913), 527 calls it a "sapore più spiccatamente cinico e neostoico che giudaico", but refers only to the text of Sextus quoted above, which is no proof of his thesis; but cf. Attridge, *First-Century Cynicism* 31f. on Cynic pacifism.

Bergk, *Philol.* 41 (1882), 595f. proposes to read εἴθε δὲ μὴ χρῴζοις ἄνομ' αἵματι μήτε δικαίως, unnecessarily; cf. ἔκνομον ἢ δίκαιον in *Or. Sib.* II 94. The reading ἔκνομα is also defended by Ludwich, *Spruchbuch* 15.

35 ἀγροῦ γειτονέοντος ἀπόσχεο, μὴ δ' ἄρ' ὑπερβῆς.
Keep off the field of your neighbour, be thus not a tresspasser.

Rossbroich 41 ("hoc praeceptum est proprium libr. Mos.") refers to Deut. XIX 14 οὐ μετακινήσεις ὅρια τοῦ πλησίον σου, XXIII 25, XXVIII 17 and similar texts. But the text is not about the non-removal of landmarks (as also Farina 37 and Seeberg, *Die beiden Wege* 98 wrongly interpret it). It is better to refer (as Young does) to Ex. XXII 4 ἐὰν δὲ καταβοσκήσῃ τις ἀγρὸν ἢ ἀμπελῶνα καὶ ἀφῇ τὸ κτῆνος αὐτοῦ καταβοσκῆσαι ἀγρὸν ἕτερον, ἀποτείσει ἐκ τοῦ ἀγροῦ αὐτοῦ κατὰ τὸ γένημα αὐτοῦ or Deut. XXIII 25 ἐὰν δὲ εἰσέλθῃς εἰς ἀμητὸν τοῦ πλησίον σου, ... δρέπανον οὐ μὴ ἐπιβάλῃς ἐπὶ τὸν ἀμητὸν τοῦ πλησίον σου (cf. v. 26). The peculiar absolute use of ὑπερβαίνειν is paralleled by I Thess. IV 6 (according to the most probable interpretation of that text, see Bauer *s.v.*), as Seeberg (*ibid.* 30) already saw. Therefore Ψ unnecessarily inserted τὸν: μὴ τὸν δ' ἄρ ὑπερβῆς.

36 [πάντων μέτρον ἄριστον, ὑπερβασίαι δ' ἀλεγειναί.]
Moderation is the best of all, excesses are grievous.

V. 36 is identical with v. 69b. Either both vv. are to be retained or v. 36 has to be athetized since 3 important mss. (L, P, V) omit it. Schmidt, *Jahrb. f. class. Phil.* 3 (1857), 516 thinks that v. 36 is a typical example of interpolation by way of word-association: ὑπερβῆς in v. 35 suggested to a reader the sentence with ὑπερβασίαι of v. 36 "aus irgendeiner Gnomensammlung". Also Bergk athetizes the verse. It clearly is an interruption between vv. 35 and 38 (also v. 37 is spurious). Ψ reads πᾶς ὅρος ἐστὶ δίκαιος, ὑπερβασίη δ' ἀλεγεινή (= *Or. Sib.* II 101), which is contextually better (see v. 35) but clearly secondary (though Kurfess, *ZNW* 1939, 179 defends it).

This verse is made up of the very famous maxim μέτρον ἄριστον and the Homeric phrase ὑπερβασίη ἀλεγεινή (*Od.* III 206; this is more probably the source of 36b than Hes. *Op.* 828 ὑπερβασίας ἀλεείνων, as

Rossbroich 55 asserts, though Eustathius (on Il. XXIII 589) quotes 36b under Hesiod's name). The formula μέτρον άριστον is generally attributed to Cleobulus, one of the Seven Sages (see e.g. Clem. Alex. *Strom*. I 61, 2; Scholia in Lucianum p. 5, 9 Rabe; Boissonade, *Anecd. Gr*. I 143f.), but sometimes to Homer (Macr. *Sat*. V 16, 6) or to Phocylides (Bachmann, *Anecd. Gr*. II 97). But, as Gerhard, *Phoinix* 269 (with notes 3 and 4) has shown, many sentences of the Seven Sages turn up again in later moralistic poets. Cf. e.g. *Carm. aur*. 38 μέτρον δ' έπι πάσιν άριστον (with the comm. of P.C. van der Horst *ad loc*.), Demophilus *Simil*. 59 (Mullach, *Fr. Phil. Gr*. I 487) and the passages referred to by Young in his *app. crit*. Also the variation καιρὸς δ' ἐπὶ πᾶσιν ἄριστος occurs, e.g. Hes. *Op*. 694, Theognis 401. Unfortunately, the text of Stobaeus' chapter ὅτι μέτρον ἄριστον (II 9) is lost. The same sentiment is expressed in a number of other ways, especially in texts where μετριότης is recommended, e.g. Democr. fr. 233 εἴ τις ὑπερβάλλοι τὸ μέτριον, τὰ ἐπιτερπέστατα ἀτερπέστατα ἂν γίγνοιτο, Aesch. *Eum*. 526ff., Pind. *Ol*. XIII 48, *Pyth*. II 34, Theogn. 331, 335, 614, 694, and the texts referred to by Schmidt, *Ethik* I 513ff., II 415f. The emphasis on moderation in Ps-Phoc. is very strong (see e.g. 69, 98, etc.). It is not strange to Jewish thought (see Bousset, *Religion* 423), but is actually a real Greek sentiment. Ps. Sal. V 17 ἱκανὸν τὸ μέτριον ἐν δικαιοσύνῃ.

In view of the uncertainty regarding the authenticity of v. 36, it is hard to say whether it is meant to be the motivation of v. 35. It looks more like a case of casual word-association.

37 [κτῆσις ὀνήσιμός ἐσθ' ὁσίων, ἀδίκων δὲ πονηρά.]

Honest acquisition is useful, but unjust acquisition is bad.

V. 37 is in only one ms. (*unus e dett*., Young) and interrupts (with v. 36) the coherence between vv. 35 and 38 (see Riessler 1319; Easton translates vv. 35, 38, [36, 37,] 39 . . .). Moreover, it is also clumsy Greek. Goram's emendation (p. 112) χρήστης χρήσιμός ἐστι φιλῶν, ἀδικῶν δ' ἀνόνητος is fanciful and unnecessary. Farina 37 compares Solon *Eleg*. I (13) 9ff. πλοῦτος δ' ὃν μὲν δῶσι θεοί, παραγίγνεται ἀνδρί | ἔμπεδος ἐκ νεάτου πυθμένος ἐς κορυφήν. | ὃν δ' ἄνδρες μετίωσιν ὑφ' ὕβριος, οὐ κατὰ κόσμον | ἔρχεται ἀλλ' ἀδίκοισ' ἔργμασι πειθόμενος | οὐκ ἐθέλων ἕπεται, ταχέως δ' ἀναμίσγεται ἄτῃ. From the O.T. one might compare Prov. XIII 11 ὕπαρξις ἐπισπουδαζομένη μετὰ ἀνομίας ἐλάσσων γίνεται, ὁ δὲ συνάγων ἑαυτῷ μετ' εὐσεβείας πληθυνθήσεται.

38 μηδέ τιν' αὐξόμενον καρπὸν λωβήσῃ ἀρούρης.

Do not damage fruits that are growing on the land.

καρπὸς ἀρούρης: Hom. *Il*. III 246, VI 142. LSJ *s.v.* λωβάομαι say: "act. λωβάω only Ps-Phoc. 38 and κατελώβησαν in Polyb. XV 33, 9." This is wrong, for λωβήσῃ is 2 sing. aor. midd. subj. LSJ must have read λωβήσῃς, which is in only one ms. (B), obviously as an emendation to avoid the hiatus. Bruck, *GPG* 155 conjectures λώβησον and says on λωβήσῃ: "activum in classicis vix reperies. Quodsi scripseris λωβήσῃ, consules Graecitati: sin servandam censueris vulgatam, ut in tali scriptore tolerabilem, notabis hoc exemplum constructionis particulae vetantis cum imperativo aoristi" (then other examples follow). But the mss. basis (L, M, P, V) of Young's text is sounder. Again Ex. XXII 5 and Deut. XXIII 25 (quoted under v. 35) might be referred to as partly parallels and possible sources. Or is this v. about weeds (cf. Matt. XIII 29f.)?

39 ἔστωσαν δ' ὁμότιμοι ἐπήλυδες ἐν πολιήταις.

Strangers should be held in equal honour with citizens.

The meaning of this verse is not easy to grasp. It may be suggested that it means that the proselytes should enjoy equal rights with the Israelites, since in Philo ἔπηλυς (= ἐπήλυτος, ἐπηλύτης) is a term for proselyte (see Bertholet, *Die Stellung . . . der Juden zu Fremden* 285-8) and he defends this view, e.g. *Spec. leg.* I 52 ἰσοτιμίαν γοῦν ἅπασιν ἐπηλύταις διδοὺς (sc. Moses) κτλ. (see Moore, *Judaism* I 327 with notes). Cf. Jeb. 47b "(the proselyte) is deemed to be an Israelite in all respects" (with the comments of Jeremias, *Jerusalem* 358ff.). See on proselytes in general Billerbeck I 355f., II 715ff., III 353ff. and the corrections by Moore, *Judaism* I 323ff.; cf. Urbach, *Sages* I 541ff., II 931ff. In that case Ps-Phoc. addresses himself to the Jews. This verse can also be read in the light of the struggle of the Jews for civic rights in Alexandria in the early Imperial period, on which see Tcherikover, *Prolegomena* in *CPJ* I 61ff. (In spite of many assertions to the contrary, the Jews did not have these rights as is convincingly shown by Tcherikover, *ibid.* 39ff.). It should be noted that in 38 A.D. Flaccus calls the Alexandrian Jews ξένοι καὶ ἐπήλυδες (Philo *In Flaccum* 54). In that case Ps-Phoc. directs himself to the heathen authorities. However, in view of vv. 40f. it is also possible that v. 39 expresses a concern for poor peasants who were forced by economic circumstances to migrate to the great cities, and who wanted to have there civic rights.

One may compare from the O.T., e.g. Lev. XIX 33f. ἐὰν δέ τις προσέλθῃ προσήλυτος ὑμῖν ἐν τῇ γῇ ὑμῶν, οὐ θλίψετε αὐτόν· ὡς ὁ αὐτόχθων ἐν ὑμῖν ἔσται ὁ προσήλυτος ὁ προσπορευόμενος πρὸς ὑμᾶς, καὶ ἀγαπήσεις αὐτὸν ὡς σεαυτόν, ὅτι προσήλυτοι ἐγενήθητε ἐν γῇ Αἰγύπτῳ. Cf. XXIV 22 δικαίωσις μία ἔσται τῷ προσηλύτῳ καὶ τῷ ἐγχωρίῳ. Ex. XXIII 9 καὶ προσήλυτον οὐ θλίψετε· ὑμεῖς γὰρ οἴδατε τὴν ψυχὴν τοῦ προσηλύτου· αὐτοὶ γὰρ προσήλυτοι ἦτε ἐν γῇ Αἰγύπτῳ. Cf. XXII 20; Deut. X 19; XXIV 17. (Gaudemet—Fascher, "Fremder", *RAC* VIII 311: "Die Milde gegenüber dem Fremden ist später oft veranlasst durch die Erinnerung an die Leiden in der ägyptischen Fremde"). In view of vv. 40f. it is very probable that such O.T. texts have inspired Ps-Phoc. to write this verse (see the Comm. on vv. 40f.). On Jewish views of strangers see also Stählin, *TWNT* V 8-14.

**40-41 πάντες γὰρ πενίης πειρώμεθα τῆς πολυπλάγκτου,
χώρης δ' οὔ τι βέβαιον ἔχει πέδον ἀνθρώποισιν.**

For we all experience the poverty that makes one wander;
and the land has nothing constant for men.

πενίης τῆς πολυπλάγκτου: Binder 71 "die Armut die uns umherwirft" (similarly my transl.). But according to some scholars this gives no good sense; see Rossbroich 41: "Has sententias auctor minime aptas et convenientes esse non vidit. Nam quid sit Judaicis advenis cum πενίᾳ πολυπλάγκτῳ non intellego. Peregrinos egenos esse necesse non est neque in LXX quicquam eiusmodi legitur". Therefore Bernays 233 n. 1 adopts the reading ξενίης of Ψ which on his view gives a much better sense (supported by Sebestyén 35, Keydel, *Jahresbericht* 230 (1931) 93 and others). Then the translation is "we all experience the status of a wandering alien". ξενίη = status of an alien (LSJ *s.v.* I 3). It is not only the context (vv. 39, 41) which seems to support this reading, but also the word πολύπλαγκτος (Homeric) that fits in better with ξενίη than with πενίη. Cf. moreover Manetho Astrol. IV 162 πουλυπλανεῖς ξενίης κελεύθους. The fact that in some texts there is a connection between poverty and wandering does not necessarily militate against ξενίης here (see e.g. the anonymous *ap.* Diog. Laert. VI 38 ἄπολις, ἄοικος, πατρίδος ἐστερημένος, πτωχός, πλανήτης, βίον ἔχων τοὐφ' ἡμέραν. Ael. *V.H.* III 29; Tyrt. 10 (6), 3-14; Solon 24, 10-12; *Gnom. Vat.*

201. Packmohr, *De Diog. Sinop. apophthegm.* 6off.). When ξενίης is read, it is clear that the O.T. passages quoted under 39 are also the source of v. 40 (Lev. XIX 34; Ex. XXIII 9 etc.). But the historical basis (the Israelites having been themselves aliens in Egypt) is here generalized into a common truth (the ἐγενήθητε or ἦτε of the Biblical texts is transposed into the timeless present πειρώμεθα). Bertholet, *Die Stellung der Israeliten und der Juden zu den Fremden* 270: "Beachtenswert ist hier ... vor allem, dass die Begründung, welche das pentateuchische Gesetz aus der Erfahrung der eigenen Geschicke des Volkes ableitete, auf eine allgemein menschliche Erfahrung ausgedehnt wird. Wir hören hier den Juden sprechen, der selber gelernt hat, wie einem in der Fremde zu Mute ist, und wie man die Ungleichheit der Stellung empfindet. Er hat daraus aber wirklich auch gelernt. Der letzte Rest von jüdischem Partikularismus ist in diesen Worten verstummt: da ist weder Grieche noch Jude" (thus also Bergk, *Gr. Lit. gesch.* II 299 n. 9; Riessler 1319 and others). Cf. also Men. *Mon.* 554 ξένους ξενίζε, καὶ σὺ γὰρ ξένος γ' ἔσῃ. However, if (as has been suggested *ad* v. 39) the background of these lines is to be seen in the position of poor peasants who from sheer necessity migrated to the city, then πενίης makes good sense. It is, after all, the best attested reading and ξενίης is a *lectio facilior*. In view of this and of the texts where poverty and wandering are combined (quoted above) πενίης might be maintained.

Only if v. 39 is about proselytes and ξενίης should be read in 40, the transition would seem to be strange. It may be explained, however, by the semantic change of גר (προσήλυτος): in the O.T. it means "resident alien", in later Jewish writings "proselyte". Such transitions are also found in rabbinic literature, e.g. the passage from Sifra Qedoshim, perek VIII 3 (on Lev. XIX 34), quoted by Moore, *Judaism* I 345: "Just as it is said in relation to Israelites, 'Thou shalt love thy neigbor as thyself', so in relation to proselytes (*gerim*) it is said, 'Thou shalt love him as thyself, for ye were strangers (*gerim*) in the land of Egypt". Cf. esp. the 4th chapter of the tractate Gerim.

In v. 41 there is also a textual problem. Some manuscripts (B, L) read χώρη, adopted by Bernays, Bergk, Sebestyén and Rossbroich (then βέβαιον and πέδον must belong together). But most probably χώρης is to be retained; then χώρης πέδον is subject of ἔχει. For this periphrastic expression cf. Aesch. *Prom.* 1 χθονὸς πέδον, Aristoph.

Nub. 573 γῆς πέδον. One could wonder whether v. 41 still belongs to the preceding lines or expresses a new thought, namely that life is living in alienation or exile, which is both a Greek and a Jewish thought. Marc. Aur. II 17, 2 ὁ δὲ βίος ... ξένου ἐπιδημία. Ps. CXVIII 19 πάροικος ἐγώ εἰμι ἐν τῇ γῇ and other texts mentioned by Rossbroich 41. But, of course, being a stranger, a wandering alien and a sojourner or an exile in this life are closely connected themes (against Rossbroich 41). See the remark of Stählin on this line of Ps-Phoc. in *TWNT* V 40. However, this line may simply be a reference to the uncertainties of a peasant's life: the unexpectedly low yield of the land, the loss of crops as the result of wars or pillaging, etc.

Vv. 40-1 are read by Ψ' with the following changes and insertions: πάντες γὰρ ξενίης πειρήσσονται πολυμόχθου | ὡς ξένοι ἀλλήλων· ξεῖνος δέ γε οὔτις ἐν ἡμῖν | ἔσσετ', ἐπεὶ πάντες βροτοὶ αἵματος ἐξ ἑνός ἐστε. | Χώρης δ' οὔ τι βέβαιον ἔχειν τόπον ἀνθρώποισιν | μηδὲ θέλῃς πλουτεῖν μηδ' εὔχεο· ἀλλὰ τόδ' εὔχου | ζῆν ἀπὸ τῶν ὀλίγων μηδέν τε ἔχοντα ἄδικον (cf. Theogn. 1155f.)

Vv. 42-47 *Love of Money and its Consequences*

42 ἡ φιλοχρημοσύνη μήτηρ κακότητος ἁπάσης.
Love of money is the mother of all evil.

This maxim was very current in antiquity in different forms, the best known of which is 1 Tim. VI. 10 ῥίζα γὰρ πάντων τῶν κακῶν ἐστιν ἡ φιλαργυρία (see Renehan, "Classical Greek Quotations in the N.T." 18f. and Hengel, *Eigentum und Reichtum* 18). Some examples of the other forms will suffice. Diog. Sin. *ap.* Diog. Laert. VI 50 τὴν φιλαργυρίαν εἶπε μητρόπολιν πάντων τῶν κακῶν. Apollodorus Com. fr. 4 (*ap.* Stob. III 16, 12, p. 482 W-H) ἀλλὰ σχεδόν τι τὸ κεφάλαιον τῶν κακῶν εἴρηκας· ἐν φιλαργυρίᾳ γὰρ πάντ' ἔνι. Hippocrates *Epist.* XVII 43 τούτων ἁπάντων αἰτίη ἡ φιλαργυρίη. *Flor. mon.* 188 (Demetrius) τὴν φιλαργυρίαν μητρόπολιν ἔλεγε πάσης κακίας. Cf. Cato *ap.* Gell. XI 2, 2 *avaritiam omnia vitia habere putabat*. *Or. Sib.* VIII 17 ἀρχὴ πᾶσι κακῶν φιλοχρημοσύνη. Polyc. *Ad Phil.* IV 1 ἀρχὴ δὲ πάντων χαλεπῶν φιλαργυρία. Cf. further the oracle in Diod. Sic. VII 12, 5; Cebes *Pinax* XIX 5; XXIII 2; XXIV 2; XXVI 2; XXXIV 3; etc. Eusebius *ap.* Stob. III 10, 28-30 (III p. 415 W-H); Bion. *ap.* Stob. III 10, 37 (III p. 417); Diog. *ap.* Stob. III 10, 45.57 (III p. 419.422) and more texts in

Stob. III 10; *Gnom. Vat.* 265 (and Sternbach *ad loc.*, 102f.); *Gnom. hom.* 2, 109b, 133, 169, 176, 194 (ed. Elter); Anon. Pyth. *Simil.* 40, 41, 43, 54 (Mullach, *Fr. Phil. Gr.* I 489f.); *Anth. Pal.* XI 270; Ovid. *Met.* I 131; Juv. *Sat.* XIV 173ff. (Cf. for the form of the expression in our line also Soph. *Phil.* 1361 ἡ γνώμη κακῶν μήτηρ. Test. Sim. V 3 ἡ πορνεία μήτηρ ἐστὶ πάντων τῶν κακῶν). Other texts can be found in Wettstein *ad* 1 Tim. VI 10; Vögtle, *Tugend- und Lasterkataloge* 201; Packmohr, *Diog. Sin. apophth.* 56ff.; Norden, "In Varronis sat. Men. observ. selectae" 338ff.; Gerhard, *Phoinix* 59ff.; Young in *app. crit.* From Jewish literature, see the long warning against φιλαργυρία in Test. Judae XVII-XIX; *Or. Sib.* III 253.641f.; the texts from Sirach mentioned below under vv. 46f.; and Philo *Spec. leg.* I 24.281; *Omn. prob.* 21; *Flacc.* 60. From early Christian literature Did. III 5 μὴ γίνου ... φιλάργυρος, Cf. II 6, V 1; II Clem. IV 3 μὴ φιλαργυρεῖν, cf. VI 4; Polyc. *Ad Phil.* IV 1.

It is not clear why Bernhardy, *Grundriss* 522, and Bergk *ad loc.* think these verses "ab hoc loco manifesto sunt alieni". That they do not contain any direct injunction is no valid argument against their authenticity. The implicit injunction is, of course, μὴ φιλαργυρεῖν. The following lines (43-7) are an explicitation of this. Ψ adds after v. 42: μὴ πόθος εἰς χρυσὸν ἢ εἰς ἄργυρον. ἐν δ' ἄρα καὶ τοῖς ἔσσεται ἀμφήκης θυμοφθόρος ἔνθα σίδηρος.

43 χρυσὸς ἀεὶ δόλος ἐστὶ καὶ ἄργυρος ἀνθρώποισιν.

Gold and silver are always a lure for men.

δόλος means here "lure, bait" (see LSJ *s.v.*). Cf. *Men. et Phil. comp.* I 232f. χρυσὸς δόλος πέφυκε καὶ γυνὴ δόλος. ἀμφότερα ταῦτα τοὺς φίλους ἐχθροὺς ποιεῖ, *Or. Sib.* VIII 18, Matt, XIII 22 ἡ ἀπάτη τοῦ πλούτου and the quotation from Anacreon *ad* vv. 44f. A negative attitude towards riches is seldom found in the O.T., almost only in Prov., e.g. XXVIII 22. The N.T. is more negative, see *IDB* IV 819 and esp. Hengel, *Eigentum und Reichtum* 31ff. On the negative attitude of Stoicism in this respect see Greeven, *Hauptproblem* 62ff. (e.g. Sen. *Ep.* 115, 10). Many texts on the theme ψόγος πλούτου are in Stob. IV 31, 53-92 (V p. 754-767 W.-H.). However, rather than only reflecting a negative view of riches, these lines warn against the dangers (see esp. 46f.) of striving after gold and silver.

44-45 χρυσέ, κακῶν ἀρχηγέ, βιοφθόρε, πάντα χαλέπτων,
εἴθε σε μὴ θνητοῖσι γενέσθαι πῆμα ποθεινόν.

Gold, originator of evil, destroyer of life, crushing all things,
would that you were not a desirable calamity to mortals!

There are several passages in Greek literature where gold is apostrophized. Anacreontea 58, 18ff. ἄπιστ', ἄπιστε χρυσέ, ... σὺ γὰρ δόλων, σύ τοι φθόνων ἔρωτ' ἔθηκας ἀνδράσιν. Eur. fr. 324 ὦ χρυσέ, κτλ. Trag. adesp. fr. 129 ὦ χρυσέ, κτλ. Palladas in *Anth. Gr.* IX 394 χρυσέ, πάτερ κολάκων, ὀδύνης καὶ φροντίδος υἱέ, καὶ τὸ ἔχειν σε φόβος, καὶ μὴ ἔχειν σ' ὀδύνη. *Paroem. Gr.* II p. 728 (L-Schn) χρυσὲ διῶκτα, τύραννε, πάντολμε, δολοπλόκε, πάντων κακῶν ἀκρόπολις, φρούριον ἀπωλείας, ἐλέπολις, ῥιψέπαλξις, σπαράκτρια τειχέων, πόλεων τειχοσείστρια, τινάκτρια δωμάτων, οἴοις κακοῖς γηγενεῖς κρεωκοπεῖς καὶ τρύχεις. Choricius *ap.* Boisonnade, *Anecd. Gr.* I 96 χρυσέ, κακῶν ἀρχηγέ (!), καὶ τῷ ἔχοντί σε φόβος, καὶ τῷ μὴ ἔχοντί σε λύπη. Cf. the apostrophe of πλοῦτος in Timocreon fr. 5 ὤφελέν σ', ὦ τυφλὲ Πλοῦτε, μήτε γῇ μήτ' ἐν θαλάσσῃ μήτ' ἐν ἠπείρῳ φανήμεν, ἀλλὰ Τάρταρόν τε ναίειν κἀχέροντα· διὰ σὲ γὰρ πάντ' ἔνι ἐν ἀνθρώποις κακά. Eur. fr. 813 ὦ πλοῦθ', κτλ. *Or. Sib.* V 231 ὕβρι, κακῶν ἀρχηγὲ καὶ ἀνθρώποις μέγα πῆμα. Kroll, *PW* XX 1, 508 compares the apostrophe of *avaritia* in Sen. *Benef.* VII 10, 1 and of θυμός in Plut. *Coh. ira* 10, 458C. A closer parallel is Prop. III 7, 1-4 *ergo sollicitae tu causa, pecunia, vitae! per te immaturum mortis adimus iter; tu vitiis hominum crudelia pabula praebes; semina curarum de capite orta tuo.* On this kind of personification see Capelle—Marrou, "Diatribe", *RAC* III 998. The epithets βιοφθόρε and πάντα χαλέπτων are explained in vv. 46-7.

εἴθε σε ... γενέσθαι is curious (Bernhardy, *Grundrisz* 23 "anstöszig"); εἴθε is seldom found with an *acc. cum inf.* Brunck, *GPG* 156 compares Eur. *Hel.* 262f. εἴθε ... λαβεῖν, but this is only a *varia lectio* (be it a *lectio difficilior*); but see *Anth. Pal.* IX 284 γαίης χθαμαλωτέρη εἴθε ... κεῖσθαι (and Renehan, *Greek Lexicographical Notes* 76 and 155). Goram's proposal (p. 95) to read εἴθε σὺ μὴ ... γένοιο has to be rejected. It has no ms. basis whatsoever.

πῆμα ποθεινόν is an oxymoron, cf. Pind. *Pyth.* II 40 καλὸν πῆμα. For θνητοῖσι ... ποθεινόν cf. *Orph. Hymn.* XXXIII 5 ... θνητοῖσι ποθεινήν (sc. Νίκην) and LX 5 ... θνητοῖσι ποθειναί (sc. Χάριτες).

V. 44 is quoted anonymously by Theodorus Prodromus (12th cent.) in his Περὶ τοὺς διὰ πενίαν βλασφημοῦντας τὴν πρόνοιαν (ed.

F.J.G. la Porte-du Theil, *Notices et Extraits des Manuscrits de la Bibliothèque Impériale* VIII 2, 1810) p. 88 and by Zonaras (12th cent.) in his *Lexicon* p. 1842 (ed. Tittmann).

46-47 σεῦ γὰρ ἕκητι μάχαι τε λεηλασίαι τε φόνοι τε,
ἐχθρὰ δὲ τέκνα γονεῦσιν ἀδελφειοί τε συναίμοις.

For your sake there are battles and plunderings and murders,
and children become the enemies of their parents and brothers (the enemies) of their kinsmen.

λεηλασίαι τε φόνοι τε: exactly the same verse-ending in *Or. Sib.* XIII 87. ἀδελφειοί = brothers and sisters, cf. Eur. *El.* 536. The curious form (ἀδελφειοί instead of the epic ἀδελφεοί) has been chosen *metri causa*, analogous to the gen. ἀδελφειοῦ which occurs sometimes in Homer. σύναιμος: in 206 Ps-Phoc. uses συνομαίμων (edd.).

These verses contain the well-known motif of the calamities caused by the love of money. They show what φιλοχρημοσύνη (42) leads up to. One often finds a kind of catalogue of such calamities. Thus the anonymous author in Stobaeus' chapter ψόγος πλούτου IV 31, 84 (V p. 764, 2ff. W-H) says of the love of money: στασιάζει μὲν οἴκους καὶ κακὸν ἆθλον ἀδελφοῖς πρόκειται, τέκνα δ' ἐχθρὰ ποιεῖ πατράσιν ἐπιθυμοῦντα τῆς περὶ τὸν πλοῦτον ἐξουσίας, αὐτοῖς δὲ τοῖς τέκνοις τοὺς γονεῖς βαρυτέρους. *Anth. Pal.* XI 270 ... ἀντὶ φόνου πενίης τ' ὀλοῆς λιμοῦ τε καὶ ὀργῆς, οἷς πάντα φθείρεις ἐκ φιλοχρημοσύνης. Lucianus *Cyn.* 15 πάντα γὰρ τὰ κακὰ τοῖς ἀνθρώποις ἐκ τῆς τούτων (sc. χρυσοῦ καὶ ἀργύρου) ἐπιθυμίας φύονται, καὶ στάσεις καὶ πόλεμοι καὶ ἐπιβουλαὶ καὶ σφαγαί (cf. Plato *Phaedo* 66C). *Or. Sib.* VIII 24ff. money is πηγὴ δυσσεβίης καὶ ἀταξίης προοδηγός, | μηχανίη πολέμων, εἰρήνης ἐχθρὰ ἀνία | ἐχθραίνουσα τέκνοις γονέας καὶ τέκνα γονεῦσιν (cf. v. 84). *Gnom. Byz.* 207 γῆν διὰ φιλαργυρίαν μετὰ πόνων γεωργεῖς, πλεῖς μετὰ κινδύνων τὴν θάλασσαν, στρατεύῃ καθ' ὥραν φονεύειν ἢ φονεύεσθαι προσδοκῶν. (See further *ad* v. 206).

The theme of v. 47 (the enmity between kinsmen) occurs also outside this context of love of money to indicate the utter depravity of the human race in a late stage of history; see Catullus LXIV 397ff.; Ovid *Metam.* I 141ff.; more texts in Kroll, *Catull* 194f. and Gerhard, *Phoinix* 15-7. In the N.T. Mk. XIII 12 παραδώσει ἀδελφὸς ἀδελφὸν εἰς θάνατον καὶ πατὴρ τέκνον, καὶ ἐπαναστήσονται τέκνα ἐπὶ γονεῖς καὶ θανατώσουσιν αὐτούς (cf. Micah VII 6 and Pap. Genev. inv. 271, col. XIII 21ff. = *Mus. Helv.* 16 (1959), 102).

It is clear that such lists have become a *topos*. In a concise form, the motif of these lines occurs in Sir., e.g. VIII 2 πολλούς γάρ ἀπώλεσεν τὸ χρυσίον, X 8 βασιλεία ἀπὸ ἔθνους εἰς ἔθνος μετάγεται διὰ . . . χρήματα, XXXI 6 πολλοὶ ἐδόθησαν εἰς πτῶμα χάριν χρυσίου. Holtzmann, in B. Stade-O. Holtzmann, *Geschichte des Volkes Israel* II (1888) 309, remarks: "Zu diesen Versen geben die Streitigkeiten im Hause jenes Grosssteuerpächters Joseph [sc. the Tobiad] die beste Illustration".

After v. 47 Ψ adds: μὴ δὲ δόλους ῥάπτειν [= v. 4a], μὴ πρὸς φίλον ἦτορ ὁπλίζειν.

Vv. 48-58 Honesty, Modesty and Self-control

48 μὴ δ' ἕτερον κεύθῃς κραδίῃ νόον ἀλλ' ἀγορεύων.

Hide not a different thought in your heart while uttering another.

On ἕτερον — ἄλλο see Sicking, *Annotationes ad Antiatticistam* (1883) 39. Obviously, the source of this verse is Hom. *Il.* IX 312f. ἐχθρὸς γάρ μοι κεῖνος ὁμῶς Ἀΐδαο πύλῃσιν, ὅς χ' ἕτερον μὲν κεύθῃ ἐνὶ φρεσίν, ἄλλο δὲ εἴπῃ. This Homeric verse is also alluded to by an anonymous Cynic *ap*. Themist. XXI 258d ἀνὴρ δ' ἄλλα κέκευθεν ἐνὶ φρεσίν, ἄλλα δὲ βάζει. The same thought is expressed by Theogn. 91f. ὃς δὲ μιῇ γλώσσῃ δίχ' ἔχει νόον, οὗτος ἑταῖρος δεινός (cf. v. 96). Soph. *O.C.* 936 τῷ νῷ θ' ὁμοίως κἀπὸ τῆς γλώσσης λέγω. Cf. Eur. *Hipp*. 413ff. On this "κεύθειν von μῦθοι und ἔπεα" see Luther, *Wahrheit und Lüge* 27ff. Cf. also Sallust. *Catil*. X 5 *aliud clausum in pectore, aliud in lingua promptum habere*. There are also close parallels in the Talmud, Pes. 113b "(God hates) one who speaks one thing with his mouth and another thing in his heart"; BM 49a "one must not speak one thing with the mouth and another with the heart". On these texts see Moore, *Judaism* II 188 and Minear, "Yes or No: the Demand for Honesty in the Early Church", *Nov. Test.* 13 (1971), 11f. The same Homeric verse may be the background of these Talmudic texts.

49 μηδ' ὡς πετροφυῆς πολύπους κατὰ χῶρον ἀμείβου.

Change not yourself according to the spot like a polyp that clings to the rock.

This line elaborates on the theme of v. 48. πετροφυής: a word of late occurrence (Ps-Dioscurides IV 90; *Or. Sib.* V 321). This verse seems to have been made by way of contrast to the famous line of

Theognis 215f. (that had become proverbial in antiquity) πουλύπου ὀργὴν ἴσχε πολυπλόκου, ὃς ποτὶ πέτρῃ, τῇ προσομιλήσῃ, τοῖος ἰδεῖν ἐφάνη. This verse of Theognis is quoted very often, e.g. by Plut. *Amic. multit.* 9, 96F, *Quaest. nat.* 19, 916C, *Sollert. anim.* 27, 978E; Athen. *Deipn.* VII 317A, XII 513D, etc. (see the passages in Young's *app. crit. ad* Theogn. 215 and esp. Peretti, *Teognide nella tradizione gnomologica* 42-49, 93-104). It was even parodied, see Philostr. *Vit. Soph.* I 5 (486) πανσόφου ὀργὴν ἴσχε Φιλοστράτου, ὃς Κλεοπάτρᾳ νῦν προσομιλήσας τοῖος ἰδεῖν ἐφάνη. The praise of the polyp as a symbol of adaptability is very often found in Greek literature. Its ability to change its colour when alarmed and to assume the colour of the ground below was well-known; see Thompson, *Glossary of Greek Fishes* 204-208, who mentions numerous illustrative passages (cf. also Köhler, *Das Tierleben im Sprichwort der Gr. und Röm.* 150; Gossen, "Polypen", *PW* XXI 2, 1791 totally neglects the literary aspects of the polyp). Some quotations may suffice. Soph. fr. 307 νόει πρὸς ἀνδρὶ σῶμα (χρῶμα cj. Bergk) πουλύπους ὅπως πέτρᾳ τραπέσθαι γνησίου φρονήματος (cf. Pind. fr. 235 (43)). Athen. VII 316-318 quotes a large number of poets on the polyp (cf. 513C-D). *Paroem. Gr.* I 298 πολύποδος ὁμοιότης· πρὸς τοὺς ἐξομοιοῦντας ἑαυτοὺς οἷς βούλονται, *ibid.* I 184 ἄλλοτε δ' ἀλλοῖον τελέθειν καὶ χώρᾳ ἕπεσθαι· ... εἴρηται δὲ ἀπὸ τῶν πολυπόδων· οὗτοι γὰρ ᾗ ἂν πλησιάσωσι πέτρᾳ φόβου κατεπείγοντος εἰς τὸ αὐτῆς εἶδος τὸ ἑαυτῶν μεταβάλλουσιν. Cf. *ibid.* II 84.204.274.616.620. Ael. *Var. hist.* I 1 ἑαυτοὺς ἐς τὴν ἐκείνων (sc. πετρῶν) μεταμορφοῦσι χρόαν. Plin. *N.H.* IX 87 *colorem mutat ad similitudinem loci* (see the whole passage 85-87 on the polyp with the comments of Cotte, *Poissons et animaux aquatiques au temps de Pline* 178-182). Cf. Oppianus *Hal.* II 232-252; Luc. *Salt.* 67; Theophr. fr. 172, 173 and 188 (on the ἐξομοιοῦσθαι of the polyp).

Bernays 210ff. thought that here a Jew opposes this Greek ideal of adaptability, of opportunism, of being πολύτροπος, "Schmiegsamkeit und Dehnbarkeit" (210). He calls Theogn. 215f. a "Grundmaxime der hellenischen Praxis" (212, cf. *ibid.* "jenes hellenische Polypenwesen"), which is diametrically opposed to the ideal of the Jewish people, "dessen Tugenden und Fehler nicht aus der farbenwechselnden Versatilität, sondern aus der entgegenstehenden Eigenschaft, aus der zähen Unbeugsamkeit entspringen" (212). Schmidt (in his review of Bernays' book in *Jahrb. f. class. Phil.* 3 (1857), 512) sees in these statements Bernays' Jewish bias and

Dieterich, *Nekyia* 180, rightly refers to Ion Trag. fr. 36 καὶ τὸν πετραῖον πλεκτάναις ἀναίμοσιν στυγῶ μεταλλακτῆρα πουλύπουν χροός "zum deutlichen Zeugnis, dass auch die entgegengesetzte Meinung [sc. against Theognis] schon in altgriechischer Weisheit vertreten war". And Rossbroich 45 points out that also Plutarch is critical of Theognis' verse (he even, wrongly, suggests that Ps-Phoc. may have known Plutarch's *Moralia*, as does Farina 39). See on this point also Gerhard, *Phoinix* 239. Lincke, who thinks that our poem is from the real Phoc., asserts (*Samaria* 55) that Theogn. 215f. is directed against (Ps-)Phoc. 49.

50 πᾶσιν δ' ἁπλόος ἴσθι, τὰ δ' ἐκ ψυχῆς ἀγόρευε.
Be sincere to all, speak what is in your heart.

There is a considerable amount of literature on the Greek and Jewish (and Christian) use of ἁπλοῦς and ἁπλότης. See e.g. Bousset, *Religion* 418ff.; Dibelius, *Jak.* 106f.; Spicq, "La vertu de la simplicité", *Rev. des sciences philos. et théol.* 22 (1933), 1-26; Hiltbrunner, *Latina Graeca* 15-105; Bacht, "Einfalt", *RAC* IV 821-840 (there more literature); and esp. Amstutz, ΑΠΛΟΤΗΣ. ἁπλοῦς (having many semantic aspects) is often used in the sense of "honest", "sincere", combined with ἀληθής — ἀλήθεια, e.g. Aesch. fr. 176 ἁπλᾶ γάρ ἐστι τῆς ἀληθείας ἔπη, Eur. *Phoen.* 469 ἁπλοῦς ὁ μῦθος τῆς ἀληθείας ἔφυ, Trag. adesp. fr. 28 μισῶ τὸν ἄνδρα τὸν διπλοῦν πεφυκότα, χρηστὸν λόγοισι, πολέμιον δὲ τοῖς τρόποις. Cf. Plato *Hipp. min.* 364e ff. Arist. *EE* III 7, 1233b38. According to Norden, *Jahrb. f. class. Phil.* Suppl. 19 (1893) 403 n.1 ἁπλοῦς and ἁπλότης "sind Schlagworte der Kyniker und Stoiker". It plays an important role in Marc. Aur. (Bacht 832). The Jewish history of the word (traced by Amstutz) begins late: one instance of ἁπλοῦς in the LXX, Prov. XI 25 ψυχὴ εὐλογουμένη πᾶσα ἁπλῆ and two instances of ἁπλότης καρδίας: Sap. Sal. I 1; 1 Chron. XXIX 17. But it is frequent in the Test. XII Patr. (Amstutz 62ff.), e.g. Test. Levi XIII 1 πορεύεσθε ἐν ἁπλότητι, and in a number of mss. the whole Test. Iss. has the title περὶ ἁπλότητος (Amstutz 74ff.). Its contrary is διψυχία (Bousset 418ff.), διγλωσσία (Hiltbrunner 89). Ἁπλότης is highly valued in Hermas, e.g. *Vis.* II 3, *Mand.* II 1 (see esp. Bacht 831-3). Amstutz 42 comments on Ps-Phoc.: "So gebraucht Ps-Phok. in seiner Lehrdichtung 48-50 ἁπλόος im Sinne von "gerade", "offen", "aufrichtig". In einer dreigliedrigen Sentenz mahnt er: Nicht birg anderen Sinn im Herzen als du aussprichst; nicht ändere opportunistisch je nach der Situation deine Äusserungen; vielmehr — in allem sei ἁπλόος; was in deinem Herzen ist, sprich aus." (Amstutz takes πᾶσιν as meaning "in all respects", which is possible, but see my translation). What Amstutz says is quite correct; it rightly demonstrates the coherence of vv. 48-50 which form a unity.

51-52 ὅστις ἑκὼν ἀδικεῖ, κακὸς ἀνήρ· ἢν δ' ὑπ' ἀνάγκης,
οὐκ ἐρέω τὸ τέλος. βουλὴ δ' εὐθύνεθ' ἑκάστου.

Whoever wrongs wilfully is a bad man; but if he does so under compulsion,
I shall not pass sentence. For it is each man's intention that is examined.

On the antithesis ἑκών — ὑπ' ἀνάγκης cf. ad v. 16. On the *brevis pro longa* in ἀνήρ see Rossbroich 9. V. 51a looks like a polemic against the Socratic maxim οὐδεὶς ἑκὼν ἁμαρτάνει (cf. e.g. Plato *Prot.* 345e1-3; *Gorg.* 509e5-6; Xen. *Mem.* IV 2, 19ff.). This rationalistic idea was widespread in antiquity; see e.g. Stobaeus' chapter II 9 (II p. 176ff. W-H) ὅτι οὐδεὶς ἑκὼν πονηρός. Cf. Ael. Arist. 34, 5 K οὐδεὶς ἑκὼν φαῦλος. Schmidt, *Ethik* I 251ff. B.A. van Groningen, *Le Grec et ses idées morales*.

The expression οὐκ ἐρέω τὸ τέλος is difficult: Riessler "den nenn ich schliesslich nicht so" (sc. schlecht); Easton "thou art guiltless" (cf. my transl.); Kurfess (*ZNW* 1939, 180) "da will ich das Ende nicht nennen"; Farina 39 "non lo diro senz' altro un malvagio"; Young (letter of 6.10.1972) "I shall not state the result/consequence(?)". It is clear that some take τὸ τέλος as an adverb (= τελέως, πάνυ); thus already Sartorius 48f. "non dico quod sit injustus prorsus". Then the object of ἐρέω is ὅτι κακὸς ἀνήρ ἐστιν (to be supplied). If τὸ τέλος is the object, then the best translation is perhaps "decision, judgment" (LSJ *s.v.* 4). Ludwich, *Spruchbuch* 18, takes τὸ τέλος with the following words: οὐκ ἐρέω· τὸ τέλος βουλὴν εὔθυνεν ἑκάστου, "(wenn aber aus Zwang,) so werde ich das nicht sagen; der Erfolg pflegt über den Rathschluss eines Jeden zu richten". A similar proposal had already been made by Wachler 10: οὐχ αἱρῶ (= damno)· τὸ τέλος κτλ. (The thoughtless emendations of Goram 109, followed by Sebestyén 36, need no comment). The most probable solution is to take τέλος as object of ἐρέω, meaning "to pass sentence". The sentence is reminiscent of the Homeric formula ἀλλ' ἔκ τοι ἐρέω, τὸ δὲ καὶ τετελεσμένον ἔσται (*Il.* II 257, *Od.* II 187, etc.).

εὐθύνεθ' (= εὐθύνεται, not εὐθύνετε) is read only by Ψ, but is no doubt right (Alexandre on *Or. Sib.* II 124: "antiquum est εὐθύνεται pro κρίνεται"; cf. LSJ *s.v.* III; the mss. read εὔθυνες, εὔθυνε, εὐθύνεται). Also βουλή is therefore preferable to βουλήν of 3 mss. (M, L, V). Rossbroich 46 rightly compares Sen. *Ep.* 95, 57 (= *SVF* III 517) *actio recta non erit, nisi recta fuerit voluntas*: *ab hac enim est actio*. Rossbroich adds rashly: "Auctorem Ps-Phoc. pendere ex Stoicorum doctrina manifestum est". But of course every well-thinking Jew could think this out. Cf. moreover Democr. fr. 62 ἀγαθὸν οὐ τὸ μὴ ἀδικεῖν, ἀλλὰ τὸ μηδὲ ἐθέλειν and the Socratic discussion on intentional and unintentional wrong-doing in Xen. *Mem.* IV 2, 19. Raspante (according to Farina 39) proposes to athetize vv. 51-2 since only here does the poet speak in the first person (singular). But that is hardly a valid argument, because the first person (plural) does occur in 40, 103 and 201.

53 μὴ γαυροῦ σοφίη μήτ' ἀλκῇ μήτ' ἐνὶ πλούτῳ.
Pride not yourself on wisdom nor on strength nor on riches.

Undoubtedly this line is a versification of Jerem. IX 22 μὴ καυχάσθω ὁ σοφὸς ἐν τῇ σοφίᾳ αὐτοῦ, καὶ μὴ καυχάσθω ὁ ἰσχυρὸς ἐν τῇ ἰσχύι αὐτοῦ, καὶ μὴ καυχάσθω ὁ πλούσιος ἐν τῷ πλούτῳ αὐτοῦ. (N.B. καυχᾶσθαι — γαυροῦσθαι, σοφία — σοφίη, ἰσχύς — ἀλκή, πλοῦτος — πλοῦτος). In almost the same form this text is also found in I Regn. II 10 (only in the LXX, not in the M.T.) μὴ καυχάσθω ὁ φρόνιμος ἐν τῇ φρονήσει αὐτοῦ, καὶ μὴ καυχάσθω ὁ δυνατὸς ἐν τῇ δυνάμει αὐτοῦ, καὶ μὴ καυχάσθω ὁ πλούσιος ἐν τῷ πλούτῳ αὐτοῦ (this text is quoted in I Clem. XIII 1). Cf. Philo *Spec. leg.* I 311 μήτ' ἐπὶ πλούτῳ μήτε δόξῃ μήτε ἡγεμονίᾳ μήτε σώματος εὐμορφίᾳ μήτε ῥώμῃ μήτε τοῖς παραπλησίοις, ἐφ' οἷς εἰώθασιν οἱ κενοὶ φρενῶν ἐπαίρεσθαι, σεμνυνθῆς (cf. *Ep. Arist.* 282 δόξῃ καὶ πλούτῳ καὶ δυνάμει). Herm. *Vis.* III 9, 6 γαυριώμενοι (*v.l.* γαυρούμενοι) ἐν τῷ πλούτῳ (cf. I 1, 8). There are also some Greek antecedents: Eur. fr. 22 τὴν δ' εὐγένειαν πρὸς θεῶν μή μοι λέγε, ἐν χρήμασιν τόδ' ἐστί, μὴ γαυροῦ, πάτερ. Cf. fr. 92 (χρήμασιν γαυρούμενος) and fr. 662 πολλοὺς δὲ πλούτῳ καὶ γένει γαυρουμένους γυνὴ κατῄσχυν' ἐν δόμοισι νηπία. Men. *Mon.* 510 μηδέποτε καυχῶ πλοῦτον ἐν δόμοις ἔχων. Men. *et Phil. comp.* I 295 ... κακῶς τε πλούτῳ καὶ τύχῃ γαυρούμενον. Pap. Florent. 367, 11 πλούτῳ γαυρωθείς. On ἐνί (*metri causa?*) *instrumentale* see Buresch, *Philol.* 51 (1892), 108ff.

54 εἷς θεός ἐστι σοφὸς δυνατός θ' ἅμα καὶ πολύολβος.

The only God is wise and mighty and at the same time rich in blessings.

There is a clear correspondence with v. 53 (σοφίη — ἀλκή — πλοῦτος); a possible translation, therefore, would be: "Only God is ..."; cf. Kroll, *PW* XX 1, 506 "bei v. 54 soll man nicht vergessen, dass εἷς "nur" heisst, und die von E. Peterson, Εἷς Θεός (Gött. 1926) behandelten Akklamationen fernhalten" (so too Farina 39 "solo Dio ..."). Indeed, εἷς may have the sense of μόνος, see LSJ s.v. 1a and cf. the Pisidian inscription first published in *Hermes* 23 (1888), 542ff. εἷς γὰρ Ζεὺς πάντων προπάτωρ. Doubtless, however, every Jew was reminded by the words εἷς θεός of his own daily Shema', in which he said (Deut. VI 4) κύριος ὁ θεὸς ἡμῶν κύριος εἷς ἐστιν (Moore, *Judaism* I 291); moreover, εἷς θεός was "geradezu terminus technicus der monotheistischen Missionspredigt" (Kerst, *ZNW* 66 (1975), 132; *ibid.* "jüdische Propagandaformel"). This justifies my translation (cf. also Geffcken's translation in Hennecke, *Neutest. Apokr.* 340: "nur der eine Gott ..."). It should be borne in mind that in their missionary activities the Jews could take pagan εἷς θεός pronouncements as a starting-point (see Hengel, *Entretiens* XVIII 315); e.g. Xenophanes fr. 23 εἷς θεός, ἔν τε θεοῖσι καὶ ἀνθρώποισι μέγιστος and the texts quoted by Norden, ΑΓΝΩΣΤΟΣ ΘΕΟΣ 244f. (for μόνος θεός see Delling, ΜΟΝΟΣ ΘΕΟΣ, *Stud. z. N.T. u. z. hell. Jud.* 391-400). Cf. Spicq *ad* 1 Tim. I 17 "les termes εἷς ou μόνος, au sens de 'supérieur à tous', sont fréquents dans les éloges ou les acclamations de l'époque". *Ep. Arist.* 132 μόνος ὁ θεός ἐστιν. Philo *Opif.* 171 θεὸς εἷς ἐστι. *Or. Sib.* III 11f. εἷς θεός ἐστι, μόναρχος ἀθέσφατος αἰθέρι ναίων αὐτοφυὴς ἀόρατος κτλ. Cf. fr. I 7f., 32; fr. III 3 ἀλλὰ θεὸς μόνος εἷς πανυπέρτατος. Ps-Soph. *ap.* Clem. Alex. *Strom.* V 113, 2 (= Denis p. 162, 20) εἷς ταῖς ἀληθείαισιν, εἷς ἐστιν θεός. "Orpheus" *ap.* Eus. *PE* XIII 12, 5 (= Denis p. 165, 1) εἷς ἔστ', αὐτογενής, ἑνὸς ἔκγονα πάντα τέτυκται. See further Bousset, *Religion* 302ff. (ch. XV "Der Monotheismus") and Peterson, ΕΙΣ ΘΕΟΣ, *passim*. For the combination of εἷς (or μόνος) with σοφός cf. Sir. I 8 εἷς ἐστιν σοφός, φοβερὸς σφόδρα. Rom. XVI 27 μόνῳ σοφῷ θεῷ. See also Heracl. fr. 32 ἓν τὸ σοφὸν μοῦνον λέγεσθαι οὐκ ἐθέλει καὶ ἐθέλει Ζηνὸς ὄνομα. Clem. Alex. *Strom.* IV 9, 1 [μοι δοκεῖ καὶ Πυθαγόρας σοφὸν μὲν εἶναι τὸν θεὸν λέγειν μόνον. Cf. Heraclides Pont. *ap.* Diog. Laert. I 12 (= fr. 87 Wehrli) μηδένα γὰρ εἶναι σοφὸν ἀλλ' ἢ θεόν (said Pythagoras). πολύολβος as a divine epithet also in Sappho fr. 133 L-P (said of Aphrodite; more texts in Rossbroich 13). Lincke's theory that the "only God" to which reference is intended in this verse is Ahura Mazda ("Phok. und die Essener" 136) needs no refutation. Alexandre's remark (*Or. Sib.* I 2 (1853), 151): "versus interpolatus (est) christiana manu" has no basis whatsoever.

55-56 μὴ δὲ παροιχομένοισι κακοῖς τρύχου τεὸν ἧπαρ·
οὐκέτι γὰρ δύναται τὸ τετυγμένον εἶναι ἄτυκτον.

Vex not your liver with bygone evils;
for what has been done can no more be undone.

παροιχόμενα κακά: Xen. *Hell.* I 4, 17. For this use of τρύχειν cf. Theogn. 913, Soph. *O.R.* 666, Sap. Sal. XI 12, XIV 15. ἧπαρ: most mss. (L, M, P, V) read ἦτορ (heart), adopted by Ludwich, *Spruchbuch* 17; this is, however, a *lectio facilior*; but cf. v. 97. Cf. τήκειν ἧπαρ in Callim. *Aitia* fr. I 8, and for the liver as the centre of emotions Soph. *Aiax* 938, Aesch. *Agam.* 432, and the use of ἧπαρ (parallel with καρδία and σπλάγχνα) in Test. Sim. II 4, II 7, IV 1; Test. Zab. II 4; Test. Gad II 1. Cf. H. L. Hagen, *Die physiologische und psychologische Bedeutung der Leber i.d. Antike*, diss. Berlin 1961. τεός and σός are also indiscriminately used in Homer. ἄτυκτος is a *hapax*.

Rossbroich 48 and Beltrami, *Riv.* 41 (1913), 532 assert that v. 56 is very typical of the *Consolationes*-literature, e.g. Plut. *Cons. ad Apoll.* 26, 115A τὸ μὲν γὰρ γεγενημένον οὐδὲ θεῷ δυνατόν ἐστι ποιῆσαι ἀγένητον. But this thought also occurs in other contexts: Theogn. 583f. ἀλλὰ τὰ μὲν προβέβηκεν, ἀμήχανόν ἐστι γενέσθαι ἀεργά. Simonides fr. 69 τὸ γὰρ γεγενημένον οὐκέτ' ἄρεκτον ἔσται. Cf. Pind. *Ol.* II 16ff.; Plato *Prot.* 324b. Hor. *Carm.* III 29, 45ff. *non tamen irritum, quodcumque retro est, efficiet, neque diffinget infectumque reddet, quod fugiens semel hora vexit.* It should be noted, however, that these lines are about evils that a man has committed himself, not about evils that one has suffered. With that proviso, Dornseiff's remark that v. 56 is "rein griechisch, und zwar sehr griechisch" (*Echtheitsfragen* 40) is right; it does not look very Jewish.

57-58 μὴ προπετὴς ἐς χεῖρα, χαλίνου δ' ἄγριον ὀργήν·
πολλάκι γὰρ πλήξας ἀέκων φόνον ἐξετέλεσσεν.

Be not rash with your hands, but bridle your wild anger.
For often someone who has dealt a blow has unintentionally committed a murder.

μὴ προπετής: supply ἴσθι, which is a rare ellips, see K-G I 42. On προπέτεια as a vice see Men. *Mon.* 631 προπέτεια πολλοῖς ἐστιν αἰτία κακῶν. Mus. Ruf. XVI (p. 86, 4ff. H.) ἐν τῇ συνουσίᾳ ἥκιστα φίλερις ὢν ἢ φίλαυτος καὶ οὔτε προπετὴς οὔτε ταραχώδης οὔτ' ὀργίλος (N.B. also here the combination with ὀργή). Prov. X 14 στόμα δὲ προπετοῦς ἐγγίζει συντριβῇ, cf. XIII 3; Sir. IX 18; 2 Tim. III 4; Acts XIX 36 (Bauer s.v.). On χείρ in the sense of "force, deed of violence" see LSJ s.v. IV.

χαλίνου δ' ἄγριον ὀργήν: Gerhard, Phoinix 70: "Im einzelnen erfreuen sich solcher Illustrierung [sc. with χαλινός] besonders die Affekte des Zorns". See Themist. XXXIV 10 τὸν θυμὸν ἐχαλίνουν (cf. Epic. fr. 485), Gnom. Byz. 253 οἱ μὲν τραχεῖς ἵπποι τοῖς χαλινοῖς, οἱ δὲ ὀξύθυμοι ἄνδρες τοῖς λογισμοῖς μετάγονται. Varro Sat. fr. 177 ... neque irato mihi habenas dedi umquam, neque cupiditati non imposui frenos. Hor. Epist. I 2, 62f. ira furor brevis est: animum rege; qui nisi paret imperat; hunc frenis, hunc tu compesce catena. On the danger of ὀργή Men. Mon. 99 βραδὺς πρὸς ὀργὴν κἀγκρατὴς φέρειν γένου (cf. James I 19!). Men. et Phil. comp. I 50 ὀργὴ δὲ δεινὰ δρᾶν ἀναγκάζει βροτούς. Boissonade, Anecd. Gr. I 120 ὀργῆς ἀπέχου καὶ θυμοῦ ἀφίστασο (cf. Col. III 8). Prov. XV 1 ὀργὴ ἀπόλλυσιν καὶ φρονίμους. Eccl. VII 10, Sir. I 22 and more texts quoted below under vv. 63f. Aboth II 10 "Be not easily provoked". For ἄγριος ὀργή see Soph. O.R. 344 δι' ὀργῆς ἥτις ἀγριωτάτη.

On v. 58 Rossbroich 49 rightly compares Did III 2 ὁδηγεῖ ... ἡ ὀργὴ πρὸς τὸν φόνον. Cf. Prov. XXV 8 μὴ πρόσπιπτε εἰς μάχην ταχέως. On unintentional murder see also above vv. 32-34.

Vv. 59-69   *Moderation in All Things*

59-60   ἔστω κοινὰ πάθη· μηδὲν μέγα μηδ' ὑπέροπλον.
οὐκ ἀγαθὸν πλεονάζον ἔφυ θνητοῖσιν ὄνειαρ.

Let your emotions be moderate, neither great nor overwhelming.
Excess, even of good, is never a boon to mortals.

κοινὰ πάθη: in v. 27 κοινὰ πάθη means "common sufferings", but here probably κοινός = μέσος (thus Bernays 206 n.1). Though LSJ give no instances of this use, this view is corroborated by the fact that ὑπέροπλος is the "Gegensatz des Maassvollen" (Schmidt, Ethik I 356). (ὑπέροπλος is an epic word, Hom. Il. XV 185, XVII 170; Or. Sib. VIII 142; also Ep. Arist. 52). Bernays' theory that this verse shows knowledge of the Aristotelian theory of μεσότης is rightly doubted by J. Freudenthal, *Die Flavius Josephus beigelegte Schrift über die Herrschaft der Vernunft* 162. Rossbroich 49: "Auctorem significare sententiam, quae graece dicitur μετριοπάθεια apertum est. ... Verbis μηδὲν μέγα significat auctor illud μηδὲν ἄγαν quod propter rem metricam adhibere non potuit". The concept of μετριοπάθεια was introduced by Crantor (*ap.* Plut. *Cons. ad Apoll.* 102D), who intended it to be a counterpart of the Stoic ἀπάθεια (Pohlenz, *Stoa* I 173). On the immoderate passionateness of the Alexandrian population see Schubart, *Ägypten* 139f.

V. 60 has the same tenor as v. 59. It is the well-known Greek motif μηδὲν ἄγαν. It is, therefore, not very probable that, as Rossbroich 50 asserts, it is about the φθόνος θεῶν (on which see below *ad* v. 71). ὄνειαρ is an epic word, equivalent to ὄφελος (see under 78).

The whole section vv. 59-69 is an exhortation to moderation in πάθη; it warns against all kinds of excesses in these matters.

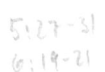

61 ἡ πολλὴ δὲ τρυφὴ πρὸς ἀμέτρους ἕλκετ' ἔρωτας

Great luxuriousness draws one to immoderate desires.

τρυφή in erotic context: Ps-Luc. *Amor.* 20: when people became homosexual ἡ πάντα τολμῶσα τρυφὴ τὴν φύσιν αὐτὴν παρενόμησεν. Philo *Somn.* I 123, *Spec. leg.* II 240 (τρυφή — ἐπιθυμίαι). Cf. Sir. XVIII 32 μὴ εὐφραίνου ἐπὶ πολλῇ τρυφῇ (see the whole context XVIII 30-XIX 3), 2 Pet. II 13 and the many warnings against τρυφή in Hermas. For ἄμετρος ἔρως cf. Ps-Plato *Epist.* VIII 354d5 ἀμέτρῳ ... ἔρωτι. Andronicus Περὶ παθῶν 4, p. 19, 10 Kreuttner λαγνεία δὲ ἐπιθυμία συνουσιῶν ἄμετρος. Philo *Mut. nom.* 214 ἡδονῆς ἀμέτρου φοράν.

Remarks on the stimulating effect of eating and drinking on sexual desires are found very frequently in Greek and Latin literature; see Hopfner, *Das Sexualleben der Griechen und Römer* I 273f. 295ff. Warnings against this are equally frequent, esp. in the Stoic-Cynic diatribe, see Gerhard, *Phoinix* 24ff., 62ff. and Oltramare, *Origines de la diatribe romaine* 272, etc. This is also a recurrent theme in Jewish literature, e.g. Philo *Agric.* 37 γαστριμαργία τοίνυν ἡ ὀπαδὸς ἐκ φύσεως ἀκολουθεῖ συνουσίας ἡδονὴ μανίαν ἔκτοπον καὶ οἶστρον ἀνεπίσχετον καὶ λύτταν ἀργαλεωτάτην ἐπιφέρουσα. Cf. *Vita Mos.* II 24; Apoc. Bar. Gr. IV 17; Sir. IX 9, and the long warning against uninhibited sexual desires as a result of immoderate use of alcohol in Test. Jud. XIV-XVI. Rabbinic texts can be found in Epstein, *Sex Laws* 113f. Cf. Clem. Alex. *Paed.* II 20, 3; 33, 1.4; 40, 1; 48, 3.

vv. 62-64   155

62 ὑψαυχεῖ δ' ὁ πολὺς πλοῦτος καὶ ἐς ὕβριν ἀέξει.
Great wealth is conceited and grows to insolence.

Farina 39 translates ὑψαυχεῖ by "genera orgoglio", but it is not transitive; ὑψαυχέω = ὑψηλοφρονέω, μεγαλαυχέω (LSJ s.v.). The strangeness of πλοῦτος being the subject of ὑψαυχεῖ is lessened when πλοῦτος is taken to mean ὁ πλούσιος, just as in v. 10 πενίην = τὸν πένητα. On the combination of arrogance and riches see 1 Tim. VI 17 τοῖς πλουσίοις ... παράγγελλε μὴ ὑψηλοφρονεῖν (cf. Herm. *Mand*. VIII 3 πολυτελείας πλούτου καὶ καυχήσεως καὶ ὑψηλοφροσύνης καὶ ὑπερηφανίας). Arrogance was seen as a great evil, Men. *Mon*. 794 ὑπερηφανία μέγιστον ἀνθρώποις κακόν. Rabbinic texts in Billerbeck II 101ff.

The relation between wealth and ὕβρις is traditional: Eur. fr. 438 ὕβριν τε τίκτει πλοῦτος (= Men. *Mon*. 792), possibly a variant of Solon fr. 5, 9 = Theogn. 153f. τίκτει τοι κόρος ὕβριν, ὅταν κακῷ ὄλβος ἕπηται ἀνθρώπῳ καὶ ὅτῳ μὴ νόος ἄρτιος ᾖ (the first part of which is often quoted by Philo; see Heinemann, *Philons Bildung* 256). Cf. Solon *ap*. Diog. Laert. I 59 τὸν μὲν κόρον ὑπὸ τοῦ πλούτου γεννᾶσθαι, τὴν δὲ ὕβριν ὑπὸ τοῦ κόρου (and again Men. *Mon*. 795 ὕβρις κακὸν μέγιστον ἀνθρώποις ἔφυ). Aristot. *Rhet*. II 16, 1390b32ff. τῷ δὲ πλούτῳ ἃ ἕπεται ἤθη, ἐπιπολῆς ἐστιν ἰδεῖν ἅπασιν· ὑβρισταὶ γὰρ καὶ ὑπερήφανοι, πάσχοντές τι ὑπὸ τῆς κτήσεως τοῦ πλούτου· ὥσπερ γὰρ ἔχοντες ἅπαντα τἀγαθὰ οὕτω διάκεινται· ὁ γὰρ πλοῦτος οἷον τιμή τις τῆς ἀξίας τῶν ἄλλων, διὸ φαίνεται ὤνια ἅπαντα εἶναι αὐτοῦ (cf. II 2, 1378b27). On this idea in Greek culture see Schmidt, *Ethik* I 267ff. and esp. J. J. Fraenkel, *Hybris* (1941); and for later rabbinic comments see Billerbeck I 827f. In general cf. also Anon. simil. 18 (in Mullach, *Fr.Phil.Gr.* I 488) οὔτε ἵππῳ χωρὶς χαλινοῦ, οὔτε πλούτῳ χωρὶς λογισμοῦ ἀσφαλῶς χρήσασθαι.

**63-64 θυμὸς ὑπερχόμενος μανίην ὀλοόφρονα τεύχει.
ὀργὴ δ' ἐστὶν ὄρεξις, ὑπερβαίνουσα δὲ μῆνις.**
Anger that steals over one causes destructive madness.
Rage is a desire, but wrath surpasses it.

V. 64b may also mean: "but if it (ὀργή) is excessive, it is wrath". ὑπερχόμενος is read by only two mss. (M, B), others have ὑπερχεόμενος, ὑπερεχόμενος, ἐπερχόμενος and ὑπαρχόμενος. Bergk and Diehl read ὑπερχύμενος "overflowing", supported by Ludwich, *Quaest*. 28. Bernays 206 n. 1 proposes θυμὸς σπερχόμενος = "jähes Aufbrausen", supported by Sebestyén 36. But ὑπέρχομαι is often used of involuntary feelings (see LSJ s.v.) and is probably right; cf. Geffcken's translation in Hennecke, *Neutest. Apokr.* 340: "Eine Begierde, die leise beginnt, ..." ὀλοόφρων is Homeric. There is a wordplay in these verses, not only with ὀργή — ὄρεξις (as Diehl rightly suggests in *app. crit.*), but also with μανίη — μῆνις (so Dornseiff, *Echtheitsfragen* 41, who sees here an indication "dass er mit Achilleus nicht einverstanden ist", *Il.* I 1). On this supposed etymological connection of μανία and μῆνις see *Etym. Magn.* p. 583, 20 τὸ δὲ μῆνις παρὰ τὴν μανίαν and the passages cited by Kreuttner in his edition of Andronicus p. 48.

The background of vv. 63-64 is the Stoic theory of the *irarum differentiae* (Sen. *De ira* I 4), on which see the synopsis in Giusta, *I dossografi di etica* II 257ff. (cf. Schmidt, *Synonymik* III 551-572). Some texts may illustrate this: Andronicus p. 17 Kr. ὀργὴ μὲν οὖν ἐστιν ἐπιθυμία τιμωρίας τοῦ ἠδικηκέναι δοκοῦντος. θυμὸς δὲ ὀργὴ ἐναρχομένη. ... μῆνις δὲ ὀργὴ εἰς παλαίωσιν ἀποτιθεμένη. Diog. Laert. VII 113f. ὀργὴ δ' ἐπιθυμία τιμωρίας τοῦ δοκοῦντος ἠδικηκέναι οὐ προσηκόντως. ... μῆνις δέ ἐστιν ὀργή τις πεπαλαιωμένη καὶ ἐπίκοτος. ... ὁ δὲ θυμός ἐστιν ὀργὴ ἀρχομένη. Stob. II 7, 10 (II p. 91 W-H) ὀργὴ μὲν οὖν ἐστιν ἐπιθυμία τιμωρήσασθαι τὸν δοκοῦντα ἠδικηκέναι παρὰ τὸ προσῆκον· θυμὸς δὲ ὀργὴ ἐναρχομένη· χόλος δὲ ὀργὴ διοιδοῦσα· μῆνις δὲ ὀργὴ εἰς παλαίωσιν ἀποτεθειμένη ἢ ἐναποκειμένη· κότος δὲ ὀργὴ ἐπιτηροῦσα καιρὸν εἰς τιμωρίαν. All types of *ira* are species of the genus ὀργή (see Diog. Laert. VII 114; Pohlenz, *Stoa* II 81; Vögtle, *Kataloge* 200). Cf. also Cic. *Tusc.* III 11, IV 21; *SVF* III 395 and other passages referred to in Kreuttner's notes and in Giusta. An early Christian example, Herm. *Mand.* V 2, 4 ἐκ τῆς ἀφροσύνης γίνεται πικρία, ἐκ δὲ τῆς πικρίας θυμός, ἐκ δὲ τοῦ θυμοῦ ὀργή, ἐκ δὲ τῆς ὀργῆς μῆνις (Joly *ad loc.* "casuistique stoicïenne"; see also Dibelius *ad loc.*). The fact that Ps-Phoc. uses ὄρεξις instead of ἐπιθυμία could well be the result of Aristotelian influence (Bernays 206 n.1); *Ars Rhet.* II 2, 1378a30 ἔστω δὴ ὀργὴ ὄρεξις ... τιμωρίας, *De anima* I 1, 403a29 ὀργή could well be defined as an ὄρεξις ἀντιλυπήσεως, but it is probably a metrical necessity. Bernays (*ibid.*) rightly remarks: "Nur hat der Phokylides das unentbehrliche Relatum [sc. the genitive after ὄρεξις] weggelassen, wahrscheinlich aus versificatorischer Not". And Rossbroich 51 points to the clumsiness of ὑπερβαίνουσα δὲ μῆνις: "Quid transgreditur ira? Supplere possis et μέτρον et χρόνον, ut sit ira inveterata". Indeed, Ps-Phoc. has composed some awkward verses in trying to render

vv. 63-65　　　　　　　　　　　157

this Stoic casuistry, but of course his ultimate concern was to warn against excesses of anger. His warning has many parallels in Biblical, Jewish and Greek literature. (In the Bible there is no difference between ὀργή and θυμός, see Büchsel, *TWNT* III 168; the terms are very frequently combined, like ὀργὴ τοῦ θυμοῦ, θυμὸς τῆς ὀργῆς). E.g. Men. gnom. pap. II 6 (p. 5 Jaekel) ζήσεις βίον κράτιστον, ἢν θυμοῦ κρατῇς. VIII 8 (p. 13 J.) θυμοῦ κράτησον, κἂν κακὴν ὀργὴν ἔχεις. XIV 16 (p. 19 J.) βλάπτει τὸν ἄνδρα θυμὸς εἰς ὀργὴν πεσών (= *Mon.* 112). Men. et Phil. comp. I 49f. ὁ θυμὸς οὔτε ῥῶσιν οὔτε νοῦν ἔχει· ὀργὴ δὲ δεινὰ δρᾶν ἀναγκάζει βροτούς. *Gnom. Byz.* 252-266 (περὶ θυμοῦ καὶ ὀργῆς). Stob. III 20 (III p. 539-556 W-H περὶ ὀργῆς). Vita Aesopi 109 (rec. W, p. 102 Perry) θυμοῦ κράτει· ἀεὶ γὰρ ὁ θυμὸς αἴτιός ἐστι τοῦ βλάπτειν. Cf. also the several treatises *De (cohibenda) ira,* e.g. of Philodemus, Seneca, Plutarch. Other texts above under v. 57. The connection between anger and madness (v. 63) is also expressed in Men. *Mon.* 503 μαινόμεθα πάντες, ὁπόταν ὀργιζώμεθα. Apollonius *ap.* Stob. III 20, 48 (III p. 549 W-H) τῆς ὀξυθυμίας τὸ ἄνθος μανία. Cic. *Tusc.* IV 77 ira . . . *dubitationem insaniae non habet.* A striking parallel is Epic. fr. 484 (= Sen. *Ep.* XVIII 14) *inmodica ira gignit insaniam.* See further Schmidt, *Ethik* I 260f., Geffcken, *Kynika* 27ff. On Jewish "Abmahnungen von Zorn" see Bousset, *Religion* 424 with n. 4 and the rabbinic texts in Billerbeck I 276-8; IV 475.1072; also Sjöberg-Stählin *TWNT* V 413-6. E.g. *Ep. Arist.* 253; Test. Dan II-IV (this whole treatise is called περὶ θυμοῦ καὶ ψεύδους); Sir. XXVII 30 μῆνις καὶ ὀργή, καὶ ταῦτά ἐστιν βδελύγματα (cf. I 22, X 18, XXIII 16, XXX 24). Prov. XV 1 ὀργὴ ἀπόλλυσιν καὶ φρονίμους. XXVII 4 ἀνελεήμων θυμὸς καὶ ὀξεῖα ὀργή. XXIX 11 ὅλον τὸν θυμὸν αὐτοῦ ἐκφέρει ἄφρων. Eph. IV 31 πικρία καὶ θυμὸς καὶ ὀργὴ καὶ κραυγὴ καὶ βλασφημία. Aboth II 10.

65 ζῆλος τῶν ἀγαθῶν ἐσθλός, φαύλων δ' ὑπέρογκος.
Zeal for good things is noble, for bad things excessive.

There are some textual difficulties in this line. Two mss. (P, V) read ἐσθλῶν ἀγαθός, which was adopted by Diehl (ἐσθλός = ἀγαθός, see Schmidt, *Ethik* I 292 and cf. vv. 66, 92); but Rossbroich 52 rightly points out the antithesis between ἀγαθός and φαῦλος (here probably neuter, not masc.) which is common among philosophers, esp. Stoics (for Stoic influence in this verse see below). The reading ὑπέρογκος is uncertain, only in one ms. (M); other mss. read ἄδηλος, ὑποεργός, ὑποεργής, δέ γε φαῦλος. Bernays 206 n.1 adopts ἄϊδηλος (supported by Bergk, Crusius, Sebestyén 36), which Ps-Phoc. also uses in v. 194, and explains ὑπέρογκος "als ein Glossem zu ἄϊδηλος". Sitzler, *Woch. f. klass. Philol.* 29 (1912), 455 proposes δὲ δυσεργής and Kurfess, *ZNW* 38 (1939), 180 n. 19 ἀπάρεστος. Both suggestions are unproven. ὑπέρογκος (occurring since Plato and Xenophon, so not Homeric as Sebestyén 36 says) may be right. It occurs seven times in the LXX. e.g. Ex. XVIII 22.26; Dan. XI 36; cf. Test. Ass. II 8 (ἡ ὑπέρογκος κακία); Jud. 16 and see Bauer *s.v.* For the usage of this line cf. Lucianus *Ind.* 17 ζῆλος τῶν ἀρίστων. Men. *Mon.* 275 ζήλου τὸν ἐσθλὸν ἄνδρα. Men. gnom. pap. IV 12 (p. 8 Jaekel) μηδὲν ὑπέρογκον ποίει. Probably this verse, like the previous ones, has a Stoic distinction as its background, see *SVF* III 413 (= Stob. II 92, 7) ζῆλος δὲ λύπη ἐπὶ τῷ ἕτερον ἐπιτυγχάνειν ὧν αὐτὸς ἐπιθυμεῖ, αὐτὸν δὲ μή· λέγεσθαι δὲ καὶ ἑτέρως ζῆλον, μακαρισμὸν ἐνδεοῦς καὶ ἔτι ἄλλως μίμησιν ὡς ἂν κρείττονος (cf. 414) and Cic. *Tusc.* IV 17 *aemulatio* (= ζῆλος) *autem dupliciter illa quidem dicitur, ut et in laude et in vitio nomen hoc sit; nam et imitatio virtutis aemulatio dicitur*, etc. Cf. Milobenski, *Der Neid in der griech. Philosophie* 113f.

Also in Did. III 2 (in the Two Ways section) θυμός, ὀργή and ζῆλος are mentioned together, but there simply in a negative sense, whereas Ps-Phoc. treats these words as *voces mediae*, like the Stoics.

66 τόλμα κακῶν ὀλοή, μέγ' ὀφέλλει δ' ἐσθλὰ πονεῦντα.

Daring in bad deeds is ruinous, but greatly strengthens a man who works at good deeds.

Farina 40 takes κακῶν as a gen. subj.: "l'audacia dei malvagi", but cf. Pind. *Nem.* VII 59 τόλμα καλῶν = courage for noble acts. Here again two kinds of τόλμα are distinguished; cf. Evenus fr. 4 πρὸς σοφίαν μὲν ἔχειν τόλμαν μάλα σύμφορόν ἐστιν, χωρὶς δὲ βλαβερὴ καὶ κακότητα φέρει. Sometimes in gnomological literature τόλμα is wholly rejected, e.g. Men *Mon.* 248 ἔστιν τὸ τολμᾶν, ὦ φίλ', ἀνδρὸς οὐ σοφοῦ, and cf. Sir. XIX 3. The emphasis on πόνος as the way to virtue (cf. v. 163b πόνος δ' ἀρετὴν μέγ' ὀφέλλει) is a Cynic trait, e.g. Diog. Laert. VI 2 and Ferguson, *Moral Values* 146-148.

67 σεμνὸς ἔρως ἀρετῆς, ὁ δὲ Κύπριδος αἶσχος ὀφέλλει.

Love of virtue is noble, but love of passion increases shame.

On Κύπρις see *ad* v. 3. Here again Ps-Phoc. renders a Stoic distinction, this time between two kinds of ἔρως; see *SVF* III 716-722, e.g.

717 τὸν δὲ ἐρωτικὸν καὶ διχῇ λέγεσθαι, τὸν μὲν κατὰ τὴν ἀρετὴν ποιὸν σπουδαῖον ὄντα, τὸν δὲ κατὰ τὴν κακίαν ἐν ψόγῳ, ὡς ἂν ἐρωτομανῇ τινα. Mostly, however, the Stoic bipartition is between ἔρως σωματικῆς συνουσίας and ἔρως φιλίας, see Kieuttner, *Andronicus* 25ff., 48f. Sometimes more than two kinds of ἔρως are distinguished(*SVF* III 718ff.). Rossbroich 53 refers to Trag. adesp. fr. 187 δισσὰ πνεύματα πνεῖς, Ἔρως. Cf. also (esp. *ad* 67b) Cic. *Tusc.* IV 68-76 (note the frequent occurrences of *flagitia, turpis*, etc. there and cf. αἶσχος in Ps-Phoc.). In the LXX ἔρως occurs only twice, Prov. VII 18 and XXX 16, both times in a negative sense (= passion).

The word ἀρετή (on which see the large collection of texts in Stob. III 1 (III pp. 3-177 W-H)) figures in the 10th (17th) fragment of the real Phocylides: ἐν δὲ δικαιοσύνῃ συλλήβδην πᾶσ' ἀρετή 'στιν (= Theogn. 147). It was proverbial in antiquity (see Dodds, *The Greeks and the Irrational* 35 n. 34 and the passages mentioned by Young *ad* Theogn. 147; add Plato *Resp.* 407a8). The relation between ἀρετή and σεμνός is traditional in gnomological literature, e.g. Ps-Isocr. *Ad. Dem.* 5 τῆς ἀρετῆς ... ἧς οὐδὲν κτῆμα σεμνότερον οὐδὲ βεβαιότερόν ἐστιν. Men. *Mon.* 69 ἀρετῆς ἁπάσης σεμνὸς ἡγεῖται λόγος (cf. Men. gnom. pap. VIII 1). This line again warns against excesses: sexual excesses bring shame upon a man.

68 ἡδὺς ἄγαν ἄφρων κικλήσκεται ἐν πολιήταις.
A man who is too simple is called foolish among the citizens.

The mss. read ἀγανόφρων, ἀγαννόφρων, ἀγαλεόφρων and ἀγωνόφρων. Bergk's conjecture ἄγαν ἄφρων is convincing. This, however, yielded different translations, e.g. Bernays 206 n.1 "der allzu Milde bekommt bei den Leuten den Namen eines Thoren". Riessler 864 "Der Strudelkopf ist bei den Bürgern hochwillkommen". Kurfess (*ZNW* 1939, 180) "Ein allzu grosser Weichling gilt als unvernünftig unter seinen Mitbürgern". The first problem is: to which word does ἄγαν belong, to ἡδύς or to ἄφρων? (Ludwich, *Spruchbuch* 21, proposed ἀγὼν ἄφρων "mit Bezug auf den erotischen Wettkampf zweier Liebenden", with reference to v. 67 and to *Anth. Pal.* IX 442, 5 where ἀγών has this sense.) The second problem is: what is the meaning of ἡδύς? On this point, too, the translations listed above differ; cf. also Rossbroich 54 "homo nimis voluptarius", Farina 40 "chi troppo indulge ai piaceri" (Easton simply omits the whole line). So some scholars see the ἡδύς as a man who is mad about pleasures (ἡδοναί), and Rossbroich 54 thinks that this line reflects

Cynic criticisms of τρυφή, referring to Crates *Epist*. 19 (p. 211 Hercher) where the ἡδὺς βίος of Odysseus is strongly censured (he rightly rejects Bernays' comparison with Aristot. *EN* IV 11, 1126a4, where the πρᾶος is criticized; Bernays' view of our author's dependence on Aristotle in this line had already been criticized by Freudenthal, *Die Flav. Jos. beigelegte Schrift* ... 163). But LSJ s.v. ἡδύς say that ἡδύς, when used of people, may mean "innocent; simple", not "voluptuary". ἡδύς was often used as an euphemism for "simple-minded, silly, foolish"; see Ps-Timaeus *Lexicon vocum Platonicarum* p. 111 (ed. D. Ruhnken — G. A. Koch, Leipzig 1828) ἡδύς· εὐήθης καὶ ἄφρων (and the editors *ad loc.*). Hence, if Ludwich's conjecture is not accepted, it seems best to take ἡδύς and ἄγαν together as meaning "too simple". But Bernhardy, *Grundrisz* 522, athetized this line as one of the very bad later additions to the poem. Though that cannot be proved, it may be right.

69-69b μέτρῳ ἔδειν, μέτρῳ δὲ πιεῖν καὶ μυθολογεύειν.
πάντων μέτρον ἄριστον, ὑπερβασίαι δ' ἀλεγειναί.

Eat and drink in moderation, be moderate in your talk.
Moderation is the best of all, excesses are grievous.

μυθολογεύειν is Homeric (*Od*. XII 450.453), meaning "to tell". (Dornseiff 41 thinks that this part of v. 69 has an anti-Homeric intention). The warning to be moderate in eating and drinking has numerous parallels both in Greek, Latin and Jewish literature (Rossbroich 54: "sapientia re vera cotidiana"); see the materials in Arbesmann, "Gefrässigkeit", *RAC* IX 345-390. Cf. also Wendland, *Philo und die kynisch-stoische Diatribe* 8-15; Hense, "Eine Menippea des Varro", *Rhein. Mus.* 61 (1906), 1-18; C. A. van Geytenbeek, *Musonius Rufus and Greek Diatribe* 98ff.; Cronbach, *IDB* II 165f. Some references will suffice: Mus. Ruf. XVIIIa (94, 6-8 H.) ἀρχὴν καὶ ὑποβολὴν τοῦ σωφρονεῖν εἶναι τὴν ἐν σίτοις καὶ ποτοῖς ἐγκράτειαν, XVIIIb (105, 7-8 H.) ἐσθίοντα δ' ἐπιμελεῖσθαι κόσμου τε καὶ μέτρου τοῦ προσήκοντος (the whole 18th treatise (p. 94-105 H.) is about exercising moderation at table). Galenus *Protr.* 16, 8 Kaibel πόνοι, σιτία, ποτά, ὕπνοι, ἀφροδισία· πάντα μέτρια. Ps-Pyth. *Carm. aur.* 33f. ἀλλὰ ποτοῦ τε μέτρον καὶ σίτου γυμνασίων τε ποιεῖσθαι. Alciphron *Epist.* III 32 οὐδεὶς τὸ μέτρῳ πίνειν ἔστεργε. Cf. Critias fr. 6, Democr. fr. 235, Heracl. *Epist.* VII p. 70, 4-5 Attridge. Boissonade *Anecd. Gr.* I 132 πῖνε μετὰ τὸ διψῆν, ἔσθιε μετὰ τὸ πεινῆν· ... ὅρος σιτίων ἔστω σοι τὸ μὴ πεινῆν. Sir. XXXI

12-31 (v. 27 ἐὰν πίνῃς ... ἐν μέτρῳ); Apoc. Bar. Gr. IV 16-17; Men. gnom. syr. 10 Schulthess (= 12, 13, 14 Audet). Jos. C. Ap. II 234 τὸ μηδὲν εἰκῇ μηδ' ὡς ἔτυχεν ἕκαστος ἐπιτεθυμηκὼς φαγεῖν ἢ πιεῖν. (For Philo see Wendland, above). Cf. in the N.T. Rom. XIII 13; XVI 18; 1 Cor. V 11; VI 10; Phil. III 19 etc. Herm. *Mand*. XII 2, 1. On the excessive luxury of the meals of the Alexandrian high society see Gussen, *Leven in Alexandrië* 91-100; Schubart, *Ägypten* 159f.

Rossbroich 54 says: "Inter moderationem cibi atque potionis subito loquitur auctor de sermone et irrupit cum vocabulo Homerico μυθολογεύειν. Versum quomodo expleret, cum nesciret, auctor tantas ineptias protulit, cf. 18, 66, 179". But cf. Sen. *Epist*. 47, 4 *intemperantia aut gulae aut linguae*; of course, eating, drinking and speaking are mentioned here as typically human activities. Moreover, μέτῳ λαλεῖν was also common in the gnomological tradition. E.g. Hes. *Op*. 719f. γλώσσης τοι θησαυρὸς ἐν ἀνθρώποισιν ἄριστος φειδωλῆς, πλείστη δὲ χάρις κατὰ μέτρον ἰούσης. Men. *Mon*. 455 λάλει τὰ μέτρια, μὴ λάλει δ' ἃ μή σε δεῖ. Boiss., *Anecd. Gr*. I 12 ἀνὴρ φρόνιμος οὐκ ἔχει πολλοὺς λόγους, τὸ γὰρ λαλεῖν περισσὰ τῆς ἀγροικίας. Sir. XIX 6, XX 7f., XXIII 7f., XXXII 7f.

V. 69b is identical with v. 36 (for commentary see there); it must be said here that it appropriately concludes this section (59-69) by summing up the whole of it (note also the climactic πάντων).

Ψ has here the following insertion: μὴ φθονερός, μὴ ἄπιστος ἔσῃ, μὴ λοίδορος ἴσθι, μηδὲ κακογνώμων, μὴ ψευδαπάτης ἀμέτρητος.

Vv. 70-96 *The Danger of Envy and Other Vices*

70 μὴ φθονέοις ἀγαθῶν ἑτάροις, μὴ μῶμον ἀνάψῃς.
Do not envy others their goods, do not fix reproach upon them.

φθόνος has two semantic aspects, sc. envy of the "have-nots" towards the "haves", and envy of the "haves" towards the "have-nots" (see W. C. van Unnik, ΑΦΘΟΝΩΣ ΜΕΤΑΔΙΔΩΜΙ, *passim*); here the first aspect is meant. Warnings against envy are common in Greek literature, e.g. Chares fr. 1 μὴ φθόνει τοῖς εὐτυχοῦσι, μὴ δοκῇς εἶναι κακός (see Young *ad loc*.), Xen. *Mem*. III 9, 8 μόνους ἔφη φθονεῖν τοὺς ἐπὶ ταῖς τῶν φίλων εὐπραξίαις ἀνιωμένους, Men. *Mon*. 52 αὐτὸς πενωθεὶς τοῖς ἔχουσι μὴ φθόνει, Mus. Ruf. XII (29, 9-11 H.) πρὸ δέ γε τοῦ ζητεῖν, ὅπως ᾧ φθονεῖ τις κακοποιήσῃ τοῦτον, τὸ σκοπεῖν ὅπως μηδὲν φθονήσῃ μηδενί, Ael. Arist. 40, p. 752 Dind. ὁ γὰρ ἔσχατον εἶναι δοκεῖ τῶν ἀνθρωπίνων ἁμαρτημάτων, ὁ φθόνος, further Dio Chrys. *Or*. 77 and 78 (Περὶ φθόνου), Anon. *Simil*. 57-60 (Mullach, *Fr. Phil. Gr*. I 490), Boissonade, *Anecd. Gr*. I 120, Cic. *Tusc*. III 20, IV 56 and the texts collected by Stobaeus in his chapter III 38 περὶ φθόνου (III p. 708-721 W-H). For comments and more materials see Schmidt, *Ethik* I 256ff.; Vögtle, *Kataloge* 200; Dover, *Popular Morality* 204f.; Hirzel, *Themis* 299ff. and esp. Milobenski, *Der Neid in der griechischen Philosophie*. Also in Jewish texts envy is frequently warned against, e.g. Tob. IV 7.16; Sir. XIV 10; Test. Sim. has as its motto περὶ φθόνου, see II 14, III 1ff., IV 5.7, etc.; also Test. Gad VII 1; *Vita Aesopi* 109 (rec. G, p. 69 Perry) τοῖς εὖ πράττουσι μὴ φθόνει, ἀλλὰ σύγχαιρε· ὁ γὰρ φθονῶν ἀγνοῶν ἑαυτὸν βλάπτει. Philo *Migr. Abr*. 183 ἀγαθότης, φθόνον μὲν τὸν μισάρετον καὶ μισόκαλον ἀπεληλακυῖα ἀφ' ἑαυτῆς, *Post. Caini* 140.150, *Agric*. 121, *Fuga* 154, etc. (all deriving from Plato *Phaedrus* 247a, see *ad* v. 71). Here one is also reminded of Philo's remark in *Flacc*. 29 οἱ δ' ὑπὸ φθόνου ῥηγνύμενοι — βάσκανον γὰρ φύσει τὸ Αἰγυπτιακόν — καὶ τὰς ἑτέρων εὐτυχίας ἰδίας ὑπελάμβανον εἶναι κακοπραγίας. Cf. *Leg. ad Gaium* 48. Men gnom. syr. 84 "Neid [חסמא = φθόνος] bewirkt Böses und Zank" (tr. Schulthess). See further Bousset, *Religion* 424 n. 5. Rabbinic material on envy (mostly expressed by the term עין רעה, "evil eye") is given by Billerbeck I 833ff. For the N.T. see Rom. I 29, Gal. V 21, Phil. I 15, 1 Tim. VI 4, Tit. III 3, 1 Pet. II 1.

μὴ μῶμον ἀνάψῃς: Bernays 207 n. 1 (following the corrector of ms. M) proposes ἀνάψῃ: "Das gangbare Activum ἀνάψῃς könnte nur heissen 'Hänge anderen keinen Schandfleck an', würde also eine neue Vorschrift ergeben und die Verbindung mit dem folgenden stören, wo wiederum nur vom Neide die Rede ist". He translates: "... auf dass du dir nicht selbst einen Schandfleck anhängest". Bergk (*ad loc*.) rejects this proposal: "neque enim invidi deterreri solent a professione sua metu ne ipsi aliorum sibi invidiam et odium concilient, sed fortiter alios vellicant: φθόνος enim et μῶμος germani sunt fratres, arctissima necessitudine coniuncti". This is right (cf. Kurfess, *ZNW* 1939, 171); moreover, μῶμον ἀνάψαι is a Homeric expression, and Homer uses it in the active, *Od*. II 86, which gives a good sense also here: do not defame your neighbour because of his goods, sc. out of envy (v. 70a). The mss. group Ψ omits vv. 70-75.

71 ἄφθονοι Οὐρανίδαι καὶ ἐν ἀλλήλοις τελέθουσιν.
The heavenly ones also are without envy toward each other.

This and the following verses give the motivation for the injunction of v. 70. Οὐρανίδαι: usually the gods (originally the sons of Uranus), just like μάκαρες in v. 75, here evidently the heavenly bodies (see v. 72). This verse has evoked much discussion (see Introd., ch. I). E.g. Dornseiff, *Echtheitsfragen* 41, says that vv. 71-5 clearly prove that the author cannot have been a Jew, since a Jew would never have called sun, moon, rivers etc. Οὐρανίδαι and μάκαρες. Sitzler, *Woch. f. klass. Philol.* 29 (1912) 451 asserts that these verses cannot have been part of the original poem because Ψ omits them. But the omission by Ψ does not prove anything (only that the interpolator was not happy with these lines). Moreover, the terms used do not imply deification of the heavenly bodies. That the heavenly bodies are gods is a common opinion in later antiquity (since Plato *Tim.* 40aff.), especially among the Stoics, e.g. *Doxogr. Gr.* 547, 9-13; see Pohlenz, *Stoa* I 82f., II 48. Since Judaism has always consistently denied the divinity of the stars, for a Jew only the idea that stars are living beings was acceptable. The ascription of personality to the parts of nature was not inconsistent with Jewish monotheism (Nock, *Essays* II 912). Thus Philo *Spec. leg.* I 13ff. explicitly says that stars are living beings, but not θεοί. (More texts of Philo against the deification of the stars in Wendland, *Therapeuten* 707 n.1). But the same Philo *Opif.* 27 says that heaven is θεῶν (!) ἐμφανῶν τε καὶ αἰσθητῶν ... οἶκος (cf. *Gig.* 8, *LA* III 104). So far a Jew could go in borrowing pagan terminology. This was facilitated by the fact that in Judaism the stars were often considered to be angels, which are living, heavenly beings (see Bousset, *Religion* 322f.). An "unorthodox", syncretistic Jew such as Artapanus went as far as attributing to Abraham the invention of astrology (texts in Denis, *Fragm.* 186ff.). And actually astrology was practised by some Jews (Hengel, *Judentum und Hellenismus* 432ff. and Wächter in *Kairos* 11 (1969), 181ff.). In view of all this, it is not too strange that Ps-Phoc. uses the terms Οὐρανίδαι and μάκαρες for the heavenly bodies (see Hengel in *Entretiens* XVIII 297).

That the heavenly bodies are here said to be ἄφθονοι may have its origin in the famous passage in Plato's *Phaedrus* 247a where it is said that φθόνος ἔξω θείου χοροῦ ἵσταται (cf. *Tim.* 29c; on the importance of these *dicta probantia* in later antiquity see e.g. W. C van Unnik, *De ἀφθονία van God* 46f.). This protest against the notion of φθόνος θεῶν is here extended to the heavenly bodies (and nature as a whole, vv. 72-74; see Hirzel, *Themis* 305 n. 5). See already Eur. *Phoen.* 543-545 νυκτὸς τ' ἀφεγγὲς βλέφαρον ἡλίου τε φῶς ἴσον βαδίζει τὸν ἐνιαύσιον κύκλον, κοὐδέτερον αὐτῶν φθόνον ἔχει νικώμενον. On the notion of φθόνος θεῶν see G. J. D. Aalders, *De oud-Griekse voorstelling van de afgunst der godheid* (1975) and the literature mentioned *ibid.* 3 n. 1.

72-74 οὐ φθονέει μήνη πολὺ κρείσσοσιν ἡλίου αὐγαῖς,
οὐ χθὼν οὐρανίοισ' ὑψώμασι νέρθεν ἐοῦσα,
οὐ ποταμοὶ πελάγεσσιν. ἀεὶ δ' ὁμόνοιαν ἔχουσιν.

The moon envies not the sun his much stronger beams,
nor the earth the heavenly heights though it is below,
nor the rivers the seas. They are always in concord.

Farina 40 says that vv. 72-4 are probably an interpolation since μάκαρες in v. 75 suits only the heavenly bodies, not the earth, rivers and seas. But in Greek literature the elements are often regarded as divine; see Lumpe, "Elementum", *RAC* IV 1081-3; cf. Hom. *Il.* III 277ff.; Hes. *Theog.* 105ff. (quoted under v. 75); Plato *Tim.* 40c (the earth as πρώτη καὶ πρεσβυτάτη θεῶν); *Men. et Phil. comp.* II 68f.; Theophilus *Ad Autol.* II 35; Sap. Sal. XIII 2. Of course, this view is not shared by Ps-Phoc., but just as in 1 Clem. XX (see below) the originally pantheistic (Stoic) thought is "zur blossen poetischen Metapher ... abgeschwächt" (Jaeger, "Echo eines unerkannten Tragikerfragments in Clemens' Brief an die Korinther", *Rhein. Mus.* 102 (1959), 340), so here our author adopts more or less naïvely this usage without worrying about its original meaning; though it must be said that the Jews often imagined the elements of nature as if they were ensouled by angels (Bousset, *Religion* 323f.). A striking parallel to our text is 1 Clem. XX, where the earth, the sea and the heavenly bodies are mentioned as examples of concord, e.g. XX 3 ἡλιός τε καὶ σελήνη, ἀστέρων τε χοροὶ κατὰ τὴν διαταγὴν αὐτοῦ ἐν ὁμονοίᾳ (!) δίχα πάσης παρεκβάσεως ἐξελίσσουσι τοὺς ἐπιτεταγμένους αὐτοῖς ὁρισμούς (see the comments of Sanders, *L' hellénisme de saint Clément de Rome* 109-142). Dio Chrys. XXXVI 55, too, speaks about the ὁμόνοια of sun, moon and stars (cf. Eur. *Phoen.* 543ff. quoted above under v. 71). Remarkably, Ginzberg, *Legends* I 23ff. (with notes V 34ff.) mentions a (late) Jewish story about the moon envying the sun. Rossbroich 57 thinks that Posidonius is the source of these verses, referring to

Cic. *Nat. deor.* II 56.97.119; III 28, but these texts speak only about the harmonious movements of heaven, which was a commonplace in later antiquity (see the rich materials collected by Pease *ad loc.*).

ὕψωμα is a late word (since Philo), often an astronomical *term. techn.* for the space above the horizon (see e.g. Lietzmann's commentary on Rom. VIII 39 and Bauer *s.v.*). On ὁμόνοια (since Thuc.) see H. Kramer, *Quid valeat ὁμόνοια in litteris Graecis*, diss. Göttingen 1914, and W. C. van Unnik, *Studies over 1 Clemens, passim*; also J. Ferguson, *Moral Values in the Ancient World* 118-132. Cf. e.g. the long passage on ὁμόνοια in Arist. *EN* IX 6, 1167a22ff. (further texts in the commentary on v. 219, and cf. *ad* 30). Originally a political term, it was transferred to the kosmos regarded as a *polis*.

75 εἰ γὰρ ἔρις μακάρεσσιν ἔην, οὐκ ἂν πόλος ἔστη.
For if there were strife among the blessed ones, heaven would not stand firm.

The word μάκαρες (mostly = the gods, in Greek literature; see C. de Heer, MAKAP, *passim*) in v. 75 has evoked the same comments as Οὐρανίδαι in v. 71, e.g. Kroll, *PW* XX 1, 508 "undenkbar im Munde eines Juden". But, as has been said *ad* v. 71, it does not mean a deification of the heavenly bodies (these are meant by μάκαρες, probably also the earth, rivers and seas, since in Hes. *Theog.* 105ff. these, too, belong to the μακάρων γένος; cf. the use of μάκαρες for the post-diluvian generation in *Or. Sib.* I 306, cf. 303). πόλος = οὐρανός, cf. Eur. fr. 839, 11; 911, 3; Timoth. fr. 2 and 13; *Or. Sib.* I 12.240, II 200.207, III 83, VIII 339, etc., also *Etym. Magn. s.v.* πόλοι quoted by Pease *ad* Cic. *Nat. deor.* II 105; cf. *polus* in Hor. *Carm.* I 28, 6; LSJ *s.v.* I 3. ἔρις is often found in connection with φθόνος (70ff.), e.g. Hes. *Op.* 24-26; in the N.T. Rom. I 29, Phil. I 15, 1 Tim. VI 4 (Spicq *ad loc.*: "Le couple φθόνος — ἔρις est constant dans la langue rhétorique et politique pour stig-. matiser les méfaits de l' envie haineuse"). Cf. also Apoc. Bar. Gr. XIII 4 φθόνοι . . . ἔρεις. *ARN* rec. A XXVIII 3: jealousy and strife. On ἔρις see further below *ad* v. 78.

76 σωφροσύνην ἀσκεῖν, αἰσχρῶν δ' ἔργων ἀπέχεσθαι.
Practise self-restraint, and abstain from shameful deeds.

The verse-order in ms. P (75, 78, 79, 80, 76, 77, 81) is caused by the presence of ἔρις in v. 75 and v. 78. σωφροσύνην ἀσκεῖν (this formula also in the pagan Eusebius *ap*. Stob. IV 23, 41) is a typically Greek virtue; σωφροσύνη is very rare in the LXX, except in the very hellenised 4 Macc., but it is a central concept in ancient Greek ethics, see esp. North, *Sophrosyne*; *Self-Knowledge and Self-Restraint in Greek Literature*, 1966; also Luck, *TWNT* VII 1094-1101; Spicq, *Ep. Past.* I 376. 409ff. Some definitions: Plato *Resp.* 430e 6-7 σωφροσύνη ἐστὶ καὶ ἡδονῶν τινων καὶ ἐπιθυμιῶν ἐγκράτεια (cf. Diog. Laert. III 91). Arist. *Ars Rhet.* I 9, 1366b13-14 σωφροσύνη δὲ ἀρετὴ δι' ἣν πρὸς τὰς ἡδονὰς τὰς τοῦ σώματος οὕτως ἔχουσιν ὡς ὁ νόμος κελεύει, ἀκολασία δὲ τοὐναντίον. Stoic definitions in *SVF* III 262ff., e.g. σωφροσύνην δ' εἶναι ἐπιστήμην αἱρετῶν καὶ φευκτῶν καὶ οὐδετέρων. Cf. 4 Macc. I 31 σωφροσύνη δὴ τοίνυν ἐστὶν ἐπικράτεια τῶν ἐπιθυμιῶν. A number of relevant texts may be found in Stob. III 5 (III p. 255-280 W.H.). In later Jewish Hellenistic literature σωφροσύνη occurs more frequently than in the LXX; see the passages from Philo and Jos. in *TWNT* VII 1098, e.g. Jos. *C. Ap.* II 195; and Test. Jos. IV 2; IX 2; X 2, 3 (this *Test.* has a subtitle περὶ σωφροσύνης). For the N.T. (esp. the Pastorals) see Bauer *s.v.*. On ἀσκεῖν (and other athletic metaphors in ethical contexts) see Spicq, *Ep. Past.* I 504f. (lit.!); e.g. Herod. I 96 δικαιοσύνην ἀσκεῖν, Plato *Resp.* 407a ἀρετὴν ἀσκεῖν. See also LSJ *s.v.* II 2. In view of the common meaning of σωφροσύνη the αἰσχρὰ ἔργα possibly are sexual sins, cf. αἰσχρόν in *Carm. Aur.* 11; but it may have a more general meaning, see Bauer *s.v.*. The term ἀπέχεσθαι (also in 6, 31, 35, 145, 149) is very frequent in Jewish and Christian paraenesis (see above *ad* 6), according to Seeberg (*Das Evangelium Christi* 125 n. 1) esp. in "Traditionsstoff". It corresponds to הרחק in the *Derek Erez* treatises, see Klein, *Katechismus* 69. As to its content v. 76 is very similar to v. 145 ἐγκρατὲς ἦτορ ἔχειν, καὶ λωβητῶν δ' ἀπέχεσθαι.

77 μὴ μιμοῦ κακότητα, Δίκη δ' ἀπόλειψον ἄμυναν.

Do not imitate evil, but leave vengeance to justice.

μὴ μιμοῦ κακότητα: 3 John 11 μὴ μιμοῦ τὸ κακόν (cf. 1 Thess. V 15 ὁρᾶτε μή τις κακὸν ἀντὶ κακοῦ τινι ἀποδῷ, Rom. XII 17; μιμεῖσθαι in this v. is almost equivalent to ἀποδιδόναι). On Δίκη (as a goddess) see Hirzel, *Themis* 138ff.; here one may print δίκη, but a kind of personification of δίκη is also found in Philo *Spec. leg.* IV 201 τὴν πάρεδρον δίκην τοῦ πάντων ἡγεμόνος (possibly inspired by Hes. *Op.* 259 or Plato *Leg.* 716a τῷ δὲ (sc. θεῷ) ἀεὶ συνέπεται δίκη τῶν ἀπολειπομένων τοῦ θείου νόμου τιμωρός), *Conf. ling.* 118 ἡ ὀπαδὸς τοῦ θεοῦ δίκη τίσεται, Omn. Prob. 89; Ps.-Diphilus ap. Clem. Alex. Strom. V 121, 1 (Denis, Fragm. p. 168, 21), and Acts XXVIII 4. The form ἀπόλειψον is important, since it is a clear indication of the late origin of this poem: it should have been ἀπόλιπε according to the grammar of classical Greek. All instances of a sigmatic aorist of λείπω are late; the earliest example is possibly λείψας in Aristoph. fr. 965 (see Sicking, Annotationes ad Antiatticam 121 and above Introd. ch. 2, p. 56). For other instances (all Hellenistic) see LSJ s.v. λείπω and P.C. van der Horst, Les vers d'or pythagoriciens 72 (on Carm. Aur. 70 ἀπολείψας, cf. Themist. Or. 25, 310d ἀπολείψειε). Keydell, Jahresbericht 272 (1941) 27: "Eine Form wie der sigmatische Aorist ἀπόλειψον ist durchaus ein schwerwiegendes Zeugnis für späte Abfassung und darf nicht beiseite geschoben werden" (here Keydell reacts to Dornseiff, Echtheitsfragen 51, who rejects Goram's (p. 111) remarks on ἀπόλειψον by saying "dieses Verbum gebraucht aber schon Homer" (!), a fine instance of Dornseiff's sloppiness). Ludwich, Quaest. 28 reads (with 2 mss.) ἀπάλειψον, "lösche durch Gerechtigkeit die Rache", unnecessarily. Cf. Test. Gad VI 7 δὸς τῷ θεῷ τὴν ἐκδίκησιν, Rom. XII 19 (cf. Deut. XXXII 35). It is notable that, whereas the Biblical and Jewish texts speak of leaving vengeance to God, Ps. Phoc. speaks of leaving it to Dike.

78 Πειθὼ μὲν γὰρ ὄνειαρ, Ἔρις δ' ἔριν ἀντιφυτεύει.
   For persuasiveness is a boon, but strife begets only strife.

Again one may print πειθώ and ἔρις without capitals, as is done by Geffcken in his edition of Or. Sib. (cf. also Paroem. Gr. II 753, where v. 78b is quoted anonymously). Four important mss. (B, M, P, V) have ὄφελος instead of ὄνειαρ (both words have the same meaning, see Boisonnade, Anecd. Gr. I 446 and above ad v. 60). Since this is metrically unsuitable, Bergk proposes ὀφέλλει, but ὄνειαρ is to be preferred as lectio difficilior. ἀντιφυτεύω (litt. to plant in turn) occurs only once elsewhere, Greg. Nyss. Hex. 2 (MG 44, 64B). For the content of this verse cf. Plato Leg. 722b5-6 ἐξὸν δυοῖν χρῆσθαι πρὸς τὰς νομοθεσίας, πειθοῖ καὶ βίᾳ. (Cf. Boiss., Anecd. I 10). Epict. Sent. 25 (35) ἐρίζειν καὶ φιλονεικεῖν πάντῃ μὲν ἀνοίκειον, μάλιστα δὲ ἐν ταῖς παρὰ πότον ὁμιλίαις ἀπρεπές. . . . ἔνθα δ' ἂν μὴ παρῇ πειθοῦς τέλος, εἰκῇ σε παρέχεις διατείνεσθαι. On the importance of πειθώ see esp. Eur. Hec. 814-820 (it is not found in LXX). Daube, N.T. and Rabbinic Judaism 348, sees the link between vv. 77 and 78 in that Ps-Phoc. "recommends sober persuasion of the wicked". ἔρις is warned of in Sir. XXVIII 11 ἔρις κατασπευδομένη ἐκκαίει πῦρ, XL 5.9, and often in the N.T., see Bauer *s.v.* (Cf. Did. III 2 μὴ γίνου ... ἐριστικός). In *Apoc. Bar. Gr.* VIII 5 and XIII 4 ἔρις is mentioned in catalogues of sins, but see earlier examples in Greek lit. in LSJ *s.v.* II. In *Test. Sal.* VIII 3.6.8 Ἔρις is an evil spirit (this may justify the capital letter in our verse), a personification as old as Homer, cf. *Il.* XI 3; XVIII 535.

79 μὴ πίστευε τάχιστα, πρὶν ἀτρεκέως πέρας ὄψει.

Trust not too quickly, before you shall see exactly the end.

πιστεύειν = to trust, see the quotation from Lührmann above *ad* v. 13. This is a common warning in gnomic literature, e.g. Boissonade, *Anecd. Gr.* I 58 μὴ τάχιστα πᾶσι πίστευε, *ibid.* 139 μὴ πᾶσιν πίστευε (= Thales, see Snell, *Leben und Meinungen* 100); Epich. fr. 13; Men. *Mon.* 460 μὴ πάντα πειρῶ πᾶσι πιστεύειν ἀεί (note the allitteration, possibly also intended by Ps. Phoc., πίστευε... πρίν... πέρας). Sir. VI 7 εἰ κτᾶσαι φίλον, ἐν πειρασμῷ κτῆσαι αὐτὸν καὶ μὴ ταχὺ ἐμπιστεύσῃς αὐτῷ, XIX 4 ὁ ταχὺ ἐμπιστεύων κοῦφος καρδίᾳ (cf. v. 15), cf. Micah VII 5. Polyc. *Phil.* VI 1 μὴ ταχέως πιστεύοντες κτλ. On ἀτρεκέως see Luther, *Wahrheit* 43ff.. Probably v. 79b means "before you know exactly what the other one is up to"; Farina 40 rightly: πέρας = le intenzioni. Cf. Theogn. 125f. οὐδὲ γὰρ εἰδείης ἀνδρὸς νόον οὐδὲ γυναικός, πρὶν πειρηθείης ὥσπερ ὑποζυγίου. Bernhardy, *Grundriss* 523, says πρίν + future indicative is "sprachlich anstössig", but see K-G II 459 n. 8.

V. 79 is the last line of the interpolation in *Or. Sib.* II.

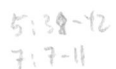

80 νικᾶν εὖ ἔρδοντας ἐπὶ πλεόνεσσι καθήκει.

It is proper to surpass your benefactors with still more benefactions.

εὖ ἔρδειν: Hom. *Il.* V 650; Theogn. 105, 368, 955. νικᾶν ἐπί + dat. is unusual (cf. Rom. XII 21 νικᾶν ἐν + dat.); Bergk's conj. ἔτι may be right; though it does not mean "on more numerous occasions" as Young thought (letter of 12-5-1973), rather: "with/by more benefactions than you have got yourself", cf. LSJ *s.v.* B III 2. On καθήκει Crouch, *Origin* 76, observes: "the author indicates familiarity with the Stoic formulation of duties"; on these καθήκοντα see e.g. Pohlenz, *Stoa* I 129-131 with the notes in II 73f. and Vögtle, *Kataloge* 215-217. But καθήκει need not be Stoic terminology, because it was the usual expression for "it is proper, it is fitting"; see Schlier in *TWNT* III 441. Crouch, *ibid*. 86, speaks about the author's "awareness of the Hellenistic duty toward benefactors", and Rossbroich 59 rightly refers to Schmidt's (*Ethik* II 370) remarks on "jene krankhafte Sucht der Griechen . . . selbst von den Freunden keine Wohltaten anzunehmen, ohne sie zu erwidern und womöglich zu überbieten". On this "utilitaristische Gegenseitigkeitsprinzip" (χάρις ἀντὶ χάριτος) see esp. Bolkestein, *Wohltätigkeit* 107, 143ff., 156ff. (158 "das Prinzip der Gegenseitigkeit (hat) eine der Grundlagen des sozialen Verkehrs der Griechen gebildet"; many texts 158ff.). In *Rhet. ad Alex*. I, 1421b37ff. Ps-Aristotle calls the principle of τοῖς εὐεργέταις χάριν ἀποδιδόναι one of the ἄγραφοι νόμοι, just like γονέας τιμᾶν. Cf. Xen. *Mem*. IV 4, 24 τοὺς εὖ ποιοῦντες ἀντευεργετεῖν οὐ πανταχοῦ νόμιμόν ἐστι; Democr.fr. 92 χάριτας δέχεσθαι χρεὼν προσκοπευόμενον κρέσσονας αὐτῶν ἀμοιβὰς ἀποδοῦναι. [Ael. Arist.] 54, p. 682 D. ὁ μὲν παρ' ὧν εὖ ἐπεπόνθει, τούτους οὐκ ἐθέλων τοῖς ἴσοις ἀμείψασθαι ἀγνωμοσύνης ἅμα καὶ ἀδικίας ἔγκλημα φέρεται. *Gnom. hom*. 179b (ed. Elter) χάριν ὀφείλειν καὶ βαρὺ φέρειν φορτίον ταὐτόν ἐστιν. In this connection, the verb νικᾶν occurs several times, just as here in Ps-Phoc., Xen. *Mem*. II 6, 35 ἔγνωκας ἀνδρὸς ἀρετὴν εἶναι νικᾶν τοὺς μὲν φίλους εὖ ποιοῦντα, *Cyrop*. V 1, 29 δὸς τοὺς ἐμὲ τιμῶντας νικῆσαί με εὖ ποιοῦντα (cf. *Ages*. IX 7 νικῴη . . . εὐεργετῶν). Ael. Arist. 40, p. 701 D. πεφύκαμεν . . . ταῖς εὐεργεσίαις πάντας ἀνθρώπους νικᾶν (cf. 13, p. 19 D. = I 88 B.; Demosth. XX 141). Cf. Ps-Isocr. *Ad Demon*. 26 αἰσχρὸν εἶναι νόμιζε . . . τῶν φίλων ἡττᾶσθαι ταῖς εὐεργεσίαις. Hierocles p. 59, 25 von Arnim(= Stob. IV 27, 20) νίκησον αὐτοῦ τὴν ἀγριότητα ταῖς εὐποιίαις. Cf. Hes. *Op*. 349f., and for νικᾶν also Rom. XII 21. That this χάρις ἀντὶ χάριτος principle had penetrated into Judaism is proved not only by Ps-Phoc. 80, but also by some texts in Josephus, on which see W. C. van Unnik in *Josephus-Studien* (*Festschrift O. Michel*) 364f. Cf. also S. C. Mott, "The Power of Giving and Receiving: Reciprocity in Hellenistic Benevolence", *Current Issues in Biblical and Patristic Interpretation* (*Festschrift M. C. Tenney*), Grand Rapids 1975, 60-72. Its consequences are illustrated by v. 152 μὴ κακὸν εὖ ἔρξῃς· σπείρειν ἴσον ἔστ' ἐνὶ πόντῳ (see the commentary there).

81-82 καλὸν ξεινίζειν ταχέως λιταῖσι τραπέζαις
ἢ πλείσταις δολίαισι βραδυνούσαις παρὰ καιρόν.

It is better to present guests with a simple meal quickly
than with a large number of elaborated courses drawn out beyond
the appropriate time (?).

καλὸν ... ἤ: better than, see K-G II 203; Blass-Debr. 245, 3; Turner, *Syntax* 31f.; Bauer *s.v.* ἤ 2b. In the LXX and N.T., this construction is a Semitism (since the Hebrew has no comparative), but there are classical parallels, e.g. Herod. IX 26 δίκαιόν ἐστι ... ἤπερ ..., Polyaenus VIII 49 καλὸν ἀποθανεῖν ἢ ζῆν, Men. *Mon.* 417 καλὸν δὲ νήφειν ἢ τὰ πολλὰ κραιπαλᾶν, *Gnom. Vat.* 39 λυσιτελεῖ δι' ἐμὲ τὸ ἀργύριον ἀπολέσθαι ἢ ἐμὲ δι' αὐτό, cf. Andocides I 125, Soph. *Aiax* 966 (?), Men. *Mon.* 306 (*v.l.*), Clitarchus *Sent.* 81 (Chadwick). In the LXX e.g. Sir XX 2 καλὸν ἐλέγξαι ἢ θυμοῦσθαι, Tob. XII 8, etc.; cf. Ep. Arist. 322 and N.T. instances in Snyder, *NTS* 23 (1976-7) 117ff.

The meaning of δολίαισι (sc. τραπέζαις) is difficult. This is the reading of all mss. Young suggests (in *app. crit.*) that δόλιος = σεσοφισμένος, but δόλιος normally means "crafty, deceitful, treacherous" and not "sophisticated, refined". Only the latter meaning would be meaningful here. Brunck's conjecture (*GPG* 159) θαλίαισι, which has won wide acceptance (Crusius, Farina and others), may therefore be right: better a quick and simple meal than extensive festivity. But see the striking opposition of λιτότης and *fraus* in Cic. *Ep. ad Fam.* VII 26, 2 *lex sumptuaria, quae videtur λιτότητα attulisse, ea mihi fraudi fuit*, and note esp. Plato's condemnation of ὀψοποιική as treacherous in *Gorg.* 464c-465a (see ἐξαπατᾷ and προσποιεῖται in 464d). Perhaps δόλιος means "looking better than it is". βραδυνούσαις παρὰ καιρόν (note παρὰ καιρόν in Phoc. fr. 6, quoted *ad* v. 83): Easton "coming too late for the hungry", Dornseiff 41 "nach langer Frist zur Unzeit geboten"; or perhaps something like "dragging on beyond due measure of time", though βραδύνειν = loiter, delay, and the opposition to ταχέως seems to favour Dornseiff's translation. Note the chiasm ταχέως — βραδυνούσαις; λιταῖσι — πλείσταις δολίαισι. On the ideal of λιτότης cf. still *Gnom. Byz.* 212, 31 ἔθιζε σεαυτὸν τῇ λιτῇ διαίτῃ ἵνα τῆς πολυτελοῦς μηδέποτε προσδεηθῇς. Perhaps this line is also inspired by Prov. XV 17 κρείσσων ξενισμὸς λαχάνων πρὸς φιλίαν καὶ χάριν ἢ παράθεσις μόσχων μετὰ ἔχθρας, though, admittedly, the element of quickness is missing here.

83 μηδέποτε χρήστης πικρὸς γένῃ ἀνδρὶ πένητι.
Never be a relentless creditor to a poor man.

The word χρήστης is used also by the real Phocylides fr. 6 καὶ τόδε Φωκυλίδεω· χρήστης κακοῦ ἔμμεναι ἀνδρός | φεύγειν, μή σέ γ' ἀνιήσῃ παρὰ καιρὸν ἀπαιτέων. But in Phoc. χρήστης means "debtor", whereas in Ps-Phoc. it means "creditor, usurer". On this question there is a scholion on Aristoph. *Nub.* 240 which runs: Φωκυλίδης ἐν μὲν τοῖς αὐτοῦ ποιήμασι κατὰ τὴν συνήθειαν τοὺς χρεωφειλέτας χρήστας καλεῖ λέγων οὕτως· (cit. Phoc. fr. 6). ἐν ἐκείνῳ μέντοι ἀντὶ τοῦ δανειστὴς λαμβάνεται· (cit. Ps-Phoc. 83). Commenting on ἐν ἐκείνῳ μέντοι Bernays 234 n. 2 says: "Diese Worte scheinen aus einer Nachweisung der Unechtheit unseres Phokylides zu stammen, denn nur so lässt sich die Wendung ἐν ἐκείνῳ μέντοι erklären; sie müssen aus einer Zeit stammen, da der echte Phokylides noch erhalten war, also aus keiner sehr späten". But W. J. W. Koster writes (in a letter of 14.10.1972) that only the first part of the scholion is a *scholion vetus*, whereas the second part (ἐν ἐκείνῳ μέντοι κτλ.) is not in any ms. and is found for the first time in Musurus' compilation of Aristophanes-scholia in the *editio Aldina* of 1498. So it was added by Musurus. (The words ἐν μὲν τοῖς αὐτοῦ ποιήμασιν, too, were added by him). It is, moreover, highly questionable whether he meant to say that he could distinguish the real Phoc. from Ps-Phoc. (thus also Bernhardy, *Grundriss* 522). See Introd., p. 39 n. 151. See further Suidas *s.v.* χρῆσται and Tzetzes on Aristoph. *Nub.* 434.

The O.T. forbids the asking of interest from Israelites, Ex. XXII 24 ἐὰν δὲ ἀργύριον ἐκδανείσῃς τῷ ἀδελφῷ τῷ πενιχρῷ παρὰ σοί, οὐκ ἔσῃ αὐτὸν κατεπείγων, οὐκ ἐπιθήσεις αὐτῷ τόκον, cf. Lev. XXV 36, Deut. XXIII 20 (see H. van Oyen, *Ethik des A.T.* 129). Also Philo forbids it, *Spec. leg.* IV 74ff. (see Heinemann, *Philons Bildung* 428f.). On the Talmudic view see Tcherikover, *CPJ* I (Proleg.) 35 n. 92; cf. Schechter, *Aspects* 230ff.; Bacher, *Agada der Tann.* I² 278f. and H. Gamoran, "Talmudic Usury Laws and Business Loans", *JSJ* 7 (1976), 129-142. Nevertheless in Egypt the Jews lent money to one another at the regular rate of interest of 24 per cent, see *CPJ* I nos. 20.24 (Sevenster, *Pagan Anti-Semitism* 77). Many Jews in the diaspora were bankers, see Bousset, *Religion* 433 (and see Taubenschlag, *Law* 341ff., 676ff. on loans and banking in Hellenistic Egypt). In view of these facts, and of the very high rate of interest (varying from 12 to 50 per cent, see Schubart, *Ägypten* 76 and Kroll, *Kultur* 93f.), this admonition was very much to the point (Kroll *ibid*. emphasizes the arbitrariness among bankers as to the height of interest). Cf. the similar warnings in *Derek Erez Rabbah* II 27 and Herm. *Mand.* VIII 10 χρεώστας μὴ θλίβειν. On πικρός cf. Men. gnom. syr. 36 (Schulthess), where מרירא (= πικρός) is used of a creditor. This word is emphasized in Ps-Phoc. It is also used of severe judges (Polyb. V 41, 3), of sycophants (Dem. XXV 45), of tyrants (Philo *Omn. prob.* 106), etc.; see the texts collected by Michaelis, *TWNT* VI 122f. and LSJ *s.v.*

84-85 μηδέ τις ὄρνιθας καλιῆς ἅμα πάντας ἑλέσθω.
μητέρα δ' ἐκπρολίποις, ἵν' ἔχῃς πάλι τῆσδε νεοσσούς.

One should not take all the birds from a nest at the same time.
But leave the mother-bird behind, in order to get young from her again.

In spite of Rossbroich 61 and Farina 41, this precept is thoroughly Jewish (Scaliger, *Animadv.* 89 "Quis ullus Graecorum hoc sanxit?"). Porphyry *Abstin.* IV 14 mentions it as a Mosaic commandment. Its source is Deut. XXII 6f. ἐὰν δὲ συναντήσῃς νοσσιᾷ ὀρνέων πρὸ προσώπου σου ἐν τῇ ὁδῷ ἢ ἐπὶ παντὶ δένδρει ἢ ἐπὶ τῆς γῆς, νεοσσοῖς ἢ ᾠοῖς, καὶ ἡ μήτηρ θάλπῃ ἐπὶ τῶν νεοσσῶν ἢ ἐπὶ τῶν ᾠῶν, οὐ λήμψῃ τὴν μητέρα μετὰ τῶν τέκνων. ἀποστολῇ ἀποστελεῖς τὴν μητέρα, τὰ δὲ παιδία λήμψῃ σεαυτῷ, ἵνα εὖ σοι γένηται καὶ πολυήμερος ἔσῃ. Wendland, *Jahrb. f. class. Phil.* Suppl. XXII (1896), 710, noticed that the same precept is also found in Philo *Hyp.*, *ap.* Eus. *PE* VIII 7,9 (p. 431, 8f. Mr.) μὴ νεοττιάν φησι κατοικίδιον ἐρημοῦν, μὴ ζῴων ἱκεσίαν οἷα ἔσθ' ὅτε προσφευγόντων ἀναιρεῖν and in Jos. *C. Ap.* II 213 ἃ δ' ὥσπερ ἱκετεύοντα προσφεύγει ταῖς οἰκίαις ἀπεῖπεν ἀνελεῖν. οὐδὲ νεοττοῖς τοὺς γονέας αὐτῶν ἐπέτρεψε συνεξαιρεῖν. Significantly, both authors add the (non O.T.) injunction that animals which appeal for help or take refuge in homes should be treated as suppliants. This indicates that both are dependent on a common source, from which Ps-Phoc., too, probably drew his material. See Crouch, *Origin* 86: "That all three authors, drawing material directly from the O.T. and working independently of one another, would include this relatively insignificant commandment in a selective survey of 'Jewish' laws is highly improbable. More probable is the suggestion that they drew from a common source" (though Crouch too easily overlooks the fact that Ps-Phoc. does not have the prohibition to kill suppliant animals). In rabbinic writings, this commandment is often quoted as the least weighty of all commandments, see the references in Crouch, *Origin* 86 n. 7. Yet it is viewed as important, e.g. *Hullin* XII 1 "The law to let the dam go from the nest is binding both in the land of Israel and outside the Land" (the whole chapter *Hullin* XII 1-5 is casuistry on Deut. XXII 6f.). On the particularly Jewish character of this verse see also Bernays 234f. (who unnecessarily emends the text) and Hadas, *Hellenistic Culture* 104. On humanity towards animals as a specific trait of the Jewish law see Philo *Virt*. 125-130.

86 μηδέποτε κρίνειν ἀδαήμονας ἄνδρας ἐάσῃς.

Never allow ignorant men to sit in judgment.

This verse may go back to Ex. XVIII 21f. (Jethro's advice) σκέψαι ἀπὸ παντὸς τοῦ λαοῦ ἄνδρας δυνατοὺς θεοσεβεῖς, . . .καὶ κρινοῦσιν τὸν λαόν or Deut. I 13 δότε ἑαυτοῖς ἄνδρας σοφοὺς καὶ ἐπιστήμονας καὶ συνετούς. Curiously enough, Rossbroich 62 denies that a Jew could advise heathen to take wise and expert judges (this is one of his arguments against Jewish authorship). This verse is possibly to be seen in the light of the situation reflected in the edict of Tiberius Julius Alexander (68 A.D.), Dittenberger *OGIS* II 669, 40ff. ἤδη δὲ τῆς πόλεως (sc. Alexandria) σχεδὸν ἀοικήτου γενομένης διὰ τὸ πλῆθος τῶν συκοφαντῶν καὶ πάσης οἰκίας συνταρασσομένης. If it reflects an inner-Jewish situation (the Alexandrian Jewish πολίτευμα had its own tribunals, see Tcherikover, *CPJ* I 32f.), then ἀδαήμων may mean someone who does not know the Torah well (cf. ἀγνοοῦντες in Jos. *Ant*. XI 129); see Jeremias, *Jerusalem* 269: "Ganz allgemein muss angenommen werden, dass, wenn eine Gemeinde bei der Besetzung des Amtes eines . . . Richters die Wahl hatte zwischen einem Laien und einem Gelehrten, der letztere vorgezogen wurde".

87 [μηδὲ δίκην δικάσῃς, πρὶν <ἂν> ἄμφω μῦθον ἀκούσῃς.]

Do not pass a judgment before you have heard the word of both parties.

This verse is given in only two inferior mss. (Young: exhibent duo dett.) For this reason and in view of Aristoph. *Vesp*. 725f. ἦ που σοφὸς ἦν ὅστις ἔφασκεν· Πρὶν ἂν ἀμφοῖν μῦθον ἀκούσῃς, οὐκ ἂν δικάσαις Diehl athetized this verse ("versus si genuinus esset, carmen esset saec. a. Chr. V"). Dornseiff, *Echtheitsfragen* 37 comments: "Die Logik dieser Athetese ist mir dunkel. Wenn nichts anderes im Wege steht, das Gedicht ins 5. Jahrh. v. Chr. zu setzen, als die mögliche Unechtheit dieser Zeile, so muss das Gedicht

auch ohne sie nicht um Jahrhunderte später entstanden sein".
Dornseiff thinks that Aristophanes' σοφός may be Phocylides, the author of our poem (in his view); but, unlike Diehl, he does not seriously consider the mss. tradition (see also Howald, *DLZ* 61 (1940), 666).

In antiquity this line is well-known and attributed to various authors (which is the case with many γνῶμαι), e.g. Hesiod, Democritus, Pittheus, Phocylides (in scholia on Lucian *Calumn.* 8). Cic. *Ep. ad Att.* VII 18 calls it a ψευδησιόδειον, see Ps-Hes. fr. 271 (= 338) μηδὲ δίκην δικάσῃς, πρὶν ἂν ἀμφοῖν μῦθον ἀκούσῃς (and Rzach *ad loc.*). Lucian *Calumn.* 8 μήτε δίκην δικάσῃς, πρὶν ἄμφω μῦθον ἀκούσῃς. Cf. further Plut. *Stoic. repugn.* 8, 1034E; Ps-Plato *Demod.* 383b-c; *Paroem. Gr.* II 759 (and n. 6 *ad loc.*), and the scholia quoted by Young *ad loc.* The minor differences in the tradition are the omission of ἄν in some readings (but πρίν can be metrically long) and the variation of ἀμφοῖν and ἄμφω (for ἄμφω as genit. see Apoll. Rhod. I 165 τῶν ἄμφω προγενέστερος). Bergk supposes that this line originally came from the Χείρωνος ὑποθῆκαι, which were commonly attributed to Hesiod in antiquity. For δίκην δικάζειν cf. Hes. *Op.* 39, Herod. V 25, etc. Goram 104 refers to Deut. XIX 16-19 as a parallel to this verse (cf. in v. 18 ἐξετάσωσιν ... ἀκριβῶς). But it is much more reminiscent of the emperor Claudius' letter to the Alexandrians where he says (*CPJ* II 153, 86-8) ἀλλὰ ἐῶσιν αὐτοὺς (sc. the Jews) τοῖς ἔθεσιν χρῆσθαι οἷς καὶ ἐπὶ τοῦ θεοῦ Σεβαστοῦ, ἅπερ καὶ ἐγὼ διάκουσας ἀμφοτέρων ἐβεβαίωσα. Cf. Sen. *Med.* 199f. *qui statuit aliquid parte inaudita altera, aequum licet statuerit, haud aequus fuit.*

88 τὴν σοφίην σοφὸς εὐθύνει, τέχνας δ' ὁμότεχνος.
    A wise man keeps straight wisdom, and a fellow-craftsman crafts.

This verse, which is quoted in the *Scholia ad Lucianum* p. 8, 20f. Rabe (οὕτω καὶ Φωκυλίδης φησί·), is very difficult to understand. Rossbroich 62 surmises that v. 88a refers to the expert judge of v. 86, and for v. 88b he compares Arist. *Vesp.* 1431 ἔρδοι τις ἣν ἕκαστος εἰδείη τέχνην, Cic. *Tusc.* I 41 *quam quisque norit artem in hac se exerceat* (which is called a Greek proverb here), Prop. II 1, 46 *qua pote quisque, in ea conterat arte diem*, Hor. *Epist.* I 14, 44 *quam scit uterque libens censebo exerceat artem.* But what is σοφός and σοφία here? Is the verse about the Stoic ideal Sage or the Jewish חכם? Does σοφία mean practical virtue, skill (cf. Wilckens, *TWNT*

VII 468), or rather theoretical virtue as opposed to τέχνη (cf. Philo *Ebr.* 88 σοφία as τέχνη τεχνῶν, Sir. IX 17 ἐν χειρὶ τεχνιτῶν ἔργον ἐπαινεσθήσεται καὶ ὁ ἡγούμενος λαοῦ σοφὸς ἐν λόγῳ αὐτοῦ)? The second possibility is more probable, since in this opposition σοφία mostly means theoretical knowledge and τέχνη practical skill. Does εὐθύνειν mean "to estimate, to appreciate" or "to keep straight, to correct"? These questions can hardly be decided. On the combination σοφίη — τέχνη cf. again Democr. fr. 59 οὔτε τέχνη οὔτε σοφίη ἐφικτόν, ἢν μὴ μάθῃ τις. Hom. *Hymn. in Herm.* 483 τέχνῃ καὶ σοφίῃ δεδαημένος and 511 ἑτέρης σοφίης ἐκμάσσατο τέχνην. On ὁμότεχνος see Bauer *s.v.* Perhaps this verse may be paraphrased thus: the wise man helps man's intellect to "go straight", just as the craftsman ensures that the repertoire of skills is also used properly; both of them, the theoretician and the practical man, ensure that things go in the approved manner, and they do not interfere with the other's business. Things should not be driven out of their course. Whether there is a reference here to the judge of v. 86, as Rossbroich suggests, is hard to say, but not impossible. The implication would then be: he who wants to administrate justice, should know what justice is.

89-90 οὐ χωρεῖ μεγάλην διδαχὴν ἀδίδακτος ἀκουή.
οὐ γὰρ δὴ νοέουσ' οἱ μηδέποτ' ἐσθλὰ μαθόντες.

An untrained ear cannot grasp important teaching;
for those who have never learned good things do not understand.

On χωρεῖν in this (late) sense cf. Matt. XIX 11f. οὐ πάντες χωροῦσιν τὸν λόγον. ... ὁ δυνάμενος χωρεῖν χωρείτω. Ps-Long. *De sublim.* IX 9 τὴν τοῦ θείου δύναμιν κατὰ τὴν ἀξίαν ἐχώρησε. Plut. *Cato min.* 64, 5 τὸ Κάτωνος φρόνημα χωρεῖν. Ditt., *Syll.* 814, 11 (67 A.D.); Jos. *C. Ap.* I 225; *Pap. Gr. Mag.* IV 729. For ἐσθλὰ μανθάνειν see Theogn. 35. Praise of παιδεία and criticism of the ἀπαίδευτος are found very frequently in Hellenistic and Jewish literature (on the importance of learning in the Hellenistic period, both with Greeks and Jews, see Hadas, *Hellenistic Culture* 69ff.), esp. in gnomic literature, e.g. Men. *Mon.* 384 κάλλιστόν ἐστι κτῆμα παιδεία βροτοῖς, *ibid.* 436 λιμὴν πέφυκε πᾶσι παιδεία βροτοῖς, *Anon. simil.* 23, 24, 26, 27, 29, 110-113 (in Mullach, *Fr. Phil. Gr.* I 489.494), *Gnom. Byz.* 220-234 (περὶ ἀπαιδεύτων καὶ ἀσυνέτων καὶ ἀνοήτων), *Gnom. homoiom.* (ed. Elter) 10a, 19b, 22, 27, 29, 29a, 39, 42, 45, 61, 67, 109c, 173, 182; more material, esp. Cynic, can be found in Gerhard,

Phoinix 121ff. and Packmohr, *Diog.* 82; cf. also Rossbroich 63 who refers to Democr. fr. 180 and Xen. *Mem.* III 6, 17 and IV 1, 3 (see also the collection of texts in Stob. II 31). The theme is very frequent in Sirach (see Bousset, *Religion* 164), e.g. XXI 14 ἔγκατα μωροῦ ὡς ἀγγεῖον συντετριμμένον καὶ πᾶσαν γνῶσιν οὐ κρατήσει. In Judaism there was a tendency to equate learning and piety (Bousset 164f.; Spicq, *Ep. Past.* I 487f.; Hengel, *Judentum und Hellenismus* 415ff.). What is meant by μεγάλη διδαχή is hard to say (the Torah?).

91 μὴ δὲ τραπεζοκόρους κόλακας ποιεῖσθαι ἑταίρους.
Make not parasitic flatterers your friends.

Most mss. (M, B, P, V) read τραπεζοφόρους, which has no sense here. τραπεζόκορος (*hapax*) = (from κορέννυμι) filling oneself at another's table, or (from κορέω) sweeping the table, epithet of parasites (LSJ *s.v.*). κόλαξ = 1. flatterer; 2. parasite. A warning against the flattering parasite is a common theme in Hellenistic literature. Rossbroich 63 "Adulatores et parasitae eodem modo atque ἀπαίδευτοι magnas agunt partes in gnomologiis et alibi". On this theme see esp. Ribbeck, *Kolax* (1884), *passim* (on the κόλαξ — παράσιτος motive esp. *ibid.* 21ff.). From the innumerable instances cf. e.g. Epict. *Sent.* 42 (48) ὥσπερ λύκος ὅμοιον κυνί, οὕτω καὶ κόλαξ καὶ μοιχὸς καὶ παράσιτος ὅμοιον φίλῳ (cf. the titles of the treatises of Plutarch Πῶς ἄν τις διακρίνειε τὸν κόλακα τοῦ φίλου and Maximus Tyr. XVIII Τίσι χωριστέον τὸν κόλακα τοῦ φίλου. This was not only a Greek theme; cf. Kroll, *Kultur* 196: "wie die Griechen eine scharfe Scheidung zwischen dem κόλαξ und dem φίλος machten, so die Römer zwischen *scurra* und *amicus*"). *Gnom. Vat.* 206 ὁ αὐτὸς (sc. Demosthenes) ἔφη τὸν κόλακα τοῦτο διαφέρειν τοῦ κόρακος (note the wordplay), ᾗ ὁ μὲν ζῶντας, ὁ δὲ νεκροὺς ἐσθίει (many parallels in Sternbach *ad loc.*). *Gnom. Byz.* 174-181 (περὶ κολάκων); *Anon. simil.* 44-48 and 121-123 (Mullach, *Fr. Phil. Gr.* I 490.494). *Floril. duo gr.* I 49 (p. 9 Schenkl). Other references to gnomologies can be found in Rossbroich 63; further Cynic maxims in Packmohr, *Diog.* 53f. Cf. also the texts collected in Stob. III 14 (III p. 468-476 W-H). On parasites in Alexandria see Clem. Alex. *Paed.* II 2, 1; 7,4. The theme is missing in Jewish literature, except for Philo *Leg. all.* II 10, III 182, *Sacrif.* 32, *Agric.* 164, *Plant.* 104-106 (!), *Migr. Abr.* 111, etc.; esp. *Leg. ad Gaium* 162 (on the Alexandrians) δεινοὶ γάρ εἰσι τὰς κολακείας. The word κόλαξ does not occur in early Christian literature, its cognates seldom.

92-94 πολλοὶ γὰρ πόσιος καὶ βρώσιός εἰσιν ἑταῖροι
καιρὸν θωπεύοντες, ἐπὴν κορέσασθαι ἔχωσιν,
ἀχθόμενοι δ' ὀλίγοις καὶ πολλοῖς πάντες ἄπληστοι.

For there are many friends of eating and drinking,
who are time-servers whenever they can satiate themselves,
but all being discontented with little and insatiable with much.

These verses give the motivation of v. 91. V. 92 has been borrowed from a gnomological tradition; see Theogn. 115 πολλοί τοι πόσιος καὶ βρώσιός εἰσιν ἑταῖροι. Rossbroich 63 "scimus ... illa aetate neminem legendo laudare locum scriptoris, sed ex florilegiis tum homines scientiam hausisse" (against Goram 103, who asserted that this verse was immediately taken over from Theognis; see also Van Groningen *ad* Theogn. 115). The expression βρῶσις καὶ πόσις (or the reverse order) is too frequent in Greek literature (since Homer) to need illustration; see Rossbroich 64 for examples (in the Bible e.g. Dan. I 10, Rom. XIV 17, Col. II 16). For the content cf. Men. *Mon.* 682 πολλοὶ τραπεζῶν, οὐ φίλων εἰσὶν φίλοι (cf. Men. gnom. syr. 47 Schulthess). Note the spiteful reiteration of ἑταίρους at the end of v. 91 in ἑταῖροι at the end of v. 92.

Ad 93: καιρὸν θωπεύειν = to be a time-server (see LSJ *s.v.* θωπ.). Cf. Floril. duo graeca I 84, p. 12 Schenkl ὁ διὰ καιρὸν εὐτυχοῦντα κολακεύων φίλον καιροῦ φίλος πέφυκεν, οὐχὶ τοῦ φίλου. κορέσασθαι: cf. τραπεζοκόρους in 91.

Ad 94: is this line construed as a chiastic antithetic parallelism (see the above translation; cf. also Lincke, *Samaria* 171 and Farina 41) or does πολλοῖς also belong to ἀχθόμενοι: "discontented with little and with much, all being (or: are) insatiable" (so Riessler 865; Binder 73; Lewis, *NTS* 13 (1966/7),55)? This second solution is equally possible. On the vice of ἀπληστία see e.g. Men. *Mon.* 386 κακὸν μέγιστον ἐν βροτοῖς ἀπληστία. *Gnom. Vat.* 536 ὁ αὐτὸς (sc. Timon) στοιχεῖα δύο ἔφη τῶν κακῶν εἶναι· ἀπληστίαν καὶ φιλοδοξίαν. Cf. Teles p. 35, 9ff. H. Ps-Heraclitus *Epist.* 2, p. 56 Attridge. Pap. Genev. inv. 271, col. VI 47-VII 13 (*Mus. Helv.* 1959, 93). Sir. XXXVII 29-31 (!). Test. Iss. VI 1. Philo *Opif.* 159, *Post.* 98, *Agric.* 58, *Ebr.* 4.6.22.122.222. Apoc. Bar. Gr. IV 16. Cf. also the texts mentioned above *ad* v. 69 (μέτρῳ ἔδειν). Note the alliterative π in the last three dactyli of v. 94.

95-96 λαῷ μὴ πίστευε, πολύτροπός ἐστιν ὅμιλος.
λαὸς <γὰρ> καὶ ὕδωρ καὶ πῦρ ἀκατάσχετα πάντα.

Trust not the people, the mob is fickle.
For the people and water and fire are all uncontrollable.

πολύτροπος: every Greek knew this word from the first line of Homer's *Od.* Dornseiff 41 comments: "Damit wird das Stichwort für Odysseus ähnlich abwertend beleuchtet wie V. 64 die Menis des Achilleus". Cf. also W. B. Stanford, *The Ulysses Theme*, Oxford 1963, 260 n. 28 and 261 n. 31 for the possible "Ulyssean implications" of the word here. This is the only instance mentioned by LSJ with an unfavourable meaning.

ἀκατάσχετος (not to be checked, uncontrollable) is a late word, occurring since the second cent. B.C., see Rossbroich 11 and Bauer *s.v.*; add Ael. Arist. 48, 65 K. ταραχὴ τῆς θαλάττης ἀκατάσχετος (it is a *varia lectio* in James III 8 where the tongue is called an ἀκατάστατον (-σχετον) κακόν). These lines are redolent of a more or less élite mentality (cf. Cronbach, *IDB* II 167) which is reminiscent of the Stoic (but not only Stoic) "mépris de la foule", on which see Bodson, *Morale sociale* 71. The unstable people is compared to the sea and the fire, e.g. Cic. *Resp.* I 65 *cave putes autem mare ullum aut flammam esse tantam, quam non facilius sit sedare quam effrenatam insolentia multitudinem*. Com. adesp. fr. 1324 δῆμος ἄστατον κακόν, καὶ θαλάσσῃ πάνθ' ὅμοιον ὑπ' ἀνέμου ῥιπίζεται. Cf. Men. gnom. pap. II 8 (p. 5 Jaekel) θάλασσα καὶ πῦρ καὶ γυνὴ τρίτον κακόν. Hor. *Carm.* I 35, 25 *volgus infidum* (cf. I 1, 7). Tac. *Hist.* I 69 *ut est vulgus mutabile* (and Heraeus *ad loc.*). *Gnom. Vat.* 121 ὁ αὐτὸς (sc. Ariston) πολυκέφαλον θηρίον εἶπεν πάντα δῆμον. More texts in Rossbroich 65 and Otto, *Sprichwörter* 378. Philo exhibits the same mentality, e.g. *Leg. ad Gaium* 67 ὄχλος γὰρ ἀνίδρυτον ἐν ἅπασι and other negative remarks on the Alexandrian mob, *ibid.* 120 (Sevenster, *Roots of Pagan Antisemitism* 24: "the rabble of Alexandria . . . had a bad reputation in the ancient world"). It is curious that Ps-Phoc. uses the word λαός in this connection instead of δῆμος or ὄχλος since in the LXX it mostly stands for Israel. γάρ was inserted by Diehl for metrical reasons (the υ of ὕδωρ is short).

Vv. 97-115 *Death and After-Life*

97 μὴ δὲ μάτην ἐπὶ πῦρ καθίσας μινύθῃς φίλον ἦτορ.
Sit not in vain beside the fire, weakening your heart.

The words μινύθειν and ἦτορ occur in combination in Homer, but there μινύθειν has an intransitive sense and ἦτορ is subject, e.g. *Od.* IV 374 μινύθει δέ τοι ἦτορ ἑταίρων, cf. Theogn. 361; but Diehl rightly compares *Od.* X 485f. οἵ μευ φθινύθουσι φίλον κῆρ ἀμφ' ἔμ' ὀδυρόμενοι. The expression φίλον ἦτορ *passim* in Homer, e.g. *Il.* V 250, XIII 84, XXI 114; Pind. *Ol.* I 4. On μή with conj. praes. as prohibition see K-G I 220 Anm. 1.

The sense of this verse is unclear. Schmidt, *Jahrb. f. class. Phil.* 3 (1857), 515f. thinks it is about sitting in sorrow by the funeral pyre, but since burning of corpses is conflicting with vv. 99ff. he regards this v. as an interpolation, caused by πῦρ in v. 96. "Wir stossen also hier auf einen der häufigen Fälle, wo ein gnomisches Gedicht dadurch erweitert wurde, dass ein Leser zu einem seiner Sätze nicht wegen irgend einer Analogie des Sinnes, sondern bloss um eines zufälligen Stichwortes willen einen in gleiches Metrum gefassten andern an den Rand setzte". Though this is a very common phenomenon indeed, it need not be the case here. Dornseiff, *Echtheitsfragen* 41f. comments: "das sieht parsisch aus", and sees a reference to a shamanistic rite here (he compares Herod. IV 73-75). Riessler 1320 says it is an "Abmahnung vor dem trauernden Hinsitzen an der Feuerstätte des Leichenbegängnisses". But πῦρ more probably means the hearth at home (see the text from Ael. Arist. quoted below). In that case it is a warning against excessive mourning (cf. v. 59 ἔστω κοινὰ πάθη). One may compare Soph. *El.* 140ff. ἀλλ' ἀπὸ τῶν μετρίων ἐπ' ἀμήχανον ἄλγος ἀεὶ στενάχουσα διόλλυσαι, ἐν αἷς ἀνάλυσίς ἐστιν οὐδεμία κακῶν. Teles p. 59, 6 H. πῶς δὲ οὐκ ἀλόγιστον καὶ ἄλλως μάταιον τὸ τελευτήσαντος τοῦ φίλου καθῆσθαι κλαίοντα καὶ λυπούμενον καὶ ἑαυτὸν προσκαταφθείροντα. Cf. esp. Ael. Arist. II 229 Behr οὐ γὰρ εἰκὸς ... ἁρπαζομένων τῶν ὄντων καθῆσθαι παρ' ἑστίᾳ (cf. ἐπὶ πῦρ καθίσας in Ps-Phoc.!) καὶ κακὸν εἶναι. Texts on μετριοπάθεια from Philo and Plut. are to be found in Wendland, *Philo* (1895) 56ff. Sir. XXXVIII 20f. μὴ δῷς εἰς λύπην τὴν καρδίαν σου, ... σεαυτὸν κακώσεις. Cf. XXX 21 and Men. gnom. syr. 100 (Schulthess).

98 μέτρα δὲ τεῦχ' ἔθ' ἑοῖσι· τὸ γὰρ μέτρον ἐστὶν ἄριστον.
Be moderate in your grief, for moderation is the best.

The text as it stands should properly be translated: "set limits to (the grief of) your family (?, or: friends)". But the text is very uncertain. All the mss. read θεοῖσι. That hardly makes sense, though some scholars have tried to translate it: Ludwich, *Quaestiones* 29 renders: "fertige Maasse (d.i. Versmaasse, Gedichte) auf die Götter" (see Kroll's criticisms in *Berl. Phil. Woch.* 25 (1905), 243); Ranston 79: "in thy religion keep the mean"; cf. Dornseiff 41f. (θεοί = the deceased, see v. 104). But these renderings are very improbable. (It might seem that the reading θεοῖσι is favoured by Aesch. *Suppl.* 1059-61 μέτριον νῦν ἔπος εὔχου· — τίνα καιρόν με διδάσκεις; — τὰ θεῶν μηδὲν ἀγάζειν, but of course this text cannot settle the matter.) Many emendations have been proposed to remove θεοῖσι, the more so since the plural θεοί looks so un-Jewish: Bernays 202 γόοισι, Bergk ποθοῖο or ποθοῖσι or (μέτρα) δ' ἔχειν κλαυθμοῖο, Schmidt (*Jahrb. f. class. Phil.* 3 (1857), 516) νέοισι, Goram 108 θανοῦσι, Crusius ἐλέοισι, and, most ingeniously, Young ἔθ' ἑοῖσι (*modum impone etiam tuis*, see his *app. crit.*). Young's proposal is most attractive, since it implies no change in the mss. tradition, but the above translation is based upon Bernays' γόοισι since that fits the context better (B.'s conjecture has gained wide acceptance, see Sebestyén, Lincke, Diehl, Farina). Then it is again a warning against excessively unrestrained expressions of grief at death (on which see Schmidt, *Ethik* II 114f.). For parallels see *ad* 97. Both lines are reminiscent of the *Consolationes*-literature.

For v. 98b see the commentary on v. 36. The position of γάρ (separating the noun from its article) is unusual, see Denniston, *Greek Particles* 95f.

99 γαῖαν ἐπιμοιρᾶσθαι ἀταρχύτοις νεκύεσσιν.
Let the unburied dead receive their share of earth.

A sentence with a late vocabulary: ἐπιμοιρᾶσθαι (occurring since the fourth cent. B.C.) = to receive as one's share; but here it has a sense not registered by LSJ *s.v.*, viz. to apportion as someone's due share. This verb often occurs in connection with burying, e.g. Moschion fr. 6, 30-32 τοὺς θανόντας ὥρισεν νόμος τύμβοις καλύπτειν κἀπιμοιρᾶσθαι κόνιν νεκροῖς ἀθάπτοις. Philo *Vita Mos.* II 283 μηδὲν μέρος ὑπολειπόμενοι τῶν σωμάτων, ὃ ταφῆς ἐπιμοιράσεται. Also ἀτάρχυτος (= unburied) is post-classical (Lycophron *Alex.* 1326). The injunction of this verse is "ein bei allen gesitteten Völkern gültiges Gesetz" (Riessler 1320). In Greek ethics, it was one of the unwritten laws (Hirzel, ΑΓΡΑΦΟΣ ΝΟΜΟΣ 65-69; Crouch, *Origin* 40ff.), see e.g. Dio Chrys. LXXVI 5. It was also one of the so-called Buzygian laws: each year the descendants of Buzyges (the legendary hero of an Attic priestly tribe) held a celebration in connection with the cult of Demeter, on which occasion curses were pronounced against those who refused to bury the dead, etc. (see J. Bernays, "Philon's Hypothetika und die Verwünschungen des Buzyges", *Ges. Abh.* I 262-282, esp. 279; Nilsson, *Gesch.* I 421 n. 1; Crouch, *Origin* 87). The original idea underlying this custom was that otherwise the soul could find no rest and might annoy people (Rohde, *Psyche* I 217, II 83.413; cf. Cumont, *After Life* 66f.). For this burial theme see Soph. *Antig.* (in its entirety); Eur. *Suppl.* 531; Pausanias I 32, 5 πάντως ὅσιον ἀνθρώπου νεκρὸν γῆ κρύψαι. Hor. *Carm.* I 28 (2) (a petition for sepulture, e.g. v. 16 *licebit iniecto ter pulvere curras*); Verg. *Aen.* VI 365. This duty is also stressed in Jewish literature (the O.T. already shows an abhorrence of leaving the dead unburied, Jer. XVI 4, XXII 19); Philo *Hyp.* in Eus. *PE* VIII 7, 7 (p. 430, 21f. Mras) μὴ ταφῆς νέκυν ἐξείργειν, ἀλλὰ καὶ γῆς αὐτοῖς ὅσον γε εἰς τὴν ὁσίαν προσεπιβάλλειν (Philo mentions it as a Buzygian law that is binding upon everyone). Jos. *C. Ap.* II 211 ἄταφον μὴ περιορᾶν. (Again, Philo, Josephus and Ps-Phoc. drew upon a common source, since it is not an explicit O.T. commandment, but note the differences in formulation; see above *ad* 84-5). This duty is very much stressed by Tobit: I 17f., II 7, IV 3, XII 12f., XIV 9. Cf. Sir. XXXVIII 16 μὴ ὑπερίδῃς τὴν ταφὴν αὐτοῦ. 5(4) Esdr. II 23 *mortuos ubi inveneris, signans commenda sepulchro*. Vit. Ad. Ev. XLVIII 6; Apoc. Mos. XL 3f., XLIII 1f. Bernays 203 compares the rules about the מת מצוה (Gittin 61a, etc.) on which see Billerbeck IV 578ff. (578: "Das Pflichtmässige der Totenbestattung trat besonders in denjenigen Bestimmungen zutage, die den sogenannten 'Pflichttoten' (מת מצוה) betrafen. Man verstand darunter einen Toten, der keine näheren Angehörigen hinterliess, die seine Bestattung zu übernehmen hatten. In diesem Fall war es Pflicht eines jeden Israeliten, einem solchen Toten den letzten Liebesdienst zu erweisen und für sein ehrenvolles Begräbnis sorgen zu helfen"). Cf. also Krauss, *Talm. Arch.* II 61f.

100-101 μὴ τύμβον φθιμένων ἀνορύξῃς μηδ' ἀθέατα
δείξῃς ἠελίῳ καὶ δαιμόνιον χόλον ὄρσῃς.

Do not dig up the grave of the deceased, neither expose
to the sun what may not be seen, lest you stir up the divine
anger.

φθίμενοι = the dead, Hom. *Od.* XXIV 436 etc. ἀνορύσσειν τάφον: Herod. I 68: Isocr. XVI 26 (ἀνορύττειν is almost a technical term in this connection, see Kroll, *PW* XX 1, 510; even more so the word τυμβωρυχία). On ἀθέατος (that may not be seen"; Christ, "Leben nach dem Tode" 140 wrongly: "unsichtbar") see Rossbroich 10f. for references. The prohibition of tomb-violation is very common in sepulchral inscriptions, see Kroll, *ibid.*, Rohde, *Psyche* II 340ff. and Parrot, *Maledictions et violations de tombes* (1939), *passim* (and the review by Nock, *JBL* 60 (1941), 88-95 = *Essays* II 527-533); also Gerner, "Tymborychia", *Zeitschr. der Savigny-Stiftung* 1941, 230ff. See e.g. the famous διάταγμα Καίσαρος (from Nazareth?) in *Suppl. Epigr. Graec.* VIII 1 (1937), nr. 13 (the Greek text also in Brown, "Violation of Sepulture in Palestine", *AJP* 52 (1931), 2 and in Parrot, *op. cit.* 65; bibliography *ibid.* 64 n. 33 and esp. Metzger, "The Nazareth Inscription Once Again", *Festschrift Kümmel* 237f.), line 1ff. ἀρέσκει μοι τάφους τύμβους τε ... μένειν ἀμετακινήτους τὸν αἰῶνα (l. 22 τυμβωρυχία). Sometimes it was believed that the well-being of a city depended upon not violating the grave of its ἥρως κτίστης; see F. Skutsch, "Sechzehnte Epode und vierte Ekloge", *Neue Jahrbücher für das klassische Altertum* 23 (1909), 24ff. (who discusses Hor. *Epod.* XVI 13f. *quaeque carent ventis et solibus ossa Quirini—nefas videre!—dissipabit insolens.* N.B. *nefas videre* = ἀθέατος; note also *solibus*). Philo *Hyp.* mentions this injunction as one of the "unwritten laws", *ap.* Eus. *PE* VIII 7, 7 (p. 430, 22f. Mras) μὴ θήκας, μὴ μνήματα ὅλως κατοιχομένων κινεῖν (this is the immediate continuation of the text quoted under v. 99, so Philo and Ps-Phoc. both have these precepts in the same order, which is probably due to their common source, see Wendland, "Therapeuten" 710). Cf. the Jewish inscription in Diehl, *Lateinische altchristliche Inschriften mit einem Anhang jüdischer Inschriften*, nr. 367, 3ff. *si quis pos ovitu me(um) arc(am) volu(erit) ap(erire), en(feret) fi(sci) vir(ibus) aur(i) lib(ram) una.* Dornseiff's (43) suggestion that (Ps-)Phoc. polemizes against the verdict of his contemporary (!) Pisistratus to remove all tombs from Delos (Herod. I 64), is to be rejected for obvious reasons.

μηδ' ἀθέατα δείξης ἠελίῳ: Demosthenes XLIII 62 mentions one of the laws of Solon prescribing ἐκφέρειν τὸν ἀποθανόντα τῇ ὑστεραίᾳ ᾗ ἂν προθῶνται, πρὶν ἥλιον ἐξέχειν and Cic. Leg. II 66 says that Demetrius of Phaleron ordered corpses to be brought out before sun-rise (ante lucem ... iussit efferri). See Rohde, Psyche I 223f. (and notes) and Stommel, "Bestattung", RAC II 204. Therefore the remark of Bousset, Religion 464 n. 2: "Die Scheu, das Sonnenlicht zu verunreinigen, ist echt orientalisch", needs to be corrected. Cf. Kroll, PW XX 1, 510, who refers to Paulus Sent. I 21, 4 qui corpus ... nudaverit et solis radiis ostenderit, piaculum committit. Other texts in Parrot, op. cit. 21 n. 32, who also mentions Jerem. VIII 1f. ἐν τῷ καιρῷ ἐκείνῳ ... ἐξοίσουσιν τὰ ὀστᾶ τῶν βασιλέων Ἰουδα ... καὶ ψύξουσιν αὐτὰ πρὸς τὸν ἥλιον, but whether the motive there is the same is dubious as in the case of Tob. II 4 ἀναιροῦμαι αὐτὸν ἐκ τῆς πλατείας καὶ εἰς ἓν τῶν οἰκιδίων μέχρι τοῦ τὸν ἥλιον δύειν καὶ θάψω αὐτόν. On δαιμόνιον χόλον cf. the deos iratos in curses in Latin tomb-inscriptions, Parrot, op. cit. 160.

Vv. 100-101 have to be read in connection with v. 102: graves were opened in order to dissect the corpses of the deceased; see Fraser, Ptolemaic Alexandria I 364, II 539.

102 οὐ καλὸν ἁρμονίην ἀναλυέμεν ἀνθρώποιο.
It is not good to dissolve the human frame.

ἁρμονίην ἀναλυέμεν: cf. Anth. Pal. VII 383 νεύρων καὶ κώλων ἔκλυτος ἁρμονίη (said of a corpse in a grave). Since this verse is to be read in connection with vv. 100-1, it is not about vivisection, but probably about dissection of cadavers (Rossbroich's scepticism as to the meaning of this verse is unjustified; Sartorius, Analysis 89 thinks it forbids suicide, but this is very improbable. If another meaning of the verse is to be considered, it might mean: do not dismember a corpse by digging it up). Graves were very likely opened sometimes in order to get material for dissection, see Edelstein, "History of Anatomy in Antiquity" 298f.; Fraser, Ptolemaic Alexandria I 364. On anatomy and dissection in antiquity see, besides the work of Edelstein and Fraser's chapter on "Alexandrian Medicine" (I 338-376, esp. 362ff.), also F. W. Bayer, "Anatomie", RAC I 430-437; F. Kudlien, "Anatomie", PW Suppl. XI 38-48 (with criticisms of Edelstein), and G. E. R. Lloyd in Südhoff's Archiv 59 (1975), 113ff. It is highly probable that dissection was practised only in Alexandria (Edelstein 251; Fraser II 539 n. 239.

"these lines [sc. Ps-Phoc. 100-102] probable indicate an Alexandrian background"), where the famous physicians Herophilus and Erasistratus inaugurated this science in the beginning of the third cent. B.C. (Edelstein, *passim*). There is some uncertainty about the question of whether it was still practised in later times. Although Kudlien 44ff. denies it, it is very likely that dissection was also done in the Roman period, albeit probably on a smaller scale and only on corpses (Fraser I 362ff.; also G. E. R. Lloyd, *Greek Science after Aristotle* (1973) 87 and J. Mansfeld, "Alcmaeon: Physikos or Physician?", *Kephalaion* (Festschrift C. J. de Vogel, Assen 1975) 31 with n. 26), From the start dissection was criticized by physicians belonging to the Empiricist and Methodist schools, on both epistemological and ethical grounds (Kudlien 45f.). But Ps-Phoc.' criticism has religious grounds and is based upon the Jewish expectation of the resurrection of the body (vv. 103-4), which was sometimes believed to be raised in the same form as it was in the tomb; see e.g. Apoc. Bar. syr. 50, 2 "the earth shall then assuredly restore the dead. ... It shall make no change in their form, but as it has received, so it shall restore them, and as I (= God) delivered them unto it, so also shall it raise them" (with the comments of Cavallin, *Life after Death* 88ff.). Parrot, *Malédictions* 166: "on semble avoir considéré que l'état du corps après la mort était en relation directe avec une existence posthume" (though this opinion was never shared by all, see Daube, *N.T. and Rabbinic Judaism* 307f.). Christ, "Das Leben nach dem Tode bei Pseudo-Phokylides" 141, thinks v. 102 is an allusion to Ez. XXXVII 7 (comparing *Or. Sib.* II 221-3) where the bones of the dead fit themselves together into a ἁρμονία (so the LXX text). "So könnte der Vers den jüdischen Brauch der Deponierung der Gebeine nach der Verwesung in Ossuarien im Auge haben. Wäre dem so, läge hier ein Beweis dafür vor, dass jene seltsamen Gebeinkästen mit der Auferstehung nichts zu tun haben, wird doch das Ossilegium in Phok. gerade aufgrund der Erwartung der Knochenauferstehung abgelehnt" (141). This interpretation seems very improbable. Ezekiel's ἁρμονία comes into being only during the process of resurrection. Moreover, there is not the slightest hint of the use of ossilegia in the text. It does emphasize the importance of the body, as do vv. 103-4.

103-104 καὶ τάχα δ' ἐκ γαίης ἐλπίζομεν ἐς φάος ἐλθεῖν
λείψαν' ἀποιχομένων· ὀπίσω δὲ θεοὶ τελέθονται.

For in fact we hope that the remains of the departed will soon come to the light again out of the earth. And afterwards they become gods.

τάχα = 1. soon; 2. perhaps, probably. In view of v. 104b the first meaning is here the most feasible (against Schmidt, *Jahrb. f. class. Phil.* 3 (1857), 516). φάος: in poetry often equivalent to "life" (see LSJ s.v. I 1b), e.g. Soph. *Phil.* 624f. ... ἐξ Ἅιδου θανὼν πρὸς φῶς ἀνελθεῖν, and, in a resurrection context, *Or. Sib.* VIII 313 καὶ τότ' ἀπὸ φθιμένων ἀναλύσας εἰς φάος ἥξει πρῶτος ἀναστάσεως (sc. Jesus), cf. I 379 αὐτὰρ ἐπὴν ἔλθῃ τρισὶν ἤμασιν ἐς φάος αὖτις, κτλ. λείψανον: frequently in plur. of the remains of the dead, e.g. Soph. *El.* 1113, *Or. Sib.* III 646. ἀποιχόμενοι = τελευτήσαντες, e.g. Pind. *Pyth.* I 93 (LSJ s.v. 3). τελέθω = to be; of the med. τελέθομαι (= to become?) LSJ cite only this instance; cf. *Or. Sib.* III 264 τελέθοντο

In vv. 103-104a a very literalistic doctrine of the resurrection is taught, which was (apart from the Sadducees) typically Jewish, and very un-Greek; see Acts XVII 32, esp. Aesch. *Eum.* 647f. ἀνδρὸς δ' ἐπειδὰν αἷμ' ἀνασπάσῃ κόνις ἅπαξ θανόντος, οὔτις ἔστ' ἀνάστασις, and Celsus in Orig. *C. Cels.* V 14; cf. Oepke, "Auferstehung", *RAC* I 931. On the motives which countered the development of a belief in the resurrection in Greek culture see Pötscher, "Die Auferstehung in der klassischen Antike", *Kairos* 7 (1965), 214f. On the resurrection of the dead as a Jewish tenet see Bousset, *Religion* 269ff.; Moore, *Judaism* II 295ff.; Billerbeck, Reg. s.v. Auferstehung; Schubert, "Die Entwicklung der Auferstehungslehre", *Bibl. Zeitschr.* 6 (1962), 177ff.; Hooke, "Life after Death; The Extra-Canonical Literature", *Exp. Times* 76 (1964/5), 273ff.; Wahle, "Die Lehren des rabbinischen Judentums über das Leben nach dem Tod", *Kairos* 14 (1972), 291ff.; Nickelsburg, *Resurrection, Immortality and Eternal Life in Intertestamental Judaism* (1972), *passim*; Cavallin, *Life After Death* I (1974), *passim* (there extensive bibliography). Starting from Is. XXVI 19 and Dan. XII 2 intertestamental and rabbinic Judaism developed the notion of bodily resurrection which, however, became a "dogma" only at the end of the first cent. A.D. (e.g. M. Sanh. X 1). Down to that time this belief existed side by side with other views on afterlife (this is proved very clearly by Cavallin's work). Also in the diaspora this conception was held (so rightly Cavallin, *op. cit.* 200 n. 8; Delling,

"Speranda Futura" 42; Bousset, *Religion* 273 wrongly treats Ps-Phoc. as an exception). Numerous texts could be mentioned (which are most easily found in Cavallin's conveniently arranged table, *op. cit.* 197). Only a few references will suffice: 1 En. XXII 13, LI 1ff.; Test. Jud. XXV 1ff.; Test. Zab. X 2; Test. Sim. VI 7; Test. Ben. X 7; 2 Macc. VII 9-14; Ps. Sal. III 11f.; 4 Ezra VII 30-2; Ps-Philo *Ant. Bibl.* III 10; Apocr. Ezek. fr. 1; Apoc. Bar. syr. L 2; Jos. *Ant.* XVIII 14; *Or. Sib.* IV 179ff; M. Sanh. X 1-3; Sanh. 91a-b; Chag. 12b (more references in the works cited above, esp. those of Schubert and Cavallin). Close verbal similarity with Ps-Phoc. 103f. is found in the famous Regina-inscription from Rome (beginning of the 2nd cent. A.D.) where we read (Frey, *Corp. Inscr. Iud.*, Nr. 476, 5f.) ... *reditura ad lumina rursum. Nam sperare potest ideo, quod surgat in aevom promissum.* Cf. ἐλπίζομεν ἐς φάος ἐλθεῖν, and see the discussion of Delling, "Speranda Futura" 39-44 and Leon, *The Jews of Ancient Rome* 248f. (Alexandre's remark (*Or. Sib.* II (1856) 406) "vox ipsa ἐλπίζομεν christianam originem aperte profitetur" is obviously wrong).

ὀπίσω δὲ θεοὶ τελέθονται: these words have evoked more discussion than any other passage in the poem. Bernays 204f. argues that these words are not only incompatible with Jewish monotheism, but are alltogether "unchristlich, unjüdisch, ungriechisch, unrömisch". Therefore he proposes to read ὀπίσω τε νέοι τελέθονται (supported by Schmidt, *Jahrb. f. class. Phil.* 3 (1857), 517 and Wendland, "Therapeuten" 712 n. 2). But ingenious though this conjecture be, it has met with much criticism. Already Frankel (rev. of Bernays, *Mon. Gesch. Wiss. Jud.* 5 (1856), 67) denies that θεοί is a proof of un-Jewishness. Bergk, *Griech. Lit. Gesch.* II 300 n. 12 says that it is not "ungriechisch" and that Ps-Phoc. wanted to accommodate himself to the Greeks after the shocking statement of the bodily resurrection. Ludwich, *Quaestiones* 30, simply says that θεοί proves that the author was not a Jew but rather a Greek. Harnack (rev. of Bernays' *Ges. Abh.* in *T.L.Z.* 10 (1885), 160) sees in v. 104b a Christian conception, referring to Theoph. *Autol.* II 27 εἰ ῥέψῃ ἐπὶ τὰ τῆς ἀθανασίας τηρήσας τὴν ἐντολὴν τοῦ θεοῦ, μισθὸν κομίσηται παρ' αὐτοῦ τὴν ἀθανασίαν καὶ γένηται θεός. This he supposed to prove the Christian origin of the poem; but later Harnack (*Gesch. der altchristl. Lit.* II 1 (1897), 589) thinks v. 104 is a (Christian) interpolation (followed by Krauss, *Jew. Enc.* X 256; Sitzler, *Woch. f. klass. Phil.* 29 (1912), 451; Kurfess, *ZNW* 38

(1939), 171 n. 4; Jervell, *Imago Dei* 28 n. 42; cf. Schürer, *Gesch. des jüd. Volkes* III⁴ 618). Rohde, *Psyche* II 378 n. 2 takes it to be a really Greek concept and to prove the syncretistic character of the poem (cf. Kroll, *PW* XX 1, 507). At the moment, nobody is inclined to athetize or emend this line (cf. Momigliano, *Bernays* 23: "None of us would eliminate an unconvenient θεοί in Ps-Phoc. by emending it into νέοι (l. 104)"). That θεοί need not be un-Jewish is rightly stressed by Hengel, *Entretiens* XVIII 297: "Das einmalige Vorkommen des Plurals θεοί (104) im Zusammenhang mit dem Hinweis auf die Auferstehung ist nicht mehr als eine freie Redeweise; ganz abgesehen von der freien Ausdrucksweise Philos, werden in Sap. Sal. und in Jos. et As. mehrfach der Fromme bzw. Joseph als υἱὸς θεοῦ bezeichnet, in Qumran werden die Engel häufig *'elim* genannt" (see also his *Der Sohn Gottes* 67-89). It should be borne in mind that many Jewish texts show a definite trend towards a blurring of the border between men who share in the resurrection and the angels. Assimilation of the immortal blessed to angels, stars and other heavenly bodies (who are called μάκαρες in vv. 75 and 163!) is often found; see the numerous examples in Cavallin, *Life After Death* I 203ff.; e.g. Apoc. Bar. syr. LI 10 "they shall be made like unto the angels, and be made equal to the stars"; 1 En. LI 1-4 "In those days shall the earth also give back that which has been entrusted to it, and ... all shall be angels in heaven". (Cf. Matt. XIII 43, XXII 30 and other texts referred to by Klijn in *JSHRZ* V 2, 156). For passages where angels are called gods or sons of God see Hengel, *Judentum und Hellenismus* 424 n. 727; Cavallin, *op. cit.* 204; Schweizer, *TWNT* VIII 355-7. See e.g. 1 QM 1, 10f.; 14, 15; 15, 14; 1 QH 7, 28; 10, 8 and cf. Luke XX 36. When the deceased were believed to become stars (which were often thought of as angels; Bousset, *Religion* 322f.) or angels, and angels were often called gods, then it is not strange that θεοί occurs here (cf. Christ, "Leben nach dem Tode bei Ps-Phok." 143: Seelen = Engel = Gestirne = Götter). Cf. further M. Smith, "The Image of God", *BJRL* 40 (1957/8), 473ff. Billerbeck II 464f. discusses some passages from rabbinic writings where some O.T. texts with *'el* or *'elohim* are even interpreted as referring to men. "Diesen Stellen darf man entnehmen, dass die Bezeichnung eines Menschen als 'Gott' für das jüdische Empfinden gerade nichts unerhörtes war" (465). Cf. *ibid.* 543 on John X 34f., where Ps. LXXXII 6 (ἐγὼ εἶπα· θεοί ἐστε) is applied to men. Add Midr. Ps. XXI 2 and the comments of Schechter, *Aspects* 47f. Dr. P. Staples suggested to me that the LXX version of 1 Sam. XXVIII 13, where the deceased Samuel seems to be called θεοί, might have played a part in this development (see Goodenough, "Greek Garments on Jewish Heroes", in A. Altmann (ed.), *Biblical Motifs*, Cambridge (Mass.) 1966, 232f.).

Of course, this usage may also have roots in non-Jewish Hellenism, where "il n'est pas rare qu'un défunt soit nommé 'dieu'" (Festugière, *Révélation* etc. III: *Les doctrines de l'âme* 140, with examples from the early Roman period *ibid.* n. 2). *Carm. Aur.* 70f. ἦν δ' ἀπολείψας σῶμα ἐς αἰθέρ' ἐλεύθερον ἔλθῃς, ἔσσεαι ἀθάνατος θεὸς ἄμβροτος, οὐκέτι θνητός (according to Bergk, *Gr. Lit. gesch.* II 300 n. 12 the source of v. 104b). *Anth. Lat.* II 975, 4 (p. 450 Bücheler-Riese) *corpore consumpto viva anima deus sum.* Diog. Laert. VIII 68f. Luc. *Hermot.* 7. Suet. *Vesp.* XXIII 4 and the texts mentioned by Lohfink, *Der Himmelfahrt Jesu* 46ff.; also Pease's edition of Cic. *Nat. deor.*, reg. s.v. deification; P.C. van der Horst, *Les vers d'or* 72ff. In v. 104b Ps-Phoc. seems to imply that there is only a resurrection of the righteous, which was a Pharisaic tenet according to Jos. *Bell.* II 163 and *Ant.* XVIII 14 (but see Billerbeck IV 1188f.).

105 ψυχαὶ γὰρ μίμνουσιν ἀκήριοι ἐν φθιμένοισιν.
For the souls remain unharmed in the deceased.

ἀκήριος = unharmed; LSJ *s.v.* say that in Ps-Phoc. 99 (read: 105) it means ἀθάνατος, free from power of the Fates (Κῆρες, the goddesses of death), but that is perhaps etymological over-interpretation (the meaning "heartless, spiritless" (from κῆρ = heart) is also improbable here). Bernhardy, *Grundrisz* II 1, 520 says that vv. 105-108 are "Verse, welche dem heidnischen Glauben allein entsprechen konnten". That is not right (see the comm. on vv. 106-108). However, belief in the immortality of the soul as an inherent quality, distinguishing it from the body that will be dissolved without any resurrection, seems to be maintained in vv. 106-108; this apparently contradicts vv. 103-104. Moreover, we may ask how v. 105 is to be harmonized with v. 108b (ἀὴρ δ' ἀνὰ πνεῦμα δέδεκται). Cavallin, *Life After Death* I 153 speaks of "the unharmonized juxtaposition of contradictory ideas about afterlife" in Ps-Phoc. But, as Nock says (*Essays* I 507 n. 19), "to press this point would be to ignore the widespread tendency of language about the afterlife to admit inconsistencies". Cavallin, *op. cit.* 202 n. 1 *et passim* observes the same phenomenon in other Jewish writings of the intertestamental period (on Ps-Phoc. p. 152f.). It should also be noted now that in Ps-Phoc. ψυχή and πνεῦμα (which is used in vv. 106 and 108) are identical, as so often in Jewish-Hellenistic literature; see Bousset, *Religion* 400f. (Wachler, *Dissertatio* 14: "πνεῦμα et ψυχή nostro sunt synonyma"). On ψυχή in Hellenistic Jewish writings in general see Dihle, *TWNT* IX 630-633. According to Rossbroich, γάρ refers to θεοὶ τελέθονται in 104. Kurfess, *ZNW* 38 (1939), 171 thinks that it refers to v. 103 (he athetizes v. 104). If vv. 103-104 have been inserted, as Harnack surmised (see *ad* 103f.), it should explain v. 102. But perhaps it only refers to ὀπίσω in v. 104 in order to explain how λείψανα can become gods.

106 πνεῦμα γάρ ἐστι θεοῦ χρῆσις θνητοῖσι καὶ εἰκών.
For the spirit is a loan from God to mortals, and his image.

For the shift from ψυχή to πνεῦμα see *ad* v. 105 and cf. the same phenomenon, in greater frequency, in Test. Abr. (rec. A) XVI-XX; and cf. Sap. Sal. IX 15 (ψυχή = νοῦς). The view that the soul/spirit or life is a loan from God is current in the Hellenistic period and occurs also in some Jewish-Hellenistic texts. In Hellenistic writings it is a "populärphilosophischer Gemeinplatz" (Rohde, *Psyche* II 394 n. 2): Cic. *Tusc.* I 93 *ea (sc. natura) quidem dedit usuram vitae tamquam pecuniae nulla praestituta die* (cf. *Resp.* I 3, 4). Lucr. III 971 *vitaque mancipio nulli datur, omnibus usu*. Macr. *Sat.* I 10, 15 *aestimaverunt antiqui animas a Iove dari et rursus post mortem eidem reddi*, Ps-Plato *Axioch.* 367b2 ὡς χρέος ἀποδιδῷ τὸ ζῆν. Ps-Plut. *Cons. ad Apoll.* 10, 106 F διὸ καὶ μοιρίδιον χρέος εἶναι λέγεται τὸ ζῆν, ὡς ἀποδοθησόμενον ὃ ἐδανείσαντο ἡμῶν οἱ προπάτορες (cf. 107A ὅταν ὁ δανείσας ἀπαιτῇ ...). Epict. I 1, 32 τότε τεθνήξομαι. πῶς; ὡς προσήκει τὸν τὰ ἀλλότρια ἀποδιδόντα (cf. IV 1, 172). *Epigr. Gr.* (ed. Kaibel) 613, 6 πνεῦμα λαβὼν δάνος οὐρανόθεν τελέσας χρόνον ἀνταπέδωκα (cf. 156, 2), 772a αὐτὸς δὲ ἀποδοὺς τὸ δάνειον τῆς ζωῆς κτλ. *Anth. Lat.* II 183 (p. 90 Büch.-Riese) *usurae vitae sortem morti reddidit*. From Jewish-Hellenistic texts: Sap. Sal. XV 8 πρὸ μικροῦ ἐκ γῆς γενηθεὶς μετ' ὀλίγον πορεύεται ἐξ ἧς ἐλήμφθη, τὸ τῆς ψυχῆς ἀπαιτηθεὶς χρέος (note also the parallel to vv. 107f.). Philo *Spec. leg.* I 295 τὸν μεταξὺ χρόνον γενέσεως καὶ θανάτου παρὰ τοῦ θεοῦ χρῆσιν λαβών, *Heres* 104 (and some more passages referred to by Wendland, "Philo und die Diatribe" 59). Jos. Bell. III 374 τῶν μὲν ἐξιόντων τοῦ βίου κατὰ τὸν τῆς φύσεως νόμον καὶ τὸ ληφθὲν παρὰ τοῦ θεοῦ χρέος ἐκτινύντων, ὅταν ὁ δοὺς κομίσασθαι θέλῃ, κτλ. The same concept lies behind Luke XII 20 τὴν ψυχήν σου ἀπαιτοῦσιν ἀπὸ σοῦ. The related notion of the soul as a deposit is found in Jos. Bell. III 272 (ψυχή = παρακαταθήκη τοῦ θεοῦ), Sextus Sent. 21 τὴν ψυχήν σου νόμιζε παραθήκην ἔχειν παρὰ θεοῦ, see further the Jewish texts in Marmorstein, "Das Motiv vom veruntreuten Depositum" 184ff. and Müller ad Apoc. Esdr. graec. VI 3 in *JSHRZ* V 2 p. 98. Bernays 203f. (too sweepingly?) says that by means of this image (of a loan) the pagan authors "wollen ... immer die Unsicherheit und Vergänglichkeit des menschlichen Daseins versinnlichen, da die Natur jeden Augenblick das dem Einzelnen auf unbestimmte Frist geliehene Leben zurückfordern könne. Der Phokylideische Spruch hingegen fasst den Geist als ein göttliches Darlehn um daraus vielmehr dessen *Ewigkeit* abzuleiten".

After this (Jewish-) Hellenistic motif there immediately follows an undeniably O.T. motif, as a kind of appendage (also stylistically): καὶ εἰκών, no doubt reflecting Gen. I 26f. ποιήσωμεν ἄνθρωπον κατ' εἰκόνα ἡμετέραν καὶ καθ' ὁμοίωσιν. ... κατ' εἰκόνα θεοῦ ἐποίησεν αὐτόν. Cf. Sap. Sal. II 23, and for the history of this motif in Judaism Jervell, *Imago Dei* (1960), 15-121 (Jervell's interpretation of our verse (*op. cit.* 28f.) is wrong: he thinks it explains v. 102 and athetizes vv. 103-4). Other examples of allusions to Gen. I 26f. omitting the preposition κατά are mentioned by Jervell, *op. cit.* 23f. Actually, in this verse not man but his spirit is an image of God. This is a well-known concept of Philo, who always makes εἰκών in Gen. I 26f. refer to man's spiritual principle, e.g. Opif. 69 ἡ δὲ εἰκὼν λέλεκται κατὰ τὸν νοῦν, Spec. Leg. I 81 τὴν ψυχὴν τὴν ἀθάνατον ἥν φασι τυπωθῆναι κατὰ τὴν εἰκόνα τοῦ ὄντος, Somn. I 74, Virt. 205, Det. pot. ins. 86, and many other passages mentioned by Baer, *Philo's Use of the Categories Male and Female* 21ff. This is a Platonic (and Stoic) view on which see Merki, "Ebenbildlichkeit", *RAC* IV 459ff. Sometimes also man as a whole is called εἰκὼν θεοῦ in Greek literature, e.g. Men. gnom. pap. II 3 (p. 5 Jäkel) γέροντα τίμα τοῦ θεοῦ τὴν εἰκόνα. Diog. Sinop. *ap*. Diog. Laert. VI 51 τοὺς ἀγαθοὺς ἄνδρας θεῶν εἰκόνας εἶναι. Cf. Lucian *Imag.* 28.

107-108 σῶμα γὰρ ἐκ γαίης ἔχομεν κἄπειτα πρὸς αὖ γῆν
λυόμενοι κόνις ἐσμέν· ἀὴρ δ' ἀνὰ πνεῦμα δέδεκται.

For we have a body out of earth, and when afterwards we are resolved
again into earth we are but dust; but the air has received our spirit.

Again an O.T. reminescense, but once more with Greek parallels: Gen. III 19 γῆ εἶ καὶ εἰς γῆν ἀπελεύσῃ. Eccles. XII 7 ... καὶ ἐπιστρέψῃ ὁ χοῦς ἐπὶ τὴν γῆν, ὡς ἦν, καὶ τὸ πνεῦμα ἐπιστρέψῃ πρὸς τὸν θεόν, ὃς ἔδωκεν αὐτό (cf. III 20 and Apoc. Esdr. graec. VII 3). Sir. XVII 1 κύριος ἔκτισεν ἐκ γῆς ἄνθρωπον καὶ πάλιν ἀπέστρεψεν αὐτὸν εἰς αὐτήν (cf. v. 32 and XL 11). Sap. Sal. XV 8 is quoted ad v. 106. The ἐκ γῆς-εἰς γῆν motif is more frequent in Greek literature (esp. in epitaphs): Xenophanes fr. 27 ἐκ γαίης γὰρ πάντα καὶ εἰς γῆν πάντα τελευτᾷ (N.B. also here the change γαίης-γῆν as in our verse). *Men. et Phil. comp.* I 113 ἀπὸ γῆς ἔφυ τὰ πάντα κεἰς γῆν οἴχεται *Epigr. Gr.* 75 (ed. Kaibel) ἐκ γαίης βλαστὼν γαῖα πάλιν γέγονα. Cf. Eur. fr. 195 and 839; *Or. Sib.* VIII 108f. These parallels show that the *varia lectio* πρὸς αὐτήν in ms. P (adopted by Crusius and Diehl, supported by Ludwich, *Spruchbuch* 21 and Rossbroich 70) is secondary, in spite of the reverse situation in 3 Kgs. XIX 3 (τὴν/ γῆν). On seemingly unelegant repetition (γαίης-γῆν) see Denniston ad Eur. *El.* 341-2. On κόνις ἐσμέν cf. Hor. *Od.* IV 7, 16 *pulvis ... sumus*; Stob. I 49, 46 quoted below, and Rossbroich 71 for more instances.

ἀὴρ δ' ἀνὰ πνεῦμα δέδεκται: poetic tmesis of the compound verb ἀναδέχομαι (= to take back); Cavallin, *Life after Death* I 155 n. 22 wrongly interprets ἀὴρ ἀνὰ as "the air above" (= αἰθήρ). That the air (mostly the higher air, aether) receives the spirit is again a very common motif in Greek and Latin literature, extensively treated by Rohde, *Psyche* II 257ff. and Waszink, "Aether", *RAC* I 150-155. Originating in philosophical schools (Diog. of Apollonia, Xenocrates) it later became a popular common-place, frequently found in epitaphs: *Corp. Inscr. Att.* I 142 αἰθὴρ μὲν ψυχὰς ὑπεδέξατο, σώματα δὲ χθῶν τῶνδε. Epich. fr. 245 γᾶ μὲν εἰς γᾶν, πνεῦμα δ' ἄνω. Eur. *Suppl.* 531ff. ἐάσατ' ἤδη γῇ καλυφθῆναι νεκρούς, | ὅθεν δ' ἕκαστον εἰς τὸ φῶς ἀφίκετο, | ἐνταῦθ' ἀπελθεῖν, πνεῦμα μὲν πρὸς αἰθέρα, | τὸ σῶμα δ' ἐς γῆν. An oracle in Stob. I 49, 46 (I p. 414 W-H) σῶμα λυθὲν ψυχήν τε λιπὸν καὶ γαῖα γενηθέν | οὐκέτι πως βιότοιο παλίνδρομον οἶδε κελεῦθον, | ἀλλὰ τὸ μὲν λυθέν ἐστι κενὴ κόνις, ἡ δὲ πρὸς αἴθρην | σκίδναται, ὁππόθεν ἦλθε, μετήορος εἰς αἰθέρ' ἁπλοῦν. *Epigr. Gr.* 41

ψυχὴν ... αἰθήρ ... ἔχει, σῶμα δὲ τύμβος, 104, 5-6 τὰ μὲν κεύθει μικρὰ κόνις ..., ψυχὴν δ' ... οὐρανὸς εὐρὺς ἔχει, 148, 2f.; 150, 8; 156, 1f.; 438; etc. Marc. Aur. IV 21 εἰ διαμένουσιν αἱ ψυχαί, πῶς αὐτὰς ... χωρεῖ ὁ ἀήρ (here ἀήρ, as in Ps-Phoc.); Cornutus *Theol. Gr.* 35 τὸν δεχόμενον τὰς ψυχὰς ἀέρα "Αιδην ... προσηγόρευσαν (the fact that this contemporary of Ps-Phoc. calls the air Hades—which was common in those days among the educated—tells against F. Christ's theory, *Theol. Zeitschr.* 31 (1975) 145, that contrasts air (with the spirit) and Hades (with the soul) in Ps-Phoc., in spite of n. 21 *ibid.*). *CIL* III 6384 *corpus habent cineres, animam sacer abstulit aer*; see the comments of Cumont, *After Life* 15, who sees here Stoic influence. Indeed the motif was very popular among Stoics (see *SVF* II 809-822); but to say that Ps-Phoc. is here wholly dependent upon Posidonius, as Rossbroich 71 does, is an exaggeration (Rohde, *Psyche* II 378 n. 2 calls Ps-Phoc. 108b Stoic). Cf. Hengel, *Judentum und Hellenismus* 228 n. 132.

109-110 πλουτῶν μὴ φείδου · μέμνησ' ὅτι θνητὸς ὑπάρχεις.
οὐκ ἔνι εἰς "Αιδην ὄλβον καὶ χρήματ' ἄγεσθαι.

When you are rich do not be sparing; remember that you are mortal.
It is impossible to take riches and money with you into Hades.

πλουτῶν: partic. of πλουτέω, not gen. plur. of πλοῦτος as Christ seems to think: "Spar nicht Reichtümer" (*Theol. Zeitschr.* 31 (1975), 140). ἔνι = ἔνεστιν, it is possible. This thought again occurs both in the O.T. and in Greek literature. Job I 21 γυμνὸς ἐξῆλθον ἐκ κοιλίας μητρός μου, γυμνὸς καὶ ἀπελεύσομαι ἐκεῖ, cf. Eccles. V 15 and Philo *Spec. Leg.* I 295. Ps. XLVIII 18 οὐκ ἐν τῷ ἀποθνῄσκειν αὐτὸν λήμψεται τὰ πάντα. Sir. XIV 13 πρίν σε τελευτῆσαι εὖ ποίει φίλῳ καὶ κατὰ τὴν ἰσχύν σου ἔκτεινον καὶ δὸς αὐτῷ (Sir. VIII 7 μνήσθητι ὅτι πάντες τελευτῶμεν). Men. gnom. syr. 65 (66; tr. Schulthess) "Wenn du Geld hast und Vermögen besitzest, so geniesse dein Geld solange du am Leben bist und dein Auge sehen und dein Fuss auftreten kann, denn sei eingedenk und sieh: In der Unterwelt kann man sein Geld nicht brauchen und der Reichtum begleitet nicht ins Totenhaus". (Christ, *ibid.* 143 stresses the affinity with the Syrian Menander here). Cf. 1 Tim. VI 7 οὐδὲν γὰρ εἰσηνέγκαμεν εἰς τὸν κόσμον, ὅτι οὐδὲ ἐξενεγκεῖν τι δυνάμεθα (and Spicq *ad loc.*). Rossbroich 71f. thinks that these verses (and the following) are typically Cynic, but that is not true, because this motif is also found outside Cynic circles; see Solon fr. 14, 7f. (= Theogn. 725f.)

τὰ γὰρ περιώσια πάντα χρήματ' ἔχων οὐδεὶς ἔρχεται εἰς 'Αΐδεω. Aesch. *Pers.* 842 τοῖς θανοῦσι πλοῦτος οὐδὲν ὠφελεῖ. Phoenix *ap.* Athen. XII 531A ἐγὼ δ' ἐς "Αιδην οὔτε χρυσὸν οὔθ' ἵππον οὔτ' ἀργυρῆν ἄμαξαν ᾠχόμην ἕλκων. Prop. III 5, 13f. *haud ullas portabis opes Acherontis ad undas*; *nudus ad infernas, stulte, vehere rates.* Sen. *Ep.* 102, 25 *non licet plus efferre quam intuleris.* Cf. *Carm. Aur.* 15f. On the changed view of Hades in later antiquity see Cumont, *After Life* 70-90.

These two lines look as if they have been more or less appended as an afterthought; their theme is not so much afterlife, but a warning against clinging too much to riches.

111 πάντες ἴσον νέκυες, ψυχῶν δὲ θεὸς βασιλεύει.

All alike are corpses, but God rules over the souls.

ἴσον: adverbial, see LSJ *s.v.* ἴσος IV 1, e.g. Soph. *O.R.* 1347. Rossbroich 47 thinks that v. 111b disrupts the connection between 111a and 112-3: "quid sibi velit supplementum ψυχῶν δὲ θεὸς βασιλεύει nescio. Animae (ψυχαί) omnino non sunt in 'Orco'! Versu 108 dixit auctor ἀὴρ δ' ἀνὰ πνεῦμα δέδεκται! Stupidus diversas opiniones permiscuit neque animadvertit se paucis versibus antea contrarium dixisse". But for such discrepancies see above *ad* v. 105. Moreover, Hades may simply be the air, see the comm. on v. 108b. The equality of all people in death is a common Hellenistic theme. Plaut. *Trin.* 493f. *aequo mendicus atque ille opulentissimus censetur censu ad Acheruntem mortuus.* Prop. III 5, 15 *victor cum victis pariter miscebitur umbris.* Sen. *Ad Marc.* XX 2 (*mors*) *exaequat omnia.* Sen. *Ep.* XCI 16 *aequat omnes cinis*; *impares nascimur, pares morimur.* Lucian *Dial. mort.* XXX 2 ἰσοτιμία γὰρ ἐν ᾅδου καὶ ὅμοιοι ἅπαντες, cf. *ibid.* I 4. *Anth. Pal.* VII 477, 3f. *Or. Sib.* VIII 107-9. Other passages in Packmohr, *Diog. Sinop.* 49f. and Greeven, *Hauptproblem* 14f. From the O.T. one may compare Job III 19 μικρὸς καὶ μέγας ἐκεῖ ἐστιν καὶ θεράπων οὐ δεδοικὼς τὸν κύριον αὐτοῦ. The formula θεὸς βασιλεύει occurs in another context also in Apoc. XI 17, XIX 6. Christ, "Leben nach dem Tode" 146 suggests that v. 111b is "eine theozentrische Beschreibung des jenseitigen ewigen Lebens". He adds: "Gottes Seelenkönigtum bedeutet doch wohl Gemeinschaft der Abgeschiedenen mit ihrem Herrscher" (cf. 144 n. 18); and then possessions (109f.) are no longer important.

112-113 κοινὰ μέλαθρα δόμων αἰώνια καὶ πατρὶς "Αιδης,
ξυνὸς χῶρος ἅπασι, πένησί τε καὶ βασιλεῦσιν.

Hades is our common eternal home and fatherland,
a common place for all, poor and kings.

δόμων seems redundant after μέλαθρα (house); therefore Bergk wanted to change the text (*Philol.* 41 (1882), 592ff. and *PLG* II[4] 96), but this poetic expression also occurs in Aesch. *Agam.* 957 (ἐς δόμων μέλαθρα). The expression "eternal home" for grave is often said to be Egyptian in origin (Cumont, *Relig. orient.* 247f.; Parrot, *Malédictions et violations de tombes* 178f.; Galling *ad* Eccles. XII 5; see Diod. Sic. I 51, 2 τοὺς δὲ τῶν τετελευτηκότων τάφους ἀϊδίους οἴκους προσαγορεύουσιν (sc. the Egyptians)), but there are several (early and late) Semitic instances, see Hoffner, *TWAT* I 635f.; Negev, *IEJ* 21 (1971), 50f.; Vattioni, *Rev. Bibl.* 78 (1971), 243f.; esp. Hoftijzer-van der Kooy, *Aramaic Texts from Deir ʿAlla* 224 (on 2, 6. I owe some of these references to Dr. Hoftijzer). Later it is found throughout the ancient world (see the numerous passages in Parrot, *op. cit.* 165-189: ch. VII "La domus aeterna", and esp. Stommel, "Domus aeterna", *RAC* IV 109-128). It is found in the O.T. in Eccles. XII 5 ἐπορεύθη ... εἰς οἶκον αἰῶνος αὐτοῦ (M.T. בית עולם), cf. Ps. XLVIII 12 and Tob. III 6; in the Murabbaʿat texts (*DJD* II 20, 7; 21, 12 בית עלמא), in the Jewish Men. gnom. syr. 22 (18; tr. Schulthess) "alle Menschen gehen ins Haus der Ewigkeit (בית עלמא)", in Jewish inscriptions, *CII* 337 (οἶκος αἰώνιος) and 523 (*domi heterne*), frequently in Latin epitaphs, *ILS* (Dessau) 7814, 7945a, 8077, 8078, 8080, 8081, 8082a, 8192, 8240, 8246, 8341 (all *domus aeterna*); Accius *ap.* Cic. *Nat. deor.* III 41 *in domum aeternam* (with Pease *ad loc.*). For κοινός and ξυνός (= κοινός) cf. *Men. et Phil. comp.* II 173 κοινὸν τὸν "Αιδην ἔσχον οἱ πάντες βροτοί, *Epigr. Gr.* 35, 4-6 κοινὸν ... θάλαμον, ... κοινὸς ταμίας.

πένησί τε καὶ βασιλεῦσι: Hor. *Od.* I 4, 13f. *pallida mors aequo pulsat pede pauperum tabernas regumque turris.* II 18, 32 *aequa tellus pauperi recluditur regumque pueris.* Cf. Lucian *Men.* 14. *Or. Sib.* II 322-4 (on Hades) οὐ γὰρ πτωχὸς ἐκεῖ, οὐ πλούσιος, οὐδὲ τύραννος, οὐ δοῦλος, οὐδ' αὖ μέγας, οὐ μικρός τις ἔτ' ἔσται, οὐ βασιλεῖς, οὐχ ἡγεμόνες· κοινῇ δ' ἅμα πάντες. Cf. VIII 110-112 and Job III 19 (quoted *ad* v. 111); for the polarity of expression cf. Test. Jud. XV 5.

114 οὐ πολὺν ἄνθρωποι ζῶμεν χρόνον, ἀλλ' ἐπίκαιρον.
We humans live not a long time but for a season.

Though the sense of ἐπίκαιρος is not quite clear here (see the various meanings in LSJ s.v.), the opposition to οὐ πολύν suggests the meaning "short, limited" (Christ, "Leben nach dem Tode" 140: "nur eine Zeitlang"; cf. LSJ s.v. II "temporary"). The sentence is a common-place with many parallels in both Greek and Jewish literature (see Rossbroich 73). Emped. fr. 2, 3f. παῦρον δὲ ζωῆς ἰδίου μέρος ἀθρήσαντες ὠκύμοροι καπνοῖο δίκην ἀρθέντες ἀπέπταν. Plut. Puer. educ. 17, 13B στιγμὴ χρόνου πᾶς ἐστιν ὁ βίος. Marc. Aur. IV 26 βραχὺς ὁ βίος. Men. et Phil. comp. I 68 ζωῆς γὰρ ἡμῖν ὀλίγος ἐμετρήθη χρόνος. Floril. duo graeca I 42 (p. 9 Schenkl). See also the collection of texts in Stob. IV 34 περὶ τοῦ βίου, ὅτι βραχὺς κτλ. From the O.T. Ps. LXXXIX 5ff., CII 15ff.; Job XIV 1f.; Is. XL 6; Sap. Sal. II 1.4, IX 5, XV 8. Cf. Men. gnom. syr. 67 (Schulthess) and Apoc. Bar. syr. XLVIII 12.

115 ψυχὴ δ' ἀθάνατος καὶ ἀγήρως ζῇ διὰ παντός.
But our soul is immortal and lives ageless forever.

One may equally well translate: "but the immortal and ageless soul lives forever". The combination ἀθάνατος καὶ ἀγήρως is Homeric: Il. II 447, VIII 539, XIII 323; Od. V 218; cf. Hes. Theog. 949. This verse is closely connected with v. 114. The view expressed here is too common to need illustration. Rohde, *Psyche* II 378 n. 2 calls v. 115 "ganz griechisch", but it is also a very common Jewish thought; see e.g. Hengel, *Judentum und Hellenismus* 357ff.; Cavallin, *Life After Death* I, *passim*; Christ, "Leben nach dem Tode" 144 n. 19; on Philo esp. Wolfson, *Philo* I 395ff. and Mayer's *Index s.v.* ἀθάνατος for references.

Vv. 116-121 *The Instability of Life*

116-117 [οὐδεὶς γινώσκει, τί μετ' αὔριον ἢ τί μεθ' ὥραν.
ἄσκοπός ἐστι βροτῶν θάνατος, τὸ δὲ μέλλον ἄδηλον.]
Nobody knows what will be after tomorrow or after an hour.
The death of mortals cannot be foreseen, and the future is uncertain.

Both verses are spurious: they occur in only one ms. (V); note also γινώσκει instead of γιγνώσκει and the Attic accusative ὥραν instead of ὥρην (which is found in v. 213). Rossbroich 73 thinks that the interpolator tried to bridge the sudden transition between vv. 115 and 118. Both vv. represent *loci communes* of ancient literature. *Ad* 116: Prov. III 28 οὐ γὰρ οἶδας τί τέξεται ἡ ἐπιοῦσα (cf. XXVII 1), Eccles. VIII 7 οὐκ ἔστιν γινώσκων τί τὸ ἐσόμενον, cf. IX 12 and Sir. XI 19. Theogn. 159f. οἶδε γὰρ οὐδεὶς ἀνθρώπων ὅ τι νὺξ χἠμέρη ἀνδρὶ τελεῖ. Men. *Mon.* 608 (= Trag. fr. adesp. 102) οὐδεὶς τὸ μέλλον ἀσφαλῶς ἐπίσταται. Men. et Phil. comp. I 204 τῆς γὰρ τύχης τὸ μέλλον οὐκ ἐπίστασαι. More references in Dibelius' commentary on James IV 14 (οὐκ ἐπίστασθε τῆς αὔριον ποία ἡ ζωὴ ὑμῶν). Cf. also the title of Varro's book *Nescis quid vesper vehat* (mentioned by Macr. *Sat.* I 7, 12). *Ad* 117: τὸ δὲ μέλλον ἄδηλον is almost proverbial; see Demosth. XV 21 ἄδηλον τὸ μέλλον ἅπασιν ἀνθρώποις. Ael. Arist. 31 p. 594 and 597 Dind.; 35 p. 102 D.; 36 p. 685 D. Philo *Jos.* 116 τὴν τοῦ μέλλοντος ἀδήλου πρόνοιαν, *Leg. ad Gaium* 322. Jos. *Ant.* VI 347 ἀδήλῳ τῷ μέλλοντι παραδόντας αὐτούς. On the theme in general cf. moreover Pind. *Ol.* XII 9, Ps-Isocr. *Ad Dem.* 29, Arist. *EN* I 10, 1101a18, Philo *LA* III 227, Sen. *Ep.* CI 4-6 and many other texts quoted by Plutarch in *Cons. ad Apoll.* 11, 107A-C.

118 μήτε κακοῖσ' ἄχθου μήτ' οὖν ἐπαγάλλεο χάρμῃ.
Let not evils dismay you nor therefore exult in success.

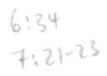

ἐπαγάλλομαι and χάρμη are both Homeric words (see LSJ); they also occur in *Or. Sib.* I 253 and 297 (cf. III 619). In vv. 118-121 again the ideal of emotional μετριότης is emphasized (cf. vv. 55, 59, 98). Exhortations to tranquillity of mind in ups and downs are frequent in gnomological literature. Theogn. 593f. μήτε κακοῖσιν ἀσῶντα λίην φρένα, μήτ' ἀγαθοῖσιν τερφθῇς ἐξαπίνης, πρὶν τέλος ἄκρον ἰδεῖν (cf. 657f.). Ps-Isocr. *Ad Dem.* 42 νόμιζε μηδὲν εἶναι τῶν ἀνθρωπίνων βέβαιον. οὕτω γὰρ οὔτ' εὐτυχῶν ἔσει περιχαρὴς οὔτε δυστυχῶν περίλυπος. Cleobulus *ap.* Diog. Laert. I 93 εὐτυχῶν μὴ ἴσθι ὑπερήφανος, ἀπορήσας μὴ ταπεινοῦ. τὰς μεταβολὰς τῆς τύχης γενναίως ἐπίστασο φέρειν (= Favorinus *gnom.* 1, *Rhein. Mus.* 35 (1880), 410). Men. *Mon.* 15 ἀνδρὸς τὰ προσπίπτοντα γενναίως φέρειν. Boissonade, *Anecd. Gr.* I 114 and 140. Plut. *Puer. educ.* 10, 7E τὸ δὲ μέγιστον, μήτ' ἐν ταῖς εὐπραγίαις περιχαρεῖς μήτ' ἐν ταῖς συμφοραῖς περιλύπους ὑπάρχειν. Cf. Cebes *Pinax* XXXI 2 μήτε χαίρειν ὅταν διδῷ μήτε ἀθυμεῖν ὅταν ἀφέληται (sc. τύχη). Cic. *Off.* I 90 *ut adversas res, sic secundas immoderate ferre levitatis est, praeclaraque est aequabilitas in omni vita et idem semper vultus eademque frons.* From Jewish literature cf. Sir. II 4 πᾶν ὃ ἐὰν ἐπαχθῇ σοι, δέξαι καὶ ἐν ἀλλάγμασιν ταπεινώσεώς σου μακροθύμησον (here, however, no counterpart to v. 118b). Vita Aes. 110 (rec. G, p. 70 Perry) ἐπὶ μεγάλῃ κτήσει μὴ χαῖρε, μηδὲ ἐπὶ μικρᾷ λυποῦ.

119-120   πολλάκις ἐν βιότῳ καὶ θαρσαλέοισιν ἄπιστον
πῆμα καὶ ἀχθομένοισι κακοῦ λύσις ἤλυθεν ἄφνω.

Many times in life incredible calamity comes suddenly to the confident and release from evil to the vexed.

These verses closely belong to the preceding (note ἄχθομαι and κακός both in 118 and in 120). Sudden changes of fortune are a recurrent theme in Greek gnomological literature. See already the prooemium of Hesiod's *Erga*. Theogn. 661ff. καὶ ἐκ κακοῦ ἐσθλὸν ἔγεντο | καὶ κακὸν ἐκ ἀγαθοῦ. καὶ τε πενιχρὸς ἀνήρ | αἶψα μάλ' ἐπλούτησε καὶ ὃς μάλα πολλὰ πέπαται | ἐξαπίνης ἀπό τοι οὖν ὤλεσε νυκτὶ μιῇ (cf. 639ff.). Archil. 58 D (= 130 W). Theodectes fr. XVI 3 N² ... τὸ μὴ βεβαίους τὰς βροτῶν εἶναι τύχας. Men. *Mon*. 577 οἷς μὲν δίδωσιν, οἷς δ' ἀφαιρεῖται τύχη, 625 ὁ βίος ἀδήλους τὰς μεταπτώσεις ἔχει, 652 πολλοὺς κακῶς πράσσοντας ὤρθωσεν τύχη, 745 τὰ θνητὰ πάντα μεταβολὰς πολλὰς ἔχει. Men. et Phil. comp. I 254f. μηδέποτε σαυτὸν δυστυχῶν ἀπελπίσῃς· καιρῶν γάρ εἰσι μεταβολαὶ καὶ τῆς τύχης, 256-7 ἂν εὐτυχῇς, ἄνθρωπε, μὴ φρόνει μέγα· πάλιν γὰρ ὄψει τῆς τύχης μετατροπήν. Many more instances in Stob. IV 41 (V p. 927-948 W-H), a chapter entitled ὅτι ἀβέβαιος ἡ τῶν ἀνθρώπων εὐπραξία μεταπιπτούσης ῥᾳδίως τῆς τύχης. Cf. also Plut. *Puer. educ*, 8, 5D and *Cons. ad Ap.* 5, 103F quoted above *ad* v. 27, and Ael. Arist. 46, p. 338 Dind. From Jewish writings Sir. XI 21 κοῦφον ἐν ὀφθαλμοῖς κυρίου διὰ τάχους ἐξάπινα πλουτίσαι πένητα. Eccles. IX 12 ὡς αὐτὰ (sc. ὄρνεα) παγιδεύονται οἱ υἱοὶ τοῦ ἀνθρώπου εἰς καιρὸν πονηρόν, ὅταν ἐπιπέσῃ ἐπ' αὐτοὺς ἄφνω (note ἐξάπινα and ἄφνω in these texts as in Ps-Phoc. 120). Cf. Men. gnom. syr. 19 and 21. See J. Krause, Ἄλλοις ἄλλος. *Untersuchungen zum Motiv des Schicksalswechsels in der griech. Dichtung*, München 1976.

121   καιρῷ λατρεύειν, μὴ δ' ἀντιπνέειν ἀνέμοισιν.

Accommodate yourself to the circumstances, do not blow against the winds.

LSJ s.v. λατρ.: καιρῷ λατρεύειν = *temporibus inservire*; cf. καιρὸν (καιροὺς) θεραπεύειν in Demosth. XVIII 307; Ael. Arist. 39 p. 743 Dind. (the texts referred to by Rossbroich 74, e.g. Sir. IV 20,

Col. IV 5, are no real parallels). ἀντιπνέειν ἀνέμοισιν: some editors (Crusius, Diehl, Farina), adopting a conjecture of Lobeck, print ἀντιπλέειν. Rossbroich 75 approves of this: "Comparatio cum ventis numquam in hominem ipsum transfertur". But that is not correct; see the texts (with metaphorical uses of πνέω and composita) collected by P. W van der Horst, "Drohung und Mord schnaubend (Acta IX 1)", *Nov. Test.* 12 (1970), 257ff. and W. J. Verdenius in *Lampas* 5 (1972), 100ff. Cf. e.g. Sappho fr. 47 (50); Aesch. *Agam.* 187.219; Soph. *Antig.* 929f.; Manetho *ap.* Jos. *C. Ap.* I 75. Brunck, *GPG* 162, remarks that one expects here indeed something about vain efforts, which is more clearly expressed by ἀντιπνέειν than by ἀντιπλέειν. Fortune is often compared to wind: Polyb. XXV 3, 9 τὰ τῆς τύχης ἀντέπνευσε. Clitomachus *ap.* Stob. IV 41, 29 (V p. 937 W-H) τοῖς εὐπλοοῦσιν ἀντιπνεύσασα ἡ τύχη ἅπαντα συγχεῖ, κᾆτα ναυαγεῖν ποιεῖ. Anon. simil. 19 (Mullach I 489) κυβερνήτου μὲν ἔργον ἀγαθοῦ εἰς τὰς τῶν πνευμάτων μεταβολὰς ἁρμόσασθαι, ἀνδρὸς δε σοφοῦ πρὸς τὰς τῆς τύχης. Cf. Teles p. 10, 4f. Hense. Lucian *Tox.* 7.

Vv. 122-131   *Speech and Wisdom, Man's Distinction*

122 μὴ μεγαληγορίῃ τρυφῶν φρένα λυσσωθείης.

Become not mad in your mind by revelling in boastfulness.

μεγαληγορίη: cf. μακραγορία, ὑπερηγορία, ὑψηγορία. λυσσόω is a *hapax*, the usual form being λυσσάω, see v. 214 λυσσῶσι. One ms. (V) reads φυσσῶν instead of τρυφῶν, which some editors (Bergk, Crusius, Diehl) have adopted in the form φυσῶν. But perhaps, as Young (letter of 12.5.1973) suggests, the reading φυσ(σ)ῶν is a mistaken gloss on τρυφῶν, abetted by a misunderstanding of the *accusativus respectus* in φρένα, which someone may have thought was the direct object of a transitive verb. For the theme cf. the many warnings against ὑπερηφανία in Greek, Jewish and Christian literature, e.g. Diod. Sic. XIII 21, 4 τοὺς ὑπερηφανοῦντας παρὰ θεοῖς μισουμένους. Sir. X 7-22 and the many examples in Bertram, *TWNT* VIII 526-530. Cf. 1 Kings II 3 μὴ καυχᾶσθε καὶ μὴ λαλεῖτε ὑψηλά, μὴ ἐξελθάτω μεγαλορρημοσύνη ἐκ τοῦ στόματος ὑμῶν.

123 εὐεπίην ἀσκεῖν, ἥτις μάλα πάντας ὀνήσει.

Practise speaking the right word, that will greatly benefit all.

On ἀσκεῖν see the notes on v. 76. Rossbroich 75 says that this precept "cum religione Iudaica nihil habet commune". He takes εὐεπίη to mean "eloquence", as does Young who in his *app. crit.* refers to Cic. *Inv.* I 2ff., where the origin and development of all civilization are attributed to eloquence; cf. Ael. Arist. 45 p. 133ff. Dind. According to Kroll (*Rhein. Mus.* 58 (1903), 578), this is a Posidonian theory. But one need not read that much into this verse. It might indeed be a slogan of an Alexandrian (?) school of rhetoric (on rhetorical training in Alexandria see R. W. Smith, *The Art of Rhetoric in Alexandria*, The Hague 1974); but more probably εὐεπίη means here something like "well-spoken, acceptable words"; cf. Soph. *O.R.* 932, where εὐεπεία = εὐφημία, and Hdt. V 50, 3. Then this verse is the positive counterpart to the warning against μεγαληγορίη in v. 122. One may compare Sir. VI 5 λάρυγξ γλυκὺς πληθυνεῖ φίλους αὐτοῦ, καὶ γλῶσσα εὔλαλος πληθυνεῖ εὐπροσήγορα, XX 13 ὁ σοφὸς ἐν λόγοις ἑαυτὸν προσφιλῆ ποιήσει, Eccles. IX 17.

124 ὅπλον τοι λόγος ἀνδρὶ τομώτερόν ἐστι σιδήρου.

Speech is to man a weapon sharper than iron.

The word or speech is often viewed as a sharp weapon both in Greek and in Jewish literature; see e.g. Ps. LVI 5 ἡ γλῶσσα αὐτῶν μάχαιρα ὀξεῖα (cf. LXIII 4). Hebr. IV 12 ζῶν γὰρ ὁ λόγος τοῦ θεοῦ καὶ ἐνεργὴς καὶ τομώτερος (!) ὑπὲρ πᾶσαν μάχαιραν (see Spicq *ad loc.*). Demetrius Phal. *ap.* Diog. Laert. V 82 ὅσον ἐν πολέμῳ δύνασθαι σίδηρον, τοσοῦτον ἐν πολιτείᾳ ἰσχύειν λόγον (= Favorinus *Sent.* 17, *Rhein, Mus.* 35 (1880), 413). Men. *Mon.* 621 ὅπλον μέγιστόν ἐστιν ἀνθρώποις λόγος. *Gnom. Vat.* 219 (on Demosthenes) ὁ αὐτὸς ἐρωτηθεὶς ποῖον μέγιστον ὅπλον εἶπε· λόγος (see Sternbach *ad loc.*). *Floril. duo graeca* I 48 (p. 9 Schenkl) ξίφους πληγὴ κουφοτέρα γλώττης. *Orph. Hymn.* XXVIII 10 γλώσσης δεινὸν ὅπλον. See further Packmohr, *Diog. Sin.* 31; Gerhard, *Phoinix* 48ff. On the shift of meaning of λόγος between 124 and 128 (from "speech" to "reason") see the commentary on v. 128.

125-128 ὅπλον ἑκάστῳ νεῖμε θεός, φύσιν ἠερόφοιτον ὄρνισιν, πώλοις ταχυτῆτ', ἀλκήν τε λέουσιν, ταύρους δ' αὐτοχύτως κέρα ἔσσεν, κέντρα μελίσσαις ἔμφυτον ἄλκαρ ἔδωκε, λόγον δ' ἔρυμ' ἀνθρώποισιν.

God allotted a weapon to every creature; the capacity to fly to birds, speed to horses, and strength to the lions; he clothed the bulls with their self-growing horns, he gave stings to the bees as their natural means of defence, but reason to man as his protection.

Note the chiasms in these lines. νεῖμε: epic aorist without augment. φύσιν ἠερόφοιτον: for this periphrastic use of φύσις (frequent in Plato) see LSJ s.v. III 5. ἀερόφοιτος is used in Aesch. fr. 282 and ἠεροφοῖτις (used by Ps-Phoc. in 171)is Homeric (Il. IX 571). πῶλος is frequently used by poets generally for ἵππος. The text of v. 127 is in disorder. Most mss. read ταύροις δ' αὐτοχύτοις κεράεσσιν, but that is syntactically impossible. Numerous emendations have been proposed. Brunck (GPG 163) ταύροις δ' αὐτοφυῆ κέρατ' ἐστίν, Bernays 217 n. 2 ταύροις δ' αὐτοφύτως κέρα ἐστίν, Goram 106 ταύροις δ' αὐτοφύτοις κεράεσσιν (!), Schmidt (Rhein. Mus. 26 (1871), 183) ταύροις δ' αὖ στόνυχας κερεαλκέσι, Hiller ταύροις δ' αὖτ' ἐφύτευσε κεράατα, see further Young's app. crit. Farina's rendering of the mss. reading by "(Dio diede ... la forza) ai tori nelle corna di cui sono forniti" (43) is unsatisfactory. Young's emendation is very ingenious and κέρα ἕσσεν may be adopted, though one expects ταύροις in view of ὄρνισιν, λέουσιν, μελίσσαις, ἀνθρώποισιν (for the construction of ἕννυμι with two accusatives see LSJ s.v.); but αὐτοχύτως (in one ms.) is difficult. αὐτόχυτος = poured out of itself, self-flowing; it is said e.g. of water in Ael. Arist. 39, 16 K. Bernays' αὐτοφύτως is the most probable solution, since the stem φυ- often occurs in this context: see ἔμφυτον in v. 128 and several passages quoted below; see esp. Plato Prot. 321a7 αὐτοφυής and Hierocles Stoicus Elem. eth. col. II 7 (p. 11 Arnim) where the bull's κέρατα are called ὅπλα συμφυᾶ.

The theme of these verses has been a common-place in Greek literature since "Protagoras" (see Plato Prot. 320d-321e). It is extensively dealt with by Dickermann, De argumentis quibusdam ... e structura hominis et animalium petitis, diss. Halle 1909, 48-73 (esp. 56-64). A great number of texts is also found in Pease's commentary on Cic. Nat. deor. II 121 and esp. 127 (II p. 875-879). The ὅπλα most frequently mentioned are ὀδόντες, κέντρα, κέρατα, ὄνυχες, ὁπλαί and ταχυτής (or ποδῶν τάχος). Some instances may suffice: Plato Prot. 320d-321e and Isocr. Nicocles 5ff. are long passages which discuss this subject, as are also Plut. De fortuna 3, 98C-E and Hierocles Stoicus col. II 3-III 52 (p. 11-19 Arnim). Philo Somn. I 103 ἀνθρώπῳ λόγος δώρημα κάλλιστον ἐδόθη παρὰ θεοῦ ... ὡς γὰρ τῶν ἄλλων ἕκαστον ζῴων ἡ φύσις οἰκείοις ἕρκεσιν ὠχύρωσε, δι' ὧν τοὺς ἐπιχειροῦντας ἀδικεῖν ἀποκρούσεται, καὶ ἀνθρώπῳ μέγιστον ἔρυμα (!) καὶ φρουρὰν ἀκαθαίρετον λόγον δέδωκε (ἔρυμα in this connection also in Cornutus Theol. Gr. 16 p. 20, 23 Lang). Cic.

Nat. deor. II 127 *cornibus tauri, apri dentibus, cursu leones, aliae fuga se, aliae occultatione tutantur*, etc. (cf. *Tusc.* V 38). *Anacreontea* XXIV 1-7 φύσις κέρατα ταύροις, ὁπλὰς δ᾽ ἔδωκεν ἵπποις, ποδωκίην λαγωοῖς, λέουσι χάσμ᾽ ὀδόντων, τοῖς ἰχθύσιν τὸ νηκτόν, τοῖς ὀρνέοις πέτασθοι, τοῖς ἀνδράσιν φρόνημα. Max. Tyr. XX 6 ὥσπερ γὰρ ἄλλο ἄλλῳ ζῴῳ ἀλέξημα ἥκει παρὰ τῆς φύσεως εἰς τὸν αὐτοῦ βίον, ὑφ᾽ οὗ σῴζεται, λέουσιν ἀλκή, κτλ. . . . ὧδε καὶ τοῖς ἀνθρώποις . . . λόγον . . . θεὸς ἔδωκε. Min. Fel. *Oct.* XVII 10 *alias armatas cornibus, alias dentibus saeptas et fundatas ungulis et spicatas aculeis aut pedum celeritate liberas aut elatione pinnarum*. See numerous other passages in Dickermann and Pease. Dickermann 58 also quotes Ps-Phoc. but reads πολλὴν ταχυτῆτ᾽ instead of πώλοις ταχυτῆτ᾽, arguing that "vulgo in hac serie non equus, sed cervus et lepus ad celeritatem illustrandam sunt adhibiti". But he is refuted by some of his own examples, e.g. Plut. *De fort.* 3, 98E κουφότατον ἵπποι καὶ ὠκύτατον and Max. Tyr. XXXI 4 τῷ ἵππων γένει . . . δρόμος.

In many texts collected by Dickermann and Pease the distinguishing weapon of man is not called λόγος, but λογισμός, νοῦς, φρόνημα, σοφία (see also Ael. Arist. 45, 17 K.). That is to say that λόγος, which seems to mean "speech" in v. 124 (in view of vv. 122-3), means "reason" in v. 128 (the following vv. too deal with σοφία). This shift of meaning cannot well be rendered in a translation, since there is no English word which covers both meanings of λόγος. It is clear that in v. 124 both semantic aspects of λόγος play a role.

In this connection it should be said that in Greek literature animals are often called ἄλογα; see Bauer *s.v.* It should also be noted that, whereas in most of the parallels from Greek literature it is nature (φύσις) that gives the "weapons", in Ps-Phoc. it is God (note the curious shift from θεός to φύσις in Philo *Somn.* I 103, quoted above).

129 [τῆς δὲ θεοπνεύστου σοφίης λόγος ἐστὶν ἄριστος.]
But speech of the divinely inspired wisdom is best.

Several scholars (Dornseiff 44ff., Bergk *ad loc.*, Ludwich, *Quaest.* 31) have rightly stressed the fact that the occurrence of θεόπνευστος in this verse does not necessarily mean that it is a Christian interpolation (see 2 Tim. III 16; Bauer *s.v.*), but its omission by two important mss. (M, B) and by Stob. (III 3, 28, where vv. 125-130 are quoted without v. 129) and its disrupting the continuity of vv.

128 and 130 strongly suggest so (curiously, Dornseiff says that v. 129 cannot be missed since it is the "gedankliche Brücke" between 128 and 130). It looks as if λόγος in 128 and σεσοφισμένος in 130 prompted the interpolator to make a (clumsy) verse containing the words λόγος and σοφία. It may be a product of Byzantine sophiology. If the verse is, nevertheless, Jewish (so e.g. Krauss, *Jew. Enc.* X 256), then it may be about the words (λόγος) of the Torah; σοφία (חכמה) = Torah, see Wilckens, *TWNT* VII 505ff. It is less probable that the verse is about the Holy Spirit, though Wisdom and Spirit are often identified in Judaism (see e.g. Kirk, "The Meaning of Wisdom in James", *NTS* 16 (1969/70), 32ff.). Already in the O.T. there is a close connection between Wisdom and Spirit, see e.g. Ex. XXXI 3 πνεῦμα θεῖον σοφίας.

130 βέλτερος ἀλκήεντος ἔφυ σεσοφισμένος ἀνήρ.
Better is a wise man than a strong one.

σοφίζειν in the LXX often renders חכם (pi. and hiph.); it is frequent in Wisdom literature. The author is induced to this theme because λόγος in v. 128 means *ratio*. The sentiment expressed is common to Greek and Jewish literature. Xenophanes fr. 2, 12 ῥώμης . . . ἀμείνων . . . σοφίη. Democr. fr. 187 σκήνεος δὲ ἰσχὺς ἄνευ λογισμοῦ ψυχὴν οὐδέν τι ἀμείνω τίθησιν. Ps-Isocr. *Ad Dem.* 6 ῥώμη δὲ μετὰ μὲν φρονήσεως ὠφέλησεν, ἄνευ δὲ ταύτης πλείω τοὺς ἔχοντας ἔβλαψε. *Gnom. Byz.* 21 (= *Flor. Mon.* 20) αἱροῦ τῇ ψυχῇ μᾶλλον ἢ τῷ σώματι ἰσχύειν, see the parallels collected by Wachsmuth *ad loc.* and cf. Herod. III 127. Prov. XXIV 5 κρείσσων σοφὸς ἰσχυροῦ. Eccles. IX 16 ἀγαθὴ σοφία ὑπὲρ δύναμιν (cf. v. 18). Rossbroich 77 surmises that this verse reflects Cynic polemics against specialization in athletics, on which see Dudley, *History of Cynicism* 87 and esp. Wendland, *Philo und die Diatribe* 43f., who mentions relevant passages from diatribes which are, however, not only Cynic. On the problem of the *brevis pro longa* α in ἀνήρ see Rossbroich 9.

131 ἀγροὺς καὶ πόλιας σοφίη καὶ νῆα κυβερνᾷ.
Wisdom directs the course of lands and cities and ships.

ἀγρούς = the country, as opposed to πόλιας, cf. Hom. *Od.* XVII 18, etc. Again σοφία might refer to the Jewish Law, though that is hardly congruous with νῆα; this, however, may have been caused by Sap. Sal. X 4 σοφία . . . τὸν δίκαιον (i.e. Noah) κυβερνήσασα, which suggests that Wisdom steered the ark of Noah. Cf. Sen.

Ep. XVI 3 (*sapientia*) *sedet ad gubernaculum et per ancipitia fluctuantium derigit cursum* (cf. also Clem. Alex. *Strom*. I 4, 25, 2 on Hesiod: ναύτην οὐκ ὀκνεῖ λέγειν σοφόν). For this metaphoric use of κυβερνᾶν see e.g. Plato *Euthyd*. 291d ἐν τῇ πρύμνῃ καθῆσθαι τῆς πόλεως πάντα κυβερνῶσα and LSJ *s.v.* Cf. D. van Nes, *Die maritime Bildersprache des Aischylos*, Groningen 1963, 122-128. On σοφία in Judaism see Wilckens, *TWNT* VII 497-510. It remains uncertain, however, what sense σοφία has for our author. It may simply be "wise deliberation". Cf. Prov. VIII 15f. where rulers are said to rule through wisdom. Cf. also above the commentary on v. 88.

Vv. 132-152   *Avoidance of Wickedness and Virtuous Life*

132-134   οὐχ ὅσιον κρύπτειν τὸν ἀτάσθαλον ἄνδρ' ἀνέλεγκτον,
ἀλλὰ χρὴ κακοεργὸν ἀποτρωπᾶσθαι ἀνάγκῃ.
πολλάκι συνθνήσκουσι κακοῖσ' οἱ συμπαρεόντες.

It is unholy to hide a wicked man so as to prevent his being brought to trial,
but one must turn away an evildoer forcibly.
Those who are with the bad often die together with them.

οὐχ ὅσιον: see Terstegen, ΕΥΣΕΒΗΣ *en* ΟΣΙΟΣ 159ff.; on p. 122 he translates this verse by "het is onverantwoordelijk . . ."; better is: „unholy; impious; unallowed", see *TWNT* V 488f., 491f. ἀνέλεγκτον is interpreted in my translation proleptically: ὥστε ἀνέλεγκτον εἶναι, but it may also be taken as a qualification of ἄνδρα. Bernays 237 says that vv. 132-3 are based upon Deut. XIII 7ff., where it is said about the man who tries to bring someone to idolatry: . . . (9) οὐ συνθελήσεις αὐτῷ καὶ οὐκ εἰσακούσῃ αὐτοῦ, καὶ οὐ φείσεται ὁ ὀφθαλμός σου ἐπ' αὐτῷ, οὐκ ἐπιποθήσεις ἐπ' αὐτῷ οὐδ' οὐ μὴ σκεπάσῃς αὐτόν· (10) ἀναγγέλλων ἀναγγελεῖς περὶ αὐτοῦ . . ., and B. comments: "Der Phokylides . . . hat es von dem jüdisch-religiösen Boden hinweg in das Gebiet der allgemeinen Criminaljustiz gezogen" (thus also Riessler 1320). It seems to be better to compare Num. XVI 26 ἀποσχίσθητε ἀπὸ τῶν σκηνῶν τῶν ἀνθρώπων τῶν σκληρῶν τούτων καὶ μὴ ἅπτεσθε ἀπὸ πάντων, ὧν ἐστιν αὐτοῖς, μὴ συναπόλησθε ἐν πάσῃ τῇ ἁμαρτίᾳ αὐτῶν. Rossbroich 78 refers to *CIG* 3044 ὅστις . . . ἢ κιξαλλεύοι ἢ κιξάλλας ὑποδέχοιτο ἢ λῃζοιτο ἢ λῃστὰς ὑποδέχοιτο . . . ἀπόλλυσθαι καὶ αὐτὸν καὶ γένος τὸ κένο (on this inscription see Schmidt, *Ethik* II 376). Reference may also be made to Dittenberger, *Sylloge* III 985, 23ff. ἐάν τις τούτων τι ποῆι ἢ ἐπιβουλεύηι, μήτε ἐπιτρέψειν μήτε παρασιωπήσειν, ἀλλ' ἐμφανιεῖν καὶ ἀμυνεῖσθαι, with the comments of Weinreich, "Stiftung" 58, who refers to Ps-Phoc. 132f. Cf. further from gnomological literature (though not strictly parallel) Men. *Mon.* 25 ἀνδρὸς πονηροῦ φεῦγε συνοδίαν ἀεί (cf. 66, 423). Boissonade, *Anecd.* I 12 ἀνδρὸς πανούργου φεῦγε τὰς ὁμιλίας, *ibid.* 158 συζῆν κακοῖσι μὴ σὺ πειρῶ τὸ σύνολον. Rossbroich 79 mentions Eur. *El.* 1355 μηδ' ἐπιόρκων μέτα συμπλείτω (see Denniston *ad loc.* and cf. Eur. *Suppl.* 226-8). Boissonade, *Anecd.* I 73 ὁ συν(ι)ὼν πονηροῖς τὴν αὐτὴν αὐτοῖς ὑποστήσεται βλάβην. Cf. the story of Bias in Diog. Laert. I 86 and other texts mentioned by Schmidt, *Ethik* I 66. Again, it is impossible to define Ps-Phoc.'s source, though it is probable that sentences of this kind derive from gnomologies. Whatever may have been the source of these verses, a Jewish origin cannot be excluded, since they reflect a really Jewish sentiment; see Nissen, *Gott und der Nächste im antiken Judentum* 318ff. ("die religiös-sittlich motivierte Feindschaft"), esp. the texts on p. 323 nn. 1013-1019 (e.g. Sir. XII 2f.; XXVIII 13; Aboth I 7; Gen. Rabba XXII 8; etc.). Later Jewish parallels to v. 134 are also mentioned by Klein, *Älteste christliche Katechismus* 152, e.g. Baba Kama 92a (a proverb) "together with the thorn the cabbage is smitten", which means that the good are punished together with the bad (see the note in the Soncino translation); cf. Negaim XII 6 and Aboth de R. Nathan (rec. A) IX 4 and XXX 3.

135-136 φωρῶν μὴ δέξῃ κλοπίμην ἄδικον παραθήκην.
ἀμφότεροι κλῶπες, καὶ ὁ δεξάμενος καὶ ὁ κλέψας.

Accept not from thieves a stolen, unlawful deposit.
Both are thieves, the one who receives as well as the one who steals.

The author's tendency towards varied diction is well illustrated by his using three different words for "thief" in these two verses: φώρ, κλώψ, κλέψας (see also *ad* v. 227). κλόπιμος is used in v. 154 in the sense of "thievish" (χεῖρες κλόπιμαι), here it means "gotten by fraud, stolen" (the word occurs only in texts from the first cent. A.D. onwards). παραθήκη (= παρακαταθήκη) is used in the LXX, e.g. Lev. V 21; see further *ad* v. 13 (where παρθεσίη is used). δεξάμενος is the usual word in this connection, see e.g. Plato *Resp.* 442e6-7 παρακαταθήκην χρυσίου ἢ ἀργυρίου δεξάμενος. Rossbroich 79 compares Prov. XXIX 24 ὃς μερίζεται κλέπτῃ μισεῖ τὴν ἑαυτοῦ ψυχήν and *Digesta* XLVII 16, 1 *pessimum genus est receptatorum, ... et praecipitur, ut perinde puniantur atque latrones. in pari causa habendi sunt qui, cum adprehendere latrones possent, pecunia accepta vel subreptorum parte dimiserunt.* Strömberg, *Greek Proverbs* 64, presumes that v. 136 renders a proverb. The proposals of Bernays, Goram and Bergk to rearrange the vv. 135-152 are all futile.

137 μοίρας πᾶσι νέμειν, ἰσότης δ' ἐν πᾶσιν ἄριστον.

Render to all their due, impartiality is best in every way.

μοίρας νέμειν: Hom. *Od.* VIII 470; Aesch. *Prom.* 294 (though in another sense). ἰσότης (cf. ἴσος in vv. 15, 111, 152, 222): equality, justice, impartiality (see the discussion of this word by Hirzel, *Themis* 228ff., 273ff.). ἰσότης played an important part in Greek ethics and politics (cf. also Stählin, *TWNT* III 346-8). Polyb. II 38, 8 δύο συνεργοῖς τοῖς ἰσχυροτάτοις, ἰσότητι καὶ φιλανθρωπίᾳ Diog. Laert. VII 126 (Zeno) ἔπονται ... τῇ δικαιοσύνῃ ἰσότης καὶ εὐγνωμοσύνη. Hence, it occurs frequently in gnomological literature, e.g. Men. *Mon.* 358 ἴσος ἴσθι πᾶσι, κἂν ὑπερέχῃς τῷ βίῳ, 362 ἰσότητα τίμα, μὴ πλεονέκτει μηδένα (cf. 366), 373 ἴσος ἴσθι κρίνων καὶ φίλους καὶ μὴ φίλους (more instances from Greek literature in Hirzel and Stählin). Great importance is attached to it by Philo, e.g. *Plant.* 122 δικαιοσύνην δὲ ἰσότης ἔτεκε, *Spec. leg.* IV 165 δύο τὰ πάντων ἄριστα· ἐν μὲν ἰσότητα κτλ. *ibid.* 231 ἔστι γὰρ ἰσότης ... μήτηρ δικαιοσύνης (for other similar passages see Heinemann, *Philons Bildung* 346f. and Fiedler, "Δικαιοσύνη" 127 nn. 1-3); cf. *Ep. Arist.* 191 and Col. IV 1. In the O.T. this concept does not play an important role.

138 ἀρχόμενος φείδου πάντων, μὴ τέρμ' ἐπιδεύῃς.

In the beginning be sparing with all things, lest in the end you come short.

τέρμα is adv. (= τέλος), see Crusius LXXIV and LSJ *s.v.* On ἐπιδεύῃς LSJ *s.v.* state: "the act. occurs only in Aeol. fut. inf. ἐπιδεύσην, *f.l.* in Sappho 2.15". But Renehan, *Greek Lexicographical Notes* 88, remarks: "This assertion is refuted by Ps-Phoc. 138". Bergk conjectured ἐπιδεύῃ, which might be right; the final -ς could be explained by influence of the adjective ἐπιδευής. If ἐπιδεύῃς is to be maintained, then it may be a freely-formed active, analogous to the new middle form τελέθονται (instead of τελέθουσι) in v. 104. The creation of active forms to middle verbs is typical of later Greek, so e.g. ἀκούσω instead of ἀκούσομαι, καταιδέω instead of καταιδέομαι, βούλω instead of βούλομαι, etc. W. J. Verdenius surmises (in a letter dated 22.7.1974) that Ps-Phoc. polemizes against Hes. *Op.* 368-9 ἀρχομένου δὲ πίθου καὶ λήγοντος κορέσασθαι, μεσσόθι φείδεσθαι· δειλὴ δ' ἐν πυθμένι φειδώ (cf. also Strömberg, *Greek Proverbs* 48).

139 μὴ κτήνους θνητοῖο βορὴν κατὰ μέτρον ἕληαι.

Take not for yourself a mortal beast's ration of food.

This translation is uncertain since the Greek text is obscure (see Bergk *ad loc.*). Most interpreters suggest that v. 139 belongs to vv. 147-8 where the eating of meat from beasts that have been torn by wild animals is forbidden (so Brunck, Rossbroich, Sitler, Beltrami, Riessler, Easton, Dornseiff, Farina); but von Blumenthal (*Gnomon* 1943, 292) rightly objects: "θνητός für τεθνηκώς schreibt sonst kein Grieche". Therefore, Deut. XIV 21 (πᾶν θνησιμαῖον οὐ φάγεσθε), often adduced in this connection, is no parallel. Scaliger, *Animadv.* 89, suggests: "quod quidem quum ex senectute et aevo maturo moritur, hic noster Phocylides vocat θνητὸν κατὰ μέτρον, mortuum secundum temporis modum et mensuram a natura praestitutam. Poetae κατὰ μοῖραν". Here the same objection applies: θνητός cannot mean "dead". Wachler, *Ps-Phoc.* 11, says: "κατὰ μέτρον conjungendum est cum κτήνους θνητοῖο, i.e. 'ne ad modum pecoris (immoderate) edas' ". Binder, *Die Elegien* etc. 75, still better renders: "Nicht entziehe dem Vieh unrechtlicherweise die Nahrung". But both Wachler and Binder leave θνητοῖο untranslated. There are two equally plausible solutions: the first is presented in the above translation; the second (suggested by Young in a letter dated 6.10.72) is to render κτήνους θνητοῖο βορήν by "the fodder of a mortal's (= man's) domestic animal" (cf. v. 141 βροτός = man). Young supports this interpretation by the following story: "Over 60 years ago my father, as a businessman in India, found his favourite horse getting too thin, and found the groom was eating the horse's food; so he dismissed him and hired a groom of a cast that was forbidden to eat a horse's food". βορὴν κατὰ μέτρον has to be taken together: the fodder by measurement = the ration of fodder. Prof. J. Mansfeld suggested to read βορὴν κατ' ἄμετρον, translating: "do not take (the meat) of a mortal animal for immoderate eating" (cf. the Homeric κατὰ δαῖτα = to eat); he compares the Pythagorean rule ἀπέχεσθαι βρωτῶν θνησειδίων τε κρεῶν in Diog. Laert. VIII 33 and v. 147 (where he also sees Pythagorean ideas). Young's interpretation looks more feasible.

140 κτῆνος δ' ἦν ἐχθροῖο πέσῃ καθ' ὁδόν, συνέγειρε.

If a beast of your enemy falls on the way, help it to rise.

συνεγείρω occurs only in Hellenistic times; the first instance is LXX Ex. XXIII 5, see below. The humane attitude towards animals expressed in v. 139 is also found in this verse. Scaliger, *Animadv.* 89, thought it was inspired by Deut. XXII 4 οὐκ ὄψῃ τὸν ὄνον τοῦ ἀδελφοῦ σου ἢ τὸν μόσχον αὐτοῦ πεπτωκότας ἐν τῇ ὁδῷ, μὴ ὑπερίδῃς αὐτούς· ἀνιστῶν ἀναστήσεις μετ' αὐτοῦ, but in Scaliger's view the author must have been a Christian "quum addidit ἐχθροῖο". This great scholar simply overlooked Ex. XXIII 5 (see Bernays 197) ἐὰν δὲ ἴδῃς τὸ ὑποζύγιον τοῦ ἐχθροῦ σου πεπτωκὸς ὑπὸ τὸν γόμον αὐτοῦ, οὐ παρελεύσῃ αὐτό, ἀλλὰ συνεγερεῖς αὐτὸ μετ' αὐτοῦ. (Rossbroich 80: "Fontem esse Exod. 23, 5 nemo est qui neget"). The same mentality is expressed in 4 Macc. II 14 and *Ep. Arist.* 227; cf. Philo *Virt.* 116-8. There are no Greek or Roman parallels (cf. Beltrami, *Riv.* 41 (1913), 535: "Ebraismo schietto").

141 πλαζόμενον δὲ βροτὸν καὶ ἀλίτροπον οὔποτ' ἐλέγξεις.

Never expose a wandering man and a sinner.

This translation is a guess, for the text is hopelessly corrupt (Bergk *ad loc.*: "multimodis hic locus corruptus"; he athetizes both 141 and 142 as clumsy interpolations). There are numerous variant readings for no less than 5 of the 7 words in this verse (see Young's *app. crit.*), the most important of which are ἀλήμονα (wanderer, rover) instead of ἀλίτροπον and ἀλύξῃς instead of ἐλέγξῃς (and μήποτε for οὔποτε). Moreover, ἀλίτροπος is a *hapax* in Greek literature (not even mentioned in LSJ). There have been made several conjectures: Bernays 238f. reads πλαζόμενόν τε βοτὸν (= beast) κατ' ἀταρπιτὸν οὔποτ' ἀλύξεις, with reference to Deut. XXII 1-3 ("when you see a fellow-countryman's ox or sheep straying, do not ignore it, but take it back to him"). Goram 112 reads πλαζόμενον δὲ βοτὸν καὶ ἀλίτροπον μήποτ' ἐλέγξῃς (and he regards ἀλίτροπος as a compound of ἀλιτρός, "sinful", and πούς, comparing μακρόπος, ἀρτίπος, πολύπος). Ludwich, *Spruchbuch* 22, proposes πλαζόμενον δὲ βροτὸν καὶ ἀλήμονα μήποτ' ἀλύξῃς (or ἀλέξῃς). Dornseiff, *Echtheitsfragen* 46 n. 2, suggests πλαζόμενον δὲ βοτὸν καὶ ἀλήμονα μήποτ' ἀλύξῃς. The first problem that has to be solved is the meaning of ἀλίτροπος, which as a *lectio difficilior* is to be preferred to ἀλήμονα. Sartorius, *Analysis* 111, takes it to derive from ἅλς (sea) and τρέπω (to turn), and translates: "marivagus, mari volutatus, in mari jactatus". This would fit in quite well with πλαζόμενον (and is to be preferred to Goram's explanation mentioned above). Young suggests (in a letter dated 6.10.1972) a derivation from ἀλιτρός and τρόπος, "of sinful ways", by haplology, comparing ἀμφορεύς from ἀμφί and φορεύς. In that case πλαζόμενον has to be interpreted metaphorically (as "an erring man"). It is not easy to decide. οὔποτ' ἐλέγξεις is a LXX type of prohibition with the future indicative (cf. οὐ φονεύσεις and the like, and see K-G I 174f.), which is preferable to μήποτ' ἐλέγξῃς since that is metrically impossible (-πον must be short). What the verse means still remains uncertain. For the literal interpretation one might compare Sen. *De ira* I 14, 3 *errantem per agros ignorantia viae melius est ad rectum iter admovere quam expellere*. For the "metaphorical" interpretation (Young) reference could be made to the Stoic theory that a bad man should be helped, not refuted, since he remains a brother; see e.g. Marc. Aur. VII 22 ἴδιον ἀνθρώπου φιλεῖν καὶ τοὺς πταίοντας, and other passages mentioned by Bodson, *Morale sociale* 114ff. (with nn. 262-268). That this view is not wholly consistent with v. 152 is no counter-argument; there are more inconsistencies in this poem. Bernays' (and Dornseiff's) interpretation (with the conj. βοτόν and ἀλύξεις) cannot, however, be ruled out; the verse would fit in very well then both with v. 140 and with v. 142. This interpretation is also supported by the fact that the source of this verse would be then Ex. XXIII 4 (rather than Deut. XXII 1ff.) while Ex. XXIII 5 is the source of v. 140. Moreover, Philo *Virt.* 116-118 deals with Ex. XXIII 4-5 and adds: thus one turns an enemy into a friend, which is a parallel to v. 142. Ps-Phoc. would seem to have the same sequence of thought as Philo. However, Philo interprets Ex. XXIII 4-5 in a metaphorical way, and a metaphorical interpretation of v. 141 also fits in excellently with v. 142. The use of ἐλέγχειν is well illustrated by *Gnom. Byz.* 59 (quoted below *ad* v. 207), where it is opposed to διορθοῦν as ὀνειδίζειν to νουθετεῖν, the one being σκληρὸν καὶ ὑβριστικόν, the other being ἤπιον καὶ φίλον.

142 βέλτερον ἀντ' ἐχθροῦ τεύχειν φίλον εὐμενέοντα.

It is better to make a gracious friend instead of an enemy.

τεύχειν is Bergk's conjecture for τυχεῖν (M, P, L, V; B τ' ἔχειν), which may be kept if one reads ἐχθροῖο with two mss. (B, L). The concern for friendship is found in the LXX only in the later Wisdom literature, e.g. Sir. VII 18 μὴ ἀλλάξῃς φίλον ἕνεκεν διαφόρου, VI 16 φίλος πιστὸς φάρμακον ζωῆς (cf. vv. 5-17 and other Wisdom texts mentioned by Crouch, *Origin* 74, and by K. Treu, "Freundschaft", *RAC* VIII 424). In Greek literature there is a high appreciation of making friends (see Bolkestein, *Wohltätigkeit* 82-84, 401 and esp. Ferguson, *Moral Values in the Ancient World* 53-75); see e.g. Diog. Laert. I 87 (Bias) ἥδιον ἔλεγε δικάζειν μεταξὺ ἐχθρῶν ἢ φίλων· τῶν μὲν γὰρ φίλων πάντως ἐχθρὸν ἔσεσθαι τὸν ἕτερον, τῶν δὲ ἐχθρῶν τὸν ἕτερον φίλον. I 91 (Cleobulus) ἔλεγέ τε τὸν φίλον δεῖν εὐεργετεῖν, ὅπως μᾶλλον ᾖ φίλος, τὸν δὲ ἐχθρὸν φίλον ποιεῖν (= *Gnom. Vat.* 370, cf. 508 with Sternbach's notes). VIII 23 (Pythagoras said) ἀλλήλοις θ' ὁμιλεῖν, ὡς τοὺς μὲν φίλους ἐχθροὺς μὴ ποιῆσαι, τοὺς δ' ἐχθροὺς φίλους ἐργάσασθαι (cf. VII 124 on Zeno, and see Pohlenz, *Stoa* I 141, II 76). Men. *Mon.* 575 οὐκ ἔστιν οὐδὲν κτῆμα κάλλιον φίλου (Young compares *Mon.* 558 ξένον προτίμα, καὶ φίλον κτήσῃ καλόν). Moschion *Gnom.* 4 (in Schenkl's ed. of Epict. p. 493) βέλτιον πολλὰ χρήματα ἀπολέσαντα ἕνα φίλον κτήσασθαι ἢ ἕνα φίλον ἀπολέσαντα πολλὰ χρήματα κτήσασθαι. *Floril. duo graeca* I 68 (p. 9 Schenkl). On Philo *Virt.* 118 see *ad* v. 141; there also comments on the connection of v. 142 with v. 141. Berger's statement (*Gesetzesauslegung Jesu* I 116) "Eine ausgeprägte Freundschaftsethik findet sich ... in jüdisch-hellenistischen Weisheitsbüchern Ps-Phokylides und Ps-Menander", is somewhat exaggerated.

143 ἀρχόμενον τὸ κακὸν κόπτειν ἕλκος τ' ἀκέσασθαι.
Nip the evil in the bud and heal the wound.

Bergk *ad loc.* rightly saw: Imitatur poeta Theogn 1133ff. Κύρνε, παροῦσι φίλοισι κακοῦ καταπαύσομεν ἀρχήν, ζητῶμεν δ' ἕλκει φάρμακα φυομένῳ. Rossbroich 80 compares Eur. fr. 32 κακῆς ἀπ' ἀρχῆς γίγνεται τέλος κακόν (on which see Strömberg, *Greek Proverbs* 39f.) and Ovid. *Rem.* 91f. *principiis obsta; sero medicina paratur, cum mala per longas convaluere moras* (quoted anonymously by Thomas a Kempis, *Imit. Christi* I 13, 21). Cf. Plut. *Coh. ira* 4, 454E-F on the containing of one's anger ἐν ἀρχῇ.

144 [ἐξ ὀλίγου σπινθῆρος ἀθέσφατος αἴθεται ὕλη.]
By a tiny spark a vast wood is set on fire.

This spurious verse (only in one ms., V) is meant as an illustration of v. 143. This sentence (a proverb?) and similar ones are very common in Greek literature, e.g. Pind. *Pyth.* III 36-8 πολλὰν δ' ὄρει πῦρ ἐξ ἑνὸς σπέρματος ἐνθορὸν ἀίστωσεν ὕλαν (cf. Solon fr. I 14f.). Eur. fr. 411, 2f. μικροῦ γὰρ ἐκ λαμπτῆρος Ἰδαῖον λέπας πρήσειεν ἄν τις (quoted by Plut. *Garrul.* 10, 507B). Other classical parallels are mentioned by Geffcken, *Kynika* 48; Rossbroich 81; Strömberg, *Proverbs* 64, and Dibelius *ad* James III 5 (who thinks that Ps-Phoc. here depends on the diatribe where fire is often an image for passions, cf. v. 145). The motif frequently occurs in Philo, e.g. *Migr. Abr.* 123 σπινθὴρ γὰρ καὶ ὁ βραχύτατος ἐντυφόμενος, ὅταν καταπνευσθεὶς ζωπυρηθῇ, μεγάλην ἐξάπτει πυράν (cf. *Somn.* II 93), *Decal.* 173 φλὸξ ἐν ὕλῃ νέμεται δαπανῶσα πάντα καὶ φθείρουσα, *Spec. leg.* IV 27 σπινθὴρ ἐντυφόμενος εἰς πολλάκις ἀνερριπίσθη καὶ μεγάλας ἐνέπρησε πόλεις (cf. 83). Cf. further Sir. XI 32 ἀπὸ σπινθῆρος πυρὸς πληθύνεται ἀνθρακιά. James III 5 ἰδοῦ ἡλίκον πῦρ ἡλίκην ὕλην ἀνάπτει (see also Ropes *ad loc.*). The interpolator used the typically epic word ἀθέσφατος (see LSJ *s.v.*).

145 [ἐγκρατὲς ἦτορ ἔχειν, καὶ λωβητῶν δ' ἀπέχεσθαι.]
Keep your heart restrained and abstain from disgraceful things.

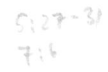

This spurious verse (again only in ms. V) says exactly the same as v. 76. δέ seems superfluous and is deleted by Keydell, *Jahresbericht* 272 (1941), 27; but see Denniston 199ff. ἐγκράτεια often lies in the sphere of sexual abstinence; it was an important concept in Greek philosophy, see Chadwick, "Enkrateia", *RAC* V 344-347, who quotes the relevant passages (e.g. Plato *Resp.* 430e, where ἐγκράτεια = σωφροσύνη; see Ps-Phoc. 76; Arist. *EN* VIII 1-10). In Philo ἐγκράτεια is the basis of all virtues, see *Somn.* I 124, *Vit. cont.* 34 (Chadwick, *ibid.* 348). See further the collection of texts in Stob. III 17 (III p. 489-512 W-H: περὶ ἐγκρατείας). In the LXX ἐγκράτεια occurs only in books that betray Hellenistic influence, e.g. 4 Macc. V 34. Cf. *Ep. Arist.* 278. In the N.T. it occurs in a catalogue of virtues in Gal. V 23; further 2 Peter I 6 (cf. 1 Cor. VII 9, IX 25; Tit. I 8). Herm. *Vis.* I 2, 4 ὁ ἐγκρατής, ὁ ἀπεχόμενος πάσης ἐπιθυμίας πονηρᾶς (= λωβητῶν in our verse, cf. also ἀπέχεσθαι with ἀπεχόμενος in Herm.). See further (besides Chadwick) Grundmann, *TWNT* II 338-340. Crouch, *Origin* 96, mistakenly thinks that λωβητῶν refers to the unclean meat of vv. 147f. For the active sense of λωβητός here cf. Soph. *Phil.* 607 αἰσχρὰ καὶ λωβήτ' ἔπη.

146 [φεῦγε κακὴν φήμην, φεῦγ' ἀνθρώπους ἀθεμίστους.]
Flee an evil report; flee lawless men.

This clumsy interpolation (again only in ms. V) probably means that one should avoid getting a bad reputation by avoiding contact with wicked people. See Pind. *Pyth*. I 99 on the importance of εὖ ἀκούειν (and Dover, *Greek Popular Morality*, s.v. reputation). Also Prov. XXII 1 αἱρετώτερον ὄνομα καλὸν ἢ πλοῦτος πολύς (other texts in Rossbroich 81). For v. 146b cf. Men. gnom. app. 3, 5 (p. 129 Jaekel) ἰδὼν πονηροὺς ἄνδρας εὐθέως φύγε. Prov. XXIV 1 μὴ ζηλώσῃς κακοὺς ἄνδρας. Men. gnom. syr. 26 (Schulthess). Lincke, *Samaria* 71, rightly compares Ps. I 1.

147-148 μὴ δέ τι θηρόβορον δαίσῃ κρέας, ἀργίποσιν δέ
λείψανα λεῖπε κυσίν· θηρῶν ἄπο θῆρες ἔδονται.
Eat no meat that is torn by wild animals, but leave the remains to the swift dogs. Animals eat from animals.

θηρόβορος: late word, occurring further only in Manetho Astrologus (fourth cent. A.D.). δαίσῃ = 2nd pers. sing. conj. aor. med. of δαίνυμι, to eat (for κρέα δαίνυσθαι see Hom. *Od*. XII 30; Herod. III 18). ἀργίποσιν ... κυσίν: Hom. *Il*. XXIV 211. λείψανα λεῖπε κυσίν: Eur. fr. 469 νόμος δὲ δείπνου λείψαν' ἐκβάλλειν κυσίν. Cf. Mark VII 28 par. Note in θηρῶν ἄπο the postposition of the preposition with ἀναστροφὴ τόνου (K-G I 554: "in der epischen, tragischen und lyrischen Dichtersprache geschieht dies häufig", there many instances). It is clear that Ps-Phoc. does his utmost to write archaic language.

This is a typically Jewish verse (so even Rossbroich 82), the source of which (as Scaliger, *Animadversiones* 89, already saw) is no doubt Ex. XXII 30 κρέας θηριάλωτον οὐκ ἔδεσθε, τῷ κυνὶ ἀπορρίψατε αὐτό (Klein, *Ält. christl. Katech*. 170, says: not Ex. XXII 30 but only Lev. XVII 15 πᾶσα ψυχή, ἥτις φάγεται θνησιμαῖον ἢ θηριάλωτον ἐν τοῖς αὐτόχθοσιν ἢ ἐν τοῖς προσηλύτοις, πλυνεῖ τὰ ἱμάτια κτλ. can have been the source of Ps-Phoc. 147f., since "dies ist die einzige Stelle im Pentateuch, in der der Eingeborene und der Fremdling in Bezug auf *nebela* und *terefa* in eine Kategorie gestellt werden". This argument has no weight; cf. moreover the mentioning of the dogs in Ex. XXII 30). The prohibition deals with *terefah* (טרפה = θηριάλωτον in LXX; often mentioned together with *nebelah*, נבלה = θνησιμαῖον), lit. "torn", sc. by wild animals. "Originally the term signified the flesh of clean beasts which had been mauled or killed by beasts of prey and so rendered unfit for food" (H. Danby, *The Mishnah* 797). Cf. Lev. XXII 8 θνησιμαῖον καὶ θηριάλωτον οὐ φάγεται μιανθῆναι αὐτὸν ἐν αὐτοῖς (cf. VII 24, XI 40, etc.). Deut. XIV 21 πᾶν θνησιμαῖον οὐ φάγεσθε. Further instances in Hatch-Redpath *s.vv.* See Philo's comments on Ex. XXII 30 and Deut. XIV 21 in *Spec. leg.* IV 119ff. (with Heinemann's remarks, *Philons Bildung* 155f.). Seeberg, *Die beiden Wege* 46ff. (esp. 50) thinks that this injunction was part of the Two Ways doctrine, but he cannot prove this (that v. 149 does belong to Two Ways material is no proof). But it was indeed one of the Noachian precepts, see Sanh. 56a. A non-Jewish parallel might be found in the Pythagorean sentence θνησιμαίων ἀπέχεσθαι, *Anon. Pyth. sent.* 41 (Mullach I 507), cf. Diog. Laert. VIII 33, quoted *ad* 139. Bernays 240 remarks: "auch hier wieder bot die griechisch-römische und die allgemeine Völkersitte doch Anhaltspunkte genug dar. Spuren eines gewissen Abscheus vor Allem von verendetem Vieh Herrührendem (κενέβρεια) finden sich vielfach bei den Classikern", but he quotes no instances. On dogs as omnivorous animals see also Ps-Phoc. 185. In antiquity dogs were viewed more favourably by Greeks and Romans (see Wright in *OCD* 294) than by Jews (see Michel in *TWNT* III 1100f.).

149 φάρμακα μὴ τεύχειν, μαγικῶν βίβλων ἀπέχεσθαι.
Make no potions, keep away from magical books.

The O.T. often warns against φαρμακεία (and φαρμακοί, e.g. Ex. XXII 18), but not against μαγεία. But these two words, which have much the same denotation, occur frequently in combination in Jewish and Christian literature. φάρμακα: Knopf *ad* Did. II 2 remarks: "Das φαρμακεύειν geht nicht nur auf das bereiten von Todesgiften, sondern auch auf das von Zaubertränken und -speisen, durch die etwa Hass und Liebe erregt wird, die Zunge eines Gerichtsgegners gebunden, die Glieder eines Kämpfers gestärkt oder gelähmt, Träume gesendet werden u.a.m.". The same could be said of μαγεύειν. For μαγικαὶ βίβλοι see e.g. Acts XIX 19 (and Conzelmann *ad loc.*, who refers to e.g. the Greek magical papyri edited by Preisendanz), and esp. the Palestinian Jewish handbook of magic (written in the Tannaitic period), published by M. Margalioth, *Sepher ha-Razim*, Jerusalem 1966. For the combination φαρμακεία (φαρμακοί, φάρμακα) and μαγεία (μάγοι, μαγεύειν) see e.g. Test. Rub. IV 9 μάγους παρεκάλεσε καὶ φάρμακα αὐτῷ προσήνεγκε.

Greek fragment of Jubil. *ap.* Epiph. *Haer.* I 3 (= p. 83, 1 Denis) φαρμακεία καὶ μαγεία, also Mart. Jes. II 5 (p. 109, 3 Denis), Test. Jac. (Copt.) fol. 184a (*ZNW* 65 (1974), 114), *Or. Sib.* I 96, Philo *Spec. leg.* III 92-103 (Heinemann, *Philons Bildung* 386ff.). On the strength of Did. II 2 οὐ μαγεύσεις, οὐ φαρμακεύσεις (cf. V 1) and Barn. XX 1 φαρμακεία, μαγεία Audet (*Didache* 140 and 150) says that this theme belongs to the Two Ways doctrine. The prohibition of magic was sometimes reckoned as one of the Noachian laws (Ginzberg, *Legends* V 93). In spite of the O.T. rules, there was much Jewish magic in antiquity; see Blau, *Das altjüdische Zauberwesen*; Bousset, *Religion* 339f.; Billerbeck IV 533ff.; Hengel, *Judentum und Hellenismus* 427-442; Urbach, *Sages* I 97ff., II 725ff.; Spicq, *Ep. Past.* I 108ff. (lit.); Nock, *Essays* I 324ff.; more lit. in Denis, *Introduction* 304f. n. 47 and Maier, *Gesch. der jüd. Rel.* 191 n. 32. A pagan denouncement of magic is found in Ditt., *Syll.* III 985, 17ff. μὴ φάρμακον πονηρὸν πρὸς ἀνθρώπους, μὴ ἐπαῳδὰς πονηρὰς μήτε γινώσκειν μήτε ἐπιτελεῖν, μὴ φίλτρον κτλ. Cf. already Plato *Leg.* 909b,933c-d, *Resp.* 364c and some other critical voices mentioned by Zintzen in *Der Kleine Pauly* V 1469f. and Mommsen, *Strafrecht* 635ff.

150 νηπιάχοις ἀταλοῖς μὴ ἄψῃ χεῖρα βιαίως.
Do not apply your hand violently to tender children.

This verse is difficult both with respect to its grammar and to its meaning. νηπιάχοις ἀταλοῖς: νηπίαχος = childish, hence: child (Hom.). ἀταλός = tender, delicate, often said of youthful persons, e.g. Hom. *Od.* XI 39 παρθενικαί τ' ἀταλαί. But three mss. (L, P, V) read ἀπαλοῖς (= tender, soft). The dative with ἄπτεσθαι is rare (mostly ἄπτ. rules a genitive), but see Pind. *Pyth.* X 28, Isthm. IV 12. ἄψῃ: two mss. (L, M) read in margin μάρψῃ (catch, take hold of, seize). χεῖρα cannot be the object of ἄψῃ (v. 186 χεῖρα βάληαι is no parallel, against Young), hence one ms. (L) reads χειρί; perhaps χεῖρα is meant as a kind of internal object or an *accus. respectus*. In view of all these uncertainties, some scholars have proposed emendations. Bernays 259 reads νηπιάχους ἀταλοὺς μὴ μάρψῃς χειρὶ βιαίᾳ. Crusius, Diehl, and Farina read νηπιάχοις ἀπαλοῖς μὴ μάρψῃς χεῖρα βιαίως. But what kind of violence or force (LSJ s.v. χείρ IV: violent measure, force) is meant here? Bernays 241 thinks that the verse forbids child-stealing (he is followed by Riessler and Easton; the latter translates· "steal not an innocent child to sell it for thine own base profit", sic!), referring to Ex.

XXI 17 ὃς ἐὰν κλέψῃ τίς τινα τῶν υἱῶν Ἰσραηλ καὶ καταδυναστεύσας αὐτὸν ἀποδῶται, καὶ εὑρεθῇ ἐν αὐτῷ, θανάτῳ τελευτάτω. But Rossbroich 83 rightly remarks: "nihil cum hoc versu simile habet". Seeberg, *Die beiden Wege* 30, says that v. 150 prohibits childmurder, wrongly referring to Did. II 2 (where paederasty and abortion are forbidden). Dornseiff, *Echtheitsfragen* 46, translates: "Vergreife dich nicht an Minderjährigen", probably interpreting the verse as directed against paedophily. That may be right, though sexual aberrations are treated in vv. 177-198. It is possibly a straightforward warning against maltreating of children; cf. Prov. I 32 ἀνθ' ὧν γὰρ ἠδίκουν νηπίους, φονευθήσονται. On the very often hard-handed chastisements of children in Judaism see Krauss, *Talm. Arch.* II 19f. and the notes *ibid.* 445f.

151 φεῦγε διχοστασίην καὶ ἔριν πολέμου προσιόντος.

Flee dissension and strife when war is drawing near.

On διχοστασίη (cf. Theogn. 78) see Schlier, *TWNT* I 511. διχοστασία occurs only once in the LXX (1 Macc. III 29), twice in the N.T. (Rom. XVI 17; Gal. V 20), but frequently in Hermas. On ἔρις see *ad* v. 78. The combination of διχοστασία and ἔρις is also found in a *varia lectio* in 1 Cor. III 3 and in 1 Clem. XLVI 5. Beltrami (*Riv.* 1913, 530) and Farina 45 point out that this is the only verse in the poem that speaks about duties towards the fatherland. But πόλεμος can mean a private quarrel, see the numerous instances quoted by Ropes and Dibelius *ad* James IV 1. However, διχοστασία mostly means (political) party-strife; see also Lewis' rendering ("Teaching of Ps-Phoc."297): "civil dissension and strife are inexcusable in time of war". We do not know whether the author alludes to a concrete historical situation (in Alexandria?; see Schubart, *Ägypten* 140ff., on the frequent party-strife in Alexandria). Does it mean that the Jews should close ranks when they are threatened by a pogrom? Young (*app. crit.*) compares Eur. *Suppl.* 949-952 ὦ ταλαίπωροι βροτῶν, τί κτᾶσθε λόγχας καὶ κατ' ἀλλήλων φόνους τίθεσθε; παύσασθ', ἀλλὰ λήξαντες πόνων ἄστη φυλάσσεθ' ἥσυχοι μεθ' ἡσύχων.

152 μὴ κακὸν εὖ ἔρξῃς· σπείρειν ἴσον ἔστ' ἐνὶ πόντῳ.

Do no good to a bad man; it is like sowing in the sea.

Bernays 213f. rightly stressed that this verse precludes a Christian origin of this poem (Farina 45 contrasts Matt. V 44). Rossbroich

84 says that it is typical of Ps-Phoc. that he is not aware that v. 152 contradicts vv. 70 and 140 (but ἐχθρός and κακός may not simply be identified). It is probable that the author here imitates Theogn. 105-108 δείλους εὖ ἔρδοντι ματαιοτάτη χάρις ἐστίν· | ἴσον καὶ σπείρειν πόντον ἁλὸς πολιῆς. | οὔτε γὰρ ἂν πόντον σπείρων βαθὺ λήιον ἀμῷς, | οὔτε κακοὺς εὖ δρῶν εὖ πάλιν ἀντιλάβοις (cf. 955f.; in Theognis, however, κακός means "ill-born"). Cf. also Ps-Isocr. *Ad Dem.* 29 τοὺς ἀγαθοὺς εὖ ποίει· καλὸς γὰρ θησαυρὸς παρ' ἀνδρὶ σπουδαίῳ χάρις ὀφειλομένη. τοὺς κακοὺς εὖ ποιῶν ὅμοια πείσει τοῖς τὰς ἀλλοτρίας κύνας σιτίζουσιν. *Gnom. hom.* 6 ἀχάριστον εὐεργετεῖν καὶ νεκρὸν μυρίζειν ἐν ἴσῳ κεῖται. Demophilus *Simil.* 55 (Mullach I 487) τὸ αὐτό ἐστιν ὄφιν ἐκτρέφειν καὶ τὸν πονηρὸν εὐεργετεῖν· παρ' οὐδετέρῳ γὰρ ἡ χάρις εὔνοιαν γεννᾷ (= *Gnom. hom.* 179b = *Flor. mon.* 51 = *Gnom. Byz.* 102, where see Wachsmuth *ad loc.* who quotes many parallels). As may be seen from these texts, this motif is well attested in the Greek gnomological tradition. Cf. Epict. II 14, 18 οἶδας τὸν εὖ ποιοῦντα ἀντευποιῆσαι καὶ τὸν κακῶς ποιοῦντα κακῶς ποιῆσαι. τί σοι λείπει; Here, again, we meet the χάρις ἀντὶ χάριτος principle ("das utilitaristische Gegenseitigkeitsprinzip", Bolkestein, *Wohltätigkeit* 107), already discussed *ad* v. 80; see the publications of Bolkestein and Mott mentioned there. W. C. van Unnik, "Die Motivierung der Feindesliebe in Lukas 6, 32-35", *Sparsa Collecta* I 121 concludes from Sir. XII 1ff. that this principle was also known in early Judaism (see e.g. XII 7 δὸς τῷ ἀγαθῷ καὶ μὴ ἀντιλάβῃ τοῦ ἁμαρτωλοῦ. For more Jewish parallels see Nissen, *Gott und der Nächste* 323 nn. 1013-1019). Luke VI 32ff. reflects Jesus' polemic against this principle. See further *ad* v. 80, and Dihle, *Goldene Regel* 109 n. 2.

σπείρειν ἴσον ἔστ' ἐνὶ πόντῳ: this is probably a proverb (Rossbroich 84); cf. Kaibel, *Epigr. Gr.* 1038, 8f. εἰς πέλαγος σπέρμα βαλεῖν καὶ γράμματα γράψαι, ἀμφότερος μόχθος τε κενὸς καὶ πρᾶξις ἄδηλος. *Paroem. Gr.* I 344, 11 εἰς ὕδωρ σπείρεις, cf. II 27 and *Or. Sib.* VIII 409. The second half of v. 152 stresses the futility of the action mentioned in the first half. It is of no use (!) at all to do good to a bad man, it yields nothing. Cf. from the O.T. Amos VI 12b "do men plough the sea with oxen?" (though not in the LXX).

Vv. 153-174 The Usefulness of Labour

153-154 ἐργάζευ μοχθῶν, ὡς ἐξ ἰδίων βιοτεύσῃς.
πᾶς γὰρ ἀεργὸς ἀνὴρ ζώει κλοπίμων ἀπὸ χειρῶν.

Work hard so that you can live from your own means;
for every idle man lives from what his hands can steal.

Verses 153-174 and 175-194 are the only two large, coherent blocks in our poem. The first block deals with the usefulness of labour (note ἐργάζειν 153, ἀεργός 154, ἔργον 159 and 162; κάματος 162, κάμνειν 171; μοχθῶν 153, μοχθεῖν 159, πολύμοχθος 170; πόνος 163, ἀριστοπόνος 171). Bernays 209 calls these 22 verses "weitaus den besten [Abschnitt] des ganzen Gedichts" (cf. Bousset, *Religion* 431 "ein schönes Lob der Arbeit und der Betriebsamkeit im allgemeinen singt der falsche Phokylides 153-174"). See on this passage esp. Bienert, *Die Arbeit* 159-164, who stresses its Jewish and un-Greek character too much.

For ἐξ ἰδίων cf. ἐκ τῶν ἰδίων in *CII* (Frey) 548; 766; also ἀπὸ τῶν ἰδίων μισθῶν in v. 157. One should not read μόχθων ὡς ἐξ ἰδίων in spite of *Or. Sib.* II 272 ἰδίων ἀπὸ μόχθων (but see Geffcken *ad loc.*) and VIII 406 ἐκ μόχθων ἰδίων. On κλόπιμος (thievish) see *ad* v. 135. The sentiment expressed in these lines is common to Hellenistic ethical thought, especially Stoicism and Cynicism, as well as to Judaism; see Hauck, "Arbeit", *RAC* I 587f. and Bergmann, "Stoische Philosophie und jüdische Frömmigkeit" 157f. On the positive valuation of labour in Judaism see also Bousset, *op. cit.* 430f.; Moore, *Judaism* II 127f., 177; Jeremias, *Jerusalem* 1f. and esp. Bienert, *Die Arbeit* 19-184. For texts see also Cronbach, "Social Ideals" 130 nn. 115-124. Ex. XX 9 ἓξ ἡμέρας ἐργᾷ καὶ ποιήσεις πάντα τὰ ἔργα σου. Ps. CIII 23 ἐξελεύσεται ἄνθρωπος ἐπὶ τὸ ἔργον αὐτοῦ καὶ ἐπὶ τὴν ἐργασίαν αὐτοῦ ἕως ἑσπέρας (cf. Ps. CXXVII 2). Prov. XXVIII 19 ὁ ἐργαζόμενος τὴν ἑαυτοῦ γῆν πλησθήσεται ἄρτων, ὁ δὲ διώκων σχολὴν πλησθήσεται πενίας (cf. XII 11). Sir. VII 15 (quoted below *ad* v. 161). Jos. *C. Ap.* II 291 (οἱ νόμοι ...) ἀργίαν καὶ πολυτέλειαν ἐξορίζοντες, αὐτάρκεις καὶ φιλοπόνους εἶναι διδάσκοντες. 2 Thess. III 10 εἴ τις οὐ θέλει ἐργάζεσθαι μηδὲ ἐσθιέτω (see the texts collected by Wettstein and Dibelius *ad loc.*, and compare Paul's own example, 2 Thess. III 7ff.). Cf. Did. XII 3, Barn. X 4. Men. gnom. syr. 77 (tr. Schulthess) "Bös ist die Trägheit, wenn einer körperlich gesund ist". Qidd. 29a "He who does not teach his son a craft, teaches him brigandage", cf. Tos. Qidd. I 11, Ab. de R.

Nathan (rec. A) XI 1. In Greek literature the theme is esp. frequent in the gnomological tradition. Hes. *Op.* 309. 311 (310 is spurious) καὶ ἐργαζόμενοι πολὺ φίλτεροι ἀθανάτοισιν. ἔργον δ' οὐδὲν ὄνειδος, ἀεργίη δέ τ' ὄνειδος. Ps-Isocr. *Ad Dem.* 40 πειρῶ τῷ ... σώματι εἶναι φιλόπονος. Antisthenes *ap.* Diog. Laert. VI 2 ὁ πόνος ἀγαθόν. Men. *Mon.* 221 ἐκ τῶν πόνων τοι τἀγάθ' αὔξεται βροτοῖς, 252 ἐν μυρίοισι τὰ καλὰ γίγνεται πόνοις, 256 ἔργοις φιλόπονος ἴσθι, μὴ λόγοις μόνον, 317 ἡ δ' ἀργία πέφυκεν ἀνθρώποις κακόν, 463 μοχθεῖν ἀνάγκη τοὺς θέλοντας εὐτυχεῖν, 811 φιλόπονος ἴσθι καὶ βίον κτήσῃ καλόν, gnom. pap. V 1 (p. 9 J.) ἐκ πονηρῶν μὴ πόριζε τὸν βίον. *Men. et Phil. comp.* I 238f. οὐκ ἔστιν εὑρεῖν τὴν τροφὴν ἄνευ κόπου. κάμνουσι πάντες τῆς ζόης ταύτης χάριν. *Floril. duo graeca* I 38 (p. 8 Schenkl). See further the numerous texts collected in Stob. III 29 (III p. 626-662 W-H) περὶ φιλοπονίας and III 30 (III p. 662-669 W-H) περὶ ἀργίας. In view of these texts, Bienert's remarks (*Die Arbeit* 161) need some qualification when he says: "Schon die ersten beiden Worte unseres Abschnittes ἐργάζευ μοχθῶν fallen auf, weil sie uneingeschränkt von jedermann eine wirtschaftliche Arbeit (ἐργάζεσθαι) fordern, die nach griechischer Anschauung nur den Banausen, den Metoiken und den Sklaven anstand". This is not valid for the Hellenistic period. Yet it may be conceded that the atmosphere of this whole passage (153-174) is more Jewish than Greek. It should be borne in mind that in antiquity the Jews were often accused of idleness and laziness because of their sabbath-rest; see Sen. *ap.* Aug. *Civ.* VI 11, Juv. *Sat.* XIV 105f. (and Mayor *ad loc.*), Tac. *Hist.* V 4 (cf. Sevenster, *Anti-Semitism* 129f.).

155 [τέχνη <γὰρ> τρέφει ἄνδρα, ἀεργὸν δ' ἴψατο λιμός.]
A craft maintains a man, but an idle man is oppressed by hunger.

This spurious line is found in only one ms. (V), obviously interpolated because of ἀεργός in v. 154 and τέχνη in v. 158. Most editors insert γάρ *metri causa*, though it is doubtlessly possible that the clumsy interpolator wrote the line without γάρ, thinking that the first syllable of τρέφει was long since it had the accent. The verb ἴπτομαι occurs only in the future tense and the aorist, but the aorist (after τρέφει) is odd in this line (gnomic ?). Cf. Men. gnom. syr. 16 (t1. Schulthess) "Hässlich ist die Trägheit; sie hungert und dürstet ...". Sir. X 27 κρείσσων ἐργαζόμενος καὶ περισσεύων ἐν πᾶσιν ἢ περιπατῶν δεξαζόμενος καὶ ἀπορῶν ἄρτων. For v. 155b cf. esp. Hes. *Op.* 302 λιμὸς γάρ τοι πάμπαν ἀεργῷ σύμφορος ἀνδρί.

156-157 μὴ δ' ἄλλου παρὰ δαιτὸς ἔδοις σκυβάλισμα τραπέζης,
ἀλλ' ἀπὸ τῶν ἰδίων μισθῶν φαγέοις ἀνυβρίστως.

Eat not the left-overs of another man's meal,
but eat without shame from what you have earned yourself.

σκυβάλισμα is a hapax, having the same meaning as σκύβαλον (a Hellenistic word, see Bauer, s.v.): refuse, rubbish, leavings, dirt, dung. For ἀπὸ τῶν ἰδίων cf. in v. 153 ἐξ ἰδίων. The text of v. 157 is hopelessly in disorder. There are variant readings for μισθῶν (e.g. βιότων, βίοτον, βροτῶν), for φαγέοις (e.g. φάγεις, φάγοις, ἄγεις, διάγοις; φαγέοις must be the optat. of a present form φαγέειν, occurring further only in the late *Anon. in Eth. Nic.* 448, 16 φαγεῖ), for ἀνυβρίστως (ἀνύβριστος). Diehl and Farina read βίοτον διάγοις ἀνύβριστος, Bernays, Bergk, Sebestyén and Crusius read βίοτον διάγοις ἀνυβρίστως, Rossbroich reads βιότων διάγοις ἀνύβριστος. In view of the mss. situation (see Young's *app. crit.*) Diehl's text seems to be the best, but any degree of certainty is excluded. Bernhardy, *Grundriss* 523, and Sitzler, *Woch. f. klass. Phil.* 29 (1912), 456 athetize the lines because of the bad Greek. Parallels and literature are mentioned *ad* vv. 153f. See also Sir. XL 28-30 ζωὴν ἐπαιτήσεως μὴ βιώσῃς· κρεῖσσον ἀποθανεῖν ἢ ἐπαιτεῖν. ἀνὴρ βλέπων εἰς τράπεζαν ἀλλοτρίαν, οὐκ ἔστιν αὐτῷ ὁ βίος ἐν λογισμῷ ζωῆς. Cf. Lk. XVI 21 and Billerbeck III 641f.; also Ev. Naz. fr. 10 . . ., *ne turpiter mendicem cibos*.

158 εἰ δέ τις οὐ δεδάηκε τέχνης, σκάπτοιτο δικέλλῃ.

And if someone has not learned a craft, he must dig with a mattock.

δεδάηκα (with genit.) is the perfect of a hypothetical δάω, aorist ἐδάην, cf. Hom. *Il.* XXI 487 πολέμοιο δαήμεναι. δίκελλα = a two-pronged fork or mattock. Digging was regarded as the hardest kind of work, mostly reserved for slaves (Charito VIII 8, 2) or uneducated workmen (Diog. Laert. VII 169). See the texts quoted by Wettstein *ad* Luke XVI 3 σκάπτειν οὐκ ἰσχύω (cf. Aristoph. *Aves* 1432 τί γὰρ πάθω; σκάπτειν γὰρ οὐκ ἐπίσταμαι). Yet even this kind of despised work must be done in order to live without shame (v. 157). Bruck, *GPG* 165, surmises that this line is a "vetus dictum". Bergk rightly rejects Goram's ἄπτοιτο δικέλλης. On τέχνη cf. Jos. *Ant.* II 283, where he mentions the φίλεργον ἐν ταῖς τέχναις of the Jewish people as a striking peculiarity.

159 ἔστι βίῳ πᾶν ἔργον, ἐπὴν μοχθεῖν ἐθέλησθα.
Life has every kind of work, if you are willing to toil.

One may equally well translate: "Every task is possible for a livelihood...", or, taking βίῳ = ἐν βίῳ (thus already Sartorius, *Analysis* 120: "est in vita varium opus"): "There is every kind of work in life ..." πᾶν = παντοῖον, παντοδαπόν, of all sorts ("allerlei Arbeit", Binder 76); see W. J. Verdenius in *Mnemosyne* 1968, 149 (on Semon. 1, 78) and Bauer *s.v.* 1αβ for instances from the N.T. Rossbroich 86 reads ἔστι βίος, πᾶν ἔργον ἐπὴν μοχθεῖν ἐθέλησθα, which is improbable. The words πᾶν ἔργον are exemplified by the two following verses.

160-161 ναυτίλος εἰ πλώειν ἐθέλεις, εὐρεῖα θάλασσα.
εἰ δὲ γεηπονίην μεθέπειν, μακραί τοι ἄρουραι.
If you want to sail and be a mariner, the sea is wide.
And if you want to cultivate land, the fields are large.

Rossbroich 86 reads ναύτιλος εἶ, πλώειν ἐθέλεις, κτλ. (following one ms. (L) and Bergk and Crusius). He asserts that this is Cynic diatribe-style, referring to Teles p. 10, 6f. Η. γέρων γέγονας· μὴ ζήτει τὰ τοῦ νέου. ἀσθενὴς πάλιν· μὴ ζήτει τὰ τοῦ ἰσχυροῦ. Cf. p. 11, 1f. and p. 52, 4f. ναυαγὸς γέγονας, εὖ τὸν ναυαγόν. πένης ἐξ εὐπόρου, εὖ τὸν πένητα. Babrius 87, 5 φίλος εἶ; τί δάκνεις; ἐχθρὸς εἶ; τί οὖν σαίνεις; Nevertheless, the parallelism of v. 160 and v. 161 (where εἰ certainly is a conjunction) makes this improbable. (Moreover, even with the reading εἰ it is "diatribe-style"; see Bultmann, *Stil* 17; e.g. Epict. III 23, 2 εἰ δολιχοδρόμος, τοιαύτη τροφή, ...· εἰ σταδιοδρόμος, πάντα ἀλλοῖα· κτλ). For Greek texts on navigation see Stob. IV 17 (IV p. 400-405 W-H) περὶ ναυτιλίας. The Jews of the O.T. were no seafarers, but in Alexandria there were not only Jews who owned boats (*CPJ* 404, 422), but also Jewish bargees and sailors (Fuchs, *Juden Ägyptens* 56; Sevenster, *Anti-Semitism* 78). γεηπονίη (= γεωπονία, farming) is highly recommended by Greek moralists (see A. C. van Geytenbeek, *Musonius Rufus* 129ff.) and already by the real Phocylides fr. 7 χρηίζων πλούτου μελέτην ἔχε πίονος ἀγροῦ. ἀγρὸν γάρ τε λέγουσιν Ἀμαλθείης κέρας εἶναι. Farina 45 sees influence of Hes. *Op.* here; that may be right, but cf. also texts like Cic. *Off.* I 151 *omnium autem rerum, ex quibus aliquid acquiritur, nihil est agri cultura melius* (cf. Cato *De agric., praef.*) and those collected by Stob. IV 15 (IV p. 376-393 W-H) περὶ γεωργίας ὅτι ἀγαθόν (esp. Mus. Ruf. XI). Agriculture is also strongly recommended in Jewish tradition (see Cronbach, "Social Ideals" 131), e.g. Sir. VII 15 μὴ μισήσῃς ἐπίπονον ἐργασίαν καὶ γεωργίαν ὑπὸ ὑψίστου ἐκτισμένην, cf. XX 28 and esp. Test. Iss. V 3-6. See the comments of Bousset, *Religion* 430ff., though his remark "das Judentum der Diaspora musste den Ackerbau von vornherein ganz aufgeben" (432) needs correction; see Fuchs, *Juden Ägyptens* 52f. Jewish landowners in Alexandria: *CPJ* 142, 145; elsewhere in Egypt: *CPJ* 234, 238, 247, 260, 272, 373, 434. (Sevenster, *Anti-Semitism* 78: "certain Jews were probably well-to-do farmers"). Bienert, *Die Arbeit* 161, says with reference to vv. 158-161: "die ... Mahnung, einen Erwerb in Landwirtschaft, Handwerk oder Handel zu suchen ... konnte man aus der griechischen Morallehre nicht entnehmen". This, again, is somewhat exaggerated.

162-163 οὐδὲν ἄνευ καμάτου πέλει ἀνδράσιν εὐπετὲς ἔργον
οὐδ' αὐτοῖς μακάρεσσι· πόνος δ' ἀρετὴν μέγ' ὀφέλλει.

There is no easy work without toil for men,
not even for the blessed themselves. But labour gives great increase to virtue.

The Greek of v. 162 is odd. One expects οὔτε ἄνευ καμάτου ... οὔτε εὐπετές or οὐδὲν ἄνευ καμάτου ... ἤ/καὶ εὐπετές. The construction as it stands is hard to explain. My translation is tentative, but gives a good sense. Curiously enough, in spite of the bad Greek, v. 162 is possibly a literal quotation of a sentence from the famous Milesian (!) Branchidae oracle (on which see Cauer, "Branchidai", *PW* III (1899), 809-813). In some scholia on Hermogenes *Rhet.* V 441 (see Bernays 209 n. 1 and Bergk *ad loc.*) the same line is quoted with the introductory formula ὁ ἐν Μιλήτῳ θεός (sc. φησιν), which is, of course, a reference to Apollo's oracle near Miletus. But this attribution is somewhat doubtful (in spite of the assertions of some scholars to the contrary). Probably these scholia derive from Syrianus' *In Hermogenem commentaria* I p. 6, 12 Rabe (where S. comments on H.'s Περὶ ἰδεῶν 266, 9 μηδὲ ἄλλο τι τῶν χρηστῶν ἐκ τοῦ ῥᾴστου παραγίνεσθαι πέφυκεν) καὶ ἐν Μιλήτῳ ὁ θεός· οὐδὲν κτλ. But in the immediately preceding and following lines Syrianus attributes a line from Epicharmus to Plato, a line from Euripides to Sophocles and a line from Archilochus again to the Milesian god (I p. 6, 10-14, see Rabe *ad loc.*). This makes the attribution of v. 162 to the oracle somewhat uncertain, to say the least. Should the attribution be right, however, then the author has drawn the text from a collection of oracles such as were current in antiquity (see Chadwick, "Florilegium", *RAC* VII 1141). Kroll, *PW* XX 508: "Dem Verfasser haben ältere Sammlungen vorgelegen; ihnen verdankt er den Branchidenspruch V. 162". The line has a proverbial character. Cf. Hes. *Op.* 289 τῆς δ' ἀρετῆς ἱδρῶτα θεοὶ προπάροιθεν ἔθηκαν. Pind. *Pyth.* XII 28 εἰ δέ τις ὄλβος ἐν ἀνθρώποισιν, ἄνευ καμάτου οὐ φαίνεται (cf. *Ol.* V 16). Epicharmus fr. 287 τῶν πόνων πωλοῦσιν ἁμῖν πάντα τἀγάθ' οἱ θεοί. Hor. *Sat.* I 9, 59f. *nil sine magno vita labore dedit mortalibus.* Cf. *Men. et Phil. comp.* I 238f. (quoted above *ad* 153f.).

V. 163a (οὐδ αὐτοῖς μακάρεσσι) is difficult. "Quam dura adiunctio!", Rossbroich 87. Why did Ps-Phoc. add these words ("inepte adiunxit", says Rossbroich)? Sebestyén 19 thinks that Ps-Phoc. polemizes against the Greek view of the Gods as ῥεῖα ζώοντες (Hom. *Il.* VI 138, *Od.* IV 805). Indeed, the ease of divine action is often mentioned in ancient literature, e.g. Eur. *Phoen.* 689 πάντα δ' εὐπετῇ θεοῖς, Ps-Aristotle *De Mundo* VI 398b12f., 400b10; Iambl. *Vita Pyth.* 139 ῥᾴδια πάντα θεῷ τελέσαι, καὶ ἀνήνυτον οὐδέν (numerous other texts are collected by Pease *ad* Cic. *ND* II 59). The verse might also be anti-Epicurean, cf. Epic. *Sent. rat.* 1 τὸ μακάριον καὶ ἄφθαρτον οὔτε αὐτὸ πράγματα ἔχει οὔτε ἄλλῳ παρέχει. Since it is improbable, however, that Ps-Phoc. speaks about gods (in the plural), and since μάκαρες in v. 75 means the forces of nature, especially the heavenly bodies, the line most probably contains a reference to the sun and the moon. Rossbroich 87 rightly compares passages where the *labores* of the heavenly bodies are spoken about, e.g. Varro *Sat.* fr. 231 *eclipsis quando fit, cur luna laboret? et si hoc ridicule credunt, dicunt quod laborant.* Cf. Cic. *Tusc.* I 92; Verg. *Georg.* II 478, *Aen.* I 742 *hic canit errantem lunam solisque labores.* The labours of the sun and the moon are the eclipses, which Ps-Phoc. points to as a model for human industry. This solution is much more probable than Bienert's (*Die Arbeit* 162), who says on μάκαρες: "Es sind vielmehr die Gesetzestreuen, die אשרי des A.T.'". Bernays 209 calls this verse "ein schlagendes Beispiel ... von der fast parodirenden Weise unseres Verfassers, Lehnsätze aus der heidnisch-classischen Litteratur seiner eigenen Religionsmeinung anzupassen", since by μάκαρες he actually means not the gods but only the servants of God.

πόνος δ' ἀρετὴν μέγ' ὀφέλλει: cf. v. 66 μέγ' ὀφέλλει δ' ἐσθλὰ πονεῦντα. The emphasis on πόνος as a requisite for ἀρετή may be Cynic; see

Dudley, *History of Cynicism* 186 etc., and see *ad* v. 66. But cf. already Eur. *Heracl.* 625 ἁ δ' ἀρετὰ βαίνει διὰ μόχθων. Rossbroich's remark that v. 163b "nihil est aliud nisi 'additamentum' versus explendi causa" is too negative. Sitzler's athetizing of v. 163 (*Woch. f. klass. Phil.* 29 (1912), 451) is also unnecessary.

164-170 μύρμηκες γαίης μυχάτους προλελοιπότες οἴκους
ἔρχονται βιότου κεχρημένοι, ὁππότ' ἄρουραι
λήια κειράμεναι καρπῶν πλήθωσιν ἀλωάς.
οἱ δ' αὐτοὶ πυροῖο νεοτριβὲς ἄχθος ἔχουσιν
ἢ κριθῶν, αἰεὶ δὲ φέρων φορέοντα διώκει,
ἐκ θέρεος ποτὶ χεῖμα βορὴν σφετέρην ἐπάγοντες
ἄτρυτοι· φῦλον δ' ὀλίγον τελέθει πολύμοχθον.

The ants having left their homes, deeply hidden under the earth,
come in their need of food, when the fields
fill the threshing floors with fruits after the crops have been reaped.
They themselves have a load of freshly threshed wheat
or barley—and bearer always follows bearer—,
and from the summer harvest they supply their food for the winter,
being indefatigable. This tiny folk is hard-working.

This passage on the ant, though in epic diction, has several traits which betray its late origin. μύχατος (since third cent. B.C.): irregular superlative of μύχιος (inward, inmost), cf. μυχοίτατος, μυχαίτατος, μυχώτατος, μυχέστατος, μύχαλος (cf. Renehan, *Greek Lexicographical Notes* 142). For the construction of ἄρουραι λήια κειράμεναι (with inner accus.) cf. *Anth. Pal.* IX 106 χθὼν πεύκας κειραμένη (see also Brunck, *GPG* 166). Usually πλήθω means "to be full"; the transitive meaning here ("to fill") occurs only in later poets (see LSJ *s.v.*; Ludwich's conj. βρίθουσιν, *Spruchbuch* 22, is unnecessary). πυροῖο ... ἢ κριθῶν: cf. the frequent combination πυροὶ καὶ κριθαί, Hom. *Od.* IX 110, XIX 112; Herod. II 36, 2, etc. (LSJ *s.v.* πυρός). αὐτοί in 167 seems difficult, see the conjectures mentioned in Young's *app. crit.* (αὐτοῖς, αὖτ' ἢ, ἤτοι). It probably means: they do it themselves and do not command others to do it for them. Or: they do it of themselves (LSJ *s.v.* I 2). νεοτριβής: LSJ *s.v.* wrongly translate "freshly ground"; it means "freshly threshed" (τρίβω). The only other occurrence listed is Soranus I 46. φέρων φορέοντα: parechesis. θέρος = (summer)harvest. ἐπάγοντες: Young compares Matt. III 12 συνάξει τὸν σῖτον αὐτοῦ εἰς τὴν ἀποθήκην (cf. VI 26, XIII 30), which is not very illustrative; cf. ἐπάγειν in Thuc. VII 60. Note the nice antithesis in v. 170 φῦλον ὀλίγον - πολύμοχθον.

Bernays 242 thinks that the book of Proverbs is the source of these lines, see VI 6-8 ἴθι πρὸς τὸν μύρμηκα, ὦ ὀκνηρέ, καὶ ζήλωσον ἰδὼν τὰς ὁδοὺς αὐτοῦ καὶ γένου ἐκείνου σοφώτερος. ἐκείνῳ γὰρ γεωργίου μὴ ὑπάρχοντος μηδὲ τὸν ἀναγκάζοντα ἔχων μηδὲ ὑπὸ δεσπότην ὢν ἑτοιμάζεται θέρους τὴν τροφὴν πολλήν τε ἐν τῷ ἀμήτῳ ποιεῖται τὴν παράθεσιν. XXX 24f. τέσσαρα δέ ἐστιν ἐλάχιστα ἐπὶ τῆς γῆς, ταῦτα δέ ἐστιν σοφώτερα τῶν σοφῶν· οἱ μύρμηκες, οἷς μὴ ἔστιν ἰσχύς, καὶ ἑτοιμάζονται θέρους τὴν τροφήν. κτλ. Cf. XXIV 25. However, Rossbroich 88 denies this and supposes Ps-Phoc. to depend here on the diatribe, referring *inter alia* to Hor. *Sat.* I 1, 33-5 *sicut parvola, nam exemplo est, magni formica laboris ore trahit quodcumque potest atque addit acervo quem struit, haud ignara ac non incauta futuri*. In Cic. *ND* I 79 and III 21 too the ant is viewed as a model of industry for men to follow (other passages in Pease's commentary *ad loc.*). See further Gerhard, *Phoinix* 27; Marx, "Ameise", *PW* I 2, 1820-2; Rech, "Ameise", *RAC* I 375-7. But in view of the fact that in vv. 171-4 Ps-Phoc. undeniably depends on the LXX version of Prov., Bernays must be right (in spite of the fact that the point of comparison in Prov. is wisdom, not toil).

171-174 κάμνει δ' ἠεροφοῖτις ἀριστοπόνος τε μέλισσα
ἠὲ πέτρης κοίλης κατὰ χηραμὸν ἢ δονάκεσσιν
ἢ δρυὸς ὠγυγίης κατὰ κοιλάδος ἔνδοθι σίμβλων
σμήνεσι μυριότρητα κατ' ἄγγεα κηροδομοῦσα.

The bee toils, traversing the air, working excellently,
either in the crevice of a hollow rock or in the reeds,
or in the hollow of an ancient oak, within their nests,
in swarms at their thousand-celled combs, building with wax.

These lines are difficult to translate since it is unclear how all the adverbial adjuncts have to be connected to the main verb or participle and to each other. Maybe they all belong to the combination of main verb plus participle: "(the bee) labours building with wax...". The language, again, is a mixture of epic diction and new forms; see E. von Leutsch, *Philol.* 22 (1865), 23f. ἠεροφοῖτις: cf. 125 ἠερόφοιτος. ἠεροφοῖτις in Hom. *Il.* IX 571, XIX 87 means "walking in darkness"; the meaning "traversing the air" is also found in *Orph. Hymn.* IX 2. ἀριστοπόνος: Pind. *Ol.* VII 51 ἀριστοπόνοις χερσί, cf. *Anth. Pal.* IX 466. πέτρης κοίλης κατὰ χηραμόν: Hom. *Il.* XXI 495 κοίλην εἰσέπτατο πέτρην, χηραμόν (said of a rock pigeon); no doubt this Homeric line was the model of v. 172. ὠγύγιος: originally from Ogyges, a mythical king of Attica; hence generally: primeval, primal, very ancient (Hes. *Theog.* 806); but also: gigantic

(Heliod. X 25). Which meaning is right here is uncertain; all the more so since Sisenna fr. 8 (*ap*. Macr. *Sat*. VI 4, 15) speaks of a *vetus atque ingens . . . arbor ilex*; ὠγύγιος means both *vetus* and *ingens*. σίμβλος is not only "beehive", but any place where bees live, e.g. in a chasm or a hollow, see Apoll. Rhod. II 130-4 (132); hence the above translation "nest". σμῆνος = swarm of bees. μυριότρητος (with numberless holes) is a *hapax*; cf. πολύτρητος in Hom. ἄγγος = vessel, *h.l.* comb. κηροδομεῖν is also a *hapax* (according to Bergk *ad loc*. κατ' ἄγγεα κηροδομοῦσα should be interpreted as ἄγγεα κατακηροδομοῦσα; that is possible).

Again it may be asked whether Ps-Phoc. depends on the LXX or on pagan Greek sources. Even Bernays did not see that the author draws here on Prov. VI 8a-c (so rightly Gerhard, *Phoinix* 27), which lines immediately follow the passage on the ant (Prov. VI 6-8; since VI 8a-c are not in the Hebrew text, it is clear that Ps-Phoc. used the LXX and not the MT): ἢ πορεύθητι πρὸς τὴν μέλισσαν καὶ μάθε ὡς ἐργάτις ἐστὶν τήν τε ἐργασίαν ὡς σεμνὴν ποιεῖται, ἧς τοὺς πόνους βασιλεῖς καὶ ἰδιῶται πρὸς ὑγίειαν προσφέρονται, ποθεινὴ δέ ἐστιν πᾶσιν καὶ ἐπίδοξος. καίπερ οὖσα τῇ ῥώμῃ ἀσθενής, τὴν σοφίαν τιμήσασα προήχθη. The combination ant-bee derives from the LXX of Prov. (thus also Bienert, *Arbeit* 162), hence Koep ("Biene", *RAC* II 275) is wrong when he asserts: "Als Symbol des Fleisses dient im Urtext der Sprüche (6, 6-8) die Ameise; die Christl. Schriftsteller haben jedoch vielfach diese Stelle von der Biene verstanden". Again Rossbroich 89 thinks that pagan Greek texts, in which the bee is praised as an example of industry, influenced Ps-Phoc. These texts are numerous indeed, see esp. Koep, "Biene" 276f. Aelian *Hist. anim*. V 12 (10-13) ἀργίαν τε καὶ ἡσυχίαν μισοῦσι, καὶ καμεῖν εἰσιν ἀγαθαί (cf. *ibid*. φιλεργίας). Hor. *Carm*. IV 2, 27ff. *apis . . . grata carpentis thyma per laborem plurimum*. Verg. *Aen*. I 430-5 *qualis apes aestate nova per florea rura | exercet sub sole labor, cum gentis adultos | educant fetus, aut cum liquentia mella | stipant et dulci distendunt nectare cellas, | aut onera accipiunt venientum, aut agmine facto | ignavum fucos pecus a praesepibus arcent* (cf. Hom. *Il*. II 87ff.). Ovid. *Ars amat*. I 93ff. is important in this connection (though this passage is not mentioned by Rossbroich); here ant and bee are mentioned together: *ut redit itque frequens longum formica per agmen, | granifero solitum cum vehit ore cibum, | aut ut apes saltusque suos et olentia nactae | pascua per flores et thyma summa volant*. Both Philo *Prov*. I 25 and Celsus *ap*. Orig.

C. Cels. IV 81 also mention the bee and the ant in combination, but they may be dependent upon the LXX. In other passages, e.g. Marc. Aur. V 1, the ant and the bee are mentioned together with other animals. So it cannot altogether be excluded that Ps-Phoc. draws on non-Jewish sources here; though it is much more likely that Prov. VI 6-8c is the source of vv. 164-174. Here again it is clear that Ps-Phoc. rewrites his sources in the light of the great poets' diction and style (cf. esp. v. 172). It is very probable that the LXX text of Prov. VI 6-8c was formed under the influence of a Hellenistic combination of ant and bee (as it is reflected in Ovid, see above). Bienert, *Die Arbeit* 162, sees here a "Synthese von jüdischem und griechischem Ethos", in which the ant is of Jewish and the bee of Greek origin.

Vv. 175-227 Marriage, Chastity and Family Life

Dibelius-Greeven (*An die Kolosser, Epheser, Philemon* 49) mention this last section of Ps-Phoc. as a parallel to the *Haustafel* in Col. III 18-IV 1; they call it "der einzige Abschnitt, in dem das Gedicht eine streng gegliederte Reihenfolge einhält". Both Ps-Phoc. and Col. III 18-IV 1 (and Eph. V 22-VI 9) deal respectively with marriage, the education of children and the treatment of slaves. Crouch, *The Origin and Intention of the Colossian Haustafel* 76, sees it as a "code", deriving from Jewish propaganda literature (see Jos. *C. Ap.* II 198-210), just like the *Haustafeln*; but see the (too sceptic) criticisms of Schrage, "Zur Ethik der neutestamentlichen Haustafeln", *NTS* 21 (1974/5), 7 n. 6 ("doch tritt das Haustafelschema nicht gerade deutlich hervor."). See further my article "Ps-Phoc. and the N.T.", *ZNW* 1978 (forthcoming). The subjects dealt with in this section remind one of the rabbinic trias "women, slaves and minors", on which see S. Zucrow, *Women, Slaves and the Ignorant in Rabbinic Literature*, Boston 1932. Berger, *Gesetzesauslegung Jesu* I 557, says that the style of this passage (μή with conj. aor. or infin.) is that of the "weisheitlicher Mahnspruch".

175-176 μὴ μείνῃς ἄγαμος, μή πως νώνυμνος ὄληαι.
δός τι φύσει καὐτός, τέκε δ' ἔμπαλιν, ὡς ἐλοχεύθης.

Remain not unmarried, lest you die nameless.
Give nature her due, beget in your turn as you were begotten.

πως: Bergk *ad loc.* "Parum commode πως additum, fortasse poeta πᾶς scripsit, quod breviter dictum pro μὴ πᾶς τεὸς οἶκος ὄληται νώνυμνος". The interchange of α and ω is paleographically quite possible, but see LSJ *s.v.* μή πως: lest in any way. νώνυμνος is epic for ἀνώνυμος, cf. Hom. *Il.* XII 70 νωνύμνους ἀπολέσθαι (!) ἀπ' Ἄργεος (cf. Sen. fr. 58 below). ὄληαι is the second person sing. of the conj. aor. med. of ὄλλυμι. δέ is here connective or explicative, not adversative (Denniston, *Greek Particles* 162ff. and Verdenius in *Mnemosyne* 1974, 32f.). λοχεύω = to bring forth, to bear, to beget (like τίκτω used of both the woman and the man).

The contents of these lines have their parallels in both Hellenistic, especially Stoic, literature and in Jewish writings. By several Stoic authors, especially Antipater of Tarsus and Musonius Rufus, marriage is strongly recommended. See Praechter, *Hierokles* 121-150 ("Zur Geschichte des Topos περὶ γάμου"); Geurts, *Het huwelijk* 1-35; Greeven, *Hauptproblem* 113-123; Leipoldt, *Die Frau* 61f.; Van Geytenbeek, *Musonius Rufus* 67f.; Oepke, "Ehe", *RAC* IV 654; Vatin, *Recherches sur le mariage* 32f. See already Hes. *Op.* 378; Zeno *ap.* Diog. Laert. VII 121 (the wise man should) γαμήσειν ... καὶ παιδοποιήσεσθαι. Antipater fr. 62 (= Stob. IV 22d, 103; *SVF* III p. 254f.) is a long text in praise of marriage as is also fr. 63 (= Stob. IV 22a, 25; *SVF* III p. 255f.); note here ... πᾶν μὲν τὸ τῇ φύσει ἐπιβάλλον σπεύδοντες ἐπιτελεῖν. Seneca fr. 58 *liberorum causa uxorem ducere, ut vel nomen nostrum non intereat* (!). Epict. III 7, 25f. ...τὰ προηγούμενα. τίνα ἐστὶ ταῦτα; πολιτεύεσθαι, γαμεῖν, παιδοποιεῖσθαι, κτλ. ... ἕκαστον τούτων δεῖ ποιεῖν, ὡς πεφύκαμεν. Mus. Ruf. XIV p. 71, 10f. H. κατὰ φύσιν δ', εἴ τι ἄλλο, καὶ τὸ γαμεῖν φαίνεται ὄν. Hierocles p. 52, 29 Arn. ἐπὶ τὸν γάμον ἐξοτρύνουσα φύσις (cf. p. 56, 15f. and *Anon. Pyth. sent.* 36 in Mullach, *Fr. Phil. Gr.* I 502). See further the texts collected in Stob. IV 22 (IV p. 494-568 W-H) περὶ γάμου and IV 24 (IV p. 600-607) ὅτι καλὸν τὸ ἔχειν παῖδας. As can be seen from these texts, the κατὰ φύσιν motif occurs frequently; see Van Geytenbeek, *Mus. Ruf.* 68 "In the later Stoics marriage is always said to be κατὰ φύσιν"; cf. also Praechter, *Hierokles* 77. This explains the φύσει in v. 176. Rossbroich's remark (89) "auctor sequitur fontes Stoicos atque Cynicos" is only partly correct since the Cynics mostly rejected marriage, see e.g. Ps-Diog. *Epist.* 47; Praechter 128f.

In their view of marriage the Stoics agreed with the Jews (see Bergmann, "Stoische Philosophie und jüdische Frömmigkeit" 158f.). Judaism heartily encouraged marital relations, for marriage was seen as a divine commandment (Gen. I 28 αὐξάνεσθε καὶ πληθύνεσθε καὶ πληρώσατε τὴν γῆν and Gen. II 24 ἕνεκεν τούτου καταλείψει ἄνθρωπος τὸν πατέρα αὐτοῦ καὶ τὴν μητέρα αὐτοῦ καὶ προσκολληθήσεται πρὸς τὴν γυναῖκα αὐτοῦ καὶ ἔσονται οἱ δύο εἰς σάρκα μίαν were the basic texts). See Billerbeck II 372ff., III 367f.; Moore, *Judaism* II 119ff.; Epstein, *Sex Laws* 14f., 141-143 (141: "Celibacy is prohibited in Jewish law. The rabbis considered procreation the first command recorded in the Bible", sc. Gen. I 28); Feldmann, *Birth Control* 46ff. ("The Mitzwah of Procreation"); Oepke, "Ehe", *RAC* IV 655f.; Nock, *Essays* II 894; Safrai in *Comp. Rer. Jud.* I 748ff. The whole passage Jeb. 61a-64a is very instructive (Jeb. VI 6 "No man may abstain from keeping the Law "Be fruitful and multiply" (Gen. I 28), unless he already has children"). Ned. 64b "a man who is childless is counted as dead". Sir. XXXVI 25; Ps-Philo *Lib. Ant. Bibl.* IX 3-6; Jos. *Ant.* IV 244. Oepke, "Ehe" 656: "Asketische Neigungen liegen dem Judentum im Ganzen fern. Freiwillige Enthaltsamkeit bleibt vereinzelt [see the criticisms on Simon ben Azzai's unmarried state, Bacher, *Tann.* I 407f.]. Ps-Phokylides verbindet Einschärfung der Vermehrung mit gewisser Zurückhaltung im Sinn der Popularphilosophie (Z. 175f., 193f.)". For Philo's view of marriage and procreation as being according to nature see esp. Heinemann, *Philon's Bildung* 261ff.

Sometimes it has been suggested that vv. 175f. allude to the "Ehescheu" in the Roman world round the beginning of the Christian era (on which see Kroll, *Kultur* 173ff. and Spicq, *Ep. Past.* I 400 n. 5); so e.g. Riessler 1320 "eine Abmahnung von der im spätern Altertum um sich greifenden Ehelosigkeit". Indeed, the emperor Augustus (during whose reign Ps-Phoc. possibly wrote) had to take measures to promote marriage and childbirth, Tac. *Ann.* III 25; see Friedländer, *Sittengeschichte* I 367ff.; Delling, "Ehegesetze", *RAC* IV 678f. Graetz, *Gesch. der Juden* III³ 633 goes so far as to date Ps-Phoc. to the early imperial period on the basis of vv. 175-6 alone.

177-178 μὴ προαγωγεύσῃς ἄλοχον σέο τέκνα μιαίνων·
οὐ γὰρ τίκτει παῖδας ὁμοίους μοιχικὰ λέκτρα.

Do not induce your wife to prostitution, defiling your children; for the adulterous bed brings not sons in your likeness.

μοιχικὰ λέκτρα: cf. *Anth. Pal.* V 302, 7 μοίχια λέκτρα. The form μοιχικός occurs only since the first cent. A.D. In the O.T. Lev. XIX

29 forbids to force one's daughter into prostitution (Preuss, "Prostitution" 275; Jagersma, *Leviticus 19*, 110f.), but nowhere the προαγωγεία of one's own wife is forbidden, probably because such things did not happen in Israel (on prostitution in Israel see Epstein, *Sex Laws* 152ff.). Berger, *Gesetzesauslegung Jesu* I 519, remarks: "Ps-Phok. 177f. ergänzt die atl Gebote um dieses Verbot", as does also Philo *Spec. leg.* III 31, who says μοιχεία and προαγωγεία are δύο τὰ μέγιστα τῶν ἀδικημάτων. Both authors were urged to give this commandment since in the early Roman empire it was not uncommon that married women prostituted themselves with the approval of their husbands. See e.g. Hor. *Carm.* III 6, 29f. *sed iussa coram non sine conscio surgit marito*, etc. and *Sat.* II 3, 237f. *tibi . . ., unde uxor media currit de nocte vocata* (cf. II 5, 75f.); Juv. *Sat.* I 55-57, VI 136-141; Sen. *Benef.* I 9, 3 and other passages from this period mentioned by Schütze, *Juvenalis ethicus* 34f.; Kroll, *Kultur* 171 (with n. 44); Thraede, "Frau", *RAC* VII 219; cf. Schubart, *Ägypten* 166.

τέκνα μιαίνων is difficult. Hermann and Herter, "Dirne", *RAC* III 1161, say that it was unpleasant to be married to a harlot since "auch den Kindern haftete leicht ein Makel an", referring to Demosth. XXII 61 τῷ δὲ παῖδας ἐκ πόρνης εἶναι, τοῦ δὲ τὸν πατέρ' ἡταιρηκέναι, τοῦ δὲ τὴν μητέρα πεπορνεῦσθαι, cf. Eupolis fr. 114 (98); Artemid. V 67 ἦν ἔρως ἑταίρας αὐτῷ, ... καὶ παῖς ἐγένετο αὐτοῖς ἐπίμωμος. But probably these words (τέκνα μιαίνων) have to be interpreted in the light of the (also obscure) verse which follows (see the γάρ in v. 178). The problem to be solved there is: what does ὁμοίους mean in this context? Does it refer to the fact that in Judaism children begotten in adultery were regarded as bastards (*mamzerim*), who did not have the same rights as the other Israelites and would perhaps not even participate in Israel's eschatological deliverance? (On this subject see Jeremias, *Jerusalem* 376ff.). Or does v. 178 imply the theory that the likeness of children to their parents was determined solely by the man's sperma (on which see Lesky-Waszink, "Embryologie", *RAC* IV 1228-1244, esp. 1233-1235). See e.g. Macr. *Sat.* V 11, 17 ... *sicut valeat ad fingendas corporis atque animi similitudines vis et natura seminis* ... and VII 16, 13 *semen est generatio ad eius ex quo est similitudinem pergens*. Rossbroich 90 thinks that the source of these verses is Hes. *Op.* 182 (on the times when Zeus will destroy the iron race) οὐδὲ πατὴρ παίδεσσιν ὁμοίιος οὐδέ τι παῖδες, *ibid.* 235 (on the country where there is justice) τίκτουσιν δὲ γυναῖκες ἐοικότα τέκνα γονεῦσιν. He also compares Hor. *Carm.* IV 5, 23 *laudantur simile prole puerperae*; cf. Theocr. XVII 43f. Whether these texts imply the same embryological theory is uncertain, as it is also in the present case. It would mean that Ps-Phoc. assumes that the children of the man who allows his wife to be a prostitute are begotten by his wife's paramours. Τέκνα μιαίνων may simply refer then to the disastrous consequences of this for the bastard children, depicted by Sir. XXIII 24f. Because the children are dissimilar to their parents, they are stigmatized. This is strikingly demonstrated in Martialis VI 39 (see Friedländer, *Darstellungen* I 285 with n. 12).

179-180 μητρυιῆς μὴ ψαῦε τὰ δεύτερα λέκτρα γονῆος·
μητέρα δ' ὡς τίμα τὴν μητέρος ἴχνια βᾶσαν.

Touch not your stepmother, your father's second wife;
but honour her as a mother, because she follows the footsteps of your mother.

Verse 179 presents grammatical difficulties. The above translation is based upon the assumption that τὰ δεύτερα λέκτρα is an apposition in the nominative to μητρυιῆς, comparable to Apoc. I 5 ἀπὸ 'Ιησοῦ Χριστοῦ, ὁ μάρτυς ὁ πιστός. See Turner, *Syntax* 314: "appositional phrases tend to be in the nom. instead of the necessary oblique case"; cf. p. 316. The main difficulty is, however, that λέκτρον is not attested as meaning "wife"; LSJ lists as the word's meanings: "bed; marriage-bed; marriage; child"; but λέχος means "bed; marriage-bed; marriage; *spouse*". Young suggests (letter of 6.10. 1972): "Do not touch your stepmother, in regard to your father's second marriage". One could also put a semicolon after ψαῦε. The second half of the verse could then be taken as a nominal phrase: "it is your father's second marriage"; so does Lincke, *Samaria* 175 (in *Anth. Pal.* IX 133 δεύτερα λέκτρα means "second marriage"). Another solution is proposed by Farina 46, who translates: "non desiderare i figli nati dalla tua matrigna", and adds a note: "i figli nati del secondo matrimonio di tuo padre, oppure i figli che la matrigna ebbe del primo marito". So he takes λέκτρα (in the sense of "children"; N.B. ms. M reads τέκνα) to be an accusative depending upon ψαῦε. Verbs meaning "to touch" mostly govern the genitive: Philo *Spec. leg.* III 32 μὴ ψαυέτω γυναικὸς ἀνήρ, Jos. *Ant.* II 57 ψαύειν γυναικός. Cf. Eur. *Hipp.* 1044 γυναικὸς θιγεῖν and 1 Cor. VII 1 γυναικὸς ἅπτεσθαι. But there are some cases with the accus., e.g. Soph. *Ant*. 961 ψαύων τὸν θεόν (more examples in K-G I 348, 7). But v. 180 makes it improbable that v. 179 forbids sexual relations with stepsisters. Moreover, in Farina's rendering δεύτερα makes no sense. Bergk tries to solve the problem very ingeniously by reading μητρυιῆς μὴ ψαῦ' ἄτε δεύτερα κτλ., with reference to Plato *Phaedrus* 275a τοῦτο γὰρ τῶν μαθόντων λήθην μὲν ἐν ψυχαῖς παρέξει . . . ἄτε . . . αὐτοὺς ὑφ' αὐτῶν ἀναμιμνησκομένους. This may well be right. Cf. K-G II 111f.

Anyhow, this verse forbids sexual relations with one's stepmother and is probably based upon Lev. XVIII 8 ἀσχημοσύνην γυναικὸς πατρός σου οὐκ ἀποκαλύψεις (cf. Lev. XX 11, Deut. XXIII 1 and 1 Cor. V 1ff.; it is also forbidden in Roman law, see Lietzmann *ad* 1 Cor. V 1). It is the first of a series that lists forbidden relations with relatives, all based upon Lev. XVIII (and XX); see Dornseiff, *Echtheitsfragen* 47 and Crouch, *Origin* 84 (on comparable lists in Jewish literature, e.g. Jos. *Ant*. III 274f., Derek Erez Rabba I 1-12, see Berger, *Gesetzesauslegung Jesu* I 316, who also mentions Ps-Phoc. 177-206; cf. Siegert, "Gottesfürchtige und Sympathisanten" 122 n. 2). The forbidden relation with a stepmother is frequently discussed in Jewish literature; see Jubil. XXXIII 10; Philo *Spec. leg*. III 20f.; Jos. *C. Ap*. II 200, *Ant*. III 274f.; Sanh. VII 4 "he that has connection with his father's wife" belongs to those "that are to be stoned"; Kerit. I 1 and other passages mentioned by Billerbeck III 343ff., esp. 349f., and Jeremias, *Jerusalem* 362 n. 95. Boissonade, *Anecd. Gr*. I 447 n. 2, thinks that 1 Cor. V 1 is the source of v. 179 and therefore declares Ps-Phoc. to be a Christian. This is obviously wrong. In some astrological treatises intercourse with one's stepmother was regarded as inevitable, as Rossbroich 91 points out. See e.g. Manetho Astrol. II 189f. ἢ καὶ μητρυιῆσιν ἑαῖς ἢ παλλακίδεσσιν σφωιτέρου γενετῆρος ὁμὸν λέχος εἰσανέβησαν, *ibid*. I 113 μητρυιαῖς μίσγοντ' ἢ παλλακίσιν γενετήρων, cf. V 205, VI 196. On ἴχνια βᾶσαν in 180 cf. Philo *Gig*. 39 κατ' ἴχνος βαίνειν, *Anth. Pal*. V 106, 3 ἐπιβαίνων ἴχνεσιν, *Od*. V 193. See further Stumpff, *TWNT* III 406f.

181 μηδέ τι παλλακίσιν πατρὸς λεχέεσσι μιγείης.
Do not have intercourse with the concubines of your father.

Nearly all mss. read μηδ' ἐπὶ, only B reads μηδέ τι, which is probably right (see Rossbroich 92). The meaning of λεχέεσσι is doubtful. Rossbroich 92 interprets πατρὸς λεχέεσσι as in apposition to παλλακίσιν (cf. λέκτρα in 179), taking λέχεα to mean "spouse" (see e.g. Eur. *El.* 481). However, it seems more probable to take λεχέεσσι as a locative dative (meaning "in bed") that goes with μιγῆναι (cf. εὐνῇ μίσγεσθαι in Hom. *Od.* I 433). This line has no O.T. counterpart, but it may be an extrapolation of Lev. XVIII 8 quoted above *ad* v. 179 (cf. Deut. XXVII 20); and see the story of Reuben's sin with Bilhah, his father's concubine in Jubil. XXXIII 1-9 and Test. Rub. III 11-15 (based upon Gen. XXXV 22); and cf. *Anth. Pal.* III 3, which is about a boy who wanted to sleep with the concubine of his father (1. 4 παλλακίδος δούλης λέκτρα προσιεμένῳ). The keeping of a concubine is taken for granted by Ps-Phoc. It was forbidden neither in the O.T. (see Baab, *IDB* I 666) nor in Jewish literature (Jeremias, *Jerusalem* 406). "Edujoth IV 8 setzt die Sitte der Nebenfrauen einfach voraus", Bousset, *Religion* 427 n. 2. In the Hellenistic world men who kept concubines were mostly widowers or divorced men, see M. de Vries, *Pallake*, Amsterdam 1927, *passim* and Vatin, *Recherches* 238 (and Index s.v. concubinage). It was a very common phenomenon never strongly condemned in antiquity. The passages from Manetho Astrol. quoted above *ad* vv. 179f. show that the stepmother and the concubine of the father are more often mentioned together. This traditional combination may have caused the insertion of this line between the otherwise "Levitic" verses. The extension of the Law so as to include the concubines of the father is indicative of the author's high morals and his respect for these women.

182 μηδὲ κασιγνήτης ἐς ἀπότροπον ἐλθέμεν εὐνήν.

Approach not the bed of your sister, a bed to turn away from.

ἀπότροπος = from which one turns away, horrible. Farina 47 rightly renders ἀπότροπος εὐνή with "il letto, che devi sempre fuggire". No doubt the basis of this verse is Lev. XVIII 9 ἀσχημοσύνην τῆς ἀδελφῆς σου ἐκ πατρός σου ἢ ἐκ μητρός σου, ἐνδογενοῦς ἢ γεγεννημένης ἔξω, οὐκ ἀποκαλύψεις ἀσχημοσύνην αὐτῆς, cf. Lev. XX 17, Deut. XXVII 22 (see the rabbinic comments on this prohibition in Kerit. I 1 and Chag. I 8; on the Noachian law character of this injunction Ginzberg, *Legends* V 92f.; on the relation between incest and the evil *jeṣer* in rabbinic literature Billerbeck IV 482). Cf. further Philo. *Spec. leg.* III 22 (Heinemann, *Philons Bildung* 279ff.). Not only in Jewish tradition was incest abhorred, it was also strongly disapproved in most Greek ethical thinking (cf. Oedipus); according to Plato Leg. 838a-b its prohibition is an άγραφος νόμος, cf. Eur. Andr. 173-5; see Delling, "Ehehindernisse", RAC IV 683 and Licht, Sexual Life 517 (516ff. on incest in Greek society; cf. Kroll, Kultur 173 on incest in republican Rome). Possibly the author has in mind here the frequent "Geschwisterehen" in Alexandria and Egypt (not only in the Ptolemaean family), on which see Taubenschlag, Law ... III n. 25 (lit.) and Vatin, Recherches 58ff. Rossbroich 92 refers to Manetho Astrol. V 206 where it is said that a certain configuration of stars κασιγνήτοις επάγει ομογάστριον εύνήν.

183   μηδέ κασιγνήτων άλόχων επί δέμνια βαίνειν.
Nor go to bed with the wives of your brothers.

Every ms. has v. 183 between vv. 194 and 195, but every editor agrees with Bernays who replaced it in this position. Its source is Lev. XVIII 16 άσχημοσύνην γυναικός άδελφοΰ σου ούκ άποκαλύψεις (cf. Lev. XX 21). Dornseiff 47 says it might equally render Lev. XVIII 18 γυναίκα επί άδελφη αύτης ού λήμψη άντίζηλον άποκαλύψαι την άσχημοσύνην αύτης έπ' αύτη έτι ζώσης αύτης. In that case, κασιγνήτων άλόχων should not be translated "the wives of your brothers", but "the sisters of your wives", which is not impossible but less probable. Beltrami's reference (Riv. 1908, 421) to Deut. XXVII 23 is wrong. See again the rabbinic comments in Kerit. I 1. The diction of v. 183 may have been inspired by Hes. Op. 328f. where the criminality of one who unjustly gathers riches is deemed as serious as that of one ός τε κασιγνήτοιο έου άνά δέμνια βαίνη κρυπταδίης ευνής άλόχου, παρακαίρια ρέζων. Rossbroich 92 again refers to Manetho Astrol. VI 204 αύτοκασιγνήτων σφετέρων συνέασιν όμεύνοις.

**184-185   μηδέ γυνή φθείρη βρέφος έμβρυον ένδοθι γαστρός,
μηδέ τεκοΰσα κυσίν ρίψη καί γυψίν έλωρα.**

A woman should not destroy the unborn babe in her belly, nor after its birth throw it before the dogs and the vultures as a prey.

φθείρη: Dioscurides Mat. med. II 163 φθείρειν έμβρυα. Cf. άποφθείρειν, to have an abortion, in Hipp. Epid. I 16 and φθορά = abortion (LSJ s.v. 5). βρέφος = foetus, cf. SVF II 222 (Chrysippus). For the diction of v. 185 cf. Hom. Il. I 4f. αύτούς δε ελώρια τεΰχε κύνεσσιν οίωνοϊσί τε πάσι, Soph. Aiax 830 ... ριφθώ κυσίν πρόβλητος οἰωνοῖς θ' ἕλωρ and Aesch. *Suppl.* 800 (where the plural ἕλωρα is also used for one single person). In 3 Regn. XX 24, too, dogs and birds are mentioned together as eaters of corpses. Abortion and the exposure of children were the current methods of "family-planning" in antiquity; see Cameron, "The Exposure of Children and Greek Ethics", *Class. Rev.* 46 (1932), 105-114; Waszink, "Abtreibung", *RAC* I 55-60; Vatin, *Recherches* 234-236; for the situation in Alexandria see Gussen, *Leven in Alexandrië* 88f., 121; on abortion techniques see Waszink on Tert. *De anima* XXV 5. Only very rarely were these practices condemned; see Dölger, "Das Lebensrecht..." 1ff.; Crahay, "Les moralistes anciens et l'avortement", *Ant. Class.* 10 (1941), 9-23, with corrections on Dölger; Van Geytenbeek, *Musonius Rufus* 78ff.; Spicq, *Ep. Past.* I 401 n. 2; cf. also Mommsen, *Strafrecht* 636f. and Taubenschlag, *Law* 138f. In most cases these condemnations came from the Stoics (who propagandized πολυτεκνία, see Praechter, *Hierokles* 84ff.), e.g. Mus. Ruf. XV (on the question εἰ πάντα τὰ γινόμενα τέκνα θρεπτέον) and Hierocles p. 55 Arn. (τὰ πάντα ἢ τά γε πλεῖστα (!) τῶν γεννωμένων ἀνατρέφειν). Cf. Juv. *Sat.* VI 596. But already in the Hippocratic *Oath* 20 we read οὐδὲ γυναικὶ πεσσὸν φθόριον δώσω. And in some Hellenistic nscriptions religious objections are voiced against abortion (see Crahay, "Moralistes" 16f.); the best known is Dittenberger, *Syll.* III 985, 20f. (about 100 B.C.) where it is forbidden to make a φθορεῖον or ἀτοκεῖον (see the extensive discussion by Weinreich, "Stiftung..." 56ff.). It is only in Jewish and Christian literature that abortion and exposure are firmly and frequently condemned. Though the Hebrew O.T. forbids neither practice, the LXX translation of Ex. XXI 22f. (on its divergence from the Hebrew text see e.g. Feldmann, *Birth Control in Jewish Law* 257f.) seems to have been a starting-point for these reflections; the text runs: ἐὰν δὲ μάχωνται δύο ἄνδρες καὶ πατάξωσιν γυναῖκα ἐν γαστρὶ ἔχουσαν, καὶ ἐξέλθῃ τὸ παιδίον αὐτῆς μὴ ἐξεικονισμένον, ἐπιζήμιον ζημιωθήσεται. καθότι ἂν ἐπιβάλῃ ὁ ἀνὴρ τῆς γυναικός, δώσει μετὰ ἀξιώματος. ἐὰν δὲ ἐξεικονισμένον ᾖν, δώσει ψυχὴν ἀντὶ ψυχῆς, κτλ. In his discussion of this text in *Spec. leg.* III 108-119, Philo derives from it not only a prohibition of ἄμβλωσις (abortion) but also of βρεφῶν ἔκθεσις (exposure) (see Wendland, *Philo* 37f. and esp. Heinemann, *Philons Bildung* 390-398); cf. *Hyp.* in Eus. *PE* VIII 7, 7 (p. 431, 1 Mras) μὴ γυναικῶν (sc. γονὴν) ἀτοκίοις καὶ ἄλλαις μηχαναῖς ἀμβλοῦν (cf. *Virt.* 131-3), and Jos. *C. Ap.* II 202 τέκνα τρέφειν ἅπαντα προσέταξεν, καὶ γυναιξὶν ἀπεῖπε μήτ' ἀμβλοῦν τὸ σπαρὲν μήτε διαφθείρειν, ἀλλ' ἢν φανείη τεκνοκτόνος ἂν εἴη. Both Philo and Josephus run here parallel to Ps-Phoc. again. This was already noticed by Wendland, "Therapeuten" 709f. (710: "Die Übereinstimmung ist um so bemerkenswerter, als entsprechende Bestimmungen in der Thorah, die sie zufällig hätten herbeiführen können, fehlen"); see also Dölger, "Lebensrecht" 20-23; Crouch, *Origin* 84f. and Nikiprowetzky, *Troisième Sibylle* 261f. If in Sap. Sal. XII 4f. (... ἔχθιστα πράσσειν, ἔργα φαρμακειῶν καὶ τελετὰς ἀνοσίους τέκνων τε φονὰς ἀνελεήμονας) φαρμακεία would mean "medicament to induce abortion" (as in Soranus *Gynaec*. I 59), then it would be the earliest Jewish instance of the dual prohibition of abortion and exposure. See *Or. Sib.* II 281f. ὅσσαι δ' ἐνὶ γαστέρι φόρτους ἐκτρώσκουσιν, ὅσοι τε τόκους ῥίπτουσιν ἀθέσμως (cf. III 765). Rabbinic texts may be found in Elon, "Abortion", *Enc. Jud.* II 99 and esp. Feldmann, *Birth Control* 251-294. This distinctive Jewish attitude was well-known to the Gentiles; see Hecataeus Abder. *ap.* Diod. Sic. XL 3, 8 and Tac. *Hist.* V 5, 3 (comments and more lit. in Stern, *Greek and Latin Authors on Jews and Judaism* I 33). This dual prohibition was taken over in early Christian literature: Did. II 2 οὐ φονεύσεις τέκνον ἐν φθορᾷ οὐδὲ γεννηθὲν ἀποκτενεῖς (= Barn. XIX 5; according to Audet, *Didache* 141, from the Two Ways doctrine), cf. V 2; Athenag. *Legatio* XXXV 6; Min. Fel. *Oct.* XXX 20; Tert. *Apol.* IX 8; cf. *Ep. ad Diogn.* V 6. See the remarks by Geffcken, *Zwei griechische Apologeten* 235. Rossbroich 92 again refers to Manetho Astrol. for counter-parallels: I 188 ἔμβρυα φθείρουσι ..., VI 98f. ἔκθετα τέκνα γονῆες ῥίπτουσ' ἐς βαθὺ κῦμα βορήν τ' ἔμεν οἰωνοῖσι, cf. IV 369.381.

186 μηδ' ἐπὶ σῇ ἀλόχῳ ἐγκύμονι χεῖρα βάληαι.

Lay not your hand upon your wife when she is pregnant.

χεῖρα(ς) βάλλειν ἐπί τινι (more common χεῖρα(ς) ἐπιβάλλειν τινί) is frequent in later Greek, mostly with a connotation of violence; see Bauer 573. The meaning of this line is disputed. Rossbroich 92 and Cameron, "Exposure" 110, say it belongs to vv. 184-5 and is still a paraphrase of Ex. XXI 22; so it forbids procuring an abortion. But Beltrami, *Riv.* 41 (1913), 540, and Crouch, *Origin* 85, think that the verse forbids sexual relations with a pregnant woman. Beltrami compares Hom. *Od.* XXI 223 where χεῖρα βάλλειν means "to embrace" (not: to have intercourse!), and Crouch refers to

Jos. C. Ap. II 202 οὐδ' εἴ τις ἐπὶ λεχοῦς φθορὰν παρέλθοι, καθαρὸς εἶναι τότε προσήκει (Thackeray translates: "none who has intercourse with a woman who is with child can be considered pure", but it must be said that this translation is far from certain). This line in Josephus immediately follows the passage on abortion and exposure quoted ad vv. 184f.; that may suggest that this interpretation is right. Moreover, it is possible to compare Jos. Bell. II 161, where it is said of the Essenes: ταῖς δ' ἐγκύμοσιν οὐχ ὁμιλοῦσιν, ἐνδεικνύμενοι τὸ μὴ δι' ἡδονὴν ἀλλὰ τέκνων χρείαν γαμεῖν (though this was not the only Jewish view; see Heinemann, Philons Bildung 271). On the other hand, the words χεῖρα βάλλειν (in spite of Beltrami's reference to Od. XXI 223) do not immediately suggest sexual intercourse. Very probably the verse simply means: treat a pregnant woman gently, do not beat her (so as to prevent a miscarriage?, v. 184). Beltrami, ibid. 540 also refers to Jos. Ant. XX 18 (on Monobazus) συγκαθεύδων δέ ποτε τῇ γαστρὶ τῆς γυναικὸς τὴν χεῖρα προσαναπαύσας ἡνίκα καθύπνωσεν, φωνῆς τινος ἔδοξεν ὑπακούειν κελευούσης αἴρειν ἀπὸ τῆς νηδύος τὴν χεῖρα καὶ μὴ θλίβειν τὸ ἐν αὐτῇ βρέφος. Though the similarity to the present line seems striking, there is probably no connection between Jos. and Ps-Phoc. here, since the element of violence is lacking in Jos.

187 μηδ' αὖ παιδογόνον τέμνειν φύσιν ἄρσενα κούρου.
Cut not a youth's masculine procreative faculty.

Four mss. (B. L, M, P) read μηδ' αὖ παιδογόνον πότε τέμνειν ἄρσενα κοῦρον (ms. L κούρου), but that is simply to eliminate φύσιν, which the copyists did not know to mean "genitals" (see Bauer s.v. 2 and Herter, "Genitalien", RAC X 3; παιδογόνος φύσις ἄρσην is a periphrasis for "male genitals"). Moreover, μηδέποτε in Ps-Phoc. (83, 86, 90) always has the aorist, not the present. Bergk changes αὖ into ἐκ: ἐκτέμνειν (here with tmesis) = to castrate. On castration in the ancient world see Licht, Sexual Life 507ff.; Hopfner, Sexualleben 382ff. and Nock, "Eunuchs in Ancient Religion", Essays I 7-15. It was more an Oriental than a Greek or Roman practice, but it penetrated into the West in the Hellenistic period with some Oriental cults, esp. the cult of the Magna Mater and Attis (see Catullus' impressive 63rd poem). Therefore, Rossbroich 93 thinks that v. 187 is a warning against this cult. But it should be borne in mind that in the Imperial period castrated boys were often used as "Lustknaben" (Hopfner, Sexualleben 418ff.). In the

O.T. castration is not explicitly forbidden, but it is forbidden by Philo (*Hyp*. in Eus. *PE* VIII 7, 7 μὴ γονὴν ἀνδρῶν ἐκτέμνοντας κτλ., according to Philo an unwritten law), Josephus (*C. Ap*. II 270f.) and in rabbinic writings (e.g. Sanh. 56b, Shabb. 110b, where it is derived from Gen. I 28 and Lev. XXII 24; other texts in Epstein, *Sex Laws* 138ff. and Billerbeck I 807). Greek law lid not prohibit castration, Roman law did so only since Domitian, see Hitzig, "Castratio", *PW* III 1772 and Hug, "Eunuchen", *PW Suppl.* III 450f. The practice, however, was generally abhorred, see e.g. Ps-Luc. *Amores* 21. Schmidt, *Jahrb. f. class. Phil.* 3 (1857), 515, says v. 187 is not in the right place here, since "es die verschiedenartige Verbote unnatürlichen Liebesgenusses in auffallender Weise unterbricht". But that is only correct on a very questionable interpretation of v. 186; hence it has no sense to replace the line.

188 μηδ' ἀλόγοις ζῴοισι βατήριον ἐς λέχος ἐλθεῖν.
Seek not sexual union with irrational animals.

ἄλογος is a fixed epitheton of animals; see Bauer *s.v.* and Verdenius in *Lampas* 1970, 99f.; βατήριον (from βατέω = to cover) is a *hapax*; LSJ *s.v.* say: βατήριον λέχος = ὀχεία (a covering, impregnating). The dative ἀλόγοις ζῴοισι is probably analogous to the dative with μείγνυσθαι. Bestiality did occur in antiquity, see e.g. Plut. *Brut. anim. rat.* 7, 990F καὶ γὰρ αἰγῶν ἐπειράθησαν ἄνδρες καὶ ὑῶν καὶ ἵππων μιγνύμενοι καὶ γυναῖκες ἄρρεσι θηρίοις ἐπεμάνησαν. But though Plutarch says it is wrong, a severe condemnation is only found in Jewish writings. In the O.T. Ex. XXII 18 πᾶν κοιμώμενον μετὰ κτήνους, θανάτῳ ἀποκτενεῖτε αὐτούς. Lev. XVIII 23 πρὸς πᾶν τετράπουν οὐ δώσεις τὴν κοίτην σου εἰς σπερματισμὸν ἐκμιανθῆναι πρὸς αὐτό, καὶ γυνὴ οὐ στήσεται πρὸς πᾶν τετράπουν βιβασθῆναι· μισερὸν γάρ ἐστιν. Cf. Lev. XX 15f.; Deut. XXVII 21. Test. Levi XVII 11 (κτηνοφθόροι in a *Lasterkatalog*); Philo *Spec. leg.* III 43-50 (Heinemann, *Philons Bildung* 284); *Or. Sib.* V 393 (against Rome) ἐν σοὶ καὶ κτηνῶν εὗρον κοίτην κακοὶ ἄνδρες. Sanh. VII 4; Kerit. I 1; Ab. zar. II 1; Jeb. 59b and many other rabbinic passages in Preuss, "Prostitution" 551f.; Billerbeck III 72f.; Epstein, *Sex Laws* 132-4. Boissonade (*Anecd. Gr.* I 447 n. 3) wrongly thought that only Christians had "canones adversus κτηνοβάτας" and that Ps-Phoc. was, therefore, a Christian.

189 μηδ' ὕβριζε γυναῖκα ἐπ' αἰσχυντοῖς λεχέεσσι.

Outrage not your wife for shameful ways of intercourse.

αἰσχυντός (shameful) is a *hapax*, cf. αἰσχυντηλός (most words with the stem αἰσχ- have something to do with inadmissible sexual practices; see LSJ p. 43). ἐπί = "for; with a view to"; LSJ B III 2 (or should we read ἐπαισχυντοῖς with ms. B?). The exact meaning of this verse is obscure (and Rossbroich's interpretation is obscure as well). There are several possibilities: 1. It is possible to read χείλεσσι with ms. P (instead of λεχέεσσι) and interpret it as cunnilingus or fellatio, as does Brunck (*GPG* 168) with reference to Aristoph. *Vesp.* 1345f. ὁρᾷς ἐγώ σ' ὡς δεξιῶς ὑφειλόμην μέλλουσαν ἤδη λεσβιᾶν (or λεσβιεῖν) τοὺς ξυμπότας. 2. It may refer to intercourse during menstruation, forbidden in Lev. XVIII 19 and XX 18 (an attractive interpretation, since this section has more parallels in Lev. XVIII and XX). Cf. Aboth de R. Nathan (rec. A) II 1-2. 3. It may prohibit all kinds of "variations" in intercourse, possibly meant by Philo *Spec. leg.* III 9 οἱ φιλογύναιοι συνουσίαις ἐπιμεμνηνότες καὶ λαγνίστερον ὁμιλοῦντες γυναιξὶν οὐκ ἀλλοτρίαις ἀλλὰ ταῖς ἑαυτῶν, though not forbidden by the rabbis, e.g. Ned. 20b "A man may do whatever he pleases with his wife"; more texts in Billerbeck III 68f. and Feldmann, *Birth Control* 155ff. (but see Derek Erez Rabba II 12). 4. It may mean: "Do not humble your wife by having extra-marital (shameful) intercourse with another woman". In that case it would simply forbid adultery (cf. γαμοκλοπέειν in v. 3). Isocrates III 40 uses λυπεῖν in this connection. 5. It may be about violating a woman in general, not one's own wife (cf. v. 198). 6. It may refer to intercourse that is not for the sake of procreation, strongly condemned by several Jewish and some Greek authors; see Wendland, "Philo und die Diatribe" 35; Heinemann, *Philons Bildung* 262ff.; Baer, *Philo's Use of the Categories Male and Female* 94f.; Meeks, "The Image of the Androgyne", *History of Religions* 13 (1973/4), 177 n. 68. The second, fifth and sixth solution would seem to be the least improbable, though the correct interpretation remains uncertain.

190 μὴ παραβῇς εὐνὰς φύσεως ἐς Κύπριν ἄθεσμον.

Transgress not for unlawful sex the natural limits of sexuality.

The diction of this line (esp. παραβαίνειν εὐνάς) is somewhat odd. εὐναὶ φύσεως = the limits set by nature to sexual activities. φύσεως

= φυσικός, gen. qualitatis (post-classical; see Blass-Debr. § 165). On Κύπρις see the commentary on vv. 3 and 67. ἄθεσμος (unlawful) is a late word (in the LXX in 3 Macc. V 12; N.T. 2 Pet. II 7 and III 17 in a similar context). In view of παραβαίνειν and ἄθεσμος, there is no doubt that the concept of νόμος φύσεως is in the background here. H. Koester, ("Nomos Physeos", *Religions in Antiquity* 521ff.) suggests that Philo was the originator of this idea. Philo also used it in sexual contexts (*ibid.* 539), so against homosexuality *Abr.* 135 ἀπαυχενίζουσι τὸν τῆς φύσεως νόμον ... ὀχείας ἐκθέσμους μεταδιώκοντες ... ἄνδρες ὄντες ἄρρεσιν ἐπιβαίνοντες. Cf. *Spec. leg.* II 50 τοῖς δὲ (sc. γεννητικοῖς) καταχρῆται πρὸς ἐκνομωτάτους οἴστρους καὶ μίξεις ἀθέσμους (!), οὐ μόνον ἀλλοτρίοις γάμοις ἐπιμεμηνώς, ἀλλὰ καὶ παιδεραστῶν καὶ βιαζόμενος τὸν ἄρρενα τῆς φύσεως χαρακτῆρα παρακόπτειν καὶ μεταβάλλειν εἰς γυναικόμορφον ἰδέαν (also III 37-42). Cf. Test. Napht. III 4 Σόδομα, ἥτις ἐνήλλαξε τάξιν φύσεως αὐτῆς. In view of these texts, and because in *Or. Sib.* V 430 παίδων Κύπρις ἄθεσμος (cf. V 166 παίδων μῖξις ἄθεσμος) clearly means homosexuality, v. 190 undoubtedly forbids homosexual relations (cf. v. 3 μήτ' ἄρσενα Κύπριν ὀρίνειν). Then v. 191 fits in very well by illustrating the implicit concept of natural law. The prohibition of homosexuality has O.T. roots, e.g. Lev. XVIII 22 μετὰ ἄρσενος οὐ κοιμηθήσῃ κοίτην γυναικός (cf. XX 13; Preuss, "Prostitution" 470). The theme often occurs in Philo (see above; more texts in Koester 539; Wendland, "Philo ..." 33ff.; Heinemann, *Philons Bildung* 283f.; Nikiprowetzky, *Troisième Sibylle* 351 n. 594), Josephus (*C. Ap.* II 199.215.273), *Or. Sib.* (II 73, III 185.596.764, IV 34, V 387 etc.), rabbinic literature (Sanh. 73a, Sukk. 29a, etc.; see Billerbeck III 70ff.), the N.T. (e.g. Rom. I 27 ἀφέντες τὴν φυσικὴν χρῆσιν τῆς θηλείας κτλ., with the φύσις motive); Did. II 2, Barn. XIX 4, etc. See *ad* v. 3.

The κατὰ/παρὰ φύσιν motive does not derive from the O.T., but from Greek philosophy (though one should bear in mind that in Judaism the order of nature and the divine Law were often identified; on that theme see M. Limbeck, *Die Ordnung des Heils*, 1971); see Plato *Leg.* 636c ἀρρένων πρὸς ἄρρενας ... παρὰ φύσιν. Mus. Ruf. XII (p. 64, 4-7 H.) συμπλοκαὶ δ' ἄλλαι αἱ μὲν κατὰ μοιχείαν παρανομώταται, καὶ μετριώτεραι τούτων οὐδὲν αἱ πρὸς ἄρρενας τοῖς ἄρρεσιν, ὅτι παρὰ φύσιν τὸ τόλμημα. Plut. *Brut. anim. rat.* 7, 990E-F; cf. Ps-Luc. *Amor.* 20 (τὴν φύσιν παρενόμησεν). More texts in Koester, *TWNT* IX 256. But strong condemnations of homosexual activities are very rare in Greek literature. Homosexuality was widely accepted; see Licht, *Sexual Life* 411-498; idem, *Sittengeschichte Griechenlands* 244-294; Dover, *Greek Popular Morality* 213ff.

191 οὐδ' αὐτοῖς θήρεσσι συνεύαδον ἄρσενες εὐναί.
For even animals are not pleased by intercourse of male with male.

συνεύαδον (to please): epic aorist (gnomicus) of *συνανδάνω (which does not occur); the only other instance is in Apoll. Rhod. III 30 (but the simplex εὔαδον occurs in Homer). This zoological error (so rightly Dornseiff, *Echtheitsfragen* 47) motivates (οὐδέ = for ... not) the prohibition of homosexuality in v. 190. It was a current opinion in Greek antiquity; see e.g. Plato *Leg.* 836c ... μάρτυρα παραγόμενος τὴν τῶν θηρίων φύσιν καὶ δεικνὺς πρὸς τὰ τοιαῦτα οὐχ ἁπτόμενον ἄρρενα ἄρρενος διὰ τὸ μὴ φύσει τοῦτο εἶναι. Plut. *Brut. anim. rat. uti* 7, 990D ὅθεν οὔτ' ἄρρενος πρὸς ἄρρεν οὔτε θήλεος πρὸς θῆλυ μῖξιν αἱ τῶν θηρίων ἐπιθυμίαι μέχρι γε νῦν ἐνηνόχασιν. Ps-Luc. *Amor.* 22 λέοντες οὐκ ἐπιμαίνονται λέουσιν κτλ. (this whole passage deals with this subject). Cf. the comparable statements in Ps-Hippocr. *Epist.* XVII 44 and Ps-Heracl. *Epist.* IX 4, which, though not dealing with homosexuality, assert that animals often are better than men. "Es war bei Kynikern und Stoikern, in alter wie in jüngerer Zeit, fast zum Dogma geworden, in dem Tier das Vorbild für alles Naturgemässe, ja auch für manche bei den Menschen verlorene Tugend gewissermassen wieder zu entdecken" (Geffcken, *Zwei griechische Apologeten* 167f., with many examples in the footnotes; see also Gerhard, *Phoinix* 51, and Attridge, *First-Century Cynicism* 33). Athenagoras *Legatio* III 1 shows that this theme was taken over in early Christian literature.

192 μηδέ τι θηλύτεραι λέχος ἀνδρῶν μιμήσαιντο.
And let not women imitate the sexual role of men.

θηλύτεραι = θήλειαι, the comparative indicating opposition rather than comparison (LSJ s.v.). A prohibition of lesbian sex is not found in the O.T. (though some rabbis deduced it from Lev. XVIII 3), but it occurs in some Jewish texts, e.g. Sanh. 65a, Jeb. 76a (with the comments of Epstein, *Sex Laws* 138, and Feldmann, *Birth Control* 125; see also Preuss, "Prostitution" 553; Billerbeck, III 69) and in the N.T., e.g. Rom. I 26 αἵ τε γὰρ θήλειαι αὐτῶν μετήλλαξαν τὴν φυσικὴν χρῆσιν εἰς τὴν παρὰ φύσιν. Cf. Apoc. Petri XI (with Dieterich, *Nekyia* 176). Rossbroich 93 again refers to Manetho Astrol. IV 358 τριβάδας τ' ἀνδρόστροφα ἔργα τελούσας. V 216 ἀνδρῶν ἔργα τέλεσσε γυναιξὶ συνευνάζουσα. On tribadism in Greek culture see Licht, *Sexual Life* 316-328; cf. esp. Luc. *Dial. meretr.* V 289ff. Criticisms of this practice are rare, see e.g. Ps-Luc. *Amor.* 20. 28 and esp. Sen. *Epist.* XCV 21 *libidine vero ne maribus quidem cedunt, pati natae; di illas deaeque male perdant! Adeo perversum commentae genus impudicitiae viros ineunt.*

193 μηδ' ἐς ἔρωτα γυναικὸς ἅπας ῥεύσῃς ἀκάθεκτον.

Do not deliver yourself wholly unto unbridled sensuality towards your wife.

On ῥέω (to yield oneself) cf. Plato *Resp.* 485d10 πρὸς τὰ μαθήματα καὶ πᾶν τὸ τοιοῦτον ἐρρυήκασιν. The word ἀκάθεκτος (ungovernable) occurs only in texts from the first cent. A.D. onwards (see Rossbroich 11). Some mss. (L, V) read ἀκάθεκτος (in the nominative) and Bergk suggests ἀκαθέκτως, but the following texts from Philo demonstrate that it belongs to ἔρωτα: *Spec. leg.* II 9 λελυττηκότες ἔρωτες ἢ ἐπιθυμίαι ἀκάθεκτοι (cf. II 193), *Jos.* 153 ταῖς ἀκαθέκτοις ἐπιθυμίαις χαριζόμενοι. On self-restraint in marriage, which was a common theme in antiquity, see *ad* v. 189 (*sub* 6) (Rossbroich 94 thinks v. 189 and v. 193 have the same theme); cf. also Sextus 231 μοιχὸς τῆς ἑαυτοῦ γυναικὸς πᾶς ὁ ἀκόλαστος. But again, as in 189, it is uncertain whether this line is about passion for women in general or for one's own wife, though the antithesis with vv. 195-7 might suggest the first alternative. Cf., however, Heinemann, *Philons Bildung* 276f. (on Jewish and Greek warnings against "masslose Befriedigung der Lust in der Ehe").

194 οὐ γὰρ ἔρως θεός ἐστι, πάθος δ' ἀΐδηλον ἁπάντων.

For "eros" is not a god, but a passion destructive of all.

ἔρως refers back to ἔρωτα in v. 193 (Schmidt, *Jahrb. f. class. Phil.* 3 (1857), 514, says that v. 194 is a gloss to v. 193 and should be athetized, unnecessarily). πάθος: in itself a neutral term, but since Zeno (Pohlenz, *Stoa* I 141ff.) used primarily in a negative sense; "besonders in der jüdischen Paränese von der konkreten Leidenschaft auf geschlechtlichem Gebiet" (Vögtle, *Tugend- und Lasterkataloge* 209). ἁπάντων is translated above as a gen. obj. depending on ἀΐδηλον, but it may be a gen. poss. to be connected with πάθος (a destructive passion of all people). This verse is directed against an overrating of sexuality, based on the divinity of Eros (possibly used as an excuse for debauchery), and expressed in many passages of Greek literature; e.g. Hes. *Theog.* 120 Ἔρος, ὅς κάλλιστος ἐν ἀθανάτοισι θεοῖσι. Eur. fr. 269 Ἔρωτα δ' ὅστις μὴ θεὸν κρίνει μέγαν | καὶ τῶν ἁπάντων δαιμόνων ὑπέρτατον, | ἢ σκαιός ἐστιν ἢ καλῶν ἄπειρος ὤν | οὐκ οἶδε τὸν μέγιστον ἀνθρώποις θεόν. Men. fr. 235 εἶτ' οὐ μέγιστός ἐστι τῶν θεῶν Ἔρως | καὶ τιμιώτατός γε τῶν πάντων πολύ; cf. Men. et Phil. comp. I 272f. See further the many texts collected by Stobaeus IV 20 (IV p. 434-480 W-H): περὶ Ἀφροδίτης. The Stoics and the Cynics polemized against this overrating of *eros*; see e.g. Antisthenes *ap.* Clem. Alex. *Strom.* II 107, 3 τόν τε ἔρωτα κακίαν φησὶ φύσεως· ἧς ἥττους ὄντες οἱ κακοδαίμονες θεὸν τὴν νόσον καλοῦσιν. δείκνυται γὰρ διὰ τούτων ἡττᾶσθαι τοὺς ἀμαθεστέρους δι' ἄγνοιαν ἡδονῆς, ἣν οὐ χρὴ προσίεσθαι, κἂν θεὸς λέγηται, τουτέστι κἂν θεόθεν ἐπὶ τὴν τῆς παιδοποιίας χρείαν δεδομένην τυγχάνῃ. Cf. some quotations from poets in Athen. XIII 562f. More texts may be found in Schneider, "Eros", *RAC* VI 309. Ps-Phoc.'s Jewish mentality is in accordance with this philosophical point of view. "Ps-Phok. verbindet Einschärfung der Vermehrung mit gewisser Zurückhaltung im Sinn der Popularphilosophie (Z. 175f. 193f.)" (Oepke, "Ehe", *RAC* IV 656).

195-197 στέργε τεὴν ἄλοχον· τί γὰρ ἡδύτερον καὶ ἄρειον
ἢ ὅταν ἀνδρὶ γυνὴ φρονέῃ φίλα γήραος ἄχρις
καὶ πόσις ᾖ ἀλόχῳ, μηδ' ἐμπέσῃ ἄνδιχα νεῖκος;

Love your own wife, for what is sweeter and better
than whenever a wife is kindly disposed towards her husband till old age
and a husband towards his wife, without strife interfering as a dividing force?

φίλα φρονέειν τινί: Hom. *Il.* IV 219. γήραος ἄχρις: cf. ἄχρι γήρως in Apollod. Com. fr. 2. ἐμπίπτω often of evils, disasters, diseases, etc. see LSJ *s.v.* 3. ἄνδιχα: adv., asunder, in twain; for the use of adverbs as expressing a result cf. K-G II 115. These lines no doubt are inspired by Hom. *Od.* VI 182-4 οὐ μὲν γὰρ τοῦ γε κρεῖσσον καὶ ἄρειον, | ἢ ὅθ' ὁμοφρονέοντε νοήμασιν οἶκον ἔχητον | ἀνὴρ ἠδὲ γυνή. These Homeric lines were frequently quoted in later antiquity to illustrate the joy of harmony in marriage, e.g. Ps-Dion. Halic. *Ars Rhet.* IV 3 ὁμόνοια πᾶσι μὲν ἀνθρώποις ἡγεῖται τῶν ἀγαθῶν, μάλιστα δὲ τοῖς γεγαμηκόσιν· καὶ εἰς τοῦτο καὶ τὸ τοῦ Ὁμήρου παραληπτέον ἐνδόξῳ κρίσει χρώμενον, ὅτι οὐδὲν μεῖζον ἀγαθὸν "ἢ ὅθ' ὁμοφρονέοντε κτλ". Plut. *Amat.* 24, 770A οὔτε γὰρ ἡδοναὶ μείζονες ἀπ' ἄλλων οὔτε χρεῖαι συνεχέστεραι πρὸς ἄλλους οὔτε φιλίας τὸ καλὸν ἑτέρας ἔνδοξον οὕτω καὶ ζηλωτόν, ὡς "ὅθ' ὁμοφρονέοντε κτλ". Hierocles Περὶ γάμου p. 54, 25-7 Arn. (= Stob. IV 22, 24 p. 505, 20-2 W-H) τί γὰρ ἂν γένοιτο "κρεῖσσον καὶ ἄρειον" κατὰ τὸν θαυμασιώτατον "Ὅμηρον, "ἢ ὅθ' κτλ.". Other texts in which this passage from Homer is quoted are mentioned by Praechter, *Hierokles* 78f. and Delling, "Ehe", *RAC* IV 691. Cf. further on the theme in general Eur. *Medea* 14f. μεγίστη γίγνεται σωτηρία, ὅταν γυνὴ πρὸς ἄνδρα μὴ διχοστατῇ. Plut. *Coniug. praec.* 2f., 138 E; 33, 142 E. Mus. Ruf. XIIIa (p. 68, 5-12 H); XIV (p. 73, 17-74, 12 H); Hierocles p. 52ff. Arn. Passages from other authors are referred to by Praechter and Delling. From Jewish literature e.g. Sir. XXVI 13-18, XXXVI 22-26; Prov. XXXI 11-12; Philo *Spec. leg.* I 138. Rabbinic parallels in Billerbeck III 610. From the N.T. one may compare Col. III 19 and Eph. V 25 (ἀγαπᾶτε τὰς γυναῖκας). W. Schrage, "Zur Ethik der neutestamentlichen Haustafeln", *NTS* 21 (1974/5), 13 says that in Ps-Phoc. "der Mann auf sein Verhältnis zur Ehefrau gar nicht angesprochen wird", and *ibid.* n. 3 "Die Frau wird dagegen in 195f. zur Liebe (στέργειν) aufgerufen". This is simply wrong.

198 μὴ δέ τις ἀμνήστευτα βίῃ κούρῃσι μιγείη.

Let no one violently have intercourse with maidens without honourable wooing.

LSJ *s.v.* ἀμνήστευτος say the word is used here adverbially and means "without honourable wooing". It seems that Ps-Phoc. borrowed this very rare word (the only other instance mentioned in LSJ is Eur. fr. 818 ἀμνήστευτος γυνή) from Ex. XXII 15 ἐὰν δὲ ἀπατήσῃ τις παρθένον ἀμνήστευτον καὶ κοιμηθῇ μετ' αὐτῆς, φερνῇ φερνιεῖ αὐτὴν αὐτῷ γυναῖκα, which is about the rape of an unbetrothed girl. Philo (*Hyp.* in Eus. *PE* VIII 7, 1) and Josephus (*C. Ap.* II 215) tighten up this injunction by stating that raping a girl is a capital crime (see Heinemann, *Philons Bildung* 286ff. for more texts), probably deducing this from Deut. XXII 23ff., which is about a girl already betrothed to another. Cf. the polemics in *Or. Sib.* II 280 against ὁπόσοι ζώνην τὴν παρθενικὴν ἀπέλυσαν (Rossbroich 93 compares Manetho Astrol. VI 174f. λάθρῃ παρθενίης ζώνην λύσαντο). Rabbinic texts on rape and seduction in Epstein, *Sex Laws* 179ff. From Greek literature one might compare Mus. Ruf. XII (64, 1f. H) ... μόνα μὲν ἀφροδίσια νομίζειν δίκαια τὰ ἐν γάμῳ καὶ ἐπὶ γενέσει παίδων συντελούμενα. The plural κούρῃσι emphasizes the generality of the rule. Bergk rightly saw that v. 198 is oddly situated between 197 and 199; he wanted to put it after 183, which is certainly a better place.

199 μὴ δὲ γυναῖκα κακὴν πολυχρήματον οἴκαδ' ἄγεσθαι.
Bring not as wife into your home a bad and wealthy woman.

Vv. 199-204 form a unity and are based upon Theogn. 183-190; see further below. πολυχρήματος: occurring since the first cent. B.C. This theme was a *topos* in Stoic and Cynic literature; see Gerhard, *Phoinix* 168f.; Praechter, *Hierokles* 82f.; Geurts, *Het Huwelijk* 85-7; Rossbroich 95. Antipater Tars. fr. 62 (= Stob. IV 22, 103) μηδ' εἰς πλοῦτον μηδ' εἰς ὀγκοῦσαν εὐγένειαν μηδ' εἰς ἄλλην χάσμην μηδεμίαν ἀποβλέπειν, μηδὲ μὰ Δία εἰς κάλλος. Nicostratus *ap.* Stob. IV 22, 102 ... ἔνιοι δὲ οὐδ' ἂν γῆμαι ἔφασαν ἄλλως γε εἰ μὴ πλουτοίη καὶ προῖκα ἐπάγοιτο πολλήν. ἀλλ' ἐνταῦθά που καὶ τὸ λαμπρὸν τοῦ δουλεύειν ἐστὶν ἰδίᾳ μὲν τῇ γυναικὶ ὑπὸ τοῦ πλούτου διατεθρυμμένῃ (with δουλεύειν ἰδίᾳ γυναικί cf. v. 200 λατρεύσεις ἀλόχῳ). Antiphanes *ap.* Stob. IV 22, 128 οὐκ ἔστιν οὐδὲν βαρύτερον τῶν φορτίων ὄντως γυναικὸς προῖκα πολλὴν φερομένης (see Stobaeus' whole chapter IV 22, 118-135, entitled ὅτι ἐν τοῖς γάμοις οὐ τὴν εὐγένειαν οὐδὲ τὸν πλοῦτον χρὴ σκοπεῖν ἀλλὰ τὸν τρόπον). Mus. Ruf. XIIIb (p. 69, 4-6 H) διὸ χρὴ τοὺς γαμοῦντας οὐκ εἰς γένος ἀφορᾶν εἰ ἐξ εὐπατριδῶν, οὐδ' εἰς χρήματα εἰ πολλὰ κέκτηνταί τινες. Hierocles p. 55 Arn. οὐ γὰρ ἐπὶ παίδων γενέσει καὶ βίου κοινωνίᾳ ἄγονται γυναῖκας ἀλλ' οἱ μὲν διὰ προικὸς ὄγκον, οἱ δὲ δι' ἐξοχὴν μορφῆς κτλ. ... τύραννον ἀντὶ γυναικὸς ἐπεισάγουσιν ἑαυτοῖς. Plut. *Amat.* 9, 754A πλοῦτον δὲ γυναικὸς αἱρεῖσθαι μὲν πρὸ ἀρετῆς ἢ γένους ἀφιλότιμον καὶ ἀνελεύθερον, cf. *Coniug. praec.* 14, 139F οὐδὲ πλουσίας γαμετῆς ὄνησις. More texts can be found in Praechter and Gerhard, also in Schmidt, *Ethik* II 167. From the gnomological tradition one may mention Theogn. 183-190 (which is quoted below in the commentary on vv. 201-204), Men. *Mon.* 154 γάμει δὲ μὴ τὴν προῖκα, τὴν γυναῖκα δέ, cf. 196 and 296. Sextus 512 χαλεπώτερον πλουσιωτέρας ἄρξεις. From Jewish literature one may (probably) compare Sir. VII 19 μὴ ἀστόχει γυναικὸς σοφῆς καὶ ἀγαθῆς· ἡ γὰρ χάρις αὐτῆς ὑπὲρ τὸ χρυσίον. Jos. *C. Ap.* II 200 γαμεῖν δὲ κελεύει (sc. ὁ νόμος) μὴ προικὶ προσέχοντας. A late rabbinic passage is mentioned by Klein, *Ältest. christl. Katech.* 100.

200 λατρεύσεις ἀλόχῳ λυγρῆς χάριν εἵνεκα φερνῆς.
  You will be a slave of your wife because of the baneful dowry.

On the pleonastic χάριν εἵνεκα see K-G I 529; cf. Plato *Leg.* 701d2 τίνος δὴ χάριν ἕνεκα ταῦτα ἐλέχθη; *Polit.* 302b9 ἅπανθ' ἕνεκα τοῦ τοιούτου πάντες δρῶμεν χάριν. Brunck, *GPG* 171f., discusses this χάριν εἵνεκα extensively and compares Soph. *Phil.* 554, where some mss. read ἀμφὶ σοῦ 'νεκα, but see K-G I 529, who quote better instances. φερνή: dowry, "Mitgift"; on the problems of φερνή, προίξ, ἕδνα, *shilluchim, mohar, nikse şon barzel, nedunja, ketubbah,* etc. see Delling, "Eheschliessung", *RAC* IV 719-731; Billerbeck II 385ff.; Jeremias, *Jerusalem* 403ff.; Krauss, *Talm. Arch.* II 43-5; Vatin, *Recherches* 190ff.; cf. also Bringmann, *Die Frau im ptolemäisch-kaiserlichen Ägypten* 25ff. In this particular case, φερνή is the marriage-portion brought in by the wife, which had to be paid back by the husband in case of divorce. When the dowry was high, that made divorce more difficult; see Taubenschlag, *Law ...* 123f.

On this theme of "Weiberherrschaft" due to "die Höhe der Mitgiften" see Schmidt, *Ethik* II 181f. and Friedländer, *Darstellungen* I 278 with nn. 5-10 (on "Pantoffelregiment reicher Frauen"). Eur. fr. 502 ὅσοι γαμοῦσι δ' ἢ γένει κρείσσους γάμους | ἢ πολλὰ χρήματ', οὐκ ἐπίστανται γαμεῖν. | τὰ τῆς γυναικὸς γὰρ κρατοῦντ' ἐν δώμασιν | δουλοῖ τὸν ἄνδρα, κοὐκέτ' ἔστ' ἐλεύθερος. | πλοῦτος δ' ἐπακτὸς ἐκ γυναικείων γάμων | ἀνόνητος· αἱ γὰρ διαλύσεις οὐ ῥᾴδιαι. Ps-Ocellus Luc. *Univ. nat.* 49 ἡ μὲν γὰρ ὑπερέχουσα πλούτῳ καὶ γένει καὶ φίλοις ἄρχειν προαιρεῖται τοῦ ἀνδρὸς παρὰ τὸν τῆς φύσεως νόμον. Plut. *Puer. educ.* 19, 13F οἵ γε μακρῷ κρείττους ἑαυτῶν λαμβάνοντες οὐ τῶν γυναικῶν ἄνδρες, τῶν δὲ προικῶν δοῦλοι λανθάνουσι γιγνόμενοι, cf. *Amat.* 7, 752E. Euripides' δουλοῖ τὸν ἄνδρα and Plutarch's δοῦλοι λανθάνουσι γιγνόμενοι well illustrate λατρεύσεις in this line (cf. also Nicostratus quoted *ad* v. 199).

201-204 ἵππους εὐγενέας διζήμεθα γειαρότας τε
  ταύρους ὑψιτένοντας, ἀτὰρ σκυλάκων πανάριστον.
  γῆμαι δ' οὐκ ἀγαθὴν ἐριδαίνομεν ἀφρονέοντες.
  οὐ δὲ γυνὴ κακὸν ἄνδρ' ἀπαναίνεται ἀφνεὸν ὄντα.

  We seek noble horses and strong-necked bulls,
  ploughers of the earth, and the very best of dogs.
  Yet we fools do not strive to marry a good wife;
  nor does a woman reject a bad man when he is rich.

ἵππος εὐγενής: Theogn. 184; Soph. *El.* 25. δίζημαι: seek out, look for. γειαρότης (plougher of earth): mostly used of men (farmers), *Anth. Pal.* IX 23, XVI 94; *Epigr. Gr.* 793, all of them post-classical texts. ὑψιτένων: with high-strained sinews, strong-necked; it is a *hapax*, but ὑψιτενέω and ὑψιτενής do occur in late authors (Oppianus, Nonnus, Theoctistes). σκύλαξ: (young) dog. ἀτάρ: often marking a strong contrast (but, nevertheless), but it may also have progressive force, with little or no idea of contrast; see Denniston, *Gr. Part.* 53. ἐριδαίνω: wrangle, quarrel; strive, compete. οὐ δὲ: it would be better to read οὐδὲ. ἀπαναίνομαι: reject. ἀφνεός (= ἀφνειός): rich; Ludwich, *Spruchbuch* 22 wants to read ἀπαναίνετ' ἀφνειὸν ἐόντα, since ὤν does not occur in Ps-Phoc., only ἐών, see vv. 73 and 134; and ἀφνειός with short first syllable does occur in Theocr. XIII 9, *Anth. Pal.* IX 678, etc. (see also Van Groningen's note on Theogn. 188).

Not until these lines does it become manifest that the source of vv. 199-204 is primarily Theogn. 183-190 κριοὺς μὲν καὶ ὄνους διζήμεθα, Κύρνε, καὶ ἵππους | εὐγενέας, καί τις βούλεται ἐξ ἀγαθῶν | βήσεσθαι· γῆμαι δὲ κακὴν κακοῦ οὐ μελεδαίνει | ἐσθλὸς ἀνήρ, ἢν οἱ χρήματα πολλὰ διδῷ, | οὐδὲ γυνὴ κακοῦ ἀνδρὸς ἀναίνεται εἶναι ἄκοιτις | πλουσίου, ἀλλ' ἀφνεὸν βούλεται ἀντ' ἀγαθοῦ. | χρήματα μὲν τιμῶσι· καὶ ἐκ κακοῦ ἐσθλὸς ἔγημε | καὶ κακὸς ἐξ ἀγαθοῦ· πλοῦτος ἔμειξε γένος (note the antithesis κακός-ἀγαθός, also in Ps-Phoc.). See the comments of Van Groningen *ad loc.* (pp. 72-4). Rossbroich 96 compares Varro *Sat.* fr. 236 *nemo est tam neglegens, quin summa diligentia eligat asinum, qui suam saliat equulam*. Cf. also *Gnom. hom.* 180 Elter οὔτε ἵππος εὐγενὴς κρίνοιτ' ἂν ὁ πολυτελῆ σκευὴν ἔχων ἀλλ' ὁ τῇ φύσει λαμπρός, οὔτε ἀνὴρ σπουδαῖος ὁ πολύτιμον οὐσίαν κεκτημένος ἀλλ' ὁ τὴν ψυχὴν γενναῖος. Ps-Phoc. seems to assume that people choose their own partners, not the girl's parents; cf. Schubart, *Ägypten* 169: "Gerade in den Eheverträgen aus Alexandreia schliessen die Frau und der Mann, nicht die Eltern, den Vertrag ab, und die Frau pflegt an erster Stelle genannt zu werden". But this was, of course, not typically Alexandrian. Moreover, the text of Theognis already reflects this situation (see Van Groningen 73).

205 μηδὲ γάμῳ γάμον ἄλλον ἄγοις ἔπι, πήματι πῆμα.

Add not marriage to marriage, calamity to calamity.

πήματι πῆμα: a very common poetic paronomasia; see e.g. the oracle in Herod. I 67 πῆμ' ἐπὶ πήματι, Soph. *Ant.* 595 πήματα ... ἐπὶ πήμασι πίπτοντ', Eur. *Or.* 1255 πήματα πήμασιν, Aelian *Var. Hist.* III 43 πῆμα δόμοις ἐπὶ πήματι βαίνει (again from an oracle),

Manetho Astrol. V 57 πῆμ' ἐπὶ πήματι δεινῷ. The construction occurs both with and without ἐπί; see further K-G I 444, 4. Some scholars have asserted that this line is contradictory to v. 175, where marriage is recommended (e.g. Kroll, *PW* XX 1, 505); therefore some want to athetize it (Schmidt, *Jahrb. f. class. Phil.* 3 (1857), 514f.; Farina 46 n. 73). But one should first determine what this verse is about. Is it about digamy (i.e. remarrying) or about bigamy (or polygamy)? A similar difficulty is presented by a passage from the Damascus Rule, *CD* IV 21, where it is condemned לקחת שתי נשים בחייהם ("to take two wives during their life-time"); that may be directed against remarrying or against bigamy; see the discussion in J. Maier, *Die Texte vom Toten Meer* II 48, and G. Vermes, "Sectarian Matrimonial Halakhah in the Damascus Rule", *JJS* 25 (1974), 197-202 (who says it is against polygamy). Both views can be defended: *a*. There was a certain tendency in some Hellenistic and Jewish circles to dissuade remarriage; see Kötting, "Digamus", *RAC* III 1016-1024. Men. et Phil. comp. I 51f. ὅστις γυναικὸς ἀποθανούσης ἐπιγαμεῖ, ὁ τοιοῦτος ὄντως οὐκ ἐπίστατ' εὐτυχεῖν. *Anth. Pal.* IX 133 εἴ τις ἅπαξ γήμας πάλι δεύτερα λέκτρα διώκει, ναυηγὸς πλώει δὶς βυθὸν ἀργαλέον. See esp. the quotations from poets in Athen. XIII 559 and Diod. Sic. XII 14. Philo *Spec. leg.* II 135 and Jos. *Ant.* XVII 349ff. can be interpreted in this sense (but contrast Josephus' own marriage life; Schürer, *History* I (1973) 46). The passages in the Pastoral Epistles about the μιᾶς γυναικὸς ἀνήρ are also to be regarded as directed against remarriage (e.g. I Tim. III 2.12; V 9; Tit. I 6 and Spicq *ad loc.*). In the early church after the New Testament period remarriage was often strongly dissuaded, see e.g. Athenag. *Leg.* XXXIII 4, who says a second marriage is εὐπρεπὴς μοιχεία (many more passages in Kötting, "Digamus" 1020f.). But it must be admitted that this sentiment about remarriage is much more Greek and Christian than Jewish; after all it had no O.T. basis (Kötting, "Digamus" 1016f.). *b*. Bigamy and polygamy was permitted in the O.T. and in Judaism (Leipoldt, *Die Frau* 111f.; Feldmann, *Birth Control* 37ff.; Jeremias, *Jerusalem* 108f.; Billerbeck III 647ff.; Danby, *Mishnah*, Reg. *s.v.* co-wife; Safrai in *Comp. Rer. Jud.* I 749). See e.g. Jos. *Bell.* I 477 ὡς ἂν ἐφειμένου τε πατρίως Ἰουδαίοις γαμεῖν πλείους, *Ant.* XVII 14 πάτριον γὰρ πλείοσιν ἐν ταὐτῷ ἡμῖν συνοικεῖν. Nevertheless, it was very unusual to have more than one wife at the same time, for understandable reasons. Hence also criticisms of this practice arose, e.g. *CD* IV 21 (see besides Vermes also Moore, *Judaism* I 202) and rabbinic texts in Billerbeck III 650; Bacher, *Agada der Tann.* I 66 and Safrai in *Comp. Rer. Jud.* I 749; e.g. Jeb. 37b. In Greek culture polygamy was also extremely unusual (see Licht, *Sexual Life* 70). Ps-Phoc. 205 may best be interpreted as dissuading this practice. But whichever interpretation is chosen, this line probably does not express a negative view of marriage as such (against Kroll).

206 μηδ' ἀμφὶ κτεάνων συνομαίμοσιν εἰς ἔριν ἔλθῃς.
Nor permit yourself strife with your kinsfolk about possessions.

συνομαίμων: Aesch. *Prom.* 410; Eur. *Hel.* 640; cf. σύναιμος in v. 47. εἰς ἔριν ἐλθεῖν τινι: cf. Herod. IX 33, 2 and Aristoph. *Ranae* 877. Rossbroich 97 says this verse has its right place between vv. 47 and 48; Sitzler, *Woch. f. klass. Phil.* 29 (1912), 456 wants to athetize it. Some mss. (M, B) do indeed omit it, and the theme is that of vv. 42-47: the dividing power of possessions; but here it seems to be about inheritances (hence συνομαίμοσιν), so that the line may be kept here. Besides the texts quoted in the commentary on vv. 42ff. cf. also Eur. *Iph. Aul.* 376f. κασιγνήτοισι γίγνεσθαι λόγους μάχας θ', ὅταν ποτ' ἐμπέσωσιν εἰς ἔριν. Isocr. *Panath.* 184 ἀποκτεῖναι δ' ἂν τολμήσαντας τοὺς ἀδελφοὺς τοὺς ἑαυτῶν καὶ τοὺς ἑταίρους καὶ τοὺς κοινωνοὺς ὥστε καὶ τἀκείνων λαβεῖν. Gerhard, *Phoinix* 17, refers to Lucian *Cyn.* 8 ἐπιβουλεύετε ἀλλήλοις διὰ ταῦτα (sc. χρήματα) καὶ φίλοις φίλοι καὶ πατράσι παῖδες καὶ γυναῖκες ἀνδράσιν. Ps-Hippocr. *Epist.* XVII 29 (p. 302 Hercher) φιλονικέοντες ἔχθρῃ πρὸς ἀλλήλους δῆριν ἔχουσι μετὰ ἀδελφέων καὶ τοκήων καὶ πολιητέων, καὶ ταῦτα ὑπὲρ τοιούτων κτημάτων ὧν οὐδὲ εἷς θανὼν δεσπότης ἐστί, ἀλληλοκτονέουσι.

207 παισὶν μὴ χαλέπαινε τεοῖσ', ἀλλ' ἤπιος εἴης.
Be not harsh with your children, but be gentle.

ἤπιος (gentle, kind): already in Homer, the word characterizes the right attitude (of fathers) towards (their) children. Hom. *Il.* XXIV 770 πατὴρ ὣς ἤπιος αἰεί, *Od.* II 47.234. See in the N.T. 1 Thess. II 7 ἐγενήθημεν ἤπιοι ἐν μέσῳ ὑμῶν, ὡς ἐὰν τρόφος θάλπῃ τὰ ἑαυτῆς τέκνα and the discussion by Malherbe, "Gentle as a Nurse. The Cynic Background to 1 Thess. 2", *Nov. Test.* 12 (1970), 203-217. This use of ἤπιος is well illustrated by *Gnom. Byz.* 59 πλεῖστον διαφέρει τὸ νουθετεῖν τοῦ ὀνειδίζειν· τὸ μὲν γὰρ ἤπιόν τε καὶ φίλον, τὸ δὲ σκληρόν τε καὶ ὑβριστικόν· καὶ τὸ μὲν διορθοῖ τοὺς ἁμαρτάνοντας, τὸ δὲ μόνον ἐλέγχει. For the sentiment cf. further Chaeremon Trag. fr. 35 πρὸς υἱὸν ὀργὴν οὐκ ἔχει χρηστὸς πατήρ (= Men. *Mon.* 635); other texts in Stob. IV 26 (p. 65off. W-H): ὁποίους τινὰς χρὴ εἶναι τοὺς πατέρας περὶ τὰ τέκνα. Eph. VI 4 μὴ παροργίζετε τὰ τέκνα ὑμῶν, ἀλλὰ ἐκτρέφετε αὐτὰ ἐν παιδείᾳ καὶ νουθεσίᾳ κυρίου (here the same μὴ ... ἀλλὰ structure as in the present line; see the comm. on v. 5). Cf. Col. III 21 οἱ πατέρες, μὴ ἐρεθίζετε τὰ τέκνα ὑμῶν. But, of course, "to be angry with" (Ps-Phoc.) is not exactly the same as "to make angry" (N.T.). The principle of v. 207 is illustrated by an interesting mitigation of a commandment in Deut. in the two following lines.

208-209 ἢν δέ τι παῖς ἀλίτῃ σε, κολουέτω υἱέα μήτηρ
ἢ καὶ πρεσβύτατοι γενεῆς ἢ δημογέροντες.

> And if a child sins against you, let the mother cut her son down to size,
> or else the elders of the family or the chiefs of the people.

ἀλιταίνω: mostly used of rather serious transgressions (see LSJ s.v.). κολουέτω (cut short, dock, curtail, prune): this reading is very uncertain, for none of the mss. has it; it is a conjecture of Bergk; the mss. read κολυέτω, (ἐσ)κρινέτω, κιρνάτω, κρινάτω (adopted by Diehl and Farina), etc. The original reading is hard to find. Keydell, *Jahresbericht* 230 (1931), 93 says: "V. 208 ist metrisch bedenklich und befriedigt auch inhaltlich nicht". Be that as it may, it has generally been assumed since Bernays (244) that these lines are a free rendering of Deut. XXI 18ff. ἐὰν δέ τινι ᾖ υἱὸς ἀπειθὴς καὶ ἐρεθιστὴς οὐχ ὑπακούων φωνὴν πατρὸς καὶ φωνὴν μητρὸς καὶ παιδεύσωσιν αὐτὸν καὶ μὴ εἰσακούῃ αὐτῶν, (19) καὶ συλλαβόντες αὐτὸν ... ἐξάξουσιν αὐτὸν ἐπὶ τὴν γερουσίαν τῆς πόλεως αὐτοῦ ... (21) λιθοβολήσουσιν αὐτὸν οἱ ἄνδρες τῆς πόλεως αὐτοῦ. "Auslegungen dieser Stelle finden sich erst in stark hellenistischen Schriften, aber immer im Zusammenhang mit dem 4. Gebot, so in Jos. C. Ap. II 206; Philo Spec. leg. II 232 (abmildernd: Gesetz als Erlaubnis, nicht als Befehl; vgl. Mk. 10, 4 par.); ... Ps-Phok. 208f; Ps-Menand. 7" (Berger, *Gesetzesauslegung Jesu* I 284). It would be better to stress the fact that, whereas Philo (over against Deut.) omits the mother's right of chastisement (see Heinemann, *Philons Bildung* 250ff.), Ps-Phoc. omits the father's right and emphasizes that of the mother. Whereas Deut. XXI 18ff. is directed against the son,

Ps-Phoc. 208f. seems to be directed against the father. Schrage, "Zur Ethik der neutestamentlichen Haustafeln" 15 n. 4 (contrasting Col. III 21/Eph. VI 4, quoted *ad* v. 207, with Philo and Josephus), rightly says: "Dabei soll gewiss nicht übersehen werden, dass sich auch Gegenstimmen gegen die harte väterliche Gewalt zu Wort melden (Ps-Phok. 207-209)". Bernays 244 thinks that this line is directed against the *patria potestas* of Roman law, referring to Sext. Emp. *Hypotyp*. III 211 παρ' ἑτέροις δὲ ὡς τυραννικὸν τοῦτο ἐκβέβληται (sc. the *patria potestas*). But a *patria potestas* in the Roman sense did not exist in Judaism; see Krauss, *Talm. Arch*. II 19f.

It may well be asked whether the δημογέροντες (already in Homer *Il*. XI 372) here refer to the Jewish γερουσία of Alexandria (N.B. δημογέροντες renders the ἐξουσία τῆς πόλεως of Deut. XXI 19). The Jewish *politeuma* of Alexandria was ruled over by a γερουσία, at least since 10 or 12 A.D. (see Schürer, *Gesch*. II⁴ 250 n. 34; Tcherikover, *CPJ* I 9 and 57; Spicq, *Ep. Past*. I 67f., esp. 68 n. 4; Stern, *Comp. Rer. Jud*. I 124; Applebaum, *ibid*. 473f.). But perhaps it does not have this technical sense here. If, however, πρεσβύτατοι γενεῆς could be rendered by "elders of the nation" (cf. זקני העם in the O.T., e.g. Ex. XIX 7), that might corroborate the opinion that a ruling authoritative body is meant here. Cf. 1 Macc. XIV 28 πρεσβύτεροι τῆς χώρας and the title πρεσβυτέριον (τοῦ λαοῦ) given to the Sanhedrin in Lk. XXII 66 and Acts XXII 5. On the term πρεσβύτεροι in general see Dibelius-Conzelmann, *Past*. 60f.

210-212 μὴ μὲν ἐπ' ἄρσενι παιδὶ τρέφειν πλοκάμους ἐπὶ χαίτης.
μὴ κορυφὴν πλέξῃς μήθ' ἄμματα λοξὰ κορύμβων.
ἄρσεσιν οὐκ ἐπέοικε κομᾶν, χλιδαναῖς δὲ γυναιξίν.

If a child is a boy, do not let locks grow on his head.
Braid not his crown nor make cross-knots at the top of his head.
Long hair is not fit for men, but for voluptuous women.

μέν = μήν, Denniston, *Gr. Part*. 362. τρέφειν πλοκάμους: Eur. *Bacch*. 494. ἄμμα = knot. λοξός = slanting, crosswise. κόρυμβος = a. uppermost point (= κορυφή); b. roll or knot of hair on the crown of the head. V. 211 has a somewhat pleonastic diction. The statement ἄρσεσιν οὐκ ἐπέοικε κομᾶν has several parallels both in Hellenistic (not Classical), Jewish, and in Christian literature. The best known text is 1 Cor. XI 14 ἀνὴρ μὲν ἐὰν κομᾷ ἀτιμία αὐτῷ ἐστιν.

The wearing of long hair by a man was often considered a sign of effemination (see Herter, "Effeminatus", *RAC* IV 629ff., esp. 632: "Am einfachsten war das Haar zu beeinflussen, das schon ohnedies weichlich sein konnte. Man liess es wachsen, so dass κομᾶν schon an sich Verdacht erregen mochte"; *ibid.* many illustrating passages). Plut. *Quaest. Rom.* 14, 267B τοῖς μὲν τὸ κείρεσθαι, ταῖς δὲ τὸ κομᾶν σύνηθές ἐστιν, cf. *Mul. virt.* 26, 261 F. Philostr. *Vit. Ap.* I 13. Ovid. *Her.* IV 75 *sint procul a nobis iuvenes ut femina compti*. Hor. *Epod.* XI 27f. *ardor ... teretis pueri, longam renodantis comam* (i.e. an *effeminatus*). Cf. Epict. III 1, 24f.; I 16, 9-14. Juv. *Sat.* II 96. Mus. Ruf. XXI (p. 116, 3ff. H) καὶ γάρ τοι δοκῶν εἶναι κόσμος οὗτος πολλὴν ἀκοσμίαν ἔχει καὶ διαφέρει οὐδὲν τοῦ καλλωπισμοῦ τοῦ τῶν γυναικῶν (Musonius does admit κομᾶν under certain circumstances; see Van Geytenbeek, *Mus. Ruf.* 119ff.). According to Gerhard, *Phoinix* 192, criticism of κομᾶν is a typically Cynic trait, but cf. Herter, *art. cit.* 632; also Kroll, *Kultur* 180 (with n. 72); Gussen, *Leven in Alexandrië* 85. 101f. (on the very effeminate hair-style of Alexandrian men, with knots, etc.). Jewish writings also protest against this practice, e.g. Philo *Spec. leg.* III 37 τὰς τῆς κεφαλῆς τρίχας ἀναπλεκόμενοι καὶ διακοσμούμενοι (= *effeminati*). Rabbinic texts in Billerbeck III 441f. and Krauss, *Talm. Arch.* II 192f.

χλιδαναῖς δὲ γυναιξίν: elaborate hairdressing in the case of women was often considered as a sign of lasciviousness (χλιδανός = luxurious, delicate, voluptuous). See e.g. Juv. *Sat.* VI 486-511. Test. Rub. V 5 λοιπὸν φεύγετε, τέκνα μου, τὴν πορνείαν, καὶ προστάσσετε ταῖς γυναιξὶν ὑμῶν καὶ ταῖς θυγατράσιν ὑμῶν, ἵνα μὴ κοσμῶσι τὰς κεφαλὰς αὐτῶν κτλ. 1 Tim. II 9 γυναῖκας ... μετὰ αἰδοῦς καὶ σωφροσύνης κοσμεῖν ἑαυτάς, μὴ ἐν πλέγμασιν κτλ. (see the materials collected by Spicq *ad loc.*); cf. 1 Pet. III 3.

213-214 παιδὸς δ' εὐμόρφου φρουρεῖν νεοτήσιον ὥρην·
πολλοὶ γὰρ λυσσῶσι πρὸς ἄρσενα μεῖξιν ἔρωτος.

Guard the youthful beauty of a comely boy;
because many rage for intercourse with a man.

εὔμορφος: see the occurrences listed by Rossbroich 13. νεοτήσιος = youthful; see Schmidt, *Synonymik* IV 30. λυσσᾶν (to rage, to be mad; cf. μαίνειν) in this connection with sexuality also in Plato *Resp.* 586c ἔρωτες λυττῶντες (cf. *Leg.* 839a), Theocr. III 47 λύσσα = raging love; cf. the terms παιδομανία, παιδομανής, etc. ἄρσενα: cf. *ad* 3. The word ἔρωτος looks pleonastic after μεῖξιν (therefore ms. M reads ἐρῶντες), but see Plato Leg. 836c πρὸς μεῖξιν ἀφροδισίων, also Alex. Lycop. 25 (p. 37, 18f. Brinkmann). The lines 213-217 exhort parents to protect their children from the immoral cravings of other people. Men. gnom. syr. 7 "Halte deinen Sohn von der Unzucht ab und deinen Sklaven vom Wirtshaus" (tr. Schulthess). On paederasty see Licht, *Sexual Life* 413ff., 492ff.; Kroll, *Kultur* 177ff.; Marrou, *Histoire de l'éducation* 55ff.; Kraus, "Paederastie", *Kleine Pauly* IV 1583f.; Kroll, *RE* XI 897ff.; E. L. de Kock, *Acta Classica* 5 (1962), 27ff.; Epstein, *Sex Laws* 134ff. Texts have been quoted *ad* vv. 3 and 190.

215-216 παρθενικὴν δὲ φύλασσε πολυκλείστοις θαλάμοισιν,
μὴ δέ μιν ἄχρι γάμων πρὸ δόμων ὀφθῆμεν ἐάσῃς.

Guard a virgin in firmly locked rooms,
and let her not be seen before the house until her wedding-day.

παρθενική: poetic for παρθένος. πολύκλειστος (closely shut) is a *hapax*. γάμοι: the plural for a single wedding occurs frequently, see Bauer *s.v.* The same applies to the plural δόμοι: e.g. Hes. *Op.* 96; cf. K-G I 18f. Young annotates to v. 215: "ut Danaae Sophocleae" (see *Ant.* 944f.). Thraede, "Frau", *RAC* VIII 200f. remarks that the locking up of women in Greek culture has often been exaggerated by modern scholars. Certainly in Alexandria women participated in public life to a high degree (cf. Bringmann, *Die Frau im ptolemäisch-kaiserlichen Ägypten* 67ff.; Gussen, *Leven in Alexandrië* 84; see, however, Vatin, *Recherches* 201f.). But this was not true of Jewish women, esp. not of unmarried girls, that Ps-Phoc. speaks about here. Philo *Spec. leg.* III 169 θηλείαις δὲ οἰκουρία καὶ ἡ ἔνδον μονή (sc. ἐφαρμόζουσι), *ibid.* 171 μηδὲν οὖν ἔξω τῶν κατὰ τὴν οἰκονομίαν πολυπραγμονείτω γυνὴ ζητοῦσα μοναυλίαν μηδ' οἷα νομὰς κατὰ τὰς ὁδοὺς ἐν ὄψεσιν ἀνδρῶν ἑτέρων ἐξεταζέσθω. *In Flacc.* 89 γύναια κατάκλειστα μηδὲ τὴν αὔλειον προερχόμενα καὶ θαλαμευόμεναι παρθένοι δι' αἰδῶ τὰς ἀνδρῶν ὄψεις καὶ τῶν οἰκειοτάτων ἐκτρεπόμενοι. 2 Macc. III 19 αἱ κατάκλειστοι τῶν παρθένων, 3 Macc. I 18 αἱ κατάκλειστοι παρθένοι ἐν θαλάμοις, 4 Macc. XVIII 7 ἐγὼ ἐγενήθην παρθένος ἁγνὴ οὐδὲ ὑπερέβην πατρικὸν οἶκον. Tcherikover, *CPJ* I 35, thinks these three texts from Macc. reflect Alexandrian circumstances. But the same rules also apply to Palestine. See Jeremias, *Jerusalem* 396: "Am liebsten sah man es, wenn die Frau, und namentlich das unverheiratete Mädchen, überhaupt nicht ausging"; *ibid.* 397: "die Jerusalemer Jungfrau aus strenggesetzlichen vornehmem Hause pflegte vor ihrer Heirat das Haus möglichst überhaupt nicht zu verlassen". Cf. also Heinemann, *Philons Bildung* 233-235. See e.g. Ket. I 8; VII 6 (on the question: when does a wife transgress the Law of Moses: "If she goes out with her hair unbound, or spins in the street, or speaks with any man"). It should also be borne in mind that the common word for a prostitute was *naphkath bārā* = she who goes out (see Jastrow, *Dictionary* 926a). One may also compare Sir. XLII 9-11 (partly quoted *ad* 217; cf. XXVI 10) and the rabbinic texts referred to by Epstein, *Sex Laws* 72. See the discussion of this whole matter by Leipoldt, *Die Frau* 92-94; Oepke, "Ehe", *RAC* IV 656, and Epstein 68-75. In the background is the idea of the Jewish father's "patria potestas" over his unmarried daughter, which was extreme (Jeremias, *Jerusalem* 399). That Ps-Phoc. reflects this idea here is remarkable in view of vv. 208-209 (see the commentary *ad loc.*). It demonstrates his concern for the intactness of the virgin before marriage.

217 κάλλος δυστήρητον ἔφυ παίδων τοκέεσσιν.
    The beauty of children is hard for their parents to guard.

V. 217 is the upshot of the four previous lines. δυστήρητος (hard to keep): a word of late provenance, cf. δυσπαρατήρητος; besides φρουρεῖν in 213 and φυλάσσειν in 215 here the third word for "to guard" appears: τηρεῖν, in δυστήρητος. Farina 48 compares Juv. *Sat.* X 295ff. *filius autem corporis egregii miseros trepidosque parentes semper habet. rara est adeo concordia formae atque pudicitiae* (cf. 289-329). Cf. also Plaut. *Epid.* 404f. *numquam nimi potest pudicitiam quisquam suae servare filiae.* From Jewish literature Sir. VII 24 θυγατέρες σοί εἰσιν; πρόσεχε τῷ σώματι αὐτῶν, and esp. XLII 9ff. θυγάτηρ πατρὶ ἀπόκρυφος ἀγρυπνία, καὶ ἡ μέριμνα αὐτῆς ἀφιστᾷ ὕπνον . . ., ἐν παρθενίᾳ, μήποτε βεβηλωθῇ καὶ ἐν τοῖς πατρικοῖς αὐτῆς ἔγκυος γένηται, κτλ. This care was obviously universal in antiquity.

218 [στέργε φίλους ἄχρις θανάτου· πίστις γὰρ ἀμείνων.]
    Love your friends till death, for faithfulness is a good thing.

This line is in only one ms. (V) and it disrupts, more or less, this passage on duties towards members of the family and kinsmen. It is spurious and may have been inserted because of φιλότης in v. 219. Rossbroich 99 says: "cum adhuc de amicis nondum locutus esset neque omnino loquatur auctor, postea aliquis illum versum inseruit". That may be right, though v. 142 speaks about the value of friendship. On πίστις (faithfulness) see the commentary on v. 13 (and the comments of Lührmann quoted there). Cf. also Polyb. XVIII 41 διεφύλαξε δὲ τὴν πρὸς πάντας τοὺς ... φίλους πίστιν. 'Αμείνων: on this kind of *comparativus pro positivo* see K-G II 305f. As already stated (*ad* v. 142), the terms φιλία and φίλος only become prominent in the later Wisdom literature of the LXX (see Treu, *RAC* VIII 424), possibly under Greek influence (Bolkestein, *Wohltätigkeit* 401). E.g. Sir. VI 14f. φίλος πιστὸς σκέπη κραταιά, ... φίλου πιστοῦ οὐκ ἔστιν ἀντάλλαγμα. See further the commentary on v. 142. Note esp. a verse of the real (?) Phocylides, fr. 17 ... οὓς δ' ἄρα τιμῶ, τούτους ἐξ ἀρχῆς μέχρι τέλους ἀγαπῶ (some scholars regard it as spurious). Another important parallel is Men. gnom. syr. 73 "Schön und vortrefflich ist die Freundschaft, die bis zum Haus des Todes ausharrt" (tr. Schulthess). Berger, *Gesetzesauslegung Jesu* I 122, has entirely misunderstood the present verse; he says that it is about "Bereitschaft, sein Leben hinzugeben" (but in view of the parallels, ἄχρις θανάτου cannot be interpreted in this way) and regards it as a Jewish forerunner of Luke XIV 26 and John XV 13, overlooking the spuriousness of this verse (as does Crouch, *Origin* 76), and giving no proof of the pre-Christian origin of the line.

219 συγγενέσιν φιλότητα νέμοις ὁσίην θ' ὁμόνοιαν.
Show love to your kinsmen and pious unanimity.

On ὅσιος see the commentary *ad* v. 1 and on ὁμόνοια *ad* v. 74. Praechter, *Hierokles* 61ff., says that love towards kinsmen is a stereotyped element in the Stoic καθήκοντα scheme; see e.g. the chapter πῶς συγγενέσι χρηστέον in Hier. p. 61, 6ff. Arn. (= Stob. IV 27, 22). In this connection, the term ὁμόνοια also occurs (though more often it is a political term), e.g. Mus. Ruf. XV (p. 81, 7f. H) ἐγὼ μὲν ἀξιοζηλότατον ἡγοῦμαι τὸν ἐπὶ πλήθει ἀδελφῶν ὁμονοούντων βιοῦντα. Men. fr. 809 (610) ὡς ἡδύ γ' ἐν ἀδελφοῖς ἐστιν ὁμονοίας ἔρως. But it is also found in Jewish texts, e.g. Sir. XXV 1 ... ὁμόνοια ἀδελφῶν καὶ φιλία τῶν πλησίον. Test. Jos. XVII 3 τέρπεται ὁ θεὸς ἐπὶ ὁμονοίᾳ ἀδελφῶν (cf. *Or. Sib.* III 375). It may be surmised that φιλότης is a poetic rendering of ἀγάπη in the LXX.

220-222 αἰδεῖσθαι πολιοκροτάφους, εἴκειν δὲ γέρουσιν
ἕδρης καὶ γεράων πάντων· γενεῇ δ' ἀτάλαντον
πρέσβυν ὁμήλικα πατρὸς ἴσαις τιμαῖσι γέραιρε.

Revere those with grey hair on the temples and yield your seat and all privileges to old persons. To an old man of equal descent and of the same age as your father give the same honours.

αἰδεῖσθαι πολιοκροτάφους: cf. Philo *Post. Caini* 181 τὴν πρὸς πρεσβυτέρους αἰδῶ, Plut. *Lib. educ.* 10, 7D (Schmidt, *Ethik* I 168: "Mit dem Namen Aidos bezeichneten die Griechen das Streben anderen, denen aus irgend einem Grunde Ehrerbietung gezollt wird, nicht wehe zu tun"); πολιοκρόταφος in Hom. *Il.* VIII 518; *Or. Sib.* I 155, etc. If ἕδρη belongs to the γέρα (privileges, prerogatives), then καί means "and generally" or "and other ..." (see W. J. Verdenius in *Mnemosyne* 1954, 38; 1956, 250; 1974, 21). ἀτάλαντος = equivalent to, like (epic usage). No doubt there is an etymological wordplay here with the words γέρουσιν-γεράων-γέραιρε. The sentiment expressed in these lines is universal in the ancient world (see Heinemann, *Philons Bildung* 256). See e.g. Lev. XIX 32 ἀπὸ προσώπου πολιοῦ ἐξαναστήσῃ καὶ τιμήσεις πρόσωπον πρεσβυτέρου (according to Bernays 245 the source of Ps-Phoc. here), cf. Gen. XXXI 35; Sir. VIII 6; Job XXXII 4. Philo *Spec. leg.* II 237ff. N.B. in 237 Philo speaks about old people as τοὺς ἥλικας ἐκείνων, sc. γονέων, which is a striking parallel to πρέσβυν ὁμήλικα πατρός in Ps-Phoc. Philo discusses this subject in the context of a discussion of the command to honour one's parents. Ps-Phoc., too, may have derived it from that commandment (which he renders in v. 8), since Josephus does so as well in *C. Ap.* II 206 καὶ παντὸς τοῦ πρεσβυτέρου τιμὴν ἔχειν τοὺς νέους φησίν (sc. ὁ νόμος). It may be a traditional derivation from the fifth commandment. Men. gnom. syr. 2 and 3 (cf. Berger, *Gesetzesauslegung Jesu* I 287). Seeberg, *Die beiden Wege* 96, refers to Herm. *Mand.* VIII 10 (where πρεσβύτας σέβεσθαι occurs in a "Tugendkatalog"), asserting without any foundation that this command is from a Jewish Two Ways document. From Greek and Latin literature e.g. Tyrt. IX 37ff. (πάντες ... εἴκουσι κτλ.), Theogn. 935f. νέοι ... χώρης εἴκουσιν, Xen. *Mem.* II 3, 16 ὁδοῦ παραχωρῆσαι τὸν νεώτερον πρεσβυτέρῳ συντυγχάνοντι πανταχοῦ νομίζεται καὶ καθήμενον ὑπαναστῆναι (cf. III 5, 15 πρεσβυτέρους αἰδέσονται). Plut. *Quom. adulat.* 15, 58B (ἕδρας εἴκων ...). Cic. *De senect.* XVIII 63 *haec enim ipsa sunt honorabilia* (sc. *seni*), ..., *salutari adpeti decedi adsurgi deduci reduci consuli*. Cf. Val. Max. II 1, 9. More texts in Bolkestein, *Wohltätigkeit* 89f. n. 6.

223 γαστρὸς ὀφειλόμενον δασμὸν παρέχειν θεράποντι.
Provide your slave with the tribute he owes to his stomach.

ὀφείλω actually governs the dative, but δασμός can be connected with a genitive, e.g. Soph. *O.R.* 36 σκληρᾶς ἀοιδοῦ δασμὸν ὃν παρείχομεν (N.B. here also παρέχειν) = the tribute we paid to the Sphinx. The following five maxims concerning the treatment of slaves were not unnecessary in antiquity. Even in Judaism "slaves were viewed as things and as the property of their masters. There were, of course, examples of good relationships between masters and slaves, but in general slaves were the most despised of people and were treated accordingly" (Crouch, *Origin* 118; cf. Stern in *Comp. Rer. Jud.* I 628). See on this matter Schmidt, *Ethik* II 203ff.; Greeven, *Hauptproblem* 28ff.; Bodson, *Morale* 112f.; Kroll, *Kultur* 204ff.; Billerbeck IV 698-744; Jeremias, *Jerusalem* 380ff.; Krauss, *Talm. Arch.* II 89ff.; Heinemann, *Philons Bildung* 337ff.; Cronbach, "Social Ideals" 146ff.; esp. Vogt, *Sklaverei und Humanität* 69-82 and Westermann, "Sklaverei", *PW Suppl.* VI (1935) 894-1068. It is conspicuous and typical of the great humanity of Ps-Phoc. that he lists only duties of masters towards slaves and not the reverse. He may have been inspired to this attitude by the Stoics; see e.g. Sen. *Epist.* 47 (the whole letter), Hierocles p. 59, 9ff. Arn., Plut. *Lib. educ.* 10, 7E and several other texts collected by Stob. IV 9 (IV p. 422-433 W-H): περὶ δεσποτῶν καὶ δούλων. But cf. also Sir. VII 20 μὴ κακώσῃς οἰκέτην ἐργαζόμενον ἐν ἀληθείᾳ and other texts quoted *ad* v. 224. In this particular verse, Ps-Phoc. admonishes the masters to give their slaves enough food. Cf. Epict. *Sent.* 24 ... κἂν ταῖς τροφαῖς ἐστιώμενος κοινωνεῖς τοῖς θεραπεύουσι τῶν παρόντων. Juv. *Sat.* XIV 126 *servorum ventres modio castigat iniquo* shows that there could be problems in this respect. Cf. also Sen. *Ep.* 47, 2-3.

224 δούλῳ τακτὰ νέμοις, ἵνα τοι καταθύμιος εἴη.
Apportion to a slave what is appointed so that he will be as you wish.

καταθύμιος = according to one's mind (see Hom. *Il.* X 383; Theogn. 617, 1238, 1283; *Anth. Pal.* V 283, IX 263; *Or. Sib.* I 264; Isaiah XLIV 9). τακτός = ordered, prescribed, fixed. Bernays 245 thinks that τακτά refers to tasks which the slave is ordered to perform; Young suggests (letter of 12.5.1973) that τακτά means fixed amounts of money (cf. LSJ *s.v.*). It may also mean the fixed amount of food already spoken about in v. 223. Bernays' proposal, however, seems the most probable one. Cf. Philo *Spec. leg.* II 90 παυσάσθωσαν οὖν οἱ λεγόμενοι δεσπόται τῶν ἐπὶ δούλοις σφοδρῶν καὶ δυσυπομονήτων ἐπιταγμάτων ... (91) καὶ οἱ θεράποντες εὐφόρως τὰ κελευσθέντα δράσουσι (cf. II 66-68; III 137-143 and *Virt.* 121-124). But, whatever τακτά may mean, emphasis is again laid upon a just and gentle treatment of the slave, in order that there may be a good relationship between master and slave. This is a common theme; see e.g. Xen. *Mem.* III 4, 9 τὸ δὲ τοὺς ὑπηκόους εὐμενεῖς ποιεῖσθαι πῶς οὐ καλὸν ἀμφοτέροις; Men. gnom. pap. XIX 10f. (p. 24 J.) ὡς ἡδὺ δούλοις δεσπότας χρηστοὺς λαβεῖν καὶ δεσπόταισι δοῦλον εὐμενῆ λαβεῖν. Mus. Ruf. XXXIII (p. 122, 9ff. H.) πειρατέον καταπληκτικὸν μᾶλλον τοῖς ὑπηκόοις ἢ φοβερὸν θεωρεῖσθαι· τῷ μὲν γὰρ σεμνότης, τῷ δὲ ἀπήνεια παρακολουθεῖ. Vit. Aes. 109 (rec. G, p. 69 Perry) δούλων σου ἐπιμελοῦ, μεταδιδοὺς αὐτοῖς ἀφ' ὧν ἔχεις, ἵνα μὴ ὡς κύριον μόνον ἐντρέπωνταί σε, ἀλλὰ καὶ ὡς εὐεργέτην τιμῶσιν (= Floril. duo graeca I 9, p. 6 Schenkl). Col. IV 1 οἱ κύριοι, τὸ δίκαιον καὶ τὴν ἰσότητα τοῖς δούλοις παρέχεσθε (cf. Eph. VI 9). Barn. XIX 7 οὐ μὴ ἐπιτάξῃς δούλῳ σου ἢ παιδίσκῃ ἐν πικρίᾳ.

225 στίγματα μὴ γράψῃς ἐπονειδίζων θεράποντα.
Insult not your slave by branding him.

ἐπονειδίζω is a *hapax* (only mentioned in the Supplement to LSJ, p. 61). In Greek and Roman antiquity it was normal practice to brand a slave only when he was a fugitive or when he had done something wrong. It was only in the later imperial period that the *stigma* was also applied as a sign of the possessor, according to Oriental customs (see Betz, *TWNT* VII 658f.). The rabbis allowed the branding of slaves in order to prevent them running away (Billerbeck III 579), but mostly a seal was hung around their necks (*ibid.* IV 718). Branding was always felt as a disgrace (Dölger, *Sphragis* 29f.); see e.g. Porph. *Vit. Pyth.* 15 Δ. λέγει δουλεῦσαι μὲν αὐτὸν τῷ Πυθ., ἐμπεσόντα δ' εἰς λῃστὰς καὶ στιχθέντα, ὅτε κατεστασιάσθη ὁ Πυθ. καὶ ἔφευγεν, δῆσαι τὸ μέτωπον διὰ τὰ στίγματα. Cf. Sen. *Benef.* IV 37 and the passages mentioned by Kroll, *Kultur* 214 n. 46. On this practice in general see e.g. Herod. V 28 ἀλλ' ἐπὴν αὖτις ἕλῃς τι δρῶντα τῶν σὺ μὴ θέλῃς, στίξον. Diod. Sic. XXXIV 2, 1 οἰκετῶν ..., οἷς ... εὐθὺς χαρακτῆρας ἐπέβαλλον καὶ στιγμὰς τοῖς σώμασιν (cf. *ibid.* 2, 27; 2, 36). Ael. Arist. XLVI p. 392 Dind. τῶν μὲν οἰκετῶν οὐδένα πώποτ' ἔστιξας τῶν σαυτοῦ. Petron. 103 *sequar ego frontes notans inscriptione sollerti, ut videamini stigmate esse puniti*; cf. 105 *vera enim stigmata credebat captivorum frontibus impressa*. Cf. also Plato Com. fr. 187, Men. *Samia* 108.310, and other passages mentioned by Bernays 246 n. 1; Dölger, *Sphragis* 23-31 and Betz, *TWNT* VII 658f. Once again Ps-Phoc.'s humane attitude is evident. (N.B. this verse has nothing to do with Lev. XIX 28).

226 δοῦλον μὴ βλάψῃς τι κακηγορέων παρ' ἄνακτι.
Do not hurt a slave by slandering him to his master.

κακηγορεῖν (speak ill of, abuse, slander): Plato *Leg.* 934e3 μηδένα κακηγορείτω μηδείς, cf. Arist. *Eth. Nic.* V 1, 1129b23. Bernays 246 (and, following him, Lincke, *Samaria* 73, Riessler 1321 and Dornseiff 48) refers to Prov. XXX 10 μὴ παραδῷς οἰκέτην εἰς χεῖρας δεσπότου. This is not a good parallel. However, the Hebrew text of Prov. XXX 10 reads: אל-תלשן עבד אל-אדנו (= do not slander a slave to his master). It looks as if Ps-Phoc. knew the Hebrew text; but it is more probable that he knew a more exact translation of Prov. here than the LXX. One might also compare Aboth II 10, where Eliezer ben Hyrkanos says: "Let the honour of thy fellow be dear to thee as thine own", a general rule, like Plato's one (see above), here applied to slaves by Ps-Phoc. Easton omits v. 226 from his translation without giving a reason.

227 λάμβανε καὶ βουλὴν παρὰ οἰκέτου εὖ φρονέοντος.
Accept advice also from a kindly disposed slave.

Note the variation in vv. 223-227: θεράπων-δοῦλος-θεράπων-δοῦλος-οἰκέτης (Bernays 246 n. 2, to avoid hiatus, unnecessarily reads δούλου here). οἰκέτης and δοῦλος, though sometimes distinguished from each other, are often synonymous (LSJ *s.v.* 2). εὖ φρονέων may also mean "judicious, prudent". Dornseiff 48 (who maintains the authenticity, and therefore the early date, of the poem) says: "in späthellenistisch-römischer Zeit, als gebildete Griechen in grosser Zahl in reichen römischen Häusern als Erzieher und Hausphilosophen lebten, wäre dieser Vers ein Witz". Although it is true that slaves were often the confidants of their masters, a passage in Seneca proves that this advice was not superfluous and certainly not a joke: *Epist.* 47, 13 *tu modo vive cum servo clementer, comiter quoque, et in sermonem illum et non numquam in necessarium admitte consilium*. On slaves as confidants see Vogt, *Sklaverei und Humanität* 69-82.

Vv. 228-230 *Epilogue*

228 ἁγνείη ψυχῆς, οὐ σώματός εἰσι καθαρμοί.

Purifications are for the purity of the soul, not (for the purity) of the body.

The above translation is based on the reading ἁγνείη, which is a conjecture of Ludwich, *Spruchbuch* 23, and makes better sense than the mss.' ἁγνείη. However, the text and meaning of this verse are rather uncertain. Young suggests (in *app. crit.*): ἁγνείη ψυχῆς σου· σώματός κτλ. = "puritas proprium est animae tuae. ad corpus pertinant purgationes (vel purgamenta)". Farina 49 reads: ἁγνείη ψυχῆς, τοῦ σώματός κτλ. = "questa è castità dell'anima, purezza del corpo". Berger, *Gesetzesauslegung Jesu* I 467, reads the text as printed by Young and translates: "die Reinheit betrifft die Seele, nicht auf den Körper beziehen sich die Reinigungen". It is also possible to read the plural ἁγνεῖαι with one ms. (P). But Bernays 247 n. 1, Bergk, Sebestyén 41 and Lincke (*Samaria* 179) athetize the verse as "zusammenhanglos" (Bernays). However, that is unnecessary and it may be suggested with Berger (*Gesetzesauslegung Jesu* I 260) that Ps-Phoc. wants to say here that all the O.T. cultic rules, which have no place in his poem, are "auf die Reinheit der Seele hin umzudeuten" (cf. Josephus' use of ἁγνεῖαι, *C. Ap.* II 198, for the cultic purifications of the Mosaic Law). It is clear that in this line there is a kind of "Spiritualisierung der Kultusbegriffe" (Wenschkewitz, 1932). See e.g. the first line of Wächter's book *Reinheitsvorschriften im griechischen Kult*: "Die kultischen Reinheitsvorschriften der Griechen zerfallen in ἁγνεῖαι und καθαρμοί. Die ἁγνεῖαι bestimmen, dass und wovon man sich vor oder während kultischer Betätigung rein halten müsse; die καθαρμοί geben die im Falle einer Verunreinigung nötigen Reinigungen an" (1f.). Many inscriptions illustrate the use of this terminology, esp. the *Lois sacrées des cités grecques*, collected by Sokolowski (1962); see e.g. the famous *lex sacra* of Cyrene (about 300 B.C.), *ibid.* nr. 115A, 1ff. Ἀπόλλων ἔχρησε· ἐς ἀεὶ καθαρμοῖς καὶ ἁγνηίαις καὶ ἱκετηίαις χρειμένος τὰν Λεβύαν οἰκέν, and the rules for ritual purity in a sanctuary on Lindos (3rd cent. A.D.), *ibid.* nr. 91, 1ff. καθαροὺς καὶ ἁγνοὺς περιρραντηρίων εἴσω καὶ τῶν τοῦ ναοῦ πυλῶν ἴναι ὅσιον, ... ἀπὸ παντὸς ἐναγοῦς, ἀνάγνου, ἀθέσμου, μὴ τὸ σῶμα μόνον ἀλλὰ καὶ τὴν ψυχὴν κεκαθαρμένους (Sokolowski *ad loc.*, p. 161: "la mention de l'âme trahit une influence philosophique et morale qui apparait dans les cultes orientaux surtout"); cf. further nr. 59, 13 and 108, 4-7 and some other instances mentioned by Weinreich, *Stiftung* 64f. and by Nilsson, *Gesch. der griech. Rel.* II 73f., 373f. See further e.g. Porph. *Abst.* II 19 δεῖ τοίνυν καθηραμένους τὸ ἦθος ἰέναι θύσοντας, ... νῦν δὲ ἐσθῆτα μὲν λαμπρὰν περὶ σῶμα μὴ καθαρὸν ἀμφιεσαμένοις οὐκ ἀρκεῖν νομίζουσιν πρὸς τὸ τῶν θυσιῶν ἁγνόν. ὅταν δὲ τὸ σῶμα μετὰ τῆς ἐσθῆτός τινες λαμπρυνάμενοι μὴ καθαρὰν κακῶν τὴν ψυχὴν ἔχοντες ἴωσιν πρὸς τὰς θυσίας, οὐδὲν διαφέρειν νομίζουσιν, ὥσπερ οὐ τῷ θειοτάτῳ γε τῶν ἐν ἡμῖν χαίροντα μάλιστα τὸν θεὸν διακειμένῳ καθαρῶς, ἅτε συγγενεῖ πεφυκότι. ἐν γοῦν Ἐπιδαύρῳ προεγέγραπτο· ἁγνὸν χρὴ ναοῖο θυώδεος ἐντὸς ἰόντα ἔμμεναι· ἁγνεία δ' ἐστὶ φρονεῖν ὅσια. Cf. *Anth. Pal.* XIV 71 ἁγνὸς πρὸς τέμενος καθαροῦ, ξένε, δαίμονος ἔρχου ψυχήν. Cic. *ND* II 71 *cultus autem deorum est optumus idemque castissimus atque sanctissimus plenissimusque pietatis, ut eos semper pura, integra, incorrupta mente et voce veneremur* (for the terminology see Pease *ad loc.*). Demoph. *Sent.* 45 (Mullach, *Fr. Phil. Gr.* I 499) ψυχῆς ἁγνῆς τόπον οἰκειότερον ἐπὶ γῆς οὐκ ἔχει θεός. Cf. Clem. Alex. *Strom.* VII 27, 4.

For the original cultic meaning of καθαρμός see Wächter, *Reinheitsvorschriften*; Rohde, *Psyche* II 69-80; Dodds, *The Greeks and the Irrational*, Index *s.v.* Plato, *Phaedo* 82d6 speaks of καθαρμὸς τῆς ψυχῆς. Empedocles' Καθαρμοί also concern the soul. Cf. Sextus 23 ἄριστον ἡγοῦ καθαρμὸν τὸ μηδένα ἀδικεῖν. See also Ep. Arist. 234 τί μέγιστόν ἐστι δόξης; ὁ δὲ εἶπε· τὸ τιμᾶν τὸν θεόν· τοῦτο δ' ἐστὶν οὐ δώροις οὐδὲ θυσίαις, ἀλλὰ ψυχῆς καθαρότητι καὶ διαλήψεως ὁσίας κτλ. This Hellenistic-Jewish text says what Ps-Phoc. means here. Cf. also Philo *Spec. leg.* III 208f. καθολικωτέραν δ' ἀπόφασιν ὁ χρησμὸς οὗτος (sc. Num. XIX 22) ἔοικέ πως δηλοῦν, οὐκ ἐπὶ σώματος αὐτὸ μόνον ἱστάμενος, ἀλλὰ ἤθη καὶ τρόπους προσδιερευνώμενος ψυχῆς. ἀκάθαρτος γὰρ κυρίως ὁ ἄδικος καὶ ἀσεβής. Compare the comments of Berger, *Gesetzesauslegung Jesu* I 467 (discussing Mark VII 15): "eine sentenzartige Formulierung von gleicher antithetischer Schärfe wie Mk. 7, 15 ist aus dem hellenistischen Judentum erhalten: Ps-Phok. 228 [text and transl.] (der Vers steht unmittelbar vor dem allgemeinen Schluss des Gedichtes in 229f. und hat daher besondere Bedeutung). ἁγνείη und καθαρμοί entsprechen sich, ψυχή und σῶμα sind entgegengesetzt. Reinheit oder Unreinheit des Körpers ist völlig belanglos, eine Beziehung zur Reinheit der Seele gibt es nicht; Reinheit der Seele allein gilt. Diese und die genannte Philostelle [*Spec. leg.* III 208-9] sind nicht zufällige Einzelzeugnisse, sondern spiegeln die auf atl. Reinheitslehren angewandte hellenistisch-jüdische Anthropologie". It should be added, however, that Ps-Phoc. (and Ep. Arist) is more radically spiritualizing than Philo (cf. Philo's οὐκ ἐπὶ σώματος μόνον with οὐ σώματος in v. 228; see Hübner's criticisms of Berger in *NTS* 22 (1975/6), 319-345, esp. 337f., and my article "Pseudo-Phocylides and the New Testament" (forthcoming)). For Ps-Phoc. the purity of the soul expresses itself in the good deeds inculcated by him in all the previous lines of the poem. See further Hauck's articles on ἁγνός κτλ. and καθαρός κτλ. in *TWNT* I 123-4 and III 416-434, who quotes other relevant texts and refers to literature (add J. Neusner, *The Idea of Purity in Ancient Judaism*, 1973, esp. 44ff.).

229-230 ταῦτα δικαιοσύνης μυστήρια, τοῖα βιεῦντες
ζωὴν ἐκτελέοιτ᾽ ἀγαθὴν μέχρι γήραος οὐδοῦ.

These are the mysteries of righteousness; living thus
may you live out a good life, right up to the treshold of old age.

ταῦτα δικαιοσύνης μυστήρια: by means of these words Ps-Phoc. summarizes the content of the whole poem. The real Phocylides also attached great importance to δικαιοσύνη, as appears from fr. 10 ἐν δὲ δικαιοσύνῃ συλλήβδην πᾶσ᾽ ἀρετή 'στιν (= Theogn. 147; on the question of priority see Van Groningen *ad loc.* and Bielohlawek, *Hypotheke* 18); cf. Arist. *Eth. Nic.* V 1, 1129b27ff. In Ps-Phoc. δικαιοσύνη is not the Greek concept of ἕξις διανεμητικὴ τοῦ κατ᾽ ἀξίαν ἑκάστῳ, but rather the Jewish צדקה, that is the right and merciful attitude to other people. When Fiedler, 'Δικαιοσύνη', *JSJ* I (1970), 120-134 asserts that Jewish-Hellenistic authors have a Greek concept of δικαιοσύνη, that is correct in the present case only insofar as this concept may include some of the aspects of ṣedaqah (think of the expression ὅσιος καὶ δίκαιος). Here in v. 229 it means the way of life as depicted in the whole poem. It should be noted that ταῦτα δικαιοσύνης κτλ. is strongly reminiscent of the first line of the poem ταῦτα δίκησ᾽ κτλ. It is an *inclusio*. Kranz, "Sphragis" 100, remarks: "Der Phokylideer verweist zuletzt zurück auf den Eingang" (Kranz mentions several examples of congruence between the beginning and the end of a poem; see further *ad* v. 1).

That the author speaks of μυστήρια in this connection does not mean that he sees Judaism as a mystery-religion. Since Plato, mystery-terminology had become more and more metaphorically used in philosophical and ethical writings, though, as Bornkamm

(*TWNT* IV 817) says, "eine völlige Profanisierung von μυστήριον nicht stattgefunden hat, vielmehr das eigentliche Gewicht dem religiösen Begriff erhalten blieb". Cf. Hegermann in: Maier-Schreiner (edd.), *Lit. und Rel. des Frühjudentums* 355: "Dabei ist die Aufnahme der Mysterientermini durch Philon kein äusserlicher Propagandatrick; vielmehr hört Philon in dieser Sprache den Geheimnisaspekt der Gotteserkenntnis ausgesprochen, die 'Mose' vermittelt". For examples of this metaphorical usage see Bornkamm, *TWNT* IV 814-817; Nock, *Essays* I 459-468, II 796-803; for Philo esp. Baer, *Philo's Use* ... 10ff. See also Hengel, *Der Sohn Gottes* 46: "(Mysteriensprache) leitet sich zwar aus der spezifisch griechischen Mysterien von Eleusis und des Dionysos her, hatte sich aber schon längst völlig verselbständigt. Sie wurde — wie das Beispiel von Artapanos, der Sapientia Salomonis und Philos zeigt — auch von der Diasporasynagoge übernommen"; also *Judentum und Hellenismus* 368 n. 570 and, on Ps-Phoc. 229f., *Pseudepigrapha* I 298 n. 1. Though, in spite of the currency of a metaphorical use of μυστήριον, the word retains something of the sense of secrecy, Ps-Phoc. sets forth these secrets for those who would read his poem. He seems to say: the secret of life is to live δικαίως, as it is described in my poem.

τοῖα = adv. neut. plur. (as τοῖον). βιεῦντες is Ionic for βιοῦντες. The Homeric phrase γήραος οὐδός (*Il.* XXII 60; *Od.* XV 246.348; Hes. *Op.* 331; etc.) had become proverbial, see e.g. Ael. Arist. XXVIII 60 Keil τὸ λεγόμενον δὴ τοῦτο ἐπὶ γήραος οὐδῷ. It is also found in Philo *Somn.* II 148.

This ending has a structural resemblence to other closing passages, e.g. *Or. Sib.* II 149ff. where the long insertion of Ps-Phoc. 5-79 in the mss-group Ψ' is followed by: οὗτος ἀγών, ταῦτ' ἐστὶν ἀέθλια, ταῦτα βραβεῖα, | τοῦτο πύλη ζωῆς καὶ εἴσοδος ἀθανασίης, | ἣν θεὸς οὐράνιος δικαιοτάτοις ἀνθρώποις | ἔστησεν νίκης ἐπαέθλιον. Ep. Barn. XXI 1 (the closing words of the Two Ways section) ὁ γὰρ ταῦτα ποιῶν ἐν τῇ βασιλείᾳ τοῦ θεοῦ δοξασθήσεται. Compared with these two texts, it is noticeable that Ps-Phoc., who also believes in life after death (vv. 103ff.), here restricts his promises to this earthly life; but this has a parallel in Herm. *Sim.* X 4, 1 *quicumque ergo in his mandatis ambulaverit, vivet et felix erit in vita sua*, and cf. Ass. Mos. XII 10. In the O.T., the blessing of a long and good life is a common theme. Dornseiff, *Echtheitsfragen* 48, says that these lines are "als Schlussvers angeregt durch den Abschluss

Lev. 19, 37", which is possible but not very probable. (N. B. Dornseiff thinks that the real Phocylides was inspired to write these lines by a sixth century B.C. Greek translation of Lev. XIX 37. A. von Blumenthal, *Gnomon* 19 (1943), 292, rightly says: "δικαιοσύνης μυστήρια wird niemand für Griechisch des 6. Jh. ausgeben".) It is better to compare (*pace* Beltrami, *Riv.* 1908, 423) Prov. XVI 31 στέφανος καυχήσεως γῆρας, ἐν δὲ ὁδοῖς δικαιοσύνης εὑρίσκεται (cf. Jos. *Ant.* VIII 314 δι' εὐσέβειαν καὶ δικαιοσύνην εἰς μακρὸν καὶ εὔδαιμον ὑπὸ τοῦ θεοῦ προήχθη γῆρας). It is also a rabbinic view; see Urbach, *Sages* 264-6. Cf. e.g. Gen. R. LIX 1 "Engage in righteousness, and you will attain to old age".

BIBLIOGRAPHY

Aalders, G. J. D., *De oud-Griekse voorstelling van de afgunst der godheid* (MKNAW, Afd. Lett., nr. 38, 2), Amsterdam 1975.
Ahlert, P.,-Kroll, W., "Phokylides", *PW(RE)* XX 1 (Stuttgart 1941), 503-510.
Ahrens, E., *Gnomen in griechischer Dichtung (Homer, Hesiod, Aeschylus)*, diss. Halle 1937.
Aland, K., "The Problem of Anonymity and Pseudonymity in Christian Literature of the First Two Centuries", *JTS* ns. 12 (1961), 39-49; in German in: K. Aland, *Studien zur Überlieferung des Neuen Testaments und seines Textes*, Berlin 1967, 24-34.
Alexandre, C., *Oracula Sibyllina*, 2 vols., Paris 1841-1856.
Alon, G., *Studies in Jewish History in the Times of the Second Temple* (in Hebrew), Tel Aviv 1967[2].
Amstutz, J., ΑΠΛΟΤΗΣ. *Eine begriffsgeschichtliche Studie zum jüdisch-christlichen Griechisch*, Bonn 1968.
Arbesmann, R., "Gefrässigkeit", *RAC* IX (1974), 345-390.
Arnim, H. von, *Hierokles' ethische Elementarlehre*, Berlin 1906.
Attridge, H. W., *First-Century Cynicism in the Epistles of Heraclitus*, Missoula 1976.
Audet, J. P., "La Sagesse de Ménandre l'Égyptien", *Rev. Bibl.* 59 (1952), 55-81.
Audet, J. P., *La Didache; Instruction des Apôtres*, Paris 1958.
Babylonian Talmud, translated into English under the editorship of I. Epstein, 18 vols., London 1935-1952.
Bach, H. J., *Jacob Bernays. Ein Beitrag zur Emanzipationsgeschichte der Juden und zur Geschichte des deutschen Geistes im neunzehnten Jahrhundert*, Tübingen 1974.
Bacher, W., *Die Agada der Tannaiten*, 2 vols., Strassburg 1903[2].
Bacher, W., *Die Agada der palästinischen Amoräer*, 3 vols., Strassburg 1892-1899.
Bacht, H., "Einfalt", *RAC* IV (1959), 821-840.
Baer, R. A., *Philo's Use of the Categories Male und Female*, Leiden 1970.
Balz, H. R., "Anonymität und Pseudepigraphie im Urchristentum", *ZThK* 66 (1969), 403-437.
Barns, J., "A New Gnomologium", *Class. Quart.* 44 (1950), 126-137; 45 (1951), 1-19.
Bauer, W., *Wörterbuch zum Neuen Testament*, Berlin 1958[5].
Bauer-Kayatz, Chr., *Einführung in die alttestamentliche Weisheit*, Neukirchen-Vluyn 1969.
Baumgartner, W., "The Wisdom Literature", in: H. H. Rowley (ed.), *The Old Testament and Modern Study*, Oxford 1951, 210-237.
Bayer, F. W., "Anatomie", *RAC* I (1950), 430-437.
Bell, H. I., *Juden und Griechen im römischen Alexandria*, Leipzig 1927[2].
Bell, H. I., *Cults and Creeds in Graeco-Roman Egypt*, Liverpool 1953.
Beltrami, A., "Ea quae apud Pseudo-Phocylidem Veteris et Novi Testamenti vestigia deprehenduntur", *Rivista di Filologia e Istruzione Classica* 36 (1908), 411-423.
Beltrami, A., "Spirito giudaico e specialmente essenico della silloge pseudo-focilidea", *ibid.* 41 (1913), 513-548.

Beltrami, A., *Studi pseudofocilidei*, Florence 1913.
Berger, K., *Die Gesetzesauslegung Jesu. Ihr historischer Hintergrund im Judentum und im Alten Testament I: Markus und Parallelen*, Neukirchen-Vluyn 1972.
Bergk, Th., "Kritische Beiträge zu dem sogenannten Phokylides", *Philol.* 41 (1882), 577-601.
Bergk, Th., *Poetae Lyrici Graeci* II, Leipzig 1882⁴.
Bergk, Th., *Anthologia Lyrici Graeca*, Leipzig 1883³.
Bergk, Th., *Griechische Literaturgeschichte* II, Berlin 1883.
Bergmann, J., *Jüdische Apologetik im neutestamentlichen Zeitalter*, Berlin 1908.
Bergmann, J., "Die Stoische Philosophie und die jüdische Frömmigkeit", in: *Judaica. Festschrift für H. Cohen*, Berlin 1912, 145-166.
Bernays, J., *Über das phokylideische Gedicht. Ein Beitrag zur hellenistischen Literatur*, Berlin 1856; repr. in Bernays' *Gesammelte Abhandlungen* I, Berlin 1885, 192-261.
Bernays, J., "Philon's Hypothetika und die Verwünschungen des Buzyges in Athen", *Ges. Abh.* I, Berlin 1885, 262-282.
Bernhardy, G., *Grundrisz der griechischen Litteratur* II 1, Halle 1867³.
Bertholet, A., *Die Stellung der Israeliten und der Juden zu den Fremden*, Freiburg i.Br.-Leipzig 1896.
Bielohlawek, K., *Hypotheke und Gnome; Untersuchungen über die griechische Weisheitsdichtung der vorhellenistischen Zeit*, Philologus Supplementband XXXII 3, Leipzig 1940.
Bienert, W., *Die Arbeit nach der Lehre der Bibel*, Stuttgart 1956².
Bigelmair, A., "Armut", *RAC* I (1950), 705-709.
Billerbeck, P., see Strack, H. L.
Binder, W., *Die Elegien des Theognis nebst Phokylides' Mahngedicht und Pythagoras' Goldenen Sprüchen; Deutsch im Versmasze der Urschriften*, Stuttgart 1859.
Black, M.,-Denis, A. M., *Apocalypsis Henochi Graece. Fragmenta pseudepigraphorum quae supersunt graeca una cum historicorum et auctorum Judaeorum hellenistarum fragmentis*, Leiden 1970.
Blank, S. H., "Wisdom", *IDB* IV (1962), 852-861.
Blau, L., *Das altjüdische Zauberwesen*, Strassbourg 1898.
Bleek, F., "Ueber die Entstehung und Zusammensetzung der uns in 8 Büchern erhaltenen Sammlung Sibyllinischer Orakel", *Theologische Zeitschrift* (Schleiermacher) 1 (1819), 120-246.
Blumenthal, A. von, review of F. Dornseiff, *Echtheitsfragen* (1939), *Gnomon* 19 (1943), 289-293.
Bodson, A., *La morale sociale des derniers stoïciens, Sénèque, Épictète et Marc Aurèle*, Paris 1967.
Boissonade, J. F., *Anecdota Graeca*, 5 vols., Paris 1829-1833.
Bolkestein, H., *Een geval van sociaal-ethisch syncretisme* (MKNAW, Afd. Lett. 72B), Amsterdam 1931.
Bolkestein, H., *Wohltätigkeit und Armenpflege im vorchristlichen Altertum. Ein Beitrag zum Problem "Moral und Gesellschaft"*, Utrecht 1939 (repr. Groningen 1967).
Bolkestein, H.,-Kalsbach, A., "Armut (Beurteilung der Armut)", *RAC* I (1950), 698-705.
Bolkestein, H.,-Schwer, W., "Almosen", *RAC* I (1950), 301-307.
Bolkestein, J. C., "Ὅσιος *en* Εὐσεβής. Bijdrage tot de godsdienstige en zedelijke terminologie van de Grieken*, diss. Utrecht, Amsterdam 1936.

Botterweck, G. J.,-Ringgren, H., *Theologisches Wörterbuch zum Alten Testament* I-..., Stuttgart-Berlin 1973-...
Bousset, W.,-Gressmann, H., *Die Religion des Judentums im späthellenistischen Zeitalter*, Tübingen 1926³ (repr. 1966).
Braun, R., *Kohelet und die frühhellenistische Popularphilosophie*, Berlin 1973.
Braude, W. G., *Jewish Proselyting in the First Five Centuries of the Common Era: The Age of the Tannaim and the Amoraim*, diss. Providence 1940.
Bringmann, L., *Die Frau im ptolemäisch-kaiserlichen Aegypten*, diss. Bonn 1939.
Brockington, L. H., "The Problem of Pseudonymity", *JTS* n.s. 4 (1953), 15-22.
Brox, N., (ed.), *Pseudepigraphie in der heidnischen und jüdisch-christlichen Antike*, Darmstadt 1977.
Brown, F. E., "Violation of Sepulture in Palestine", *AJP* 52 (1931), 1-29.
Brunck, R. F. Ph., *Gnomici Poetae Graeci*, Strassburg 1784, Leipzig 1817².
Bultmann, R., *Der Stil der paulinischen Predigt und die kynisch-stoische Diatribe*, Göttingen 1910.
Buresch, K., "Kritischer Brief über die falschen Sibyllinen", *Philol.* 51 (1892), 84-112.
Burkert, W., *Zum altgriechischen Mitleidsbegriff*, diss. Erlangen 1955.
Cameron, A., "The Exposure of Children and Greek Ethics", *Class. Rev.* 46 (1932), 105-114.
Capelle, W.,-Marrou, H. I., "Diatribe", *RAC* III (1957), 990-1009.
Carrington, Ph., *The Primitive Christian Catechism*, Cambridge 1940.
Castanien, D. G., "Quevedo's Translation of the Pseudo-Phocylides", *Philological Quarterly* 40 (1961), 44-52.
Cauer, F., "Branchidai", *PW* (*RE*) III (1899), 809-813.
Causse, A., "La propagande juive et l'hellénisme", *RHPhR* 3 (1923), 397-414.
Cavallin, H. C. C., *Life After Death. Paul's Argument for the Resurrection of the Dead in 1 Cor. 15, Part I: An Enquiry into the Jewish Background*, Lund 1974.
Chadwick, H., *The Sentences of Sextus*, Cambridge 1959.
Chadwick, H., "Enkrateia", *RAC* V (1962), 343-365.
Chadwick, H., "Florilegium", *RAC* VII (1969), 1131-1160.
Charles, R. H., (ed.), *The Apocrypha and Pseudepigrapha of the Old Testament*, 2 vols., Oxford 1913.
Charlesworth, J. H., *The Pseudepigrapha and Modern Research*, Missoula 1976.
Christ, F., "Das Leben nach dem Tode bei Pseudo-Phokylides", *Theologische Zeitschrift* (Basel) 31 (1975), 140-149.
Christ, W. von,-Schmid, W.,-Stählin, O., *Geschichte der griechischen Litteratur*, 2 vols., München 1920-1924.
Cohen, A., (ed.), *The Minor Tractates of the Talmud*, 2 vols., London 1965.
Cohen, H., *Religion der Vernunft aus den Quellen des Judentums*, Frankfurt 1929².
Cohn, L., review of J. Raspante, *Sulla composizione e sull' autore del carme Pseudofocilideo* (1913), *Sokrates* 3 (1915), 234-237.
Colpe, C., "Antisemitismus", *Der Kleine Pauly* I (1964), 400-402.
Colson, F. H., "Quintilian I 9 and the 'Chria' in Ancient Education", *Class. Rev.* 35 (1921), 150-154.
Conybeare, F. C.,-Harris, J. R.,-Smith Lewis, A., *The Story of Aḥikar from the Syriac, Arabic, Armenian, Ethiopic, Greek and Slavonic Versions*, London 1898.

Conzelmann, H., *Der erste Brief an die Korinther*, Göttingen 1969.
Cotte, H. J., *Poissons et animaux aquatiques au temps de Pline. Commentaire sur le livre IX de l'Histoire Naturelle de Pline*, diss. Aix 1944.
Crahay, R., "Les moralistes anciens et l'avortement", *Ant. Class.* 10 (1941), 9-23.
Crenshaw, J. L., (ed.), *Studies in Ancient Israelite Wisdom*, New York 1976.
Croiset, A.,-Croiset, M., *Histoire de la littérature grecque*, 5 vols., Paris 1887-1899.
Cronbach, A., "The Social Ideals of the Apocrypha and Pseudepigrapha", *HUCA* 18 (1944), 119-156.
Cronbach, A., "Ethics in Noncanonical Jewish Writings", *IDB* II (1962), 161-167.
Crouch, J. E., *The Origin and Intention of the Colossian Haustafel*, Göttingen 1972.
Crusius, O., "Elegie", *PW (RE)* V (1905), 2260-2307.
Crusius, O., *Anthologia Lyrica Graeca*, Leipzig 1907.
Cumont, F., *After Life in Roman Paganism*, New Haven 1922.
Cumont, F., *Les religions orientales dans le paganisme romain*, Paris 1929[4].
Dalbert, P., *Die Theologie der hellenistisch-jüdischen Missionsliteratur*, Hamburg 1954.
Danby, H., *The Mishnah*, Oxford 1933.
Daube, D., *The New Testament and Rabbinic Judaism*, London 1956.
Davies, W. D., *Paul and Rabbinic Judaism*, London 1955[2].
Delling, G., "Ehebruch", "Ehegesetze", "Ehehindernisse", "Eheleben", "Ehescheidung", "Eheschliessung", *RAC* IV (1959), 666-730.
Delling, G., *Bibliographie zur jüdisch-hellenistischen und intertestamentarischen Literatur 1900-1965*, Berlin 1969, 1975[2].
Delling, G., "Speranda Futura. Jüdische Grabinschriften Italiens über das Geschick nach dem Tode", *Studien zum Neuen Testament und zum hellenistischen Judentum*, Göttingen 1970, 39-44.
Delling, G., "Josephus und die heidnischen Religionen", *ibid* 45-52.
Delling, G., "ΜΟΝΟΣ ΘΕΟΣ", *ibid.* 391-400.
Delling, G., "Perspektiven der Erforschung des hellenistischen Judentums", *HUCA* 45 (1974), 133-176.
Denis, A. M., *Introduction aux pseudépigraphes grecs d'Ancien Testament*, Leiden 1970.
Denis, A. M., see Black, M.
Denniston, J. D., *The Greek Particles*, Oxford 1954[2].
Dibelius, M.,-Greeven, H., *An die Kolosser, Epheser, an Philemon*, Tübingen 1953[3].
Dibelius, M.,-Greeven, H., *Der Brief des Jakobus*, Göttingen 1964[11].
Dibelius, M.,-Conzelmann, H., *Die Pastoralbriefe*, Tübingen 1966[4].
Dickerman, S. O., *De argumentis quibusdam apud Xenophontem, Platonem, Aristotelem obviis e structura hominis et animalium petitis*, diss. Halle 1909.
Diehl, E., *Anthologia Lyrica Graeca*, 2 vols., Leipzig 1923.
Dieterich, A., *Nekyia. Beiträge zur Erklärung der neuentdeckten Petrusapokalypse*, Leipzig 1913[2] (= 1893[1]; repr. Darmstadt 1969).
Dieterich, A., "Griechische und römische Religion", *ARW* 8 (1905), 474-510.
Dietrich, E. L., "Die "Religion Noahs", ihre Herkunft und ihre Bedeutung", *ZRGG* 1 (1948), 301-315.
Dihle, A., *Die Goldene Regel. Eine Einführung in die Geschichte der antiken und frühchristlichen Vulgärethik*, Göttingen 1962.
Dihle, A., "Ethik", *RAC* VI (1966), 646-796.

Dihle, A., *Der Kanon der Zwei Tugenden*, Köln 1968.
Dittenberger, W., *Sylloge inscriptionum graecarum*, 4 vols., 1915-1924³.
Dodds, E. R., *The Greeks and the Irrational*, Berkeley-Los Angeles 1951.
Dölger, F. J., *Sphragis. Eine altchristliche Taufbezeichnung in ihren Beziehungen zur profanen und religiösen Kultur des Altertums*, Paderborn 1911.
Dölger, F. J., "Das Lebensrecht des ungeborenen Kindes und die Fruchtabtreibung in der Bewertung der heidnischen und christlichen Antike", *Antike und Christentum* IV, Münster 1934 (1975²), 1-61.
Dornseiff, F., *Echtheitsfragen antik-griechischer Literatur. Rettungen des Theognis, Phokylides, Hekataios, Choirilos*, Berlin 1939.
Dornseiff, F., *Antike und alter Orient. Kleine Schriften* I, Leipzig 1959².
Dossios, N. G., "Über einige Varianten zu den Pseudophocylidea", *Philol.* 56 (1897), 616-620.
Dossios, N. G., *Quelques variantes dans les Phokylideia d'après un manuscrit du 17ᵉ siècle de Janina (Epire)*, Le Puy-en-Velay 1914.
Dover, K. J., *Greek Popular Morality in the Time of Plato and Aristotle*, Oxford 1975.
Duchesne-Guillemin, J., *The Western Response to Zoroaster*, Oxford 1958.
Dudley, D. R., *A History of Cynicism from Diogenes to the 6ᵗʰ Century A.D.*, London 1937.
Easton, B. S., "Pseudo-Phocylides", *Anglican Theological Review* 14 (1932), 222-228.
Easton, B. S., "New Testament Ethical Lists", *JBL* 51 (1932), 1-12.
Eckermann, N., "Phokylides", in: J. S. Ersch-J. G. Gruber (edd.), *Allgemeine Encyklopädie der Wissenschaften und Künste*, Section III, Band 24 (1848), 482-485.
Edelstein, L., "History of Anatomy in Antiquity", *Ancient Medicine*, Baltimore 1967, 247-301.
Edmonds, J. M., *Elegy and Iambus* (LCL), 2 vols., London 1931.
Edmonds, J. M., *The Fragments of Attic Comedy*, 4 vols., Leiden 1957-1961.
Eissfeldt, O., *Einleitung in das Alte Testament*, Tübingen 1964³.
McEleney, N. J., "Conversion, Circumcision and the Law", *NTS* 20 (1973-4), 319-341.
Elter, A., *De gnomologiorum Graecorum historia atque origine commentatio*, 9 Programme der Universität Bonn 1893-1896.
Elter, A., *De gnomologiorum Graecorum historia atque origine commentationis ramenta*, Bonn 1897.
Elter, A., *Gnomica Homoiomata*, 5 vols., Bonn 1900-1904.
Eltester, W., review of F. Dornseiff, *Echtheitsfragen* (1939), *ZNW* 39 (1940), 243.
Encyclopaedia Judaica, ed. C. Roth, 16 vols., Jerusalem 1971-1972.
Epstein, L. M., *Sex Laws and Customs in Judaism*, New York 1948.
Fabricius, J. A., *Codex Pseudepigraphus Veteris Testamenti*, 2 vols., Hamburg 1722-1723².
Fabricius, J. A., *Bibliotheca Graeca* I, Hamburg 1790⁴.
Farina, A., *Silloge pseudofocilidea*, Naples 1962.
Feldmann, D. M., *Birth Control in Jewish Law. Marital Relations, Contraception and Abortion as Set Forth in the Classic Texts of Jewish Law*, New York-London 1973³.
Feldman, L. H., "Jewish 'Sympathizers' in Classical Literature and Inscriptions", *Transactions of the American Philological Association* 81 (1950), 200-208.

Feldman, L. H., "The Orthodoxy of the Jews in Hellenistic Egypt", *Jewish Social Studies* 22 (1960), 215-237.
Ferguson, J., *Moral Values in the Ancient World*, London 1958.
Festugière, A. J., *La révélation d'Hermès Trismégiste III: Les doctrines de l'âme*, Paris 1953.
Feuling, J. B.,-Goodwin, H. D., *Phocylides. Poem of Admonition*, Andover (Mass.) 1879.
Fiebig, P., "Phokylides", *RGG* IV² (1930), 1239.
Fiedler, M., "Δικαιοσύνη in der diaspora-jüdischen und intertestamentarischen Literatur", *JSJ* 1 (1970), 120-143.
Finkelstein, L., "Some examples of Maccabean Halaka", *JBL* 49 (1930), 20-42.
Fraenkel, J. J., *Hybris*, diss. Utrecht 1941.
Frankel, Z., review of J. Bernays, *Ueber das phokylideische Gedicht* (1856), *MGWJ* 5 (1856), 66-71.
Franyó, Z.,-Snell, B.,-Maehler, H., *Frühgriechische Lyriker I*, Berlin 1971.
Fraser, P. M., *Ptolemaic Alexandria*, 3 vols., Oxford 1972.
Freedman, H.,-Simon, M., *Midrash Rabba*, 10 vols., London 1939.
Freudenthal, J., *Die Flavius Josephus beigelegte Schrift über die Herrschaft der Vernunft (IV Makkabäerbuch), eine Predigt aus dem ersten nachchristlichen Jahrhundert*, Breslau 1869.
Freudenthal, J., *Alexander Polyhistor (= Hellenistische Studien I-II)*, Breslau 1875.
Freudenthal, J., "Zu Phavorinus und der mittelalterlichen Florilegienliteratur", *Rhein. Mus.* 35 (1880), 408-430.
Frezza, P., Παρακαταθήκη, *Symbolae R. Taubenschlag dedicatae I*, Warsaw 1956, 139-172.
Friedländer, L., *Darstellungen aus der Sittengeschichte Roms*, 4 vols., Leipzig 1919-1921⁹.
Friedländer, M., *Geschichte der jüdischen Apologetik als Vorgeschichte des Christentums*, Zürich 1903.
Friedländer, P., Ὑποθῆκαι, *Hermes* 48 (1913), 558-616.
Fuchs, L., *Die Juden Ägyptens in ptolemäischer und römischer Zeit*, Wien 1924.
Fürst, J., *Bibliotheca Judaica. Bibliographisches Handbuch umfassend die Druckwerke der jüdischen Literatur einschliesslich der über Juden und Judenthum veröffentlichten Schriften*, 3 vols., Leipzig 1849-1863.
Funk, F. X., *Doctrina duodecim apostolorum. Canones apostolorum ecclesiastici ac reliquae doctrinae de duabus viis expositiones veteres*, Tübingen 1887.
Funk, F. X.,-Bihlmeyer, K., *Die apostolischen Väter*, Tübingen 1956².
Galling, K., "Stand und Aufgabe der Koheletforschung", *ThR* N.F. 6 (1934), 355-373.
Galling, K., "Prediger", *PW(RE)* XXII 2 (1954), 1827-1831.
Galling, K., *Der Prediger*, in: *Die fünf Megilloth*, Tübingen 1969.
Gaudemet, J.,-Fascher, E., "Fremder", *RAC* VIII (1973), 306-347.
Geffcken, J., *Die Oracula Sibyllina*, Leipzig 1902.
Geffcken, J., "Christliche Sibyllinen", in: E. Hennecke (ed.), *Neutestamentliche Apokryphen*, Tübingen-Leipzig 1904, 318-345.
Geffcken, J., *Zwei griechische Apologeten*, Leipzig 1907 (repr. Hildesheim 1970).
Geffcken, J., *Kynika und Verwandtes*, Heidelberg 1909.
Geiger, A., review of J. Bernays, *Ueber das phokylideische Gedicht* (1856), *Jüdische Zeitschrift für Wissenschaft und Leben* 4 (1866), 52-59.

Gemser, B., *Sprüche Salomos*, Tübingen 1963².
Gerhard, G. A., *Phoinix von Kolophon*, Leipzig 1909.
Gerner, E., "Tymborychia", *Zeitschrift der Savigny-Stiftung für Rechtsgeschichte, Roman. Abt.* 61 (1941), 230-275.
Geurts, N., *Het huwelijk bij de Griekse en Romeinse moralisten*, diss. Utrecht, Amsterdam 1928.
Geytenbeek, A. C. van, *Musonius Rufus and Greek Diatribe*, Assen 1963.
Gildemeister, J., "Pythagorassprüche in syrischer Überlieferung", *Hermes* 4 (1870), 81-98.
Ginzberg, L., *The Legends of the Jews*, 7 vols., Philadelphia 1909-1938.
Giusta, M., *I dossografi di etica*, 2 vols., Turin 1962-1967.
Glatzer, N. N., *Hillel the Elder. The Emergence of Classical Judaism*, New York 1966.
Görler, W., ΜΕΝΑΝΔΡΟΥ ΓΝΩΜΑΙ, diss. Berlin 1963.
Goram, O., "De Pseudo-Phocylide", *Philol.* 14 (1859), 91-112.
Gossen, H., "Polypen", *PW(RE)* XXI 2 (1952), 1791-1797.
Graetz, H., *Geschichte der Juden* III, Leipzig 1878³.
Greeven, H., *Das Hauptproblem der Sozialethik in der neueren Stoa und im Urchristentum*, diss. Greifswald, Gütersloh 1935.
Groningen, B. A. van, "Le Grec et ses idées morales", *Acta Congressus Madvigiani II: Formation of the Mind, Forms of Thought, Moral Ideas*, Copenhagen 1958, 57-117.
Groningen, B. A. van, *Théognis. Le premier livre édité avec un commentaire*, Amsterdam 1966.
Guignebert, Ch., *Le monde juif vers le temps de Jésus*, Paris 1935.
Gussen, P. J. G., *Het leven in Alexandrië volgens de cultuurhistorische gegevens in de Paedagogus (boek II en III) van Clemens Alexandrinus*, diss. Leiden, Assen 1955.
Guttmann, M., *Das Judentum und seine Umwelt*, Berlin 1927.
Hadas, M., *Hellenistic Culture; Fusion and Diffusion*, New York 1959.
Harnack, A. von, review of J. Bernays, *Gesammelte Abhandlungen* (1885), *TLZ* 10 (1885), 159-161.
Harnack, A. von, *Geschichte der altchristlichen Literatur*, 4 vols., Leipzig 1893-1904.
Harnack, A. von, *Die Apostellehre und die jüdischen beiden Wege*, Leipzig 1896².
Harris, J. R., *The Teaching of the Apostles and the Sibylline Books*, Cambridge 1885.
Harris, J. R., *The Teaching of the Apostles*, London-Baltimore 1887.
Hart, A., "Die Pseudo-Phokylideia und Theognis im Codex Venetus Marcianus 522", *Neue Jahrbücher für classische Philologie* 14 (1868), 331-336.
Hatch, E.,-Redpath, H. A., *A Concordance to the Septuagint*, 3 vols., Oxford 1897-1906 (repr. Graz 1954).
Hauck, F., "Arbeit", *RAC* I (1950), 585-590.
Heer, C. de, ΜΑΚΑΡ - ΕΥΔΑΙΜΩΝ - ΟΛΒΙΟΣ - ΕΥΤΥΧΗΣ, diss. Utrecht 1968.
Heinemann, I., "Die Lehre vom ungeschriebenen Gesetz im jüdischen Schrifttum", *HUCA* 4 (1927), 149-171.
Heinemann, I., "Antisemitismus", *PW(RE)* Suppl. V (1931), 3-43.
Heinemann, I., *Philons griechische und jüdische Bildung. Kulturvergleichende Untersuchungen zu Philons Darstellung der jüdischen Gesetze*, Breslau 1932 (repr. Hildesheim 1962).

Heinrici, C. F. G., "Die urchristliche Ueberlieferung und das Neue Testament", in: *Theologische Abhandlungen Carl von Weizsäcker gewidmet*, Freiburg-in-Br. 1892, 321-352.
Hempel, J., "Ethics in the Old Testament", *IDB* II (1962), 153-161.
Hengel, M., "Anonymität, Pseudepigraphie und 'literarische Fälschung' in der jüdisch-hellenistischen Literatur", in: *Pseudepigrapha I* (*Entretiens de la Fondation Hardt* XVIII), Vandoeuvres-Geneva 1972, 231-329.
Hengel, M., *Eigentum und Reichtum in der frühen Kirche*, Stuttgart 1973.
Hengel, M., *Judentum und Hellenismus. Studien zu ihrer Begegnung unter besonderer Berücksichtigung Palästinas bis zur Mitte des 2. Jh. v. Chr.*, Tübingen 1973².
Hengel, M., *Der Sohn Gottes. Die Entstehung der Christologie und die jüdisch-hellenistische Religionsgeschichte*, Tübingen 1975.
Hengel, M., *Juden, Griechen und Barbaren. Aspekte der Hellenisierung des Judentums in vorchristlicher Zeit*, Stuttgart 1976.
Hense, O., "Eine Menippea des Varro", *Rhein. Mus.* 61 (1906), 1-18.
Hermann, A.,-Herter, H., "Dirne", *RAC* III (1957), 1149-1213.
Herter, H., review of F. Dornseiff, *Echtheitsfragen* (1939), *TLZ* 66 (1941), 17-19.
Herter, H., "Effeminatus", *RAC* IV (1959), 620-650.
Hewett, W., *The Preceptive Poem of Phocylides, One of the Less Greek Poets, Translated into English Verse*, Watford 1840.
Hiller, E.,-Crusius, O., *Anthologia Lyrica*, Leipzig 1913.
Hiltbrunner, O., *Latina Graeca*, Bern 1958.
Hirzel, R., ΑΓΡΑΦΟΣ ΝΟΜΟΣ, Abhandl. der königl. sächsischen Gesellsch. der Wiss., Phil.-hist. Classe XX 1, Leipzig 1900.
Hirzel, R., *Der Eid. Ein Beitrag zu seiner Geschichte*, Leipzig 1902.
Hirzel, R., *Themis, Dike und Verwandtes*, Leipzig 1907.
Hoftijzer, J.,-Kooy, G. van der, *Aramaic Texts from Deir Alla*, Leiden 1976.
Hollerbach, H. R., *Zur Bedeutung des Wortes* χρεῖα, diss. Köln 1964.
Holwerda, D., *Scholia vetera in Nubes*, Groningen 1977.
Hommel, H., "Juden und Christen im kaiserzeitlichen Milet", *Istanbuler Mitteilungen* 25 (1975), 167-195.
Hooke, S. H., "Life After Death: The Extra-Canonical Literature", *Expository Times* 76 (1964/5), 273-276.
Hopfner, Th., *Das Sexualleben der Griechen und Römer* I 1, Prag 1938 (repr. New York 1975).
Hopfner, Th., "Abstinenz", *RAC* I (1950), 41-44.
Horna, K., "Gnome, Gnomendichtung, Gnomologien", *PW(RE)* Suppl. VI (1935), 74-90.
Horowitz, J., "Entwicklung des alexandrinischen Judentums unter dem Einflusse Philos", in: *Judaica. Festschrift für H. Cohen*, Berlin 1912, 535-567.
Horst, P. C. van der, *Les vers d'or pythagoriciens*, diss. Leiden 1932.
Horst, P. W. van der, "Drohung und Mord schnaubend (Acta IX1)", *Nov. Test.* 12 (1970), 257-269.
Horst, P. W. van der, "Pseudo-Phocylides and the New Testament" *ZNW* 69 (1978) (forthcoming).
Howald, E., review of F. Dornseiff, *Echtheitsfragen* (1939), *Deutsche Literaturzeitung* 61 (1940), 663-668.
Hübner, H., "Markus VII 1-23 und das 'jüdisch-hellenistische' Gesetzesverständnis", *NTS* 22 (1975/6), 319-345.
Hurwitz, M. S., "Pseudo-Phocylides", *Enc. Jud.* XIII (1971), 1335-6.
Jackson Knight, W. F., *Elysion. Ancient Greek and Roman Beliefs Concerning Life After Death*, London 1970.

Jaeger, W., "Echo eines unerkannten Tragikerfragments in Clemens' Brief an die Korinther", *Rhein. Mus.* 102 (1959), 330-340.
Jaekel, S., *Menandri Sententiae*, Leipzig 1964.
Jastrow, M., *A Dictionary of the Targumim, the Talmuds and the Midrashic Literature*, New York 1903.
Jellicoe, S., *The Septuagint and Modern Study*, Oxford 1968.
Jenni, E.,-Westermann, C., *Theologisches Handwörterbuch zum Alten Testament*, 2 vols., München-Zürich 1971-1976.
Jeremias, J., *Jerusalem zur Zeit Jesu*, Göttingen 1962³.
Jervell, J., *Imago Dei. Gen. I 26f. im Spätjudentum, in der Gnosis und in den paulinischen Briefen*, Göttingen 1960.
Joly, R., *Hermas. Le Pasteur*, Paris 1968².
Kaibel, G., *Epigrammata graeca ex lapidibus conlecta*, Berlin 1878.
Kaibel, G., "Inschriften aus Pisidien", *Hermes* 23 (1888), 532-545.
Kamlah, E., *Die Form der katalogischen Paränese im Neuen Testament*, Tübingen 1964.
Kamlah, E., "Frömmigkeit und Tugend. Die Gesetzesapologie des Josephus in c. Ap. 2, 145-195", in: *Josephus-Studien für O. Michel*, Göttingen 1974, 220-232.
Kautzsch, E., (ed.), *Die Apokryphen und Pseudepigraphen des Alten Testaments*, 2 vols, Tübingen 1900 (repr. Darmstadt 1962).
Kerst, R., "1 Kor. 8, 6 — ein vorpaulinisches Taufbekenntnis?", *ZNW* 66 (1975), 130-139.
Keydell, R., "Die griechische Poesie der Kaiserzeit", *Jahresberichte über die Fortschritte der Altertumswissenschaften* 230 (1931), 41-161; ibid. 272 (1941), 1-71.
Keydell, R., "Phokylides", *Der kleine Pauly* IV (1971), 806-7.
Kirk, J. A., "The Meaning of Wisdom in James", *NTS* 16 (1969/70), 24-38.
Kittel, G., *Die Probleme des palästinischen Spätjudentums und das Urchristentum*, Stuttgart 1926.
Klauser, Th.,-Labriolle, P. de, "Apophthegma", *RAC* I (1950), 545-550.
Klein, G., *Der älteste christliche Katechismus und die jüdische Propagandaliteratur*, Berlin 1909.
Klopfenstein, M. A., *Die Lüge nach dem Alten Testament*, Zürich 1964.
Klijn, A. F. J., "Die Ethik des Neuen Testaments", *Nederlands Theologisch Tijdschrift* 24 (1970), 241-249.
Knopf, R., *Die Lehre der zwölf Apostel. Die zwei Clemensbriefe*, Tübingen 1920.
Köhler, C. S., *Das Tierleben im Sprichwort der Griechen und Römer*, Leipzig 1881.
Koep, L., "Biene", *RAC* II (1954), 274-282.
Koep, L.,-Stommel, E.,-Kollwitz, J., "Bestattung", *RAC* II (1954), 194-219.
Koester, H., "Nomos Physeos. The Concept of Natural Law in Greek Thought", in: *Religions in Antiquity (Essays in Memory of E. R. Goodenough)*, Leiden 1968, 521-541.
Kötting, B., "Digamus", *RAC* III (1957), 1016-1024.
Kranz, W., "Sphragis. Ichform und Namensiegel als Eingangs- und Schluszmotiv antiker Dichtung", *Rhein. Mus.* 104 (1961), 3-46; 97-124 (repr. in his *Kleine Schriften* (1967), 27-78).
Krauss, S., "Les préceptes des Noachides", *REJ* 47 (1903), 32-40.
Krauss, S., "Pseudo-Phocylides", *The Jewish Encyclopedia* X (1905), 255-6.
Krauss, S., *Talmudische Archäologie*, 3 vols., Leipzig 1910-1912.
Kreuttner, X., *Andronici qui fertur libelli* Περὶ παθῶν *pars prior de affectibus*, Heidelberg 1885.

Kroll, W., "Zur Ueberlieferung der Pseudophocylidea", *Rhein. Mus.* 47 (1892), 457-461.
Kroll, W., "Studien über Ciceros Schrift De Oratore", *Rhein. Mus.* 58 (1903), 552-597.
Kroll, W., review of A. Ludwich, *Über das Spruchbuch des falschen Phokylides* (1904) and *Quaestionum pseudophocylidearum pars altera* (1904), *Berliner Philologische Wochenschrift* 25 (1905), 241-3.
Kroll, W., *Die Kultur der ciceronischen Zeit*, Wiesbaden 1933 (repr. Darmstadt 1963).
Kroll, W., "Pseudo-Phokylides", see P. Ahlert.
Kroll, W., "Aphrodisiacum", *RAC* I (1950), 496-501.
Krüger, P., *Philo und Josephus als Apologeten des Judentums*, Leipzig 1906.
Kudlien, F., "Anatomie", *PW(RE)* Suppl. XI (1968), 38-48.
Kühner, R.,-Gerth, B., *Ausführliche Grammatik der griechischen Sprache*, 2. *Teil: Satzlehre*, 2 vols., Hannover-Leipzig 1898-1904³ (repr. Darmstadt 1966).
Kümmel, W. G., (ed.), *Jüdische Schriften aus hellenistisch-römischer Zeit*, 6 vols., Gütersloh 1973-...
Kuhn, K. G.,-Stegemann, H., "Proselyten", *PW(RE)* Suppl. IX (1962), 1248-1283.
Kurfess, A., "Das Mahngedicht des sogenannten Phokylides im zweiten Buch der Oracula Sibyllina", *ZNW* 38 (1939), 171-181.
Kurfess, A., "Oracula Sibyllina I/II", *ZNW* 40 (1941), 151-165.
Kurfess, A., *Sibyllinische Weissagungen*, München 1951.
Lake, K., "Proselytes and God-Fearers", in: F. J. Foakes Jackson-K. Lake (edd.), *The Beginnings of Christianity* V, London 1933, 74-96.
Lausberg, H., *Handbuch der literarischen Rhetorik*, 2 vols., München 1960.
Leipoldt, J., "Antisemitismus", *RAC* I (1950), 469-476.
Leipoldt, J., *Die Frau in der antiken Welt und im Urchristentum*, Leipzig 1955².
Leipoldt, J.,-Grundmann, W., (edd.), *Umwelt des Urchristentums*, 3 vols., Berlin 1967-1970².
Lenz, F. W., "Über die Problematik der Echtheitskritik", *Das Altertum* 8 (1962), 218-228.
Leon, H. J., *The Jews of Ancient Rome*, Philadelphia 1960.
Lesky, A., *Geschichte der griechischen Literatur*, Bern 1971³.
Lesky, E.,-Waszink, J. H., "Embryologie", *RAC* IV (1959), 1228-1244.
Leutsch, E. von, "Ein Gedicht des Theognis", *Philol.* 22 (1865), 17-29.
Leutsch, E. von,-Schneidewin, F. G., *Corpus Paroemiographorum Graecorum*, 2 vols., Göttingen 1839-1851 (repr. Hildesheim 1965).
Levy, I., *Recherches Esséniennes et Pythagoriciennes*, Paris 1965.
Lewis, J. J., "The Teaching of the Pseudo-Phocylidea", *The London Quarterly and Holborn Review*, October 1953, 295-298.
Lewis, J. J., "The Table-talk Section in the Letter of Aristeas", *NTS* 13 (1967/8), 53-56.
Liagre Böhl, F. M. Th. de, "Die Juden im Urteil der griechischen und römischen Schriftsteller", *Opera Minora*, Groningen 1953, 101-133.
Licht, H., *Sexual Life in Ancient Greece*, London 1932 (= 1971¹⁰).
Licht, H., *Sittengeschichte Griechenlands*, Hamburg 1968.
Liddell, H. G.,-Scott, R.,-Jones, H. S., *A Greek-English Lexicon*, Oxford 1940⁹ (*A Supplement* by E. A. Barber, Oxford 1968).
Lifshitz, B., "Du nouveau sur les 'Sympathisants'", *JSJ* 1 (1970), 77-84.
Limbeck, M., *Die Ordnung des Heils. Zum Gesetzesverständnis des Frühjudentums*, Düsseldorf 1971.

Lincke, K. F. A., *Samaria und seine Propheten*, Tübingen-Leipzig 1903.
Lincke, K. F. A., "Phokylides und die Essener", *Die Grenzboten* (*Zeitschrift für Politik, Literatur und Kunst*) 68 (1909), 128-138.
Lincke, K. F. A., "Phokylides, Isokrates und der Dekalog", *Philol.* 70 (1911), 438-442.
Lloyd, G., "Alcmaion and the Early History of Dissection", *Sudhoffs Archiv* 59 (1975), 113-147.
Lohfink, G., *Der Himmelfahrt Jesu*, München 1971.
Lohse, E., "Pseudo-Phokylides", *RGG* V³ (1961), 362.
Lohse, E., *Umwelt des Neuen Testaments*, Göttingen 1971.
Ludwich, A., *Lectiones Pseudo-Phocylideae*, Königsberg 1892.
Ludwich, A., review of A. A. Zanolli, *De Pseudophocylidea* (1903), *Berliner Philologische Wochenschrift* 23 (1903), 1153-55.
Ludwich, A., "Über das Spruchbuch des falschen Phokylides", *Programm Königsberg*, Königsberg 1904, 1-26.
Ludwich, A., "Quaestionum pseudophocylidearum pars altera", *ibid.* 27-32.
Lührmann, D., "Pistis im Judentum", *ZNW* 64 (1973), 19-38.
Lumpe, A., "Elementum", *RAC* IV (1959), 1073-1100.
Luther, W., *Wahrheit und Lüge im ältesten Griechentum*, Leipzig 1935.
McCown, C. C., *The Testament of Solomon*, Leipzig 1922.
Maier, J., *Die Texte vom Toten Meer*, 2 vols., München-Basel 1960.
Maier, J., *Geschichte der jüdischen Religion*, Berlin 1972.
Maier, J.,-Schreiner, J., (edd.), *Literatur und Religion des Frühjudentums*, Würzburg 1973.
Malherbe, A. J., "Gentle as a Nurse. The Cynic Background to 1 Thess. 2", *Nov. Test.* 12 (1970), 203-217.
Malherbe, A. J., "Hellenistic Moralists and the New Testament", in: H. Temporini (ed.), *Aufstieg und Niedergang der römischen Welt* II (forthcoming).
Marcus, R., "A Selected Bibliography (1920-1945) of the Jews in the Hellenistic-Roman Period", *Proceedings of the American Academy for Jewish Research* 16 (1946/7), 97-181.
Marcus, R., "The *Sebomenoi* in Josephus", *Jewish Social Studies* 14 (1952), 247-250.
Marmorstein, A., "Das Motiv vom veruntreuten Depositum in der jüdischen Volkskunde", *MGWJ* 78 (1934), 183-195.
Marmorstein, A., "A Greek Lyric and a Hebrew Poet", *JQR* 37 (1946/7), 169-173.
Marrou, H. I., *Histoire de l'éducation dans l'antiquité*, Paris 1960⁵.
Martin, V., "Un recueil de diatribes cyniques. Pap. Genev. inv. 271", *Museum Helveticum* 16 (1959), 77-115.
Matthews, I. G., *The Jewish Apologetic to the Grecian World in the Apocryphal and Pseudepigraphical Literature*, Chicago 1914.
Mayer, G., *Index Philoneus*, Berlin-New York 1974.
Meeks, W. A., "The Image of the Androgyne", *History of Religions* 13 (1973/4), 165-208.
Meineke, A., *Ioannis Stobaei Florilegium* IV, Leipzig 1859.
Merki, H., "Ebenbildlichkeit", *RAC* IV (1959), 459-479.
Metzger, B. M., "Literary Forgeries and Canonical Pseudepigrapha", *JBL* 91 (1972), 3-24.
Metzger, B. M., "The Nazareth Inscription Once Again", in: *Jesus und Paulus* (*Festschrift fur W. G. Kümmel*), Göttingen 1975, 221-238.
Meyer, E., *Ursprung und Anfänge des Christentums*, 3 vols., Stuttgart-Berlin 1923-5 (repr. Darmstadt 1962).

Milobenski, E., *Der Neid in der griechischen Philosophie*, Wiesbaden 1964.
Minear, P. S., "Yes or No: The Demand for Honesty in the Early Church", *Nov. Test.* 13 (1971), 1-13.
Momigliano, A., *Jacob Bernays*, Mededelingen der Koninklijke Nederlandse Akademie van Wetenschappen, Afdeling Letterkunde, Nieuwe Reeks XXXII 5, Amsterdam 1969.
Momigliano, A., *Alien Wisdom. The Limits of Hellenization*, Cambridge 1975.
Mommsen, Th., *Römisches Strafrecht*, Leipzig 1899.
Moore, G. F., *Judaism in the First Centuries of the Christian Era. The Age of the Tannaim*, 3 vols., Cambridge (Mass.) 1927-1930.
Mott, S. C., "The Power of Giving and Receiving: Reciprocity in Hellenistic Benevolence", in: *Current Issues in Biblical and Patristic Interpretation (Studies in Honour of M. C. Tenney)*, Grand Rapids 1975, 60-72.
Murphy, R. E., "Form Criticism and Wisdom Literature", *CBQ* 31 (1969), 478-483.
Mussies, G., *The Morphology of Koine Greek as Used in the Apocalypse of John*, Leiden 1971.
Mynors, R. A. B., "Didactic Poetry, Greek", *OCD* (1949), 277-278.
Nauck, A., *Tragicorum Graecorum Fragmenta*, Leipzig 1889².
Negev, A., "A Nabatean Epitaph from Trans-Jordan", *Israel Exploration Journal* 21 (1971), 50-52.
Nestle, W.,-Liebich, W., *Geschichte der griechischen Literatur*, 2 vols., Berlin 1961-1963³.
Neusner, J., *Rabbinic Traditions about the Pharisees before 70*, 3 vols., Leiden 1971.
Neusner, J., *The Idea of Purity in Ancient Judaism*, Leiden 1973.
Nickel, J., *Phokylides' Mahngedicht in metrischer Übersetzung*, Mainz 1833.
Nickelsburg, G. W. E., *Resurrection, Immortality and Eternal Life in Intertestamental Judaism*, Cambridge (Mass.) 1972.
Nikiprowetzky, V., *La troisième Sibylle*, Paris-Den Haag 1970.
Nilsson, M. P., *Geschichte der griechischen Religion* II, München 1961².
Nissen, A., *Gott und der Nächste im antiken Judentum. Untersuchungen zum Doppelgebot der Liebe*, Tübingen 1974.
Nock, A. D., "The Question of Jewish Mysteries", *Essays on Religion and the Ancient World* I, Oxford 1972, 459-469.
Nock, A. D., "Tomb Violation and Pontifical Law", *ibid.* II 527-533.
Nock, A. D., "Philo and Hellenistic Philosophy", *ibid.* II 559-565.
Nock, A. D., "Religious Symbols and Symbolism", *ibid.* II 877-919.
Nock, A. D., "Isopoliteia and the Jews", *ibid.* II 960-962.
Norden, E., "Beiträge zur Geschichte der griechischen Philosophie", *Jahrbücher für classische Philologie* Suppl. 19, 2 (1893), 365-462.
Norden, E., *Agnostos Theos. Untersuchungen zur Formengeschichte religiöser Rede*, Leipzig 1923² (repr. Darmstadt 1956).
North, H., *Sophrosyne. Self-Knowledge and Self-Restraint in Greek Literature*, Ithaca 1966.
Oepke, A., "Auferstehung (des Menschen)", *RAC* I (1950), 930-938.
Oepke, A., "Ehe", *RAC* IV (1959), 650-666.
Oltramare, A., *Les origines de la diatribe romaine*, diss. Geneva 1926.
Otto, A., *Die Sprichwörter und sprichwörtlichen Redensarten der Römer*, Leipzig 1890 (repr. Hildesheim 1962).
Oyen, H. van, *Ethik des Alten Testaments*, Gütersloh 1967.
Pack, R. A., *The Greek and Latin Literary Texts from Greco-Roman Egypt*, Ann Arbor 1952.

Packmohr, A., *De Diogenis Sinopensis apophthegmatis quaestiones selectae*, diss. Münster 1913.
Palmer, L. R., "Greek Dialects", *OCD* (1949), 271-2.
Pape, W.,-Benseler, G., *Wörterbuch der griechischen Eigennamen*, 2 vols., Braunschweig 1911³ (repr. Graz 1959).
Parrot, A., *Malédictions et violations de tombes*, Paris 1939.
Pelletier, A., *Lettre d'Aristée à Philocrate*, Paris 1962.
Peretti, A., *Teognide nella tradizione gnomologica*, Pisa 1953.
Peterson, E., ΕΙΣ ΘΕΟΣ. *Epigraphische, formgeschichtliche und religionsgeschichtliche Untersuchungen*, Göttingen 1926.
Pötscher, W., "Die Auferstehung in der klassischen Antike", *Kairos* 7 (1965), 208-215.
Pohlenz, M., *Die Stoa. Geschichte einer geistigen Bewegung*, 2 vols., Göttingen 1970-1972⁴.
Polster, G., "Der kleine Talmudtraktat über die Proselyten", ΑΓΓΕΛΟΣ 2 (1926), 1-38.
Porte-du Theil, F. J. G. la, "Theodorus Prodromus Περὶ τοὺς διὰ πενίαν βλασφημοῦντας τὴν πρόνοιαν", *Notices et Extraits des Manuscrits de la Bibliothèque Impériale* VIII 2 (1810), 78-88.
Praechter, K., *Hierokles der Stoiker*, Leipzig 1901.
Preuss, J., "Prostitution und sexuelle Perversitäten nach Bibel und Talmud", *Monatshefte für praktische Dermatologie* 43 (1906), 271-279; 342-345; 376-381; 470-477; 549-555.
Pseudepigrapha I: Pseudopythagorica — Lettres de Platon — Littérature pseudépigraphique juive; Entretiens sur l'antiquité classique XVIII, Vandœuvres-Geneva 1972.
Rad, G. von, *Weisheit in Israel*, Neukirchen 1970.
Ranston, H., *Ecclesiastes and Early Greek Wisdom Literature*, London 1925.
Rappaport, U., "Bibliography of Works on Jewish History in the Hellenistic and Roman Periods 1946-1970", in: B. Oded *et al.* (edd.), *Studies in the History of the Jewish People and the Land of Israel* II, Haifa 1972, 247-321.
Raspante, J., *Sulla composizione e sull' autore del carme pseudophocilideo*, Catania 1913.
Rech, P., "Ameise", *RAC* I (1950), 375-377.
Reicke, B., *Die Zehn Worte in Geschichte und Gegenwart*, Tübingen 1973.
Renehan, R., "Classical Greek Quotations in the New Testament", in: *The Heritage of the Early Church* (Festschrift G. V. Florovsky), Rome 1973, 17-46.
Renehan, R., *Greek Lexicographical Notes. A Critical Supplement to the Greek-English Lexicon of Liddell-Scott-Jones*, Göttingen 1975.
Ribbeck, O., *Kolax*, Abhandl. der sächs. Ges. der Wiss., phil.-hist. Classe 9, Leipzig 1884, 1-113.
Richter, W., *Recht und Ethos. Versuch einer Ortung des weisheitlichen Mahnspruches*, München 1966.
Riessler, P., *Altjüdisches Schrifttum auszerhalb der Bibel*, Augsburg 1928.
Robinson, J. M., "Logoi Sophon", in: H. Koester-J. M. Robinson, *Entwicklungslinien durch die Welt des frühen Christentums*, Tübingen 1971, 70-106.
Rohde, E., *Psyche. Seelencult und Unsterblichkeitsglaube der Griechen*, 2 vols., Leipzig-Tübingen 1898² (repr. Darmstadt 1961)
Rohde, U. A., *De veterum poetarum sapientia gnomica*, 2 vols., Havniae 1800.

Rordorf, W., "Un chapitre d'éthique judéo-chrétienne: les deux voies", *RSR* 60 (1972), 109-128.
Rose, H. J., "Pseudepigraphic Literature", *OCD* (1949), 743.
Rosenthal, F., "Sedaka, Charity", *HUCA* 23 (1950/1), 411-430.
Rossbroich, M., *De Pseudo-Phocylideis*, diss. Münster 1910.
Rostovtzeff, M., *The Social and Economic History of the Hellenistic World*, 3 vols., Oxford 1941.
Rostovtzeff, M., *The Social and Economic History of the Roman Empire*, 2 vols., Oxford 1957².
Rudisch, F., "Zur Überlieferung der Pseudophocylidea", *Wiener Studien* 35 (1913), 386-388.
Ruhl, L., *De mortuorum iudicio*, Giessen 1903.
Safrai, S.,-Stern, M., (edd.), *Compendia Rerum Judaicarum ad Novum Testamentum* I 1 + 2: *The Jewish People in the First Century*, Assen 1974-6.
Sanders, E. P., *Paul and Palestinian Judaism*, London 1977.
Sanders, L., *L'hellénisme de saint Clément de Rome et le paulinisme*, Louvain 1943.
Sartorius, G., *Analysis grammatica et familiaris expositio carminum Phocylidis et Pythagorae in usum adolescentiae Graecorum literarum studiosae*, Görlitz 1617.
Scaliger, J. J., *Animadversiones in Chronologica Eusebii*, in: *Thesaurus Temporum*, Leiden 1606 (Amsterdam 1608²).
Schäfer, K. T., "Aposteldekret", *RAC* I (1950), 555-558.
Schechter, S., *Aspects of Rabbinic Theology*, New York 1909 (repr. 1961).
Schenkl, H., *Florilegia duo graeca*, Wien 1888.
Schier, I. A., *Phocylidis ... carmina cum selectis adnotationibus aliquot doctorum virorum Graece et Latine*, Leipzig 1751.
Schmalzriedt, E., *Peri Physeos. Zur Frühgeschichte der Buchtitel*, München 1970.
Schmid, H. H., *Wesen und Geschichte der Weisheit*, Berlin 1966.
Schmid, J., "Pseudo-Phokylides", *LThK* VIII (1963), 867-868.
Schmid, W.,-Stählin, O., *Geschichte der griechischen Literatur*, 5 vols., München 1929-1948.
Schmidt, J. H. H., *Synonymik der griechischen Sprache*, 4 vols., Leipzig 1876-1886 (repr. Amsterdam 1969).
Schmidt, L., review of J. Bernays, *Ueber das phokylideische Gedicht* (1856), *Jahrbücher für classische Philologie* 3 (1857), 510-519.
Schmidt, L., *Die Ethik der alten Griechen*, 2 vols., Berlin 1882.
Schmidt, M., "Verbesserungsvorschläge zu schwierigen Stellen griechischer Schriftsteller", *Rhein. Mus.* 26 (1871), 161-234.
Schneider, C., "Phokylides", *BHH* III (1966), 1463-1464.
Schneider, C., "Eros", *RAC* VI (1966), 306-312.
Schneider, C., *Kulturgeschichte des Hellenismus*, 2 vols., München 1967-1969.
Schoeps, H. J., *Paulus. Die Theologie des Apostels im Lichte der jüdischen Religionsgeschichte*, Tübingen 1959.
Schrage, W., *Die konkreten Einzelgebote in der paulinischen Paränese*, Gütersloh 1961.
Schrage, W., "Zur Ethik der neutestamentlichen Haustafeln", *NTS* 21 (1974/5), 1-22.
Schubart, W., "Alexandria", *RAC* I (1950), 271-283.
Schubart, W., *Ägypten von Alexander dem Groszen bis auf Mohammed*, Berlin 1922.

Schubert, K., "Die Entwicklung der Auferstehungslehre von der nachexilischen bis zur frührabbinischen Zeit", *Biblische Zeitschrift* NF 6 (1962), 177-214.
Schürer, E., review of K. Lincke, *Samaria und seine Propheten* (1903), *TLZ* 28 (1903), 708-710.
Schürer, E., *Geschichte des jüdischen Volkes im Zeitalter Jesu Christi*, 3 vols., Leipzig 1901-1909⁴.
Schürer, E., *The History of the Jewish People in the Age of Jesus Christ*, rev. and ed. by G. Vermes and F. Millar, I, Edinburgh 1973.
Schulthess, F., "Die Sprüche des Menander aus dem Syrischen übersetzt", *ZAW* 32 (1912), 199-244.
Schwartz, J., "Die Rolle Alexandrias bei der Verbreitung orientalischen Gedankenguts", *ZPE* 1 (1967), 197-217.
Schwer, W., "Armenpflege", *RAC* I (1950), 689-698.
Schwer, W., "Barmherzigkeit", *RAC* I (1950), 1200-1207.
Scott, R. B. Y., "The Study of the Wisdom Literature", *Interpretation* 24 (1970), 20-45.
Scott, R. B. Y., *The Way of Wisdom in the Old Testament*, New York 1971.
Sebestyén, K., *A Pseudo-Phokylides*, Budapest 1895.
Seeberg, A., *Der Katechismus der Urchristenheit*, Leipzig 1903 (repr. München 1966).
Seeberg, A., *Das Evangelium Christi*, Leipzig 1905.
Seeberg, A., *Die beiden Wege und das Aposteldekret*, Leipzig 1906.
Seeberg, A., *Die Didache des Judentums und der Urchristenheit*, Leipzig 1908.
Selwyn, E. G., *The First Epistle of St. Peter*, London 1946.
Sevenster, J. N., "Antisemitisme in Alexandrië in de eerste eeuw na Christus" *Rondom het Woord* 15 (1975), 10-23.
Sevenster, J. N., *The Roots of Pagan Anti-Semitism in the Ancient World*, Leiden 1975.
Sicking, L. J., *Annotationes ad Antiatticistam*, diss. Utrecht 1883.
Siegert, F., "Gottesfürchtige und Sympathisanten", *JSJ* 4 (1973), 109-164.
Sint, J. A., *Pseudonymität im Altertum. Ihre Formen und ihre Gründe*, Innsbruck 1960.
Sitzler, J., "Zu den griechischen Elegikern", *Jahrbücher für classische Philologie* 30 (1884), 48-53.
Sitzler, J., review of M. Rossbroich, *De Pseudo-Phocylideis* (1910), *Wochenschrift für klassische Philologie* 29 (1912), 449-457.
Sitzler, J., review of J. Raspante, *Sulla composizione* etc. (1913), *Wochenschrift für klassische Philologie* 33 (1916), 699-702.
Skemp, J. B., "Service to the Needy in the Graeco-Roman World", in *Service in Christ* (FS K. Barth 1966), 17-26.
Skutsch, F., "Sechzehnte Epode und vierte Ekloge", *Neue Jahrbücher für das klassische Altertum* 23 (1909), 23-35.
Smallwood, E. M., *Philonis Alexandrini Legatio ad Gaium*, Leiden 1970².
Smith, M., "The Image of God: Notes on the Hellenization of Judaism", *Bulletin of the John Rylands Library* 40 (1957/8), 473-512.
Smith, R. W., *The Art of Rhetoric in Alexandria*, Den Haag 1974.
Snell, B., *Leben und Meinungen der Sieben Weisen*, München 1938.
Sokolowski, F., *Lois sacrées des cités grecques*, Paris 1962.
Spengel, L., *Rhetores Graeci*, 3 vols., Leipzig 1853-56 (repr. Frankfurt 1966).
Speyer, W., "Religiöse Pseudepigraphie und literarische Fälschung", *Jahrbuch für Antike und Christentum* 8/9 (1965/6), 88-125.
Speyer, W., "Fälschung (literarische)", *RAC* VII (1969), 236-277.

Speyer, W., *Die literarische Fälschung im heidnischen und christlichen Altertum*, München 1971.
Spicq, C., *Les épitres pastorales*, Paris 1969⁴.
Spinner, S., *Herkunft, Entstehung und antike Umwelt des hebräischen Volkes*, Vienna 1933.
Spoerri, W., "Gnome", *Der kleine Pauly* II (1967), 822-829.
Stählin, O., "Die hellenistisch-jüdische Litteratur", in: W. Schmid-O. Stählin, *Gesch. der griech. Lit.* II 1, München 1920⁶, 535-656.
Stern, M., *Greek and Latin Authors on Jews and Judaism* I, Jerusalem 1974
Sternbach, L., *Gnomologium Vaticanum*, Berlin 1963 (orig. in *Wiener Studien* 9-11 (1887-1889)).
Stommel, E., "Domus Aeterna", *RAC* IV (1959), 109-128.
Strack, H. L.,-Billerbeck, P., *Kommentar zum Neuen Testament aus Talmud und Midrasch*, 5 vols., München 1922-1928.
Strathmann, H., "Askese", *RAC* I (1950), 749-758.
Strömberg, R., *Greek Proverbs. A Collection of Proverbs and Proverbial Phrases Which Are Not Listed by the Ancient and Byzantine Paroemiographers*, Göteborg 1954.
Strugnell, J.,-Attridge, H., "The Epistles of Heraclitus and the Jewish Pseudepigrapha: A Warning", *HTR* 64 (1971), 411-413.
Susemihl, F., *Geschichte der griechischen Litteratur in der Alexandrinerzeit* 2 vols., Leipzig 1891-1892 (repr. 1965).
Svensson, A., *Der Gebrauch des bestimmten Artikels in der nachklassischen griechischen Epik*, Lund 1937.
Sylburg, F., *Epicae elegiacaeque minorum poetarum gnomae*, Frankfurt 1591 (= *Theognidis, Phocylidis, Pythagorae, Solonis et aliorum poemata gnomica*, Utrecht 1659).
Taubenschlag, R., *The Law of Greco-Roman Egypt in the Light of the Papyri*, Warsaw 1955².
Tcherikover, V. A., "Jewish Apologetic Literature Reconsidered", *Symbolae R. Taubenschlag dedicatae III* (= *Eos* 48 (1956)), Wratislawa-Warsaw 1957, 169-193.
Tcherikover, V. A., "The Ideology of the Letter of Aristeas", *HTR* 51 (1958), 59-85.
Tcherikover, V. A., *Hellenistic Civilization and the Jews*, Philadelphia 1966².
Tcherikover, V. A.,-Fuks, A., *Corpus Papyrorum Judaicorum*, 3 vols., Cambridge (Mass.) 1957-1964.
Terstegen, W. J., ΕΥΣΕΒΗΣ *en* ΟΣΙΟΣ *in het Grieksch taalgebruik na de 4ᵉ eeuw*, diss. Utrecht 1941.
Thompson, D' A. W., *A Glossary of Greek Fishes*, London 1947.
Thraede, K., "Frau", *RAC* VIII (1973), 197-269.
Thyen, H., *Der Stil der jüdisch-hellenistischen Homilie*, Göttingen 1955.
Treu, K., "Die Bedeutung des griechischen für die Juden im römischen Reich", in *Festschrift E. Ivanka*, Salzburg 1973, 123-144.
Überweg, F.,-Praechter, K., *Die Philosophie des Altertums*, Berlin 1926¹² (repr. Darmstadt 1961).
Unnik, W. C. van, *Studies over de zogenaamde eerste brief van Clemens:* 1. *Het litteraire genre*. Amsterdam 1970 (MKNAW, Afd. Lett. XXXIII 4).
Unnik, W. C. van, ΑΦΘΟΝΩΣ ΜΕΤΑΔΙΔΩΜΙ (Mededelingen van de Koninklijke Vlaamse Academie van Wetenschappen, Afd. Lett. 33, 4), Brussel 1971.
Unnik, W. C. van, *De ἀφθονία van God in de oudchristelijke literatuur* (MKNAW, Afd. Lett. XXXVI 2), Amsterdam 1973.

Unnik, W. C. van, "Die Motivierung der Feindesliebe in Lukas VI 32-35", *Sparsa Collecta* I, Leiden 1973, 111-126.
Unnik, W. C. van, "Josephus' Account of the Story of Israel's Sin with alien Women in the Country of Midian (Num. 25, 1ff.)", in: *Travels in the World of the Old Testament (Studies presented to M. A. Beek)*, Assen 1974, 241-261.
Urbach, E. E., *The Sages. Their Concepts and Beliefs*, 2 vols., Jerusalem 1975.
Valk, M. H. A. L. H. van der, "Zum Worte ὅσιος", *Mnemosyne* ser. III, 10 (1942), 113-140.
Vatin, C., *Recherches sur le mariage et la condition de la femme mariée à l'époque hellénistique*, Paris 1970.
Vattioni, F., "Tripolitana I et Tobie III 6", *Rev. Bib.* 78 (1971), 242-246.
Vaux, R. de, *Hoe het oude Israël leefde*, 2 vols., Roermond 1960.
Verdenius, W. J., "KAI, 'and generally' ", *Mnemosyne* IV 7 (1954), 38.
Verdenius, W. J., review of J. D. Denniston, *The Greek Particles* (1954), *Mnemosyne* IV 9 (1956), 248-252.
Verdenius, W. J., "Notes on Menander's *Epitrepontes*", *Mnemosyne* IV 27 (1974), 17-43.
Vögtle, A., *Die Tugend- und Lasterkataloge im Neuen Testament*, Münster 1936.
Vögtle, A., "Achtlasterlehre", *RAC* I (1950), 74-79.
Vögtle, A., "Affekt", *RAC* I (1950), 160-173.
Vogt, J., *Sklaverei und Humanität. Studien zur antiken Sklaverei und ihrer Erforschung*, Wiesbaden 1965.
Volkmann, R., *Die Rhetorik der Griechen und Römer*, Leipzig 1885².
Vossius, I., *De Oraculis Sibyllinis*, London 1685.
Vries, M. de, *Pallake*, diss. Utrecht, Amsterdam 1927.
Wachler, L., *Dissertatio inauguralis philologica de Pseudo-Phocylide*, Rinteln 1788.
Wachsmuth, C., *Studien zu den griechischen Florilegien*, Berlin 1882.
Wachsmuth, C.,-Hense, O., *Stobaei Anthologium*, 5 vols., Berlin 1884-1912.
Wackernagel, J., *Sprachliche Untersuchungen zu Homer*, Göttingen 1916.
Wächter, L., "Astrologie und Schicksalsglaube im rabbinischen Judentum", *Kairos* 11 (1969), 181-200.
Wächter, Th., *Reinheitsvorschriften im griechischen Kult*, Giessen 1910.
Wahl, C. A., *Clavis librorum Veteris Testamenti apocryphorum philologica*, Leipzig 1853 (repr. Graz 1972 with an appended *Index verborum in libris pseudepigraphis usurpatorum* by J. B. Bauer).
Wahle, H., "Die Lehren des rabbinischen Judentums über das Leben nach dem Tod", *Kairos* 14 (1972), 291-309.
Walter, N., *Der Thoraausleger Aristobulos. Untersuchungen zu seinen Fragmenten und zu pseudepigraphischen Resten der jüdisch-hellenistischen Literatur*, Berlin 1964.
Walter, N., "Frühe Begegnungen zwischen jüdischem Glauben und hellenistischer Bildung", in: E. C. Welskopf (ed.), *Neue Beiträge zur Geschichte der alten Welt* I, Berlin 1964, 367-378.
Waszink, J. H., "Abtreibung", *RAC* I (1950), 55-60.
Waszink, J. H., "Aether", *RAC* I (1950), 150-158.
Waszink, J. H., "Embryologie", see E. Lesky.
Wedderburn, A. J. M., "Philo's Heavenly Man", *Nov. Test.* 15 (1973), 301-326.
Wefelmeier, C., *Die Sentenzensammlung der Demonicea*, diss. Köln, Athens 1962.

Weinreich, O., *Stiftung und Kultsatzungen eines Privatheiligtums in Philadelphia in Lydien*, Sitzungsber. der Heidelberger Akad. der Wiss., Phil.-hist. Klasse 16, 1919.
Weiss, H. F., "Zur Frage der historischen Voraussetzungen der Begegnung von Antike und Christentum", *Klio* 43-45 (1965), 307-328.
Weiss, H. F., *Untersuchungen zur Kosmologie des hellenistischen und palästinischen Judentums*, Berlin 1966.
Wendland, P., *Quaestiones Musonianae*, diss. Berlin 1886.
Wendland, P., reviews of A. Elter, *Gnomica* I (1892), *TLZ* 18 (1893), 492-494 and *Berl. Philol. Wochenschr.* 13 (1893), 229-235.
Wendland, P., reviews of A. Elter, *De gnom. graec. hist. atque orig.* (1893ff.), *Byzantinische Zeitschrift* 2 (1893), 325-328 and 6 (1897), 445-449.
Wendland, P., "Philo und die kynisch-stoische Diatribe", in: P. Wendland-O. Kern, *Beiträge zur Geschichte der griechischen Philosophie und Religion*, Berlin 1895, 1-75.
Wendland, P., "Die Therapeuten und die philonische Schrift vom beschaulichen Leben", *Jahrbücher für class. Philol.* Suppl. Bd. 22 (1896), 693-772.
Wendland, P., *Anaximenes von Lampsakos*, Berlin 1905.
Wendland, P., *Die hellenistisch-römische Kultur in ihren Beziehungen zu Judentum und Christentum*, Tübingen 1912$^{2-3}$.
Wenschkewitz, H., "Die Spiritualisierung der Kultusbegriffe Tempel, Priester und Opfer im Neuen Testament", ΑΓΓΕΛΟΣ 4 (1932), 70-230.
Westermann, C., "Weisheit im Sprichwort", in: *Schalom. Festschrift für A. Jepsen*, Berlin 1971, 73-85.
Wettstein, J. J., *Novum Testamentum Graecum*, 2 vols., Amsterdam 1751-1752 (repr. Graz 1962).
Wibbing, S., *Die Tugend- und Lasterkataloge im Neuen Testament*, Berlin 1959.
Wifstrand, A., "Stylistic Problems in the Epistles of James and Peter", *Studia Theologica* 1 (1947/8), 170-182.
Wilpert, P., "Begierde", *RAC* II (1954), 62-78.
Wolfson, H., *Philo*, 2 vols., Cambridge (Mass.) 1948^2.
Young, D., *Theognis, Ps-Pythagoras, Ps-Phocylides, Chares, Anonymi Aulodia, fragmentum teleiambicum*, Leipzig 1961, 1971^2.
Zanolli, A. A., *De Pseudophocylidea*, Venice 1902.
Zeller, E., *Die Philosophie der Griechen in ihrer geschichtlichen Entwicklung* III, 2 vols., Leipzig 1923^5 (repr. Darmstadt 1963).
Ziebarth, E., *Aus der antiken Schule*, Bonn 1913^2.
Ziebarth, E., *Aus dem griechischen Schulwesen*, Leipzig 1914^2.
Zintzen, C., "Zauberei", *Der kleine Pauly* V (1975), 1460-1472.

CONCORDANCE

ἀγαθός 60, 65, 70, 203, 230
ἄγαμος 175
ἄγαν 68
ἄγγος 174
ἀγήρως 115
ἁγνείη 228
ἀγνώς 16
ἀγορεύω 7, 48, 50
ἄγριος 57
ἀγρός 35, 131
ἄγω 110, 199, 205
ἀδαήμων 86
ἀδελφειός 47
ἄδηλος 25, 117
ἀδίδακτος 89
ἀδικέω 21(2), 51
ἄδικος 5, 10, 37, 135
ἀεί 43, 74 cf. αἰεί
ἀέκων 58
ἀέξω 62
ἀεργός 154, 155
ἀήρ 108
ἀθάνατος 115
ἀθέατος 100
ἀθέμιστος 146
ἄθεσμος 190
ἀθέσφατος 144
αἰδέομαι 220
ἀΐδηλος 194
Ἀΐδης 110, 112
αἰεί 168
αἴθω 144
αἷμα 4, 31
αἱρέω 18, 84, 139
αἶσχος 67
αἰσχρός 76
αἰσχυντός 189
αἰώνιος 112
ἀκάθεκτος 193
ἀκατάσχετος 96
ἀκέομαι 143
ἀκήριος 105
ἀκουή 89
ἀκούω 87
ἀλεγεινός 36, 69β
ἀλιταίνω 208
ἀλίτροπος 141
ἄλκαρ 128

ἀλκή 53, 126
ἀλκήεις 130
ἀλλά 5, 15, 32, 114, 133, 157, 207
ἀλλήλος 71
ἄλλος 48, 156, 205
ἀλλότριος 6
ἄλογος 188
ἄλοχος 177, 183, 186, 195, 197, 200
ἀλωή 166
ἅμα 54, 84
ἄμβροτος 17
ἀμείβω 49
ἀμείνων 218
ἄμετρος 61
ἅμμα 211
ἀμνήστευτος 198
ἄμυνα 32, 77
ἀμφί 206
ἀμφιβάλλω 32
ἀμφότεροι 136
ἄμφω 87
ἄν 75, 87
ἀνά 108
ἀνάγκη 51, 133
ἀναλύω 102
ἄναξ 226
ἀνάπτω 70
ἄνδιχα 197
ἄνεμος 121
ἀνήρ 2, 26, 51, 83, 86, 124, 130, 154, 155, 162, 192, 196, 204
ἀνέλεγκτος 132
ἄνευ 162
ἄνθρωπος 41, 43, 102, 114, 128, 146
ἀνορύσσω 100
ἀντί 142
ἀντιπνέω 121
ἀντιφυτεύω 78
ἀνύβριστος 157
ἀπαναίνομαι 204
ἅπας 14, 30, 42, 113, 193, 194 cf. πᾶς
ἀπερίστατος 26
ἀπέχομαι 6, 31, 35, 76, 145, 149
ἄπιστος 119
ἄπληστος 94

ἁπλόος 50
ἀπό 148, 154, 157
ἀποίχομαι 104
ἀποκτείνω 34
ἀπολείπω 77
ἀποτρωπάω 133
ἀπότροπος 182
ἅπτω 150
ἄρα 35
ἀργίπους 147
ἄργυρος 43
ἀρείων 195
ἀρετή 67, 163
ἀριστοπόνος 171
ἄριστος 36, 69β, 98, 129, 137
ἀρκέω 6
ἁρμονίη 102
ἄρουρα 38, 161, 165
ἄρσην 3, 187, 191, 210, 212, 214
ἀρχηγός 44
ἄρχομαι 138, 143
ἀσκέω 76, 123
ἄσκοπος 117
ἄστατος 27
ἄστεγος 24
ἀτάλαντος 221
ἀταλός 150
ἀτάρ 202
ἀτάρχυτος 99
ἀτάσθαλος 132
ἀτρεκής 79
ἄτρυτος 170
ἄτυκτος 56
αὖ 107, 187
αὐγή 72
αὔξω 38
αὔριον 22, 116
αὐτός 163, 167, 176, 191
αὐτόχυτος (-φυτος) 127
ἄφθονος 71
ἀφνεός 204
ἄφνω 120
ἀφρονέω 203
ἄφρων 68
ἄχθομαι 94, 118, 120
ἄχθος 167
ἄχρι 216
ἄχρις 196, 218

βάζω 7
βαίνω 180, 183
βάλλω 186
βασιλεύς 113

βασιλεύω 111
βατήριος 188
βέβαιος 41
βέλτερος 130, 142
βίαιος 150
βίβλος 149
βίη 198
βίος 27, 30, 159
βιοτεύω 5, 153
βίοτος 119, 165
βιοφθόρος 44
βιόω 229
βλάπτω 226
βορή 139, 169
βούλευμα 1
βουλή 52, 227
βραβεύω 12
βραδύνω 82
βρέφος 184
βροτός 117, 141
βρῶσις 92

γαῖα 99, 103, 107, 164 cf. γῆ
γαμοκλοπέω 3
γάμος 205(2), 216
γαμέω 203
γάρ 34, 40, 46, 56, 58, 75, 78, 90,
    92, 96, 98, 105, 106, 107, 154,
    155, 178, 194, 195, 214, 218
γαστήρ 184, 223
γαυρόω 53
γειαρότης 201
γειτονέω 35
γενεή 209, 221
γεηπονίη 161
γεραίρω 222
γέρας 221
γέρων 220
γῆ 107 cf. γαῖα
γῆρας 196, 230
γίγνομαι 45, 83
γινώσκω 116
γλῶσσα 20
γονεύς 8, 47, 179
γράφω 225
γυνή 184, 189, 193, 196, 199, 204,
    212
γύψ 185

δαιμόνιος 101
δαίνυμι 147
δαίς 156
δασμός 223

CONCORDANCE

δέ 7, 8, 9, 13, 14, 16, 22(2), 26, 31, 33, 35, 36, 37, 39, 41, 47, 48, 50 (2), 51, 52, 55, 57, 61, 62, 64(2), 65, 66, 67, 69, 69β, 74, 76, 77, 78, 85, 88, 91, 94, 97, 98, 103, 104, 108, 111, 115, 117, 121, 127, 128, 129, 137, 140, 141, 145, 147 (2), 155, 156, 158, 161, 163, 167, 168, 170, 171, 176, 180, 194, 198, 199, 203, 204, 208, 212, 213, 215, 216, 220, 221
δεδάηκα 158
δείκνυμι 101
δέμνιον 183
δεύτερος 179
δέχομαι 24, 108, 135, 136
δή 90
δημογέρων 209
διά 115
διδαχή 89
δίδωμι 19, 22, 26, 29, 128, 176
δίζημαι 201
δικάζω 11(2), 87
δίκαιος 9, 12, 14, 33
δικαιοσύνη 229
δίκελλα 158
δίκη (Δίκη) 1, 77, 87
διχοστασίη 151
διώκω 168
δόλιος 82
δόλος 4, 43
δόμος 112, 216
δόναξ 172
δοῦλος 224, 226
δρῦς 173
δύναμαι 56
δυνατός 54
δυστήρητος 217
δῶρον 2

ἐάω 21, 86, 216
ἐγκρατής 145
ἐγκύμων 186
ἕδρη 221
ἔδω 69, 148, 156
ἐθέλω 21, 159, 160
εἰ 75, 158, 160, 161
εἰδωλόθυτος 31
εἴθε 33, 45
εἴκω 220
εἰκών 106
εἰμί 25, 30, 37, 39, 43, 50, 56, 59, 64, 73, 75, 92, 95, 98, 106, 108, 117, 124, 129, 152, 159, 194, 204, 207, 224, 228
εἵνεκα 200
εἰς 24, 110, 206 cf. ἐς
εἷς 54
ἐκ 50, 103, 107, 169 cf. ἐξ
ἕκαστος 52, 125
ἕκητι 46
ἔκνομος 33
ἐκπρολείπω 85
ἐκτελέω 58, 230
ἑκών 16, 51 (16 ἑκοντί)
ἐλέγχω 141
ἔλεος 23
ἕλκος 143
ἕλκω 9, 15, 61
ἐλπίζω 103
ἔλωρον 185
ἔμβρυον 184
ἔμπαλιν 176
ἐμπίπτω 197
ἔμφυτος 128
ἐν 13, 20, 39, 68, 71, 105, 119, 137 cf. ἐνί
ἔνδοθι 173, 184
ἔνι 110
ἐνί 53, 152
ἕννυμι 127
ἐξ 5, 144, 153
ἑός 6, 98
ἐπαγάλλομαι 118
ἐπάγω 169
ἐπαράσιμος 18
ἐπεί 25
ἔπειτα 107
ἐπέοικα 212
ἔπηλυς 39
ἐπήν 93, 159
ἐπί 80, 97, 183, 186, 205, 210(2)
ἐπιδεύω 138
ἐπίκαιρος 114
ἐπίμετρον 14
ἐπιμοιράομαι 99
ἐπιορκέω 16
ἐπονειδίζω 225
ἐργάζομαι 153
ἔργον 76, 159, 162
ἔρδω 80, 152
ἐριδαίνω 203
ἔρις (Ἔρις) 75, 78(2), 151, 206
ἔρυμα 128
ἔρχομαι 22, 103, 120, 165, 182, 188, 206

ἔρως 61, 67, 193, 194, 214
ἐς 9, 32, 57, 62, 103, 182, 188, 190, 193
ἐσθλός 65, 66, 90
ἑταῖρος 91, 92
ἑτερόζυγος 15
ἕτερος (ἕταρος) 48, 70
ἐτήτυμος 7
ἔτι 98
εὖ 80, 152, 227
εὐγενής 201
εὐεπίη 123
εὐθύ 22
εὐθύνω 52, 88
εὐμενέω 142
εὔμορφος 213
εὐνή 182, 190, 191
εὐπετής 162
εὐρύς 160
ἐχθρός 34, 47, 140, 142
ἔχω 20, 28, 41, 74, 85, 93, 107, 145, 167

ζῆλος 65
ζῶ 114, 115, 154
ζωή 230
ζῷον 188

ἤ (comp.) 82, 196
ἤ (disiunct.) 116, 168, 172 (2 × : ἠὲ ... ἤ), 173, 209(2)
ἡδύς 68, 195
ἠεροφοῖτις 171
ἠερόφοιτος 125
ἥλιος (ἠέλιος) 72, 101
ἦν 11, 34, 51, 140, 208
ἧπαρ 55
ἤπιος 207
ἦτορ 97, 145

θάλαμος 215
θάλασσα 160
θάνατος 117, 218
θαρσαλέος 119
θεόπνευστος 129
θεός 1, 8, 11, 17, 29, 54, 104, 106, 111, 125, 194
θεράπων 223, 225
θέρος 169
θῆλυς 192
θήρ 148(2), 191
θηρόβορος 147
θλίβω 19

θνητός 45, 60, 106, 109, 139
θυμός 63
θωπεύω 93

ἴδιος 153, 157
ἵνα 85, 224
ἵππος 201
*ἵπτομαι 155 (ἴψατο)
ἴσος 15, 111, 152, 222
ἰσότης 137
ἵστημι 75
ἴσχω 20
ἴχνιον 180

καθαρμός 228
καθήκω 80
καθίζω 97
καί 6, 24, 30, 43, 54, 62, 69, 71, 92, 94, 96(2), 101, 103, 106, 107, 110, 112, 113, 115, 119, 120, 131(2), 136(2), 141, 145, 151, 176, 185, 195, 197, 209, 221, 227
καιρός 82, 93, 121
κακηγορέω 226
κακοεργός 133
κακός 11 (-ὧς), 44, 51, 55, 66, 118, 120, 134, 143, 146, 152, 199, 204
κακότης 42, 77
καλιή 84
κάλλος 217
καλός 14, 81, 102
κάματος 162
κάμνω 171
καρπός 38, 166
κασίγνητος 183
κασιγνήτη 182
κατά 49, 139, 140, 172, 173, 174
καταθύμιος 224
κείρω 166
κέντρον 127
κέρας 127
κεύθω 48
κηροδομέω 174
κικλήσκω 68
κλέπτω 18, 136
κλόπιμος 135, 154
κλώψ 136
κοιλάς 173
κοῖλος 172
κοινός 27, 30, 59, 112
κόλαξ 91
κολούω 208
κομάω 212

κόνις 108
κόπτω 143
κορέννυμι 93
κόρυμβος 211
κορυφή 211
κούρη 198
κοῦρος 187
κραδίη 48
κρέας 147
κρείσσων 72
κριθή 168
κρίνω 10, 86
κρίσις 9
κρούω 15
κρυπτός 20
κρύπτω 132
κτέανον 206
κτῆνος 139, 140
κτῆσις 37
κυβερνάω 131
Κύπρις 3, 67, 190
κύων 148, 185

λαμβάνω 227
λαός 95, 96
λατρεύω 121, 200
λέγω 22 (εἴπῃς), 52 (ἐρέω)
λεηλασίη 46
λείπω 148
λείψανον 104, 148
λέκτρον 178, 179
λέχος 181, 188, 189, 192
λέων 126
λήϊον 166
λιμός 155
λιτός 81
λόγος 20, 124, 128, 129
λοξός 211
λοχεύω 176
λυγρός 200
λύσις 120
λυσσάω 122, 214
λύω 108
λωβάω 38
λωβητός 145

μαγικός 149
μάκαρ 75, 163
μακρός 161
μάλα 123
μανθάνω 90
μανίη 63
μαρτυρίη 12

μάτην 97
μάχη 46
μεγαληγορίη 122
μέγας 59, 66, 89, 163
μεθέπω 161
μείγνυμι 181, 198
μεῖξις 214
μέλαθρον 112
μέλισσα 127, 171
μέλλω 117
μέν 78, 210
μένω 175
μετά 116(2)
μετέπειτα 8, 11
μέτρον 14, 36, 69(2), 69β, 98(2), 139
μέχρι 230
μή 5, 7, 9, 10(2), 15, 16, 18, 19, 22,
   31, 32, 33, 35, 45, 48, 53, 55, 57,
   70(2), 77, 79, 91, 95, 97, 100,
   109, 121, 122, 135, 138, 139, 147,
   149, 150, 152, 156, 175(2), 177,
   179, 190, 198, 199, 207, 210, 211,
   216, 225, 226
μηδέ 38, 49, 59, 84, 87, 100, 181,
   182, 183, 184, 185, 186, 187, 188,
   189, 192, 193, 197, 205, 206
μηδέν 59
μηδέποτε 83, 86, 90
μήνη 72
μῆνις 64
μήτε 3(2), 4(2), 16(2), 21(2), 33(2),
   53(2), 118(2), 211
μήτηρ 42, 85, 180(2), 208
μητρυιή 179
μιαίνω 4, 34, 177
μιμέομαι 77, 192
μιμνήσκω 109
μίμνω 105
μιν 216
μινύθω 97
μισθός 19, 157
μοῖρα 137
μοιχικός 178
μοχθέω 19, 153, 159
μυθολογεύω 69
μῦθος 87
μυριότρητος 174
μύρμηξ 164
μυστήριον 229
μύχατος 164
μῶμος 70

ναυηγός 25

ναῦς 131
ναυτίλος 160
νεῖκος 197
νέκυς 99, 111
νέμω 9, 14, 125, 137, 219, 224
νεοσσός 85
νεοτήσιος 213
νεοτριβής 167
νέρθεν 73
νηπίαχος 150
νικάω 50
νοέω 90
νόος 20, 48
νώνυμνος 175

ξεινίζω 81
ξενίη (?) 40
ξίφος 32
ξυνός 113

ὁ, ἡ, τό 2, 7, 12, 14, 27, 30, 32, 40, 42, 50, 52, 56, 61, 62, 65, 67, 88, 90, 98, 117, 129, 132, 134, 136(2), 143, 157, 167, 179, 180
ὅδε 85
ὁδηγέω 24
ὁδός 140
οἴκαδε 199
οἰκέτης 227
οἶκος 24, 164
οἰκτίρω 25
ὄλβιος 2
ὄλβος 27, 110
ὀλίγος 94, 144, 170
ὄλλυμι 175
ὀλοή 66
ὀλοόφρων 63
ὁμῆλιξ 222
ὅμιλος 95
ὄμνυμι 17
ὅμοιος 178
ὁμόνοια 74, 219
ὁμότεχνος 88
ὁμότιμος 39
ὁμόφρων 30
ὄνειαρ 60, 78
ὀνήσιμος 37
ὀνίνημι 123
ὀπίσω 104
ὅπλον 124, 125
ὁππότε 165
ὁράω 79, 216
ὀργή 57, 64

ὀρέγω 28
ὄρεξις 64
ὀρίνω 3
ὄρνις 84, 126
ὄρνυμι 101
ὅς, ἥ, ὅ 29, 197
ὅσιος 1, 5, 37, 132, 219
ὅστις 17, 18, 51, 123
ὅταν 196
ὅτι 109
οὐ 41, 72, 73, 74, 89, 90, 102, 114, 158, 178, 194, 204, 228 cf. οὐκ
οὐκ 52, 60, 75, 110, 132, 203, 212
οὐδέ 163, 191
οὐδείς 116, 162
οὐδός 230
οὐκέτι 56
οὖν 21, 118
οὔποτε 141
οὐρανίδης 71
οὐράνιος 73
οὗτος 1, 29, 229
ὀφείλω 223
ὀφέλλω 66, 67, 163

πάθος 27, 59, 194
παιδογόνος 187
παῖς 178, 207, 208, 210, 213, 217
πάλι 85
παλλακίς 181
πανάριστος 202
παρά 6, 82, 156, 226, 227
παραβαίνω 190
παραθήκη 135
πάρειμι (?) 6
παρέχω 23, 29, 223
παρθενική 215
παρθεσίη 13
παροίχομαι 55
πᾶς 7, 9, 13, 27, 30, 36, 40, 44, 50, 69β, 84, 94, 96, 111, 115, 123, 137(2), 138, 154, 159, 221
πατήρ 181, 222
πατρίς 112
πέδον 41
πειθώ 78
πειράομαι 40
πέλαγος 74
πέλω 162
πένης 19, 83, 113
πενητεύω 28
πενίη 10, 40 (?)
πέρας 79

CONCORDANCE

πέτρη 172
πετροφυής 49
πῆμα 45, 120, 205(2)
πικρός 83
πίνω 69
πίπτω 26, 140
πιστεύω 79, 95
πίστις 13, 218
πλάζω 141
πλείων, πλεῖστος 80, 82
πλέκω 211
πλεονάζω 60
πλήθω 166
πληρόω 23
πλήσσω 58
πλόκαμος 210
πλόος 25
πλουτέω 5, 109
πλοῦτος 28, 53, 62
πλώω 160
πνεῦμα 106, 108
ποθεινός 45
ποιέω 91
πόλεμος 151
πολιήτης 39, 68
πολιοκρόταφος 220
πόλις 131
πολλάκι 58, 134
πολλάκις 119
πόλος 75
πολύκλειστος 215
πολύμοχθος 170
πολύολβος 54
πολύπλαγκτος 40
πολύπους 49
πολύς 61, 62, 72, 92, 94, 114, 214
πολύτροπος 95
πολυχρήματος 119
πονέω 66
πονηρός 37
πόνος 163
πόντος 152
πόσις I 197
πόσις II 92
ποταμός 74
ποτί 169
πρέσβυς 209, 222
πρίν 79, 87
πρό 216
προαγωγεύω 177
προλείπω 164
προπετής 57
πρός 32, 61, 107, 214

πρόσειμι 151
πρόσωπον 10
πρῶτος 8
πτωχός 22
πῦρ 96, 97
πυρός 167
πῶλος 126
πως 175

ῥάπτω 4
ῥέω 193
ῥίπτω 10, 185

σεμνός 67
σίδηρος 124
σίμβλος 173
σκάπτω 158
σκυβάλισμα 156
σκύλαξ 202
σμῆνος 174
σός 28, 186 cf. τεός
σοφίζω 130
σοφίη 53, 88, 129, 131
σοφός 2, 54, 88
σπείρω 152
σπέρμα 18
σπινθήρ 144
σταθμός 15
στέργω 195, 218
στίγμα 225
στυγέω 17
σύ 8, 11(2), 23, 29, 34, 45, 46, 161, 177, 208, 224
συγγενής 219
συμπάρειμι 134
σύναιμος 47
*συνανδάνω 191 (συνεύαδον)
συνεγείρω 140
συνθνήσκω 134
συνομαίμων 206
σφέτερος 169
σώζω 26
σῶμα 107, 228
σωφροσύνη 76

τακτός 224
ταῦρος 127, 202
ταχύς 79, 81, 103
ταχυτής 126
τε 46(3), 47, 54, 113, 126, 143, 171, 201, 219
τέκνον 47, 177
τελέθω 71, 104, 170

τέλος 52
τέμνω 187
τεός 55, 195, 207
τέρμα 138
τεύχω 56, 63, 98, 142, 149
τέχνη 88, 155, 158
τηρέω 13
τίκτω 176, 178, 185
τιμάω 8, 180
τιμή 222
τις, τι 38, 41, 84, 147, 158, 176, 181, 192
τίς, τί 116(2), 195
τοι 124
τοῖος 229
τοκεύς 217
τόλμα 66
τομός 124
τράπεζα 81, 156
τραπεζόκορος 91
τρέφω 155, 210
τροχός 27
τρυφάω 122
τρυφή 61
τρύχω 55
τύμβος 100
τυφλός 24

ὑβρίζω 189
ὕβρις 62
ὕδωρ 96
υἱός 208
ὕλη 144
ὑπάρχω 109
ὑπερβαίνω 35, 64
ὑπερβασίη 36, 69β
ὑπέρογκος 65
ὑπέροπλον 59
ὑπέρχομαι 63
ὑπό 51
ὑψαυχέω 62
ὑψιτένων 202
ὕψωμα 73

φαίνω 1
φαγέω 31, 157
φάος 103
φάρμακον 149
φαῦλος 65
φείδομαι 109, 138
φερνή 200
φέρω 168
φεύγω 12, 146(2), 151

φήμη 146
φθείρω 184
φθίνω 100, 105
φθονέω 70, 72
φίλος 97, 142, 196, 218
φιλότης 219
φιλοχρημοσύνη 42
φόνος 32, 46, 58
φορέω 168
φρήν 20, 122
φρονέω 196, 227
φρουρέω 213
φυλάσσω 13, 215
φῦλον 170
φύσις 125, 176, 187, 190
φύω 60, 130, 217
Φωκυλίδης 2
φώρ 135

χαίτη 210
χαλεπαίνω 207
χαλέπτω 44
χαλινόω 57
χάρις 9, 200
χάρμη 118
χεῖμα 169
χείρ 4, 23, 26, 28, 34, 57, 150, 154, 186
χηραμός 172
χθών 73
χλιδανός 212
χόλος 101
χράομαι 165
χρή 133
χρῄζω 23, 29, 33
χρῆμα 110
χρῆσις 106
χρήστης 83
χρόνος 114
χρυσός 43, 44
χωρέω 89
χώρη 41
χῶρος 49, 113

ψαύω 179
ψευδής 12
ψεύδορκος 17
ψεῦδος 7
ψυχή 50, 105, 111, 115, 228

ὠγύγιος 173
ὥρη 116, 213
ὡς 49, 176
ὥς 108

INDEX OF SUBJECTS DISCUSSED IN THE COMMENTARY

The numbers refer not to the pages of the book but to the lines of the poem. The topics discussed in the Introduction can easily be found by consulting to the individual chapter headings.

abortion 184
acquisition 37
active forms created to middle verbs 138
adultery 3, 178, 189
after-life 103ff.
agriculture 160-1
air, aether (as place of the spirit of the dead) 108
alien, status of an, 40-1
alms 23
anatomy 102
anger 57-8, 63-4
animals as examples 191
ant 164-70
apostrophizing of gold 44-5
athletics, polemics against, 130
avoidance of evildoers 132-4

banking 83
beast 139, 140
beauty of children 213-7
bee 171-4
benefaction 80, 152
bestiality 188
bigamy 205
birds 84-5
blessed ones 75
blind, the, 24
blood, eating of, 31
bloodshed 4
boastfulness 122
branding 225
bridle one's anger 57-8
Buzygian laws 99

castration 187
celibacy 175-6
changes of fortune 119-20
children 207ff.
closing passages 229-30
concord 74
concubines 181
contentment 6
creditor 83

daring 66
deification of the dead 104
deposit 13, 135-6
digging up graves 100-1
dissection 102
dissension 151
dogs 148, 184
dowry 200

eating and drinking 69
eclipses 163
effemination 210-2
elders of the people 209
élite mentality 95-6
embryology 177-8
emotions 59
enmity between kinsmen 47
envy 70-4
equality of all people in death 111
eros 194
eternal home 112
evil report 146
excessive mourning 97-8
exposure of children 185

faith(fulness) 13, 218
false witness 12
farming 161
fickleness 95-6
field 35
fire 96, 97, 144
flatterers 91
food sacrificed to idols 31
forbidden degrees 179-83
friend(ship) 142, 218
fruits 38

gentleness 207
god 11, 29, 54, 106, 111
gold 43-5

Hades 110, 112-3
hairdressing 210-2
Haustafel 175-227
hearing both parties 87

290   INDEX OF SUBJECTS DISCUSSED IN THE COMMENTARY

heavenly bodies   71, 72-4
heavenly ones   71
helpless, the,   26
homeless, the,   24
homosexuality   3, 190, 191, 213-4
honesty   48-50
honouring of God   8
honouring of one's parents   8
hunger   155
hybris   62

idleness   153-5
image of God   106
impartiality   9, 137
immortality of the soul   115
incest   182, 183
injustice   21
insatiability   94
insolence, see *hybris*
instability of life   116ff.
intentional and unintentional wrong-
   doing   51-2
intercourse during menstruation   189
intercourse with animals   188
interest   83
irarum differentiae   63-4

judgement   9, 10, 11, 86, 87
justice   9, 12, 14, 21

killing   32-4

labour   153ff.
labourer   19
land   41
lesbian sex   192
liver (as centre of emotions)   55-6
locking up of women   215-6
long hair   210-2
love   195-7, 218, 219
love of money   42ff.
luxuriousness   61
luxury   69
lying   7

madness   63-4
magic, Jewish,   149
magical books   149
marriage   175-6, 205
marriage with a rich woman   199ff.
measures   14
mitigation of a commandment   208-9
mob   95-6

moderation   36, 59-60, 69, 98
murder   46, 58
mystery-terminology   229-30

natural means of defence   125-8
nature   175-6, 190
nautical metaphor   131
navigation   25
needy, the,   23, 29

opportunism   49
oracle of the Branchidae   162
overrating of sexuality   194

pacifism   32-4
paederasty   213-4
parasites   91-4
partiality   9-10
passion   67, 194
payment   19
perjury   16-7
persuasiveness   78
polyp   49
poor, the,   10, 19, 22, 23, 28, 29, 83,
   113
poverty   40-1
pregnancy   186
pride   53
proselytes   39
prosperity, unstability of,   27
prostitution   177-8
protection   32-4
purifications   228
purity   228

rage   64
rape   198
rashness   57
ration of fodder   139
reason   128
receiver   136
relentlessness   83
remarrying   205
respect for elderly persons   220-2
resurrection of the body   102, 103-4
righteousness   229-30

sailing   160
seeds   18
self-restraint   76, 145, 193
sexual abstinence   145
sexual desires   61
sexual sins   177ff.

INDEX OF SUBJECTS DISCUSSED IN THE COMMENTARY

shipwrecked, the, 25
shortness of life 114
simple meal 81-2
sincerity 50
sinner 140
slandering 226
slaves 223-7
Solomon, epithet of, 1-2
soul 105, 106, 111, 115, 228
speech 123ff.
sphragis 1-2
spirit 106, 107-8
spirit as a loan and image of God 106
spiritualization of O.T. commandments 228
stain 4, 32-4
stepmother 179-80
Stoic casuistry 63-4, 65, 67
strangers 39
strife 75, 78, 151, 197, 206
suffering 27
surpassing of your benefactors 80
sword 32-4

terefah 147-8
toil 162-3
tongue, taking heed of the, 20
tranquillity of mind 118
trust 79, 95-6
truth, speaking of the, 7

unanimity among kinsmen 219
unburied dead, duty to bury, 99
uncertainty of the future 116-7
uneducated, the, 89-90
unstability of life 27, 119-20
unwritten laws 8, 80, 99, 100
usury 83
utilitarianism 80, 152

vain efforts 121
variations in intercourse 189
vengeance 77
violation 189, 198
violence 150
virginity 13, 215-6
virtue 67

wealth 5, 28, 62, 109-10
weapon 124-8
weighing 15
wheel, life as a, 27
wiles 4
willful wrongdoing 51-2
wisdom 129, 131
wise, the, 88, 130
wordplay, etymological, 63-4, 220-2
work 153ff.
wrath 64

zeal 65

INDEX OF BIBLICAL PASSAGES

The numbers refer not to the pages of this book but to the lines of the poem.
(All O.T. references are to the LXX).

Genesis		11, 40	147f.	5, 16	8
1, 26f.	106	17, 10	31	5, 17	3
1, 28	175f., 187	17, 15	147f.	5, 18	4
2, 24	175f.	18, 3	192	5, 19	5
3, 19	107f.	18, 8	179f., 181	5, 20	12
31, 35	220-2	18, 9	182	5, 21	6
35, 22	181	18, 16	183	6, 4	54
		18, 18	183	6, 5	8
Exodus		18, 19	189	10, 19	39
		18, 22	3, 190	12, 16	31
18, 21f.	86	18, 23	188	12, 23-5	31
18, 22	65	19, 3	8	13, 7-10	132-4
18, 26	65	19, 9f.	22	15, 11	28
19, 7	208f.	19, 11	13	15, 14	29
20, 7	16f.	19, 12	16f.	15, 23	31
20, 12	8	19, 13	5, 19, 22	16, 18-20	9
20, 13	3	19, 14	24	16, 19	10
20, 14	5	19, 15	9, 10	19, 14	35
20, 15	4	19, 16	21, 32-4	19, 15-9	12, 87
20, 16	12	19, 17	20	21, 18-21	208f.
20, 17	6	19, 19	14f.	22, 1-3	141
21, 14	4	19, 26	31	22, 4	140
21, 17	18, 150	19, 28	225	22, 6f.	84f.
21, 22f.	184f., 186	19, 29	177f.	22, 22-4	3
22, 4	35, 38	19, 32	220-2	22, 23f.	198
22, 6-12	13	19, 33f.	39	23, 1	179f.
22, 15	198	19, 34	40	23, 20	83
22, 18	149, 188	19, 35f.	14f.	23, 25	35, 38
22, 20	39	20, 11	179f.	24, 7	18
22, 24	83	20, 13	3, 190	24, 14	19
22, 30	147f.	20, 15f.	188	24, 17	39
23, 1-3	9	20, 17	182	25, 14	14f.
23, 3	10	20, 18	189	27, 17	18, 35
23, 4	141	20, 21	183	27, 18	24
23, 5	140	22, 8	147f.	27, 21	187
23, 6	10	22, 24	187	27, 22	182
23, 7	21	24, 22	39	27, 24	4
23, 9	39, 40f.	25, 36	83	32, 35	77
31, 3	129				
		Numbers		1 Kings	
Leviticus		15, 29f.	16f.	2, 3	122
3, 19	31	16, 26	132-4	2, 10	53
5, 20-26	13	Deuteronomy		3 Kings	
5, 21	135f.				
7, 24	147f.	1, 17	9, 10	19, 3	108
7, 26	31	5, 11	16f.	20, 24	184f.

INDEX OF BIBLICAL PASSAGES

1 Chronicles	
29, 17	50

Judith	
8, 23	9
10, 8	9

Tobith	
1, 17ff.	99
2, 3ff.	99
2, 4	100f.
4, 3ff.	8
4, 7	70
4, 14	19
4, 16	23, 70
12, 8	81f.
12, 12f.	99
14, 12f.	99

1 Maccabees	
3, 29	151
14, 28	208f.

2 Maccabees	
3, 19	215f.
7, 9-14	103f.

3 Maccabees	
1, 18	215f.
5, 12	190

4 Maccabees	
1, 31	76
2, 14	140
5, 2	31
5, 34	145
18, 7	215f.

Psalms	
1, 1	146
48, 18	109f.
50, 11	10
56, 5	124
63, 4	124
70, 9	10
82, 6	104
89, 5ff.	114
102, 15ff.	114
103, 23	153f.
118, 19	40f.
127, 2	153f.

Proverbs	
1, 7f.	8
1, 32	150
3, 27f.	22, 23
3, 28	116f.
5, 20	3
6, 6-8	164-170
6, 8a-c	171-4
6, 24	3
6, 29	3
7, 1	8
7, 5	9
7, 18	67
10, 14	57f.
11, 1	14f.
11, 25	50
12, 11	153f.
13, 3	57f.
13, 11	37
14, 21	19
14, 31	19
15, 1	57f., 63f.
15, 17	81f.
16, 11	14f.
16, 31	229f.
17, 5	19
17, 15	11
18, 5	10
19, 26	8
20, 10	14f.
20, 23	14f.
21, 3	7
21, 13	26
21, 23	20
21, 26	23
21, 28	12
22, 1	146
22, 22	10, 19, 26
23, 22-5	8
24, 1	146
24, 5	130
24, 23	10
24, 25	164ff.
25, 8	57f.
25, 18	12
27, 1	116f.
27, 4	63f.
27, 10	218
28, 19	153f.
28, 22	43
28, 24	8
29, 11	63f.
29, 24	135f.
30, 10	226
30, 16	67
30, 24	164ff.
31, 9	10
31, 11f.	195ff.
31, 20	28

Ecclesiastes	
3, 20	107f.
5, 1	20
5, 15	109f.
7, 10	57f.
8, 7	116f.
9, 12	116f., 119f.
9, 16	130
9, 17	123
11, 9	11
12, 5	112
12, 7	107f.

Job	
1, 21	109f.
3, 19	111, 112f.
14, 1f.	114
20, 15	5
29, 18	24
31, 32	24
32, 4	220-2

Wisdom of Solomon	
1, 1	50
2, 1	114
2, 4	114
2, 23	106
9, 5	114
9, 15	106
10, 4	131
12, 4f.	184f.
14, 25f.	3f.
14, 28f.	16f.
15, 8	106, 107f., 114

Sirach	
1, 8	54
1, 14ff.	8
1, 22	57f., 63f.
2, 4	118
3, 1-16	8
4, 1-6	10, 19
4, 1	23
4, 3	22
4, 27	10
6, 5-17	142
6, 5	123
6, 7	79

6, 14f.	218	30, 21	97	Ezekiel	
6, 16	142	30, 24	63f.	12, 24	9
7, 13	7	31, 6	46f.	18, 6	31
7, 15	153f., 160f.	31, 12-31	69	18, 7	13
7, 18	142	32, 7f.	69	18, 11	31
7, 19	199	36, 22-26	195ff.	18, 15	31
7, 20	223	36, 25	175f.	18, 19-21	23
7, 24	217	37, 29-31	92-4	22, 9	31
7, 27-31	8	38, 16	99	37, 7	102
7, 32	23, 28	38, 20f.	97	45, 10	14f.
8, 2	46f.	40, 5	78		
8, 6	220-2	40, 9	78	Daniel	
8, 7	109f.	40, 11	107f.	1, 10	92-4
9, 9	3, 61	40, 28-30	156f.	11, 36	65
9, 17	88	42, 4	14f.	12, 2	103f.
9, 18	57f.	42, 9-11	215f., 217		
10, 7-22	122	Psalms of Solomon		Matthew	
10, 8	46f.			3, 12	164ff.
10, 18	63f.	3, 11f.	103f.	5, 33	16f.
11, 7	9	4, 4	16f.	5, 44	152
11, 19	116f.	5, 17	36	7, 2	11
11, 21	119f.	Hosea		13, 22	43
11, 32	144			13, 29f.	38
12, 1ff.	152	7, 12	11	13, 43	104
14, 10	70	9, 1-6	11	15, 14	24
14, 13	109f.	12, 8	14f.	19, 11f.	89f.
16, 8	10	Amos		22, 16	10
17, 1	107f.			22, 30	104
18, 32	61	1, 3ff.	11	26, 52	32-4
19, 3	66	6, 12	152		
19, 4	79	8, 4	10, 19	Mark	
19, 6	69	8, 4ff.	14f.	7, 15	228
19, 10	20	Micah		7, 21f.	6
19, 13-7	9			7, 22	4
20, 2	81f.	6, 11	14f.	7, 28	148
20, 5	20	7, 5	79	13, 12	46f.
20, 7f.	69	7, 6	46f.		
20, 13	123	Zechariah		Luke	
20, 24-6	7			3, 11	28
20, 28	160f.	8, 16	7	3, 14	6
21, 14	89f.	Isaiah		6, 32ff.	152
21, 26	20			6, 37	11
23, 7f.	69	26, 19	103f.	6, 38	14f.
23, 11	16f.	40, 6	114	6, 39	24
23, 16	63f.	44, 9	224	10, 7	19
23, 24	177f.	58, 7	24	12, 20	106
25, 1	219	Jeremiah		16, 3	158
26, 10	215f.			16, 21	156f.
26, 13-8	195ff.	6, 16-21	11	18, 20	3f.
27, 30	63f.	8, 1f.	100f.	20, 36	104
28, 11	78	9, 22	53	22, 66	208f.
29, 1f.	23	16, 4	99		
29, 8f.	23	22, 19	99		

INDEX OF BIBLICAL PASSAGES

John		Ephesians		2 Timothy	
7, 24	9	4, 19	6	3, 4	57f.
10, 34f.	104	4, 25	7	3, 16	129
17, 12	13	4, 31	63f.		
Acts		5, 3	6	Titus	
2, 45	30	5, 5	6	1, 6	205
15, 29	31	5, 25	195-7	3, 3	70
19, 19	149	6, 2	8		
19, 36	57f.	6, 4	207	Hebrews	
21, 25	31	6, 9	224	4, 12	124
22, 5	208f.	Philippians		13, 2	24
28, 4	77	1, 15	70, 75	13, 5	6
Romans		3, 19	69	James	
1, 26	192	Colossians		1, 19	20, 57f.
1, 27	3, 190	2, 16	92-4	2, 11	3f.
1, 29	70, 75	3, 8	57f.	3, 1ff.	20
2, 19	24	3, 19	195-7	3, 5	144
8, 39	72-4	3, 21	207	3, 6	27
12, 13	24	4, 1	137, 224	3, 8	95f.
12, 17	77			4, 14	116f.
12, 19	77	1 Thessalonians		5, 4	19
12, 21	80	2, 7	207	5, 12	16f.
13, 9	3f.	4, 6	35	1 Peter	
13, 13	69	5, 15	77	1, 17	10
14, 17	92-4	2 Thessalonians		2, 1	70
16, 17	151	3, 10	153f.	3, 3	212
16, 18	69			2 Peter	
16, 27	54	1 Timothy		1, 6	145
1 Corinthians		1, 9f.	3f.	2, 7	190
3, 3	151	1, 10	3, 16f., 18	2, 13	61
5, 1ff.	179f.	2, 9	212	3, 17	190
5, 11	69	3, 2	205	3 John	
6, 10	69	3, 12	205	11	77
7, 1	179f.	5, 9	205	Apocalypse	
7, 9	145	5, 18	19	1, 5	179f.
8, 1.4.7.10	31	6, 4	70, 75	2, 14	31
9, 25	145	6, 6	6	2, 20	31
10, 19	31	6, 7	109f.	11, 17	111
11, 14	210-2	6, 8	6	19, 6	111
Galatians		6, 10	42		
5, 20	151	6, 17	62		
5, 21	70				
5, 23	145				